International Conference on Development of Digital Economy (ICDDE 2024)

SHS Web of Conferences Volume 188 (2024)

Shanghai, China
15 – 17 March 2024

Editor:

Azlina Md Yassin

ISBN: 978-1-7138-9560-2

Printed from e-media with permission by:

Curran Associates, Inc.
57 Morehouse Lane
Red Hook, NY 12571

Some format issues inherent in the e-media version may also appear in this print version.

For additional information, please contact EDP Sciences – Web of Conferences
at the address below.

EDP Sciences – Web of Conferences
17, Avenue du Hoggar
Parc d'Activité de Courtabœuf
BP 112
F-91944 Les Ulis Cedex A
France

Phone: +33 (0) 1 69 18 75 75
Fax: +33 (0) 1 69 28 84 91

contact-edps@webofconferences.org

Additional copies of this publication are available from:

Curran Associates, Inc.
57 Morehouse Lane
Red Hook, NY 12571 USA
Phone: 845-758-0400
Fax: 845-758-2633
Email: curran@proceedings.com
Web: www.proceedings.com

TABLE OF CONTENTS

DIGITAL FINANCE ANALYSIS AND RESEARCH

INTERNATIONAL ECONOMIC STUDIES

BUSINESS MANAGEMENT AND STRATEGY

edp sciences

Web of Conferences

Statement of Peer review

In submitting conference proceedings to *Web of Conferences*, the editors of the proceedings certify to the Publisher that

1. They adhere to its **Policy on Publishing Integrity** in order to safeguard good scientific practice in publishing.
2. All articles have been subjected to peer review administered by the proceedings editors.
3. Reviews have been conducted by expert referees, who have been requested to provide unbiased and constructive comments aimed, whenever possible, at improving the work.
4. Proceedings editors have taken all reasonable steps to ensure the quality of the materials they publish and their decision to accept or reject a paper for publication has been based only on the merits of the work and the relevance to the journal.

Title, date and place of the conference

2024 International Conference on Development of Digital Economy (ICDDE 2024)
March 15th-17th, 2024
Shanghai, China

Proceedings editor(s):

PROF. MADYA DR. AZLINA BINTI MD YASSIN
DEPUTY DEAN (ACADEMIC & INTERNATIONAL),Faculty of Technology and Business Management, University Tun Hussein Onn Malaysia (UTHM)

Date and editor's signature

March 19th, 2024

SHS Web of Conferences **188**, 01001 (2024) https://doi.org/10.1051/shsconf/202418801001
ICDDE 2024

Analysis of Currency Risk Hedging Strategies in Multinational Companies: A Case Study of the 2022 Russo-Ukrainian War and Surge in US Dollar Exchange Rate

Yikai Huang*

College of Economics, Shenzhen University, Shenzhen, 518060, China

Abstract. The volatility of exchange rates due to frequent global events is one of today's hot topics. The profitability of large multinational corporations is highly correlated with exchange rates. This paper primarily takes a case study approach, focusing on the combination of global events and large multinational corporations, integrated with the strategic optimization of commodity swaps. The ultimate goal is to develop innovative strategies for large multinational corporations to hedge against foreign exchange risk. The first case of the article focuses on the analysis of the Russian Ruble exchange rate, which first fell and then rose from February to August 2022, and Coca-Cola HBC modifies cash and debt to account for foreign exchange swings. The second case assesses the financial impact of a spike in the U.S. dollar exchange rate in 2022, where Coca-Cola reduces its assets in financial derivatives designated as hedges and significantly increases its liabilities to offset them. In addition, the study also presents a novel strategy that mixes forward foreign currency contracts with commodity futures. Reduce risk by securing profits ahead of time. This comprehensive analysis aims to provide companies with insightful and actionable strategies for managing the complexity and uncertainty of currency market volatility.

1 Introduction

In 2022, the global economy faced significant challenges, including the Russo-Ukrainian war and significant currency fluctuations, particularly the rise of the U.S. dollar. These developments had a profound impact on both global financial markets [1, 2] and multinational corporate strategies.

This thesis examines these dynamics, focusing on two aspects: the impact of the Russo-Ukrainian war on the Russian ruble and Coca-Cola HBC's strategic response; the other is the impact of the rise of the US dollar on Coca-Cola Company, highlighting its currency hedging tactics. This analysis aims to shed light on the direct impact of international political-economic events on global companies and the adaptability of multinational corporations to macroeconomic volatility.

2 Case Description

2.1 Case 1: The 2022 Ukrainian Crisis: Economic and Geopolitical Impacts and Their Effect on Global Markets and Coca-Cola HBC

The Ukrainian crisis of 2022 is a complicated and multifaceted global event with far-reaching political and economic consequences. Russia's launch of a large-scale military operation against Ukraine on February 24, 2022, significantly escalated an already tense situation in eastern Ukraine that had been ongoing since 2014 [3]. This crisis is rooted in a complex web of factors, encompassing historical, political, security, and geopolitical dimensions. At its core are Russia's fears of NATO's eastward expansion, Ukraine's ambitions to deepen ties with Western powers, especially the EU and NATO, and Russia's and Ukraine's contrasting cultural and historical identities.

During the Russia-Ukraine conflict, the United States imposed strict economic sanctions targeting key Russian sectors such as banking [4]. At the same time, these Western nations provided Ukraine with crucial military and humanitarian aid. As a countermeasure, Russia responded by restricting its energy exports and seeking to strengthen its economic ties with alternative global partners, most notably China [5].

As Russia is a major global supplier of oil and gas, the crisis has led to a significant increase in energy prices. Western sanctions against Russia and a rethinking of its energy dependence have led to a major restructuring of the global energy market. Both Russia and Ukraine are major global exporters of wheat and other grains. Wars have disrupted production and exports in these areas, causing global food prices to rise [5].

* Corresponding author: 2021022041@email.szu.edu.cn

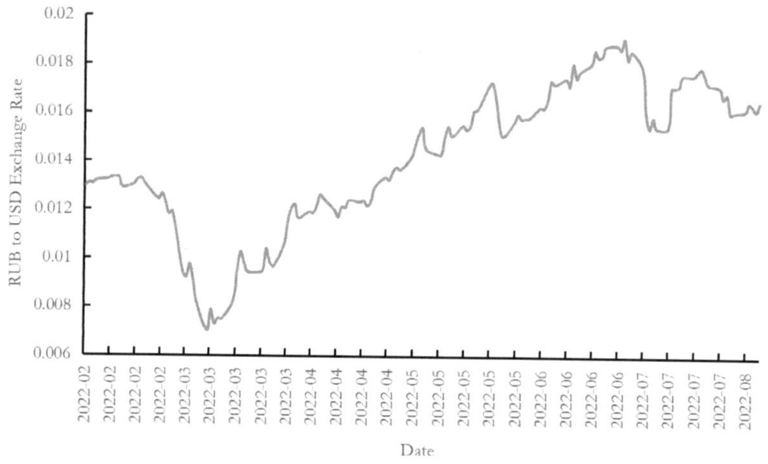

Fig. 1. RUB To USD Exchange Rate from 2022-02-01 to 2022-08-05
Data source: www.investing.com
Photo credit: Original

Fig. 1, which plots the exchange rate of the Russian ruble against the U.S. dollar, shows a sharp decline in the value of the ruble beginning on February 24, 2022, coinciding with the start of the Russia-Ukraine conflict. After this initial plunge, the ruble began a gradual recovery beginning in early March, eventually surpassing its pre-conflict value by mid-April.

Coca-Cola HBC's operations in Russia were impacted by the crisis between Russia and Ukraine. Coca-Cola stated in March 2022 that it was stopping its business in Russia [6], which had a significant negative impact on Coca-Cola HBC, one of the company's main bottlers. At the same time, the significant fluctuation of the ruble exchange rate also exposes Coca-Cola HBC to some foreign exchange risk.

2.2 Case 2: Soaring Dollar Rate Spurs U.S. Firms to Currency Hedge in 2022

The US Federal Reserve sharply increased interest rates in 2022 in an effort to fight inflation in the face of continued conflicts and a volatile world. Influenced by a variety of factors, the dollar experienced significant appreciation, reaching its highest level in two decades (please see Fig. 2).

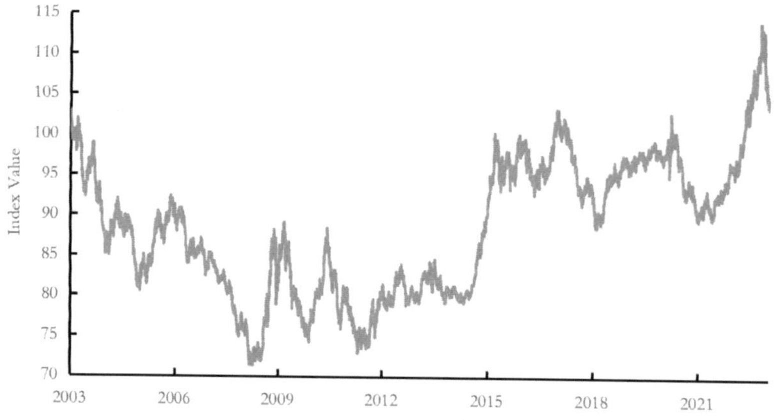

Fig. 2. ICE US Dollar Index from 2003 to 2023
Data source: Yahoo Finance
Photo credit: Original

The rise in the value of the dollar has serious implications for large multinational corporations. Essentially, for large U.S.-based multinationals, the appreciation of the dollar depreciates the foreign currency earnings of their overseas operations relative to the dollar when converted back into U.S. dollars. This has a significant impact on the profits of these companies. As a result, U.S. companies are forced to adopt currency hedging strategies.

2.3 Dynamics of the foreign exchange market and economic consequences

The following article will make a specific analysis of the two cases mentioned before.

2.3.1 Changes in exchange rate fluctuations of the Rouble and the impact on Coca-Cola HBCs

The ruble exchange rate experienced three stages of depreciation, recovery and appreciation in the period from February to August 2022.

The sharp drop in the ruble coincided with the start of the Ukrainian crisis in 2022. Investors and markets often assume that conflict leads to instability, especially when it involves a large economy like Russia. This has led investors to sell the ruble and shift assets to currencies that are perceived as safer, such as the dollar or euro.

In parallel, Europe and the United States imposed a series of sanctions on Russia. This included the announcement on February 27 that Europe and the United States would ban some Russian banks from using the SWIFT system [5]. The move was a direct hit on Russia's financial system [7]. It not only increases the risk of capital outflows from Russia, but also has a direct impact on Russian exports, especially oil and gas. This has affected Russia's government revenues and the value of its currency, leading in part to a sharp depreciation of the Russian ruble.

The rebound and recovery after the significant drop is related to Russia's counter-sanctions measures. On April 1, 2022, Putin announced the enforcement of mandatory payment in rubles for natural gas [8]. Approximately 33% of the natural gas used in Europe comes from Russia [9]. The policy of mandatory ruble purchases is beneficial in strengthening the ruble and increasing its currency value. This has greatly influenced the recovery of the ruble exchange rate. After Putin's announcement, Fig. 1 shows that the Russian ruble had already recovered to its pre-war level.

The subsequent appreciation of the ruble (almost tripling from its low to its high) is related to Russia's counter-sanctions policy in February and March. Russia's counter-sanctions included both domestic and international measures. Domestically, Russia adopted counter-sanctions legislation, which required citizens to sell any foreign exchange profits they received from dealing with non-residents (see Fig. 3). The international measures have already been mentioned in Section 2.3.1. Under the combined influence of these internal and external factors, Russia stabilized the value of the ruble and prevented capital outflows. These factors included market expectations and the speculative and arbitrage mentality of investors, which ultimately drove the ruble's appreciation.

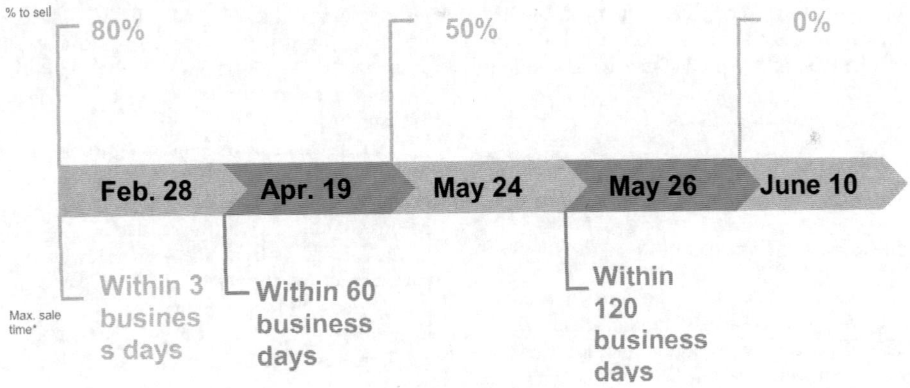

Fig. 3. The specific event requirements of the 'Citizens should sell any foreign exchange profits they received from dealing with non-residents' law

Source: ALRUD. (2022, July 21). Overview of Russian counter-sanctions measures. Retrieved from https://www.alrud.com. [10]

On the one hand, the volatility of the ruble exchange rate has created income instability for Coca-Cola HBC. This is because Coca-Cola HBC, a company headquartered in Switzerland, must convert its rouble earnings in Russia into euros. Therefore, the drastic fluctuation of the ruble poses a significant currency risk for Coca-Cola HBC. On the other hand, the Russian-Ukrainian conflict has a broad international impact, accompanied by sanctions and countermeasures. As a large multinational company, Coca-Cola HBC's ecosystem is closely linked to the policies of various countries. As a result, other countries' sanctions policies against Russia have a significant impact on Coca-Cola HBC's business.

2.3.2 Variations in the US dollar's value in foreign currencies and their effects on the Coca-Cola Company

In 2022, the dollar rose steadily, mainly due to the Federal Reserve's consistent interest rate hikes [2] and pessimistic market expectations. At one point, it reached its highest level in 20 years (please see Fig. 4).

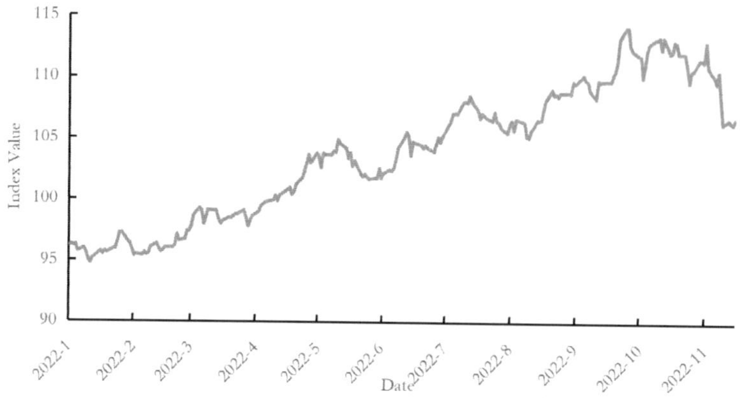

Fig. 4. ICE US Dollar Index 2022

Data source: Yahoo Finance
Photo credit: Original

As a large multinational corporation with operations around the world, the Coca-Cola Company has been significantly impacted by the strengthening of the U.S. dollar. Headquartered in the United States, the Coca-Cola Company's foreign currency earnings from its overseas operations depreciated significantly against the dollar. This created challenges in maintaining profitability. In addition, the Company has substantial holdings in cash and cash equivalents as well as other interests in domestic and foreign banks and financial organizations. Due to currency fluctuations and global events, the company also faced risks associated with the default or failure of counterparty financial institutions [11].

2.4 Strategies and their economic consequences

2.4.1 Coca-Cola HBC Strategy

First, on the business side, as a result of the United States' sanctions policy against Russia, many U.S. multinationals have announced the suspension of their operations in Russia. Coca-Cola's production and marketing are banned in Russia as a result of this. Coca-Cola HBC primarily manufactures, bottles and distributes The Coca-Cola Company's products in certain regions. The Coca-Cola Company's decision to halt operations in Russia has had a big effect on Coca-Cola HBC's activities there. In response, Coca-Cola HBC suspended Coca-Cola orders and canceled all investments in Russia. Coca-Cola HBC in Russia was transformed into a locally managed, self-sufficient company focused on the production, bottling and distribution of local brands. In accordance with the Board-approved treasury policy, Coca-Cola HBC stuck to its goal of hedging between 25% and 80% of rolling 12-month estimated transactional foreign currency exposure [6].

Second, in terms of the Russian ruble exchange rate, the strengthening of the ruble after March positively impacted Coca-Cola HBC's sales in Russia. Coca-Cola HBC's volume sales in Russia declined by 41%, mainly in the second half of the year. However, the strong performance of the ruble provided the company with unexpected currency gains. In addition, with the integration of Multon, Coca-Cola HBC's comparable EBIT in Russia in 2022 actually exceeded that of 2021 [6].

Table 1. Comparison of Coca-Cola HBC's other comprehensive income between 2022 and 2021

	2022			2021		
Item	Prior to taxes € million	Income tax € million	after taxes € million	Prior to taxes € million	Income tax € million	after taxes € million
The expenditure of hedging	(3.5)	-	(3.5)	(2.7)	-	(2.7)
Hedging for cash flow	34.6	(3.9)	30.7	69.5	(9.5)	60
Translation of foreign currencies (losses)/gains	(252.6)	-	(252.6)	73.6	-	73.6
Decrease in equity investment valuation at fair value via other comprehensive income	(0.1)	-	(0.1)	-	-	-
Realistic profits	26	1.8	27.8	16.1	(6.1)	10
Part of other total revenue	34.2	-	34.2	14.6	-	14.6

from investments made using the equity method						
Reclassification of the portion of other comprehensive income from equity method assets that resulted from a business combination to the income statement	145.2	-	145.2	-	-	-
Other comprehensive (loss)/income	(16.2)	(2.1)	(18.3)	171.1	(15.6)	155.5

Data source: Coca-Cola HBC. (2022). 2022 Integrated Annual Report. Retrieved from https://www.coca-colahellenic.com/en/investor-relations/2022-integrated-annual-report [6]

It is noteworthy that Coca-Cola HBC's foreign currency translation decreased significantly in 2022 compared to 2021(see Table.1). The amount of foreign currency translation losses reached 252.6 million euros in 2022, which is largely related to the Russian ruble.

To manage the significant volatility of the Russian ruble, Coca-Cola HBC reduced its current ruble-denominated borrowings in 2022 (from €57.2 million in 2021 to €2.2 million). This significantly reduced the liability risk associated with ruble volatility. In addition, repaying debt when the ruble exchange rate is low can be somewhat profitable.

After recovering from a low, the Russian ruble offered arbitrage opportunities during its appreciation. In response, Coca-Cola HBC took advantage of this by increasing its Russian ruble cash holdings for speculative purposes (from 9.5 million euros in 2021 to 96.4 million euros in 2022.

2.4.2 Coca-Cola Strategy

The Coca-Cola Company's net operating revenues from operations outside of the US reached $27.6 billion in 2022. It was necessary to convert these foreign currency-denominated revenues into US dollars. Nonetheless, the profitability of foreign currency revenues was significantly impacted by the rising of the US dollar. Of course, the weakness of some currencies would be offset by the strength of others, but there was still a significant risk. To manage this risk, The Coca-Cola Company lessened its net exposure to foreign exchange volatility by utilizing financial derivatives. The Company also maintained a prudent level of debt. The company increased its return on equity to shareholders by lowering its cost of capital through the utilization of debt financing [11].

Table 2. Financial statement of derivative instruments designated as hedging tools by The Coca-Cola Company (unit: USD)

Derivatives Designated as Hedging Instruments	Balance Sheet Location	31-Dec-22	31-Dec-21
Assets:			
Foreign currency contracts	Prepaid expenses and other current assets	126 $	151
Foreign currency contracts	Other noncurrent assets	13	27
Interest rate contracts	Prepaid expenses and other current assets	—	1
Interest rate contracts	Other noncurrent assets	—	282
Total assets		139 $	461
Liabilities:			
Foreign currency contracts	Accounts payable and accrued expenses	54 $	15
Foreign currency contracts	Other noncurrent liabilities	108	17
Commodity contracts	Accounts payable and accrued expenses	2	—
Interest rate contracts	Other noncurrent liabilities	1,676	14
Total liabilities		1,840 $	46

Data source: The Coca-Cola Company. (2022). 2022 Form 10-K Annual Report. Retrieved from https://investors.coca-colacompany.com/financial-information/financial-results [11]

From an asset perspective, Table 2 provides relevant information. Compared to 2021, the Coca-Cola Company's assets designated for hedge accounting in derivative instruments decreased by $322 million in 2022. The anticipation that the value of the US dollar will appreciate more, lowering the value of other currencies in relation to the US dollar, is the reason for a more thorough explanation. Coca-Cola reduced its prepaid expenses for foreign currency contracts to avoid paying more U.S. dollars after the currency devaluation. Therefore, Coca-Cola's reduction in derivative assets can be interpreted as an effort to minimize potential losses due to fluctuations in the U.S. dollar exchange rate.

From a liability perspective, the Coca-Cola Company's liabilities designated for hedge accounting in derivative instruments increased significantly by $1,794 million in 2022. This increase was most pronounced in the other long-term liability portion of interest rate contracts, which increased by $1,662 million. By fixing interest rates and increasing the amount of long-term debt in interest rate contracts, the Company is better able to manage the risk of future fluctuations in the U.S. dollar exchange rate and reduce future financing costs.

Furthermore, the Coca-Cola Company uses derivative financial instruments to lower its net exposure to changes in foreign exchange rates rather than for trading reasons. The Company keeps an eye on a combination of short-term and long-term debt, as well as debt with fixed and variable rates. Additionally, the Company manages its exposure to interest rate changes by periodically entering into interest rate swap agreements. The Coca-Cola Company had $11.37 billion in notional value of foreign exchange derivatives as of December 31, 2022 [11].

3 Optimization

In the above text, a common risk point for both multinational companies is the significant fluctuation of foreign currency revenues from overseas operations when converted into their domestic currency. As a result, even if there are no significant changes in the supply and demand for a product in a particular overseas region, i.e. the foreign currency value of the product remains relatively stable, the conversion into the domestic currency can still result in significant fluctuations.

The basic process of a commodity swap is as follows [12]. Suppose a commodity producer sells product X. However, due to significant fluctuations in the price of product X, the producer's profits are unstable. Therefore, the producer finds a counterparty to enter into a commodity swap. The specific operation involves the producer exchanging the sales revenue received during the contract period with the counterparty at an average price agreed in the contract. This serves to hedge the risk

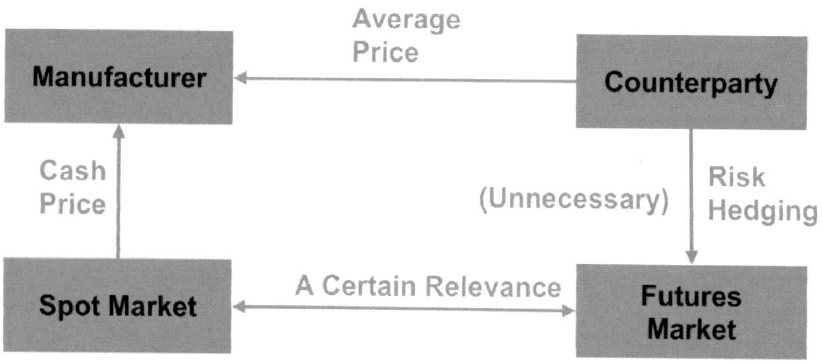

Fig. 5. Basic process of commodity swapping

Photo credit: Original

In the multinational case discussed above, the paper's strategy involves incorporating foreign exchange forwards into commodity swaps to lock in profits. The specific operation is as follows. Suppose the commodity producer can consistently generate a value of 1000 in foreign currency sales in the region before a major event occurs. This foreign currency revenue of 1000 can be exchanged for 1000X dollars at the launch of the period's exchange rate. After the major event, on the one hand, the producer's foreign currency income during this period is 1000-Y (mainly a negative impact). This income is then converted into $(1000 - Y) * (X - Z)$ dollars at the currency rate at the conclusion of the duration (this project refers to the actual currency rate at the conclusion of the duration, represented in calculations as the forward rate). Both $1000 - Y$ and $(1000 - Y) * (X - Z)$ dollars are the company's expected revenues. Next, a counterparty is found to agree on an average price. (For example, $\frac{[(1000-Y)+1000]}{2} * \frac{(X-Z)+X}{2}$) The specific strategy for setting the average price is determined by the particular event, company, and commodity using statistical methods. This article provides only the direction of the strategy and does not perform a detailed price analysis.

4 Conclusion

This paper examines two global events. The first event is the outbreak of the Russian-Ukrainian war in 2022. The international community placed sanctions on Russia, and Russia responded with its own penalties. This significantly affected the exchange rate of the ruble. In response, Coca-Cola HBC changed the content of its business in Russia and hedged its risk by reducing its rouble-denominated liabilities and increasing its rouble-denominated cash and cash equivalents. The second event was the rise in the U.S. dollar exchange rate in 2022 due to the Federal Reserve's continuous interest rate hikes to combat hyperinflation, as well as a variety of global events. This has had a significant impact on The Coca-Cola Company's profitability due to the large amount of foreign currency revenue it generates. As a result, the Coca-Cola Company reduced its assets designated as hedging derivatives and significantly increased its liabilities designated as hedging derivatives to hedge against foreign currency fluctuations. Finally, the research proposes an optimized hedging strategy using commodity swap strategies in managing risk exposure. This optimized strategy, based on the standard commodity swap, incorporates foreign exchange factors, thus adding two variables. This approach can effectively reduce potential losses and foreign exchange fluctuation risks arising from global events in business operations.

This paper only discusses the general direction of using commodity swaps for risk hedging. In the future, models of commodity swaps may be developed based on specific cases in conjunction with econometrics.

References

1. J. Xu, K. Khan, & Y. Cao. Conflict and exchange rate valuation: Evidence from the Russia-Ukraine conflict. Heliyon, 9, e16527 (2023).
2. B. Martucci, Fed's interest rate hikes in 2022 & 2023 – What the July hike means for you. https://www.moneycrashers.com
3. P. Havlik. Economic consequences of the ukraine conflict. Wiiw Policy Notes (2014).
4. U.S. Department of the Treasury, U.S. Treasury announces unprecedented & expansive sanctions against Russia, imposing swift and severe economic costs. https://home.treasury.gov/news/press-releases/jy0608
5. Q. Chen, & Y. Wang. From the Russo-Ukrainian Conflict to Financial War and Its Risk Implications. FFD, 124 (2022).
6. Coca-Cola HBC, 2022 Integrated Annual Report. https://www.coca-colahellenic.com
7. E. Orhan. The effects of the Russia-Ukraine war on global trade. JITLL, 8(1), 141-146 (2022).
8. Reuters, Putin says Russian gas must be paid in roubles from Friday. https://www.reuters.com/business/energy/
9. R. J. Anderson. Europe's Dependence on Russian Natural Gas: Perspectives and Recommendations for a Long-term Strategy (Vol. 42). (George C. Marshall European Center for Security Studies, 2008).
10. Alrud. Overview of Russian counter-sanctions measures. (2022).
11. The Coca-Cola Company, 2022 Form 10-K Annual Report. https://investors.coca-colacompany.com
12. Z Lou. Research on derivatives promoting the innovation of commodity financial services (Master's thesis, Zhejiang University) (2021).

The Improvement Path for Credit ABS of Commercial Banks—A Case Study of China Construction Bank

Zhiming Qu[1,*]

[1]Finance,School of Business, East China University of Political Science and Law, Shanghai, 201620, China

Abstract. This article focuses on the current state of asset securitization in China Construction Bank (CCB). It conducts an in-depth analysis of two areas, namely non-performing asset securitization and green asset securitization, and explores suitable improvement approaches for these two domains. The analysis analyzed the basic information of China Construction Bank's asset securitization, including market share and other relevant factors, and takes into account the domestic and international development status and historical path, and incorporates mainstream views in academia to propose practical and significant solutions.For non-performing asset securitization, the main improvements are targeted towards the credit enhancement system and methods. The suggested approaches include the introduction of insurance and risk diversification mechanisms, as well as market adjustments to enhance the credit enhancement capabilities of non-performing asset securitization.Regarding green asset securitization, the focus lies on the pricing system as the domestic market is still in its early stages of development. The suggested methods involve improving the foundation, establishing standards, and enhancing awareness.

1 Introduction

1.1 Research background

Since 2012, the revival of credit Asset-Backed Securities (ABS) has played a significant role in China's commercial banking sector. Over the past eleven years, ABS has adhered to asset credit as its core, entering a phase of high-quality ABS, maintaining "zero defaults" and "zero risk events." It has continued to innovate, promoting product diversification in the bond market, and its role in serving the real economy and preventing and resolving financial risks has become increasingly prominent. In the field of commercial banking, green asset securitization has received attention and continues to develop. In contrast, non-performing asset securitization remains in a stable growth state as an important means for banks to handle non-performing assets.

ABS plays a crucial role in commercial banks by diversifying their funding sources. By packaging credit assets into securitized products, commercial banks can transform them into tradable assets, thus gaining access to a wider range of funding sources. This diversified financing method helps lower commercial banks' funding costs and enhances their resilience to risks, as shown in Figure 1.

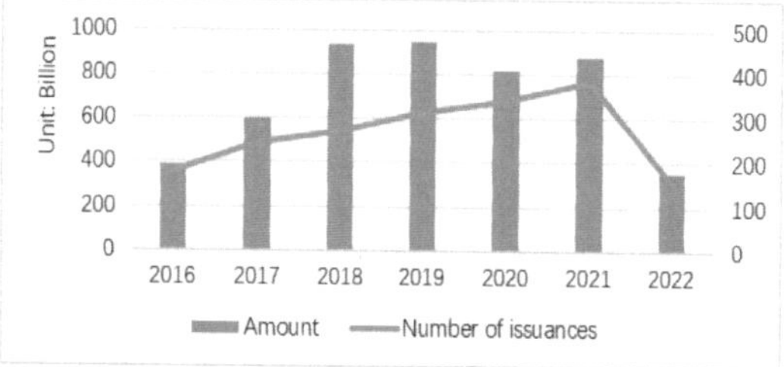

Fig 1. Amount and number of credit ABS issuances (Photo credit: Origin)

Furthermore, ABS provides commercial banks with an effective tool for managing non-performing assets. Non-performing asset securitization, as a vital approach, helps commercial banks transfer non-performing assets off their books, reducing the burden of such assets and improving asset quality. By packaging non-performing assets into securitized products, commercial banks can sell them to other investors, facilitating the swift clearance of assets and the retrieval of funds, thereby enhancing the banks' asset efficiency.

Additionally, ABS plays a significant role in the field of green finance, especially in green asset securitization. With the growing global emphasis on environmental protection, commercial banks increasingly focus on developing green finance. Commercial banks can attract more social capital to support environmental projects and drive sustainable development by packaging green assets into securitized products. This enhances the banks' social image and reputation and brings new business opportunities and profit potential.

* Corresponding author: 210529010152@ecupl.edu.cn

In summary, ABS has multiple roles in the commercial banking sector. It diversifies funding sources, helps commercial banks reduce financing costs, and enhances risk resilience. ABS also provides an effective tool for managing non-performing assets, alleviating the burden of such assets, and improving asset quality. Furthermore, ABS's development in the field of green finance presents new opportunities for commercial banks. As ABS continues to innovate and evolve, its role in serving the real economy and preventing and resolving financial risks will become increasingly prominent, providing robust support for the sustainable development of commercial banks.

1.2 Literature review

Tao Jiacheng and others conducted a study based on data from 42 listed banks in China and concluded that asset securitization can enhance banks' profitability. They found that this can be achieved by increasing the proportion of non-interest income in the profit structure, reducing risk exposure, and alleviating capital constraints [1]. Similar conclusions were drawn by Senfeng Gou using an improved DuPont analysis method, and it was observed that the benefits of asset securitization are even greater for larger commercial banks or those with more active asset securitization activities [2,3]. Zhang Jianghong provided a detailed explanation of the advantages of non-performing asset securitization, highlighting how this measure enables commercial banks to effectively address the negative impact and issues caused by non-performing assets on the entire socio-economic system, thus improving commercial banks' liquidity and capital adequacy [4]. Song Xiaoling and others explored the positive impact of green credit ABS on bank profitability based on the Equator Principles. However, it should be noted that domestic green credit ABS is still in its developmental stage and differs from more mature systems abroad, necessitating continued efforts towards its vigorous development.

1.3 Research gap

Previous research has primarily focused on the overall theoretical benefits of asset securitization, with limited quantitative analysis on specific projects such as non-performing and green asset securitization. This is mainly because these two types of ABS (Asset-Backed Securities) are still in the developmental stage in China. Moreover, several empirical analyses have indicated that the current credit asset securitization of non-performing and green assets may somewhat hinder the profitability of listed commercial banks.

This paper aims to utilize existing data and theories, taking China Construction Bank, which has the largest volume of ABS in the domestic market, as an example. The objective is to analyze the potential benefits of non-performing assets and green asset credit ABS on the profitability of commercial banks. Furthermore, further research and promotion of credit asset securitization in these two areas are crucial for fostering financial market stability and sustainable development.

1.4 Research framework

Firstly, non-performing asset securitization can effectively transfer and diversify the risks associated with non-performing assets, thereby enhancing commercial banks' asset quality and overall risk management capabilities. Packaging non-performing assets into securitized products makes it possible to attract more investors, thereby increasing liquidity and market activity. Additionally, non-performing asset securitization can alleviate capital constraints for commercial banks, releasing capital supply and providing more lending and investment opportunities, consequently promoting profitability.

Secondly, green asset securitization is important as an emerging financial instrument in promoting sustainable development and environmental protection. Packaging green credits into securitized products can attract more funds to flow into green industries and projects, facilitating the growth of the green economy. Compared to traditional credit models, green asset securitization offers higher flexibility and liquidity, providing commercial banks more opportunities to participate in the green finance market, expand their business scope, and enhance profitability.

2 Case description

China Construction Bank, one of the major commercial banks in China, has significant experience and market share in credit asset securitization. The bank actively participates in credit asset securitization, packaging credit assets into securities products and issuing them to investors, thereby achieving risk transfer and fund retrieval. China Construction Bank has a wide range of product lines in credit asset securitization, covering various loans and debt assets.

Non-performing asset securitization involves transforming non-performing assets, such as non-performing loans, of banks or other financial institutions into securities products to attract investors and diversify risks. In China, the non-performing asset securitization market is still developing but has made certain progress. China Construction Bank ranks first in both the total amount and the number of issuances of Non-Performing Asset Credit Asset-Backed Securities (ABS). Wang supports the promotion of sustainable development through the securitization of non-performing assets in China, considering it as one of the important issues currently faced by the academic community and regulatory authorities. As one of the significant domestic issuers of non-performing asset securitization, China Construction Bank actively promotes the development of non-performing asset securitization business to alleviate the pressure of non-performing assets on the bank.

With its leading position in the market, China Construction Bank plays a crucial role in securitizing non-performing assets. By converting non-performing assets into tradable securities, the bank can attract investors and effectively manage and mitigate the risks associated with these assets. This contributes to the bank's overall risk management strategy and helps to reduce the impact of non-performing assets on its balance sheet, as shown in Figure 2.

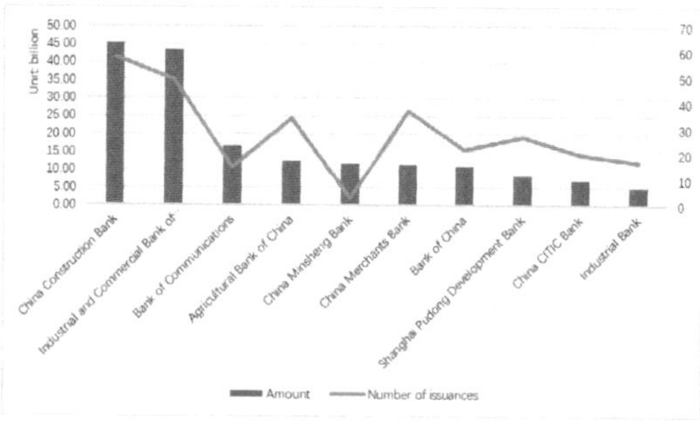

Fig 2. Top Ten Issuers of Non-Performing Asset Credit ABS (Photo credit: Origin)

Green credit securitization refers to packaging green loans or debt assets related to environmental protection and sustainable development into securities products for issuance. Amit also argues that commercial banks can enhance profitability and promote diversified operations by choosing to securitize green assets [5,6]. In China, green finance and credit securitization receive government support and promotion. China Construction Bank ranked second among the top six banks in terms of green loan balance in 2022. The bank actively responds to national policies and promotes the development of green loan securitization business. By issuing green loan securitization products, China Construction Bank can attract more funds to green industries and projects, facilitating sustainable development and environmental protection.

China Construction Bank's proactive efforts and achievements in green finance are evident. As a significant financial institution, China Construction Bank responds to national policies and strives to promote green loan securitization business development, as shown in Figure.

Overall, China Construction Bank actively participates and plays an important role in credit asset securitization, non-performing asset securitization, and green credit securitization. These securitization businesses help improve the bank's asset quality, risk management capabilities, and profitability while promoting the development of the financial market and achieving sustainable economic growth.

3 Analysis on the problems

3.1 Problem 1. non-performing asset securitization

The non-performing loan (NPL) balance of China Construction Bank is experiencing stable growth. This stable increase in NPL balance may challenge the bank's risk-bearing capacity. Through non-performing asset securitization, China Construction Bank can transfer the NPLs to other investors, achieving risk diversification and assisting in capital retrieval and asset value realization. By packaging the NPLs into securitized products and selling them to investors, China Construction Bank can swiftly recover funds from a portion or the entirety of the NPLs, thereby enhancing the capital return rate and capital adequacy ratio.

In non-performing asset securitization, the credit enhancement theory of asset securitization plays a crucial role. How to implement credit enhancement for non-performing assets determines whether banks can attract funds from institutional investors and capital markets, provide new funding sources, and increase the bank's financing channels and fund flexibility.

Internal Enhancement: Internal enhancement refers to classifying different assets within the structure of non-performing asset securitization to achieve credit enhancement for investors. By dividing non-performing assets into different priority levels of securities, such as senior, subordinated, subordinated, subordinated, and underlying securities, internal enhancement ensures that senior securities have priority repayment rights while subordinated and underlying securities bear higher risks.

External Enhancement: External enhancement refers to providing additional credit enhancement protection by introducing third-party guarantors or credit enhancement institutions. In this case, the issuer of non-performing asset securitization purchases additional guarantees or credit enhancements to enhance the credit quality of the securitized products and boost investor confidence. These guarantors or credit enhancement institutions typically have higher credit ratings and stronger repayment abilities, thereby providing a higher level of credit enhancement.

Both internal and external enhancements aim to improve the credit quality of non-performing asset securitization products, attract more investor participation, and reduce overall risk levels.

In domestic non-performing asset securitization, credit enhancement measures are primarily focused on the senior/subordinated structure. Cao Mengqiao also acknowledges that one of the important ways to enhance non-performing asset securitization in Chinese commercial banks is through improving credit enhancement measures [7]. This approach somewhat simplifies the credit enhancement process but may result in lower market liquidity for the subordinated securities. Due to the higher risk associated with subordinated securities, fewer investors may be willing to purchase them, thus limiting their marketability. Additionally, this concentration of risk in subordinated securities can be a concern. If the subordinated securities face a higher risk of default, it could have negative implications for the entire securitization product.

3.2 Problem 2. green asset securitization

The core advantage of green asset securitization lies in its ability to help China Construction Bank optimize its balance sheet and risk management. Liu analyzed the transformative impact of asset securitization on the business of commercial banks from the perspective of asset securitization [8]. By packaging green credit assets into securitized products, Construction Bank can transfer them off its balance sheet, reducing its exposure to risks associated with green credit. Xia Yong et al. analyzed the green social reputation of banks and concluded that commercial banks can enhance their green reputation through the development of green credit [9]. Fu further found that this impact is particularly significant for large banks operating within the context of public ownership in China [10]. In this article, China Construction Bank fulfills these prerequisites. By actively participating in the green asset securitization market, Construction Bank can expand its business scale and market share in green finance, enhancing its brand image and reputation. It also enables construction banks to obtain lower financing costs, as investors generally perceive green projects to have lower risks and better long-term returns. Moreover, green attributes can lead to lower financing costs for credit-based assets in the same category, as shown in Figure 3.

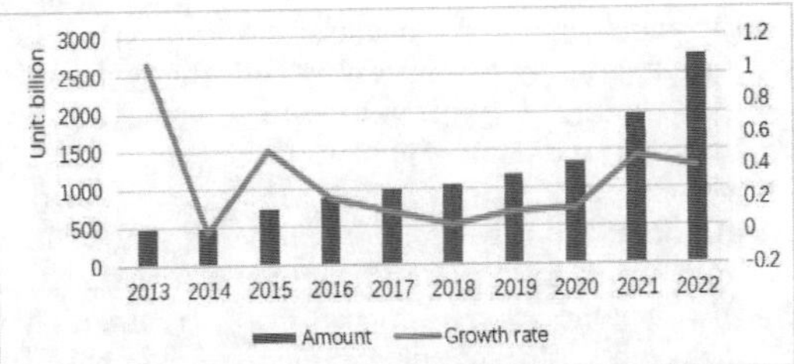

Fig 3. Green credit balance and growth rate of China Construction Bank
(Photo credit: Origin)

The domestic green credit asset securitization started relatively late and is still in development, leaving room for improvement in several aspects. In terms of pricing green credit asset-backed securities (ABS), the domestic market mostly relies on static cash flow discounting and static spread methods, lacking a clear and unified pricing approach. Prices are typically determined through issuance inquiries. In contrast, foreign markets tend to favor option-adjusted spread (OAS) methodology, incorporating the possibilities of early exercise and prepayment into the pricing model to achieve fairer pricing.

The static cash flow discounting method discounts future cash flows based on projections but fails to account for green credit assets' unique attributes and risk factors. The static spread method relies on the spread levels of similar securities in the market, but it does not adequately reflect the additional value and environmental impact of green credit assets.

In comparison, the OAS methodology comprehensively considers the characteristics of green credit assets. Incorporating the possibilities of early exercise and prepayment into the pricing model ensures a more equitable pricing approach. The OAS methodology better captures the flexibility and potential future returns of green credit assets, providing a more accurate pricing benchmark.

Therefore, there is room for improvement in pricing within the domestic green credit asset securitization market. Establishing a clear and unified pricing approach is necessary, drawing on foreign practices and experiences and introducing pricing models that comprehensively consider factors such as the OAS methodology. This will enhance transparency, fairness, and market participants' confidence in green credit asset securitization, further promoting the development of green finance and the market's maturity.

The lack of consideration for green factors in the pricing system is evident. The novelty of green asset securitization lies in its green value, which is not reflected in the existing pricing models. It still follows the same pricing approach as ordinary asset-backed securities. This can be observed in two aspects:

Firstly, the reference benchmark for issuance prices continues to be the ordinary government bond interest rate. However, in the international development of green finance, many countries have taken measures to establish more applicable green bond benchmark interest rates. There are two specific models. One is France's "online point selection" approach, which aims to establish a green benchmark government bond comparable to the pricing benchmark of ordinary government bonds. The second model, represented by Germany, constructs a green government bond yield curve with slightly lower yields compared to ordinary government bonds. In contrast, China has not yet formed any green bond interest rate benchmarks, and the green value cannot be reflected, which will have a certain impact on the financing effectiveness of green projects.

Secondly, the green features are not reflected in the credit rating of green asset-backed securities. Unlike ordinary asset-backed securities, green asset securitization has additional environmental benefits and risks. There are strict restrictions on the approval and use of green projects. If there are violations in fund utilization or severe environmental pollution, they will face severe penalties from relevant regulatory authorities, undoubtedly increasing credit risks. In 2020, China issued the "Green Bond Credit Rating Guidelines (Trial)" for the first time, proposing the consideration of ESG factors in credit ratings. However, this program is currently being tested in the green finance reform and innovation pilot zones and has not been widely promoted.

4 Suggestions

4.1 Solution to credit enhancement in commercial bank's non-performing asset securitization

Chen pointed out that the key future reform and development direction for non-performing asset securitization in China is optimizing the structure of non-performing asset securitization products [11]. This not only helps to reduce issuance costs but also enhances market transparency. Credit enhancement in the securitization of non-performing assets by commercial banks can be improved and refined through several methods.

The first one is diversified credit enhancement structures. Introduce more layers of credit enhancement structures, such as super senior, senior, subordinated tranches, and other derivative instruments, to increase the credit rating of the securities and reduce risks. This can attract more investors and enhance the market value of the securities.

The introduction of some helpful mechanisms, such as insurance mechanisms, can also help. Commercial banks can consider introducing insurance mechanisms to enhance credit enhancement. By purchasing credit insurance or utilizing guarantees from insurance institutions, the credit rating of the securities can be improved, providing stronger protection for investors. Another one is to Establish risk diversification mechanisms. Commercial banks can diversify their non-performing asset portfolios by combining different types of non-performing assets. This helps to reduce overall risk and increase the credit rating of the securities, thereby boosting investor confidence. By engaging third-party rating agencies, commercial banks can engage independent third-party rating agencies to assess and rate the non-performing assets, increasing the credibility and impartiality of the credit ratings. Liu and Kang believe that this is due to the improvement of market support measures [12].

Moreover, there are some things the bank and the market should pay attention to. Information disclosure for non-performing asset-backed securities should be strengthened, providing comprehensive, accurate, and transparent information to increase investor trust. They can strengthen risk management and monitoring as well. They should establish robust risk management systems to monitor the risk profile of non-performing asset-backed securities and implement appropriate risk control measures to ensure the sustainability and effectiveness of credit enhancement.

By implementing these improvement and refinement methods, commercial banks can further enhance the credit enhancement of non-performing asset securitization, mitigate risks, increase investor confidence, and better meet market demands.

4.2 Solution to pricing issues in commercial bank's green asset securitization

Taking into account the suggestions proposed by Yao and the current early stage of the development of green asset securitization in Chinese commercial banks, the following are some suggestions and improvement measures for addressing pricing issues in green asset securitization [13].

Establishing a green asset pricing model is an apparent way to approve green asset securitization. Commercial banks can develop a pricing model specifically for green assets, taking into account their characteristics and risk factors to more accurately determine the pricing of securities. Such a model can assess and price green assets based on environmental impact, sustainability, market demand, and future cash flows.

Another solution is enhancing data collection and analysis of green assets. Commercial banks can strengthen their capabilities in collecting and analyzing data related to green assets. By establishing comprehensive green asset databases that include environmental data, energy efficiency data, financial data of green projects, etc., it is better to assess the value and risks of green assets and provide a more reliable pricing basis.

Considering market demand and investor preferences, Commercial banks should consider the changing market demand and investor preferences during the pricing process. As the market for green asset securitization is relatively new, investors may have different perceptions and preferences regarding its risks and returns. Therefore, commercial banks should closely monitor market trends, and investor needs to adjust pricing strategies to attract a wider range of investors.

Commercial banks can also seek input from external rating agencies. They collaborate with independent external rating agencies to obtain their pricing recommendations and opinions on green asset securitization products. This can provide more objective and independent perspectives, thereby improving the accuracy and credibility of pricing.

It is also important to improve the accuracy of risk pricing simultaneously. Commercial banks should fully consider the risk characteristics of green assets and employ appropriate risk pricing methods during the pricing process. This includes considering environmental risks, legal and regulatory risks, technological risks, etc., to ensure that the pricing aligns with the level of risks involved.

By implementing these improvement measures, commercial banks can enhance pricing accuracy in green asset securitization, mitigate risks, and attract more investors to participate in the green finance market.

5 Conclusion

By analyzing the current situation of non-performing asset securitization and green asset securitization in China Construction Bank (CCB), the following conclusions can be drawn:

Firstly, some areas can be improved regarding non-performing asset securitization in CCB. One of the key issues is optimizing the internal structure of credit enhancement. Taking into account the mainstream methods of credit enhancement and structural improvement both domestically and internationally, as well as CCB's position as one of the six largest banks in China and the largest issuer of non-performing asset securitization, recommendations for improvement can be proposed.

Secondly, for the development stage of green asset securitization in domestic commercial banks, CCB can refer to the well-established asset securitization systems in foreign countries. An effective improvement approach for CCB would be to enhance the pricing system.

This article focuses on two specific areas within CCB's asset securitization. By optimizing the securitization process, CCB can enhance operational efficiency, reduce risk exposure, and promote innovation and diversified development. Leading the development of non-performing asset securitization and green asset securitization in domestic commercial banks, non-performing asset securitization helps banks clean up their non-performing assets, improve asset quality, enhance profitability, and strengthen risk management capabilities. Green asset securitization facilitates commercial banks' participation in the green finance market, enabling them to engage in green lending and investments, expand their business scope, and enhance market competitiveness. Optimizing the securitization process elevates the industry's professional standards and risk management capabilities, fostering sustainable development.

This article lacks the use of primary data, and the availability of specific data on CCB's securitization products is limited. Therefore, the characteristics of the two types of products can only be summarized in a general manner, which may result in less precise features. In the future, more detailed and accurate data can be obtained through surveys and interviews to enhance the analysis.

References

1. J. C. Tao, S. Y. Zhang. Market Modern, (19): 130-133 (2023).
2. L. Gou. Shanxi Univer of Finance and Economics, (2023)
3. J. H. Zhang. Times Finance, (01): 76-78+95 (2023)
4. X. Song, X. Deng & R. Wu. International Journal of Financial Studies (2019)
5. Y. Wang. International Journal of Social Sciences and Economic Management, **3** (4): 20-29 (2022)
6. A. Ghosh. Journal of Financial Innovation in Banking, 2(1):1-28 (2018)
7. M. Q. Cao. Small and Medium-sized Enterprise Management and Technology (Mid-monthly), **11**, 85-87 (2021)
8. Z. Y. Liu. China Management Informatization, **25**(2), 144-146 (2022)
9. Research Group of the Shizuishan City Center Branch of the People's Bank of China. Financial Development Review, (07), 32-44 (2022)
10. X. Y. Fu. Investment and Entrepreneurship, **33**(04), 215-219 (2022)
11. S. X. Chen. China Business Review, (20), 89-91 (2021)
12. T. Liu, K. Kang. Journal of Tianjin Normal University (Social Sciences), (04), 94-100 (2022)
13. Y. Yao. [Master's thesis]. Anhui University of Finance and Economics (2021)

Comparative Analysis of S&P 500 and NASDAQ: A Machine Learning Approach to Understanding Differential Market Sensitivity and Growth Stocks

Cheng Lin[1,*]

[1]School of Finance, Zhejiang University of Finance & Economics, Hangzhou, 310018, China

Abstract. The purpose of this study is to gain a deeper understanding of the dynamics and market sensitivity of technology stocks by constructing and predicting random stock portfolios in the S&P500 and NASDAQ indices using machine learning models. The article employs a rolling time window cross-validation approach to train the models, ensuring optimization based on continuously updated data. By comparing the predicted results with actual outcomes, the article analyze whether technology stocks possess characteristics of growth stocks and how key events impact the price fluctuations of technology stocks. The results also indicate the need to dynamically adjust the learning rate based on market characteristics, volatility, trends, and other factors to enhance the adaptability of the machine learning models in different conditions and better uncover the latent information within diverse data samples. Overall, the findings of this study underscore the importance of dynamically adjusting the learning rate of machine learning models under various market conditions, providing a fresh perspective for financial application research. Future research can further explore and develop cutting-edge methods related to optimizing the learning rate of models, such as adaptive learning rates, multi-task learning, and incremental learning, to more effectively cope with different market situations and similar issues in other fields.

1 Introduction

With the rapid development of financial markets, the analysis and prediction of stock markets have become hot topics of research. In particular, the stocks of technology and growth companies, such as many companies listed on NASDAQ, have attracted widespread attention. Therefore, understanding the dynamics, market sensitivity of these technology stocks, and their differences with other standard stocks, as well as their sensitivity to different market conditions, is crucial [1].

Previous and current research has extensively used various machine learning methods to predict and analyze stock markets. For example, some studies have used neural networks, decision trees, and random forests to predict changes in stock prices or indices [2]. In previous research, it observed that market fluctuations can affect the learning rate of machine learning models. This suggests that different markets may require different learning rates to optimize model performance [3].

Influenced by many factors, the market sensitivity shows a strong temporal change. The learning results of many machine learning models have large deviation and low accuracy, which is caused by the inherent limitations of the corresponding methods to accurately outline the dynamic characteristics of financial market trends [4]. To address this issue, this paper considers adopting validation methods more suited to the characteristics of time series data. Rolling Time Window Cross-Validation is an effective method that accommodates the sequential and dependent nature of time series [5]. In this approach, training sets are adjusted through continuously moving time windows, ensuring that models are always predicated on the most current data.

The aim of this study is to construct and predict random stock portfolios from the S&P 500 and NASDAQ indices using machine learning models, in order to understand the dynamics and market sensitivity of technology stocks, as well as the intrinsic relationship between market sensitivity and the learning rate of machine learning models [6, 7]. Specifically, it employed a walking-forward machine learning model to build and predict investment portfolios randomly selected from the S&P 500 and NASDAQ indices, and hoped to analyze whether technology stocks conform to the characteristics of growth stocks by comparing predicted results with actual results during three significant moments that greatly affected technology stocks. Additionally, it explored how these critical events affected the price fluctuations of technology stocks, the distinct features of technology stocks and standard stocks in prediction, and whether there exists a particular requirement for market sensitivity to the learning rate of machine learning models. It hopes to reveal insights that are beneficial for future research.

* Corresponding author: cheng_lin@zufe.edu.cn

Many machine learning methods in financial applications face the problem of overfitting or underfitting [8]. This is often due to the improper adjustment of the model's learning rate. Therefore, it is necessary to incorporate hyperparameter optimization techniques into the model [7, 9]. While some advanced methods, such as adaptive learning rates and incremental learning, have been proposed to address this issue, how to dynamically adjust for different market conditions remains a challenge [10, 11].

This research conclusion further confirms the viewpoint that it is necessary to dynamically adjust the learning rate according to the characteristics, volatility, trends, and other factors of the market for different market sensitivities. This not only improves the model's adaptive ability under different conditions, but also better explores the underlying patterns of different data samples. Therefore, when training machine learning models, it is necessary to dynamically adjust the learning rate α according to the specific characteristics of different markets to ensure the effectiveness of the model in application. In addition, this study can also promote the development of the machine learning field by demonstrating its effectiveness in financial applications and improving its generalization performance through dynamic adjustment of the learning rate.

2. Methodology

2.1 Data preprocessing

This study first ensured reproducibility of results by setting a random seed, and generated a sample of 50 assets comprising components of both the S&P 500 and NASDAQ 100 indices.

The data collection and processing procedure involved the following steps:

1. Obtaining the composition lists of the S&P 500 and NASDAQ 100 from Wikipedia, and randomly selecting a subset as the sample.
2. Utilizing the yfinance library to download price data for the chosen stocks, covering a time span from January 1st, 2015 to June 30th, 2023.
3. Conducting data cleaning and processing, including calculation of daily returns, and employing box plot methods to handle outlier values, thus ensuring data quality and accuracy.
4. Computing and resampling 20-day returns and daily returns.

Notably, despite successfully downloading data for 50 randomly selected stocks, there were instances of failed downloads due to the time frame within the sample; some stocks were either not listed or had been suspended or delisted.

These processed data form a crucial foundation for the subsequent model construction and portfolio building. This data report provides a clear overview of the data collection, downloading, and processing procedures, laying the groundwork for further research.

2.2 Model establishment and evaluation

The establishment and optimization of the model is a key step in this study. It adopted the Walking Forward Machine Learning method and used Ridge regression model for prediction. The following will detail the process of model establishment and the process of model hyperparameter optimization and evaluation.

2.2.1 Model establishment

This paper first defines a time sliding window method to control the size of the training set. By setting variable sliding window sizes, it can adjust the minimum time period of the training set to ensure that the model has sufficient data for training. Next, it selected a set of hyperparameters (alpha_values) as tuning parameters for the Ridge regression model. These hyperparameters will be adjusted in the subsequent model optimization process. It uses the train_and_evaluate_model function to implement model training and evaluation. The function accepts the data of training set and testing set as inputs, and trains the model by iterating over different alpha values. In each time sliding window, it takes one stock as the target variable (y) and use the returns of other stocks as feature variables (x) to train the model. By adjusting the hyperparameter alpha, it obtained the optimal model with the smallest mean squared error (MSE).

2.2.2 Hyperparameter optimization

This paper optimizes the model by traversing through different training set sizes. For each training set size, it trained the model using the train_and_evaluate_model function and selected the best alpha with the minimum MSE. For each training set size, it calculated the prediction results of the model, and calculated the MSE and the MAE of the prediction results. By comparing the MSE with different alpha values, it chose the best alpha with the minimum MSE as the hyperparameter of the model. At the same time, it also used the MSE and the MAE as evaluation indicators to evaluate the performance of the model and observe the training process of the model by drawing the learning curve.

2.2.3 Model evaluation

This paper used the MSE as a metric to evaluate the model performance. MSE measures the average squared error between the predicted and actual values of the model and can reflect the accuracy and accuracy of the model. Furthermore, it can use other evaluation metrics such as MAE to further evaluate the model performance. MAE measures the mean absolute error between the model predicted and actual values and can provide a more comprehensive assessment of the model error.

Through the above modeling and optimization process, it obtained a predictive model based on S&P500 data, and selected the optimal model through hyperparameter tuning and evaluation metrics. This model can be used to predict stock returns and provide important references for investment decisions.

2.2.4 Portfolio construction

Based on the predictive results of the model, it can construct investment portfolios. The specific steps include the following:

Using CVXPY library for portfolio optimization: it utilizes predicted stock returns and covariance matrix to optimize investment portfolios. By minimizing the volatility of portfolios and satisfying some constraint conditions such as weight sum of 1 and non-negative weights, it can obtain the optimal weight for investment portfolios.

Portfolio backtesting: Apply each time window's portfolio weight to each stock's daily return rate to calculate the cumulative return of the portfolio. At the same time, this paper also compares it with the cumulative return of a benchmark index (such as SPY) to evaluate the performance of the portfolio. Through the above investment portfolio construction process, it can make effective investment decisions based on the predictive results of the model and evaluate the return of investment portfolios.

3 Data analysis

3.1 MSE & MAE in the process modelling evaluation

In the modeling of the S&P 500 index, a comparison between MSE and MAE indicates that after 200 samples, the reduction in MAE becomes minimal, suggesting limited benefits from additional data in terms of decreasing the mean absolute error (see Figure 1). The stability observed in MSE across the sample range may suggest sensitivity to specific patterns or noise within the data, or insufficient information in the training data for further error reduction. Future research should explore strategies to mitigate the impact of noise on the model. The current model's performance appears to have reached a threshold, indicating a need to consider model improvements or alternative approaches for enhancing predictive accuracy.

This phenomenon also applies to return forecasts for the NASDAQ index. Does this indicate that for this method, a sample size of 200 is a limit? To further increase accuracy, this paper recommends expanding the time window.

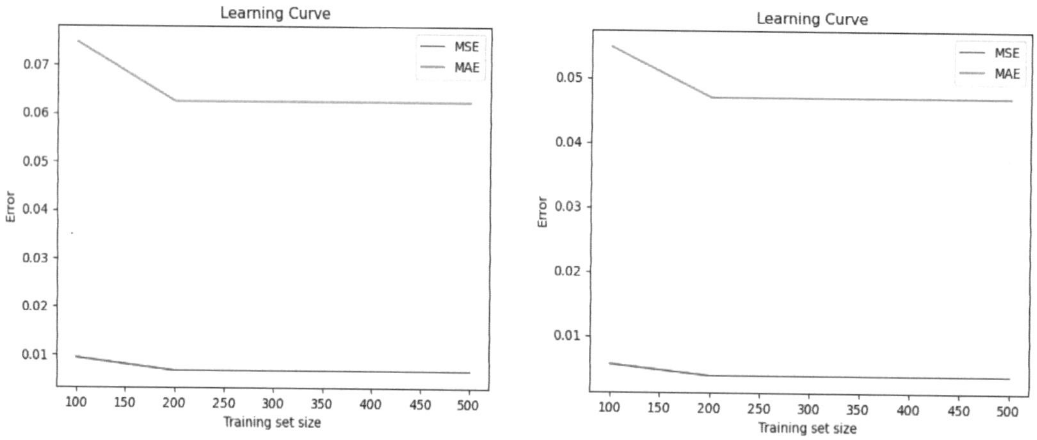

(a) S&P 500 (b) NASDAQ

Fig. 1. The MSE & MAE learning curve (Photo/Picture credit: Original).

Simultaneously, through different alpha values, it can get the best alpha values adapted to the corresponding data set to represent the best model parameters for model training. It has derived different ridge alpha values for the two indices: 0.01 for the S&P 500 and 1 for NASDAQ. The alpha parameter, also known as the regularization parameter, controls the degree of constraint on the model's weights. Different alpha values affect how closely the model fits the data and its ability to generalize to new data. Thus, it can speculate that NASDAQ stocks, being more heavily weighted towards technology stocks with potentially greater price volatility, require a larger alpha. In contrast, the S&P 500, which includes a broader range of industries, may be relatively more stable and thus require a smaller alpha. This indirectly supports the theory mentioned at the beginning.

3.2 S&P 500 and NASDAQ prediction vs returns display

This paper has developed a code to dynamically display a comparative trend graph of actual versus predicted results for a randomly selected stock from the pool of 50. This chart presents the actual and predicted returns of a particular stock over time. The solid blue line represents the actual returns, while the orange dashed line represents the predicted returns. Here is an analysis of the chart:

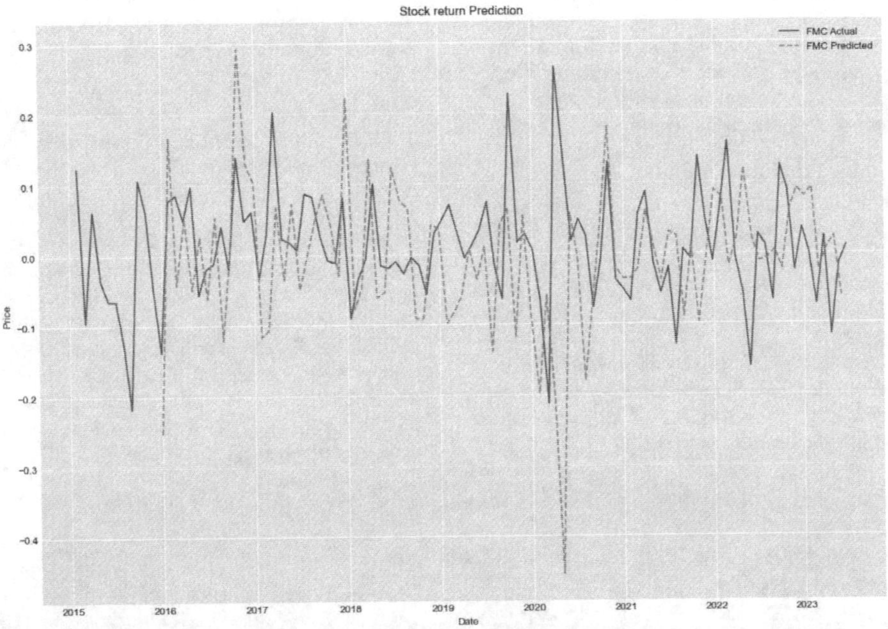

Fig. 2. Stock return forecast in SPY index (Photo/Picture credit: Original).

Figure 2 demonstrates the fluctuations of stock return rates over time, indicating a high degree of instability. In some periods, such as early 2018 and early 2021, the prediction aligns closely with the actual trend. However, in other periods, particularly at the beginning of 2020 and mid-2022, there are significant discrepancies between the prediction and the actual values, suggesting that the model fails to accurately predict the stock's performance during these times.

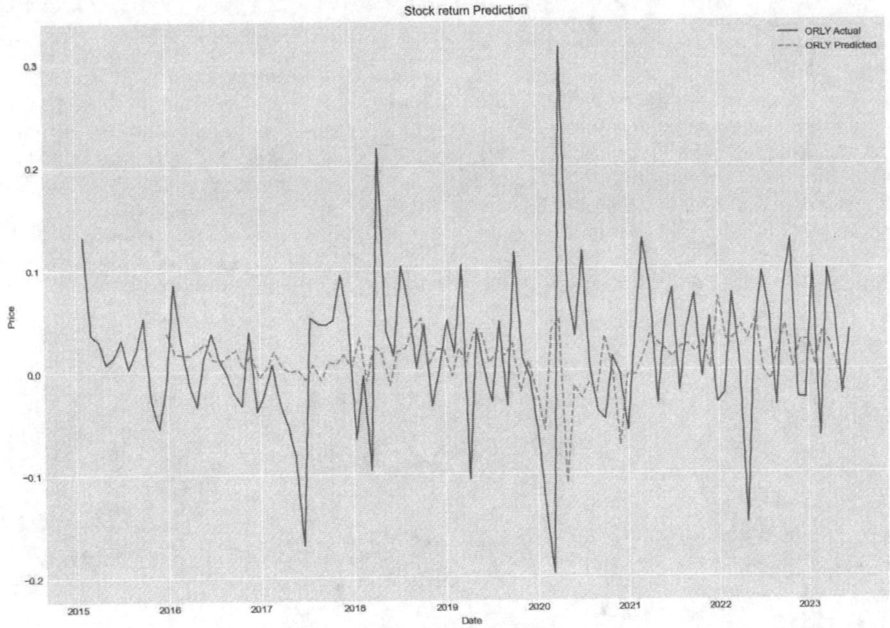

Fig. 3. Stock return forecast in NASDAQ index (Photo/Picture credit: Original).

In comparing predictive outcomes with the SPY index and those with the NASDAQ, it is evident that predictions for the S&P 500 are more accurate (see Figure 3). Observationally, the NASDAQ exhibits significantly greater volatility, a factor not anticipated by the model. This highlights the need for future improvements in the forecasting approach for high-volatility data, such as the application of differencing methods.

Predictions seem to align with actual data in certain periods. However, there are intervals, especially in early 2020 and early 2022, where the prediction significantly deviates from reality, suggesting that the model failed to accurately foresee the stock's behavior during volatile periods in both the SPY and NASDAQ 100 Indices.

A sharp decline in actual return rates is observable at the beginning of 2020, likely related to market turbulence caused by the global COVID-19 pandemic. The predictive line failed to capture this downturn, possibly due to the model not accounting for the impact of such rare events.

To improve the model's predictive power, it may be necessary to consider more complex time-series models, such as ARIMA or GARCH, or to incorporate macroeconomic indicators as predictive variables. Furthermore, it is essential to consider whether the model includes mechanisms to adapt to extreme market events and whether special modeling for such events is required.

3.3 S&P 500 and NASDAQ portfolio weights pie charts comparison

This paper will select three significant moments that greatly impacted tech stocks: the Facebook lawsuit in December 2018, the public registration opening of OpenAI in November 2022. The White house disclosed that there might be potential further regulation targeting artificial intelligence products in May 2023. It intends to explore how these pivotal events influenced the price movements of tech stocks and evaluate the effectiveness of the Walking Forward Model in predicting the outcomes of these black swan events.

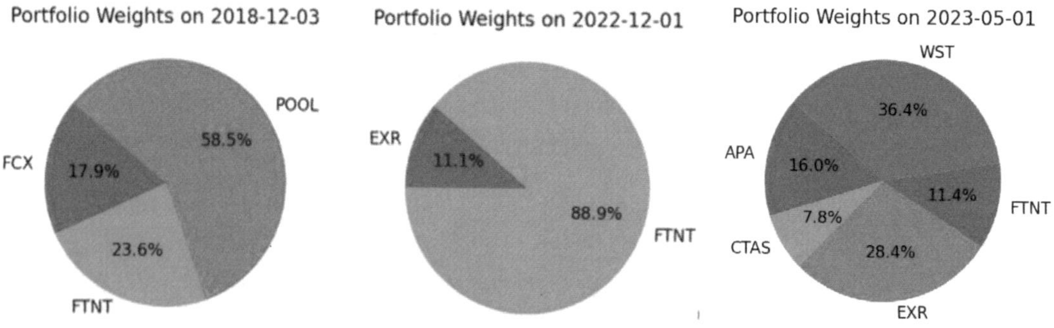

(a) Dec. 3rd, 2018 (b) Dec. 1st, 2022 (c) May 1st, 2023

Fig. 4. S&P 500 weights on 3 time points (Photo/Picture credit: Original).

SPY index portfolio (see Figure 4): Despite the selection of three tech-related milestones, the S&P 500's top ten constituents are tech-centric firms such as Apple, Microsoft, Amazon, Tesla, Alphabet A and C shares, Berkshire Hathaway B, UnitedHealth, Nvidia, and Johnson & Johnson. Yet, none of these tech-linked stocks were included in the portfolios at these specific times. The debut of OpenAI didn't result in a direct inclusion of Microsoft in the portfolio. This could be due to covariance constraints designed to minimize risk rather than increase the weight of tech stocks. During this period, a mining company was allocated instead, a decision that requires further analysis.

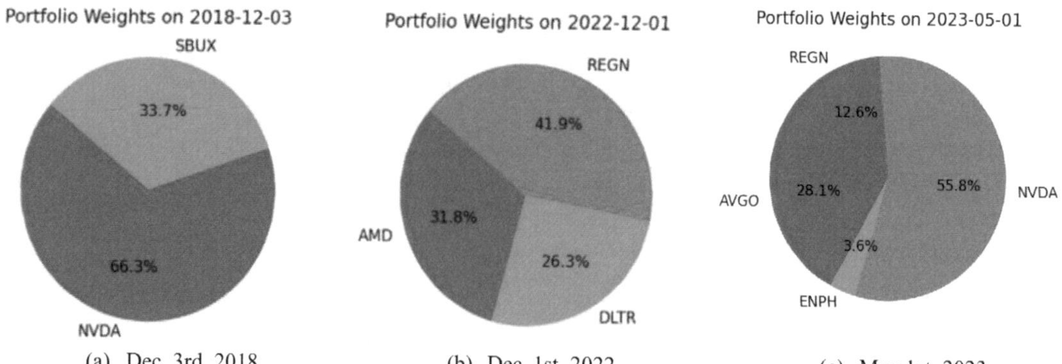

(a) Dec. 3rd, 2018 (b) Dec. 1st, 2022 (c) May 1st, 2023

Fig. 5. NASDAQ weights on 3 time points (Photo/Picture credit: Original).

NASDAQ index portfolio (see Figure 5)： At the time of OpenAI's release, the portfolio opted for an 31.8% stake in AMD, a computer chip company, focusing on designing the CPU and other computer components, also chose a retail company and a biotechnology company. Overall, there are no companies

https://doi.org/10.1051/shsconf/202418801003

directly related to the OpenAI supply chain. This indicates that the event did not significantly influence the optimal portfolio outcome. Additionally, the forecasting failed to predict the severe volatility trend in tech stocks and the impact of market fluctuations, leading to a discrepancy between the projected and actualized portfolio returns. At all three time points, despite including some technology-related stocks, more than 50% of the portfolio composition is actually unrelated to OpenAI. Overall, the portfolio tends to rely on companies with a tangible economy, such as e-commerce retail, energy development, and branded coffee

3.4 Portfolio compared to benchmark

Figure 6 indicates that the portfolios of both indices have surpassed their benchmark indexes, with the S&P 500 aligned with the SPY ETF and the NASDAQ with the QQQ ETF. However, it harbours doubts about the accuracy of these predictions in practice. This is due in part to questions about whether the forecasted results can genuinely align with actual prices, and the adjustment of the learning rate during the model building process is not enough to have real insight into the underlying information of the data, and also because the simplicity of the model's factors may not account for market risks, potentially resulting in forecast biases.

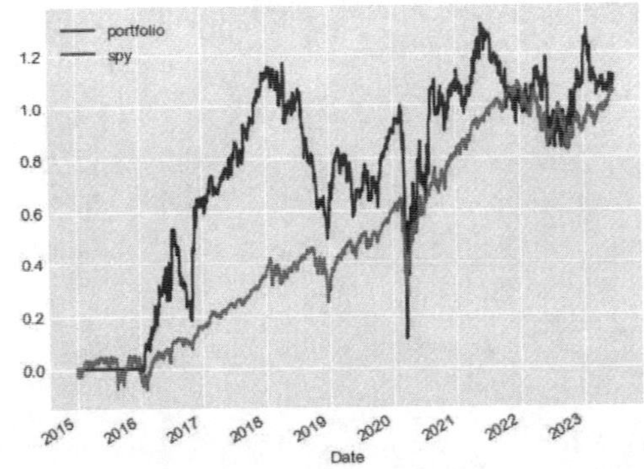

(a) S&P 500

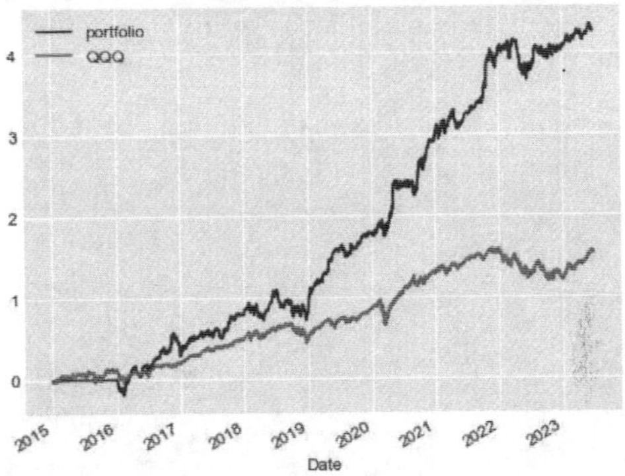

(b) NASDAQ

Fig. 6. Portfolio return benchmarking (Photo/Picture credit: Original).

4 Conclusion

Through the simulations and forecasts, this paper has substantiated the initial hypothesis that technology stocks exhibit greater volatility. This study of three specific time points indicates that these events have an impact on short-term fluctuations but do not affect the long-term investment strategy. The portfolio still favors companies with solid industrial foundations in the long run, such as those in energy, brick-and-mortar e-commerce, automotive manufacturing, and the healthcare sector. This outcome may be attributed to the use of covariance constraints to hedge risks, leading to the exclusion of stocks with high returns but also high risks.

In addition, the results show that facing the sensitivity of different markets, it is necessary to make dynamic fine adjustment to the learning rate based on market characteristics, volatility, trend and other factors, so as to improve the automatic fitness of the model under different conditions, so as to better mine the underlying information of different data samples. Therefore, in the training process of the machine learning model, the learning rate alpha should be dynamically adjusted according to the specific characteristics of different markets to ensure the effectiveness of the model in its application. This has important implications for investors, policy makers, and market analysts who can use these insights to develop more effective investment strategies, make informed decisions, and better understand market dynamics.

Overall, the results of this paper emphasize the importance of dynamically adjusting the learning rate of machine learning models to improve the model generalization performance in various market conditions. This provides a new perspective for future research on financial applications, where the model performance can be optimized by more finely adjusting the learning rate. In the future, more research is expected to focus on the application and development of some relevant cutting-edge methods, such as adaptive learning rate, multi-task learning, incremental learning and other methods, to adjust the learning rate of machine learning models more effectively, so as to better cope with different market situations and similar problems in other fields.

References

1. R. Zhang, SF 11, 5 (2018).
2. D. Shah, H. Isah, F. Zulkernine, IJFR, 7 (2), 26 (2019).
3. Y. Wu, et al., *Unmysterious the learning rate strategy for high-precision training of deep neural networks* in the Proceeding of IEEE Big Data (Big Data), 1971-1980 (2019).
4. B. Liu, MET (09), 83-87 (2022).
5. L. Li, F. Noorian, M. Moss, W. Leong, *Rolling window time series prediction using MapReduce* in

https://doi.org/10.1051/shsconf/202418801003

the Proceedings of the 2014 IEEE 15th International Conference on Information Reuse and Integration (IEEE IRI 2014), 757-764 (2014).

6. W. Galbraith, S. Zernov, AFE, 19(13), 1019-1028 (2009).
7. R. Chen, Master's dissertation on CSI 300 prediction model research based on SSA-LSTM-LightGBM, Guangxi University for Nationalities (2023).
8. J. Klaas, Machine learning for finance: principles and practice for financial insiders. Packt Publishing (2019).
9. H. Li, D. Song, J. Kong, et al., Hyperparameter optimization technology evaluation of traditional machine learning model. computer science (2023).
10. S. Yang, AS 11 (2021).
11. A. Folly, *A Brief Survey of Group-based Incremental Learning Algorithms* in the Proceedings of IEEE Seminar Series on Computational Intelligence (SSCI), 339-344 (2019).

A study of the correlation between volatility and risk diversification control in options and futures markets

Chengfan Yang[1,*]

[1]School of Finace and Investment, Guangdong University of Finace, Guangzhou, Guangdong Province, 510521, China

Abstract. With the continuous development of financial derivatives, many enterprises increasingly prefer using financial derivatives such as options and futures when hedging their risks. However, in the process of using them, many enterprises do not use them as a tool for risk hedging but instead use them for hedging or even try to achieve short-term wealth appreciation through options and futures trading, which is contrary to the original intention of enterprises to use financial derivatives. At the same time, financial derivatives are affected by market volatility. Without professionals to carry out risk control, it will be a double-edged sword; using bad will become a sword to stab at the enterprise. This paper adopts the illustrative method and literature research method to analyse the impact of market volatility and the importance of risk control of options futures by taking the example of the German metal company trying to hedge through options futures in 1993, which ultimately caused the enterprise to fall into difficulties.

1 Introduction

Modern options and futures are indispensable financial derivatives used for risk control in today's financial market trading. In modern times, futures and options trading has been further developed and standardised to become important tools in the financial markets. The futures and options market provides producers, consumers, and investors with a platform for risk hedging, price discovery, and speculative trading. It plays an important role in the stability and development of the modern economy. Modern options futures trading began around the end of the 19th century and the beginning of the 20th century with several landmark events. The Chicago Board of Trade (CBOT), founded in 1848, was one of the world's first futures exchanges. Initially, the CBOT was primarily designed to provide trading in agricultural futures to help farmers and merchants hedge their exposure to price fluctuations. As industrialisation grew, so did the demand for industrial commodities and metals in the financial markets. In order to hedge against fluctuations in the prices of these commodities, futures exchanges began to offer more types of futures contracts, including metals and energy. Options trading is a relatively recent development but has a long history. In the early 1900s, options trading began to take off on exchanges such as the Chicago Derivatives Exchange (CME). Options contracts give investors the right to buy or sell the underlying asset at a specific price at a certain time. In 1973, the Chicago Board Options Exchange (CBOE) was established, which marked the formal formation of the options trading market. With the development of computer technology, the emergence of electronic trading platforms has revolutionised futures and options trading, making it more efficient and convenient. Overall, the origins of modern futures and options markets can be traced back to the 19th and early 20th centuries in the U.S. Over time, these markets have continued to grow and become an integral part of the global financial market. Although risk is hedged due to options futures, many firms in the market still fail to hedge or control risk due to market uncertainty. Due to the uncertainty of the market, options and futures also have large market volatility, and many firms face great market uncertainty while using options and futures for risk hedging [1]. Therefore, studying market volatility and risk control of options and futures is important to enterprises and can help them create better risk control strategies for their conditions. It is of great business value for individual companies to avoid unnecessary costs and reduce risks.

The analysis by Frank Asche et al. concluded that market volatility is divided into implied volatility and actual volatility, the use of implied volatility to predict future changes in commodity prices, and the relationship between implied volatility and actual volatility. The research results show implied volatility can be used as an effective risk management tool to help traders better control the risk of futures and options trading [2]. Meanwhile, a dynamic hedging strategy based on stochastic volatility is proposed by Man-man Zhu et al. 2021, which can effectively reduce trading risk in futures and options trading. The research results show that the strategy can achieve good risk management effects under different market conditions [3]. This shows a strong correlation between market volatility and risk control management. Not only that, market volatility can also predict the risk faced by the enterprise and make a more

* Corresponding author: 221526150@m.gduf.edu.cn

reasonable response program. Lars Stentoft 2015, studied the impact of market volatility on futures and options trading and proposed a trading strategy based on implied volatility, which can help traders better respond to changes in market volatility and risk management [4]. Most scholars have only studied the arbitrage of option futures, and only a few have studied the correlation between market volatility of option futures and risk control management and the impact between the two.

This paper first takes the failure of futures trading of a German metal company in 1993 as a case to analyse the impact of market volatility on risk control, which shows that option futures hedging risk does not only look at the company itself but also needs to be analysed from the macro point of view of the market. The case is then used to illustrate the risks inherent in options and futures and the impact of market volatility on risk control, showing that risk control is not 100%. Finally, the theories provide insights and warnings to companies that need to control risk.

2 Case description

The case of Deutsche Metallbau is a story of failed risk management in financial derivatives trading. German Metals is a long-established industrial group dealing in metals, energy, and other products. Its U.S. subsidiary, MGRM, entered into several long-term supply contracts with a number of oil retailers in 1993, promising to supply petrol, heating oil, and jet fuel at fixed prices. These contracts also included an option that allowed the retailers to terminate the contracts and receive cash compensation if the market price was higher than the contracted price. In order to hedge against the risk of rising oil prices, MGRM employed a hedging strategy in the futures and storefront markets by buying large quantities of short-term oil futures contracts and swaps that it continually rolled over. In this manner, MGRM hoped to lock in future profits while taking advantage of the market's law of spot premiums to earn basis differentials. However, MGRM's hedging strategy encountered a series of problems that led to large losses. First, in late 1993, there was a sharp decline in oil prices, causing MGRM to incur large floating losses on its long futures contracts and swap agreements. Although future gains on the supply contracts could offset these losses, MGRM was required to make significant margin calls under the day-ahead settlement rules. Secondly, the spot premium pattern of the market has changed to a spot discount situation, where the spot price is lower than the futures price. This means that MGRM has to pay for closing losses when it rolls over and post in cash to cover the change in basis differentials. Again, because MGRM's futures position was too large, accounting for 20% of the total crude oil futures position on the New York Mercantile Exchange (NYMEX), the exchange decided to cancel MGRM's "hedging privilege" and double the margin. This put further pressure on MGRM. Finally, the Supervisory Board of Deutsche Metallbau, which did not understand MGRM's hedging strategy and regarded it as speculative, decided to close out MGRM's futures position and cancel the supply contract. This decision occurred at the most undesirable time, causing MGRM to forgo future supply contract gains and pay liquidated damages. It is estimated that MGRM lost $1.3 billion on the futures and swaps trades, more than half of Deutsche Metallbau's capital, and nearly caused the company to go bankrupt.

3 Analysis on the problems

3.1 The status of investments in futures trading

In addition to trading spot, futures, and options on commodity exchanges for its own industrial group, Deutsche Gesellschaft für Metallwirtschaft (DGM) also offers brokerage services to other businesses engaged in hedging, arbitrage, and speculative trading. It also trades in the over-the-counter market with counterparties acting as market makers. Oil commodities trading is the area of expertise for Deutsche Metals AG's U.S. subsidiary, MG REFINING AND MARKETING (henceforth referred to as "Deutsche Metals"). Deutsche Metals signed a deal to trade oil commodities with a client in the summer of 1993. "MG REFINING AND MARKETING signed a long-term supply agreement with its client in the summer of 1993.

This was unique because it combined a special supply contract with a financial derivative element. "Deutsche Metals committed to providing aviation fuel, heating oil, and automotive oil to oil retailers in the United States (henceforth referred to as "customers") at a fixed price for a period of ten years, with a portion of the supply to be delivered in regular quantities and a portion to be delivered at a time to be decided by the customer. The remaining portion of the supply will be delivered at the user's decision. Unlike typical long-term contracts that adjust for inflation, the contract ensures a fixed supply price for an extended period. Delivery time and quantity are uncertain. The financial derivative component gives the customer the right to choose whether to require Deutsche Metals to pay the difference between the spot price and contract price for the entire 10-year contract term. If the global oil spot price exceeds the contract price, the customer can choose whether to force Deutsche Metals to settle the contract by paying the difference in cash for the undelivered oil.

At the end of the contract, the contract was priced at $3 to $5 above the spot market price, which was attractive to the supply side. And crucially, German Metal Construction had to accept the terms of the contract. Subsequently, Deutsche Metallbau was confident in relying on its extensive trading experience in the global commodity markets and was even more assured of its technical capabilities in financial derivatives trading. As a result, German Metal Construction developed a hedging strategy in an attempt to hedge against the risk of changes in the price of oil by purchasing standardized futures contracts for oil on the New York Mercantile Exchange and swapping them on the over-the-counter market, thereby transferring the price risk arising from the contracts with its customers.

Although the firm's approach was theoretically and practically appropriate, the hedging strategy failed.

3.2 Reasons for analysis based on the characteristics of options futures trading

When the contract came up for renewal, Deutsche Metallurgical had to swallow the cost of closing the position and inject cash to bridge the widening spread between spot premiums and spot discounts. At this critical juncture, the New York Mercantile Exchange (NYMEX) proposed doubling initial margins for oil futures contracts, further compounding Deutsche Metallurgical's financial woes. With cash flow constraints and limited financial resources, the company struggled to meet the exorbitant margin requirements and the cost of rolling over contracts. Creditors and shareholders began to lose faith, reluctant to extend further loans or invest. This uncertainty led to major shareholders questioning the company's resilience in weathering the crisis. As a result, Deutsche Metallurgical—once a proud pillar of the German industrial landscape—teetered on the brink of bankruptcy, sending tremors throughout the industry.

3.3 Causes of the problem

Firstly, Deutsche Metallbau lacks a thorough understanding of the nature of futures trading. As a highly technical activity, financial derivatives trading involves various stages such as design, trading, clearing, and performance, which poses new management challenges for companies that produce and consume these contracts. It should be noted that financial derivatives trading has dual characteristics: it can be used for hedging to avoid risks, and at the same time, it can also be a tool for speculation by taking on high risks to pursue high returns. The dual nature makes it particularly difficult to accurately judge the nature and risks of a trade [5]. Many cases have shown that some people often trade speculatively in the name of hedging to gain personal benefits. Therefore, senior management must have sufficient professional knowledge or rely on the support of professional technical personnel to make independent and objective judgments on the nature of derivative transactions that could significantly impact the enterprise's overall risk [6].

However, Deutsche Metallbau demonstrates a clear speculative mentality in futures trading, completely ignoring market volatility. The company lacks sufficient technical support to hedge risks, and senior management handles futures trading too casually, ultimately leading to huge losses.

Using financial derivatives for hedging usually requires the help of complex mathematical models. The key is to accurately measure the correlation between the current price of goods and the price of derivative contracts selected. If the correlation measurement is inaccurate, the risk of hedging failure will increase. The G30 has conducted in-depth research on the technical level and issues of global financial derivatives trading and recommends that rigorous testing must be carried out before practical applications of hedging design. In the case of Deutsche Metallbau, the hedging design models did not undergo rigorous testing, and there were significant problems with key technical parameters such as coverage, term matching, and risk prevention of basis swaps. In addition, potential liquidity risks and credit risks were not properly handled, which seriously affected the evaluation and implementation of the hedging strategy.

Finally, issues that arise in the later stages of futures management are partly attributed to the limitations of traditional accounting techniques. Traditional accounting techniques cannot timely reflect the profits and losses of trading positions.

It is important for businesses to understand how to manage the financing and profit/loss issues associated with hedging. Once the hedging position is established and the design is perfect, the loss on one side will always be balanced by the profit on the other side, regardless of market price changes. However, traditional financial accounting statements often fail to provide a clear and complete picture of the true profit, loss, and risk associated with derivative transactions. This, coupled with the fact that many managers, investors, and creditors may not have a comprehensive understanding of the concept of hedging, can lead to misinformation and only focusing on the loss side.

Therefore, it is essential for business stakeholders to gain a better understanding of hedging methods and their implications. In the case of Deutsche Metallbau, a lack of communication between management, shareholders, and other stakeholders about hedging long-term oil supply contracts led to management conflicts that ultimately had catastrophic consequences. To avoid such situations, businesses need to ensure that all relevant parties are well-informed and understand the purpose and risks associated with hedging strategies [7].

4 Suggestions

4.1 Establish a risk management system

The objective of risk management optimisation of the OTC commodity options business of the enterprise is to establish a comprehensive proactive and intelligent risk management system through the joint participation of the enterprise management and all employees, to ensure that the OTC commodity options business of the enterprise complies with the relevant laws and regulations, regulatory provisions, self-regulatory rules and requirements of the enterprise regulations, and to realise the maximisation of the value of the enterprise is to promote the enterprise on the premise that the overall risk is measurable, controllable and affordable, to Comprehensive implementation of development strategies and the achievement of business objectives, to promote the company to continuously strengthen the awareness of risk management, take the initiative to form a good risk management culture, to ensure that the regulatory requirements, the group's decision-making and deployment and the company's business management objectives are effectively implemented [8].

It is necessary to objectively analyse the current situation of the enterprise's economic operation. On this basis, should be hired in options and futures trading and risk avoidance of relevant technical personnel, focusing on the relevant tail hedging strategy, not only by the senior management's own decision to make decisions that affect the operation of the entire enterprise [9]. At the same time, a large enterprise should retain its customers and have the right to know the company's decision-making, not to arbitrage for the company's senior management, which can only play a negative role in the life of a company.

4.2 Professional staff to carry out risk control and operations

Facing up to the nature of the use of options and futures in the enterprise, the use of options and futures needs to be related to professional staff to carry out risk control and a series of operations. Critical attitude to the relevant opinions of senior management, the board of directors of the enterprise should be independent of a new regulatory authority to manage it, and at the same time to give high authority to isolate it from the senior management, can not influence the impact of relevant decisions, so as to ensure the normal operation of the enterprise and the rights and interests of shareholders and customers. It is also important to utilise market volatility, supplemented by the appropriate use of relevant data tools, for risk control management [10].

4.3 Improvement of accounting standards and traditional accounting

First, the Activity-Based Costing (ABC) method was introduced: traditional accounting focuses only on direct and indirect costs, ignoring activity-based costs. Introducing the ABC method can allocate costs more accurately and help companies better understand the impact of different activities on costs, thus enabling more effective cost control and decision-making.

Second, introducing performance evaluation indicators: Traditional accounting mainly focuses on financial indicators and ignores the impact of non-financial indicators on business performance. The introduction of performance evaluation indicators can more comprehensively assess the performance of the enterprise, including customer satisfaction, employee satisfaction, product quality, and other non-financial indicators, to help enterprises more comprehensively understand their competitive advantages and disadvantages.

Third, introducing environmental accounting: Traditional accounting often ignores the impact of the enterprise on the environment and the impact of the environment on the enterprise. The introduction of environmental accounting can help enterprises understand their environmental costs and risks more comprehensively to plan and manage the development of enterprises.

Fourth, introducing risk management accounting: Traditional accounting focuses only on historical data, ignoring future risks and uncertainties. Introducing risk management accounting can help companies better understand future risks and uncertainties and thus better plan and respond to future challenges.

5 Conclusion

This paper focuses on the collapse of the futures hedging strategy of Deutsche Metallbau in 1993 as an example to analyse the impact of market volatility and risk control of options futures on the whole strategy. Due to the limited technological development in those years, some of the tools for risk control were not yet intelligent; at the same time, the detailed nature of the traditional accounting techniques also contributed to the disaster, which led to the solution strategies proposed in this paper. Many techniques are now being realised, but the revelations are still significant for most who use option futures for risk hedging. These strategies can reduce, in most cases, the subjective and objective risks associated with implementing risk controls that companies can address. On this basis, they can also remind companies that when using options futures, they should be clear about the purpose of their use and follow the basic principle of maximising the company's interests rather than simply hedging for a small group of people. However, due to the diversity and uncertainty of the market, many factors are not considered in other conditions ideal to solve the existing problems.

References

1. N. H. Chen. Small and medium-sized enterprise management and science and technology (upper ten journal), (08):39-40 (2021)
2. A. Frank, E. D. Roy & S. Marie. Wild Fish, Aquaculture Economics & Management, **19**: 3, 316-335 (2015)
3. M. M. Zhu. Shanghai Jiao Tong University (2021).
4. J. Zhao, Y. D. Xue. Hebei Industrial Science and Technology, **26**(06):513-518 (2009)
5. S. Chen. 21st Century Business Herald, 2022-12-01(002) (2022)
6. K. Chen. Mall Modernisation, (24):83-84 (2019)
7. C. Song, J. Feng, Y. S. Jiang. China Petroleum and Chemical Industry, (09):52-56 (2021)
8. H. G. Xiao. Shandong University (2023)
9. L. S. Li, M. Zhou, W. X. Zhao. Securities Market Herald, (06):54-66 (2023)
10. X. B. Lian. Northeast University of Finance and Economics (2016)

Enterprise Futures Hedging Risk Management -Take the Qingshan Holdings' Nickel Futures Incident on the LME as an Example

Zunhao Xia[1,*]

[1]School of Business, Guangxi University, Nanning, 530004, China

Abstract. When conducting international commodity trade, companies have to face changes in the prices of raw materials and finished products. Particularly in the context of a volatile international situation and increasingly complex geopolitics, enterprises are often inclined to engage in hedging activities to mitigate price risks. Establishing and improving risk management in hedging to promote enterprises' smooth trade business is significant. Good risk management can ensure the long-term and stable development of enterprises. This paper conducts a case study through the March 2022 nickel futures price surge event on the London Metal Exchange. Through the huge loss of Tsingshan Group in the transaction, the cause of the event and the corresponding suggestions are put forward. The causes of the problems are analyzed from the macro-environmental and micro factors of the exchange and the enterprise, and the solutions are put forward. This paper has a certain reference value for similar enterprises to improve their hedging risk management ability.

1 Introduction

1.1 Research background

As global economic integration progresses, the significance of commodity supply chains in the international arena has grown even more prominent. Due to the complexity of the global situation and the impact of geopolitics, there has been an increase in price fluctuations of commodities, making companies more susceptible to the risks of price volatility in raw materials and finished products. In the current volatile international situation, international commodity trade is more likely than before to be affected by the macro environment and unforeseen events.

In the first quarter of 2022, there was a collective surge in commodity prices. The S&P Goldman Sachs Commodity Index (GSCI), a barometer for global raw material prices, witnessed a remarkable increase of nearly 34%, marking the largest surge since 1990. Meanwhile, the rapid development of electric vehicles and renewable energy equipment has boosted the demand for metals such as aluminum, nickel, and lithium. The International Monetary Fund (IMF) estimated that the global economic growth rate 2022 will be 3.4%, showing a significant decline compared to the 6.2% growth rate in 2021. The World Bank had projected a drop in global economic growth for 2022 to be 2.9%, compared to the 5.9% growth rate recorded in 2021.

Many companies use futures for hedging to avoid price risk, but there are some unavoidable risks. In particular, the frequent occurrence of black swan events in recent years has led to an increase in price volatility factors in the international futures market, making it necessary for enterprises to consider and face more diversified risks when using futures for hedging. If companies do not implement hedging programs according to the right principles, they are prone to face greater risk exposure. At the same time, problems such as incomplete risk control and inadequate regulatory systems may cause enterprises to incur huge losses in participating in hedging.

Therefore, risk management throughout the entire process of hedging becomes particularly important for optimizing corporate hedging strategies, mitigating price risks, and enhancing the company's overall risk management capabilities. For core companies with large volumes, their losses in hedging often hit the entire supply chain and industrial chain. For these important enterprises, having good risk management and corresponding countermeasures play an important role in enhancing the stability of supply and demand in the whole market and promoting the development of the industry. This paper will study and explore how to strengthen enterprises' risk management on futures hedging and propose corresponding countermeasures.

1.2 Literature review

Bartram & Jiang found that firms' hedging behavior reduces their exposure to price risk and increases firm value [1,2]. By estimating the efficiency of futures

* Corresponding author: 2031200525@st.gxu.edu.cn

hedging, Xiang & Wang & Ling found that the hedging efficiency of most hedging programs was above 90%, and the ability of the futures market to serve the real economy was gradually enhanced [3]. Zhu & Han proposed that futures played an important role in promoting the quality development of the real economy, but at the same time, they believed that the current futures market was not perfect and there were many problems and put forward a series of measures to improve it [4]. Li & Duo analyzed the risks that may arise when enterprises carry out hedging business and pointed out that there are inherent risks and extrinsic risks in the process of hedging, and at the same time, put forward the corresponding countermeasures according to these risks [5]. Cao & Tang take the crude oil hedging loss of a wholly-owned subsidiary of a Chinese state-owned enterprise as an example to analyze the reasons for the failure of financial derivatives hedging in large enterprises and put forward relevant countermeasures [6].

1.3 Research gap

Most scholars analyze the effect of hedging to avoid price risk by studying enterprises' hedging behavior and further exploring the value that hedging can play in enterprises. It was found that companies can better avoid the risk of price fluctuations in raw materials and finished goods by hedging. And the case study proves that hedging has a high efficiency of value preservation. Some articles prove that the correct use of hedging can promote the high-quality development of the real economy. Meanwhile, most scholars take the possible risks in the conventional financial derivatives market as the starting point, point out some risks that enterprises may face when hedging business, and put forward corresponding suggestions. Few scholars focus on enterprise failure cases under the influence of black swan events. They analyzed the macro background that led to the failure of enterprise hedging, the failure of the enterprise's own management, and improper risk management of hedging, and they put forward corresponding countermeasures.

1.4 Research framework

This paper focuses on the case study method. e the nickel futures price surge in the London Metal Exchange (LME) as a case study. This paper will analyze the reasons for the failure of Tsingshan Group's hedging business using futures and the risk management problems it faced and propose relevant opinions according to the problems. First is a specific description of the incident of the surge of nickel futures price in the LME. Second, the futures hedging issues and risks in this case will be analyzed. Finally, corresponding countermeasures are proposed based on the different issues analyzed.

2 Case description

2.1 Nickel prices on the London Metal Exchange (LME) experienced a sharp surge

In March 2022, the nickel futures prices on the LME experienced an epic surge, causing a sensation in the international financial markets. During this period, the LME had to halt trading twice and implemented a series of emergency adjustments.

In 2021 and early 2022, the nickel prices on the LME remained relatively stable at around $20,000 per metric ton. However, by the end of February 2022, the conflict between Russia and Ukraine escalated, leading to a series of sanctions imposed by Western countries on Russia. Market concerns about possible restrictions on trade and delivery of related resource goods have triggered significant volatility in global commodity prices. From March 1 to 4th, nickel prices on the LME saw a continuous upward trend for four consecutive trading days, with the highest price surpassing $30,000 per metric ton. Then, on March 7th and 8th, the front-month nickel futures contract on the LME broke historical records, reaching a peak increase of 250%. On March 7, nickel futures opened at $29,770 and briefly surged to a historic high of $55,000 during intraday trading. During overnight trading on March 8, nickel futures continued to skyrocket, breaking the $100,000 mark and reaching a peak price of $101,365, as shown in Figure 1.

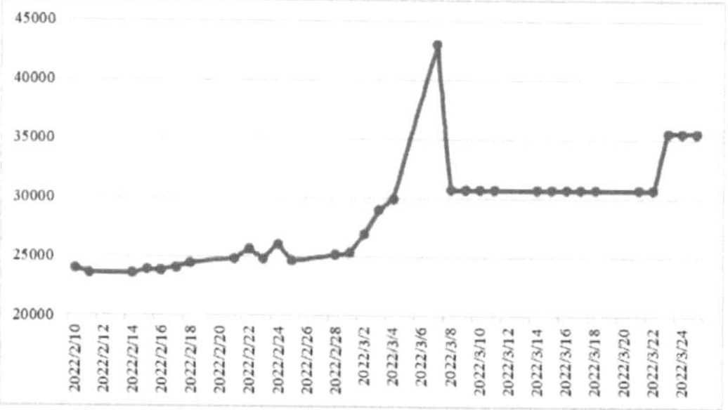

Fig 1. LME Nickel Official Prices (Shown in US$)
(Photo credit: Origin)

2.2 Tsingshan group suffers massive losses

Tsingshan Holding Group Co, as a producer of metal nickel, held a global market share of 18% in 2020. Tsingshan Group adopted a future hedging strategy by taking short positions in nickel futures to hedge against the risk of metal nickel price fluctuations.

Taking the market speculation of 150,000-200,000 tons of short positions, Tsingshan Group's selling price for the position opened before March 6, 2022, is about $25,000 per ton, and based on the highest price of $101,000 per ton that appeared on March 8, its floating loss will reach $11.4 billion - $15.2 billion. According to hedging, if Tsingshan Group has sufficient underlying goods, the profit of spot delivery on the expiration date has been locked in advance, and the company only needs to make physical delivery. However, Tsingshan Group faced a problem: they did not have enough delivery commodities and failed to move their positions in time. On March 15, 2022, Tsingshan Group announced it had reached a silent agreement with a consortium of futures banking creditors. During the silent period, participating futures banks agreed not to close out Tsingshan's positions or require additional margin on existing positions. As an integral part of the agreement, Tsingshan Group is expected to gradually reduce its existing positions reasonably and orderly as abnormal market conditions subside. However, it is already certain that Tsingshan Group has incurred losses that cannot be reversed.

3 Analysis on the problems

3.1 Macro reasons

3.1.1 Russia-Ukraine conflict leads to panic in nickel futures market

In February 2022, the conflict between Russia and Ukraine escalated, leading to a series of sanctions imposed by Western countries against Russia. As a major global producer and exporter of nickel, Russia accounts for 8% of the world's nickel supply, and its production of electrolytic nickel exceeds 20% of the global total. Russia plays a significant role in the nickel supply chain. Although the West's policy of sanctions against Russia did not directly restrict Russia's non-ferrous metal export trade, the main supply side of nickel brought the potential risk of non-negligible impact and public opinion.

The policy of sanctions against Russia implemented by Western countries increases the liquidity risk of the nickel spot. The liquidity risk of nickel spots triggered panic in the nickel trading market, exacerbate the possibility of a shortage of LME nickel stocks and the risk of a run on the LME, creating the conditions for nickel prices to rise. Market participants are concerned about the instability of the nickel supply. As a result, they are taking measures to address the potential nickel shortages. The interaction of this panic and investor behavior has driven volatility in the nickel futures market, resulting in high prices.

Although, in recent years, Russia's nickel production in the global market has seen a gradual decline from the LME standard delivery goods - electrolytic nickel-Russia's Norilsk nickel industry accounted for about 15% of the global electrolytic nickel production. The sanctions imposed by the West on Russia have worsened the conditions for Russian electrolytic nickel to enter the LME delivery market. This situation poses a potential risk for the sharp surge in nickel futures on the LME.

3.1.2 Nickel supply and demand support nickel prices rose steadily

Nickel is widely used in various sectors, such as stainless steel production, electroplating, and batteries. With the continuous reform and upgrading of the manufacturing industry, the demand for nickel has steadily increased [7]. As a crucial non-ferrous metal supporting the new energy sector, the demand for nickel has been steadily rising in line with the rapid development and expansion of the new energy industry. According to data compiled by the Nickel Institute in 2022, nickel accounts for a significant proportion of global usage across various sectors. Specifically, nickel's usage in stainless steel production constitutes 70% of global consumption. Other alloys account for 16%, electroplating layers represent 8%, and nickel consumption in the battery sector amounts to 5%. Despite the relatively low proportion of nickel demand in the battery sector, the continuous increase in demand for electric vehicles and the promotion of high-nickel batteries have accelerated the growth of nickel demand in the new energy sector. New energy batteries are poised to be a driving force for long-term and stable future nickel demand growth.

Despite Indonesia's abundant reserves of nickel resources and increased production of nickel pig iron and ferronickel, its output remains limited. This has resulted in a global nickel supply that can only meet the growing demand for nickel. The supply and demand dynamics in the global nickel market have led to a sustained increase in nickel prices. Investors and market participants anticipate that the supply gap will continue to persist. This supply and demand scenario supports a steady rise in nickel prices from 2016 to 2022. Against the backdrop of tight supply and surging demand, global nickel stocks continue to fall. And since 2021, nickel stocks on the LME have declined month by month to low levels. The above factors provide inherent conditions for the surge in nickel futures.

3.2 Micro reasons

3.2.1 Strict limitations on LME nickel futures standard delivery brands

In the LME nickel futures contract, only Class I electrolytic nickel with a minimum purity of 99.8% can be used for future delivery. Galaxy Futures Commodity Research Institute of non-ferrous R & D report shows that in 2012, Class I nickel accounted for 51%, Class II nickel accounted for 38%, while in 2021, Class I nickel, Class II nickel accounted for 31.4% and 63.6%, respectively. The proportion of Class I nickel products available for future delivery continues to decline, while the production of high-ice nickel, nickel pig iron, etc., is rising yearly. However, many forms of nickel, such as Class II nickel, nickel salts, high-ice nickel, and ferronickel, are not deliverable on the LME. The demand for risk management of nickel industry chain chain-related production enterprises, especially ferronickel and other non-standard goods, continues to increase. The hedging demand has increased substantially. This has led to a continuous increase in trading volume in the nickel futures market while the supply of electrolytic nickel remains relatively stable. The growth rate of hedging volume for nickel futures is significantly higher than that of electrolytic nickel supply, and Tsingshan Group falls into this category. The existing design of LME futures contracts has struggled to keep up with the significant changes in the global nickel industry. The growing demand for hedging non-standard nickel products and the insufficient supply of pure nickel has created a contradiction, resulting in the potential for speculative trading in LME nickel.

Indeed, while Tsingshan Group possesses a significant nickel production capacity in Indonesia, a considerable portion of its products may not qualify as standard delivery brands in LME nickel futures. This situation means that shorting nickel futures on the LME does not provide a complete hedge for the nickel products produced by the Tsingshan Group. As a non-standard asset, hedging operations using futures contracts may not perfectly align with Tsingshan Group's main product portfolio. The underlying assets of the futures contracts held by the company do not fully match its primary products. This situation makes the hedging behavior of Tsingshan Group naturally exist in the face of the risk of physical delivery not being completed or even forced position behavior.

3.2.2 Tsingshan Group holds an excessive short position in nickel futures

Indonesia is rich in nickel resources, and Tsingshan Group has invested in many nickel production plants in Indonesia to achieve its goal of producing nickel at low cost. Tsingshan Group, the world's No. 1 nickel producer in 2021, said it will continue to increase its investment in Indonesia's nickel industry. According to their claims, Tsingshan Group expects to produce an estimated 600,000 metric tons of nickel equivalent in 2021, 850,000 metric tons in 2022, and 1.1 million in 2023. The announced production forecast by Tsingshan Group represents a significant portion of the global nickel supply, directly impacting the global nickel supply market. The substantial increase in these production forecasts has significantly boosted the supply in the nickel market. However, global economic conditions have been sluggish at the same time, leading to a decrease in market expectations for the demand side of the nickel market. Therefore, Tsingshan Group predicts that nickel metal prices will continue to decline in the future market. To ensure stability in the spot market and hedge against the risk of falling nickel prices, Tsingshan Group has actively taken on a significant short position in nickel futures. However, the number of futures short positions the group holds exceeds its holdings in the spot market. If trading in the futures market fails, Tsingshan Group's production capacity may not be able to withstand the consequences, and the risk exposure may exceed the company's capacity to bear it.

4 Suggestions

4.1 Improvement of enterprise risk awareness

As a financial derivative, a hedging business has its own market rules. Enterprises carrying out hedging business to hedge price risks should follow the market rules of futures to carry out business. Enterprises should consider their situation in the spot market, but more importantly, they should not blindly rely on their spot market advantages and reduce the emphasis on the risk management of hedging business. When the Russia-Ukraine conflict broke out, it buried the hidden danger of blocked spot delivery of electrolyzed nickel. The risk sensitivity of futures market participants catalyzes increased volatility in the nickel futures market. When hedging, enterprises should not ignore macrogeopolitical factors but also consider the role of market participants in promoting the market.

4.2 Strengthen strategic risk management at the decision-making level

Strategic risk management is the highest promoter in enterprise risk management. Strengthening risk management and control at the strategic level often makes risk management more effective with less effort [8]. The upward price trend of nickel had already appeared before this incident. The continuous innovation and commercialization of the global new energy field has put higher supply demand on the supply side of nickel. Enterprises should face future development and serve the enterprise strategy when managing risk. Risk management programs related to industry trends need to be continually enhanced. Enterprises need to strengthen cross-management, improve market monitoring and early warning capabilities, and establish a multi-level risk early warning system.

4.3 Flexibly use a variety of financial derivatives to diversify hedging risks

Futures trading adopts the mark-to-market system on a daily basis, also known as the daily debt-free system and daily settlement system [9]. Although Tsingshan Holdings mainly conducts transactions with LME member banks in the over-the-counter market, there is still great pressure on member banks to call margin in case of market emergencies. The strict margin system and mark-to-market system of futures markets require high liquidity for futures trading. In contrast, non-standardized financial derivatives such as forward contracts and swaps do not have this requirement. In addition to futures, companies can also use derivative instruments such as forward contracts, swaps, and options to hedge their risks. By combining various financial derivatives, it can better avoid the strict restrictions of the exchange on standard delivery products.

Tsingshan's hedging positions are on the LME, exposing it to the London market. China's futures market implements penetrating supervision, with a specially set up margin supervision center, and the risk system is the world's leading [10]. If Tsingshan can carry out part of the position hedging in the Chinese market, it can reduce the hedging risk accordingly. Enterprises should also be careful not to concentrate risks in one market when hedging. In extreme cases, there will often be no buffer.

4.4 Match positions as required and build an early warning system for closing positions and delivery

Enterprises should reasonably control the scale of hedging when conducting hedging business, especially when there is no perfect match between the underlying futures asset and the spot. Enterprises should make full use of futures and options tools to protect positions in hedging. At the same time, they should strengthen the observation and adjustment of risk exposure and make the futures positions follow the spot positions for liquidity management.

Enterprises should formulate risk early warning measures, and when extreme situations occur in the futures market, they should be able to close positions or deliver in time to alleviate position risks. Position risk is assessed by taking into account risk events that may occur and analyzing the potential impact of the events. Risk assessment for the delivery and closing of positions is carried out dynamically in accordance with the enterprise's business conditions and risk tolerance. In order to avoid bad consequences such as forced positions and unbearable risk to enterprises, enterprises should do a good job formulating risk response measures and constantly improving their risk response-ability.

5 Conclusion

Enterprises can effectively avoid the price risk of raw materials and finished products by hedging, but they will encounter many unexpected situations when carrying out hedging business. The impact of geopolitical and world turmoil has led to very volatile prices for nickel futures on the LME. Strict restrictions on the delivery of products on futures exchanges can make it quite limiting for enterprises to use the underlying product for hedging. Enterprises actively hold unreasonable amounts of futures positions, laying the groundwork for failure to complete delivery. In order to better manage hedging risk, enterprises should first establish risk awareness and formulate hedging strategies based on their own conditions. Moreover, it is necessary to clarify the enterprise's strategic objectives and improve the risk control ability of the strategic decision-making layer. When the underlying futures are severely restricted, look for a combination of multiple financial derivative instruments to diversify the hedging risk. Enterprises should establish reasonable hedging positions according to demand and improve the early warning mechanism for closing and delivery.

This paper analyzes the risks encountered by enterprises in the process of hedging to avoid the risk of price fluctuations of raw materials and finished products under the background of international turmoil and geopolitical influence, puts forward corresponding countermeasures and suggestions, and bridges the gap in the analysis of the complexity of the world situation in conventional hedging operations; and helps real enterprises to establish risk management principles when conducting hedging operations and enables companies to consider diversification risks in a multifaceted manner and to avoid situations where they are exposed to large risk exposures. It also promotes establishing comprehensive risk control and sound regulatory systems by real enterprises and improves the reaction speed and response-ability to deal with hedging risks.

This paper focuses on qualitative research through the case of the Tsingshan Nickel incident, missing the use and analysis of data. Future research can conduct more in-depth research through data investigation and game model derivation of enterprise hedging business.

References

1. J. Xiuzhen, Q. Lin. Journal of Shanghai Jiao Tong University, 471-473+478 (2005)
2. S. M. Bartram, G. W. Brown, J. Conrad. Financial Development, **46**(4),967-999 (2011)
3. X. Gede, W. Yang, L. Xinjie, J. Tingting. Financial Development, **2**, 40-46 (2019)
4. Z. Zhao lin, H. Xue guang. Academic Journal of Zhongzhou, **7**, 33-37 (2022)
5. L. Ai hua, D. Yuyang. China Collective Economy, **4**, 91-92 (2022)
6. C. Guojun, T. Jiayi. Financial Accounting, **7**, 13-17 (2019)
7. G. Futures. Nickel fundamental weekly analysis. Retrieved from https://www.yhqh.com.cn/upload/cn/uploadfile/2023/1022/20231022082116194.pdf (2023)
8. L. Weian, D. Wentao. Journal of Audit & Economics, **28**(04), 3-12 (2013)
9. F. Junhui, Z. Weiguo, D. Qian, K. Wentao. Journal of Management Science, **24**(03), 86-93 (2011)
10. X. Quanwei. Researches in Chinese Economic History, **02**, 146-159 (2018)

The impact of digital economy on consumption and education industry: Taking China as an example

Huiyu Chen*

School of International Education, Wuhan University of Technology, Wuhan, Hubei Province, 430070, China

Abstract. Looking around the world, a new round of scientific and technological revolution and industrial transformation is developing in depth. The digital economy has become an important factor affecting global resource allocation, industrial structure, and the international division of labor. Promoting the development of the digital economy has become an important strategic direction for most countries. The digital economy is shining brightly in daily consumption, education, and other fields. This article uses macro, meso, and micro education to conduct a detailed analysis of the market structure and impact of the digital economy on daily consumption and education and discovers the electrification of digital consumption and digital education. The study found that the pain points of digital consumption include insufficient protection of consumer privacy, uneven quality of digital consumption, and insufficient supervision of digital consumption. The pain points of digital education are the difficulty in acquiring customers, the high cost of acquiring customers, and the need to improve teaching quality and rapidly expand the market. Conflicts and limited online teaching formats lead to low accuracy in performance testing.

1 Introduction

Digital technology has become more and more interwoven into the process of economic and social growth across a range of industries in recent years as innovations have been accelerated by the Internet, big data, cloud computing, artificial intelligence, blockchain, and other technologies. The digital economy in China has essentially progressed through three stages: the gestation of technology, the explosive growth stage, and the integration and coordination stage, which involves deepening application, standardizing development, and promoting inclusive sharing [1]. Digital technology is of great significance to life consumption, tourism, travel, game education, etc., and has greatly changed the development pattern of these fields. Now, this article will take China as an example to make a more detailed analysis of the impact of the digital economy on life consumption and education from macro, meso, and micro perspectives.

2 Daily consumption

2.1. Macroscopic

2.1.1 Policy

Regarding everyday consumption, the Chinese government aggressively advances the role of the digital economy in daily consumption while actively adhering to current trends. According to the State Council's notification on the release of the "14th Five-Year Plan" digital economy development plan, my nation's digital economy will advance to a new stage of inclusive sharing, standardized development, and deepening application during this time.

Table 1 Main indicators of digital economy development during "the fourteenth five-year plan"

Index	2020	2025	Property
The proportion of GDP that the digital economy's key industries' added value represents. (%)	7.8	10	Anticipation
Number of IPv6 active users (100 million households)	4.6	8	Anticipation
Amount of people using gigabit broadband (10,000 households)	640	6000	Anticipation
The size of the information technology services and software industry (trillion yuan)	8.16	14	Anticipation

* Corresponding author: 2016141414001@stu.scu.edu.cn

Table 1 Main indicators of digital economy development during "the fourteenth five-year plan" (continuous)

Application penetration rate of industrial websites (%)	14.7	45	Anticipation
National online retail sales (trillion yuan)	11.76	17	Anticipation
E-commerce transaction scale (trillion yuan)	37.21	46	Anticipation
Number of real-name users of online government services (billion)	4	8	Anticipation

Data source: Ma [2]

According to Table 1, China's outlook for the development of the digital economy during the 14th Five-Year Plan shows that within 5 years, the number of gigabit broadband users will increase nearly 10 times, the user base of the digital economy will continue to expand, and online retail sales and electronic business transactions will also grow. This indicates that in the next few years, the combination of the digital economy and daily consumption will develop rapidly and achieve healthy growth. It can be seen that the Chinese government has a positive and standardized attitude towards digital consumption. China is actively seizing the opportunities of the times and vigorously developing the role of the digital economy in consumption.

2.1.2 Economics

Consumption channels: China's e-commerce sales in 2020 amounted to 11.76 trillion yuan, indicating a 10.9% rise over 2019. Of these, 24.9% of all retail sales of consumer products were made through the sale of physical items through online channels, with 9.76 trillion yuan in sales. China has 782 million online shoppers as of December 2020, up 72.15 million from March 2020; this represents 79.1% of all Internet users in the country.

Online retail stimulates both the urban and rural consumption cycles in terms of the domestic consumption cycle. Cross-border e-commerce contributes to the stabilization of foreign trade in relation to the twin cycles of domestic and international trade. Furthermore, internet live streaming has rapidly developed into a new digital business model based on "online traffic + physical consumption". With 66.2% of live streaming e-commerce users buying live streaming items, live streaming e-commerce has grown in popularity among consumers [3].

Living and Purchase Patterns: People have decided to stay at home more frequently as a result of the pandemic, which has driven up demand for internet services. The growth of the digital economy has become a crucial strategy in recent years for many nations looking to expedite economic recovery. In light of these factors, the fast advancement of digital consumption has encouraged the modification and modernization of digital consumption models. People's habits and consumption patterns are increasingly shifting as a result of digital consumption [4].

Consumption disparity between rural and urban dwellers and consumption structure optimization: The digital economy has considerably tapped into the spending potential of rural dwellers, fueled by new digital economy forms represented by these technologies and influenced by developing technologies like big data, artificial intelligence, and mobile Internet. It is evident that consumer demand has gotten more diverse, which has resulted in ongoing modifications and improvements to the structure of consumption. Additionally, the digital economy can not only greatly improve the production and service efficiency of enterprises but also significantly expand the employment scale of enterprises. This, in turn, improves labor productivity and production quality, thereby promoting the adjustment of the income distribution structure, increasing the effective demand of residents, and improving the consumption level and standard, thereby promoting the transformation and upgrading of the consumption structure [4].

Many fresh forms of consumption have been partially expanded as a result of certain changes in the living conditions and consumption patterns of both urban and rural populations. Due in large part to the ongoing advancements in contemporary communication technology and the Internet, even urban and rural populations may make payments and utilize mobile phone and computer clients [5].

2.1.3 Social

Digital consumption can help transform urban space: Many cities have recognized the potential of digital consumption and strongly support the development of related new business formats. Taking Ningbo as an example, during the Information Consumption Experience Day event in October 2021, Ningbo showcased 27 digital consumption experience interactive projects, encompassing consumption scenarios such as communications, medical care, people's livelihood, finance, and entertainment. The city also unveiled the Ningbo Mobile Tianning flagship, which includes 13 municipal-level information consumption experience centers, such as the Ningbo Smart City Science and Technology Museum, to cultivate and guide citizens in digital consumption. According to the head of the Ningbo Municipal Economic and Information Bureau, the establishment of an information consumption experience center will accelerate the advancement of information technology products and services to the upper echelons of the industrial chain in addition to offering rich, new digital life experiences that will foster the growth of digital consumption. People's awareness of knowledge, sense of gain, enjoyment, and security in the sphere of consuming are therefore improved as a result [6].

Digital consumption has also become an essential starting point for leveraging rural consumption upgrades and aiding rural revitalization. With the development of digital rural construction, the divide between urban and rural regions is closing and digital consumption is rising quickly in rural areas. As an illustration, consider internet purchasing. In China, rural online retail sales were 180 billion yuan in 2014; by 2020, they had grown to 1.79 trillion yuan. More than 130,000 village-level e-commerce service sites and over 2,000 county-level e-commerce public service and logistics distribution facilities have been constructed nationwide. With a 97.6% coverage percentage, express delivery outlets have reached over 30,000 towns and villages across the country. The increasing use of digital consumption in rural regions has improved the shopping experience for villagers by giving them access to a wider variety of higher-quality items [6].

2.1.4 Technology

It is impossible to distinguish the encouragement of information infrastructure development from the advancement and growth of China's digital consumption. China ranks first across the globe in the scope of information infrastructure building, according to the "White Paper on China's Digital Economy Development". More new technology being used means more chances to enhance digital consumption. China has the greatest 4G and optical fiber networks in the world. By the end of 2020, 96% of households have access to fixed broadband. With over 200 million 5G terminal connections and 718,000 5G base stations constructed, the 5G network development is the fastest and largest in the world [6].

2.2. Mesocosm (value chain)

2.2.1 Digital technology

Currently, new digital technologies such as big data, the Internet of Things, artificial intelligence, and blockchain are profoundly reshaping the "people-goods-field" of the retail industry, continuously driving the evolution of business models, operating rules, and competition. Digital consumption is becoming a new growth pole [7].

As the process of digitalization accelerates, on the one hand, the digitalization of production and manufacturing-end infrastructure has significantly improved, and digital technology is aiding in the further opening and sharing of the retail value chain. On the other hand, data accumulated on the sales and consumer side has become an essential production factor, driving supply chain innovation and promoting the empowerment and traction of the retail industry. While promoting the transformation of the industrial structure, digitalization can better meet the personalized needs of consumers, reshape the customized value chain with demand as the core, and bring about ecological changes in the entire retail industry [7].

A relatively representative product of the development of digital technology is the digital renminbi. The director of the Digital Currency Research Institute of the People's Bank of China said, "Digital RMB will coexist with traditional electronic payment tools for a long time." China has always supported the coordinated development of various payment methods. Digital RMB and general electronic payment tools exist in different dimensions and are both complementary and different.

2.2.2 Digital products and services

In recent years, with the development of smart terminals and mobile Internet, upgraded business formats such as social e-commerce and live broadcast e-commerce have been further spawned. With digital empowerment, users' scenario needs are more diverse and integrated, which also calls for the retail supply industry to be more intelligent and precise. Social e-commerce uses social media to drive sales and has become one of the hottest business trends in China. It is also an important disruptive force.

Today, mass Chinese consumers spend more than 7 hours a day on the mobile Internet, which is a fifth more than before the COVID-19 crisis. Of these 7 hours, about 2/3 are spent on social or content applications. More and more users are beginning to seek information from social media, key opinion leaders/key opinion consumers (KOL/KOC), and friends to make purchase decisions [8].

In China, there are a total of five types of social e-commerce prototypes, which are [8]:

Social traffic-draining platforms - KOL and KOC guide consumers to emerging e-commerce platforms or brand stores.

Social marketing e-commerce platform - KOL and KOC guide customers to e-commerce brand stores.

Social bargaining e-commerce - each new customer can enjoy a lower price to encourage social sharing of products.

Community group buying/S2B2C - Incentivize consumers and small businesses to sell to their circle of friends or social circles through commissions.

Social DTC - Brands and KOL/KOC interact directly with consumers in the WeChat group operated by the brand and achieve sales through the brand's own platform or WeChat mini program.

2.2.3 Digital marketing (trends)

With the gradual improvement of consumers' status and the increasing communication points with consumers under new retail, the operating model of brands has gradually transformed from traditional product and channel management to a consumer-centered operation model. The wave of digitalization transformation provides new opportunities for brands to deeply tap into consumer assets.

In actual business, people face many challenges in truly implementing "consumer-centeredness." First of all, the number of actual points of contact between brands and end consumers is limited, making it difficult to carry out direct and effective communication in a systematic manner. Therefore, for most brands, "consumer-centered" is more of an ideal and goal, with little impact on actual business. Guidance is still relatively limited.

In transforming the concept of "consumer-centered" from theory into practice, new retail platforms represented by Tmall have done a relatively good job. Based on the new generation of big data, the Internet of Things, AI, and other technologies, Alibaba has systematically integrated the information of more than 600 million consumers in its ecosystem through Uni-D. It also fully records every touchpoint in the consumer journey, allowing brands to communicate with a large number of consumers in a timely and effective manner and understand the specific needs of each type of consumer. This truly enables brands to carry out various businesses such as product research and development, marketing promotion, and category planning with consumers at the center [9].

2.3. Microscopic

2.3.1 Consumer characteristics

In today's era, with the rapid development of Internet technology, the channels through which people obtain information are becoming increasingly diversified. In this case, consumption concepts tend to be rational, consumption touchpoints are fragmented, and decision-making paths are decentralized. Consumption is not downgraded; rather, individuals are making smarter choices. Consumers are becoming more pragmatic and rational, with more people making purchasing decisions based on real needs, comprehensive exploration, and thorough comparison.

It can be seen from Table 2 that people have diverse consumption concepts. About 40% of people pursue brands and products that they need or that are cost-effective. Among the decision-making factors, people first pay attention to the quality of the product, followed by functionality, and finally cost-effectiveness. In the case of price comparison, when faced with different products, consumers will compare prices based on current information channels to obtain the most satisfactory products and prices. There are very few people who do not compare prices, accounting for only 6% of the total. Therefore, while people choose to consume digitally, about one-third of them search for coupons before shopping to get the best price.

Table 2 Influencing factors of consumer consumption

Consumption attitudes		Decision factors	Price comparison		Coupon favor	
41%	I buy everything I really need	In food and beverage, clothing, shoes and hats, beauty and cosmetics Consumer research on three major categories of personal care, quality is decided by consumers. The top 1 factors and check rates are: 14%, 14%, 12%	31 %	"I will carefully compare the prices of all products" [maximum]	32%	"Before I shop, I continually search for discounts." [maximum]
36%	I am willing to look for brands and products with the best value for money		6%	"Almost never compare prices" [minimum]	7%	"I won't pay attention to coupons" [minimum]

2.3.2 Environment

In 2022, the per capita disposable income of Chinese residents will be 24,538 yuan, showing a steady increase (please see Fig. 1). China currently has the world's largest and fastest-growing middle-income group, with more than 400 million people in 2017. According to McKinsey's prediction, there will be an additional 71 million middle-class families in the next three years [10].

Although China is the second-largest consumer market and the largest online retail market globally, according to World Bank standards (2020-2021), it is an upper-middle-income country (GNI reached the standard for the first time in 2010 and exceeded the average level for the first time in 2019). However, consumer desires are suppressed, and the residents' consumption rate has long been lower than the average level of the same group [10].

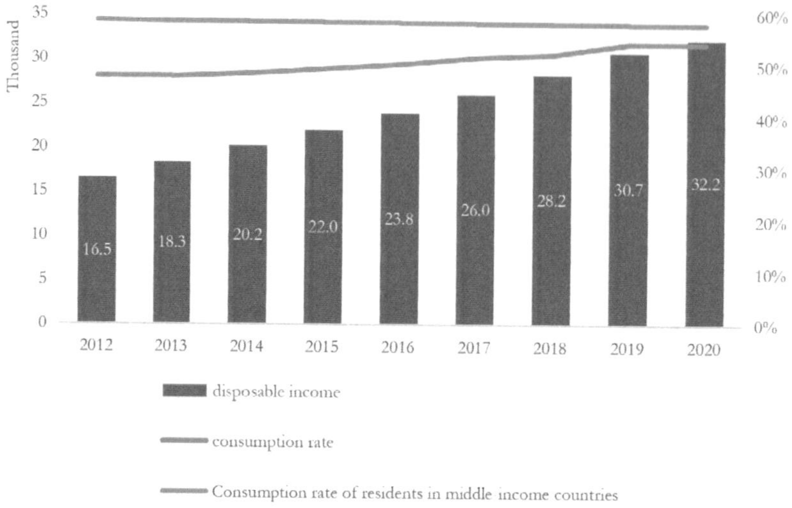

Fig. 1. Consumption and income level of Chinese residents

Photo credit: Original

The Ministry of Commerce has designated 2023 as the "Year to Boost Consumption," and restoring and expanding consumption has been prioritized. With continued efforts to expand domestic demand, policies and measures to promote consumption, and the gradual recovery of offline consumption scenes, China's consumer economy will gradually pick up. The epidemic has entered a new stage of prevention and control, and the normalization of production and life is expected to restore consumer confidence.

Table 3 Investigation into the reasons for the decline in consumption willingness of Chinese residents

	Decreased demand for goods due to the impact of the epidemic	The epidemic affects shopping /going out
Prime factor	23%	14%
Top three important factors	58%	43%

As can be seen from Table 3, in the survey on the reasons for the decline in consumption willingness, the impact of the epidemic has been selected as the top reason many times. From the perspective of the epidemic affecting the reduction in demand for goods, the epidemic is the main factor, accounting for 23%, and contributes to 58% of the top three important factors. From the perspective of the epidemic affecting shopping and travel, the epidemic is the main factor, accounting for 14%, ranking among the top three important factors. Overall, important factors accounted for 43%.

2.3.3 Information channels

Figure 2 shows that the channels through which consumers obtain information vary in different regions. Search engines, live broadcast rooms, and public accounts/video accounts all have a high proportion of selections, all above 60%. Secondly, short videos, e-commerce apps, social networking media, shopping mall stores, and official websites have a very high proportion influencing consumer decision-making, all above 10%.

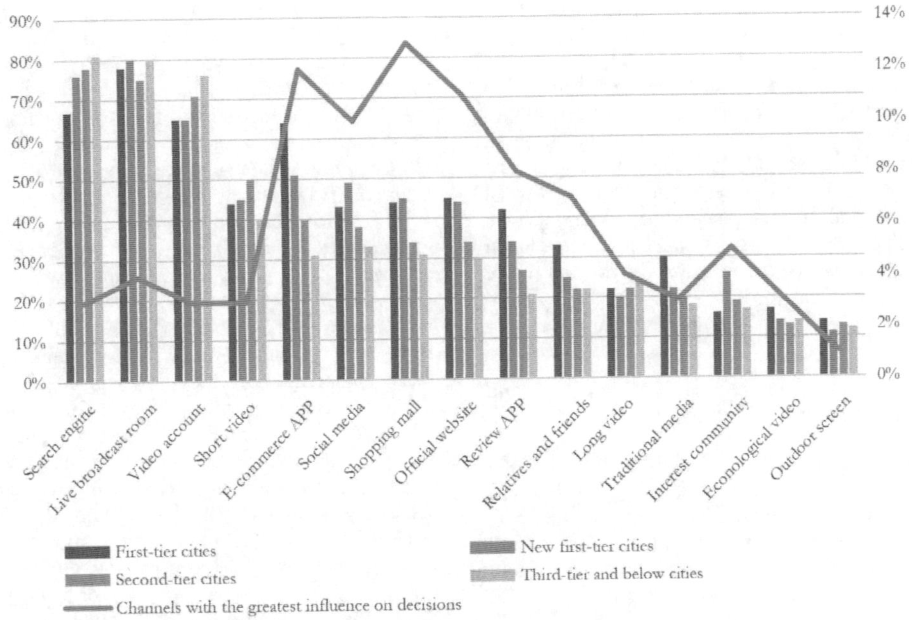

Fig. 2. Channels through which consumers obtain information and decision-making factors

Photo credit: Original

In addition, people should innovate digital consumption supervision methods, smooth the production-circulation-consumption cycle, strengthen data security and privacy protection, and better maintain digital consumption order. This includes building a digital consumption ecology to protect the legitimate rights and interests of consumers.

2.3.4 Pain points

Inadequate protection of buyer privacy: While the rapid growth of the digital marketplace necessitates the acquisition of vast amounts of user data to generate scale impacts, doing so also raises the possibility of personal information leaks.

Three variables contribute to the difficulty in safeguarding privacy. Initially, there is a great deal of knowledge asymmetry between users and data obtaining organizations. The collection of users' privacy and the purposes for which it is utilized are unknown to them. It is nearly impossible to retrieve the compromised privacy, secondly. One cannot retrieve compromised user privacy because digital information is widely copied, saved, and shared. Lastly, the extent of the harm resulting from privacy breaches is hard to quantify. Policies defending user privacy are quite hazy since there isn't a consensus regarding the worth of users' personal data. Cross-border data flows have raised the concern of privacy leakage [11].

The quality of digital consumption is uneven and breeds new problems: With the continuous development of new consumption, the industry has not only extended old problems in traditional consumption such as uneven product quality and difficult-to-guarantee after-sales service, but it has also given rise to new problems such as big data maturity, privacy leakage, and data security. The second issue is the abuse of market dominance, with repeated prohibitions on monopoly agreements, data blocking, "expiration," and refusal to trade. Finally, unfair competition behaviors such as counterfeiting, false propaganda, and fraud still exist [12].

2.4. Suggestions & outlook

At present, the digital economy is booming worldwide, and digital consumption has become an indispensable part of economic development. Regarding the further development direction of digital consumption, this article puts forward the following suggestions:

2.4.1 Improve the online market supervision system

During the development period of the online market, some behavioral activities with negative externalities are prevalent, harming the rights and interests of consumers. In recent years, some monopolistic behaviors, unfair competition, and abuse of market dominance have disrupted the market order. Therefore, it is recommended that the state introduce relevant policies to strengthen the internal ecological governance of platforms and urge platform companies to standardize rule establishment, data processing, algorithm formulation, and other behaviors. This will help standardize the order of online market competition and guide the healthy development of the digital economy.

2.4.2 Formulating a more secure and private digital consumption environment

It is essential to set up and maintain a system of security protection for digital consumption, raise the bar for security technology in digital consumption, apply technologies like face recognition, firewalls, and encrypted transmission, and strengthen user capabilities for data encryption and digital identity authentication. Furthermore, care should be taken to create and strengthen the system for protecting users' privacy when consuming digital content, make clear the rights and responsibilities of each party when consuming digital content, uphold users' freedom to know and make choices about their privacy, and increase users' awareness of and capacity for protecting their privacy.

2.4.3 Improving the balance of services and experiences in digital consumption

Along with increasing technological innovation in digital consumption, relevant enterprises need to develop new models, formats, and scenarios for digital consumption, enhance the quality of services provided and the overall digital consumption experience, and cater to the various and individual needs of digital consumption.

3 Education

3.1 Macroscopic

3.1.1 Policy

The "14th Five-Year Plan for Digital Economy Development" released by the State Council recently, included the following recommendations in column 8: improve network security protection capabilities, advance smart education, and encourage the orderly and intelligent upgrade of infrastructure. Additionally, it seeks to encourage the development of new educational infrastructure and a top-notch system of education support [2].

Secondly, the report of the 20th National Congress of the Communist Party of China made, for the first time, a "three-in-one" overall arrangement and deployment of education, science and technology, and talents. It included "promoting the digitalization of education" in the report and incorporated "building an educational power" into the goals of my country's development in 2035 as an overall goal [13].

But in July 2021, the General Office of the State Council and the General Office of the Communist Party of China released a statement titled "Opinions on Further Reducing the Homework Burden and Off-Campus Training Burden of Students in Compulsory Education." It suggested "double reduction," or lessening the amount of homework assigned to students enrolled in both off-campus training programs and required schooling. The Ministry of Education's Party Leadership Group considers it to be the "No. 1 Project."

3.1.2 Economic

The national fiscal education funds in China invested a total of 21.4 trillion yuan between 2018 and 2022, with an average annual growth rate of 7%. The percentage of GDP has consistently maintained over 4%, according to data from the Ministry of Education's Finance Department. In my nation, the number of full-time teachers climbed at an average annual growth rate of 3% from 16.7285 million in 2018 to 18.8036 million in 2022. In the same time frame, national fiscal education expenditures for teacher salaries and benefits rose by an average of 8% annually, making up 61% of the total and increasing by 2.4 percentage points to 63.4% [14]. The nation will spend 513.7 billion yuan, 2.6801 billion yuan, 955.6 billion yuan, and 1.6397 billion yuan on preschool education, compulsory education, high school education, and higher education, respectively, in 2022—an increase of 3%, 6.7%, 8.5%, and 8.5%, correspondingly, across the previous year. Kindergartens, regular elementary schools, regular junior high schools, regular high schools, secondary vocational schools, and regular colleges and universities all saw increases in their overall per-student education costs over the prior year of 7.3%, 5.2%, 3.6%, 2.8%, 1.2%, and 1.3%, in that proper order [15].

The state also attaches great importance to remote and backward areas. From 2018 to 2023, the central government has allocated a total of 85.5 billion yuan to continue supporting the implementation of relevant plans and policies to guide teachers to take root in rural areas and serve the grassroots. There will be further implementation of the special post plan to support a large number of college graduates to teach in rural schools in the central and western regions. Implementation of the "Three Regions" Talent Plan teacher special project and the Silver Age Lecture Plan, encouraging outstanding teachers and retired teachers to teach in poverty-stricken areas, ethnic minority areas, old revolutionary areas, and border areas, to promote schools in the central and western regions and underdeveloped areas to improve the quality of education and teaching [14].

From 2018 to 2023, the central government has allocated a total of 17.6 billion yuan to focus on strengthening the capacity building of teachers and improving education and teaching standards. The government will continue to implement the "National Training Plan" to train more than 1 million principals and teachers every year, significantly improving the level of rural school principals in running schools, running schools, and teacher education and teaching [14].

All things considered, China has consistently placed a high value on education and invests a substantial sum of money annually to support it, with annual spending increasing steadily. The nation will nextly proceed to unwaveringly carry out the decisions and agreements made by the State Council and the Party Central Committee regarding the prioritization of education development and investment, as well as the full realization of the contribution that education investment makes to development, equity, reform, and quality improvement in the building of an educational power. It carries out the strategy for developing education priorities and serves as a policy guiding body.

3.1.3 Social

A high percentage of Internet use promotes the growth of digital education: Based on Figure 3, it is evident that the population of Internet users in my nation is increasing gradually. The number of Internet users is steadily increasing as a result of the nation's accelerating Internet infrastructure building, improved information accessible services, and digital aging. By the end of 2022, there were 1.067 billion Internet users in my nation, up 3.44% from the previous year, with a 75.6% Internet penetration rate.

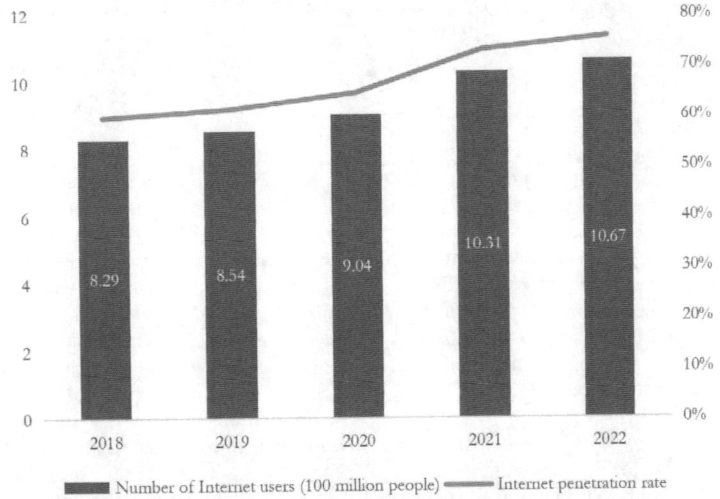

Fig. 3. China's Internet penetration rate and user base from 2018 to 2022

Photo credit: Original

The need for education is rising daily, and the nation's educational system is developing in an orderly manner. Furthermore, statistics given by the Ministry of Education indicates that there will be 518,500 schools nationwide in 2022, spanning all levels and categories. The country's student population makes up a sizable share, the scope of higher education and compulsory education has grown, and the need for education in society is rising. The need for talent and the nature of education have changed significantly as a result of the big data, blockchain, artificial intelligence, and other technologies developing so quickly. These changes have progressively altered the idea, culture, and ecology of education. There is now a greater need for digital education.

3.1.4 Technology

Infrastructure is becoming increasingly complete: Nowadays, the percentage of schools with Internet connectivity at all levels and types has reached 100%, with more than three-quarters of schools having wireless network coverage, and 99.5% of schools equipped with multimedia classrooms. The new education infrastructure is gradually advancing, and the construction of private education networks is actively deployed to promote the application of network technologies such as 5G and IPv6. Various regions are accelerating the construction of teaching environments such as intelligent interactive classrooms and virtual simulation laboratories, strengthening the connection and integration of physical space and virtual space, and promoting iterative upgrades of educational infrastructure [16].

High-quality resources achieve inclusive sharing: The national smart education public service platform continues to enrich the supply of high-quality resources, actively expand functional applications, and strengthen the supply of important public service products in the field of education. At present, the platform has brought together more than 44,000 primary and secondary school resources, over 1,300 vocational education professional teaching resource libraries, 27,000 high-quality university MOOCs, and online special resources such as "Shuren Classroom" to provide teachers, students, and social learners with a "one-stop" service. It has basically built the world's largest education and teaching resource library [16].

3.2 Mesocosm

The scope of digital education is very broad. Here, this paper only focuses on the field that accounts for the largest proportion of digital education—online education. The industry chain analysis of online education mainly discusses the value creation and delivery process of digital education from the three links of upstream, midstream, and downstream.

Table 4 Online education industry chain structure

Upstream industry	Midstream industry	Downstream industry
Resource supply	Online education	Demand users
Course development Course production Production of teaching aid materials Teacher development	Early childhood education K12 subject training Advanced education Vocational education Language education General quality education	B-side users
Online education technology support		Schools Businesses Educational institutions
Cloud services Platform construction Tool development System docking		C-side users Individual learner

Digital education's fundamental support system is known as the upstream link, and its content is its source of content resources. The creation of teaching aids, the hiring of instructors, and the development and production of online course materials are within the purview of content resource providers. In meantime, e-learning technology support offers systems, platform building, tool development, and online education cloud services for pertinent organizations and businesses, among other services [17].

The core and major part of online education, comprising different platforms, institutions, and businesses that may offer online education, is the central link in the chain of the online education sector. Early childhood education, K–12 subject instruction, higher education, vocational training, language instruction, and other high-quality education are all often covered via online learning in China (see Table 4). The consumers who desire online education are downstream. In China, the demand for online education may be broadly classified into two groups: C-end users, who are mostly individual students, and B-end users, who include businesses, educational institutions, and schools [17].

Schools are important demanders of digital education and need to use digital technologies and platforms to achieve personalized, intelligent, and systematic education. Individuals are the ultimate beneficiaries of digital education and need to use digital technologies and platforms to achieve lifelong learning and self-development.

3.3 Microscopic

3.3.1 Competitive landscape of online education

There are various participants in online education in my country. Upstream suppliers of live broadcast technology, intelligent voice, and comprehensive solutions provide technical support. Midstream online education startups continue to emerge and blossom in various subdivisions. To speed up the industrial chain, offline education institutions like New Oriental and TAL are setting up product matrices and hopping on the Internet wave. Online education has advanced significantly in the quality and vocational education sectors, despite a significant decline in demand from downstream consumers in the K12 subject training and education sector as a result of the "double reduction" strategy [18].

When the competitive environment of the online education sector is analyzed using Porter's "Five Forces" model, it is evident that the online education manufacturing sector faces somewhat intense rivalry. One of the "five forces" influencing the Chinese online learning market is [18]:

(1) Competition among existing competitors is relatively fierce: Although my country's K12 education sector is experiencing a cold spell, competition in vocational education, quality education, and other sectors has intensified.

(2) The upstream bargaining power is strong: Online education is based on cloud computing, video technology, and other software and hardware, and the update speed is fast, so the upstream bargaining power is strong.

(3) Robust downstream negotiating power: The online education sector is highly segmented, with numerous players operating in each, leading to a high level of product uniformity.

(4) The online education sector has average entrance hurdles and does not necessitate stringent technological constraints, making potential newcomers a danger. Although K12 education is no longer as profitable as it once was, there is still some attraction to the sector overall. Data indicates that a significant amount of cash has been drawn to the online education sector due to its enormous expansion potential. A total of 49 investments and financings totaling 14.34 billion yuan—a 48.29% year-over-year increase—occurred in the online education sector in the first half of 2020 (see Fig. 4).

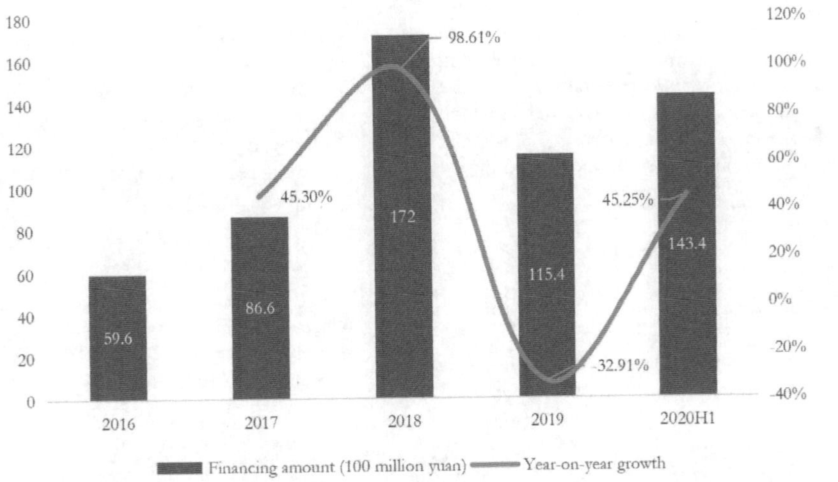

Fig. 4. The amount and growth rate of online education investment and financing in China from 2016 to 2020 H1

Photo credit: Original

(5) The risk of substitutes is greater: On the one hand, my country promotes after-school services in schools and occupies a considerable part of the extracurricular training market; on the other hand, as the output of free educational content on short video platforms such as Bilibili and Douyin becomes more and more high-quality, it will have a certain impact on online education companies.

3.3.2 Pain point analysis

Difficulty in acquiring customers and high cost of acquiring customers: The cost of acquiring customers in the online education industry is much higher than that of offline institutions, and the customer acquisition cycle is relatively long. Factors that parents need to consider when choosing an institution include reputation, cost-effectiveness, and service effectiveness, etc. These will all play a role to a certain extent, making it more difficult to acquire customers in the online education industry. Compared with the tangible products and services of offline institutions, choosing online education institutions will increase the safety risks of parents to a certain extent. The multifaceted superposition of the above factors has led to the difficulty and high cost of acquiring customers in the online education industry.

Improving teaching quality conflicts with rapid market expansion: In order to maintain market demand, various online courses neglected to consolidate their own educational concepts while maintaining a rapid update speed. This made it difficult to effectively integrate resources. Moreover, the most important indicator in the personnel evaluation system of online education institutions is often the continuation rate, making it difficult for teachers to concentrate on polishing their own standards. The final result is a waste of a lot of resources [19].

There are limitations to the online teaching approach, and test scores are not very accurate: PPT, text, and video instruction continue to dominate modern online learning environments, despite a slow but steady diversification of features. As such, the interplay and cross-referencing of educational materials are crucial. In Q&A portions while studying online, there are typically neither questions nor answers [19].

3.4 Suggestions & outlook

3.4.1 Raise the threshold for online quality education and strengthen supervision

In recent years, the online education industry has witnessed the simultaneous growth of large enterprises and small workshops, leading to endless educational problems. To further promote the development of the entire online quality education, it is necessary to formulate access standards for online quality education institutions and strictly control the teaching conditions and teaching content of online education institutions [19].

3.4.2 Focus on the training and construction of teachers

In order to further promote the development of the industry, the next step of reform should focus on increasing teaching research and teacher training and improving the training mechanism within the enterprise. At the same time, relevant government departments must also establish certain teaching quality standards to standardize the development of teachers' teaching activities and coordinate multiple platforms to supervise the quality of teachers' teaching [19].

3.4.3 Innovative teaching methods and methods of digital education

Digital education should be student-centered, focusing on cultivating students' innovative abilities and comprehensive qualities. It should adopt problem-oriented, project-based, inquiry-based, and cooperative teaching methods to enhance students' independent learning and cooperative learning abilities. Making full use of digital technology and resources to achieve personalized, intelligent, and scenario-based teaching can improve the effectiveness and interest of education. This approach aims to build an open and shared digital teaching environment.

4 Conclusion

Clearly, digital transformation is the craze of the moment. Concerning digital consumption, upgraded formats like social e-commerce and live streaming e-commerce have significantly improved consumers' spending power in recent years. However, digital consumption faces challenges such as insufficient user privacy protection, uneven product quality, and a lack of market supervision. This article recommends improving the online market supervision system by introducing relevant policies to strengthen the internal ecological governance of platforms. Additionally, it suggests enhancing the security and privacy protection of digital consumption through establishing and improving the security protection system and paying attention to the establishment and improvement of the privacy protection system. Moreover, it advocates for improving the balanced service and experience in digital consumption by increasing technological innovation to enhance the market vitality.

As for digital education, mainly online education, there are still various pain points. Therefore, digital education should improve thresholds for online quality education and strengthen supervision by formulating access standards for online quality education institutions. It should also focus on teacher training and construction, setting up certain teaching quality standards to standardize the development of teacher teaching activities. Lastly, it suggests coordinating multi-platform supervision of teacher teaching quality and advocating for innovative digital education teaching methods, such as a student-centered approach.

References

1. Y. Guo.(2023). Encourage the digital economy's growth in a high-quality manner and establish fresh catalysts for economic expansion. Economic Aspect, 23(12), 23-26.
2. J. Ma. Notice of the State Council on Issuing the “14th Five-Year Plan” Digital Economy Development Plan_Macroeconomics_Chinese Government Network. https://www.gov.cn/zhengce/content/2022-01/12/content_5667817.htm
3. Y. Cao. (2023). "China Internet Development Report (2023)" published. China Industry News. 23(3), 1.
4. X. Liu. New consumption trends in the digital economy era. Governance. 21(4), 16-18
5. H. Sun, P. Song. Research on the trend characteristics and dynamic mechanism of the transformation and upgrading of urban and rural residents’ consumption structure. XSS, (2), 57-65 (2022).
6. Z. Li.(2022). New technology and business models——A fresh look at digital consumer life. People's Daily Overseas Edition. 22(5), 1-3
7. J. Gu. Digital transformation fosters superior retail company development. Annual Conference Voice.
8. Caleb B, David P, H. Ye, B. Lan, Z. Li, Y. Chen.(2021) McKinsey China Consumer Special Issue. Leverage the power of social e-commerce to promote business growth in China – McKinsey Greater China.
9. Y. Liu, F. Zheng, C. Xie, C. Li, S. Sun, Y. Xu. (2022) Tmall & Bain. Digital transformation centered on brand consumers under new retail.
10. Fxbaogao. 2023 Omni-channel Consumer Digital Operation Guide. Hangzhou: Digital Cloud Marketing Academy (2023).
11. B. Shao, Z. Li, M. Ma. (2023) Concerns about consumer privacy protection in e-commerce and solutions in the big data age. "Internet Security Research and Usage". 23 (9), 126.
12. D. Wang. Enhance the effectiveness of market supervision in response to changes in the macroeconomic situation. CP, (3): 101-103 (2022).
13. J. Cao. (2023) Aggressively advance the strategic national action plan for education digitalization and quicken the building of an educational power. China Education Network. 23(6), 12.
14. Ministry of Education. The cumulative national financial investment in education from 2018 to 2022 is 21.4 trillion yuan - Government Portal of the Ministry of Education of the People's Republic of China. http://www.moe.gov.cn/fbh/live/2023/55499/mtbd/202309/t20230901_1077763.html
15. J. Cao. The total investment in education funding in 2022 is 6,134.4 billion yuan - The People's Republic of China Ministry of Education's official. http://www.moe.gov.cn/jyb_xwfb/s5147/202307/t20230703_1066834.html
16. B. Liu, R. Shang. (2023) Encouraging the modernization of higher education through digitalization: An analysis of China's higher education system's digital transformation plan in the age of digital intelligence. Forum for Education and Culture. 23(6),1-10.
17. Forward-looking Industry Research Institute. Analysis of the current status of the industrial chain and regional market structure of China's online education industry in 2021 K12 online education is developing rapidly_ Forward-looking trends. https://bg.qianzhan.com/trends/detail/506/210827-6917c7b0.html

https://doi.org/10.1051/shsconf/202418801006

18. P. Li. (2022) Forward-looking Industry Research Institute. Insight 2022: The competitive environment and market share of China's online education sector. Industry depth.
19. X. Xu, Y. Lan, Y. Wang. Opportunities and challenges of online education under the new coronavirus epidemic. MCI, 32, 129-130 (2020).

Investment Weightings of Technology and Traditional Stocks: Investor Choice and Risk Management

Chenxing Li[1,*]

[1]Faculty of Science and Engineering, University of Liverpool, Liverpool, L69 3BX, United Kingdom

Abstract. In the era of big data, the financial landscape is undergoing transformative changes through the integration of advanced technologies. This research delves into the dynamic realm of asset portfolios within the information technology industry, traditional sectors, and amalgamated portfolios containing popular giant stocks. Employing Python and machine learning, the study focuses on predicting expected returns, comparing and analyzing diverse portfolios to identify optimal investment strategies for risk management. Evaluation metrics include annual return, annual volatility, Sharpe ratio, and statistical charts. The findings highlight the lucrative potential of investing in the information technology sector, revealing an impressive annual return rate of 40.1%. In contrast, traditional industry portfolios not only underperform but also exhibit high-risk profiles and diminished returns. This research underscores the critical role of technological advancements and data-driven methodologies in shaping contemporary financial strategies for robust portfolio management. his research advocates for the strategic incorporation of technology-driven insights in financial decision-making, emphasizing the significant outperformance potential of information technology portfolios in navigating the complexities of modern investment.

1 Introduction

During this age of constant development in the financial markets, quantitative trading has become a common practice. For example, in their study conducted in 2019, Chakrabarty and Biswas employed the strategic Markowitz portfolio optimization approach to construct a portfolio using the stock performance of eight companies [1]. The outcome yielded favorable investment returns. Investors also tend to use quantitative method to allocate their investment. According to the research of Goodell et al., the integration of AI and ML is fundamentally reshaping the landscape of trading and investment choices [2]. The quantitative portfolio allocation which is based on machine learning is gradually accepted by the investors.

In the finical industry, AI is widely used to manage portfolio. Beccalli et al. used AI to manage portfolio and discuss the ethics problems [3]. What's more, Nawrocka used neural networks for portfolio creation and trading strategies [4]. Even in 2002, Chan et al. applied artificial intelligence to portfolio management [5]. Therefore, using artificial intelligence for portfolio research has become a trend and hot topic.

During this research, researchers has divided random stock data into three groups as three different types of portfolio strategies. These three sets of data respectively include the following types of stocks: 30 traditional stocks, 30 technology stocks and a hybrid strategy of 30 traditional and technology stocks. The primary goal is to identify a suitable investment strategy, with the central challenge revolving around predicting the movements of the three stock portfolios [6]. In this research, machine learning will be employed to ascertain the optimal weights for the stocks.

2 Methodology

This section primarily focuses on presenting the experimental code, comprising four components: Data, Model, Portfolio Construction, and Portfolio Simulation. As mentioned earlier, the experimental data spans from January 1, 2015, to June 30, 2023, and is segmented into three portfolios: technological, traditional, and mixed. Each portfolio consists of 30 randomly selected stocks from the S&P500. The technological portfolio specifically encompasses stocks from the 'Information Technology' industry as categorized by S&P500. The traditional portfolio encompasses various traditional industries, such as industrials, healthcare, financials, materials, and others. All selections within this category are made randomly and are cross-checked by human review to ensure the absence of any controversial enterprises regarding industry classification. Examples include Google, Amazon, and Tesla, which are confirmed through human verification.

As for the "Mixed" portfolio, it consists of 20 randomly selected stocks from various industries, with an additional inclusion of 10 hot stocks to simulate fund manager selection. The list of hot stocks includes codes like NVDA, TSLA, QCOM, MSFT, NFLX, ADBE,

* Corresponding author: C.Li105@student.liverpool.ac.uk

AMD, AMZN, GOOG, and META. Following the data handling phase, the next step is the Model component.

The research team opted for the "Walking Forward Machine Learning Model." The walk-forward approach differs somewhat from traditional machine learning and may prove more fitting for dynamic market changes in terms of its modelling. In each iteration, the walking forward model is trained on known historical data and subsequently applied to predict the next time point or period. The actual results are then disclosed, and the model is updated with this new data before making the subsequent prediction. This process simulates real-time application, mirroring a scenario where each prediction is generated after the model has observed the latest data [7]. Nevertheless, traditional machine learning cross-validation proves unsuitable for the dynamic nature of the market due to several reasons. Firstly, in conventional machine learning, the dataset is typically divided into a training set and a test set. The model is trained on the entire training set and then assessed on the test set. Secondly, the model is trained only once on the training set without any simulation of model updates upon encountering new data. In essence, the fixed dataset and one-time training of traditional cross-validation methods make them ill-suited to adapt to market changes. For model fitting the team used Ridge regression. This kind of regression is an extension of linear regression that solves the problem by adding a regularization term to the cost function (loss function). The goal of Ridge regression is to minimize this cost function. The inclusion of regularization encourages the model to favor smaller parameter values during the data fitting process, effectively minimizing the risk of overfitting [8]. Through the manipulation of the regularization parameter alpha, experiments gain the ability to regulate the model's sensitivity to regularization.

Next part is about Portfolio Construction. It primarily delves into convex optimization problems utilizing the CVXPY library for portfolio optimization. The team configured the problem to maximize portfolio return while minimizing portfolio volatility. Moreover, the optimal weights derived from the convex optimization problem are applied to ascertain the optimal weights at the current time point. In essence, convex optimization is employed to dynamically calculate the weights of various assets, leveraging predicted returns and the covariance matrix.

3 Empirical results

Historical data for these stocks is downloaded using the "yfinance" library and the returns of these stocks are calculated and forecasted using the rolling window method.

The graphical results are mainly: (1) Calculate the return of the portfolio and plot the cumulative return curve. (2) Output the portfolio backtesting results using the "pyfolio" library.

3.1 Tech-stock portfolio

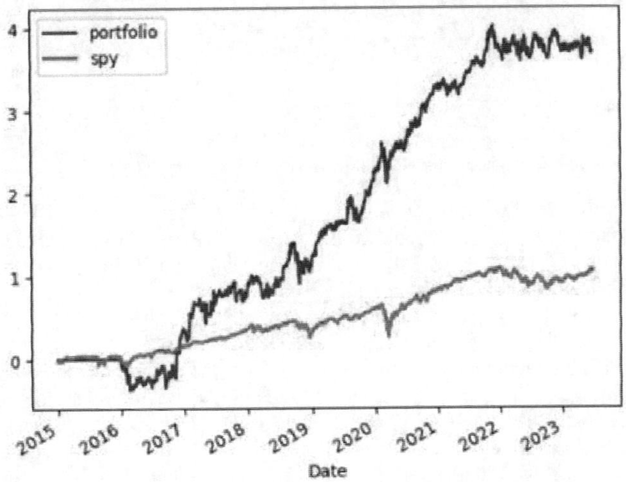

Fig. 1. Tech-stock portfolio return (Photo/Picture credit: Original).

In Figure 1 and Table 1, several key metrics are evident. The strategy demonstrates an annualized return of approximately 45.5%, while the total portfolio achieves a cumulative return of about 1,558.4% over the specified period. The portfolio's volatility is around 48.8% per year, indicating a potential monthly return fluctuation within a range of ±48.8%. The Sharpe ratio stands at 1.01, implying that the return per unit of risk taken surpasses the assumed risk-free rate (considered as 0%) by a factor of approximately 1.01 [9]. The Calmar ratio is 1.04, signifying that the investment return exceeds the risk-free rate plus one standard deviation of 4%. The maximum drawdown reaches a low of -43.7%, indicating a decline of 43.7% at its lowest point during this period. The maximum loss from a market peak to a market nadir, commonly called the maximum.

 https://doi.org/10.1051/shsconf/202418801007

Table 1. Tech-stock portfolio result.

	Backtest
Annual return	40.1%
Cumulative return	1,558.4%
Annual volatility	48.8%
Sharpe ratio	1.01
Calmar ratio	1.04
Max drawdown	-43.7%
Omega ratio	1.20
Sortino	1.51
Kurtosis	5.88
Tail ratio	1.05
Daily value at risk	-6.0%

Drawdown (MDD), measures how sustained one's losses can be [10]. The Omega ratio is 1.20, suggesting an expected excess return of 120 basis points (or 1.2%) annually for the portfolio. The Sortino ratio is 1.51, meaning the portfolio's return on each unit of downside risk taken surpasses the risk-free rate plus 1.51 standard deviations. The portfolio exhibits no significant bias, as its skewness is close to zero. With a kurtosis of 5.88, its return distribution is considerably flatter than a normal distribution. The tail ratio is 1.05, indicating a slight right-skewness at the top of the return distribution. The portfolio's daily value at risk is -6.0%, suggesting an expected probability of a 6% loss under normal market conditions.

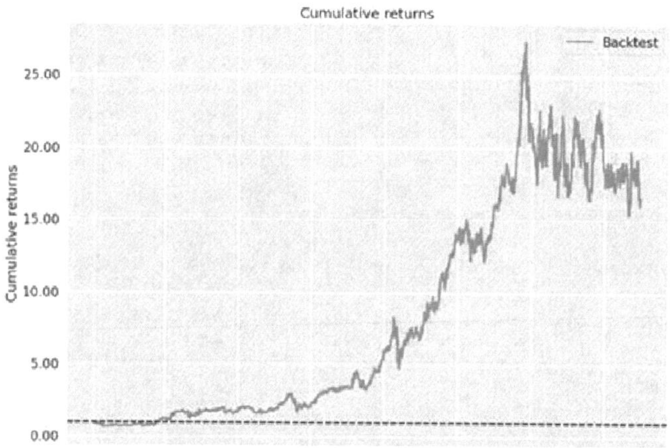

Fig. 2. Tech-stock cumulative return (Photo/Picture credit: Original).

Figure 2 illustrates the cumulative return over time, representing the total return of the investment or portfolio as time passes. This graph is useful for evaluating how well an investment performs, comparing different strategies, and analyzing the relationship between risk and return. According to the graph, the portfolio starts with an initial value of around 0.00 on the time axis, indicating no profit or loss initially. The highest point on the graph, situated beyond 25.00 on the time axis, reflects a cumulative return of 2500%. To put it simply, if the initial investment was $100, the portfolio would be valued at $2500 at that specific point in time. This visual representation provides a clear picture of how the investment evolves over the specified timeframe.

Figure 3(a) is rolling Sharpe Ratio (6 months): this is a line graph showing the Sharpe Ratio recalculated over 6 months. The portfolio's risk varies and reaches a peak (approximately 5.00) in the later months of the year, suggesting a gradual improvement in the portfolio's risk-adjusted return. Moreover, the average Sharpe ratio consistently exceeds 1.

Figure 3(b) is the percentage of underwater area, showing the portion of the portfolio's market value on a given day that is less than the initial market value. This chart aids in assessing the maximum decrease in the portfolio's value over time and quantifying the losses at different percentage levels. In the timeframe from 2022 to 2023, the portfolio experienced a more significant decline, exceeding 40%, and this decline persisted for an extended duration with substantial decreases.

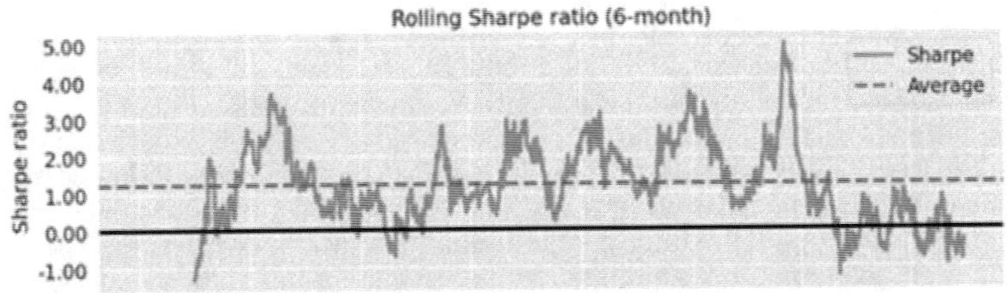

(a) Rolling Sharpe ratio

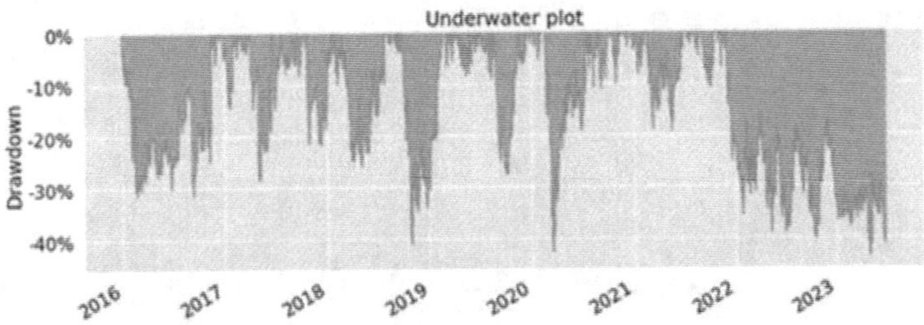

(b) Underwater plot

Fig. 3. Tech-stock rolling Sharpe ratio and the underwater plot (Photo/Picture credit: Original).

3.2 Traditional stock portfolio

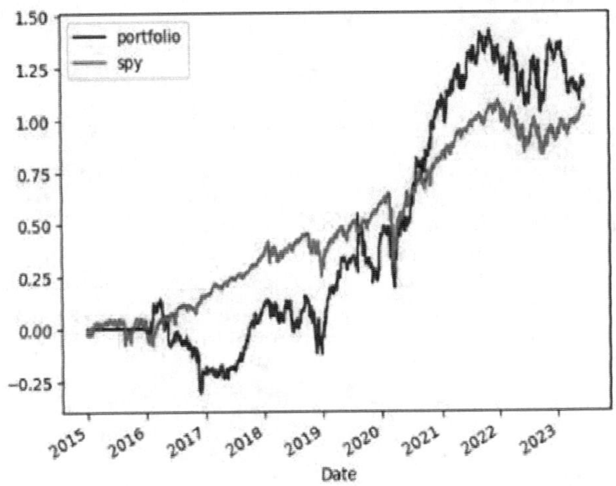

Fig. 4. Traditional stock portfolio return (Photo/Picture credit: Original).

Table 2. Traditional stock portfolio result.

	Backtest
Annual return	12.0%
Cumulative return	134.3%
Annual volatility	29.5%
Sharpe ratio	0.53
Calmar ratio	0.31
Max drawdown	-38.3%
Omega ratio	1.10
Sortino	0.80
Skewness	1.01
Kurtosis	18.90
Tail ratio	1.01
Daily value at risk	-3.7%

In Figure 4 and Table 2, the portfolio shows an annualized return of 12.0%. This implies that if someone had invested in this portfolio since December 31, 2015, the annual return on investment would have been 12.0%. As of June 29, 2023, the cumulative return for the portfolio is 134.3%. The annualized volatility is 29.5%, suggesting that the portfolio's prices have experienced higher fluctuations during this period, indicating a greater level of risk. The Sharpe ratio is 0.53, meaning that for every 1 unit of risk assumed, the portfolio earns an additional 0.53 units of return. The max drawdown, at -38.3%, represents the most significant loss the portfolio faced over the past few years. An Omega ratio of 1.10 indicates the excess return the portfolio has generated while enduring certain losses. The fact that it's greater than 1 suggests higher volatility compared to market levels and increased risk. The Sortino ratio of 0.80 indicates that the portfolio earns a higher excess return when exposed to a unit of downside risk. A skewness of 1.01 suggests a positively skewed return distribution, implying a longer right-hand tail and the possibility of some extreme positive returns. The kurtosis of 18.90 indicates a return distribution much steeper than the normal distribution. The tailed ratio of 1.01 suggests a slightly higher probability of the portfolio's return distribution being in the left tail compared to the normal distribution. The daily value at risk of -3.7% signifies the maximum potential daily loss the portfolio could incur.

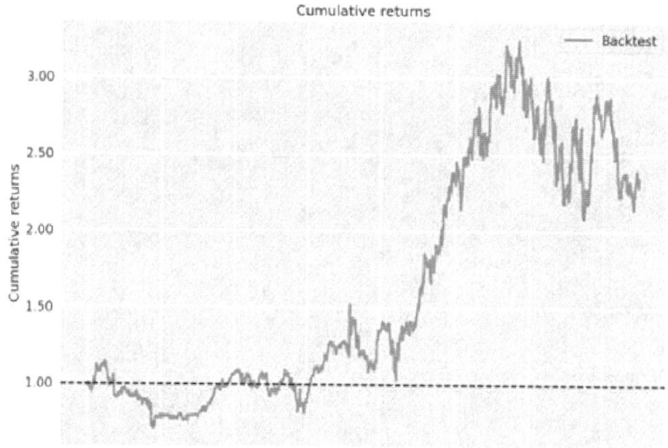

Fig. 5. Traditional portfolio cumulative returns (Photo/Picture credit: Original).

In Figure 5, the portfolio starts with an initial value of 1.00. The peak on the time axis reaches 3.00, signifying a cumulative return of 300%. To put it differently, if the initial investment were $100, the portfolio's value at this specific point would be $300.

Figure 6(a) shows the rolling Sharpe ratio peaks (above 4.00) during the early and middle periods, fluctuating slightly in the later periods and frequently dipping below 0. Additionally, the average Sharpe ratio is less than 1. Figure 6(b) demonstrates a greater occurrence of assets declining below their initial market value in the years 2017, 2018, 2020, and 2023. Notably, in 2017, assets below the market value constituted 40% of the portfolio, indicating a more substantial decline during that particular period.

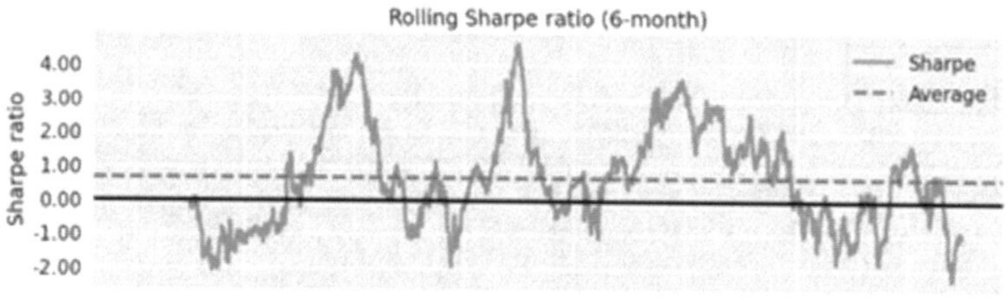

(a) Rolling Sharpe ratio

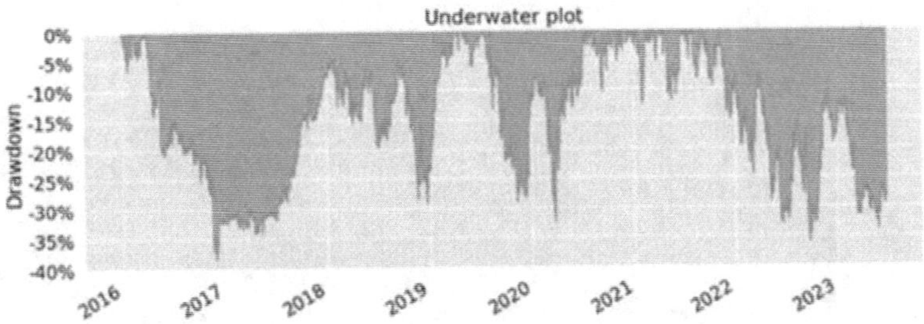

(b) Underwater plot

Fig. 6. Traditional portfolio rolling Sharpe ratio and the underwater plot (Photo/Picture credit: Original).

3.3 Mixed stock portfolio

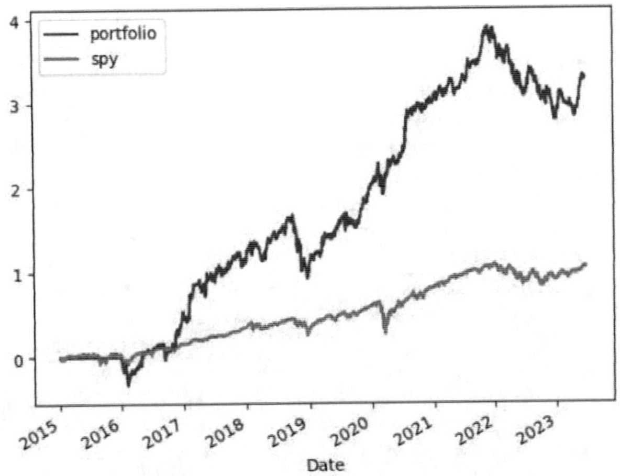

Fig. 7. Mixed stock portfolio return (Photo/Picture credit: Original).

Table 3. Mixed stock portfolio result.

	Backtest
Annual return	40.1%
Cumulative return	1145.6%
Annual volatility	45.0%
Sharpe ratio	0.97
Calmar ratio	0.56
Max drawdown	-71.7%
Omega ratio	1.19
Sortino	1.46
Skewness	0.17
Kurtosis	5.10
Tail ratio	1.15
Daily value at risk	-5.5%

In Figure 7 and Table 3, the portfolio has an annualized return of 40.1%. The cumulative return is 1145.6%. The extent of the portfolio's annualized volatility is 45.0% showing the range of price changes. The Sharpe ratio is 0.97 which is smaller than 1 and means the diversity is not very well. The Calmar ratio is 0.56, indicating a higher risk. The max drawdown which is the largest decline in the portfolio's history, is -71.7% in this portfolio. The Omega ratio is 1.19 which is bigger than 1, indicating higher volatility than market levels and higher risk. 1.46 of the Sortino ratio means that taking 1 unit of downside risk can result in a return of 1.46 units. The skewness is 0.17, indicating the portfolio is relatively symmetrical and only slight leftward deviation. The kurtosis is 5.10 meaning that the shape of the return distribution is much steeper than normal. The tail ratio of 1.15 has a higher probability falls in the left tail rather. The daily value at risk that describes the maximum loss could face per day is -5.5%.

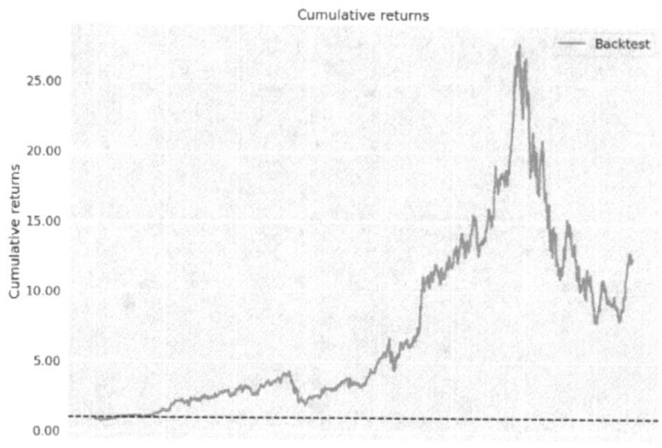

Fig. 8. Mixed portfolio cumulative returns (Photo/Picture credit: Original).

In Figure 8, the manifestation of cumulative return of the mixed stock is similar to that of tech-stock. The initial value of the portfolio is around 0.00, indicating no gain or loss. The highest point of the portfolio on the time axis is over 25.00, indicating a cumulative return of 2500%. This means that if the initial investment was $100, then at this point in time, the investment is worth $2500.

Figure 9(a) shows that the rolling Sharpe ratio fluctuates more gently, for the most part above the average ratio, with only a few instances where it falls below 0. In addition, the average Sharpe ratio is close to 1.

Figure 9(b) shows that the portion of the portfolio's market capitalization on a given day that is lower than the initial market capitalization is small, and only in 2019 and 2023 is the situation more pronounced, with a larger portion of the market capitalization loss.

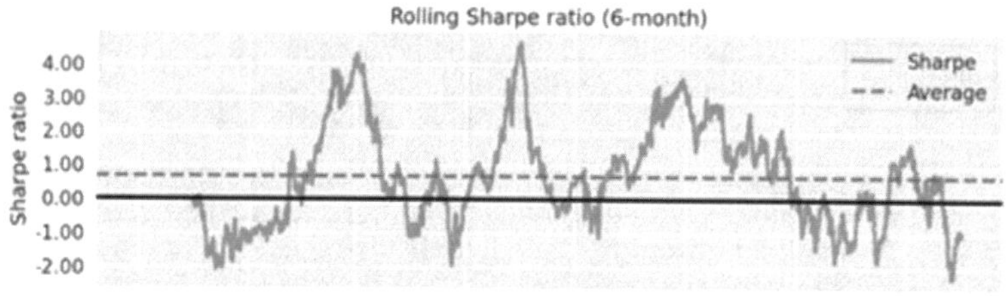

(a) Rolling Sharpe ratio

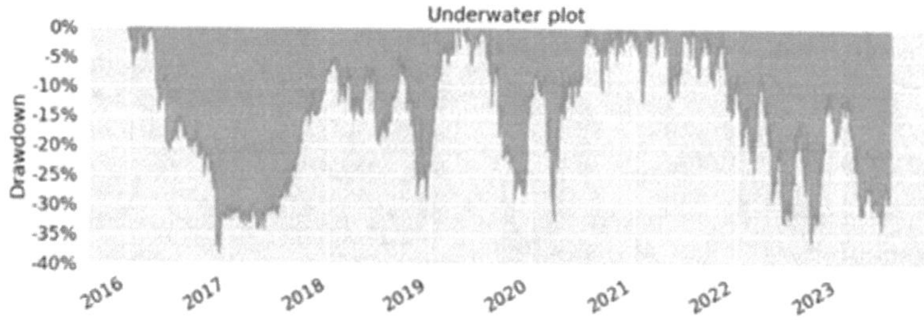

(b) Underwater plot

Fig. 9. Mixed stock portfolio rolling Sharpe Ratio and the underwater plot (Photo/Picture credit: Original).

3.4 Comparison

The results include predictions of the technical, traditional, and mixed portfolios, each with a specified alpha value. This part will focus on analyzing and comparing the differences between the three results.

The first portfolio which needs to analyze is tech-portfolio. From the Graph 1, it has shown numerous useful information. From a temporal standpoint, the tech portfolio did not initially outperform the SPX500. However, two years later, it experienced explosive growth that far surpassed the market. This trend persisted until 2021 before showing signs of slowing down. In the last three years, the market exhibited fluctuations. Solely based on visual observations, the tech portfolio appears to be an outstanding investment at the moment. Table 1 reinforces this perspective, indicating an annual return rate of 40%, a cumulative return rate of 1558%, and an average Sharpe ratio of 1.01. Furthermore, Graph 3 illustrates numerous instances where the Sharpe ratio exceeds 4. Despite an annual volatility of 48.8%, most of the fluctuations, as depicted visually, are positive and consistently increasing. However, it's crucial to note that the maximum retracement has reached 43.7%, and the Daily Value at Risk has peaked at 6%. In summary, the tech portfolio represents a high-risk, high-reward investment.

The second portfolio which needs to analyze is traditional portfolio. Evaluating the statistical charts, the performance of the traditional portfolio appears less promising, as it consistently falls short of outperforming the market. It took six years from the outset to marginally surpass the market. During most of this period, its performance lagged behind, dealing a significant blow to investor confidence. It's highly likely that investors abandoned this portfolio a few years ago, opting instead for investments in the SPX500 index. By focusing solely on the data in Table 2, the traditional portfolio seems relatively stable, boasting a 12% annual return, a 29.5% annual fluctuation, and a maximum drawdown of only 38.3%. Indeed, when considering only these metrics, it appears more stable than the tech portfolio. However, this slight advantage in volatility comes at a cost—the cumulative return is significantly lower than that of the previous asset portfolio, and the risk remains considerable. The modest 5% reduction in the maximum drawdown results in prolonged underperformance compared to the market, with returns several times inferior to those of the tech portfolio. Clearly, the traditional portfolio exhibits high risk and low return characteristics.

The third portfolio is mixed portfolio. Considering the rate of return, the mixed portfolio stands out noticeably. Its returns are only slightly less than the first portfolio, and the Sharpe ratio has also reached 0.97. However, the portfolio's volatility and maximum drawdown rate are substantial, with the maximum drawdown even reaching 71.7%. In summary, the mixed portfolio represents a high-risk, high-return investment positioned between the tech portfolio and the traditional portfolio.

Based on the analyses of the three investment portfolios, the tech portfolio shows the highest performance according to the Sharpe ratio, followed by the mixed portfolio and, finally, the traditional portfolio.

3.5 Cumulative returns vs. holding period returns

In the section dedicated to portfolio simulation and backtesting, the returns of the portfolio are represented by both the blue and green lines in the result graphs, such as Graph 4 and Graph 5. However, their trends exhibit slight variations, which can be ascribed to the utilization of two distinct methods for calculating returns, as evident in the provided code. The blue line illustrates cumulative returns derived through "cumsum", while the green line depicts holding period returns calculated using "cumprod".

Cumulative return signifies the overall return across a specific time span and can be computed utilizing the "cumsum" function. This function adds up the returns at each time point, yielding the cumulative return over the entire designated time period.

Holding period return, on the other hand, refers to the total return over a specific holding period of an investment. It can be calculated using "cumprod", where the returns at each time point are multiplied together to obtain the overall return over the holding period.

The computation of cumulative return presupposes a consistent principal amount. As such, the cumulative return for an investment signifies the overall gain or loss the investment has experienced over time, without considering the specific duration of the investment. In contrast, holding period return operates on the assumption of a growing principal over time. Consequently, holding period return exhibits exponential growth, while the growth of cumulative return appears comparatively subdued. Based solely on the observable trends in the chart, holding period return appears more favorable than cumulative return in the short term.

4 Conclusion

Based on the research findings, opting for an all-tech asset allocation appears to be the optimal choice given the same level of risk. Contrary to common investor beliefs, investing in traditional industries doesn't seem to translate into less risky or more stable returns; moreover, it might pose challenges for investments to outperform the market. Even a blend of technology stocks, traditional industries, and currently popular technology giants, as seen in the mixed portfolio, did not achieve the anticipated level of stability in fluctuations, despite yielding substantial returns. These outcomes serve as a reminder for investors to consider industries with promising development prospects. Simultaneously, the existence of traditional portfolios underscores that elevated risks do not necessarily equate to higher returns. Investors should use a cautious attitude and scientific concepts to make investments based on the market environment.

An inherent assumption in the code section involves liquidating all assets at the close of each month and reconstructing the portfolio at the start of the month. This practice is infrequent in actual trading scenarios, potentially introducing bias to the predictions. When computing the covariance matrix, it simplifies the model by abstracting it from the training data, utilizing the entire dataset instead. If the model were optimized using solely the training data, it might yield different outcomes.

Regarding the choice of asset portfolio data, relying solely on the information technology industry for constructing the tech-portfolio may seem somewhat limited. It would be beneficial to include recently popular AI-related companies, as certain entities excel in AI applications without being classified under the information technology industry—Tesla being a notable

https://doi.org/10.1051/shsconf/202418801007

example. Moreover, given the random selection of companies, including numerous traditional industries, there is a challenge in ensuring the exclusion of companies from declining traditional sectors. This potential inclusion might adversely impact the performance of the traditional portfolio or mixed portfolio.

Although this study reveals the investment results for different types of portfolios, it also has some limitations and shortcomings. If research can classify the investment industries more carefully, set up more control groups and change the machine learning algorithm, paper may get more results. In addition, it is hoped that machine learning can be more widely used in related research.

References

1. N. Chakrabarty and S. Biswas, Strategic markowitz portfolio optimization (smpo): a portfolio return booster, 2019 9th Annual Information Technology, Electromechanical Engineering and Microelectronics Conference (IEMECON), pp. 196-200 (2019).
2. J. W. Goodell, S. Kumar, W. M. Lim, & D. Pattnaik. JBEF, 32, 100577 (2021).
3. E. Beccalli, V. Elliot, & F. Virili. Artificial intelligence and ethics in portfolio management. In Lecture notes in information systems and organisation, pp. 19–30 (2020).
4. D. Nawrocka. Machine learning for trading and portfolio management using Python. Berlin School of Economics and Law (2018).
5. E. M. H. Chan, C. W. Wong, W. Tse, B. K. Cheung, & G. Y. N. Tang. Artificial intelligence in portfolio management. In Springer eBooks, pp. 403–409 (2002).
6. Z. Tang & G. Gupta. Stock investment strategies and portfolio analysis. In Advances in intelligent systems and computing, pp. 397–406 (2022).
7. P. B. C. Gray. Stock prediction with ml: walk-forward modeling. The Alpha Scientist (2018).
8. C. Saunders, A. Gammerman, & V. Vovk. Ridge regression learning algorithm in dual variables. International Conference on Machine Learning, 515–521 (1998).
9. W. F. Sharpe. JPM, 21(1), 49–58 (1994).
10. M. Magdon-Ismail & A. F. Atiya. RM, 17(10), 99-102 (2004).

Risk Management in Derivatives Markets: Integrating Advanced Hedging Strategies with Empirical Analysis

Fengshuo Liu[1,*]

[1]College of Information Science and Engineering/College of Artificial Intelligence, China University of Petroleum (Beijing), Chengbei Street, Beijing, 102249, China

Abstract. This study provides a comprehensive analysis of hedging strategies in the Chinese 50ETF options market, emphasizing dynamic hedging, Value at Risk (VaR), and machine learning-based approaches. Each strategy is meticulously evaluated against various market conditions, revealing distinct strengths and weaknesses. Dynamic hedging proves cost-effective in stable markets but struggles in high volatility scenarios, limiting its risk reduction capacity. Conversely, the VaR model, while reducing risk effectively under extreme conditions, may lead to over-hedging in calmer markets due to high costs and dependence on historical data. Machine learning strategies excel in adapting to complex and nonlinear market dynamics, though their effectiveness is contingent on data accuracy and model robustness. The study highlights the criticality of aligning strategies with market specifics and investor risk profiles, advocating for adaptable risk management in the fluctuating realm of financial derivatives. It provides empirical insights into modern hedging methods, offering practical guidance for their application in dynamic financial markets.

1 Introduction

1.1 Research background

Under the influence of globalization and technological advancement, financial markets are fraught with complexity and uncertainty, undergoing unprecedented transformations. In an uncertain financial environment, risk management becomes crucial for optimizing portfolio management [1]. The Chinese 50ETF options market, as a typical emerging market, has rapid growth and high volatility, highlighting the importance of efficient risk management strategies. In recent years, this market has shown significant growth and diversification trends, including surges in trading volume, diversification of participants, and increasing complexity of market structures. These changes bring substantial business opportunities and significantly increase market risks, especially for derivatives, a highly leveraged financial instrument. Traditional risk management and hedging strategies are severely challenged when faced with such market conditions. This study explores and evaluates advanced hedging strategies suitable for such markets, like dynamic hedging, VaR-based risk management, and strategies incorporating the latest machine learning technologies. Discussion and implementation of these methods are crucial for understanding and controlling the complexity of the derivatives market, offering vital theoretical and practical support for the stability and sustainable development of financial markets.

These hedging strategies hold significant commercial value, as they can improve market efficiency and transparency, reduce systemic risks, and have notable social value. They help protect investor interests and promote the stable development of financial markets. Moreover, with the ongoing evolution of global financial markets, particularly the rise of new areas like cryptocurrencies, the hedging strategies explored in this study have significant practical significance for the current market and offer a forward-looking perspective for addressing future market uncertainties and risks. Therefore, this research focuses on solving current issues and future financial market trends, carrying profound significance.

1.2 Literature review

Rao delved deeply into the key role of financial derivatives (such as futures, options, and swaps) in risk management [2]. He highlighted that the proper use of these tools could effectively manage risks, reduce costs, and enhance returns. He also emphasized understanding the complexity of these derivative instruments in practical operation, providing a theoretical reference for analyzing hedging strategies and evaluating their adaptability and effectiveness under different market conditions.

Sajjad et al. thoroughly investigated the application of derivatives in Pakistan's financial service industry, especially in hedging systemic and non-systemic risks [3]. They introduced the basics of derivatives and

* Corresponding author: 2022216078@student.cup.edu.cn

https://doi.org/10.1051/shsconf/202418801008

analyzed their practical market applications, offering an international perspective. This is crucial for understanding and comparing the applicability and effectiveness of derivative hedging strategies in different market environments. Particularly for the Chinese 50ETF options market focused on in this paper, their study provides insights into the implementation of hedging strategies under different market backgrounds, aiding in the global context evaluation and refinement of the research.

Arenas-Falótico and Scudiero explored the historical development, standardization elements, and role in risk management of futures contracts [4]. Their research provided a detailed theoretical background for understanding how futures contracts are effective risk management tools. This supports the dynamic hedging and VaR models discussed in this paper, especially in analyzing the effectiveness and limitations of futures contracts as hedging tools. Their in-depth analysis aids in understanding and evaluating the potential advantages and risks of applying these hedging tools in the Chinese 50ETF options market.

Cao et al. explored new gamma and vega hedging methods in financial markets using deep learning technology [5]. They introduced advanced distributed reinforcement learning algorithms, providing theoretical and practical bases for incorporating machine learning into hedging strategies. This is highly relevant to the machine learning-based hedging strategies discussed in this paper, especially when studying their application in the Chinese 50ETF options market. Their research proves the feasibility of using high-tech hedging strategies and provides theoretical support and empirical basis for exploring similar high-tech methods in this paper.

Zhang and Yin studied the hedging strategies of stock index futures in the Chinese market, particularly in ambiguity aversion [6]. Their empirical data and strategy analysis offer an in-depth perspective for understanding and applying hedging strategies. They provide a valuable reference for studying hedging strategies in the Chinese 50ETF options market, especially when considering market participants' attitudes toward risk and behavioral responses. Their empirical approach and focus on the Chinese market provide important region-specific perspectives and empirical support for this paper.

1.3 Research framework

The framework of this study focuses on exploring in-depth risk management strategies for the Chinese 50ETF options market. Firstly, this paper will systematically review the theoretical basis of market risk management, particularly dynamic hedging strategies, VaR models, and machine learning-based methods, analyzing their application and limitations in current literature. Secondly, this study will employ empirical analysis methods, collecting and analyzing market data to assess the performance of different risk management strategies in reducing market risks, cost-effectiveness, and execution efficiency. Additionally, the impact of market changes on the effectiveness of these strategies will be considered, comparing the adaptability and effectiveness of different strategies under various market conditions. Finally, this study proposes optimized and customized risk management strategy recommendations based on market conditions and investors' risk preferences, promoting a close integration of theory and practice. The research results will aid in understanding the practical challenges of current market risk management and provide significant theoretical and practical guidance for strategy optimization and future research in financial markets.

2 Market analysis and hedging strategy formulation

2.1 Data collection and preprocessing

This study extracted relevant Chinese 50ETF options market data from the Tonghuashun iFinD financial data terminal. The dataset covers trading information from January 2022 to March 2023, focusing on 18 option products over 164 trading days for in-depth analysis. As one of China's most active options trading markets, the 50ETF options market, with its high liquidity and significant volatility, provides an ideal experimental basis for constructing hedging strategies, enhancing their practical application and adaptability.

After importing the data, the initial steps included data cleansing—removing rows with missing values and duplicate records—and standardizing the dataset to ensure consistency across different variables. Subsequently, the study calculated the logarithmic returns of each option, an essential indicator for measuring market volatility. To eliminate non-stationarity in the data, first-order differencing was performed. Finally, short-term, medium-term, and long-term moving averages were calculated to effectively identify market price trends, providing crucial technical reference for subsequent hedging strategy formulation.

2.2. Market characteristic analysis

The study used the standard deviation of logarithmic returns to estimate the market's historical volatility. Assuming 252 trading days per year, the calculated historical volatility was 14.38%. This rate reflects the level of market volatility during the study period. Notably, higher volatility often suggests higher risks but offers investors higher potential returns. This market characteristic is crucial for options traders, as it directly impacts the formulation of trading strategies and risk management.

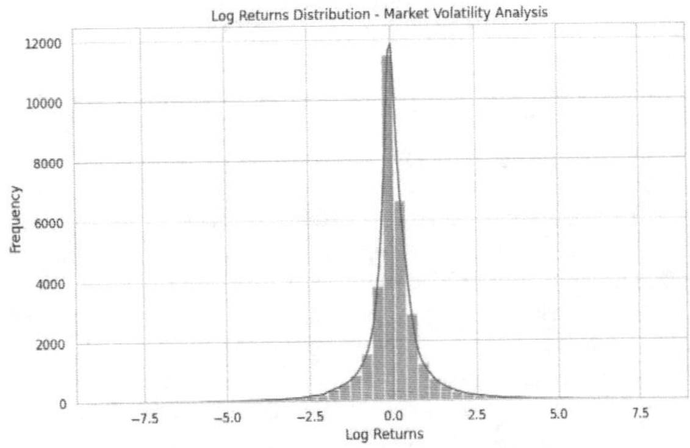

Fig 1. Market Volatility Analysis (Photo credit: Origin)

As shown in Figure 1, the market volatility analysis indicated that most logarithmic returns during the selected period were concentrated near zero, suggesting relative market stability with a low frequency of extreme returns. The distribution of returns, approximating a normal distribution with a peak near the center, indicates frequent small fluctuations in the market. However, the thicker tails on both sides of the distribution suggest a higher likelihood of extreme market movements compared to a normal distribution.

Moreover, the study utilized moving averages to analyze price trends. Moving averages, calculated by assigning equal or predefined weights to time series data, summarize the overall patterns of time series over a given period and forecast trends [7]. This paper selected 20-day, 50-day, and 100-day windows to represent short-term, medium-term, and long-term trends. Analysis revealed that market prices showed variable trends at different timescales, sometimes upward, sometimes downward, and at times remaining flat, indicating the market's high complexity and the need for flexible hedging strategies, as shown in Figure 2.

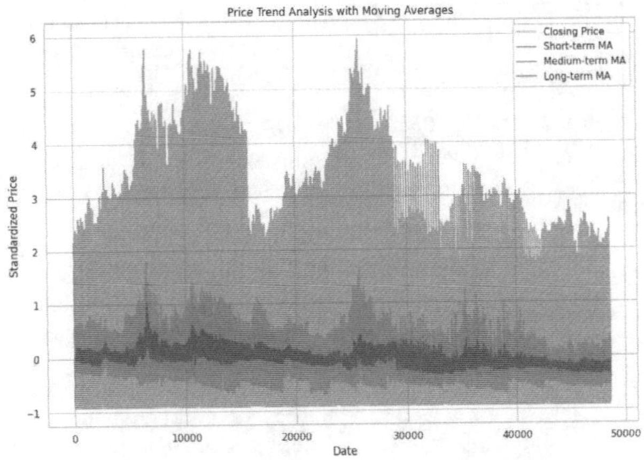

Fig 2. Price Trend Analysis (Photo credit: Origin)

Moving averages showed a smoothed trend of market prices. Short-term MAs indicated more frequent fluctuations, while long-term MAs showed a steadier trend. Price trend analysis is invaluable in determining market entry and exit points and is crucial for formulating dynamic hedging strategies.

2.3 Establishment and simulation of hedging strategies

Dynamic Hedging: Delta dynamic hedging, or delta-neutral hedging, involves constructing a delta-neutral portfolio and continually adjusting its composition over time or as asset prices change to maintain a portfolio delta of zero [8]. This paper used the Black-Scholes option pricing model to calculate the Delta value of options, assuming a risk-free rate of 0.01. Hedging was conducted daily, recording hedging costs and cumulative hedging expenses.

Value at Risk (VaR): A historical simulation-based VaR model was established. VaR represents the maximum expected loss of a financial asset or portfolio over a given confidence level and time period [9]. The model calculates the maximum potential loss at a given confidence level based on the distribution of historical logarithmic returns. This paper used a 95% confidence level, implying a 5% probability that actual losses would exceed the VaR value. The number of times the VaR was exceeded, and the cumulative excess loss over VaR was recorded.

Machine Learning Hedging: Used machine learning technology to predict market movements and formulate corresponding hedging strategies. The study applied the ARIMA (Autoregressive Integrated Moving Average) model for time series forecasting of differenced data. An ARIMA model is labeled as an ARIMA (p, d, q) model, where p represents the number of autoregressive terms, d is the number of differences, and q is the number of moving averages [10]. The model parameters used here were (5,1,2), indicating a fifth-order autoregressive, first-order difference, and second-order moving average. The data was divided into an 80% training set and a 20% test set, with the model fitted using the training set and predictions made using the test set. Prediction errors and accuracy were recorded.

Strategy Simulation: The study simulated these strategies on historical data, recording and comparing metrics such as hedging costs, risk reduction, and efficiency. It assumed a fixed hedging cost of 100 units per hedge, defined risk reduction as either the maximum single-day loss avoided or the product of prediction accuracy and total actual losses, and efficiency as the ratio of risk reduction to hedging costs.

3 Empirical analysis

Table 1. The results of running the Delta hedging strategy

Total Hedging Cost	1563.2822418670517
Average Daily Hedging Cost	0.03249053812463996
Max Single-Day Loss	-0.4531493071200352
Estimated Risk Reduction	0.4531493071200352
Hedging Efficiency	0.00028987043732987854

Table 2. The results of running the VaR strategy

Historical VaR (95%)	1.010912483730049
Number of Exceedances	2417
Estimated Risk Reduction	4729.532876154398
Estimated Hedging Cost	241700

Table 3. The results of running the ARIMA model strategy-ADF Test on Differenced Series

ADF Statistic	-16.220511819816352
p-value	3.902237590331006e-29
Critical Values 1%	-3.4325899226553007
Critical Values 5%	-2.862529648766977
Critical Values 10%	-2.5672968177028945
Test MSE	0.002
Test MAE	0.029
Test MAPE	107.036%

Table 4. The results of running the ARIMA model strategy-Performance Metrics

Hedging Cost	32400
Estimated Risk Reduction	9.267882711864406
Hedging Efficiency	0.0002860457627118644

According to Table 1 to Table 4, this chapter explores the application and effectiveness of different hedging strategies in the Chinese 50ETF options market by analyzing data from four tables and theoretical analysis. The applicability and limitations of dynamic hedging, the Value at Risk (VaR) model, and machine learning hedging strategies are summarized as follows:

Firstly, the dynamic hedging strategy analysis indicates that it has the lowest hedging cost but shows the weakest performance in risk reduction and hedging efficiency. This strategy performs well in markets with lower volatility and smaller price movements. However, in markets with higher volatility and significant price changes, this strategy may struggle to reduce risk effectively and could even lead to substantial losses. Additionally, dynamic hedging requires frequent position adjustments, increasing transaction costs and operational complexity.

Secondly, according to data from Table 2, the Value at Risk (VaR) model incurs the highest hedging cost but excels in risk reduction. It is suitable for markets with high volatility and significant price changes, helping to reduce risk effectively. However, markets with lower volatility and smaller price movements may lead to over-hedging, thereby increasing hedging costs. It's important to note that the VaR model relies on historical data and may not accurately predict sudden market changes, leading to ineffective or insufficient hedging.

Lastly, the machine learning hedging strategy has higher hedging efficiency than the other two strategies. This strategy applies particularly to markets with high volatility and complex, nonlinear price movements. It can analyze a large amount of data and fully utilize machine learning technology's powerful fitting and predictive capabilities to capture subtle changes in market dynamics, devising more precise and adaptive hedging plans. However, machine learning hedging also faces several limitations, such as model stability and interpretability, data quality and availability, and the costs and time associated with model training and updates.

Overall, the effectiveness of hedging strategies depends greatly on the specific characteristics of the market conditions. Investors and risk managers need to choose the appropriate strategy based on market characteristics and risk preferences. Understanding the performance and limitations of different hedging strategies under various market conditions is crucial for formulating effective risk management strategies.

4 Results presentation and discussion

4.1 Data visualization

This section presents the performance of different hedging strategies through several key charts based on the data analyzed in previous sections. These charts provide visual evidence of the effectiveness of the strategies, further supporting our empirical analysis.

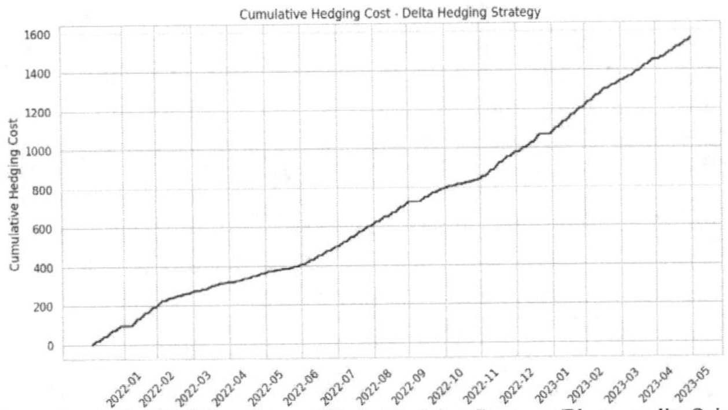

Fig 3. Cumulative Hedging Costs of Delta Hedging Strategy (Photo credit: Origin)

Figure 3 reveals the cumulative hedging costs of the Delta hedging strategy over the entire study period. The chart shows a nearly linear increase in hedging costs over time. This trend reflects the impact of market volatility, necessitating frequent adjustments in hedging positions, thus leading to cumulative costs. This visualization highlights the potential costs of dynamic hedging in high-volatility markets.

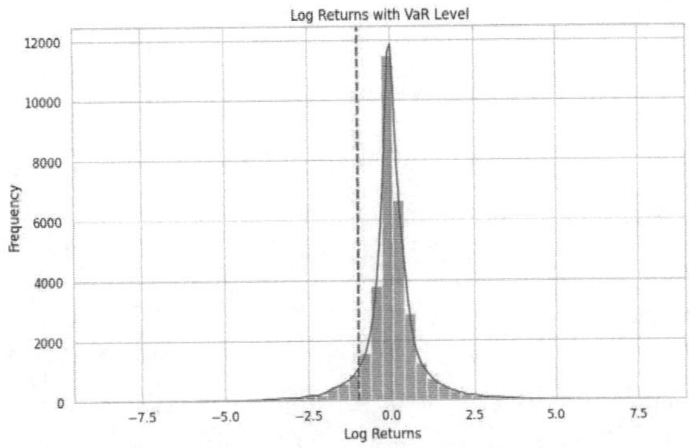

Fig 4. Market Log Returns and VaR Levels (Photo credit: Origin)

Figure 4 displays the distribution of market log returns and the VaR levels. The VaR level, indicated by the red dashed line, highlights the boundary of predicted losses by the model. The portion exceeding the red line represents actual losses exceeding the VaR model's predictions, showcasing the extreme loss events beyond the VaR level the model fails to cover.

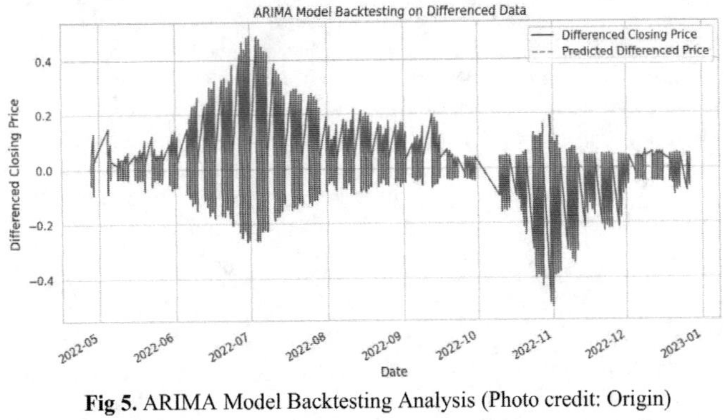

Fig 5. ARIMA Model Backtesting Analysis (Photo credit: Origin)

Figure 5, through the backtesting results of the ARIMA model, demonstrates the model's ability to capture market price trends. Although the model's prediction accuracy is not high in certain periods (especially during periods of significant price fluctuations), it generally simulates market trends well most of the time. This analysis highlights the potential of time series models in market forecasting, indicating the need for further parameter adjustments and more complex models to improve prediction accuracy.

Through the analysis of these charts, we can more clearly understand the advantages and limitations of different hedging strategies, providing valuable perspectives for decision-makers. These visual results support our quantitative analysis and guide future hedging strategies and model improvements.

4.2 Strategy evaluation

Based on the analysis conducted earlier, this section evaluates the specific performance and applicability of dynamic hedging, the Value at Risk (VaR) model, and machine learning hedging strategies. These evaluations rely on the existing theoretical framework and a detailed analysis of actual market data, aiming to provide a more comprehensive perspective.

Firstly, although the dynamic hedging strategy shows lower hedging costs in low-volatility markets, its ability to reduce risk is limited in high-volatility markets. This has been validated in practical market applications. Moreover, this strategy requires continuous position adjustments, possibly increasing transaction costs and operational complexity. Therefore, market volatility characteristics must be considered when choosing dynamic hedging. Secondly, the VaR model excels in risk reduction, especially in highly volatile market environments, but its high hedging costs and reliance on historical data may lead to poor hedging effectiveness in some situations. This suggests carefully considering market conditions and applicability is necessary when applying the VaR model. Lastly, the machine learning hedging strategy shows advantages in hedging efficiency, particularly suitable for complex, nonlinear market environments. Nonetheless, the effectiveness of this strategy is limited by model stability and data quality and requires continuous model training and updates. Therefore, constant optimization of the model is necessary in practical applications to adapt to market changes.

In conclusion, each hedging strategy has its applicable scenarios and limitations. Investors and risk managers need to consider specific market characteristics and their risk preferences when choosing hedging strategies. Additionally, as market environments continually evolve, hedging strategies also need ongoing adjustment and optimization to adapt to new market conditions.

5 Conclusion

5.1 Key findings

This study delved into the application and effectiveness of three main hedging strategies in the Chinese 50ETF options market: dynamic hedging, the Value at Risk (VaR) model and machine learning-based hedging strategies. Through comprehensive analysis of these strategies under various market conditions, the study revealed each strategy's specific advantages and limitations.

The findings indicate that while each strategy has value in specific market environments, their performances vary across different market dynamics. Dynamic hedging shows advantages in low-volatility markets due to its low cost but has limited risk reduction capability in high-volatility environments. The VaR model effectively reduces risk under extreme market conditions but may lead to over-hedging in stable markets due to its high hedging cost and reliance on historical data. Concurrently, machine learning hedging strategies perform well in complex market environments but are limited by the model's accuracy and data quality. These findings emphasize the need to consider the market's specific characteristics and investors' risk preferences when selecting and applying hedging strategies. No single strategy is optimal in all situations; choices and adjustments must be made based on specific market environments and objectives. The conclusions of this study provide valuable perspectives for market participants, aiding them in making more informed decisions in complex and volatile financial environments.

This study offers an empirical basis for understanding and applying different hedging strategies and provides practical guidance for risk managers facing market uncertainties. By thoroughly analyzing and understanding the strengths and limitations of these strategies, investors and risk managers can more effectively manage market risks and achieve more robust investment returns.

5.2 Future research directions

While this study provides a comprehensive assessment of hedging strategies in the Chinese 50ETF options market, many directions merit deeper exploration in the field of hedging strategies, especially against the backdrop of constantly evolving financial markets. Future research could focus on optimizing strategy combinations to adapt to market diversity and uncertainty. This includes finding the optimal balance among dynamic hedging, VaR models, and machine learning strategies and developing new hybrid strategies to better cope with rapid market changes. For instance, strategies could dynamically adjust parameters or weights based on market volatility and trends or use multi-level hedging to address different risk levels and expected returns. Considering trading costs, market impact, liquidity risk, and hedging errors can further refine the evaluation of the effectiveness of hedging strategies.

With the rise of emerging markets, especially areas like cryptocurrencies, exploring the applicability and effectiveness of existing hedging strategies in these markets becomes increasingly important. Future research should assess how these strategies perform against emerging markets' unique challenges and opportunities and explore how to adjust or develop new strategies to meet these markets' unique needs. Moreover, considering the potential and limitations of machine learning hedging strategies, future research should focus on applying more advanced data analysis methods and machine learning models, such as deep learning, reinforcement learning, and ensemble learning, to enhance model prediction and generalization capabilities, thereby improving the accuracy and market adaptability of hedging strategies. Additionally, incorporating more feature variables, such as technical indicators, fundamental factors, and market sentiment, can enhance the models' input information and interpretability. Furthermore, understanding the impact of evolving regulatory policies and market structures on the effectiveness of hedging strategies is equally important. Future studies should focus on the influence of regulatory framework changes, market participant behaviors, and market structure adjustments on the choice and implementation of hedging strategies to better adapt to market environments and formulate effective risk management strategies.

In summary, future research will continue to explore how to achieve effective risk management amidst the complexity and uncertainty of financial markets. By continually adapting to market evolutions and leveraging emerging technologies, more advanced and comprehensive solutions for risk management can be developed, thereby promoting the stability and healthy development of financial markets.

References

1. S. Hammoudeh & M. McAleer. The North American Journal of Economics and Finance, **25**, 109-115 (2013)
2. G. S. Rao. International Journal of Advanced Research in Management and Social Sciences, **1**(4), 55-60 (2012)
3. F. Sajjad, U. Noreen & K. Zaman. Middle-East Journal of Scientific Research, **18**(6), 748-758 (2013)
4. A. J. Arenas-Falótico & E. ScudieroAiBi Revista de Investigación, Administración e Ingeniería, **11**(3), 42-51 (2023)
5. J. Cao, J. Chen, S. Farghadani, J. Hull, Z. Poulos, Z. Wang & J. Yuan. Frontiers in Artificial Intelligence, 6, 1129370 (2023)
6. Z. Jinqing, & Y. Yiwen. Financial Research, **503**(5), 170-188 (2022)
7. S. Yaqian, C. Chaoran & Qu. Hao. Journal of Nanjing University (Natural Sciences), **58**(4), 649-657 (2022)
8. C. Ziying. Research and Optimization of Gold Option Hedging Strategies Based on Dynamic Delta Hedging (Master's Thesis, Shanghai University)
9. Z. Haitao, W. Xiaoxing, Z. Shufeng & W. Hanying. China Securities and Futures (06), 52-65 (2023)
10. J. Fattah, L. Ezzine, Z. Aman, H. El Moussami & A. Lachhab. International Journal of Engineering Business Management, 10, 1847979018808673 (2018)

Portfolio Optimization Based on Markowitz Investment Theory and Monte Carlo Simulation

Senfan Ding[1,*]

[1]School of Computer Science and Information Engineering, Hefei University of Technology, Xuancheng, 242000, China

Abstract. In the current global economic recovery, the market still has a certain degree of volatility, in the case of volatility or bad market how to go to the portfolio and optimize it is a very critical task. In this paper, based on Markowitz's investment theory, Monte Carlo algorithm is applied to achieve portfolio optimization, which is verified by the dataset of five A-share data selected as a representative dataset in the period of global epidemic. For the model and the algorithm, good results are achieved for the objective market, and the market conditions are successfully represented; for the portfolio optimization, the high-risk and high-return portfolio with the highest Sharpe ratio is finally found, and compared with the portfolio with minimized risk, and the portfolio with the highest Sharpe ratio is concluded as the optimal portfolio for this experiment, which is the optimal portfolio for this experiment, and should not be pursued for low risk but will be the best portfolio for this experiment in the turbulent and downturn market. In a volatile and depressed market, it should not be pursued for low risk but will result in a loss of return, and it should be maximized with a certain degree of volatility.

1 Introduction

In recent years, the global economy has been recovering amid volatility, but due to the recurrence of epidemics and supply chain bottlenecks, the growth rate will gradually fall back to the norm, and inflationary pressures will intensify, increasing the risk of global "stagflation". Monetary policy tightening in developed economies, cross-border capital flow back to the United States, the dollar index and U.S. bond yields rose, offshore dollar liquidity tightened, financial market volatility risk [1].

China's economy has shown a "V"-shaped trend, with an annual growth rate of around 3.2%, under the impact of a variety of domestic and international factors that exceeded expectations [2]. The soundness of China's financial system has been fully assessed. The soundness of China's financial system was comprehensively assessed, and the financial system persisted in serving the real economy, preventing and controlling financial risks, and deepening financial reforms, creating a favourable monetary and financial environment for promoting high-quality economic development. The global financial system is still facing a high degree of uncertainty, and the banking sector is still feeling tremendous pressure in its operations. Credit risk and liquidity risk appeared particularly prominent, while sluggish demand for credit led to higher lending standards, which in turn slowed the expansion of banks' asset size. Financial market volatility showed a divergent trend, and banks encountered some obstacles in capital replenishment. In addition, the recovery of non-interest-bearing business has been unsatisfactory, resulting in a decline in the overall profitability of banks. This series of factors together constitute the complex challenges facing the banking industry today [3].

Against this market backdrop, it is particularly important for individual investors to make good portfolio decisions and optimize them accordingly. In more volatile markets, portfolio optimization is of utmost importance as it is important to adopt the right portfolio to maximize the benefits. Portfolio optimization has always been a challenging proposition in finance and management. Portfolio optimization helps in portfolio selection in volatile market conditions [4]. Numerous intelligent algorithms based on artificial intelligence and machine learning have been used for optimization, such as the Bayesian network model proposed by Shenoy is well suited for scenarios that combine qualitative and quantitative information [5]. Among the classical approaches, there are many fruitful models, like the multi-stage portfolio optimization using var as a risk measure proposed by Xu, et al. has advantages in short-term investment, but for long-term investment, there are more uncertainties [6]. Cong and Oosterlee also proposed a Monte Carlo-based multi-period mean-variance portfolio optimization model, which obtains more satisfactory allocations under the constraints of control variables for dynamic portfolio management problems [7]. Shadabfar and Cheng also used a probabilistic approach for optimal portfolio selection using hybrid Monte Carlo simulation and Markowitz model and finally achieved good results [8]. Monte Carlo algorithm has been a widely used mathematical

* Corresponding author: 2021218369@mail.hfut.edu.cn

method for stochastic simulation of complex systems in the financial field, which can simulate the consideration of changes in different influencing factors, provide a reliable reference for asset allocation, and finally achieve portfolio optimization. Some traditional techniques, the efficient frontier and the Monte Carlo simulation are classical methods used in portfolio optimization and are the basis of the methodology of this paper [9, 10].

In this paper, it is through the Monte Carlo model, based on Markowitz's portfolio theory by calculating the Sharpe ratio and other indicators to finally find the efficient frontier to achieve the optimization of the portfolio, and at the same time, the corresponding visualization is carried out to prove that the modeling algorithm has usability and reliability on the given data set.

2 Methodology

2.1 Data selection

The dataset studied in this paper comes from tushare, imported through the code writing interface, and studied the data in the five stocks '002955.SZ' - Honghe Technology, '300033.SZ' - Flush, '601127.SH' - Sailix, '002594.SZ' - BYD, '603000 .SH' - People's Daily, five stocks for the period from January 1, 2019 to December 31, 2022, for this particular period, the characteristics of the A-share data also simultaneously make the results more relevant.

2.2 Modeling

2.2.1 Markowitz portfolio theory

The "mean and variance portfolio model" proposed by Markowitz in 1952 is to analyze the mean and variance of the returns of individual stocks in a portfolio of assets under the conditions of prohibition of securities financing and absence of risk-free borrowing, to find out the effective boundary of the portfolio, i.e., the portfolio with the smallest variance under a certain level of return, and to select a portfolio from it. investment portfolio.

The methodology for realizing this model includes the following steps.

Definition of Return and Risk: The expected return of a portfolio as a measure of return and the variance as a measure of risk.

Risk-Return Tradeoff: Finding the portfolio that maximizes expected return for a given level of risk or minimizes risk for a given level of expected return by solving a quadratic programming problem.

Analysis of Correlation Characteristics: A measure that analyzes the extent to which a portfolio's expected and probable returns deviate from their expectations, using variance as the primary tool of analysis.

Identification of Efficient Portfolios: Identify theoretically feasible efficient portfolios by properly analyzing a security's expected return, the variance of the return, and the interrelationship of the security's return with other securities.

$$
\begin{aligned}
&\tilde{r} = (\tilde{r_1}, \dots, \tilde{r_n}) \\
&E(\tilde{r}) = \left(E(\tilde{r_1}), \dots, E(\tilde{r_n})\right) \\
&\sigma^2(\tilde{r}) = \left(\sigma^2(\tilde{r_1}), \dots, \sigma^2(\tilde{r_n})\right) \\
&V = \left(\operatorname{cov}\left(\tilde{r_i}, \tilde{r_j}\right)\right) \\
&W = (W_1, \dots, W_n), W'1 = 1W' = 1 \\
&\tilde{r_p} = W'\tilde{r} \\
&E\left(\tilde{r_p}\right) = W'E(\tilde{r}) \\
&\sigma^2\left(\tilde{r_p}\right) = W'VW
\end{aligned} \tag{1}
$$

Portfolio returns:

$$
\mathrm{r_p} = (\mathrm{W_1} - \mathrm{W_0})/\mathrm{W_0} \Rightarrow \mathrm{W_0}\left(1 + \mathrm{r_p}\right) = \mathrm{W_1} \tag{2}
$$

The utility function of the investor:

$$
\mathrm{u(W)} = \mathrm{a} + \mathrm{bW} + \mathrm{CW}^2 \tag{3}
$$

$\tilde{r}$ represents the gain vector, and $E(\tilde{r})$ represents the expectation vector, and $\sigma^2(\tilde{r})$ represents the variance vector, and V represents the covariance matrix. W represents the weight vector. $\tilde{r_p}$ represents the portfolio return. $E\left(\tilde{r_p}\right)$ represents the portfolio expectation, and $\sigma^2\left(\tilde{r_p}\right)$ represents the portfolio variance, and the above are the formulas used in Markowitz's theory to compute it.

2.2.2 Monte Carlo algorithm

The basic idea: when the problem is to solve the probability of the occurrence of a random event, or the expected value of a random variable, through some kind of "experiment" method, the frequency of the occurrence of such events to estimate the probability of this random event, or to get some of the numerical characteristics of this random variable, and will be the solution to the problem.

First of all, it is necessary to set the necessary parameters of the model, including the standard deviation of the simulated returns σ_{δ}, the total amount of funds M, the benchmark interest rate μ and so on.

Generate a sample of random numbers by Monte Carlo algorithm for a given stock market:

Determine the n dimensional white noise vector based on the model parameters:

$$
\epsilon = (\epsilon_1, \cdots, \epsilon_n)^T \tag{4}
$$

Calculations $\sigma_{\epsilon}^{-2}\exp\left(-r\tau + 0.5\tau' V_{\epsilon}(\tau)/\lambda\right)$ where r is the prime rate and τ is the time scale. $V_{\epsilon}(\tau)$ is the covariance matrix between the two future time scales and λ is the parameter of the Poisson harmonic curve.

For each time scale t, compute the Monte Carlo distribution corresponding to the expected return.

$$r_{ij}(t)=\frac{1}{\sqrt{N}}\left(\mu_j+\sum_{l-1}^{N-1}\frac{1}{\sqrt{N-l}}\psi\left(l-\frac{(t-1)N}{N}\right)\left(\sigma_\epsilon r_j(t+(l-1)\Delta t)+\sqrt{N-l}\sigma_i r_j(t)\right)\right)+\epsilon_j(t) \quad (5)$$

Calculate the rate of return:

$$Rate\ of\ return=\frac{current\ price-purchase\ price}{purchase\ price} \quad (6)$$

Calculate volatility:

$$\sigma_p=\sqrt{\frac{1}{n-1}\sum_{i=1}^{n}\left(P_i-\bar{P}\right)^2}\times\sqrt{252} \quad (7)$$

Assume that $P_1, P_2 \ldots P_n$ is a continuous stock price and that 252 days is the number of trading days in a year.

Calculate the Sharpe ratio:

$$R_p=\left(\frac{current\ price/_{puchase\ price}}{n}\right)^{\frac{1}{year}}-1 \quad (8)$$

$$Sharp\ ratio=\frac{R_p-R_f}{\sigma_p} \quad (9)$$

Where R_p is the annualized rate of return, R_f is the risk-free rate, andσ_p is the annual volatility.

Sharpe ratio, volatility, and yield are three of the most important metrics essential to the application of the Monte Carlo algorithm based on Markowitz's investment theory, and the final efficient frontier will be derived from a combination of them.

3 Empirical results

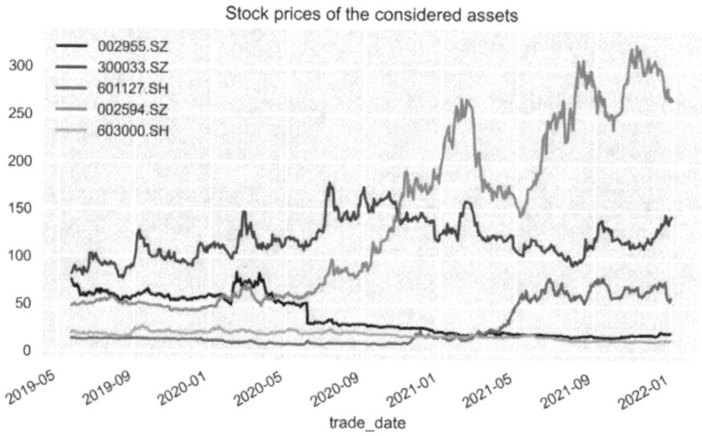

Fig. 1. Visualization of data for several stocks (Photo/Picture credit: Original).

For the overall data visualization between May 2019 and January 2022 as shown in Figure 1, it can be seen that until May 2020 the stock prices of the five stocks were significantly lower due to the objective impact and influence of the global epidemic on the financial markets at that time. After that, 002594.SZ (BYD) with a large surge, 300033.SZ (Flush) is a slight increase to maintain a certain degree of stability; in January 2021 after 601127.SH (Sailix) also had a more significant increase, but after May 2020 002955.SZ (Hong and Technology) and 603000.SH (People's Daily) but a slight downward trend.) are on a slight downward trend. Overall, these five stocks are unstable and highly variable over the time implied by the dataset, a characteristic that leads to some error or uncertainty in finding efficient frontiers later on, and will require the Monte Carlo algorithm to simulate much more often.

Table 1. Portfolio Performance (a).

Start date	End date	Total months	Annual return	Cumulative returns	Annual volatility	Sharp ratio	Calmar ratio	Stability
2021-12-30	2019-05-23	30	-8.4%	-20.0%	32.4%	-0.11	-0.21	0.45

Table 2. Portfolio Performance (b).

Max drawdown	Omega ratio	Sortino ratio	Skew	Kurtosis	Tail ratio	Daily value at risk
-40.7%	0.98	-0.17	0.70	2.53	1.00	-4.1%

Derived from a function in python that creates a simple portfolio performance are shown in Tables 1 and 2. Firstly, the Cumulative and Annual Returns are both negative and the Cumulative Return of -20.0% is a testament to the volatility of the financial markets and the high level of disruption to all aspects of trading during this period. The annual volatility of 32.4% indicates a high level of risk; the Sharpe Ratio is negative, indicating poor balance and excessive risk; the Kalmar Ratio is negative, indicating poor return performance based on the maximum retracement; the maximum retracement of -40.7% is a good indication of a large relative peak-to-trough loss over a period of time that experienced a large movement; and the Omega Ratio is close to 1, indicating a positive return over a period of time that experienced a large movement. suggests that the portfolio performs better during the time period of positive returns and is a more appropriate portfolio; the Sortino Ratio is negative, suggesting that it performs poorly during downside volatility; the skewness of 0.7 indicates some right skewness, suggesting that the chances of a positive return are slightly higher than a negative one; the kurtosis is 2.53, which suggests that the portfolio has a high degree of spikiness relative to a normal distribution, with a potentially heavier tail; and a negative value of the daily value-at-risk is indicates that the maximum degree of loss is not low.

Overall, there was a high exposure to risk during the backtesting period and an overall underperformance of returns (see Figure 2). The investment strategy needs to be carefully evaluated and adjustments need to be made to improve portfolio performance and risk management.

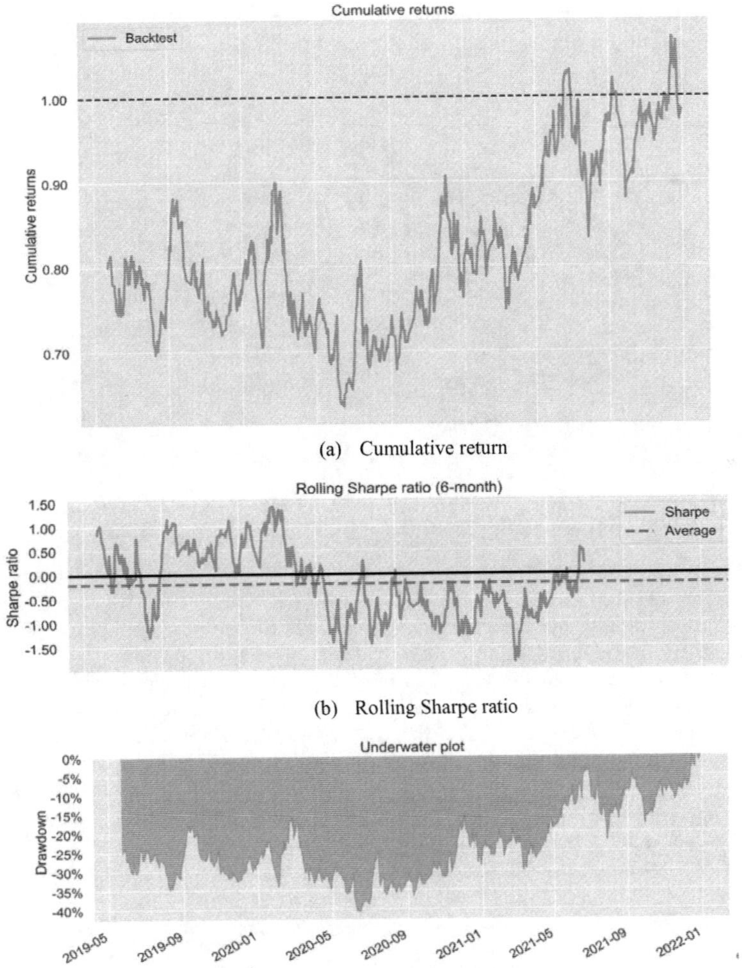

(a) Cumulative return

(b) Rolling Sharpe ratio

(c) Underwater plot

Fig. 2. Performance of investment portfolio (Photo/Picture credit: Original).

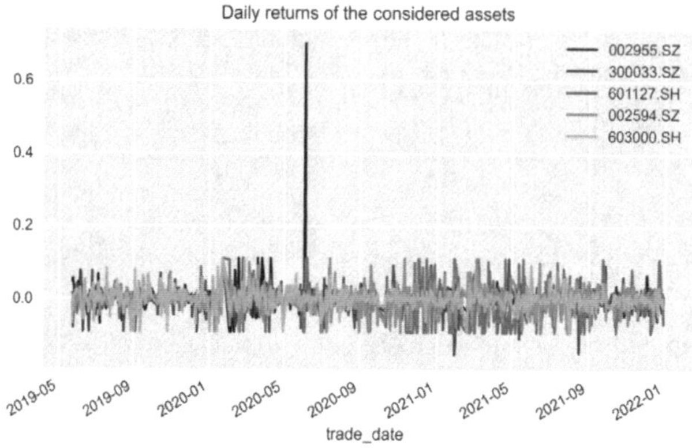

Fig. 3. Daily returns of the considered assets (Photo/Picture credit: Original).

As can be seen from Figure 3 for this period, several stocks have returned above and below 0 and have never had higher returns, again illustrating the slump and turmoil in the market during this period. Therefore, portfolio and portfolio optimization will become even more important.

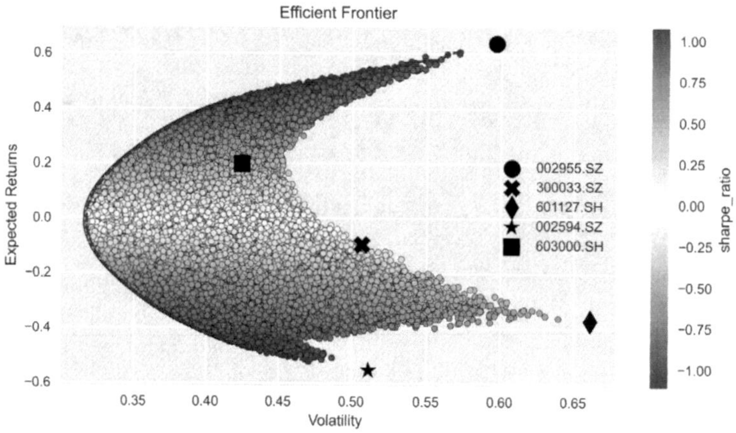

Fig. 4. Efficient frontier map corresponding to five stocks (Photo/Picture credit: Original).

Each point in Figure 4 represents a portfolio, the x-axis represents volatility, and the y-axis represents the income i.e. return. Also portfolios with higher Sharpe ratios are usually more efficient. Meanwhile, the black dots corresponding to the five stocks are their performance as separate assets in terms of return and risk. It can be seen that for the stock 002955.SZ, it has the best return despite the higher volatility. As can be seen from Figure 1, its stock price is relatively stable and has declined somewhat, which suggests that it is and is more likely to contribute to a high-quality portfolio; compared to 002955.SZ, 603000.SH and 300033.SZ ensured a certain level of return with lower volatility, while the two 002594.SZ and 601127.SH performed SZ and 601127.SH are poor, in the case of volatility is not low return is still not optimistic.

From here it is already basically clear how the five stocks corresponded to the situation during this period, in general the performance is relatively bad, the higher volatility represents the instability of the market, the low returns indicate the slump during this period, the pursuit of certain returns can only be carried out in a risky situation.

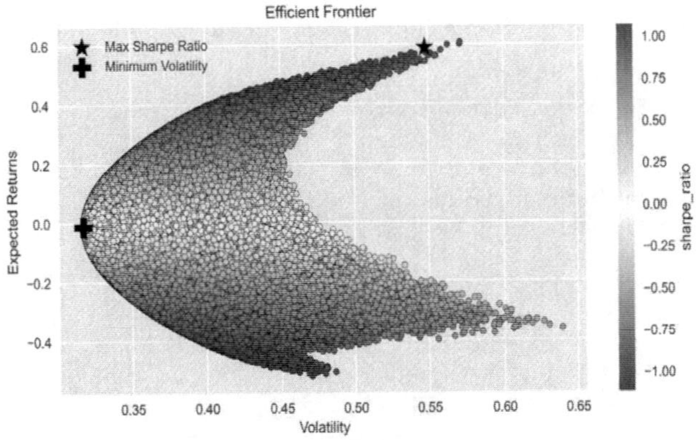

Fig. 5. Two key portfolios (Photo/Picture credit: Original).

Figure 5 is the most important one in the whole portfolio optimization and the result of the portfolio optimization. In the experimental calculations carried out in this paper, the proportion of each stock in the portfolio corresponding to the maximum Sharpe ratio and the proportion of each stock in the minimum risk are calculated as follows:

Maximum Sharpe Ratio portfolio: returns: 58.97% volatility: 54.82% sharpe ratio: 107.57

Weights: 002955.SZ: 89.75% 300033.SZ: 0.57% 601127.SH: 0.21% 002594.SZ: 0.16% 603000.SH: 9.31

Analyzing this result, for this particular period, the return alone at 58.97% is already among the better performers in the market, and a volatility higher than 50% indicates a higher risk and requires careful consideration. In terms of its weight allocation, the vast majority of the percentage is given to 002955.SZ, while the others account for very little. It can be seen that Honghe Technology has a better performance in Figure 4, with the highest return but also higher risk, which makes the portfolio when the Sharpe Ratio is the highest when the portfolio is exposed to greater risk and high sensitivity for this stock, which will affect the performance of the entire portfolio once it receives the impact may lead to the worst case scenario of high risk and low return. 603000 has the same weighting as 002955.SZ in Figure 4, except 002955.SZ has the same weighting as 002955.SZ, which has the same weighting as 002955.SZ. Figure 4 has the best overall performance except for 002955, which guarantees low volatility and relatively high returns, but if extreme returns are sought, it should be the second target, and is therefore the second in the portfolio. For the other underperforming stocks, it is correct and factual to consider a lower percentage. Overall, the returns were significant but accompanied by a high degree of concentration and risk.

For a portfolio that minimizes risk, the calculations are as follows:

Minimum Volatility portfolio : returns: -1.25% volatility: 31.75% sharpe_ratio: -3.95

Weights: 002955.SZ: 17.73% 300033.SZ: 15.60% 601127.SH: 12.50% 002594.SZ: 22.93% 603000.SH: 31.24%.

In this portfolio, the order of percentage is 603000>002594>002955>300033>601127, which is in line with the return-risk profile of each stock in Figure 4. For 603000, its risk is the lowest and its return is guaranteed, but for 002594, it is actually biased, its performance is the worst, but in order to ensure a lower risk still occupies a large proportion, which directly leads to the final overall return is negative and the indicators are not good. From these results, it is easy to see that the portfolio actually underperformed as the returns were negative even when risk was minimized and the volatility was not kept low and the Sharpe ratio was negative. Although a more even distribution of stocks would have avoided concentration, it was not a good portfolio with the goal of high return and low risk. During this period of time, even if one were to aim for low risk, one would still incur losses. Overall, it was not a good investment choice to pursue low risk at the cost of poorer returns.

In summary, the impact of the global epidemic and certain international factors, these five stocks have been affected by the more serious, and they as a few of the typical A-share stocks also shows that the market downturn at the time, in the optimization of the portfolio can only get high-risk and high-return portfolio, and did not achieve the ideal low-risk and high-return optimal portfolio.

4 Conclusion

Based on the above experimental data, it can be concluded that the Monte Carlo algorithm based on Markowitz's investment theory successfully demonstrates the financial market downturn and turbulence during this special period and optimizes the portfolios for the five stocks, and finally obtains the optimal high-risk-high-return portfolio with the highest Sharpe ratio. For this special period of time, this paper does not introduce the risk factor model, which may lead to a certain degree of randomness or bias in the results, the future will consider adding the risk model to the portfolio optimization, so that in the case of multiple condition constraints can still be found in a variety of market environments, that is, to optimize the portfolio; in

https://doi.org/10.1051/shsconf/202418801009

addition to the selection of the data set is also very important, this experiment is specially Selected this special period of data for portfolio optimization, obviously, there is a certain degree of difficulty, and finally arrived at the minimization of risk portfolio has a certain degree of irrationality, in the face of such a market situation still want to pursue low returns and high yield is obviously unrealistic, and even in the case of minimizing the risk of the yield is still negative, it can be imagined that this period of time is not optimistic about the market situation, should be taken more appropriate investment measures. More appropriate investment measures and allocations should be adopted.

Algorithmic models, also due to the specificity of the market, resulting in even the Monte Carlo algorithm in the number of simulations as high as 10 to the seventh power still failed to find a better portfolio, so consider the applicability of the model for such a special market is not particularly ideal. Currently many intelligent artificial intelligence and machine learning model algorithms are more advanced and reasonable, the future will carry out research on the application of deep learning or machine learning algorithms model for portfolio optimization, especially in the processing of time series data above the more advantageous, the results will be more accurate.

References

1. Bank of China. 2023 Fourth Quarter Economic and Financial Outlook Report. https://www.boc.cn/aboutboc/bi1/202310/t20231008_23843447.html.
2. Bank of China. Economic and Financial Outlook Report for the Third Quarter of 2023. https://www.boc.cn/aboutboc/bi1/202211/t20221130_22168786.html.
3. Bank of China. Economic and Financial Outlook Report for the Third Quarter of 2023. https://www.boc.cn/aboutboc/bi1/202307/t20230703_23314068.html.
4. A. Gunjan, & S. Bhattacharyya. AIR, 56, 3847-3886 (2023).
5. C. Shenoy, & P. P. Shenoy. Bayesian network models of portfolio risk and return. MIT Press (2000).
6. C. Xu, J. Wang, & N. Shiba, IJIC, 3(3), 709-724 (2007).
7. F. Cong, & C. W. Oosterlee. JEDC, 64, 23-38 (2016).
8. M. Shadabfar, & L. Cheng. AEJ, 59(5), 3381-3393 (2020).
9. M. J. Best, & J. Hlouskova. MMOR, 52(2), 195-212 (2000).
10. M. Pedersen. SSRN 2438121 (2014).

Trends in China's pharmaceutical market during the COVID-19 epidemic

Shilin Nie*

Faculty of Social Sciences and Law, University of Bristol, Bristol, BS8 1TH, United of Kingdom

Abstract. The COVID-19 epidemic has had a significant impact on the Chinese pharmaceutical market, leading to substantial changes in demand, production, supply, and market size. This study aims to analyze the impact on the Chinese pharmaceutical market by examining the evolving market trends during the COVID-19 epidemic. Through relevant literature and data, the following conclusions are drawn: the Chinese pharmaceutical market has undergone significant changes in demand, production, supply, price, and scale due to the epidemic. These factors not only posed considerable challenges to the Chinese pharmaceutical market during the epidemic, prompting the government and enterprises to implement a series of policies to overcome these difficulties, but also presented opportunities and challenges for the development of the Chinese pharmaceutical market. Based on the above analyses, this paper proposes some innovations and suggestions, for example the government should put forward some policies to manage market price fluctuations in some special period, and the state should also cultivate and introduce more innovative talents to help the country innovate in science and technology.

1 Introduction

In December 2019, unexplained pneumonia was first reported in Wuhan, Hubei Province, China, causing national concern and worry. On January 7, 2020, China identified a novel coronavirus as the causative agent of the outbreak and began notifying the World Health Organization (WHO). As one of the largest pharmaceutical markets in the world, China has also faced tremendous changes and challenges during this outbreak. China's pharmaceutical market has exhibited different trends in the nearly three years since the outbreak developed.

This paper will analyze the impact of the COVID-19 epidemic on the Chinese pharmaceutical market and its changing trends. The study aims to analyze the changing trends in China's pharmaceutical market during the COVID-19 epidemic, providing a scientific basis and practical experience for the development of the pharmaceutical industry. Moreover, it aims to offer targeted references and decision-making support for the government, industry, and enterprises.

The rest of the paper is arranged as follows: the second part analyzes the impact of the COVID-19 epidemic on the Chinese pharmaceutical market in terms of demand, production, supply, and price changes. The third part examines the trends of the Chinese pharmaceutical market during the epidemic, focusing on market size, product structure, and scientific and technological innovation in pharmaceuticals. The fourth part is the conclusion, which mainly summarizes the key points of the second and third parts and puts forward some views and suggestions.

2 Impact of the Covid-19 epidemic on the Chinese pharmaceutical market

2.1 Impact of the epidemic on demand for pharmaceuticals

The outbreak of the epidemic resulted in many people getting infected, causing the demand for healthcare resources to skyrocket. The epidemic has led to a significant increase in the demand for pharmaceuticals, healthcare, and medicines. Medical supplies such as masks, disinfectants, and protective clothing were in short supply, leading to a tight supply of medical equipment and drugs. According to statistics, the resumption rate of factories across the country under the impact of the epidemic was 70%, and not considering the less affected primary industry, the demand for masks reached 390 million per day based on the calculation that each person in the country used one mask per day [1]. During the epidemic, the transaction value of supplies related to epidemic prevention and protection sold through the Internet increased dozens of times [2]. In addition, the epidemic triggered a focus on immune system strengthening and health maintenance, increasing the demand for nutraceuticals and healthy foods. Increased awareness of prevention and control among the population has also boosted traffic in pharmacies and healthcare facilities.

* Corresponding author: uf23112@bristol.ac.uk

2.2 Impact of the epidemic on pharmaceutical production and supply

The outbreak had a significant impact on pharmaceutical production and supply chains. Due to the widespread spread of the outbreak and China's policy on controlling the outbreak, which required controlling the movement of people, many pharmaceutical companies' production lines and factories were forced to shut down or reduce their production. During this period, about 37 pharmaceutical factories producing active ingredients in China were closed down [3]. This leading to a decrease in production capacity and a shortage of pharmaceutical products. At the same time, the transport of raw materials and medicines needed by the pharmaceutical factories was obstructed due to the isolation of people and restrictions on traffic control during the epidemic, further causing tensions in the supply chain. This left hospitals and patients facing difficulties in obtaining medicines.

As time passed and the epidemic was controlled, pharmaceutical production gradually returned to normal, with many companies implementing preventive and control measures, resuming production lines, and increasing production to meet market demand. In mid-to-late February 2020, several companies switched production to address tight supplies. Despite a reduction in the number of production days compared to the previous month, the production of masks and medical masks still increased by 2.9 times and 3.5 times year-on-year. Additionally, the output of disinfection products such as alcohol, medical instruments, and equipment like forehead thermometers increased by more than 15% [4].

Simultaneously, banks and the government took a series of measures, such as expanding financial support for the production of medical supplies to help enterprises through difficult times. On January 31, 2020, the People's Bank of China (PBOC) issued an emergency notice to provide loans of 300 billion yuan to enterprises directly involved in the production, transport, and sale of crucial epidemic prevention medical and living supplies [5]. At the same time, based on the unique refinancing project provided by the PBOC, the Central Finance and Economics Commission (CFEC) issued a specific refinancing program aligned with the bank's policy on the production of medical supplies. Moreover, the People's Bank of China provides a particular refinancing program, offering a central financial rate of 50% to provide interest support for enterprises supporting epidemic prevention and control work in pharmaceutical products and medical equipment. After confirmation and audit by provincial financial departments, companies can apply for interest support [6].

2.3 Impact of the epidemic on pharmaceutical prices

Firstly, the prices of some medicines and medical resources have skyrocketed due to surges in demand and shortages in supply. Particularly at the beginning of the outbreak, the demand for such medicines and resources increased dramatically throughout the country, and the scarcity of the products needed was attributed to the shortage of raw materials, the limited production capacity of pharmaceutical companies, and transport difficulties. As a result, suppliers were forced to raise prices to meet market demand, leading to a spike in the price of some scarce materials. In the early stage of the outbreak, the prices of heat-clearing and detoxifying herbs rose due to the surge in demand, with the price of honeysuckle rising from RMB 180 to RMB 240, Panax quinquefolium from RMB 15 to RMB 25, forsythia from RMB 53 to RMB 68, and Scutellaria baicalensis from RMB 22 to RMB 28 in a short period (please see Figure 1) [7]. The increase in the price of these raw materials led to a simultaneous increase in the price of medicines.

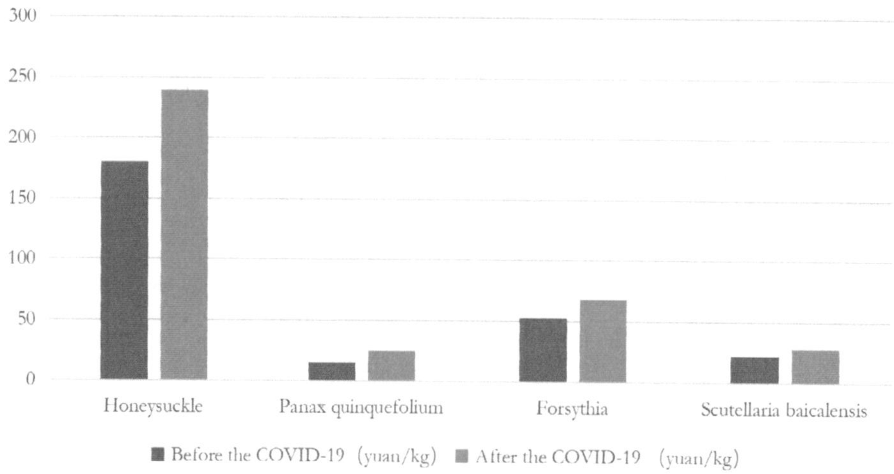

Fig. 1. Changes in the price of medicinal materials before and after the outbreak of the epidemic
Data source: https://baijiahao.baidu.com/s?id=1776661990635756312&wfr=spider&for=pc
Photo credit: Original

Prices of pharmaceutical products have gradually stabilized as the epidemic has been brought under control, the supply of medicines has stabilized, and the state has implemented price control measures to limit the extent of price increases. The government and the state's efforts to regulate the market and maintain social stability, along with controlling the extent of price increases, and the increased production capacity, and more efficient transport and supply chain management measures taken by pharmaceutical manufacturers and suppliers have helped balance supply and demand. This has led to a gradual return to normalized prices for pharmaceutical products.

3 Changing trends in China's pharmaceutical market

3.1 Trends in the size of the pharmaceutical market

During the COVID-19 epidemic, China's pharmaceutical market size exhibited a significant growth trend. The outbreak of the epidemic led to a higher demand for healthcare, resulting in a surge in demand for medicines, medical devices, protective gear, and even immune-boosting products such as health supplements. Since the beginning of 2020, the market size of China's mask industry has experienced explosive growth, reaching 244.416 billion yuan, an increase of nearly 400 times compared to 2019. As the epidemic is almost over in 2022, the market size of China's mask industry is projected to be about 65.25 billion yuan (please see Figure 2) [8].

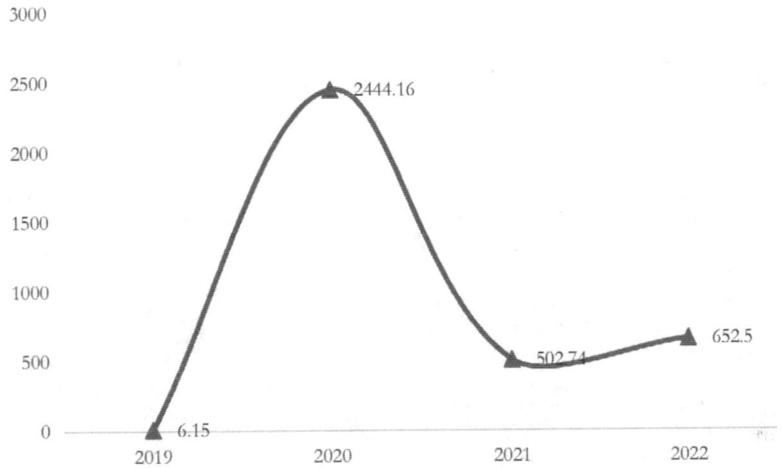

Fig. 2. The scale of China's mask industry from 2019 to 2022
Data source: https://www.chinabaogao.com/baogao/202303/627420.html
Photo credit: Original

3.2 Trends in the restructuring of pharmaceutical product mix

After the outbreak of COVID-19, the demand for antipyretics, antivirals, and other medicines to protect against COVID-19 viruses increased, and research and development of new products, such as vaccines, were emphasized. Simultaneously, the demand for respiratory-related drugs surged during the outbreak. As the COVID-19 virus primarily spreads through the respiratory tract and significantly impacts the respiratory system, the supply and demand for respiratory-related drugs, such as antiviral drugs, anti-infective drugs, and bronchodilators, were strained. Pharmaceutical companies increased the productivity of such drugs to meet market demand.

3.3 Changing trends in pharmaceutical science and technology innovation

During the COVID-19 epidemic, pharmaceutical science and technology innovation received further impetus and attention. Significant breakthroughs were made in developing new vaccines and other innovations in medical technology. Research institutes and pharmaceutical companies nationwide intensified their R&D efforts, ushering in a new chapter in medical research. According to the progress of global COVID-19 vaccine research and development published in the Nature Journal's sub-issue "Nature Reviews: Drug Discovery" in April 2020, a total of 19 countries or regions around the world were involved in vaccine research and development, with a total of 115 Covid-19 vaccines in the pipeline, while China alone accounted for 14 R&D teams. As of May 2022, 34 Covid-19 vaccines have been approved for clinical trials in China [9]. Overall, the development of COVID-19 vaccines in China is at the forefront of the world.

At the same time, the application of technologies such as artificial intelligence and big data has become increasingly widespread. The development of artificial intelligence is rapid and has a significant influence on the field of chemical medicine. The influence of artificial intelligence on medicine is mainly divided into two directions: traditional Chinese medicine and modern Western medicine. Currently, some negative public opinion in society has created a particular obstacle to the development of Chinese medicine. However, if researchers can combine artificial intelligence and Chinese medicine through artificial intelligence to assist in the actual application of Chinese medicine, the judgment and processing of Chinese medicine become more credible, which will be of great significance to the development of Chinese medicine. In terms of Western modern medicine, artificial intelligence, after deep learning, can accurately feature learning by deep convolutional neural networks to identify specific targets of a given image. For example, the COVID-19 pneumonia AI evaluation system can accurately analyze CT images, which significantly contributed to the epidemic. In this regard, AI relies on powerful logical analysis capabilities that can identify omissions and flaws in human research [10].

Big data analytics can provide vast medical data to support decision-making and innovation. Applying these technologies not only accelerates the speed of pharmaceutical R&D but also improves the quality and accuracy of the results.

4 Conclusion

During the COVID-19 outbreak, the Chinese pharmaceutical market experienced dramatic changes. The COVID-19 virus significantly increased the demand for protective gear and medicines, and uncertainties such as the need for factories to shut down after the outbreak led to a lack of supply in the market, affecting prices in the Chinese pharmaceutical market. These changes created a series of challenges and opportunities for the Chinese pharmaceutical market, necessitating pharmaceutical companies and the government to strengthen cooperation and develop targeted policies and strategies to cope with the changes brought about by the outbreak.

During the COVID-19 epidemic, the Chinese pharmaceutical market also underwent significant trends. These changes were reflected in alterations to the size of the pharmaceutical market, shifts in the structure of pharmaceutical products, and changes in pharmaceutical science and technology innovation. The surge in demand for medical drugs and protective products led to a clear growth trend in the size of the Chinese pharmaceutical market during this period. Additionally, it resulted in dramatic changes in the structure of medical products on the market.

Simultaneously, with the development of the epidemic over time, the Chinese pharmaceutical market has implemented a series of innovations, such as research on the COVID-19 vaccine, providing a reference for the future development of the Chinese pharmaceutical market. Pharmaceutical companies need innovative thinking and keen insight to seize market opportunities, address market challenges, and continually adjust their strategies to promote the sustainable development of the pharmaceutical market.

References

1. Z, Liu. Mask equipment: large gap between supply and demand, strong demand for equipment. https://down2.51pdf.cn/online/viewer.asp?rnd=200224164922366
2. T, Lin. Short-term impact of the epidemic on the retail market is large, the long-term positive trend in consumption has not changed. https://www.stats.gov.cn/sj/sjjd/202302/t20230202_1896310.html
3. C. M. Bookwalter. Drug shortages amid the COVID-19 pandemic. US Pharm. 46(2): 25-8 (2021).
4. W, Zhang, Industrial production was significantly reduced by the impact of the epidemic Medical living materials and basic industries to ensure strong protection. https://www.stats.gov.cn/sj/sjjd/202302/t20230202_1896312.html
5. Zhang, Z. A., Pang, C., & Tsoi, V. Covid-19: Chinese Government Financial Assistance measures. White & Case LLP.
6. The Central People's Government of the People's Republic of China. Circular on Supporting Financial Strengthening Services to Do a Good Job in Preventing and Controlling the Pneumonia Epidemic of New Coronavirus Infections. https://www.gov.cn/zhengce/zhengceku/2020-02/03/content_5474105.htm
7. Matters of vision. How long will the drug market be on fire, and how long will it take to find opportunities in the mountains and the waves. https://baijiahao.baidu.com/s?id=1776661990635756312&wfr=spider&for=pc
8. W. Guanyan. China Mask Industry Development Trend Research and Future Investment Research Report (2023-2030).
9. C. H. Song. K. W. Yao. Economic analysis of co-development - Insights based on Covid-19 vaccine development. BE, (04): 141-142+159 (2023)..
10. R, Yang. The Important Role and Prospect of Artificial Intelligence in Pharmaceuticals. STEM (01),23-25 (2022).

The impact of brake failure rights protection event on Tesla Motors: stock prediction based on ARIMA model

Yifei Tang*

School of Economics and Business Administration, Chongqing University, Chongqing Municipality, 400044, China

Abstract. On April 19, 2021, the Shanghai Auto Show witnessed a rights protection incident involving Tesla's brake failure. The arrogant official response has eroded consumer trust and had a detrimental impact on Tesla's operational performance. This article employs the ARIMA model to analyze Tesla's stock price data, selecting data from a year prior to and following the incident. The forecast findings are analyzed to determine the impact of the event on Tesla's stock prices, followed by advice for investors on decision-making. According to this article, Tesla's stock prices were significantly negatively impacted by the rights protection incident. Meanwhile, policy lags and the absence of a weak efficient market could be blamed for the notable shift in stock price that occurred only starting on the seventh day of the event. This suggests that investors could leverage the interval of time between the occurrence of the event and the occurrence of stock price variations to their advantage when managing their investments.

1 Introduction

Tesla, as a publicly traded company specializing in automobiles, is known for its four super factories, providing ultra-high production capacity. It has successively launched four models in the Model series and offers various charging services for its new energy vehicles. The innovative energy model and structural design of automobiles have led to a continuous increase in sales. However, Tesla's development history is also marked by constant controversy.

Since 2021, Tesla has faced multiple major accidents [1]. In January 2021, a Tesla Model 3 car, purchased just six days earlier, experienced a circuit malfunction while using Tesla's official supercharging station. On May 3rd, a Tesla car crashed into a wall in an underground parking lot in Guangzhou, China, and the airbags did not deploy. The continuous occurrence of accidents has heightened consumer concerns about Tesla's safety [2,3].

In April 2021, a car owner staged a "roof protection" incident at the Shanghai Auto Show, further thrusting Tesla into the forefront of public opinion. On April 19, 2021, during the first Media Day of the exhibition, a Tesla owner stood on the roof of a Tesla car, shouting "Tesla brake failure" to assert her rights, drawing a crowd of media and onlookers. The white T-shirt she wore had the words "brake failure" printed on it. According to media reports, the car owner's father failed to brake while driving the Tesla Model 3, causing a rear-end collision that nearly resulted in the death of her entire family [1]. What further fueled her anger was Tesla's manufacturer refusing to return the car and provide compensation. This led her to choose the extreme measure of standing on the roof of the car at the show to protect her rights. Subsequently, various critical voices about Tesla surfaced on the internet [2].

Research indicates that when companies experience a black swan event, external investors tend to adopt a bearish stance on the company's stock [4]. Simultaneously, existing shareholders and other stakeholders may harbor doubts about the company's corporate governance capabilities, thereby influencing corresponding investment decisions [5]. Consequently, companies should actively respond by sending positive signals to the market [5].

However, Tesla Vice President Tao Lin emphasized in response to media inquiries that "all the public opinion was caused by this lady." Tesla's insincere crisis PR, haughty reactions from upper management, and slow fixes were the catalyst for a crisis of consumer trust, resulting in a sharp decline in Tesla's market share. Only 25,845 cars were traded in Tesla China in the first quarter following the incident, a 27% drop from the prior quarter. Among these, only 6,264 copies of the Model 3 involved in this rights protection event were sold, a significant drop of around 75% from the previous period.

Previous research has primarily focused on the series of public opinion impacts caused by Tesla's inappropriate public relations strategy, undermining consumer confidence and leading to a sharp drop in sales, thereby affecting short-term business indicators [6]. As a listed company, stock information theory determines that the volatility of stock prices can better reflect the fundamental impact on Tesla [7]. To fill the gap, this article will compare the differences between stock fluctuations and predicted values after the roof rights protection event, analyze whether the event has an impact on Tesla's stock prices and the degree of impact,

* Corresponding author: 20216130@stu.cqu.edu.cn

and provide decision-making recommendations to investors.

The remaining part of this article is structured as follows: Section 2 will introduce the data sources and model design. Section 3 will comprehensively discuss the ARIMA model and its results. Firstly, it will explain the basis for determining the order of the ARIMA model, and then analyze and explain the stock prediction results based on the time series background. The discussion on the implications of this study for investor investment decisions and how policymakers can understand the research findings will be presented in Section 4. Finally, Section 5 will briefly reiterate the main conclusions of this article.

2 Research methods and model design

2.1 Data sources

Investing is one of the authoritative stock data query websites in China, so this paper used this website to collect the Tesla stock price information needed for our research [8]. This study collected the closing price data of Tesla stock on each trading day from April 19, 2020, to April 19, 2022, covering one year before and after the "Roof Rights Protection" event. There are a total of 505 sets of data per day and 105 sets of data per week.

2.2 Model design

The ARIMA model is developed based on the ARMA model [9]. Unlike the ARMA model used for modeling stationary time series, ARIMA can be employed to model non-stationary time series by performing differencing on non-stationary sequences [10]. The ARIMA (p, d, q) model is denoted as:

$$\begin{cases} \Phi(B)\nabla^d x_t = c + \Theta(B)\varepsilon_t \\ E(\varepsilon_t) = 0, Var(\varepsilon_t) = \sigma_t^2, E(\varepsilon_t\varepsilon_u) = 0, u \neq t \\ E(x_u\varepsilon_t) = 0, \forall u < t \end{cases} \quad (1)$$

In equation (1), $\nabla^d = (1-B)^d$ 、 $\Phi(B) = 1-\phi_1 B-\phi_2 B^2-\ldots\phi_p B^p$ is the autoregressive coefficient polynomial of the stationary reversible ARMA (p, q) model; D in the model is the order of the difference; $\Theta(B) = 1-\theta_1 B-\ldots-\theta_q B^q$ is the moving smoothing coefficient polynomial of the stationary reversible ARMA (p, q) model; $\{\varepsilon_t\}$ is a zero mean white noise sequence.

2.3 Augmented Dickey Fuller test

After summarizing and formatting data in Excel, use Stata MP 16 software to process the sequence. Perform stationarity tests on the daily and weekly sequences of Tesla's stock closing price. ADF (Augmented Dickey Fuller test), also known as unit root test, determines whether a time series has a unit root [11]. A time series without a unit root is stationary, while a time series with a unit root is non-stationary [11]. The null hypothesis of the ADF test has a unit root. If the p-value obtained is less than a confidence level of 5%, it indicates that there is at least 95% confidence that the time series is stationary. If the sequence is not stationary, perform natural logarithmic transformation and differencing on the sequence until it is stationary and can pass the ADF test.

Table 1 Weak stationarity test

	t (Test Statistic)	MacKinnon approximate p-value for Z(t)
	Daily	
Ln index	-1.523	0.8212
1st order difference	-11.675	0.0000
2nd order difference	-21.478	0.0000
	Weekly	
Ln index	-1.652	0.7713
1st order difference	-5.640	0.0000
2nd order difference	-8.655	0.0000

Table 1 shows that the second-order differenced sequences are stationary because the p-values for both the daily and weekly sequences are 0.000, which is less than 0.05.

2.4 Establishment of ARIMA model

After obtaining a stable time series, follow the three steps for modeling and prediction:

1) Model ordering and fitting: Determine the model parameters p (autoregressive order), d (number of differences required to transform the original time series into a stationary time series), and q (moving average order) based on the ACF and PACF plots [11,12]. Select the optimal parameters to fit the model. Try to start with smaller parameters and gradually increase them if the goodness of fit is poor.

2) Perform a residual test on the fitting model to ensure that the residuals conform to the assumption of white noise and validate the effectiveness of the model [10,11].

3) Prediction: After establishing the model, predict Tesla's stock price for the next 9 days and two weeks, respectively. Analyze the deviation between the predicted and actual values on different trading days under daily and weekly forecasts, as well as the reasons.

3 Empirical results and analysis

3.1 Order determination

As the model order obtained from the first-order differenced sequence of the stock price was too high, there is a risk of non-convergence in residual sequences, which could affect the goodness of fit of the model [10]. Therefore, although the first-order differenced sequences of daily and weekly degrees satisfy the condition of sequence stationarity (p, q), this study chooses the p, q values from second-order differenced sequences to determine the order. According to Table 1, the p-value of the 2nd order differenced sequence of Tesla's stock closing price is less than the significance level of 0.05, hence rejecting the null hypothesis. Therefore, this sequence is considered to be a white noise sequence at a 95% confidence interval, and the model is effective. The difference order is 2, which is obtained from part 2.3.

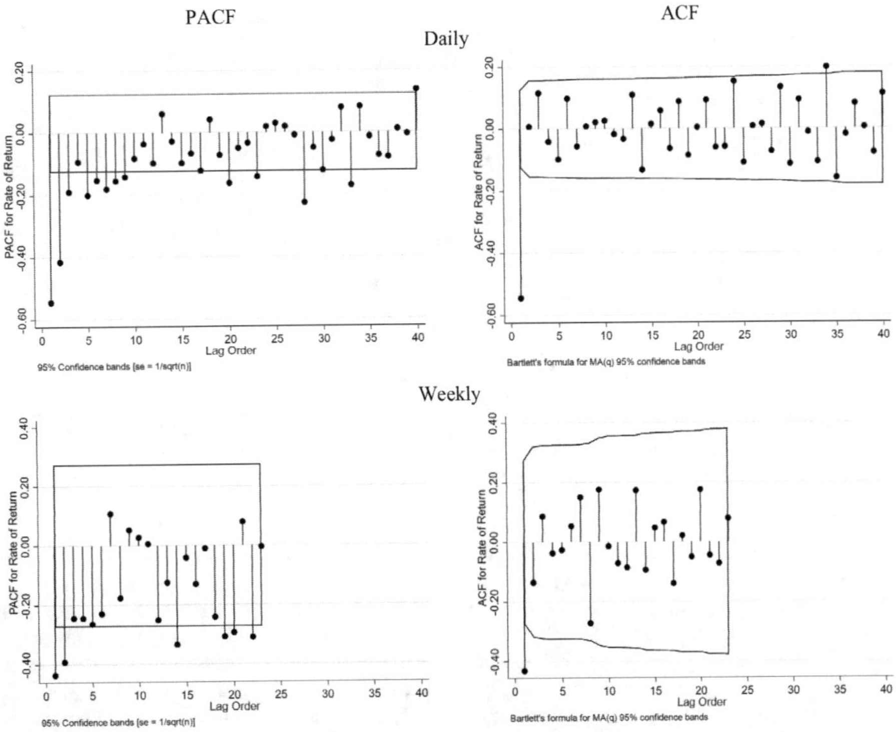

Fig. 1. ARMA (p, q) identification

Photo credit: Original

For the daily second-order differenced sequence, set p=9 and q=1 to establish a model and predict Tesla's closing price for the next 9 trading days. For the weekly second-order differenced sequence, set p=2 and q=1 to establish a model and predict Tesla's closing price for the next two weeks. To verify the accuracy of the model fitting, residual testing was performed on the prediction results. The initial assumption was that the residual sequence of the model was a white noise sequence, with a significance level of 0.1. The test results are shown in Table 2.

Table 2 Residual test

Model	Portmanteau (Q) statistic	Prob > chi2
Daily-ARIMA(9,2,1)	43.7690	0.3146
Weekly-ARIMA(2,2,1)	23.1027	0.9851

The P-value of Daily ARIMA (9,2,1) is 0.3146, which is greater than the significance level of 0.1. The P-value of Weekly ARIMA (2,2,1) is 0.9851, also greater than the significance level of 0.1. Therefore, this part accepts the null hypothesis that the residual sequence is white noise. The residuals of the daily and weekly sequence prediction models established using ARIMA conform to the assumption of white noise, indicating the effectiveness of the model.

3.2 Results and explanation

Draw trend charts of Tesla's stock closing price based on the predicted results.

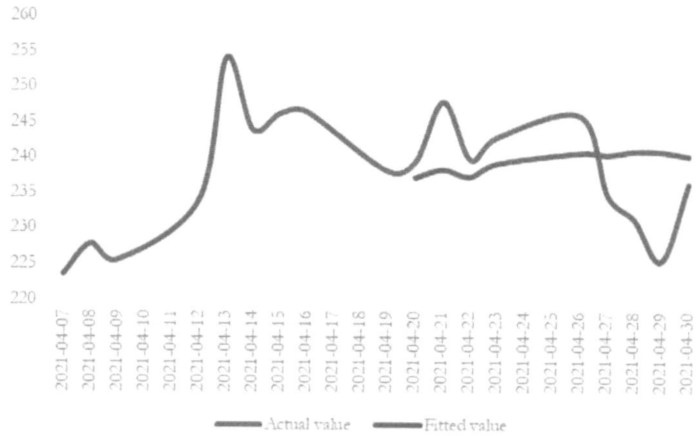

Fig. 2. Actual value and fitted value, daily

Photo credit: Original

As shown in Figure 2, under the daily and weekly models, with the event date of April 19, 2021, as the time node, there was no significant deviation between the predicted and actual values of Tesla's stock closing price from April 20, 2021, to April 25, 2021. However, starting from April 26, 2021, there was a significant deviation between the predicted and actual values of Tesla's stock closing price. From April 20, 2021, to April 25, 2021, the daily forecast of Tesla's stock closing price fluctuated almost in the same direction as the actual value, but the amplitude was relatively small, consistently within the range of 235-240. From April 26, 2021, to April 29, 2021, the predicted value remained almost at a level, while the actual value plummeted from 245 to 225. The weekly predicted value and actual value curve are smoother compared to the daily value, but there is also a significant deviation in almost the same time period. This indicates that the "roof rights protection" incident at the Shanghai Auto Show had a significant negative impact on Tesla's stock price, and this impact suddenly became apparent 7 days after the incident occurred.

There are several reasons why Tesla's stock has lagged behind in responding to the rights protection incident. Firstly, there is a policy lag effect in stock price fluctuations [13]. When a specific event occurs that will affect the stock price, the stock market cannot immediately adjust the stock price due to the influence of laws, regulations, and local policies [13]. The time difference between the time when the event occurred and the time when the stock price was adjusted accordingly is known as the policy lag. The reasons for delayed stock price fluctuations can also be analyzed from the perspective of market efficiency [7]. Research has shown that the lower the efficiency of the market, the more difficult it is for securities prices to accurately and quickly reflect changes in the intrinsic value of securities [14]. In a weakly efficient market, stock prices can fully reflect all historical information; that is, future trends in stock prices are independent of past events [15]. Mo Yixian and Zhou Lemin used an autocorrelation regression model to verify that historical information in today's era still has an impact on current stock returns, and the market has not yet reached weak efficiency [16]. This explains why the rights protection incident that occurred on April 19, 2021, still has an impact on stock prices from April 26, 2021, onwards.

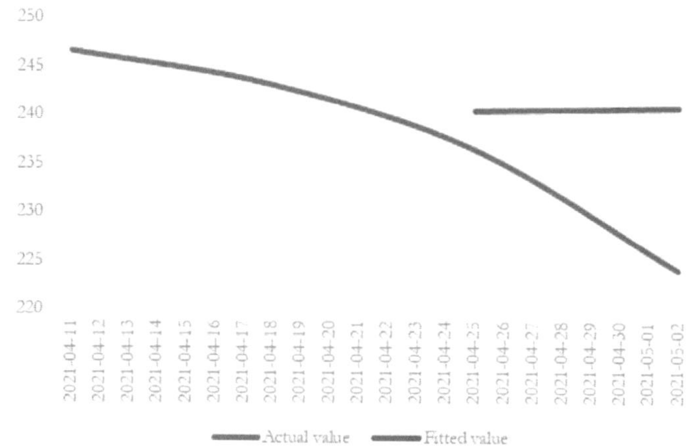

Fig. 3. Actual value and fitted value, Weekly
Photo credit: Original

4 Conclusion

This article aims to study the impact of the rights protection incident involving a Tesla car owner at the Shanghai Auto Show on Tesla's stock price and provide recommendations for investor decision-making by analyzing the reasons for stock price changes. The article primarily uses the ARIMA model to process relevant data, employing daily and weekly Tesla stock closing price sequences to predict the short-term trend of stock price changes. The prediction results indicate that within about 7 days of the event, stock prices were not significantly affected. However, after 7 days, there was a sharp decline in stock prices. This suggests that the rights protection incident has a significant negative impact on Tesla's stock price. Meanwhile, the delayed response of stock prices may be related to policy delays and the stock market not achieving weak efficiency.

While existing research mainly discusses the impact of Tesla's public relations errors on consumer confidence, the decline in business performance, and the negative effects on brand reputation, this article focuses on the impact on its stock price fluctuations. The ARIMA model used in this study has limitations in fitting accuracy when establishing high-order models. Therefore, this method can only study the short-term impact of the event. To compensate for limitations, future research can focus on whether the rights protection event has a long-term impact on Tesla's stock price.

Tesla Motors has been facing numerous vehicle safety and after-sales issues in recent years. An uncompromising and arrogant attitude will not only worsen the trust relationship between the brand and consumers, affecting the business performance of the enterprise, but also cause investors to lose confidence, which is not conducive to Tesla's long-term development. Therefore, only by maintaining a positive attitude towards consumers and actively investigating and resolving after-sales issues can the brand's image be restored in front of the public and investor confidence be regained.

Investors can utilize the time difference between public information disclosure and stock price changes to manage their investments. On the one hand, they should closely monitor relevant news and make rational decisions based on public opinion and personal experience. For a black swan event that is suspected to affect reputation, leading investors to anticipate a stock price decline, they should sell the stock in a timely manner before any adjustments are made to the stock price.

References

1. Y. S. Li. IFM, (05):54-56 (2021).
2. L. L. Wang et al. CM, (06):36 (2021).
3. M. L. Xu. PRM, (06):4 (2021).
4. J. Z. Fan. FE, (11):31-32 (2013).
5. G. Li. Research on "Black Swan" Phenomenon Performance Forecast in A-share Listed Company. Xi'an Shiyou University, (2021).
6. R. D. Li, Q. Feng, Y. Li. et al. JUSS:1-8 (2023).
7. Q. Q. Yang, J. Hu, L. D. Zhang. et al. JHUT, 15(03):1-13+49 (2023).
8. Investing. https://cn.investing.com/
9. S. Khan, H. IJACSA, 11(7) (2020).
10. X. D. Huang. Research on Stock Price Index Prediction Based on Time Series and Deep Learning Model. STBU, 2023.
11. M. T. Huang. NJKJ ,44(03):61-62 (2023).
12. Q. Xing. Stock Price Forecasting Analysis Based on Deep Learning Hybrid Models. SU, (2023).
13. T. Chen. CSS, (12):10-17 (2004).
14. Y. C. Zhan. JCU, 29(05):30-33 (2019).
15. Y. T. Guo YT. MC, (02):48-49 (2019).
16. Y. X. Mo YX., L. M. JSLUAF, (01):60-72 (2020).

Determinants on Successful Investment of Venture Capitalist

Tianyu Gui[1,*]

[1]School of Finance, Zhongnan University of Economics and Law, Wuhan, 430073, China

Abstract. Venture capital (VC) has transcended its Silicon Valley origins to become a global force shaping the innovation and economic landscape. It is imperative to recognize the critical role of VC and improve its success rate. Employing the "jockey-horse-meadow" model, this paper identifies three crucial determinants influencing VC success: the entrepreneurial team, strategic approach and business model, and the market context. Delving into specific sub-points, the paper underscores the unique significance of each determinant, substantiating their pivotal roles in shaping VC outcomes. This research not only contributes insights into the success dynamics of VCs but also serves as a valuable reference for startups seeking financing and development. Additionally, it offers guidance to investors navigating the selection process, aiding them in identifying startups with genuine potential for impactful investment. By shedding light on these fundamental factors, this paper enriches the discourse surrounding VC success, fostering a more informed and strategic approach in the dynamic world of venture capital.

1 Introduction

Venture Capital (VC) represents a funding avenue where investors support startups and small businesses perceived to possess significant long-term growth prospects. VCs excel at addressing a crucial challenge in market economies: bridging the gap between innovative entrepreneurs lacking financial resources and investors equipped with capital but lacking visionary ideas. The remedy, as proposed by theoretical frameworks and substantiated through prior empirical investigations into VC practices, encompasses distinct measures undertaken by VCs to overcome this funding disparity [1].

Venture capital (VC) has its roots dating back to the early 20th century. Initially concentrated in the United States, particularly in the Silicon Valley region renowned for its tech innovation and vibrant startup scene, early venture capitalists were often affluent individuals or family enterprises seeking high-risk, high-reward opportunities. In the 1950s and 1960s, as technology rapidly advanced, venture capital emerged as a pivotal force driving technological innovation and nascent industries. Venture capital firms began to gain prominence, focusing on supporting startups that faced challenges securing funds within traditional financial systems. During this period, the focus of venture capital was primarily on emerging fields like semiconductors and computer technology. The 1970s and 1980s marked further development in the venture capital industry. Large institutional investors and banks also entered the scene, contributing to the maturation and scaling of the venture capital market. The 1990s witnessed the advent of the internet, injecting new vitality into venture capital. A plethora of internet startups emerged, and venture capital quickly became the preferred means for entrepreneurs to secure funding.

In 21century, the venture capital ecosystem has continued to grow globally. Not only in the United States but also in other regions such as Europe and Asia, independent and flourishing venture capital ecosystems have taken shape. The critical role of venture capital in driving innovation, economic growth, and employment is increasingly recognized by governments and the business community worldwide. In summary, venture capital has evolved from its initial small-scale practices to become a key financial instrument globally, supporting innovation and driving economic development.

Despite its importance, venture capital has a very low success rate. Throughout its long history, the factors that contribute to the success of venture capital have been one of the main topics of study. There is now a wide range of research on venture capital success factors, this literature has underscored the importance of the entrepreneurial team, financial deal, legal environment, financial market context, the tax system, public spending on research and development and degree of information [2, 3]. Thus, this article focuses on three main determinants on successful VC: entrepreneurial team, strategy and business model, market context. These factors are based on "jockey-horse" framework developed by Kaplan, Sensoy and Stromberg. The entrepreneurial team is the "jockey", the strategy and business model are the "horse" while the market context is a "meadow" where horse run [1].

The following three sections will specify why entrepreneurial team, strategy and business model, and market context are key determinants of venture capital success.

* Corresponding author: 202121030250@stu.zuel.edu.cn

https://doi.org/10.1051/shsconf/202418801012

2 Entrepreneurial team (jockey)

In the fast-paced world of venture capital (VC), the success of an investment is intricately tied to the entrepreneurial team steering the startup. The entrepreneurial team serves as the nucleus, influencing the vision, strategy, and execution of the venture. This essay delves into how the composition, skills, and dynamics of an entrepreneurial team significantly shape and impact the success of venture capital investments.

2.1 Board composition and complementary skills

The success of an entrepreneurial firm is closely linked to the team's dynamics, composition, and turnover, as these factors play a crucial role in introducing fresh perspectives and insights to the organization [4].

The composition of an entrepreneurial team is a critical factor that plays a pivotal role in both attracting and retaining venture capital. Investors meticulously assess the diversity of skills, experiences, and backgrounds within a team to gauge its ability to navigate challenges and capitalize on opportunities. A well-rounded team possesses the versatility needed to adapt to the ever-evolving business landscape. For instance, a blend of technical expertise, industry knowledge, and strong business acumen can form a comprehensive approach to problem-solving.

Investors also seek a delicate balance within the team, looking for a mix of risk-takers and risk-mitigators. A successful entrepreneurial team must be innovative and forward-thinking while also having the ability to manage and mitigate risks effectively. This balance instils confidence in venture capitalists, enhancing the likelihood of a positive outcome for their investment.

The synergy among team members and their complementary skills is crucial in significantly impacting venture capital success. A team where each member brings a unique set of skills, such as marketing, finance, technology, and operations, is better equipped to address multifaceted challenges. This diversity ensures that the startup adopts a comprehensive and strategic approach to its development and growth. Venture capitalists view a cohesive team with complementary skills as a risk-mitigation strategy. A well-coordinated team can efficiently allocate resources, make informed decisions, and navigate uncertainties, thereby increasing the probability of success in the fiercely competitive business environment.

2.2 Leadership and vision

According to the study, venture capitalists place significant importance on management-related criteria, with particular emphasis on the track record of founders and the diversity of backgrounds within the startup's core team as pivotal factors [5].

Leadership within an entrepreneurial team is instrumental in steering the venture towards success. Visionary leaders who can inspire and motivate their team create a positive and driven organizational culture. This culture, in turn, fosters innovation and resilience, critical elements in the startup ecosystem. Venture capitalists recognize the importance of strong leadership and a compelling vision. A leader who can articulate a clear and ambitious vision not only attracts investment but also aligns the team towards a common goal. The ability to communicate this vision effectively is often considered a key indicator of a team's potential for success.

2.3 Dynamic collaboration

Dynamic collaboration and communication among team members are essential for a venture's success. The study indicates that relational capabilities not only result in the addition of founding team members but also contribute to growth in sales and employment [6]. Venture capitalists closely assess the team's ability to work together harmoniously, exchange ideas, and adapt to evolving circumstances. Effective communication fosters a collaborative environment where knowledge is shared, and decisions are made collectively.

Investors acknowledge that a cohesive team is better equipped to address challenges and pivot when necessary. The success of a venture capital investment is significantly influenced by the entrepreneurial team's adaptability in navigating market changes and unforeseen obstacles.

In conclusion, the success of venture capital investments is deeply intertwined with the entrepreneurial team driving the startup. The composition of the team, the complementarity of skills, effective leadership, and dynamic collaboration all play pivotal roles in influencing venture capital success. Investors are not merely investing in a product or service; they are investing in the collective capability of the entrepreneurial team to navigate challenges, innovate, and ultimately realize the full potential of the venture.

As the venture capital landscape continues to evolve, the significance of a strong and capable entrepreneurial team will remain a cornerstone of successful investments. In an environment where uncertainty is the norm, the entrepreneurial team serves as the bedrock upon which successful venture capital endeavours are built. It is the alchemy of diverse skills, visionary leadership, and collaborative spirit that propels ventures towards success, making the entrepreneurial team an indispensable factor in the dynamic world of venture capital.

3 Strategy and business model (horse)

The findings unveil a positive correlation between a startup founder's innovative business model and robust social networking, indicating that such startups are more likely to exhibit superior performance metrics such as sales volume, employment rates, return on equity (ROE), return on investment (ROI), among others [7]. This section will delve into the startup's strategy and business model, exploring their influence on the success of venture capital investments.

3.1 Clear business model

The success of venture capital investments hinges on the presence of a transparent and workable business model. Venture capitalists actively pursue startups that exhibit a clear trajectory toward profitability, thereby improving the prospects of a successful exit strategy. Primarily, a well-defined business model must encompass both Revenue Generation and Scalability.

Venture capitalists are typically more inclined to invest in ventures capable of generating substantial revenue. A clear business model should efficiently translate products or services into sources of profit, achieved through various means such as direct sales, subscription models, or advertising revenue. The choice of business model is highly positively correlated with success in securing investment as well as success, and A higher survival rate is notably associated with two business model patterns, namely Freemium and Subscription, while four patterns—Cross Selling, Hidden Revenue, Layer Player, and No Frills—are significantly correlated with a lower survival rate [8].

Also, a good business model should be scalable. Venture capitalists often seek business models with rapid scalability potential. This involves the ability of a business to achieve scale within a short timeframe. Businesses with scalability are more likely to realize significant returns on investment within the time frame that investors are focused on. Thus, they are favoured by venture capitalists for financial support.

3.2 Differentiation and competitive advantage

The strategy of a business should focus on creating unique value propositions and establishing a competitive advantage. This is the same crucial factor that venture capitalists consider, including the Unique Value Proposition and Barriers to Entry.

A core component of a business strategy is creating a unique value proposition. This implies that the products or services offered by the business stand out in the market, catering to the unique needs of customers. This enhances customer stickiness to reach a wider consumer base. Value specificity is one of the fundamentals of a company's ability to gain a foothold in the marketplace. Venture capitalists are more inclined to invest in ventures that can distinguish themselves in a competitive market.

While possessing special value, the startup should also consider how to establish barriers to entry to protect itself from the impacts of intense competition. This may include technological patents, unique datasets, a strong brand, and more. The presence of barriers to entry makes it challenging for other businesses to easily replicate the success model, increasing the attractiveness of the investment.

3.3 Market potential

The success of venture capital often relies on the market potential that a business chooses. This includes the size and growth prospects of the market and the position of the business within that market.

Venture capitalists typically look for businesses operating in large and continually growing markets. Such markets offer more opportunities, allowing businesses to achieve substantial revenue and providing investors with higher potential returns. A business strategy should precisely define and target the specific segment of the market that the business aims to serve. Venture capitalists are interested in whether a business can accurately grasp and meet the needs of this market segment. By precisely defining the addressable market, businesses can better achieve an increase in market share.

3.4 Integrated impact

These three factors intertwine and collectively influence the success of venture capital. For instance, a business might possess a clear business model, but without a unique value proposition and market potential, its attractiveness diminishes. Conversely, even with enormous market potential, a business may struggle to achieve successful venture capital if its business model lacks clarity or competitive advantage.

Throughout the venture capital process, investors typically conduct in-depth analyses of a business's strategy and business model to evaluate potential returns and risks. Therefore, founders and management teams should dedicate themselves to developing an appealing business model, emphasizing a unique value proposition, and seeking growth opportunities in potentially vast markets.

In conclusion, the key to venture capital success lies in the strategy and business model of a business. These two factors complement each other, propelling businesses to stand out in a competitive market and create substantial returns for investors. Therefore, entrepreneurs and investors alike should thoroughly understand and prioritize these key factors to collectively drive innovation and business development.

4 Market context (meadow)

Venture capital success is profoundly influenced by the market context in which startups operate. This market context encompasses various factors, including macroeconomic conditions, legal and regulatory landscapes, and cultural influences. This discussion delves into how these three aspects contribute to or hinder the success of venture capital investments.

4.1 Macroeconomic conditions

Macroeconomic factors play a pivotal role in shaping the landscape for venture capital investments. The overall health of the economy, inflation rates, and interest rates can impact the availability of funds, investor confidence, and the willingness of startups to take risks. During periods of economic expansion, venture capital tends to flow more readily as investors are optimistic about growth opportunities. Conversely, economic downturns can lead to a tightening of investment, increased risk aversion, and a more challenging environment for startups to secure funding. Through a comparative examination of the financial crisis and an economic boom, the empirical results of the comprehensive analysis assert that the United States venture capital markets exhibit significant correlations with the broader macroeconomy in specific dimensions. Changes in the macroeconomic landscape have a pronounced impact on venture risk levels, consequently resulting in risk mitigation or, conversely, risk augmentation. These outcomes are contingent upon investors' risk preferences and the defined risk-to-reward ratio [9].

The size and stability of the market also influence venture capital success. A large and stable market provides greater opportunities for startups to scale and achieve significant returns. Economic indicators such as consumer spending, GDP growth, and unemployment rates are closely monitored by venture capitalists to assess the overall market context and potential for success.

4.2 Legal and regulatory landscape

The legal and regulatory environment is a critical determinant of venture capital success. Different jurisdictions have varying laws and regulations that can either facilitate or impede the growth of startups. Various factors, including intellectual property protection, contract enforcement, and the overall ease of conducting business, play pivotal roles in determining the appeal of a market for venture capital. Research indicates that cross-country variations in legality, encompassing legal origin and accounting standards, exert a substantial influence on the governance structure of investments in the venture capital industry. Robust legal frameworks contribute to expedited deal screening and origination, an increased likelihood of syndication, reduced chances of potentially detrimental co-investments, and a smoother facilitation of investor board representation [10].

In addition, regulatory changes can have a profound impact on certain industries. For example, emerging technologies may face evolving regulatory frameworks that can either foster innovation or create barriers to entry. Venture capitalists need to stay abreast of legal developments to anticipate potential risks and opportunities associated with their investments.

Moreover, compliance with regulations is essential for startups seeking venture capital. Companies that navigate the legal landscape effectively are more likely to gain the trust of investors and operate sustainably. Regulatory clarity and a supportive legal environment contribute to a positive market context for venture capital investments.

4.3 Cultural influences

Cultural factors significantly shape the success of venture capital investments. Cultural nuances can impact consumer behaviour, market acceptance of products or services, and the overall business environment. Understanding the cultural context is crucial for startups to tailor their strategies and offerings to local preferences. In some cultures, risk-taking and entrepreneurship are highly encouraged, fostering an environment conducive to innovation and venture capital success. Conversely, conservative cultural attitudes may pose challenges for startups introducing disruptive technologies or unconventional business models.

Cultural diversity also plays a role in the success of global venture capital investments. Investors need to navigate and understand the cultural differences in various markets to make informed decisions. In contrast to the risk-sharing motive, a heightened cultural disparity between investor countries and their invested companies is linked to smaller venture capital (VC) syndicates. This phenomenon is primarily driven by reduced representation of local investors in syndicates led by foreign VCs. However, specific syndication strategies related to cultural disparities, such as involving locally experienced foreign VCs or syndicate members from culturally similar countries, correlate with increased participation of local VCs offering valuable monitoring services. Further research indicates that these culture-linked syndication approaches significantly align with VC financing and monitoring strategies in cross-border investments, influencing their ultimate success [11]. Establishing effective communication and building relationships with local partners are vital for overcoming cultural barriers and ensuring the success of venture capital endeavours.

In conclusion, the success of venture capital investments is intricately tied to the market context, encompassing macroeconomic conditions, legal and regulatory landscapes, and cultural influences. Investors must carefully evaluate these factors to make informed decisions, mitigate risks, and capitalize on opportunities. By understanding and navigating the complexities of the market environment, venture capitalists can enhance their chances of backing successful startups and achieving robust returns on their investments.

5 Conclusion

In conclusion, the three factors in the "jockey-horse-meadow" model, namely the entrepreneurial team, strategy and business model, and market context, play a very important role in the success of VCs. These three factors are indispensable, just like the success of VC is a jockey driving a horse in the meadow, which requires good driving skills of the jockey, a strong horse, and a flat and wide meadow. The composition of the entrepreneurial team, leadership, vision, and complementary competencies proved to be the key factors for a successful team; a clear business model, special value and competitive advantages, and market potential proved to be the key factors for a successful entrepreneurial project; and macroeconomic conditions, laws and regulations, and cultural influences also proved to be important contextual factors affecting the success of entrepreneurial investments. Only when good jockeys,

https://doi.org/10.1051/shsconf/202418801012

sturdy horses, and vast meadows are all met at the same time is a startup team most likely to get financing as well as succeed in their venture. The limitation of this article is that it does not fully include other possible influencing factors, and it is hoped that future articles will analyse the determinants of VC success in complete detail.

References

1. P. A. Gompers, W. Gornall, S. N. Kaplan, et al., JFE, 135(1), 169-190 (2020).
2. J. Lerner and J. Tåg, ICC, 22(1), 153-182 (2013).
3. E. G. S. Félix, C. P. Pires, and M. A. Gulamhussen, J Financ Serv Res, 44, 259–279 (2013).
4. C. M. Beckman, M. D. Burton, and C. O'Reilly, JBV, 22(2), 147-173 (2007).
5. R. Eugster and M. J. Kendzia, ABR, 10(12), 132-144 (2022).
6. J. Brinckmann and M. Hoegl, SEJ, 5(1), 37-57 (2011).
7. S. C. Lee, W. H. Lim, and E. K. Suh, JDS, 12(6), 81-88 (2014).
8. J. Weking, T. P. Böttcher, S. Hermes, et al., *Does Business Model Matter for Startup Success? A Quantitative Analysis* in the Proceedings of 27th European Conference on Information Systems, ECIS, 6.
9. P. Kuosmanen, Macroeconomic impact on venture markets: Does the correlation exist? University of VAASA (2022).
10. D. Cumming, D. Schmidt, and U. Walz, JBV, 25(1), 54-72 (2010).
11. N. Dai and R. Nahata, JIBS, 47, 140-169 (2016).

ESG Practice of Medical Device Companies and its Impact on Corporate Performance: Taking Mindray as an Example

Ziyue Chen[1,*]

[1]School of Economics and Management, Beijing University of Chemical Technology, Beijing, 100029, China

Abstract. In the context of China's "dual carbon" goal, the concept of Environment, Social and Governance (ESG) has attracted more and more attention, and enterprises have turned their attention to ESG in the process of thinking about how to transform to a new model of sustainable development. At the same time, with the aging population and the continuous progress of medical technology, the medical device industry shows a trend of rapid development. Researchers found that good ESG practices have a positive impact on enterprise performance. However, most of the studies are empirical studies based on big data samples, while there are few case studies on specific companies. As a leading enterprise in the medical device industry, Mindray has made continuous efforts in green development, social responsibility and corporate governance, and has achieved excellent performance in ESG transparency and ESG performance evaluation. Therefore, this study takes Mindray as the research object, adopts literature research method and case study method to analyze its ESG practice path and its impact on corporate performance. The study found that Mindray Medical's ESG practices performed well, and its good ESG practices had a positive impact on both its non-financial performance and financial performance, which was conducive to its sustainable and healthy development.

1 Introduction

Sustainable development has always been an important concept of China's development. The proposal of China's "dual carbon" goal points out the development direction for enterprises, promotes enterprises to accelerate the transformation of development mode, integrate the concept of green, environmental protection and low-carbon into business activities, and promote the sustainable development of enterprises. Therefore, more and more enterprises are turning their attention to Environment, Social and Governance (ESG). ESG is short for environment, society and governance. It is a corporate governance evaluation system that takes into account economic benefits, environmental and social impacts. It is an important standard to measure whether an enterprise has environmental awareness and can undertake social responsibilities. In the research on ESG and enterprise green development, Wang found that the improvement of enterprise ESG performance can effectively convey positive signals, strengthen risk smoothing ability, and stimulate the vitality of green innovation, so as to improve the level of low-carbon and green transformation of enterprises [1]. Yu kai found that ESG performance has a positive impact on corporate green innovation and total factor productivity, which can promote the green development of enterprises by improving the external information environment [2]. In the research on the impact of ESG performance on corporate reputation, Li and Cui found that the improvement of ESG performance can send positive signals to different stakeholders, thus enhancing the image and status of enterprises in various market players and affecting corporate reputation [3]. Li et al. found that good ESG performance can improve corporate reputation and ease financing constraints, enhance the cohesion of enterprises to customers or suppliers, and thus enhance the discourse power in the supply chain [4]. In the study on the relationship between ESG and corporate investment and financing, Yang et al. found that the improvement of corporate ESG performance can reduce inefficient investment behaviour and reduce the cost of equity capital [5]. Fang found that the overall ESG performance of enterprises was conducive to alleviating the green financing constraints of enterprises [6]. Mahmood found that ESG performance can promote the acquisition of commercial credit financing (CCF) by promoting green innovation, improving social reputation and reducing operational risks [7]. In terms of corporate financial risks, S. Muttanachai and L. D. Jin both found that the improvement of ESG performance can reduce corporate financial risks, improve financial conditions and constrain financial irregularities [8, 9]. From a comprehensive perspective, Liu found that ESG performance can promote the improvement of corporate financial performance by reducing corporate financing constraints [10]. Kim and Li, & Peng all found that there is a positive correlation between ESG disclosure and enterprise performance [11, 12]. ESG performance has a positive impact on the profitability of enterprises, and

* Corresponding author: 2021060133@buct.edu.cn

the impact is more significant for enterprises with larger scale [13]. Kaiser found that good ESG performance can increase the value of enterprises [14]. To sum up, the disclosure and performance improvement of ESG can promote the green and sustainable development of enterprises, and play a positive role in promoting the reputation of enterprises. At the same time, the improvement of ESG performance can effectively promote the improvement of corporate financing efficiency, reduce financial risks and financing costs, and have a significant positive role in promoting corporate financial performance.

As a leading enterprise in the medical device industry, Mindray actively implements ESG strategy, integrates sustainable development management into its daily management structure, and establishes a comprehensive sustainable development management system. Mindray has been awarded the title of "2022 ESG TOP20 Competitiveness of China's Listed Pharmaceutical Companies". Therefore, this paper takes Mindray as the research object to analyse its ESG practice path and the impact of its ESG performance on corporate performance.

This paper uses two research methods: literature research and case study. The literature research method is adopted to sort out the literature from all aspects of the impact of ESG practices on enterprise performance, laying a theoretical foundation for the research of this paper. At the same time, the single case study method is used to discuss the impact of Mindray Medical ESG practice path and enterprise performance.

This study aims to directly reflect the relationship and influence between the two through case analysis of ESG practice paths and benefits of specific medical device enterprises, fill the gap of specific case studies of ESG implementation of medical device enterprises, and provide certain theoretical basis for enterprise management to practice ESG concepts.

2 Mindray ESG practice case

2.1 Introduction to Mindray

Shenzhen Mindray Bio-Medical Electronics Co., Ltd. was formally established on January 25, 1999, listed on the GEM of Shenzhen Stock Exchange in October 2018 (A-share: 300760), and has been continuously disclosing social responsibility reports since 2018. The company is mainly engaged in the research and development, manufacturing, marketing and service of medical devices, always customer demand-oriented, committed to providing quality products and services for global medical institutions. The company integrates innovation, closely responds to clinical needs, and supports medical institutions to provide quality medical services, thus helping to improve medical conditions and reduce medical costs around the world. After years of development, the company has become the largest medical equipment and solution provider in China and the world's leading. Headquartered in Shenzhen, China, the company has subsidiaries in about 40 countries, and has established a R&D (Researching and Development) innovation platform based on global resource allocation, forming a huge global R&D, marketing and service network. Mindray always adheres to the core values of "customer-oriented, people-oriented, rigorous and pragmatic, and proactive", keeps in mind the corporate mission of "popularizing high-end technology and enabling more people to share quality life care", and firmly roots the concept of sustainable development in every link of the value chain of business activities. Through the deep integration of its own business with the sustainable development goals, committed to making lasting contributions to a quality and healthy future.

2.2 Mindray ESG management

Mindray has integrated sustainability management into its daily management structure and established a comprehensive sustainability management system including the board of directors, the strategy and sustainability committee, and the ESG executive committee. In order to coordinate all business and functional departments to jointly promote the implementation of the company's sustainable development strategy and policy, the company has set up six sub-committees in the ESG executive committee to standardize corporate governance, innovation-driven future, collaborative development of business chain, promote green development, sustainable workplace and common prosperity, rooted in the six areas of Mindray's sustainable development strategy. The concept of sustainable development will be firmly rooted in the whole value chain of business activities, and actively practice social responsibility.

Under the guidance of the strategy and sustainability committee of the board of directors, the ESG executive committee and the ESG system management team continue to pay attention to ESG-related risks of the group and formulate reasonable ESG risk mitigation plans to ensure that the company actively fulfils corporate social responsibilities in operation and is committed to achieving sustainable development goals. In the process of daily business operation and management, the company implements the responsibility of sustainable development management from top to bottom, and actively fulfils corporate social responsibility. At the same time, performance indicators such as carbon emission, quality management, product safety, human capital development and technological innovation will be set up, and these ESG performance indicators will be linked to the remuneration of relevant directors and senior management.

2.3 ESG practice of Mindray

(1) Environmental dimension: Mindray adheres to the strategic layout of green manufacturing, integrates the green concept into production and operation, and adheres to the road of innovative green medical treatment. In the process of product research and development, it practices the concept of energy-saving and recyclable design and

development, improve the added value of products through green product patents, and protect the environment with innovative technologies. At the same time, it actively practices carbon emission and energy management, water resources management, pollution discharge and noise management, sticks to the bottom line of compliance, adopts a series of emission reduction measures, conducts regular environmental monitoring, promotes pollutant reduction and promotes green development.

(2) Social dimension: Mindray has established an integrated supply chain architecture suitable for the company and a customer demand-oriented product delivery system, focusing on improving the management ability of product quality and safety, and actively carrying out customer service collaborative management, timely understanding and meeting customer needs, and improving customer satisfaction. In addition, Mindray implements the whole life cycle management of suppliers, improves the communication and cooperation between upstream and downstream suppliers, improves the efficiency of problem solving, and wins the trust of relevant stakeholders. At the same time, Mindray adheres to the management of responsible marketing, and takes effective measures to crack down on counterfeit products, maintain the image of the enterprise, and improve the brand reputation. In addition, Mindray adheres to the talent development concept of "making Mindray a lifelong university for employees", establishes a sound talent training system, and adheres to diversity and equal opportunity, protects the rights and interests of employees, and undertakes social responsibilities.

(3) Governance dimension: Mindray has continuously improved its governance structure, established a professional ESG executive committee and ESG system management group, and provided training on ESG-related topics and sharing of excellent ESG management practice cases of global peers for board members, so as to strengthen their professional ability in ESG governance. At the same time, the company pays attention to improving internal and external risk management capabilities, establishes an effective business ethics and compliance governance structure, which is supervised and reviewed by the board of directors, and sets up a compliance committee as the discussion and decision-making body for business ethics and compliance business management. In addition, it pays attention to the maintenance and management of investor relations, takes the initiative to carry out investor relations management activities, listens to investors' opinions and suggestions, and timely responds to investors' demands.

2.4 Mindray ESG rating

The higher the ESG rating is, the smaller the potential ESG risk of the enterprise is, the better the ESG performance of the company is, the higher the transparency of key ESG data disclosure is, and the higher the sustainable development ability is. Different institutions score the performance of enterprises in various indicators through indicators at all levels. In all scoring types, the ESG score of Mindray is generally higher than that of most peer enterprises, and the rating is almost above A, especially in the rating of China Securities Index and China Securities Index, which both reach AAA. This means that Mindray pays more attention to ESG practices than its peers, and has excellent ESG performance, less potential ESG risks, and higher sustainable development ability, which is more likely to be favoured by investors.

3 The impact of Mindray ESG practice on corporate performance

3.1 Impact of ESG practice on non-financial performance

Based on the fact that Mindray main production base is the Guang Ming production plant, this paper takes the Guang Ming production plant as the object to analyze the changes of its main environmental performance indicators. Mindray adheres to the principle of energy saving and consumption reduction, low carbon and environmental protection, and is committed to building a sustainable green and environmental protection enterprise. Taking green development as a key part of the company's high-quality development in the new era, Mindray complies with national and local laws and regulations on environmental protection and emission indicators, and effectively protects and improves the environment by relying on the company's advanced technology and scientific management means. Reduce negative impact on the environment. As shown in Table 1, the emission concentration of each major pollutant of Mindray showed a decreasing trend during the period from 2018 to 2022, and all met the emission standards. At the same time, Mindray has achieved 100% wastewater and waste gas discharge standards from 2018 to 2022. It can be seen that Mindray has been effective in environmental protection.

Table 1. Main environmental performance indicators of Mindray.

Main environmental performance indicators	2018	2019	2020	2021	2022
Chemical oxygen demand emission concentration (mg/L)	109	52	40.6	26.24	14.833
Five days biochemical oxygen demand emission concentration (mg/L)	50.6	11.4	14.21	4.9	5.375

https://doi.org/10.1051/shsconf/202418801013

Ammonia nitrogen emission concentration (mg/L)	1.88	1.45	6.51	0.644	0.186
Total phosphorus emission concentration (mg/L)	0.65	0.42	0.118	0.220	0.015
Emission concentration of anionic surfactant (mg/L)	0.79	0.4	0.158	0.2	0.13

3.2 Improvement of corporate reputation

In recent years, Mindray has always adhered to the practice of social responsibility, stayed true to the original aspiration of "becoming the core force to protect human health", and made efforts to sustainable development in all aspects. It adheres to integrated innovation, complies with the needs of the era of low-carbon development and green development, manages and monitors business links, so as to reduce the negative impact on the environment and move forward to a low-carbon circular economy. At the same time, it adheres to customer-oriented, deeply cultivates the field of medical devices, and wins the respect and trust of global customers. In addition, it adheres to the development concept of serving the society, actively returns to the society, practices social responsibility and shapes a responsible corporate image while becoming bigger and stronger. With the gradual deepening of Mindray ESG practice, the improvement of the quantity and quality of accumulated honours obtained by the company has brought about a promotion effect on the reputation of the enterprise. As shown in Table 2, these are the major honours Mindray has received since 2018. These honours convey the positive side of Mindray to investors and the public, reflect the company's good performance and operating conditions, and thus increase the company's visibility and enhance its brand reputation.

Table 2. Honors Received by Mindray from 2018 to 2022.

2018	"Top 10 New Media Communication Rankings for Healthy China Brands" and "Annual Responsibility Brand for Healthy China" titles
2019	Ranked 415th among the Top 500 Chinese Manufacturing Enterprises in 2019, The first Deloitte China "Private Enterprise Excellent Management Company" award
2020	Ranked 331th among the Top 500 Chinese Manufacturing Enterprises in 2020, International Humanitarian Assistance Contribution Award, National (China) Product and Service Quality Integrity Demonstration Enterprise
2021	Ranked 305th among the Top 500 Chinese Manufacturing Enterprises in 2021, Outstanding ESG case in China, Most Social Responsibility Award, The 12th China Listed Companies Investor Relations Forum Tian ma Award for Best Investor Relations of Chinese Listed Companies
2022	Ranked 312th among the Top 500 Chinese Manufacturing Enterprises in 2021,2022 Top 20 ESG Competitiveness of China's Listed Pharmaceutical Companies,2021-2022 Best ESG Award,2022 Corporate Excellence in Social Responsibility Award,2022 Ivy Spring Award Smart Medical Enterprise of the Year

Source: Shenzhen Mindray Biomedical Electronics Co., Ltd. 2018-2022 Social Responsibility Report

3.3 Innovation performance

Innovation is the endogenous driving force of enterprises, which can enhance the core competitiveness of enterprises, promote the sustainable and healthy development of enterprises, and achieve greater revenue and market share. This paper selects four indicators of Mindray's R&D investment from 2018 to 2022, the total number of R&D personnel, the proportion of R&D personnel and the cumulative number of patents applied to reflect the innovation performance of the enterprise. Mindray adheres to customer demand-oriented, integrated innovation, independent research and development to master the core technology, committed to the development of market-leading products, to create excellent core competitiveness. As can be seen from Table 3, Mindray's R&D investment increased year by year from 2018 to 2022, insisting on maintaining high R&D investment on the basis of high quality. R&d team is an important guarantee for enterprise innovation ability, which can provide strong innovation power and R&D strength guarantee for enterprises. Mindray attaches great importance to the cultivation of R&D talents. The total number of R&D personnel in the enterprise increases year by year, and the proportion of R&D personnel is relatively stable at about 24%. At the same time, the cumulative number of patents applied by enterprises is also gradually increasing, with a steady annual increase, which indicates that Mindray has stable professional experimental ability, internal control and management ability, and good innovation ability.

Table 3. Innovation Performance of Mindray Medical from 2018 to 2022.

Year	**R&D investment (RMB billion)**	**Total number of R&D personnel**	**R&D personnel proportion**	**Accumulated number of patent applications**
2018	1.42	2258	24.45%	-

2019	1.65	2508	25.50%	4873
2020	2.10	3070	25.94%	6412
2021	2.73	3492	23.78%	7418
2022	3.19	3927	24.40%	8670

Source: Shenzhen Mindray Biomedical Electronics Co., Ltd. Annual Report 2018-2022

3.4 Increase in market share

Market share is also the market share, which refers to the proportion of the sales volume of a certain category in the market of similar products of a certain enterprise. The higher the market share is, the stronger the competitiveness of the enterprise is. This paper selects the ratio of Mindray's total medical device revenue (CNY 100 million) to the medical device market size (CNY 100 million) to represent Mindray's market share in the medical device industry. It can be seen from Figure 1 that since 2018, the market share of Mindray has gradually increased, from 2.60% in 2018 to 3.15% in 2022. It can be seen that since Mindray carried out ESG practice, the profitability and sustainable development ability of Mindray have been gradually improved, which is conducive to expanding its popularity and influence.

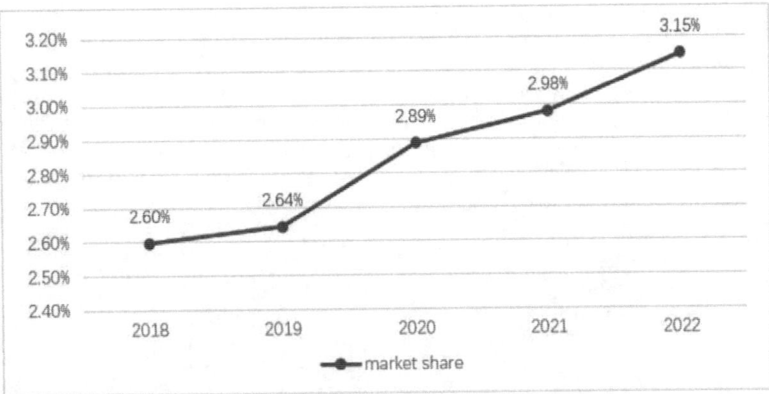

Source:: Frost&sullivan and Shenzhen Mindray Biomedical Electronics Co., Ltd. Annual Report 2018-2022

Fig. 1. Mindray's market share from 2018 to 2022 (Picture/Photo credit: Original).

4 Impact of ESG practice on financial performance

4.1 Growth analysis

Mindray attaches great importance to the deep integration of long-term development strategy and sustainable development concept of the group, and promotes long-term development of the enterprise through active ESG practice. Mindray conducts supplier life cycle management, promotes communication and collaboration with suppliers, and takes the initiative to carry out a series of investor relations management activities to enhance stakeholder confidence. At the same time, Mindray insists on innovating green healthcare, improving product research and development capabilities and product quality, coupled with its efficient internal governance and risk management, which effectively reduces the governance cost of the enterprise and promotes long-term sustainable development. In addition, Mindray has established a product delivery system based on customer needs. It pays attention to product quality and safety management while fully considering customer needs, and wins customer trust, thus promoting the development of the company. In addition, Mindray also implements responsible marketing management to combat counterfeit products, maintain brand image and enhance brand reputation, thus promoting the development of the enterprise. It can be seen that Mindray's ESG practice has contributed to the improvement of the company's growth ability in all aspects.

Operating income is the main operating results of an enterprise, which can intuitively reflect the development ability and growth rate of an enterprise, and reflect the change of enterprise scale. As can be seen from Figure 2, the operating revenue of Mindray has grown steadily in the past six years, showing a continuous upward trend, increasing by nearly three times from 2017 to 2022.

https://doi.org/10.1051/shsconf/202418801013

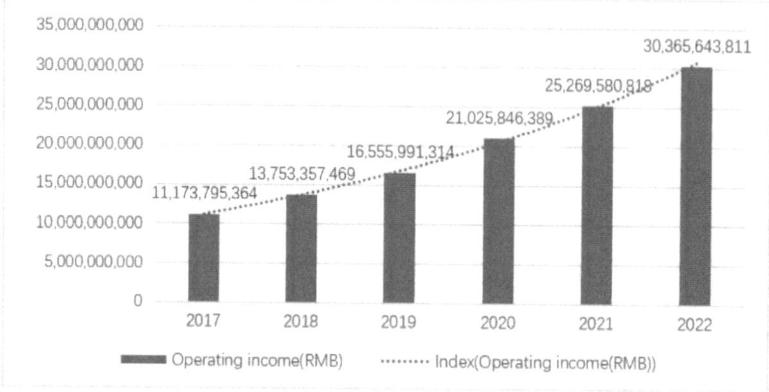

Source: Shenzhen Mindray Biomedical Electronics Co., Ltd. Annual Report 2018-2022

Fig. 2. Mindray's operating income trend from 2017 to 2022 (Picture/Photo credit: Original).

The difference between operating cash net flow and net profit can reveal the quality of net profit and reflect the health of enterprise development. First, as shown in Figure 3, the difference between Mindray's net operating cash flow and net profit is very small, and the two indicators are almost the same, indicating that Mindray's net profit earning ability is good, profitability is good, and it has real growth. At the same time, it can also be seen from Figure 3 that Mindray's net operating cash flow and net profit are gradually increasing from 2017 to 2022, reflecting its healthy development. The changing trend of the above indicators shows that Mindray's development ability and health are gradually improved after ESG practice, and it has a good growth ability.

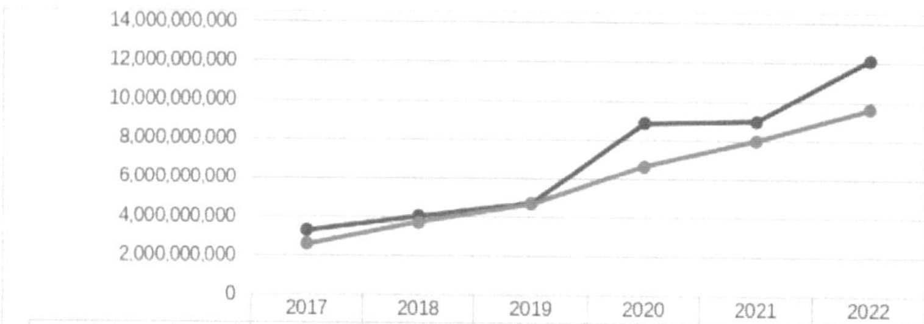

	2017	2018	2019	2020	2021	2022
Net operating cash flow(RMB)	3,300,366,91	4,034,585,37	4,721,794,91	8,870,109,84	8,998,649,17	12,141,147,8
Net profit(RMB)	2,601,191,05	3,725,741,91	4,684,816,79	6,659,603,29	8,004,045,87	9,610,716,81

Source: Shenzhen Mindray Biomedical Electronics Co., Ltd. Annual Report 2018-2022

Fig. 3. Comparison of Mindray's net operating cashflow and net profit (Picture/Photo credit: Original).

4.2 Profitability analysis

Good ESG performance can enhance the image of the enterprise, thus enhancing the market share of the enterprise, improving the product profit margin, and further enhancing the profitability of the enterprise. Through ESG practices such as good product quality, supplier life cycle management and investor relationship management, Mindray sends positive signals to different stakeholders, generates social publicity effect among consumers and investors, improves its reputation and brand influence, and promotes sales volume. At the same time, Mindray adheres to green innovation, actively adjusts the energy structure, reduces energy consumption, reduces the cost of environmental regulation, obtains more new market opportunities, and improves profitability. In addition, Mindray's transparent ESG disclosure regularly reduces the cost for investors to search for corporate information, thus relieving the pressure of financing constraints, enabling enterprises to have more funds to invest in innovation projects, improve innovation performance, enhance their core competitiveness to a certain extent, and increase profitability.

Profitability refers to the comprehensive ability of an enterprise to obtain profits and realize capital appreciation. In this paper, the profitability of Mindray is analysed by the three indicators of earnings cash guarantee multiple, net profit margin on sales and return on assets (ROA). The following is Mindray's profitability analysis.

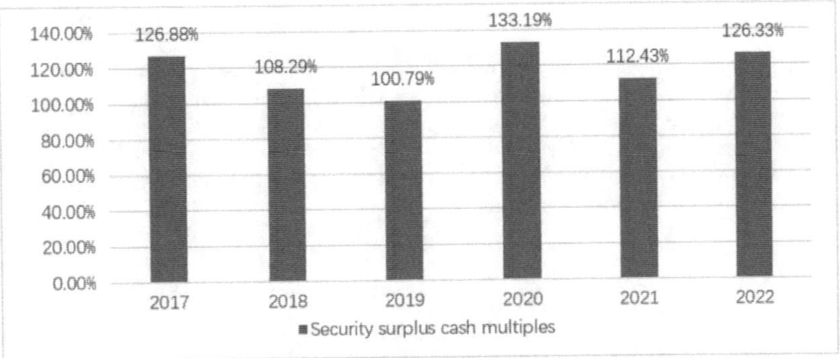

Source: Shenzhen Mindray Biomedical Electronics Co., Ltd. Annual Report 2018-2022

Fig. 4. Trend of Mindray's Security Surplus Cash multiples.

Surplus cash guarantee multiple is the ratio of net operating cash flow to net profit in a certain period of time, which reflects the guarantee degree of cash income in the net profit of an enterprise. As shown in Figure 4, Mindray maintained a relatively stable trend of earnings cash guarantee multiple from 2017 to 2022. The average earnings cash guarantee multiple for six years was 117.98%, and both the annual earnings cash guarantee multiple and the average earnings cash guarantee multiple were greater than 100%, indicating that the company's net profit was guaranteed by cash. The company's earnings are of good quality.

Table 4. Comparison of Mindray's profitability analysis indicators.

Year	Sales net profit ratio (%)	Industry average sales net profit ratio (%)	Return on asset (%)	Industry average return on asset (%)
2017	23.28	13.40	18.98	6.52
2018	27.09	15.69	20.66	7.88
2019	28.30	15.73	19.83	8.06
2020	31.67	27.75	22.60	15.87
2021	31.67	27.27	22.42	15.08
2022	31.65	24.48	22.65	13.49

Source: Shenzhen Mindray Biomedical Electronics Co., Ltd. Annual Report 2018-2022

The net profit margin of sales is the proportion of the net profit in the operating income of the enterprise in the operating activities, which can reflect the change of the profit status of the enterprise and the operating efficiency of the enterprise. As can be seen from Table 4, the net profit margin on sales of Mindray keeps an increasing trend, and from 2017 to 2022, the net profit margin on sales is higher than the average value of the industry every year, reflecting Mindray's performance in the whole industry and is in the forefront.

Return on assets (ROA) is the ratio of a company's net profit to its total assets, which reflects the efficiency and ability of a company in using its total assets to create profits. As can be seen from Table 4, from 2017 to 2022, Mindray's return on assets has never been lower than 18%, and the value is relatively stable, and the return on assets has been higher than the average level of the industry for six years, perhaps this is the benefit brought by its ESG practice. This means Mindray has better financial stability and can effectively use assets to create profits.

The above indicators show that Mindray has high profitability, which is higher than the average level of the industry due to its ESG practices.

4.3 Solvency analysis

From the above analysis of profitability and growth capacity, it can be seen that Mindray's good ESG performance has increased the sales volume of its products, increased its market share in the medical device industry, reduced financing constraints, gained the trust of relevant stakeholders and the support and subsidy of the government, and alleviated the problem of information asymmetry. In addition, Mindray's supplier life cycle management enhances the cooperation between upstream and downstream enterprises, making the collection of receivables easier, thus helping to improve the solvency of enterprises. At the same time,

Mindray, on the one hand, formulated a reasonable ESG risk mitigation plan, constantly improved the internal business environment of the enterprise, and reduced the occurrence of financial risks from the source. On the other hand, it pays attention to the training of employees, emphasizes diversification and equal opportunity, improves the satisfaction of employees, reduces the quit rate, reduces the cost caused by personnel turnover, so as to avoid the occurrence of financial risks caused by excessive human expenditure, and further improves the solvency of enterprises.

Debt paying ability refers to the ability of an enterprise to repay its debts when due, which can be reflected by the financial status of the enterprise. This paper will analyse the solvency of Mindray from four perspectives: asset-liability ratio, current ratio, quick ratio and equity ratio.

Source: Shenzhen Mindray Biomedical Electronics Co., Ltd. Annual Report 2018-2022

Fig. 5. Trend of Mindray's Asset Liability Ratio (Picture/Photo credit: Original).

The asset-liability ratio refers to the ratio between total liabilities and total assets; generally speaking, the asset-liability ratio is between 40% and 60%, which is a reasonable range. As shown in Figure 5, the asset-liability ratio of Mindray in 2017 was 53.91%, higher than that of the following years, but still less than 60%, which is within a reasonable range. With the deepening of ESG practice, the asset-liability ratio of enterprises shows a downward trend. It can be seen that with the continuous promotion of ESG practice, the asset-liability ratio of Mindray gradually decreases and remains in the ideal range, indicating that Mindray has almost no debt repayment risk and debt repayment is guaranteed.

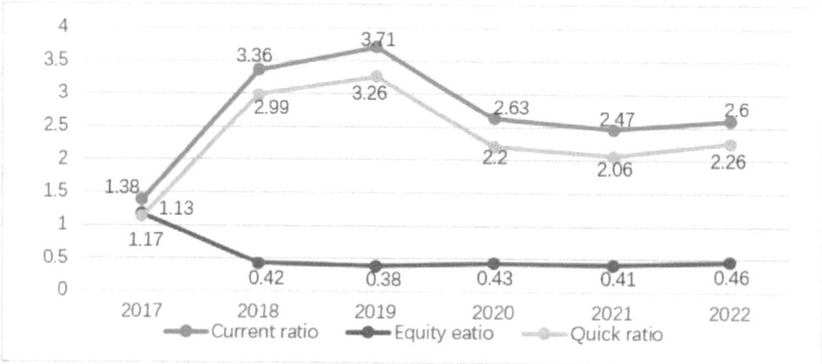

Source: Shenzhen Mindray Biomedical Electronics Co., Ltd. Annual Report 2018-2022

Fig. 6. Mindray's solvency analysis (Picture/Photo credit: Original).

Current ratio is the ratio of current assets to current liabilities, which can measure the short-term solvency of an enterprise. Generally speaking, it can be seen from Figure 6 that the liquidity ratio of Mindray in 2017 was 1.38%, which was slightly low and the risk of debt repayment was high. However, since 2018, it has been higher than 2 for five consecutive years, indicating strong short-term debt paying ability and resistance to risks. This is because the effect of ESG practices has a certain lag, but it also shows that the impact of ESG practices on the solvency of enterprises is long-term.

Quick ratio is the ratio of quick assets to current liabilities of an enterprise. If the quick-freezing ratio of an enterprise can be maintained at about 1, it can be said that the short-term solvency of the enterprise is reliably guaranteed. As can be seen from Figure 6, Mindray's quick ratio is all greater than 1, and in the period from 2018 to 2022, its quick ratio is all greater than 2, which indicates that Mindray's working capital is very restructured and it has strong solvency. And with the continuous advancement of ESG practice, Mindray shows stronger solvency.

https://doi.org/10.1051/shsconf/202418801013

Equity ratio refers to the ratio between total liabilities and shareholders' equity of an enterprise, which can measure the long-term solvency of an enterprise and reflect the stability of the basic financial structure. As shown in Figure 6, Mindray's equity ratio shows a downward trend and is stable at less than 0.5 between 2018 and 2022. Generally speaking, an equity ratio of 1 can indicate that the long-term debt paying ability of the enterprise is guaranteed, while the equity ratio of Mindray in the past five years is less than 0.5, which is enough to show that its basic financial structure is stable and its debt paying ability is strong.

To sum up, Mindray has very low leverage risk and excellent performance in debt repayment and risk resistance.

4.4 Operating capacity analysis

The first is the internal governance of the enterprise. Mindray adheres to compliance operation, establishes an effective internal management framework and sets up three lines of defence of compliance management on a global scale, so as to promote the improvement of internal governance capacity and thus improve operational capacity. At the same time, Mindray's supplier life cycle management and business chain collaborative management promote the management of the supply chain and its business process management, thus improving its operational capabilities. In addition, as mentioned above, Mindray's ESG practices effectively reduce financial risks, thus further improving its operating capacity.

Operating capacity refers to the ability of an enterprise to effectively manage and use assets, liabilities and funds in daily business activities. It reflects the operating efficiency and profitability of the enterprise, which is of great significance to the development of the enterprise and the acquisition of sustainable competitive advantage. This paper will discuss the operating capacity of Mindray from two perspectives of deposit operation cycle and accounts receivable turnover, and analyse the days of accounts receivable turnover and the average situation of the industry in which Mindray is located.

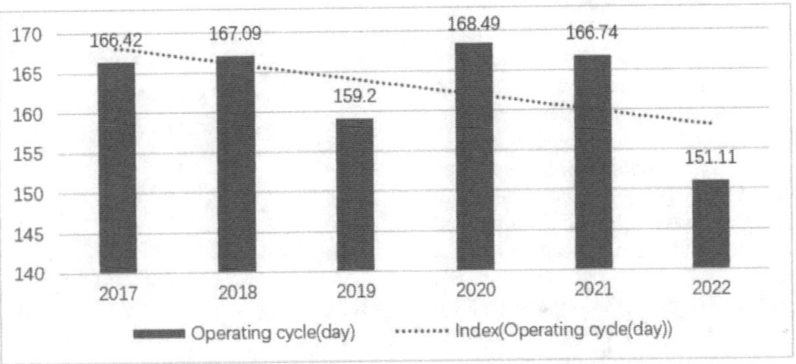

Source: Shenzhen Mindray Biomedical Electronics Co., Ltd. Annual Report 2018-2022

Fig. 7. Mindray's operating cycle trend (Picture/Photo credit: Original).

The length of the operating cycle determines the demand for current assets of an enterprise, and the shorter operating cycle reflects the effective operation management. It can be seen from Figure 7 that the operating cycle of Mindray generally shows a downward trend, which means that the capital turnover rate of Mindray is also improving, the capital turnover speed is improving, and the operating capacity of the enterprise is also constantly improving.

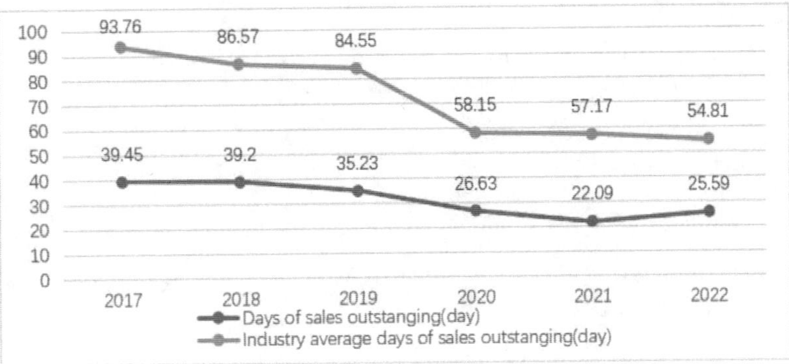

Source: Shenzhen Mindray Biomedical Electronics Co., Ltd. Annual Report 2018-2022

Fig. 8. Analysis of Mindray's operational capabilities (Picture/Photo credit: Original).

The shorter the accounts receivable turnover days, the higher the efficiency of the use of working capital of the enterprise. It can be seen from Figure 8 that Mindray's accounts receivable turnover days show a downward trend, and from 2017 to 2022, its turnover days are lower than the industry average accounts receivable turnover days, which shows that Mindray has a good fund recovery status and good asset flow. In general, it can be seen from the above indicators that Mindray's operating capacity is constantly improving with the in-depth development of ESG practice.

5 Conclusions

This paper selects Mindray as a case company, and studying its ESG practice path and its impact on corporate performance. According to research, Mindray's ESG practice has a good overall effect, and its ESG practice has a positive impact on both non-financial and financial performance of the enterprise. Through the good practice performance in the environment, society and governance, it has achieved good environmental benefits, created a responsible corporate image, increased brand awareness, improved corporate reputation, and promoted the improvement of innovation performance and market share. At the same time, the improvement of Mindray ESG practice enhances the confidence of relevant stakeholders, wins the trust of customers, improves brand reputation, and can effectively reduce governance costs, thus contributing to the improvement of enterprise growth ability and improving the profitability and operating capacity of the enterprise. In addition, Mindray's good ESG performance can reduce financing constraints, reduce financial risks, improve the equity governance structure, improve governance capacity, and thus improve the solvency and operational capacity of the enterprise.

For enterprises, they should actively respond to China's "dual carbon" policy, establish ESG management concept, and integrate ESG concept into all links of enterprise production and operation, so as to promote sustainable and healthy development of enterprises. Use ESG practice to promote the green transformation and upgrading of enterprises, improve the ability to fulfill social responsibility, improve governance and risk prevention ability, so as to improve the brand image, enhance the operation ability of enterprises, and promote sustainable and healthy development.

For external investors of enterprises, they should establish ESG investment concepts. When making investment decisions, the ESG performance of enterprises should be taken into consideration, the evaluation dimensions should be expanded, and both financial and non-financial performance of enterprises should be taken into account, so as to have a better understanding of the sustainable development ability of enterprises and improve the possibility of obtaining long-term investment returns.

For the government and other relevant departments, it is necessary to further improve the ESG information disclosure mechanism and ESG evaluation system, so as to achieve a win-win situation between ESG governance and the "dual carbon" strategy and promote sustainable development.

References

1. F. Wang. CFE, 1, 1-14 (2023).
2. E. Z. W. Yukai. IRFA, 91 (2024).
3. L. Li, L. Cui, EE, (11), 28-39 (2023).
4. Y. Li, Y. Wu, & X. Tian, JFE, 49(08),153-168 (2023).
5. B. Yang, T. Wei, M. Zhang, et al., JSU, 45(10), 101-109 (2023).
6. H. Fang, SJ, 15(14), (2023)
7. M. F. Mahmood, ESPRI, 30(35), 83961-83974 (2023).
8. S. Muttanachai, CBM, 10(1), (2023).
9. L. D. Jin, SJ, 15(13), (2023).
10. X. Z. Liu, JGEBF, 5(10), (2023).
11. S. Kim, Z. C. Li, SJ, 05(06), (2023).
12. Y. S. C. Peng, JEM, 345118829-118829 (2023).
13. S. Kim, Z. C. Li, SJ, 13(07), (2023).
14. G. F. A. Kaiser, GFJ, 38, 45-64 (2017).

https://doi.org/10.1051/shsconf/202418801014

The Different Impact of Covid-19 Pandemic on Catering and Pharmaceutical Industry in China: Evidence from Time Series Model

Yiran Dai*

Adam Smith Business School, University of Glasgow, Glasgow, G12 8QQ, United Kingdom

Abstract. Covid-19 pandemic is a huge setback for the global economy. This essay investigates the distinct impacts of the COVID-19 pandemic on China's catering and pharmaceutical industries using time series models. It highlights how the pandemic differently influenced these sectors, with the catering industry experiencing a significant downturn and the pharmaceutical industry showing a surge in demand for medical products and services. The paper employs indices to represent industry situations, analyzes stock prices' volatility, and predicts closing prices without the pandemic's impact. The study utilizes the ARIMA model for forecasting and empirical analysis, revealing how the pandemic accelerated trends in these industries and its varying effects on them. This research offers insights into industry-specific impacts of global crises and provides valuable perspectives for policymakers, investors, and researchers in understanding economic effects during health emergencies. The results indicated that the covid-19 pandemic had a negative impact on catering industry and the stock price was much lower than expected. While it had a relatively positive effects on pharmaceutical industry since the huge demand of medicine and other related supplies.

1 Introduction

The COVID-19 pandemic, emerging in late 2019, rapidly evolved into a global crisis, profoundly affecting economies and industries worldwide. At the same time, China's industries are facing many challenges during this period. Before the pandemic, China's catering industry had developed rapidly, in contrast, the healthcare industry has been in a more stable way. Based on information from the National Statistics Bureau of China, the catering industry experienced a consistent compound annual growth rate of 10.67% over the past decade. In the last five years, its annual output value represented about 4.7% of the national GDP. Specifically, in 2019, the industry's revenue hit 5.89 trillion RMB, marking a 17.7% increase from the prior year. This growth rate surpassed the national GDP growth rate by roughly 11% [1]. In 2019, the size of China's pharmaceutical market was US$149.8 billion, with expectations to grow at a CAGR of more than 12% between 2019 and 2029. Before the COVID-19 pandemic, China's pharmaceutical industry was undergoing significant growth and development. As the world's second-largest pharmaceutical market, China was a strategic priority for many global players in the industry. The Chinese pharmaceutical industry was characterized by a healthy pace of growth, with market growth remaining in mid-single figures over the years leading up to 2020 [2].

The impact from covid-19 pandemic is global. Utilizing the Global Trade Analysis Project (GTAP) CGE model, Park et al. from the Asian Development Bank conducted an analysis of the worldwide economic impacts of COVID-19 as of May 2020. Their approach factored in variations in trading costs, productivity shocks, and fiscal stimulus measures to estimate the pandemic's economic consequences under scenarios of both short- and long-term containment. According to their findings, global GDP could potentially fluctuate between a decrease of 6.4% and 9.7%. Specifically, Asia (excluding China) might see GDP reductions ranging from 4.6% to 7.2%, while China's GDP could decline by 7.5% to 11.2% [3]. The pandemic has greatly impacted traditionally robust sectors such as petroleum, finance, real estate, and accommodation and catering. These industries have experienced significant challenges due to the pandemic, leading to a diminished role in the overall economic network [4].

The arrival of the pandemic brings both accelerated and pause button to these two industries. Statistics reveal that the catering industry was the second most impacted sector during the COVID-19 pandemic. The industry experienced a severe downturn, particularly evident during traditional peak periods like New Year's Eve dinners, which saw a dramatic decline in subscriptions due to the outbreak. The restrictions on dining out and general movement significantly affected restaurants, leading to substantial financial losses. During the first

* Corresponding author: 2016141491004@stu.scu.edu.cn

six months of 2020, China experienced a significant 32.8% year-on-year drop in its national catering revenue, a decline that was 42.2 percentage points steeper than the decrease recorded in the same period of the previous year. For larger establishments, revenues fell by 30.2% year-on-year. Overall, 2020 catering revenues were down by 16.6% from the previous year. The industry faced mounting pressures from unsold food stock, high operating costs, and dwindling profits, pushing it into a severe survival crisis [5]. However, the pandemic significantly increased public demand for medical products and services. There was a surge in the need for antiviral and antibacterial medications, traditional Chinese medicines, and protective gear like masks, disinfectants, ventilators, and oxygen generators. Alibaba International Station reported substantial increases in supplying medical protective equipment. The demand for such items in March showed a growth rate three times higher than the previous year, with a 300% increase in Europe. Additionally, the pandemic boosted the demand for online medical consultations, pharmaceutical delivery, and retail services [6]. In order to delve deeper into the impact on these two industries, we use index to represent the industry situation. Indexes serve as measures of risk and reward that change over time, providing a standard for evaluating performance, understanding its drivers, and making improvements. Following the introduction of the Capital Asset Pricing Model (CAPM), indexes have become instrumental in creating passive investment vehicles and in forming the foundation for portfolio management. [7]. This paper highlights the significance of the catering and pharmaceutical sectors in China, noting their differing states of development and market dynamics prior to the pandemic, focus on the trend of two indices and construct an appropriate model to make the comparison.

2 Research design

2.1 Data acquisition

This paper uses cn.Investing.com to search and obtain indices data for the catering and pharmaceutical industries, in detail, SZHCI can be used to represent the fluctuation for catering and SZHCSI for pharmaceutical industry [8]. This study focuses on the daily opening and closing prices and weekly opening and closing prices and stock returns that calculated by dividing the difference between closing prices during the Covid-19 period (from 2019/1/1 to 2020/1/24). The data are used to analysis the volatility of stock prices in both sectors and make a prediction of the closing prices without the impact of Covid-19 based on the previous data. In order to make a clearer model, we use ln(1+x) to edit the data and construct the model by STATA. It can show the difference of two industries by comparing their performances through the model.

2.2 ADF unit root test

The ADF test, commonly employed to assess stationarity in time series data, operates under the null hypothesis that the time series possesses a unit root, which suggests non-stationarity. In this study, the first step is to input the data includes indices for both the catering and pharmaceutical industries with values for daily and weekly timeframes into STATA to perform ADF test. Then it can get t-value and p-value for ln () indices. As indicated in Table 1, the p-value for the 1st and 2nd log-returns is 0, which falls below the threshold of 0.1. This outcome is enable to dismiss the null hypothesis, indicating that the model is both stable and feasible. It suggests that the model may be well-suited for the data being analyzed.

Table 1 Weak stationarity test

Variables	t	p
	Catering, daily	
Ln index	-2.196	0.4923
1st order difference	-11.118	0.0000
2nd order difference	-20.397	0.0000
	Catering, weekly	
Ln index	-2.203	0.4880
1st order difference	-3.826	0.0153
2nd order difference	-7.307	0.0000
	Pharmaceutical, daily	
Ln index	-2.806	0.1946
1st order difference	-12.675	0.0000
2nd order difference	-20.933	0.0000
	Pharmaceutical, weekly	
Ln index	-2.372	0.3945
1st order difference	-3.913	0.0116
2nd order difference	-7.228	0.0000

2.3 ARIMA Model

ARIMA, an acronym for Autoregressive Integrated Moving Average, is a model used in statistical analysis to forecast data in time series. It combines three key components: autoregression (AR), differencing (I), and moving average (MA). The AR part involves using past values to predict future values, the I part involves differencing the series to make it stationary, and the MA part uses past forecast errors in the prediction equation. This model is particularly effective for analyzing and forecasting time series data where the data points are sequentially dependent. They are particularly useful for short-term forecasting and have applications in various areas, including stock market analysis, economic forecasting, and sales prediction. ARIMA(p,d,q) can be expressed as follow:

$$\left(1-\sum_{i=1}^{p}\varphi i-L^{i}\right)(1-L)^{d}Xt=(1+\sum_{i=1}^{q}\theta iL^{i})\varepsilon t \tag{1}$$

In this formula, 'p' represents the order of the Autoregressive (AR) component as determined by the Partial Autocorrelation Function (PACF) model, 'q' denotes the order of the Moving Average (MA) component as identified by the Autocorrelation Function (ACF) model, and 'd' signifies the degree of differencing.

3 Empirical results and analysis

3.1 Order of ARIMA model

To find out the order of the stock return in logarithm, PACF and ACF models can derive the lag orders for AR(p) and MA(q). At first use the 1st order difference to print the graphics of PACF and ACF and find the order is too high. Then it can apply 2nd order difference to the model and the results are as follows.

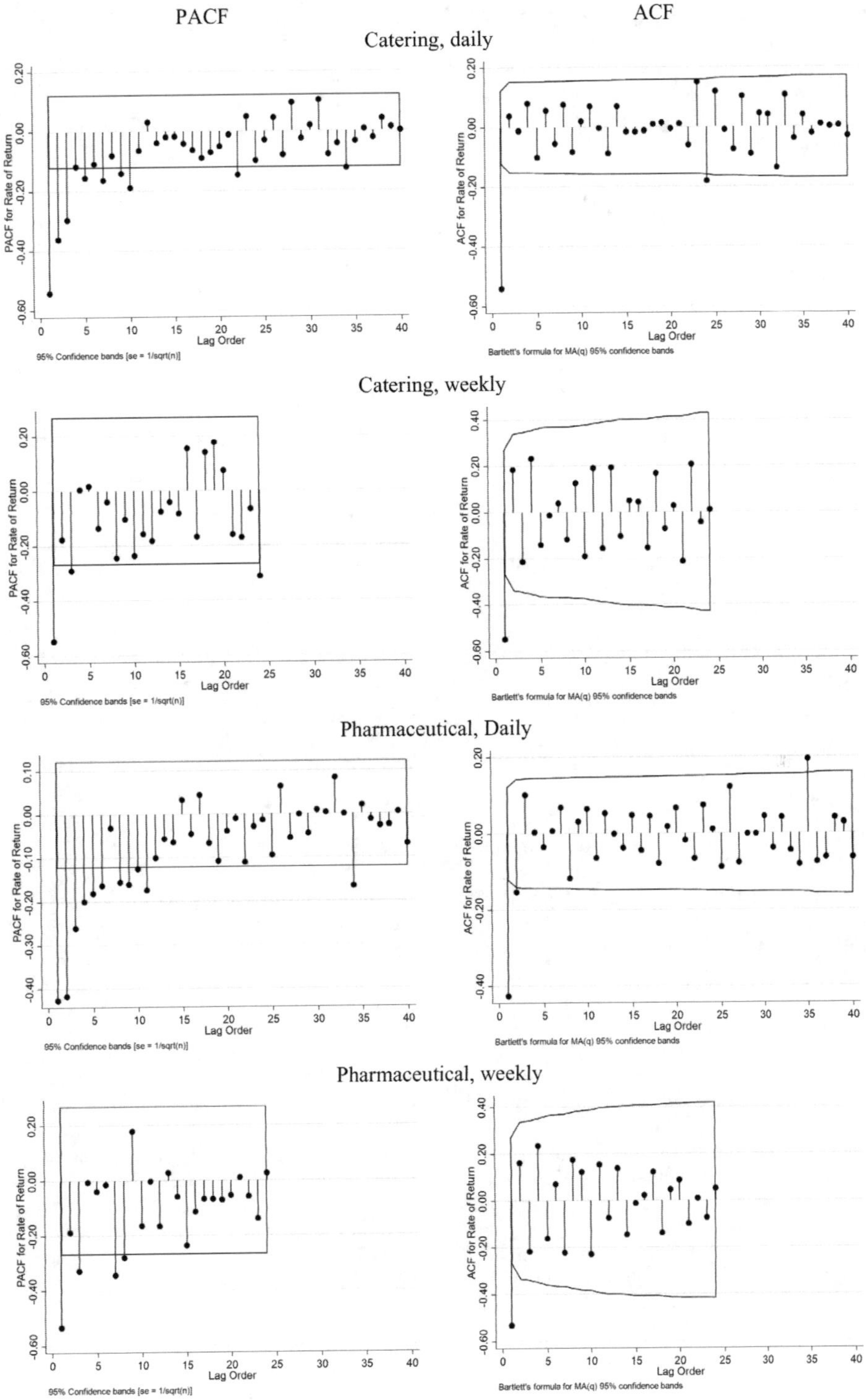

Fig. 1. ARMA (p, q) identification

Photo credit: Original

 https://doi.org/10.1051/shsconf/202418801014

In the first row in Figure 1, it shows that lag order of AR(p) is 10 and MA(q) is 1 which is the first part beyond the critical value. In the second row, it shows the lag order of AR(p) is 3 and MA(q) is 1. In the third row, it shows the lag order of AR(p) is 9 and MA(q) is 2. In the last row, it shows the lag order of AR(p) is 7 and MA(q) is 1.

Then the residual test can check if the residuals (differences between observed and predicted values) behave like white noise, meaning they are randomly distributed and have no autocorrelation.

Table 2 Residual test

Model	Portmanteau (Q) statistic	Prob > chi2
Catering, daily-ARIMA(10,2,1)	27.0491	0.9413
Catering, weekly-ARIMA(3,2,1)	22.5731	0.5451
Pharmaceutical, daily-ARIMA(9,2,2)	*24.8738*	0.9707
Pharmaceutical, weekly-ARIMA(7,2,1)	17.4123	0.8306

From Table 2, the residuals show no patterns or correlations, it typically indicates that the model has adequately captured the underlying structure of the time series data, suggesting that the model has successfully accounted for the systematic information in the data.

3.2 Prediction and interpretation of results

The ARIMA model then can predict the data based on the indices closing prices from 2019/1/1 to 2020/1/24 as fitted value and compare the fitted value with the actual data.

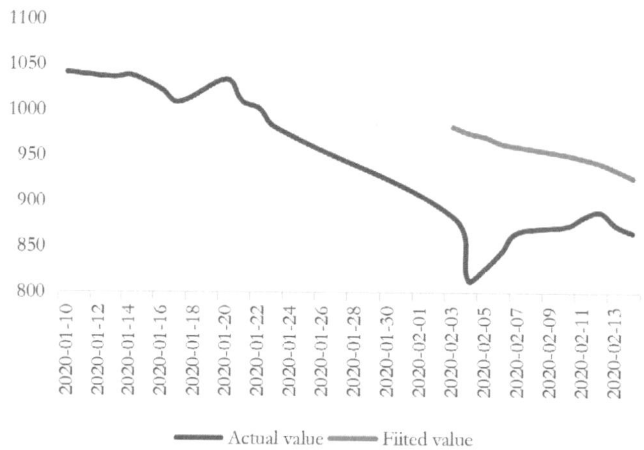

Fig. 2. Actual value and fitted value, Catering-daily
Photo credit: Original

From Figure 2 and Figure 3, the catering index in China initially reflected these challenges. Stock prices of companies in the catering industry faced a sharp decline as investors reacted to the sudden and substantial revenue losses experienced by businesses in the sector. There is a sharp decline between 2020-1-22 and 2022-1-23, that the price was from 1001.91 to 981.11 and the price was continue to decrease to the bottom 812.89 on 2020-2-5. The Evergrande research institute has reported that the epidemic led to a significant impact on the catering industry. Specifically, the retail sales in this sector experienced a loss of approximately 500 billion yuan during just seven days of the Spring Festival. The pandemic's effect on the industry was profound, with 93% of catering businesses opting to shut down their stores. Among these, 73% closed all their outlets, 8% shut down over 80% of their locations, and 7% closed less than half of their stores [9]. The changes on weekly closing stock prices gives a clearer demonstration of this decline. This decline in share prices contributed to a negative trend in the catering index. As the actual stock prices of catering experienced a significant and rapid drop and it displayed heightened volatility during the early stages of the pandemic. While the fitted line shows a relatively steady decline, this may have been influenced by the closing of the stock market during the Spring Festival of China. The pandemic led to widespread lockdowns and social distancing measures, which significantly impacted businesses that rely on customer physical presence, like the catering industry. This resulted in fluctuations in the catering index, reflecting reduced consumer spending and operational challenges for restaurants and related services.

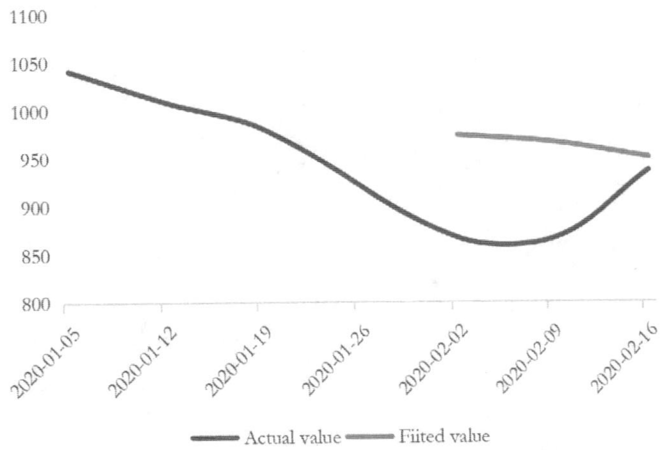

Fig. 3. Actual value and fitted value, Catering-weekly
Photo credit: Original

From Figure 4 and Figure 5, it shows that COVID-19 positively impacted the pharmaceutical index in China. The actual value is much higher than the fitted value as they should act without the impact of pandemic.

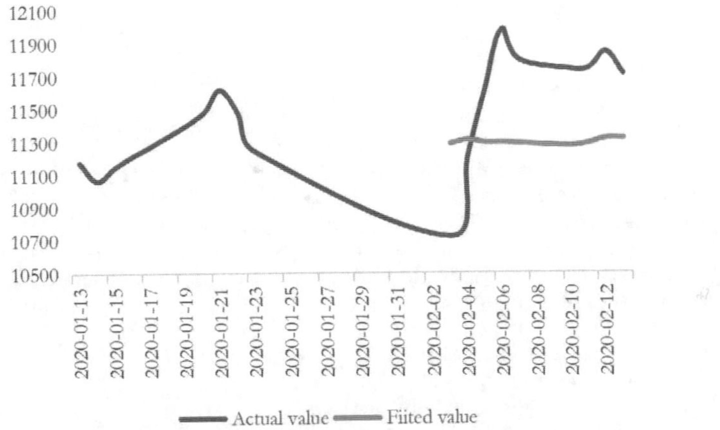

Fig. 4. Actual value and fitted value, Pharmaceutical -daily
Photo credit: Original

The prices of pharmaceutical index decreased first from 11,481. It may because of the reduced Trading volume and the Chinese New Year period often comes with a pause in corporate and governmental economic activities, which might affect market expectations about economic growth and corporate earnings, thereby impacting stock prices. Whie from 2020-2-4, the beginning of the pandemic, there has been a significant increase, well above the pre-New Year's prices. The pandemic led to increased demand for medical products and services, including pharmaceuticals, personal protective equipment, and healthcare supplies. This surge in demand was reflected in a rise in the pharmaceutical index, indicating growth and resilience in this sector during the pandemic, in contrast to many other industries that faced downturns. The pharmaceutical industry's performance highlights its critical role and increased consumer reliance during health crises. It indicates that the investment attitude toward the pharmaceutical industry in China during the COVID-19 pandemic has been generally positive and has seen significant growth since when an outbreak of an infectious disease is declared, investing in medical companies can be an effective strategy to mitigate risks [10].

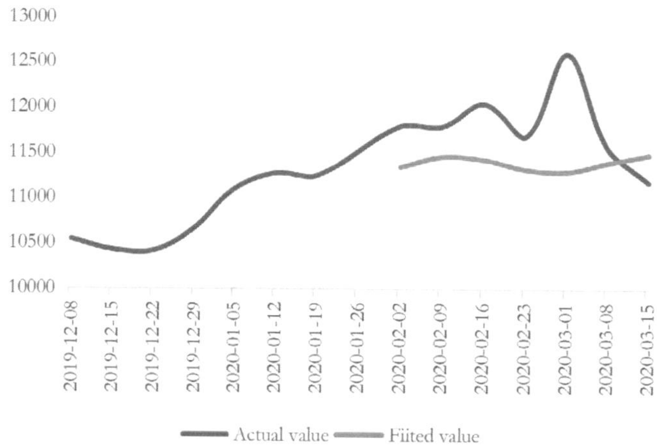

Fig. 5. Actual value and fitted value, Pharmaceutical -weekly
Photo credit: Original

4 Conclusion

This paper's findings show unique insights into the impact of COVID-19 on the catering and pharmaceutical industries. Unlike existing literatures, which broadly focuses on the overall economic impact of the pandemic, this study provides a nuanced comparison between two distinct sectors. The implications for research are significant, offering a detailed case study for understanding industry-specific impacts of global crises. Policymakers can leverage these findings to tailor responses and support mechanisms for different sectors. Investors, on the other hand, can use this analysis to make informed decisions, recognizing the varying resilience and vulnerabilities within different market segments. This paper thus contributes valuable perspectives to the existing body of knowledge on the economic effects of the pandemic.

The aim of this study is to investigate the different impacts of the coronavirus pandemic period on the restaurant and pharmaceutical industries in terms of utilization, stock returns and stock volatility through ARIMA models. This study draws its conclusions after conducting an empirical investigation. The paper demonstrates that the catering and pharmaceutical industries have very different impacts during the epidemic period. Compared to the pre-epidemic period, the catering industry was extremely impacted and volatile, while the pharmaceutical industry showed a growing trend. This is due to the fact that policies during the epidemic limited the growth of the restaurant industry, while the demand for healthcare services boosted the healthcare industry. With the end of the epidemic, the industry will eventually weaken and return to normal with the general trend of the stock market.

References

1. National Bureau of Statistics. https://data.stats.gov.cn/index.htm
2. F. L. Deu, S. Tang, and G. Zhou. Biopharma in China: Insights into a market at a crossroads, McKinsey & Company. https://www.mckinsey.com/industries/life-sciences/our-insights/biopharma-in-china-insights-into-a-market-at-a-crossroads
3. W. McKibbin. and R. Fernando. The global economic impacts of the COVID-19 pandemic, EM, 129: 106551 (2023).
4. Y. Han. The impact of the COVID-19 pandemic on China's economic structure: An input–output approach, SCED, 63: 181–195 (2022).
5. C. Zhang, J. Jiang, H. Jin, & T. Chen. The impact of COVID-19 on consumers' psychological behavior based on data mining for online user comments in the catering industry in China. IJERPH, 18(8): 4178 (2021).
6. H. Liu. The Impact of the Coronavirus on Chinese Pharmaceutical Industry. ICFIED, 2021, 51-56 (2021).
7. A. W. Lo. (2015). What is an index?. Available at SSRN 2672755.
8. Investing. https://cn.investing.com
9. X. Xiong. and R. Yao. Strategic analysis of the catering industry under covid-19: A case study in China, E3S Web of Conferences, 253: 01047 (2021).
10. M. Donadelli, R. Kizys. and M. Riedel. Dangerous infectious diseases: Bad news for main street, good news for wall street?, JFM, 35: 84–103 (2017).

SHS Web of Conferences **188**, 01015 (2024) https://doi.org/10.1051/shsconf/202418801015
ICDDE 2024

Study on Financial Risk and Countermeasures in Enterprise Mergers and Acquisitions--Take LVMH's Acquisition of Tiffany as an Example

Yanfei Fu[1,*]

[1]School of Economics and Business Administration, Beijing Normal University, Beijing, 100875, China

Abstract. M&A is an important approach for enterprises to achieve industrial upgrading and scale effect, reduce operating costs, and promote the diversified development of enterprises. The financial risks that often appear in the process of M&A are the key to the success of M&A and the reorganization of enterprises. Existing equity and economic problems make enterprises easily fall into financial disputes and cause huge losses. Investment and mergers are important ways for enterprises to expand scale, enter new markets, and acquire new technologies or mature brands. Through investment and merger, market share can be increased, competitiveness can be enhanced, and the financial statements of enterprises can be enhanced, but risks in merger and acquisition are also accompanied. Through the case study of LVMH Group's merger and acquisition of Tiffany, this paper will analyze the financial risks and countermeasures in the merger and acquisition and extract feasible and effective measures from LVMH Group's treatment methods to help both parties control the risks in the merger process and achieve the purpose of merger and acquisition.

1 Introduction

M&A is an important approach for enterprises to achieve industrial upgrading and scale effect, reduce operating costs, and promote the diversified development of enterprises [1]. The financial risks that often appear in the process of M&A are the key to the success of M&A and the reorganization of enterprises. Existing equity and economic problems make enterprises easily fall into financial disputes and cause huge losses.

Based on previous studies, this study will take the case of M&A between LVMH and Tiffany as an example, conducting quantitative and qualitative analysis of several types of financial risks that may occur in the M&A process according to the performance of the financial statements of both parties and understanding the specific causes and potential problems of financial risks, and find effective prevention and control strategies through specific cases.

2 Case description

2.1. M&A background

LVMH Group's 2019 financial report shows that operating income increased by 15% compared with 2018, and net profit increased by 9%. The revenue structure shows that the revenue of the leather goods sector accounts for the vast majority of the operating income of the LVMH group, which is about 41%, but the revenue of the watch jewelry sector accounts for only 8%. According to the official website, there are only six brands in the LVMH watch and jewelry sector: Tag Heuer, Hublot, Zenith, Bulgari, Chammel, and Fred.

As a classic brand in the field of jewelry and watches, Tiffany has an irreplaceable influence on product design and brand image. However, since 2016, Tiffany's performance has continued to decline, especially in the second quarter of 2019. Global same-store sales fell 3% from last year, about twice as much as expected, and sales fell into a regressive state in Japan and Europe except for a slight increase in China. Under such an environment, it is a good time for LVMH Group to acquire Tiffany [2].

2.2 M&A motivation

Due to the special nature of the luxury industry, brand effect is an important intangible asset, so the acquisition of high-value brands can effectively enhance brand influence, and merger and acquisition is an important way to obtain it [2]. Although LVMH Group has become the world's largest luxury goods group, there is still a big gap in the field of jewelry watches compared with other competitors. LVMH jewelry brands are mostly acquired, but its competitors, Van Cleef & Arpels, Cartier, and other brands under Richemont Group, have higher brand awareness and market experience, and the revenue growth and scale in the field of jewelry watches far exceeds the value of LVMH Group's jewelry watch business. As a result, Tiffany, which is well-known and

* Corresponding author: 202111998360@mail.bnu.edu.com

influential in the field of jewelry watches, has received the attention of LVMH Group.

2.3 M&A progress

LVMH announced that it would acquire Tiffany for $135 per share for a total of about $16.2 billion in November 2019. However, the United States announced in July 2020 that it planned to impose 25% tariffs on French imports of cosmetics and other goods, so LVMH Group announced in September that it would postpone the acquisition of Tiffany. Subsequently, the two sides began to sue each other for the "feud" plot: Tiffany first sued LVMH for failing to complete the acquisition on time and tried to renegotiate the acquisition price. Not long after that, LVMH also chose to sue, accusing Tiffany of mismanagement during the new coronavirus outbreak to shrink its revenue, and applied to cancel the transaction at the original price. On October 29, 2020, the acquisition made progress. LVMH announced that it had reached an agreement with Tiffany on the modification of the merger agreement, and the acquisition price was adjusted to $131.5 per share under the condition that the remaining terms remained unchanged, completing the acquisition at a total price of $15.8 billion [3]. In the end, the acquisition was officially completed on January 7, 2021.

3 Analysis

3.1 Theoretical basis

3.1.1 Information asymmetry theory

The theory of information asymmetry refers to the difference in understanding of relevant information among different groups in the market economy. Those with sufficient information are often at an advantage, while those with poor information are often at a disadvantage. At the same time, the theory points out that the seller knows more about the commodity information than the buyer in the market. The party with more information can benefit by providing reliable information to the party with less information; One of the buyers and sellers with less information will try to obtain information from the other [4].

3.1.2 Synergistic effect theory

Synergy takes into account the resource integration and synergy between the two parties after the completion of the merger or acquisition to maximize the value of resources, while the focus of this study is the financial embodiment of enterprises to achieve reasonable tax avoidance or reduce the cost of capital through merger and acquisition.

3.2 Financial risk analysis

The financial risk of M&A is divided into two stages: strategic investment and performance process acquisition [5]. Next, from the perspective of the financial risks that are prone to occur in the two stages -- valuation risk and integration risk, this paper analyzes the financial risks in M&A and the coping policies of LVMH Group.

3.2.1 Valuation risk analysis

The essence of M&A is the transfer of corporate control, and the process is reflected in that the M&A party judges the market valuation of the transferring enterprise through advanced market research and decision analysis and negotiates with the transferring to reach an agreement on the M&A price. From the perspective of the acquirer, if the valuation is too low, it is easy to reduce the cooperation willingness of the transferring and reduce the success rate of the merger. Suppose the valuation is too high and exceeds the actual value of the enterprise. In that case, the enterprise will increase the capital cost and find it difficult to reap the expected benefits, and even lead to serious consequences such as the rupture of the enterprise's capital chain, which will affect the subsequent production and respect activities of the enterprise [6].

In the merger and acquisition case between LVMH and Tiffany, the cooperation was terminated due to differences in valuation and pricing, which was related to the information asymmetry between the two parties to a certain extent. The decrease in the acquisition price from $135 per share to $131.50 per share is related to many factors, including Tiffany's operating performance during the acquisition negotiations, and LVMH Group's knowledge of Tiffany's revenue performance becomes the key to pricing. According to Tiffany's financial report data before the acquisition, Tiffany suffered a huge loss in revenue and profit in the first quarter of 2020, and although there was a rebound in the second and third quarters, it was far less than the revenue performance in the fourth quarter of 2019, as shown in Table 1.

Table 1. Four quarters of net profit of Tiffany

	2019 Q4	2020 Q1	2020 Q2	2020 Q3
Profit (units: billion)	269	-92.8	63.7	179.5

The choice of valuation method often affects the formation of pricing risk. Revenue-based free cash flow method is applied to the acquisition price of LVMH Group, and the change curve in Figure 1 is obtained after sample fitting.

 https://doi.org/10.1051/shsconf/202418801015

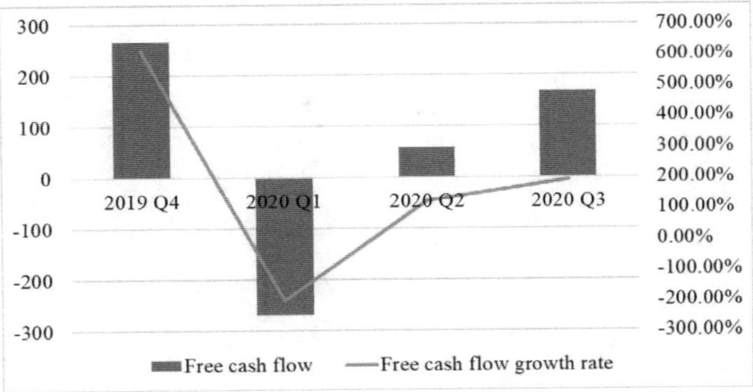

Fig 1. Tiffany's free cash flow from 2019 Q4 to 2020 Q3
(Photo credit :Original)

In the first quarter of 2020, Tiffany's cash flow showed a dramatic decline, which is closely related to Tiffany's sluggish performance; Although there was a small recovery in the last two quarters, it was difficult to return to the level before epidemic. Free cash flow reflects the future debt repayment and profitability of the enterprise. Tiffany's earnings performance in the first half of 20 years made it difficult for the two parties to continue the cooperation, but the subsequent return of earnings and revaluation made the cooperation between the two parties successfully reached.

3.2.2 Integrated risk analysis

Financial integration risk refers to the hidden danger of disputes arising from the inconsistency of corporate culture, organizational management form, business process, and functional division of department personnel during business integration, resulting in the failure of the enterprise to effectively integrate business and resources within the expected time, which has an impact on the profitability level and the development of production and business activities in subsequent stages [6]. If integration risks are effectively prevented, effective synergies can be achieved in future development. In response to this risk, LVMH chose to send LV chairman and CEO Michael Burke, who will also serve as chairman of Tiffany, LV in the United States and the brand's global commercial activities. Anthony Ledru will serve as CEO of Tiffany. The two are responsible for operating Tiffany and said it plans to overhaul its design team.

In the comparison of the performance in 2021 and 2020, the jewelry and watch business is the brightest business segment of the LVMH Group in 2021, which has to be attributed to the great merger and acquisition of Century of Tiffany. This jewelry brand with pure American genes achieved the growth of three indicators of revenue, profit, and cash flow in the first year after joining the LVMH family and led jewelry watches to become the third largest business segment of LVMH, with the revenue proportion increasing from 7.5% in 2020 to 14.0%. The share of profits increased from 3.6% in 2020 to 9.8% [7].

4 Suggestion

In the scheme of risk control in the pricing of M&A projects, the enterprise can adopt several control measurements, including making clear merger and acquisition strategy and transfer research, optimizing evaluation methods, evaluating their own resources' joint ability, and entrusting professional institutions [6].

4.1 Make M&A strategy clear

The objectives of M&A and reorganization of enterprises have the characteristics of diversification, and the common objectives include expanding business areas and forming scale synergies. Due to the differences in M&A prices and work priorities under different targets, enterprises must determine M&A targets based on their actual conditions and formulate clear M&A strategies to guide the follow-up work. For example, in this case, LVMH is trying to expand the field of jewelry watches and form synergies through mergers and acquisitions, so it needs to focus on the value the transfer can create in terms of performance, brand effect, and resource allocation.

4.2 Conduct thorough due diligence

According to the case of the LVMH merger and acquisition of Tiffany, there is a general information asymmetry between the acquirer and the transferring, which often leads to the regret or willingness of the acquirer to give up the acquisition during the merger and acquisition process. Therefore, to ensure the smooth progress of the merger and the rights and interests of both parties and avoid the premium of the merger price, it is necessary to grasp the transfer's real production and operation conditions fully. In this regard, in the investigation process, enterprises should collect as much information as possible from all aspects of the enterprise, starting from the internal and external environment of the enterprise, verify the status and value of assets, especially intangible assets, analyze the geographical advantages and brand effect of the acquired enterprise, verify the actual value of the acquired enterprise, and eliminate the impact of information asymmetry. It is also necessary to pay special attention to the situation of corporate debt, do a good job in debt analysis, and prevent the deliberate concealment by the target company from causing great interference to the judgment of corporate value and future profitability, fully understand the core value of the target company, and know yourself and the other [8].

4.3 Optimizing valuation method

Enterprises should choose valuation methods according to M&A conditions and strategic objectives. For example, if the main goal of M&A is to improve profit, the cash flow method can be preferred to determine the present value of the enterprise. Suppose similar M&A activities of brands are active. In that case, a group of enterprises with high similarity can be selected as samples to set price-earnings ratio, enterprise value income, and other indicators, and the comparative valuation method can be used to accurately evaluate the market value of M&A objects under sample reference.

4.4 Entrusting professional agency

Enterprises need to collect more information about the target enterprise, choose the most appropriate valuation method in the face of multiple valuation methods, and hire professional intermediaries to reduce valuation risks [9]. Compared with LVMH, a large-scale group with rich experience in mergers and acquisitions, professional institutions are more suitable for enterprises with limited scale or lack of experience in mergers and acquisitions and can obtain more objective and reasonable evaluation prices by entrusting a third party to carry out market research and enterprise value estimation on their behalf.

4.5 Financial integration risk control

According to the preliminary research results, after the completion of the merger and acquisition, the enterprise needs to build a new financial management structure, and on the premise of ensuring normal work, reduce the management structure levels, merge departments with similar functions, and explain relevant matters to the original employees in advance. At the same time, in terms of the integration of assets and liabilities, the disposal plan of various assets should be formulated in advance according to the actual situation, and the financing assets should be quickly put into the newly launched production and operation activities [10].

5 Conclusion

M&A is an important approach for enterprises to achieve industrial upgrading and scale effect, reduce operating costs, and promote the diversified development of enterprises. In the merger and acquisition process, enterprises will get higher benefits but also face many potential financial risks in the negotiation process and integration period. In the case of analysis of M&A between LVMH and Tiffany, it can be seen from the obstacles encountered in the merger process, and the financial integration after the completion of the merger that financial risks run through the whole process of the merger and reorganization of enterprises, and the effect of risk control has a profound impact on the success rate of the merger and the production and operation of enterprises. The same goes for leading enterprises in the luxury industry. Enterprises in the same field and other fields should also improve various financial risks in the M&A process, actively implement pricing and financial integration risks, and help enterprises achieve the expected M&A objectives and maximize the synergistic benefits after the M&A.

References

1. Sun. HF. Chinese Agricultural Accounting, **33** (22):127-129 (2023)
2. Li. Xj, Xue. YJ, Cui. CM. Time of Fortune, (03):84 (2020)
3. Beijing News, $15.8 billion! LVMH completed the acquisition of Tiffany and the two sides had a "breakup war". January 8, 2021.Retrieved on November 21, 2023. Retrieved from:https://baijiahao.baidu.com/s?id=1688303236204700178&wfr=spider&for=pc
4. Wang. ZY. Financial risk analysis of T Company's merger and acquisition of S Company based on Analytic Hierarchy Process. Hebei Normal University (2023)
5. Jian.GQ, Meng. YM. Hebei Enterprises, (10):24-26 (2023)
6. Peng Q. China's Collective Economy, (17): 140-143 (2023)
7. Fu.Y, Zhang. XM. Chinese gemstone, (2):245-247 (2022)
8. Yu.ZH, Bai.JH. Cooperative economy and Technology, (16): 98-100 (2023)
9. Huang. E, Li. MY, Xu. J. Cooperative Economy and Technology, (22): 109-111 (2023)
10. Lin.QS. International Business Accounting, (16):79-82 (2023)

Pair Tarding and Residual Risk: A Case Study Based on the China's Securities Firm

Jiaxin Chen*

School of Mathematics and Physics, Xi'an Jiaotong-Liverpool University, Suzhou, 215123, China

Abstract. With the development of the financial field, there are more and more hedging strategies accompanied by an increasing number of residual risks in these strategies. These risks are generally ignored by people, resulting in losses. This paper begins with CITIC Securities, the leader in China's securities industry, and analyzes its large-scale paired trading case, spreading spreads in the A-stock market. Firstly, at the macro trading level, this paper finds that there are still credit risks and liquidity risks in the trading of this investment portfolio by referring to the prospectus of CITIC Securities' bond offering. It puts forward relevant suggestions to reduce these risks. Next, the focus shifts to the analysis of the portfolio strategy itself. The paper identifies four risk points: stock price rise in advance, abnormal events, reduced hedging opportunities, and market irrationality. It also provides suggestions on how to mitigate losses caused by these remaining risks. For example, setting up profit and loss points, establishing relevant departments to control the remaining risk points, maintaining good customer credit, and improving the company's credit rating.

1 Introduction

CITIC Securities is a comprehensive industry leader and the only securities company in China with assets exceeding one trillion yuan. It has garnered a wide reputation and a strong brand advantage in the domestic market. It was the first in the industry to propose and practice asset management business, which, along with investment banking, brokerage, and proprietary investment, constitutes the company's main business. Additionally, as an investment advisory company, CITIC Securities tailors various financial service solutions for clients, including a variety of financial derivatives business, such as options, futures, and hedging [1].

This paper primarily studies the matching trading case of CITIC Securities in the A-share market and analyzes its residual risk. From the perspective of transaction motivation, matching transactions can be divided into two types: spread widening and spread convergence [2].

Spread convergent pair trading involves taking two fundamentally similar stocks that historically satisfy a long-term equilibrium relationship. It assumes no recent events have affected significant changes in stock prices. When the price difference between the two stocks is greater than the transaction cost, buy low-priced stocks and short high-priced stocks simultaneously, and close the position after waiting for the price difference to fall [2]. Convergent spread trading has shown a broad prospect in the A-share market. Research by Mai and Wang found that from January 1, 2004, to December 31, 2010, using the method of spread convergence on data pairs composed of stocks with complete data in the Shanghai Stock Exchange 50 and Shenzhen Stock Exchange 40 yielded positive returns in both markets after deducting transaction costs. The maximum positive returns, 6.43%, were obtained in the Shenzhen market using the FTBD method [3].

Due to the special events of individual stocks, the long-term equilibrium relationship between two stocks (or indexes and stocks) may be destroyed, resulting in an enlarged price spread. Therefore, it is necessary to select representative stocks or sector indexes and establish a long-short paired investment portfolio to earn profits [2].

This paper studies the large-scale paired trading mode in which representative stocks of the industry are selected, and long-short paired investment portfolios are established with individual stocks to offset industry risks and obtain stable excess returns.

2 Case description

On the evening of April 20, 2011, Tasly announced that two new drugs had recently obtained the new drug certificate and drug registration approval documents issued by the China Food and Drug Administration. The news was clearly positive for Tasly, but it was not enough to propel the stock into an independent rally. If you had bought Tasly based on the announcement information, the investment would have suffered a loss of nearly 8% between April 20 and April 28. Moreover, due to the general underperformance of pharmaceutical stocks, after two months of holding, as of June 20, the stock was still down 2.2% on that day.

* Corresponding author: Jiaxin.Chen21@student.xjtlu.edu.cn

Choosing to trade long-short pairs and selecting Guangzhou Pharmaceutical, in the same industry as Tasly, as a counterparty among the underlying securities available for sale, would have resulted in a gain of 3.6% when the share price was adjusted after the announcement (as of April 28). Two months later (June 20), the cumulative profit was 13% [2].

3 Residual risks at the macro trading Level

The long-short pairing portfolio effectively uses representative stocks of the sector to hedge industry risks, thus obtaining stable excess returns. However, there are still some residual risks in the portfolio. From the perspective of macro trading, as a securities company, CITIC Securities mainly faces industry risks in the following four aspects: financial risk, operational risk, management risk, and policy risk [4].

Financial risk can be divided into the following three aspects, namely credit risk, liquidity risk, and fair value change risk of corporate financial investment assets. These three points will not affect whether the portfolio itself is profitable, but for the actual operation, if there is a client participating in the portfolio, there may be two risks, such as credit risk and liquidity risk.

The credit risk of the portfolio with convergent spread mainly comes from three aspects: First, when trading the portfolio, there is a fund gap, and CITIC Securities is responsible for settlement on behalf of customers, which will cause the risk of loss. The second is to buy the portfolio in the form of securities financing such as margin financing and stock pledge repurchase. On the maturity date, if the customer fails to perform the contract, it can cause risks.

The company selected in the three portfolios has the credit risk that financial fraud has not been detected, which is illustrated here (Case: Chaori Company announced a forecast of 2011 profit of more than 8200w yuan one week before the bond issuance, making its bonds sought after by the securities market, but amended the announcement one week after the bond issuance, and the revised profit was 142 million yuan less than before) [5]. If this event occurs in the portfolio, the original good news is directly converted into a negative, which will directly violate the spread and expand the large pair trading strategy, resulting in an immeasurable loss.

Furthermore, if there are behaviors of OTC derivatives transactions such as interest rate swaps, stock income swaps, OTC, and forward transactions in portfolio transactions, there will be the possibility of counterparty default and the risk of counterparty default (Case: Company A and Sekwang Shipyard of Korea signed a shipbuilding contract on October 31, 2008, and settled in the form of progress payment in advance. The ship was scheduled to be delivered in February 2011, but two years after the implementation of the project, the ship was not delivered, and Sekwang Shipyard suddenly applied for bankruptcy protection).

Liquidity risk refers to the risk that a company cannot obtain sufficient funds at a reasonable cost in time to repay maturing debts, fulfill other payment obligations, and meet the capital needs of normal business operations [4]. The drying up of liquidity in financial markets led to the 2008 global financial crisis [7].

If the commissioning party is produced, it may lead to the first and second types of credit risk, the generation of customer credit risk, and the possible liquidity risk. If the investment portfolio involves over-the-counter transactions, it will lead to the emergence of the fourth type of credit risk in the credit risk, counterparty credit risk. Operating risks, management risks, and policy risks related to the securities industry are not closely related to the portfolio.

For credit risk, CITIC Securities may establish a set of internal credit rating systems to evaluate the credit of customers, counterparties, and portfolio companies, restrict the investment of customers with low credit or require them to provide collateral for a guarantee, and require them to pay sufficient margin to reduce the risk of credit failure. Citic Securities can conduct due diligence on portfolio companies to reduce the risk of undetected financial fraud. For counterparties with low credit, they should reduce the amount of transactions with them, reduce the proportion of such transactions, and try to trade with counterparties with high credit ratings. In addition, CITIC Securities can establish a sound legal department to pursue the breach of trust, so as to reduce the breach rate of customers and counterparties and reduce the possibility of bad debts. For liquidity risks, CITIC Securities can increase the reserve fund, establish good cooperative relations with a number of banks, increase the credit limit of its own assets, and maintain a low asset liability ratio and sufficient cash flow.

4. Residual risk of the portfolio itself

From the perspective of the portfolio itself, the remaining risk points in this case mainly lie in the following four aspects: stock price rise in advance, abnormal events, reduction of hedging opportunities, and market irrationality.

The early rise in share prices means that some of the excess gains may have been reflected in share prices before the information was made public.

For example, the annual financial report released by Jiuan Medical on January 20 shows that the performance of Jiuan Medical increased by 243.46% to 364.68% compared with the same period of the previous year [8]. This should have been obvious good news for Jiuan Medical, and the stock price should have risen in response to this positive development.

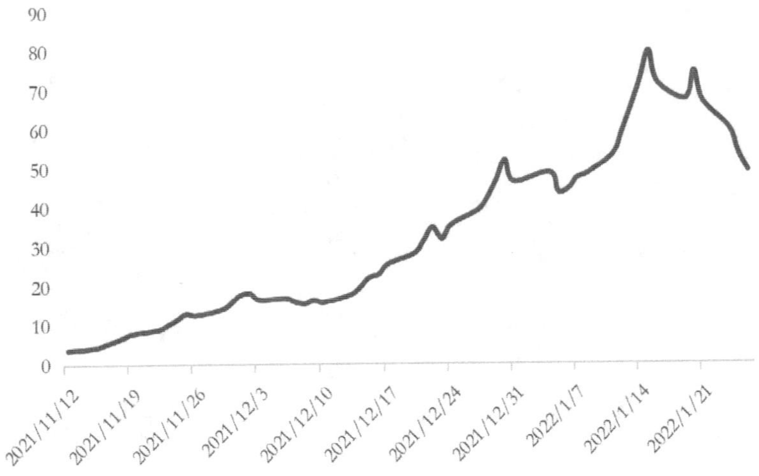

Fig. 1. Jiuan medical stock prices

Data source: Straight flush
Photo credit: Original

Instead of rising, the stock price fell nearly 30 percent the following week. As can be seen from Figure 1, in the two months before the announcement of annual results, the stock price of Jiuan Medical rose nearly tenfold. Due to the sharp rise in the early stage, the early cashing of excess earnings, and even the cashing of overdraft, the stock price of Jiuan Medical fell in the week after the announcement of annual results.

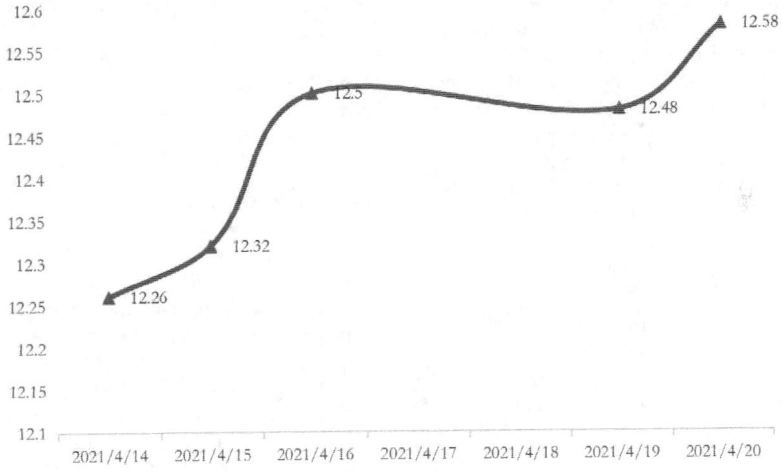

Fig. 2. Changes in Tasly stock prices

Data source: Straight flush
Photo credit: Original

It can be seen from Figure 2 that from April 15 to April 20, Tasly experienced an obvious slight rise in the days before the good news came out, and this slight rise may be a form of early cashing of excess returns.

Secondly, after opening a position, either side of the hedge portfolio is susceptible to unusual events. Here are two cases (Case 1: On March 8, 2022, due to the dual impact of the Russia-Ukraine conflict and Qingshan Holding Group's short cover, the nickel price, which was originally trading at $10,000 to $20,000, soared by $30,000 in a few minutes and even reached a sky-high price of 100,000 yuan per ton at 6 o'clock on the same day. Without government supervision, this incident would be completely out of control, and Qingshan Holding Group would directly face bankruptcy [9].

Additionally, on November 21, 2023, Douyu issued an announcement confirming that the CEO of Douyu was arrested for casino crimes, and Douyu's stock price fell by more than 20% in a week (see Fig. 3), constituting a shocking decline [10]. If a similar event occurs, the short side rises, and the long side falls sharply, leading to unpredictable losses.

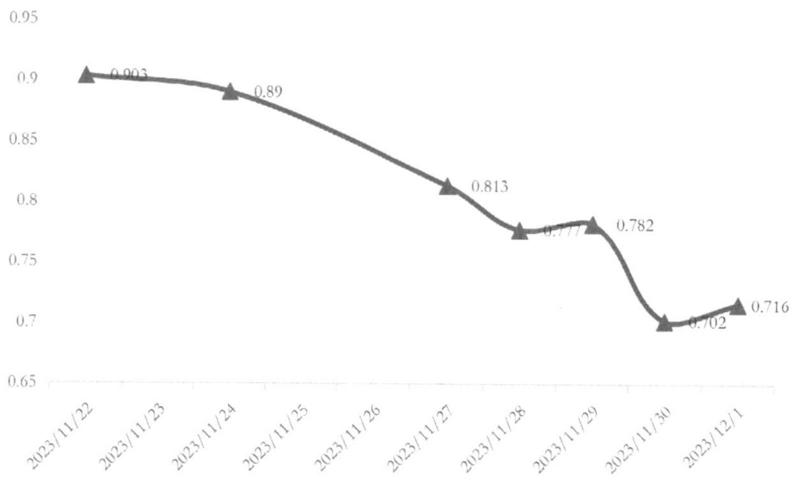

Fig. 3. Changes in Douyu stock prices

Data source: Straight flush

Photo credit: Original

Third, if too many participants adopt similar strategies, the opportunities for hedging trades will be greatly reduced (similar to arbitrage, if there are too many participants, then the arbitrage space will be reduced).

Fourth, long-term irrationality or short-term sudden changes in the market may occur. Some malicious short selling can lead to the decline of stocks in the portfolio that were originally long, and some own-index events. For example, on December 8, 2022, the bizarre flash collapse of Ketobiology fell directly from -1.5% to -20.01% in the late bidding stage for one second, with the last trading volume being 942 lots and a transaction amount of about 2.25 million lots. After a similar short-term sudden flash collapse, it may lead to a reduction in customer confidence and forced liquidation, resulting in losses. Customer credit will be reduced.

To anticipate the stock price rising in advance, investors can observe the change in the stock price before the good news is released. If there is a significant rise before the good news comes out, people need to incorporate this part of the rise into the portfolio and make a judgment on the future stock price rise space according to the rising stock price and the degree of good news.

For abnormal events, CITIC Securities may establish a risk control department and set up a risk limit. The risk control department should monitor the relevant influencing factors of the investment portfolio daily. When abnormal events occur and the risk level exceeds the established limit, the risk control department should take timely measures.

In situations where too many participants adopt similar strategies before adopting a long-short paired portfolio, the investment department of CITIC Securities may evaluate the portfolio to see if there is still profit space. If there is, investors need to set up a good stop profit and stop loss to maintain profit.

In the case of long-term irrationality or short-term sudden changes in the market, CITIC Securities can set up a good stop loss and take timely action against malicious short selling to prevent the expansion of losses. In the case of short-term sudden changes, relevant countermeasures should be taken immediately, the cause of sudden changes investigated to avoid risks and prevent further expansion of losses. The client should be provided with timely relief.

For the risk of timely stop loss, in the case of oolong events, timely explanation, increasing customer confidence, and maintaining their own credit are essential.

5 Conclusion

In general, CITIC Securities holds a significant advantage in scale and is the first securities company in China with an asset scale exceeding one trillion yuan. It expands a large paired investment portfolio by utilizing price spreads and establishes a long-short paired investment portfolio with individual stocks using representative stocks of the industry they are in, thus offsetting industry risks and achieving a stable paired trading mode of excess returns. It can effectively reduce the impact of sectors on dividends and systemic risks. However, there are still some remaining risks in this portfolio.

Firstly, by analyzing the industry risks faced by CITIC Securities, this paper finds that there are still credit risks and liquidity risks in this portfolio from the perspective of macro trading and puts forward relevant suggestions to mitigate these risks. Then, the focus shifts to the analysis of the portfolio strategy itself, identifying four risk points: stock price rise in advance, abnormal events, reduced hedging opportunities, and market irrationality. Combined with case analysis, the paper provides relevant suggestions to minimize the risk of this investment.

In summary, spreading a large paired portfolio is a simple and low-risk trading strategy. This type of long-short paired trading portfolio can reduce the impact of market fluctuations on good or bad news and has wide applicability. However, it also needs to consider influencing factors such as credit risk, liquidity risk, stock price rise in advance, abnormal events, reduction of hedging opportunities, and market irrationality. CITIC Securities can establish relevant departments to control the remaining risks, maintain a low asset liability ratio and sufficient cash flow, set up profit and loss points for the investment portfolio, maintain good customer credit, and upgrade the company's credit rating.

References

1. Citic Securities. Company introduction [EB/OL]. [2023-12-25]. www.cs.ecitic.com/newsite/AboutUs/
2. L Dong, Y Gaojian. Citic Securities - Hedging Strategy Research and Product Design: Practice and Case Study of A-share Market matching trading.
3. M Yongguan, W Susheng. JMR, 26 (01):30-40 (2014`).
4. CITIC securities. In 2023 raised through issuance of corporate bonds for professional institutional investors public instruction register (draft).
5. L Yali, Z Wenqing, X Ang. Southwest Finance, (07):39-45 (2018).
6. W Qiang, L Zhicui, Y Juan. MM, (03):50-52 (2012).
7. L Yali. SF, (05):12-20 (2019).
8. Andon Health Co., LTD. 2021 annual performance forecast.
9. Z Xu, H Kuangyuan. CSF, (4): 44-51 (2022).
10. DOYO Co., LTD. Fffering the latest chief executive and chief operating conditions. https://www.10jqka.com.cn

https://doi.org/10.1051/shsconf/202418801017

Behavioral Finance: Several Key Effects of Investor Decision-Making

Shicheng Yi[1,*]

[1]School of Finance, Zhejiang University of Finance & Economics, Hangzhou, 310018, China

Abstract. This paper examines the field of behavioral finance. First, a review of the behavioral finance literature will highlight the key findings and theories that have emerged in this field. Second, this paper will also discuss the practical applications of behavioral finance, including how it can be applied to improve investment decisions and reduce cognitive biases. Finally, several future research directions that may further advance the field of behavioral finance are analyzed, such as exploring the role of emotions in financial decision-making and examining the impact of social factors on investor behavior, pointing out shortcomings and making extensions to current research in this field. This paper will specifically analyze behavioral finance in terms of loss aversion, market anomalies, framing effect and endowment effect, revealing the psychological bias and cognitive bias of human beings in the process of financial decision-making, and providing new perspectives and methods for understanding the operating mechanism of the financial market and investment strategies.

1 Introduction

Behavioral finance is a discipline that combines psychology and finance to comprehend the decision-making approach of investors and traders, and it focuses on human decision-making behavior in the financial market and the influencing factors that lead to a certain outcome. Behavioral finance has a wide range of applications. In terms of specific applications in the investment field, it can help investors identify cognitive biases and emotional influences so as to better formulate investment strategies. In terms of asset pricing, the drinking of behavioral finance can reveal the mechanism and law of market price formation and provide investors with more accurate asset pricing reference. In short, behavioral finance explains, researches and predicts the future development of the financial market from the behavior of micro-individuals as well as the psychological motivation that generates such behavior.

In traditional finance theory, investors are usually assumed to be rational, able to accurately assess risk and return and make optimal decisions. However, in reality, numerous psychological, emotional, and cognitive biases often cause them to deviate from a rational investment path.

Investors often show a tendency to overconfidence, they overestimate their ability to avoid risk and judge in the investment, perceiving that their decision-making is at a low-risk level, higher than the average market accuracy. However, overconfidence may lead to investors to ignore the potential risks, or turn a blind eye to possible losses, and ultimately lead to investment losses. Further, there is the herd effect on investors. The herding effect, also known as crowd effect, is frequently employed in economics to describe the propensity of economic agents to follow the collective. The herd's view is enough to make investors lose their rational understanding, blindly go with the tide without considering their own objective investment circumstances and risk tolerance, and make irrational investment decisions. In addition , there are loss aversion and framing effects that affect the outcome of a decision, which will be discussed in later work.

2. Loss aversion

Loss aversion, which denotes the phenomenon that individuals tend to attach greater emotional significance to potential losses compared to equivalent gains, they feel the pain of losses more intensely than the pleasure of gains. This phenomenon is due to a preference of the human psyche when faced with a decision, where people are more inclined to protect the benefits they already have rather than actively pursue gains.

Loss aversion, as a psychological concept, has its roots deep in the landmark 1979 treatise Prospect Theory: An Analysis of Decision under Risk by Israeli psychologists Daniel Kahneman and Amos Tversky [1, 2]. In this article, it is elaborated that people tend to show strong aversion and avoidance tendencies when faced with potential losses. This theory not only reveals the complex psychological dynamics of the human decision-making process, but also profoundly influences subsequent behavioral finance research. With the depth of research, the concept of loss aversion has gradually

* Corresponding author: yi03@zufe.edu.cn

demonstrated its strong explanatory power and application value in a variety of fields.

Kahneman and Tversky quantitatively analyzed the ratio between the pain from losses and the pleasantness of gains in terms of investor sentiment, market inertia and stock market forecasts. The findings suggest that the pain from losses is at least twice as great as the pleasure from gains. This finding provides an important theoretical basis for further research on loss aversion.

In the field of investment, investors tend to show excessive caution and conservatism in the face of possible financial losses, a phenomenon that is precisely the reflection of loss aversion in investment behavior. Shi, et al. studied the trading behavior and trading strategies of investors in China, a developing country, and analyzed the trading data covering 68.41 million investors (individuals and institutions) who traded A-share stocks on the Shenzhen Stock Exchange within a five-year interval [3]. The conclusions show that loss aversion is related to the average market value of investors' holdings, where the group with an average monthly market value of less than one million shares, which also dominates the number of investors, is loss averse, i.e., it tends to sell when the share price rises sharply and to hold when the share price falls sharply. The other groups, i.e., the medium individuals with market capitalization between $1 million and $10 million and the large individuals with market capitalization greater than $10 million, are risk averse, and stock price fluctuations will be the reason why they will reduce the frequency of their buying and selling transactions.

In the insurance field, the reason why people are willing to pay premiums to avoid potential risks and losses is also closely related to loss aversion. The influence of the loss aversion on the likelihood of purchasing commercial health insurance through a probit model and found that when the decision reference point is established in the uninsured framework, the higher the degree of loss aversion of consumers, the lower the likelihood of purchasing health insurance. In contrast, in the presence of an insurance reference point, consumers' loss aversion is positively correlated with the demand for social health insurance. That is, the more loss aversion people have, the more they will tend to purchase social health insurance. This result is consistent with the predictions of prospect theory, as well as with the phenomenon of loss aversion leading to status quo bias.

Specifically, prospect theory suggests that people care more about losses than equally sized gains. Thus, when people consider whether to purchase social health insurance, their decision-making reference point is the state of being uninsured, i.e., the losses they might suffer without insurance. If people are more averse, they are more inclined to purchase health insurance to avoid the risk of potential losses. This tendency is especially obvious in the social environment of universal coverage.

As for the financing mechanism, Xie, et al. examine the influence of loss aversion under consignment contracts on the preference of financing mechanism and the setting of financing conditions [4]. By building a game model, the results show that retailers' preference between direct and secured financing is acutely sensitive to their degree of disinclination to loss, carefully considering the impact it may have on their decision-making process. Provided that the retailer's reluctance to incur losses surpasses a certain limit, they will choose secured financing over direct financing. In the event that both the producer's production costs and the intensity of loss aversion are significantly high, the choice between direct and secured financing has the same outcome for profit-maximizing retailers. In sum, loss aversion behavior may significantly affect the financial parameter settings of each mechanism.

3 Market anomalies

3.1 Momentum effect

Initially posited by Jegadeesh and Titman in their 1993 study, the momentum effect is a concept which describes the trend inertia of stock prices in the short run, i.e., in the past period of time, stocks that have exhibited higher yields are anticipated to maintain their superior performance in the future, whereas stocks that have generated lower yields are anticipated to continue underperforming. This phenomenon reflects market investors' preference for stock price trends and expectations of trend continuation in their trading decisions.

The short-term momentum effect exists primarily because investors underreact when faced with market information. When there is positive or negative news in the market, investors often need a period of time to understand and digest the information and make investment decisions accordingly. During this process, stock prices tend to continue to follow the original trend up or down.

After Jegadeesh and Titman's study of return data from the U.S. stock market found this effect, several studies by Griffin and others have confirmed that momentum strategies can deliver stable and widespread returns in several European and American stock markets [5, 6]. In contrast, in some emerging markets such as Korea and Taiwan, the overall profitability of momentum strategies is not as good as in most developed stock markets. The study of the momentum effect in markets other than the above two stock markets is somewhat controversial, with monthly and annual data yielding significantly different momentum effect returns than weekly data. In this regard, Gao, et al. provide an in-depth examination of the formation mechanism of the momentum effect, and they argue that there is a difference in the formation mechanism of the momentum effect in the winners' and losers' portfolios [7]. In the winner portfolio, the momentum effect is mainly influenced by investors' psychological "fear of stock price reversal". In the losers' portfolio, the momentum effect mainly stems from the delayed reaction of bad news in the stock price due to the shorting restriction.

From the perspective of behavioral finance, the behavioral bias of investors is the main reason for the momentum effect. Currently, there are mainly theoretical explanations such as underreaction, overreaction and positive feedback model. Among them, underreaction refers to investors' underreaction to information, which leads to a time lag in stock price movements, thus generating the momentum effect. Overreaction, on the other hand, is when investors are overconfident in private information, leading to a sustained rise or fall in stock prices. Positive feedback mode refers to the fact that stocks that have risen or fallen in price in the previous period will continue to rise or fall in response to positive feedback trades in which investors "buy up and kill down". However, existing research lacks direct evidence of the impact of these behavioral biases on momentum portfolio returns.

It should be noted that although the short-term momentum effect can provide valuable investment information under certain circumstances, investors should still carefully assess the market situation and their own risk tolerance when utilizing this effect to formulate their investment strategies, in order to avoid the risks associated with blindly following the herd or over-trading.

3.2 Reversal effect

In behavioral finance, the reversal effect refers to the phenomenon that after a period of rising or falling stock prices, a reverse trend may occur in the future. The concept of reversal effect can be traced back to 1985, when De Bondt and Thaler found in their study that investors show excessive pessimism towards a portfolio of past losers and excessive optimism towards a portfolio of past winners [8]. This overreaction can cause prices to deviate from their fundamental values and eventually lead to reversals.

In a later study, Jegadeesh and Lehmann found that the reversal effect also exists in investments with maturities of one month or less [9]. This suggests that the reversal effect exists not only in long-term investments but also in short-term investments.

In addition, some scholars have developed models to predict the reversal effect in stock prices. Wurgler and Zhuravskaya showed that the reversal effect can be explained by a model containing a factor representing past price behavior and a factor representing reversal behavior [10]. Such a model can explain why past price behavior affects future price behavior and the causes of the reversal effect.

For China, an emerging market that is relatively unregulated, the reversal effect requires further research by scholars. Lu and Zou find that small-company stocks have a weaker tendency of price inertia relative to large-company stocks, i.e., small-company stocks are more prone to price reversals [11]. This phenomenon may be due to the relatively low liquidity of small company stocks and the lack of attention from market participants, resulting in their prices being more susceptible to market sentiment and short-term trading. In addition, stocks with high turnover have weaker price inertia trends relative to stocks with low turnover. This may be due to the fact that stocks with high turnover usually have higher market attention and more investor participation, and thus are more susceptible to market sentiment and trading behavior, and thus more prone to price reversals.

These studies provide an important theoretical basis and empirical support for understanding investors' behavioral biases and the reversal effect of stock prices. However, despite the progress that has been made, the reversal effect, as a currently active area of research, has yet to be explored and explored in depth in more of its dimensions.

In practice, investors need to be aware of the risk of price reversal in small-company stocks and stocks with high turnover and take proper risk management measures. In addition, investors need to further study and understand the impact of market sentiment, trading behavior, and company fundamentals on stock prices in order to better grasp investment opportunities and risk management strategies.

4 Framing effect

Kahneman and Tversky first proposed the concept of framing effect [12]. Framing effect refers to the phenomenon that the decision maker's preference for the same issue and the decision result differ under different expressions or frameworks. In behavioral finance, the framing effect is used to explain how investors make different decisions when faced with similar but differently formulated investment options. Specifically, when the same investment problem is presented to investors in different ways, even if the nature of the problem is the same, investors may have different expectations, judgments, and risk perceptions due to the different descriptions, which may lead them to make different decisions.

Information asymmetry and framing effects are closely related in finance. In the presence of information asymmetry, investors rely more on available information to make decisions, and this information is often presented in a particular frame. As a result, changes in framing may lead to different interpretations and assessments of the same basic information by investors. When investors are faced with information asymmetry, they may be more vulnerable to framing effects because their interpretations and decisions about information may be influenced by the way it is presented. investors to make inconsistent decisions between similar risks and rewards, which in turn affects the effectiveness and stability of the market.

Emotional and cognitive biases play an important role in investment decisions. The interaction of framing effects and incidental emotions has a complex impact on investment decisions. Under the gain frame, participants preferred riskier investment options, whereas under the loss frame, they preferred safer options. Under the gain frame, euphoria caused participants to be more myopic and ignore the advantages of the riskier investment option, whereas under the loss frame, euphoria had the opposite effect, causing participants to value the advantages of the riskier investment option more highly. Under fearful emotions, the framing effect on investment decisions, on the other hand, showed no significant regularity.

Mitigating the impact of framing effects on investment decisions is an important issue for investors and the stable functioning of financial markets. To mitigate this problem, decision support systems can be used to provide investors with comprehensive, accurate and timely information and analysis results, assisting investors to make more rational and scientific investment decisions of the system. Through the data integration and analysis capabilities of decision support systems and based on advanced data analysis techniques and financial theories, analytical models suitable for specific investment objectives and risk preferences are constructed. These models can provide insights into investment opportunities and help investors understand potential risks and returns.

Further research needs to focus on how to help investors pay more attention to their emotional and cognitive biases and learn how to manage them so that they can make more disciplined and "optimal" decisions rather than just focusing on the causes of risk-seeking and risk-averse behaviors.

5. The endowment effect

The endowment effect, i.e., once an individual owns an asset, he or she tends to assess the value of that asset at a higher level than he or she would have done if he or she did not own it, thus creating a tendency to be reluctant to give it up or trade it was first proposed by Thaler [13]. This concept is of special importance in financial economics as it relates to a number of core topics such as asset pricing, market efficiency and investor behavior.

In terms of theoretical framework, the endowment effect is in tension with traditional financial theories such as expected utility theory and the capital asset pricing model. Traditional theories suggest that investors are rational and will evaluate assets based on risk-adjusted expected returns. However, the endowment effect suggests that investors have emotional attachments and irrational preferences for assets they already hold, which may lead to distortions in market prices and inefficient resource allocation. Research in the field of finance consistently shows that the endowment effect has a significant impact on investors' trading behavior, asset pricing, and market efficiency. For example, investors tend to overvalue stocks or other financial assets they already hold and are reluctant to sell even when faced with negative information, which may lead to under- or over-reaction in the market.

Discussing the problem of risk management bias and correction for commercial banks, Huang, by combining behavioral finance with commercial bank risk management, found that there are biases in commercial bank risk management, mainly due to the existence of irrationality and susceptibility to emotions and will of risk managers as limited rational individuals [14]. In addition, risk managers also have some special psychological and behavioral characteristics, such as a stronger tendency of risk aversion in work decision-making, a weaker tendency to avoid business losses, a stronger herd behavior and a tendency to initiate work innovation, these behavioral characteristics lead to risk management bias. The test of risk management bias reveals that risk managers have irrational behavioral characteristics in their behavioral decision-making process, and these behavioral characteristics affect risk management effectiveness.

However, the current study still faces some challenges. Firstly, the relationship between the endowment effect and other concepts in behavioral finance (e.g., representativeness inspiration, availability inspiration, etc.) has not been fully clarified. Secondly, how to effectively apply the theoretical and empirical findings of the endowment effect to the practice of financial markets and policy making remains an urgent issue.

Combining interdisciplinary approaches such as neuroeconomics and experimental economics, future research can further reveal the neurobiological basis and psychological mechanism of the endowment effect, as well as its performance in different market environments and investor groups. This will provide important theoretical and practical guidance for financial market regulation, investment strategy development and investor education.

6. Conclusion

Based on the perspective of behavioral finance, this paper reviews the key concepts of loss aversion, momentum effect, reversal effect, framing effect and endowment effect, and describes and evaluates the related research results at home and abroad. These concepts reveal the psychological and behavioral biases of investors in the decision-making process, and are important for understanding the operating mechanism of financial markets and predicting market trends. However, the current research mainly focuses on the description and explanation of specific phenomena, and there is a relative lack of research on the interactions between phenomena and the overall impact. Future research can explore the dynamic mechanisms and influencing factors behind these behavioral financial phenomena in greater depth with the help of quantitative models, providing new perspectives and methods for financial market stability and efficiency improvement. The development and application of quantitative models will provide more precise and comprehensive analytical tools for theoretical and empirical research in behavioral finance. Future research needs to pay further attention to the interactions and dynamic evolution of these phenomena and strengthen the application of quantitative models in behavioral finance research.

In summary, this paper reviews key concepts in behavioral finance, including loss aversion, momentum effect, reversal effect, framing effect, and endowment effect. While current research primarily describes these phenomena, there is a need for deeper exploration of their interactions and overall impact. Future studies should employ quantitative models to uncover dynamic mechanisms and influencing factors, providing new insights for enhancing financial market stability and efficiency. Emphasizing the development and application of quantitative models will contribute to more precise analytical tools, advancing both theoretical and empirical research in behavioral finance.

Reference

1. A. Tversky, D. Kahneman, Journal of Risk and Uncertainty. 5, 297–323 (1992).
2. D. Kahneman, A. Tversky, Econ. 47, 263 (1979).
3. Y. Shi, Z. Li, and W. Chen, FR, 11, 129-142 (2009).
4. W. Xie, H. Yu, Y. Zhong, Y. Zhou, EJOR, 314, 206–228 (2024).
5. N. Jegadeesh, S. Titman, JF, 48, 65–91 (1993).
6. J. M. Griffin, X. Ji, J. S. Martin, JF, 58, 2515–2547 (2003).
7. Q. Gao, C. Hu, and X. Yan, FR, (02), 97-107 (2014).
8. W. F. M. De Bondt, R. H. Thaler, JF, 40, 793–805 (1985).
9. N. Jegadeesh, JF, 45, 881–898 (1990).
10. J. Wurgler, E. Zhuravskaya, JB, 75, 583–608 (2002).
11. Z. Lu and H. Zou, Study on the Inertia and Reversal Effects in the Chinese Stock Market (2007).
12. D. Kahneman, A. Tversky, AP, 39, 341–350 (1984).
13. R. H. Thaler, JEBO, 1, 39–60 (1980).
14. S. Huang, NCE, (03), 105-108 (2017).

SHS Web of Conferences 188, 01018 (2024) https://doi.org/10.1051/shsconf/202418801018
ICDDE 2024

An Study on the Causes and Consequences of the SVB Collapse

Haonan Chen[1,*]

[1]Rosedale Global High School, Beijing, 102199, China

Abstract. This comprehensive study delves into the nuanced causes and repercussions surrounding the failure of Silicon Valley Banks(SVB), scrutinizing both external and internal factors. Internally, the demise is attributed to mismanagement of assets and liabilities, coupled with flaws in the business model. Externally, the Federal Reserve's interest rate hike and relaxed financial regulations during the Trump era are identified as pivotal triggers. Post-bankruptcy, the rapid acquisition and sale of SVB, First Total Bank, and Signature Bank temporarily alleviate risks within the US banking sector. Regulatory authorities respond by fortifying rules, enhancing industry resilience but simultaneously tightening loan conditions, potentially intensifying economic downturn pressures. Presently, market confidence is on the mend due to regulatory influence, limiting systemic risks. However, the looming 2023 interest rate hike poses a threat, particularly with tight monetary policies. Small and medium-sized US banks, heavily invested in commercial real estate, face heightened vulnerability, potentially precipitating a downward spiral in property prices. Drawing lessons from Lehman Brothers, the study advocates for a balanced approach to monetary policy, emphasizing financial stability, improved risk management by regulators, and ongoing efforts to avert and mitigate future financial crises.

1 Introduction

In 2007, as the US housing market began to collapse, the value of subprime mortgages fell sharply. The value of Lehman's assets began to fall sharply because of its large holdings of assets related to real estate. In 2008, with the tightening of the US credit market and the further decline of asset value, Lehman Brothers faced great financial pressure, which directly caused investors' confidence in Lehman Brothers to begin to falter, resulting in a sharp decline in its stock price in the short term [1]. On September 15 of the same year, Lehman Brothers formally filed for bankruptcy protection, which was one of the largest in U.S. history. The systemic risk generated by the failure of Lehman Brothers, which at the time triggered great uncertainty and panic in global financial markets and caused the US credit market to almost freeze up, went far beyond this. This panic quickly spread to the entire financial system because of the close linkages between financial institutions. And the effects were not confined to the United States, but quickly spread around the world, causing a sharp slowdown in economic growth and rising unemployment around the world. Numerous governments, such as China's, have implemented bailout plans to strengthen their financial systems. Additionally, the worldwide economic downturn has exposed underlying issues within the global financial structure. After the crisis, the US government passed a number of laws and policies, such as the Dodd-Frank Act, to strengthen financial regulation and reduce future systemic risks [2].

Unfortunately, the United States has once again experienced a tragic event after 15 years. On March 8st, 2023, SVB Financial Group made an announcement regarding the sale of assets worth $21 billion which resulted in a financial loss of $1.8 billion for the company. This turn of events is disheartening. Additionally, they issued $15 billion in convertible bonds and emergency new shares to raise $2.25 billion [3]. Naturally, this announcement garnered significant attention from the market. The unconventional actions taken by SVB raised concerns among depositors who feared potential risks faced by these institutions. Consequently, many depositors began withdrawing their funds due to liquidity concerns. By March 9st, client requests for cash amounted to a staggering $42 billion and panic selling ensued in relation to the bank's stocks. As a result of insolvency issues on March 10th , According to a study conducted by Ali et al., SVB has recently encountered financial challenges and is currently facing the possibility of closure, as indicated by the California Department of Financial Protection and Innovation [4]. This development not only marks the largest bank downfall since the 2008 financial crisis but also emerges as one of the most notable failures in American history. Shortly after this crisis at SVB unfolded within two months' time frame; First Total experienced its own liquidity run which led to its swift takeover. It is important to note that First Total was even

* Corresponding author: gjjybj_gjyk@xdf.cn

larger and more diversified than No.16 SVB whose collapse initiated a chain reaction affecting larger and more influential banks. Given this context, this paper aims to delve into an extensive analysis exploring both causes and consequences surrounding the crisis at SVB while examining potential systemic risks that may arise from such failure events [5].

2 Causes of the SVB collapse

Based on the information provided by the Federal Deposit Insurance Corporation (FDIC),there are more than 4,700 banks in the United States, including many "problem banks" with weak financial, operational or managerial performance. Among these banks, SVB became the first large bank to have a crisis, which was closely related to its own asset-liability management problems.

Through the analysis of the interest rate environment, the author found that the continuous and rapid interest rate hike measures of the Federal Reserve led to the rapid tightening of market liquidity, especially the financing environment of start-ups had a serious impact. During 2020-2021, SVB achieved rapid growth in the scale of assets and liabilities, with assets growing from US $71 billion in 2019 to US $211.5 billion in 2021, including a single annual growth rate of 83% in 2021, and the amount of liabilities rose significantly, going up from US $64.4 billion in 2019 to reach a staggering US $194.9 billion by 2021.This change benefited from the quantitative easing policy of the Federal Reserve, the significant increase in market risk appetite, and the enhanced financing capacity of scientific and technological innovative enterprises [6]. In these two years, these enterprises have obtained a large amount of funds.

2.1 Internal factors

When analyzing the liability structure of SVB, it can be seen that it has a clear difference compared to other banks. SVB 's liabilities are relatively short-term and concentrated, and its deposits account for a large proportion of liabilities, exceeding 90% in some years. Demand deposits accounted for 65 percent of the total in 2021, three times that of 2019. Of the time deposits, $5.586 billion came from domestic customers, of which 83 percent were due within three months. In addition, the industry distribution of deposit customers of SVB is also very concentrated. By the end of 2022, 63% of deposits come from technology, life science and health enterprises, 13% from PE/VC institutions, and only 6% from private banks, which indicates that the customer group of SVB is highly homogeneous, mainly science and technology innovation enterprises or venture capital institutions. Since 2021, SVB has experienced a large-scale increase in debt. However, due to the very low interest rate in the first two years, enterprises' demand for time deposits is not strong, and the deposit industry concentration is too high, science and technology innovation enterprises have a high demand for funds in the start-up period and are more inclined to use demand or short-term deposits, resulting in the short-term debt structure of SVB. It is worth noting that SVB has benefited significantly from the downward interest rate cycle, achieving rapid expansion in the past two years and ranking 14th in debt in the United States in 2021. However, as the rate hike cycle arrives, it is the most liquid demand deposits that are hit first, with SVB seeing a $45.1 billion decline in demand deposits in 2022. With the rapid growth of debt scale, SVB's assets have also increased significantly, with a compound growth rate of nearly 40% in the past five years, with asset growth doubling in 2021. However, in contrast, the growth rate of customer loans and advances was slower than that of total assets, with its proportion falling from nearly 50% in 2018 to 35% in 2022, indicating that although the rapid growth of liabilities brought a large cash inflow, there was not enough loan demand to accept this cash, resulting in a large amount of idle funds. By combining the financial statements of SVB, it can be found that for these idle funds, the bank adopted a relatively aggressive investment strategy. Between 2020 and 2021, SVB's asset growth came mainly from two types of investments: available-for-sale investments, which doubled in 2020; The second is to hold maturing investments. As of the end of 2022, 94% of held-to-maturity (HTM) assets were assets with maturities of more than 10 years, while mortgage-backed securities (MBS) assets had negative convexity, that is, as interest rates rose, the duration of assets was extended, resulting in large unrealized losses.

SVB saw demand deposits fall by $45.1 billion in 2022 as the funding environment for startups became tougher at the start of the 2022 rate hike cycle, causing them to start withdrawing deposits to maintain daily operations. In order to replenish its liquidity, SVB increased its short-term borrowing by $13.5 billion, but this was not enough to offset the loss of deposits on the liability side, leading the bank to sell assets. In addition, most of SVB's deposit customers are corporate customers, whose accounts are insured up to $250,000. But the majority of SVB's deposits aren't insured, with 88% of them uninsured as of 2022, making it more vulnerable to a run in the event of liquidity problems. On the asset side, due to the large increase of SVB's holdings of available for sale (AFS) and hold to maturity (HTM) assets in the past two years, when the interest rate hike cycle arrives, the duration of these two types of assets is rapidly extended, resulting in a large number of unrealized losses, which further leads to SVB triggering a chain reaction in the market when selling assets.

SVB 's business model is highly linked to the technology innovation industry and commercial real estate. The technology innovation sector is characterized by a high level of risk, whereas the growth of commercial real estate is closely tied to the extent of economic well-being, both of which are extremely sensitive to changes in the economic cycle. After the outbreak of the pandemic, the demand for remote working surged, which promoted the prosperity of the technology and innovation industry, with a large amount of funds flowing in and converted into bank deposits [7]. However, with the aggressive interest rate hike by the

https://doi.org/10.1051/shsconf/202418801018

Federal Reserve and the slowdown of the US economic growth, the boom period of the technology innovation industry and venture capital ended, and the technology innovation companies began to consume deposits to maintain operations, resulting in a rapid loss of bank deposits. At the same time, remote working has reduced demand for commercial real estate, especially office buildings, leading to a marked decline in U.S. commercial property prices last year. SVB is highly related to these industries, and its customer base covers nearly half of the high-tech. SVB's operations are closely intertwined with science and technology innovation enterprises as well as venture capital funds, particularly those in the United States that receive support from venture capitalists, providing a full range of services from financing to investment and merger for these enterprises, and building a service chain of the whole life cycle. In order to improve returns and realize risk hedging, SVB also innovated the business model of "investment and loan linkage", that is, while providing loans to enterprises, it made equity investments directly or indirectly, or lent to investment funds to magnify returns. This model effectively reduces information asymmetry and broadens the income channel. However, this also makes the investment end closely bound to the science and technology innovation enterprises, which lays a hidden danger for the risk exposure of SVB and becomes an important reason why SVB is the first to experience a crisis among many regional banks.

2.2 External factors

In early 2020, the global spread of the COVID-19 pandemic prompted the Federal Reserve to take action in response to concerns about both public health and the economy. In March, they applied reductions in interest rates of 0.5% and 1% correspondingly, followed by initiating a new round of quantitative easing at the end of that month. Quantitative easing involves the central bank purchasing significant amounts of national bonds or medium- to long-term bonds in order to inject liquidity into the market and maintain low interest rates, thereby stimulating economic growth. This policy is often colloquially referred to as 'increasing money supply' within financial circles. By increasing market liquidity through quantitative easing, it encourages businesses to seek financing opportunities, thus fostering a positive economic cycle. To ensure low interest rates are sustained, central banks typically acquire large volumes of long-duration bonds which helps alleviate liquidity pressures. Compared to conventional monetary policies, quantitative easing is more assertive and can potentially result in excessive money circulation leading to inflationary issues; therefore countries tend to exercise caution when implementing such measures. The United States continued its implementation of this round of quantitative easing until late 2021. Throughout these two years marked by quantitative easing (QE), there was a notable surge in inflation levels within the United States with consumer price index (CPI) reaching its peak at 9.1% year-on-year in July 2022.

Affected by persistently high inflation, the Federal Reserve began a cycle of rapid interest rate increases in early 2022. In one year, the federal funds rate was raised from 0.25% to 5.25%, a cumulative increase of 5 percentage points. Such continuous and rapid interest rate hikes led to the deterioration of financing conditions, especially for technology and innovation enterprises, which became extremely severe. With external financing channels blocked, these companies can only supplement the cash flow of daily operations by withdrawing bank deposits, which has triggered a wave of withdrawals by science and technology innovation companies. Initial public offerings in the U.S. totaled just $21.8 billion in 2022, compared with the $85.4 billion raised in 2020 and the $153.5 billion raised in 2021. In addition, the US banking industry also saw negative deposit growth in 2022, with $17.77 trillion of deposits outstanding at the end of the year, down 0.98 percent year on year. On the whole, the completely different monetary policies in the United States in the past three years have resulted in excessive liquidity in the early stage, and a large number of funds have poured into technology and innovative enterprises. However, these enterprises have a long return on investment period, and after the deterioration of financing environment, they can only continue to replenish working capital by withdrawing deposits, which in turn affects the stability of the liability side of the bank.

The deregulation of financial regulations under Trump laid the groundwork for the crisis, mainly in the following aspects:

First, a relaxed regulatory culture: In response to the Economic Growth, Deregulation, and Consumer Protection Act of 2018, the Federal Reserve's regulatory culture shifted to focus more on reducing the burden on banks and requiring more evidence in the regulatory decision-making process, which led supervisors to tend to delay decisions or even avoid actions. At the same time, the financial and human resources allocated to the financial supervision department also appear insufficient.

Second, regulatory easing: In July 2018, the Federal Reserve raised its definition of a "large bank" from $50 billion to $100 billion in total assets, a change that delayed SVB's inclusion in the "large bank" category by three years.

Third, poor regulatory implementation: Although the Federal Reserve upgraded SVB's regulatory classification from "regional bank" to "large Bank" in May 2021, it did not send the results of its first regulatory rating to SVB until August 2022, which contained important information about deficiencies in SVB 's governance and internal controls. Because of the long transition period for regulatory upgrades, the first stress test that SVB was supposed to undergo after it was upgraded to a large bank was not conducted until the time of its failure.

Together, these factors constituted weaknesses in the financial regulatory system that set the stage for SVBs and the financial crisis that followed.

3 Consequences of the SVB collapse

The regional banks in the United States were significantly affected by the unexpected downfall of SVB. In addition, affected by the rapid depletion of cash flow of SVB, the US financial market experienced severe turmoil. Many banks represented by the First Total Bank achieved rapid expansion due to excessive reliance on unstable financing sources, which were quickly identified as potential risk points by the market. In a sign that the risk of a run is spreading, shares in the banks tumbled and trading in several were suspended. The downfall of SVB was not just a single incident, but revealed deeper problems across the financial system.

Affected by the downfall of SVB and the failure of Signature Bank in New York and First Total Bank faced severe crises. In recent years, Signature Bank has been heavily involved in crypto assets, while First Total Bank primarily focuses on commercial real estate lending [8]. To attract California's high net worth population, First Total Bank offers loans at significantly lower interest rates compared to the industry average. These distinctive characteristics contribute to why these three banks were among the first to encounter risks among regional banks [9]. Notably, the failure of First Total Bank became the failure of the bank that ranks second in terms of size in American history and played a significant role in triggering a chain reaction of systemic risk following SVBs' collapse. Unlike SVB's sudden collapse, market scrutiny closely monitored First Total Bank's risk exposure from March until its closure in May [10]. Consequently, market analysis gradually leaned towards an inevitable outcome - the bank's collapse. First Total Bank, established in 1985 in San Francisco, California, operates as a state non-Federal Reserve member bank under the supervision of both the FDIC and the California Financial regulator. Its core focus lies in offering deposit and loan services for residential, commercial, and personal purposes to affluent individuals. Additionally, it provides private wealth management solutions. As of the conclusion of 2022, First Total Bank ranked as the fourteenth largest financial institution in the United States with total assets amounting to $212.6 billion and deposits totalling $176.4 billion; uninsured deposits accounted for approximately 67.4% of this figure. Unfortunately, following SVB's collapse, First Total experienced a significant decline in its stock price along with a surge in deposit withdrawals due to substantial losses incurred from mortgage and securities assets. The bank witnessed an alarming decrease from $123 to $12 per share between March 1st and March 20st - representing a staggering drop exceeding 90%. On April 24th, market concerns were further exacerbated when First Total Bank disclosed that it had suffered a loss of $100 billion worth of deposits during Q1. Consequently, its shares plummeted to $3.50 between April 25st and April 28th - signifying an astonishing depreciation of value by approximately 97% thus far into the year 2023.

First Republic Bank made several attempts to save itself during the crisis, but the situation was difficult to reverse. On March 16, 2023, JPMorgan Chase and 10 other large banks jointly injected $30 billion of deposits into First Total Bank to stabilize market confidence. However, the money was nowhere near enough to compensate the bank for rapidly losing deposits. To obtain the necessary liquidity, First Total borrowed from several sources: $63.5 billion from the Federal Reserve's discount window, $13.8 billion from the Bank Time Financing Program (BTFP), and an additional $14.1 billion from the Federal Home Loan Bank. By the end of the first quarter, about 45 per cent of the bank's financing had been replaced by government funds, up from just 7 per cent at the end of the previous year, according to market estimates. The funds were funded at a cost of between 4.8 per cent and 5.0 per cent, well above the bank's deposit taking cost of 1.4 per cent, while its asset-side return was just 3.7 per cent. This meant that although First Total was still able to eke out a living on government borrowing, it was no longer profitable and would face mounting losses if it continued to operate, making liquidation a highly likely outcome. This shows the severity of the situation of the First Republic Bank in the crisis, even with the support of the government and other banks, it was difficult to restore its financial health.

In the emergency case of First Total Bank's collapse, the U.S. government did not provide full deposit protection for the bank, but adopted a cost-sharing approach to facilitate its takeover. Before the collapse, First Total approached multiple potential buyers, but because even a free purchase would mean taking a large capital loss, no bank was willing to buy First Total on market terms. To find buyers quickly and reduce volatility in the market, regulators had to step in and cover some of the costs [11]. On May 1, 2023, the California Department of Financial Protection and Innovation announced the closure of First Total Bank and appointed the Federal Deposit Insurance Corporation (FDIC) as receiver. On the same day, the FDIC and JPMorgan reached a buy-and-take agreement. Under the deal, JPMorgan agreed to take on $92 billion in deposits, $173 billion in loans and $30 billion in securities from First Concord. The FDIC will provide loss-sharing on the home mortgage and commercial real estate loans and support JPMorgan with about $50 billion in five-year fixed-rate financing [12]. The cost borne by the FDIC is estimated at $13 billion. This action demonstrated the flexibility and determination of supervisory authorities in responding to major banking crises, as well as their key role in stabilizing financial markets and protecting the interests of depositors.

In order to prevent the bankruptcy of SVB from becoming the trigger for serious systemic risks, the US government together with relevant regulators quickly discussed the feasibility of a new round of financial regulatory reform, hoping to further strengthen the resilience of the banking industry through financial regulatory reform. But such tightening could constrain bank lending, adding to downward pressure on the economy.

At a U.S. Senate hearing in May to review financial regulation, the mentioned entities include the Federal Reserve, the Federal Deposit Insurance Corporation, and the Office of the Comptroller of the Currency, and the California and New York state financial regulators all expressed their determination to establish stronger oversight and regulatory frameworks. This was a direct response to the recent banking crisis, particularly the failures of SVB and First Total Bank. In July, Mr. Barr, the Fed's vice chairman for financial supervision, proposed reforms centered on strengthening bank capital levels, which are expected to increase capital ratios by about 2 percentage points for banks with $100 billion or more in total assets. The Fed also plans to remove certain regulatory exemptions put in place in 2019, reinstate a requirement that all banks with $100bn in total assets take losses on available-for-sale securities into account when calculating their capital needs, expand the coverage of stress tests and speed up implementation of measures such as Basel III. Greater capital discipline would be good for the resilience of the US banking sector, particularly for those previously under-regulated banks with assets in the $100bn - $250bn range. However, higher capital adequacy ratios may also limit the lending capacity of banks, especially during economic downturns, which may have certain procyclical effects. Although it may take a long time from the proposal to the actual implementation, the release of reform proposals has already started to influence the behavior of the banking sector, which is trying to strengthen capital accumulation and adopt a more prudent attitude in granting loans. These measures can also help prevent future financial crises and improve the stability and safety of the banking sector as a whole.

4 Conclusion

This study provides an in-depth analysis of the causes and consequences of the failure of SVB. For the reasons of bankruptcy, this paper analyzes from two aspects: external factors and internal factors. This paper argues that the internal factors behind the bankruptcy and collapse of SVB are mainly due to the poor management of its assets and liabilities, and some shortcomings in its business model. As for the external factors, this paper believes that the interest rate hike by the Federal Reserve and the financial regulation relaxation in the Trump era are the main reasons for the bankruptcy of SVB. As for the consequences of the bankruptcy of SVB, this paper argues that after the rapid takeover and sale of SVB, First Total Bank and Signature Bank, the risks of the US banking industry are cleared in the short term. At the same time, the US regulatory authorities further strengthened the regulatory rules after the bankruptcy of SVB, which effectively enhanced the resilience of the banking industry, but also encouraged banks to tighten loan conditions, objectively increasing the downward pressure on the economy. However, for now, the confidence of the US financial market has gradually recovered under the influence of regulatory policies, risk contagion has been effectively suppressed, and the probability of systemic risks breaking out in the short term is small.

Indeed, the certainty that the Fed will continue to raise interest rates in 2023 could pose further downside risks to the economy, especially in the current context of tight monetary policy. Due to their large exposure to the commercial real estate sector, small and medium-sized banks in the United States are particularly sensitive to the adjustment of commercial real estate prices during the economic downturn, which will increase the financial pressure of banks if there is a significant adjustment in the valuation of commercial real estate in the future. Already, some regional banks are selling commercial-property loans at a discount to stem losses after the Silicon Valley collapse. If there is a sharp correction in commercial property valuations, more US banks could sell assets at a loss, which in severe cases could lead to a downward spiral in commercial property prices that could be a trigger for systemic risk. It can be seen from the cases of Lehman Brothers Bank and SVB that the crisis of regional banks in the United States cannot be avoided only by strengthening supervision. The most fundamental solution lies in properly handling the relationship between monetary policy and financial stability, and solving the drastic adjustment of macro environment caused by the relaxation and tightening of financial policy. And give greater consideration to the maintenance of financial stability during significant shifts in monetary policy. This requires taking into account the impact on financial stability in the formulation and implementation of monetary policy, as well as measures to reduce it if necessary. At the same time, regulators need to continuously improve their ability to identify and manage risks and ensure the overall stability of the banking system, so as to prevent and mitigate possible financial crises in the future.

References

1. E. Bouri, R. Nekhili, H. Kinateder, T. Choudhury, FRL, 55, 103845 (2023).
2. M. K. Hassan, M. Kamran, H. G. Djajadikerta, T. Choudhury, PBFJ, 73, 101768 (2022).
3. C. RamíRez, P. A. Shively, JMCB, 44, 433–455 (2012).
4. S. Ali, F. Moussa, M. Youssef, FRL, 58, 104352 (2023).
5. K. Liu, JFEP, 13, 424–441 (2020).
6. M. Akhtaruzzaman, S. Boubaker, A. Sensoy, FRL, 38, 101604 (2021).
7. H. Miyajima, Y. Yafeh, JBF, 31, 2866–2885 (2007).
8. A. Dutta, L. C. Voumik, A. Ramamoorthy, S. Ray, A. Raihan, JRFM, 16, 216 (2023).
9. F. Allen, D. Gale, JPE, 108, 1–33 (2000).
10. M. Pericoli, M. Sbracia, JES, 17, 571–608 (2003).
11. J. A. Batten, T. Choudhury, H. Kinateder, N. Wagner, AOR, 330+335–360 (2022).
12. N. Mansley, Z. Wang, X. Weng, W. Zhang, Int. Rev. Financ. Anal. 86, 102499 (2023).

Behavioral Finance: The impact of Investor Expectations on the Financial Markets

Hanzhi Wang[1,*]

[1]Shanghai Starriver Bilingual School, Shanghai, 201108, China

Abstract. This paper explores the profound impact of investor behavior, driven by cognitive biases such as loss aversion, the framing effect, and the endowment effect, on financial markets. The presence of these biases introduces market anomalies and long-term reversals, challenging the efficiency of the market. While valuable insights are gained from studying investor behavior, limitations must be considered. Individual variations in psychological traits and decision-making processes may render these theories inapplicable to all investors. Historical data, a primary tool for analyzing behavior, may not reliably predict future market trends. Quantifying cognitive biases and measuring their impact presents challenges due to the subjective nature of psychological factors. Additionally, limited sample sizes in some studies may compromise the generalizability of findings. Despite these constraints, understanding investor behavior remains paramount for unraveling market dynamics and shaping informed investment strategies. The paper underscores the need to acknowledge these limitations while appreciating the nuanced role of cognitive biases in financial markets.

1 Introduction

The study of financial markets has been a cornerstone of economic research for decades. Traditional theories have long championed the concept of efficient markets, where prices reflect all available information. The Efficient Market Hypothesis (EMH), particularly influential in the 1970s, posited that securities' prices in financial markets are always at their fair value, making it impossible to consistently outperform the market through expert stock selection or market timing [1]. However, the steadfastness of this theory began to wane as anomalies and patterns of excess volatility emerged, particularly noted in the 1980s, which led to the burgeoning field of behavioral finance. Researchers like Shiller have chronicled the journey from a staunch belief in market efficiency to acknowledging the nuances and the value of behavioral theories in finance [1].

Yet, a gap remains in comprehensively understanding how investor expectations, characterized by cognitive biases and emotional reactions, influence market dynamics. While financial anomalies have been extensively documented, the mechanisms through which investor psychology, particularly loss aversion, impacts market efficiency are not fully understood. This is surprising given the potential implications for both market predictability and investment strategy. Current literature suggests that irrational investor behavior can indeed have significant effects on market efficiency, challenging the traditional EMH [2].

This paper aims to deepen the exploration of behavioral finance by investigating the impact of loss aversion on financial market anomalies, specifically short-term momentum and long-term reversal, as well as the framing effect. By employing a refined predictive model that integrates behavioral factors overlooked in previous research, this study seeks to elucidate how investor expectations shape market movements. This approach is not only theoretically robust, but it also offers practical insights into market behavior that could be advantageous for financial practitioners.

In summary, this paper will present a structured examination of the following: the Efficient Market Theory, the correlation between irrational investors and market efficiency, and the influence of investor behavior on market anomalies. A detailed methodology is utilized to explore these phenomena, with significant findings highlighting the complex interplay between psychology and market efficiency. This investigation is poised to fill the research void by offering a nuanced perspective on how investor expectations can lead to predictable patterns within financial markets, ultimately challenging the notion of market efficiency.

2 Loss aversion

Loss aversion is a cognitive bias characterized by the principle that individuals feel the pain of a loss more acutely than the pleasure of an equivalent gain. This phenomenon is central to behavioral finance and has significant implications for investor behavior and market dynamics.

The impact of loss aversion extends deeply into the psyche of financial decision-making. Empirical studies have shown that when faced with potential losses, investors exhibit a tendency to become risk-averse, often

* Corresponding author: 1910831234@mail.sit.edu.cn

irrationally holding on to losing investments to avoid realizing losses, while conversely, quickly liquidating profitable positions to secure gains [3, 4]. This behavior is driven by the disproportionate weight given to the fear of loss over the potential for an equal amount of gain. Loss aversion can therefore lead investors to make choices that are not aligned with their long-term financial interests or the fundamental values of the assets they hold.

In the context of financial markets, the decision-making processes influenced by loss aversion can contribute to several market anomalies. For example, the disposition effect, a behavioral bias where investors are prone to sell winners too early and ride losers too long, is a direct consequence of loss aversion [3]. This effect can result in the momentum and reversal patterns observed in asset prices, as investors react to short-term fluctuations and over-correct in the long term.

Moreover, loss aversion has been linked to the under-performance of individual investors compared to market benchmarks. The analysis of trading records and investment returns indicates that the more actively individuals trade, influenced by loss aversion, the poorer their performance tends to be, suggesting that this bias can be detrimental to wealth accumulation [3].

Research utilizing comprehensive data sets and psychological models has further reinforced that loss aversion can distort investor expectations and lead to systematic deviations from optimal investment behavior [3, 4]. This divergence from rationality is essential in understanding the mechanisms behind price formation and the efficiency of financial markets. The studies demonstrate that the pain of losses is felt more intensely and weighs more heavily in decision-making than the satisfaction of an equivalent gain. As such, loss aversion not only impacts individual investment choices but also has broader implications for market behavior and efficiency, challenging traditional financial theories which assume rational actors.

In summary, loss aversion plays a pivotal role in shaping investor expectations and financial decision-making. The tendency to avoid losses more strongly than to seek gains can result in predictable yet inefficient market outcomes. Recognizing and understanding the influence of loss aversion is paramount for both individual investors aiming to optimize their investment strategies and for economists seeking to elucidate the complexities of market behavior.

3 Market anomalies

3.1 Momentum

Short-term momentum in market anomalies refers to the phenomenon where stocks or assets that have performed well in the recent past continue to outperform in the near future. It is a manifestation of investor behavior driven by cognitive biases and emotional reactions, including loss aversion. Loss aversion leads investors to hold on to winning stocks for longer periods to avoid selling at a loss and quickly liquidate profitable positions to secure gains.

Zaremba delves into the momentum effect within global equity markets, scrutinizing anomalies at the country level. The study encompasses 78 countries over the period from 1995 to 2015, investigating 40 potential cross-sectional inter-market anomalies, including some that have not been previously explored. The results offer compelling support for the notion that anomalies demonstrating strong performance in the preceding 6-12 months are likely to outperform in the future. Additionally, the returns on strategies at the individual country level display minimal correlation, implying that creating a portfolio based on historically top-performing strategies can be advantageous for global investors [5].

The research methodology entails employing sorting procedures to assemble portfolios of countries with equal and capitalization weights, subsequently evaluating their performance using both country-level and stock-level asset-pricing models. The investigation identifies the most resilient effects and constructs portfolios of anomalies with equal weights. To validate cross-sectional patterns linked to the past performance of portfolios, Patton and Timmerman's monotonic relationship tests are applied [5].

Another relevant study by Dhankar and Maheshwari places emphasis on behavioral-based explanations for the momentum anomaly [6]. The paper discusses the ongoing debate surrounding the profitability of momentum strategies and evaluates various authors' work on possible causes of the effect. It contributes to the literature on behavioral finance, which seeks to understand financial markets through a paradigm shift from neoclassical assumptions towards incorporating investor irrationality and cognitive biases [6].

3.2 Reversal

Long-term reversal refers to the phenomenon where stocks or assets that have performed poorly over a period eventually outperform in the longer run. This behavior impacts decision-making as it suggests that investors' initial reactions to information may be overextended, leading to subsequent corrections in asset prices. It implies that investors, driven by expectations built on past performance, may push prices away from fundamental values, only for these to correct over time.

The essence of long-term reversal lies in the psychological tendencies of market participants. Investors react to new information by updating their expectations, and these revised expectations can lead to significant price movements. However, due to cognitive biases like anchoring or the representativeness heuristic, investors often overreact to new information in the short term, leading to price movements that deviate from the assets' fundamental values. Over time, as emotions wane and rational analysis prevails, prices tend to revert, reflecting a more accurate assessment of the assets' intrinsic value. This adjustment manifests as a long-term reversal.

The influence of long-term reversal extends to the mechanisms of financial decision-making. Investors, driven by recency biases, might give undue weight to short-term performance when evaluating investments. This can lead to suboptimal strategies, such as the tendency to chase past performance, resulting in buying high and selling low—actions contrary to sound investment principles.

In the realm of financial markets, the decision-making shaped by long-term reversal contributes to distinctive patterns in asset pricing. For instance, the contrarian investment strategy, which involves buying underperforming assets and selling outperformers, is predicated on the principle of long-term reversal [7, 8]. This strategy assumes that the market will eventually correct the mispricing caused by investor overreaction, leading to the observed phenomenon where poor performers eventually outperform.

Additionally, long-term reversal has been linked with market inefficiencies. While traditional finance models assume markets are efficient and assets are fairly priced, the persistence of long-term reversal suggests that psychological biases can lead to systematic mispricing that savvy investors can exploit [7, 8]. Some argues that long-term return anomalies do not necessarily refute market efficiency. It suggests that both overreaction and underreaction to information are as common and that long-term return anomalies are sensitive to methodological approaches. This study utilizes event studies and considers the lag in price adjustments to information. The key conclusion is that the evidence against market efficiency from long-term return studies is fragile and that many anomalies are not robust to changes in methodology. This supports the main theme by showing how investor expectations, when tested with different methods, may not conclusively lead to persistent anomalies, thus questioning the impact of such expectations on financial markets [7].

While other explores long-term return reversals across international equity markets, introducing a late-stage contrarian strategy that identifies securities ready to reverse based on recent short-term performance. This study is particularly relevant as it provides evidence of reversal in both developed and emerging markets. By focusing on recent short-term performance to select contrarian securities, this research shows that investor expectations based on past performance can lead to profitable opportunities when such expectations result in mispricing, which then corrects over time. This supports the essay's theme by demonstrating a practical application of how investor expectations, when misaligned with long-term fundamentals, can impact financial markets [8].

These studies underline the fact that investor reactions to new information can be extreme and short-sighted, with a gradual realignment of prices over the long term as the market absorbs and accurately reflects all available information. Consequently, long-term reversal not only affects individual investment decisions but also has pervasive implications for broader market behavior and the concept of market efficiency, challenging the conventional wisdom of rational market behavior.

In summary, the momentum effect is a pivotal aspect of behavioral finance, influencing investor expectations, market anomalies, and price formation. Understanding the influence of the momentum effect is crucial for investors seeking to optimize their strategies and for economists aiming to comprehend the complexities of market behavior. Nonetheless, long-term reversal is a critical concept in behavioral finance that challenges traditional market efficiency theories. The reviewed literature indicates that investor expectations, shaped by behavioral biases, can lead to market anomalies, although these anomalies' persistence and implications for market inefficiency are debatable. The impact of investor expectations on financial markets is evident but must be understood within the context of methodological rigor and the dynamic nature of market forces.

4 Framing effect

The framing effect, defined as the influence of how information is presented or framed on people's choices and decisions, plays a significant role in behavioral finance, shaping investment behaviors and influencing financial wellbeing.

One study focused on the impact of framing effect on investment behaviors and financial wellbeing [9]. The research, conducted in Pakistan, utilized Structural Equation Modeling to analyze data collected from 344 respondents. The study found that the framing effect could adversely influence financial wellbeing. Moreover, the research revealed the mediating role of investment behaviors between framing effect and financial wellbeing, contributing to the field of behavioral finance.

A different investigation delved into how the method of elicitation shapes return expectations [10]. The study revealed a notable impact of the elicitation mode on the forecasts. Surveys that inquired about anticipated future stock prices were observed to yield expectations more inclined towards mean reversion compared to surveys directly seeking future returns. This observation supports behavioral theories regarding investor expectation formation, particularly those grounded in the representativeness heuristic.

In the context of financial market surveys, the mode of eliciting return expectations can profoundly influence the results. Surveys asking for future stock price levels tend to produce different expectations compared to those directly asking for future returns. This insight is crucial, as survey results are influential in academia and practice, often shaping economic policy debates and corporate decisions.

The influence of the framing effect extends to the realm of investment decision-making. The manner in which information regarding an investment opportunity is presented—whether as a prospective gain or a prospective loss—holds substantial sway over investor behavior. This phenomenon is closely tied to the notion of loss aversion, wherein individuals tend to assign greater importance to potential losses than equivalent gains, thereby impacting their choices in investment decisions.

In summary, the framing effect has substantial implications for investment behaviors and financial wellbeing. The way information is presented can significantly influence decision-making, investor expectations, and market outcomes. Understanding the influence of framing effect is crucial for investors, policymakers, and researchers, as it sheds light on the complexities of decision-making and the behavioral biases that influence financial markets.

These studies contribute to the body of knowledge in behavioral finance, emphasizing the need to consider the framing effect and its implications for investment behaviors and financial wellbeing. Recognizing the impact of framing effect is essential for developing more comprehensive and effective strategies for investment decision-making and policy formulation in the financial realm.

5 Endowment effect

The endowment effect is a cognitive bias that causes individuals to ascribe more value to things merely because they own them. This bias suggests that the act of owning an item increases its subjective value, which can distort an individual's valuation of the asset.

In financial markets, the endowment effect can have a profound impact on trading behavior and asset valuation. Investors affected by this bias may demand a higher price to part with an asset than the maximum price they are willing to pay to acquire it, if they do not own it. This can lead to pricing inefficiencies, where the market price does not reflect true asset value but is rather inflated by the subjective valuations of current owners.

The study by Furche and Johnstone provides empirical evidence of the endowment effect in stock market order placements [11]. They found that on the Australian Stock Exchange, sell orders were placed further from the market compared to buy orders, indicating that sellers, due to the endowment effect, valued their shares higher than potential buyers did. This asymmetry was more pronounced among private clients than institutional investors, suggesting that less sophisticated market participants are more prone to the endowment effect. This finding aligns with behavioral finance theories that predict individuals will not always act in economically rational ways.

Furthermore, the classroom experiment replicates the endowment effect in a controlled environment, demonstrating its relevance in educational settings and its potential impact on learning behavioral finance [12]. The experiment showed that students valued items they owned higher than the same items when they did not own them, thus illustrating the practical implications of the endowment effect in shaping financial decisions and expectations.

The endowment effect supports the essay's theme by illustrating how investor expectations, shaped by psychological ownership, can significantly affect financial markets. The tendency of investors to overvalue assets they own contributes to market inefficiencies and challenges the assumption of rational behavior in economic theory. Such biases in valuation and trading behavior affect market liquidity, lead to potential asset mispricing, and can influence the dynamics of the market overall. The endowment effect, therefore, provides a clear example of how psychological factors, specifically ownership feelings, can distort investor expectations and, subsequently, market outcomes.

The literature supports the notion that the endowment effect influences financial decision-making. While traditional financial theories assume rational actors who value assets solely based on objective criteria, behavioral finance, through studies like those by Furche and Johnstone, reveals that subjective experience of ownership can alter this valuation [11]. The classroom experiment further reinforces the concept that even when made aware of their biases, individuals still succumb to them, which underscores the potency of the endowment effect in real-world financial scenarios [12].

In conclusion, the endowment effect is a fundamental concept in behavioral finance, providing insight into the non-rational ways in which investor expectations can shape financial market dynamics. By understanding this bias, market participants and educators can better anticipate and mitigate its impact on investment strategies and market efficiency.

6 Conclusion

Investor behavior, influenced by cognitive biases such as loss aversion, the framing effect, and the endowment effect, plays a significant role in financial markets. These biases can lead to market anomalies and long-term reversals, challenging the efficient market hypothesis and impacting market prices.

While the study of investor behavior and cognitive biases offers valuable insights into financial markets, there are certain limitations to consider. Firstly, these theories may not hold true for all investors as individuals vary in their psychological traits and decision-making processes. Secondly, relying on historical data to analyze investor behavior may not always accurately predict future market behavior. Additionally, quantifying cognitive biases and measuring their impact can be challenging, considering the subjective nature of psychological factors. Moreover, the sample sizes in some studies might be limited, which could affect the generalizability of the findings.

The intricate interplay between investor behavior and cognitive biases introduces a nuanced dimension to financial markets, challenging the traditional notions of market efficiency. While the identified biases such as loss aversion, the framing effect, and the endowment effect can instigate market anomalies and long-term reversals, a comprehensive understanding requires careful consideration of the limitations inherent in the study of investor behavior. Individual variations in psychological traits and decision-making processes may undermine the universality of these theories, and the reliance on historical data presents a potential obstacle to accurately predicting future market behavior. Moreover, the subjective nature of psychological factors and the challenges in quantifying biases may introduce complexities in measuring their true impact. Despite these limitations, recognizing and delving into investor behavior is indispensable for unraveling the intricacies of market dynamics and formulating informed investment strategies in an ever-evolving financial landscape.

All in all, investor behavior influenced by cognitive biases can significantly influence financial markets by giving rise to market anomalies and long-term reversals. However, it is important to acknowledge the limitations of these theories, recognizing that not all investors may exhibit the same biases and that historical data cannot always predict future market outcomes. Nonetheless, understanding and studying investor behavior remains crucial for comprehending market dynamics and informing investment strategies.

Reference

1. R. J. Shiller, JEP, 17, 83–104 (2003).
2. K. Daniel, S. Titman, FAJ, 55, 28–40 (1999).
3. A. Tversky, D. Kahneman, The Quarterly Journal of Economics. 106, 1039–1061 (1991).
4. N. Barberis, R. H. Thaler, A survey of behavioral finance (Handbook of The Economics of Finance, 2003).
5. A. Zaremba, EIER, 31, 703–721 (2018).
6. R. Dhankar, & S. Maheshwari, SSRN 2785520 (2016).
7. M. Malin, G. N. Bornholt, JIFM, 25, 1–17 (2013).
8. E. F. Fama, JFE, 49(3), 283-306 (1998).
9. E. Otuteye, & M. Siddiquee, BFJ, 7(2), 123-135 (2014).
10. M. Glaser, T. Langer, J. Reynders, M. Weber, EFR, 11, 325–357 (2007).
11. A. Furche, D. Johnstone, JBF, 7, 145–154 (2006).
12. J. Itzkowitz, J. Itzkowitz, AFE (2020).

A Study of Factors Influencing Investor Expectations in the Capital Market

Yuxuan He[1,*]

[1]School of Economics and Finance, Guangdong University of Foreign Studies, Guangzhou, 510006, China

Abstract. This paper examines three key factors that influence investor expectations: company announcements, market seasonality and environment, and social and corporate governance (ESG). It shows that these factors individually and jointly have a significant impact on investor behavior and market dynamics. Corporate announcements serve as an important source of information that directly influences investor behavior and expectations, while market seasonality demonstrates cyclical patterns in investor expectations. Meanwhile, ESG investments reflect investors' concerns about corporate performance in environmental protection, social responsibility, and governance. While research on these factors has been more extensive, further research is needed to combine these factors with other market dynamics and to quantify their impact on long-term investment decisions and market trends. This study aims to provide a comprehensive understanding of the diverse factors that influence investor expectations by analyzing these factors in an integrated manner. This not only provides insights for investors and market analysts, but also provides important information for policymakers in guiding the market and formulating policies.

1 Introduction

In global financial markets, the formation and changes in investor expectations have a profound impact on market dynamics. Investment decisions, asset pricing and market volatility are largely driven by investors' expectations of future developments. These expectations not only reflect the interpretation of current market information, but also involve predictions of future trends. Understanding the key factors influencing investor expectations is therefore essential for predicting market direction, guiding investment strategies and shaping effective regulatory policies.

This paper focuses on three factors that primarily influence investor expectations: company announcements, market seasonality and environment, and social and corporate governance (ESG). Corporate announcements, such as earnings releases and major trades, are important sources of information for the market and directly affect investor behavior and expectations [1]. Seasonal factors, such as the holiday effect or the earnings cycle, have been shown to have a significant impact on stock returns and market volatility, revealing seasonal patterns in investor expectations [2]. Meanwhile, ESG investment, as an emerging investment trend, reflects investors' concerns about corporate performance in environmental protection, social responsibility, and governance, which are increasingly important factors influencing investment decisions and expectations [3].

While there has been extensive research on the factors affecting investor expectations, the existing literature still contains gaps or shortcomings in certain key areas. First, the immediate impact of corporate announcements on investor expectations has been widely recognized as an important source of market information. However, how to quantify the impact of these announcements on long-term investment decisions and market trends, especially when interacting with other market dynamics, has yet to be thoroughly investigated [1]. Second, although the effects of market seasonality are widely observed, research on how seasonality interacts with other market factors, especially in influencing investors' long-term expectations, remains limited [2]. For example, whether seasonality effects coincide with the timing of firm-specific announcements and how this overlap affects investor reactions and expectations remain to be explored in greater depth. Finally, ESG factors have become an important component of investment decisions in recent years. However, there has been insufficient research on how to combine the impact of ESG factors with traditional financial metrics and how these factors interact with seasonal patterns in the market and company announcements to influence investor expectations [3].

Therefore, the purpose of this study is to fill these research gaps by providing a comprehensive perspective on the multiple factors that influence investor expectations by considering company announcements, market seasonality, and ESG together. Through an in-depth analysis of corporate announcements, market seasonality, and ESG factors, this study will explore how these factors individually and collectively contribute to investor expectations and how they affect the overall

* Corresponding author: 20221704951@gdufs.edu.cn

performance of the market. This comprehensive exploration not only provides investors and market analysts with a foundation of insights to help them better understand market dynamics and predict market movements, but also provides policymakers with important information on how to more effectively navigate markets and formulate policies. It also promotes a deeper understanding of financial market behavior and provides practical strategies and solutions for dealing with the constant changes in the markets.

2. Announcement

In the financial markets, Announcement refers to a formal statement issued by a company about its business, financial position, strategy or other important matters. These announcements usually cover a wide range of formats such as financial reports, major transactions, mergers and acquisitions, management changes, new product launches or the signing of major contracts. Corporate announcements play a vital role in the stock market and the financial ecosystem as a whole by serving as an important source of information in the market, conveying key information to investors, analysts and other market participants. These announcements directly influence investors' judgments and predictions about a company's future performance. For example, financial reports provide key data on a company's operational efficiency and profitability, helping investors to assess a company's value and growth potential. Announcements of major transactions or mergers and acquisitions, on the other hand, may signal a significant shift in the company's business, with implications for the company's future market position and competitiveness. Management changes may reflect a change in the company's strategic direction or the stability of its internal management, which in turn affects investors' perceptions of the company's governance structure and decision-making efficiency. Because these announcements provide critical information about a company's current situation and future prospects, they play a central role in the investor decision-making process. Investors rely on this information to construct and adjust their investment strategies, assess investment risks, and make buy, hold, or sell decisions. As a result, company announcements not only affect the performance of individual stocks, but may also have a wide-ranging impact on the market as a whole, including share price volatility, market sentiment and investment trends.

The impact of corporate announcements on market reactions has been a central theme in the field of financial research. Historically, major corporate announcements, such as acquisitions, mergers, or significant financial changes, have often led to dramatic stock price fluctuations. For example, research has analyzed how an earnings warning announcement by a large company significantly affects its stock price in a short period of time, which in turn affects the market performance of the entire industry [1]. In addition, announcements about management changes often have an immediate impact on investor confidence and future expectations of the company, which is reflected in the movement of stock prices and increased trading volume [1]. Theoretically, information asymmetry and market efficiency are two key concepts to explain the impact of corporate announcements. The information asymmetry theory suggests that announcements can reduce information asymmetry due to the inequality of information between company management and external investors, thus affecting investor expectations and behavior. Market efficiency theory, on the other hand, emphasizes how information from announcements is quickly reflected in stock prices, revealing the market's ability to absorb and react to new information [1]. Existing studies have shown the diversity of the impact of corporate announcements on the stock market. On the one hand, positive announcements, such as earnings reports that exceed expectations, usually lead to an increase in stock prices, while negative news may lead to a decrease in stock prices [1]. On the other hand, market reaction to announcements is also affected by factors such as investor sentiment, market environment and complexity of announcement content. In addition, it is also found that even expected announcements may trigger asymmetric responses in the market, suggesting that the market's reaction to announcements depends not only on the content of the announcements themselves, but is also related to the expectations and interpretations of market participants [1].

Corporate announcements have a significant impact on investors' information acquisition, processing and expectation formation. Corporate announcements provide investors with key information about a company's operations, financial position, and strategic direction. For example, increased stock market volatility and changes in stock market returns can affect investors' expectations. These changes are usually communicated through company announcements, allowing investors to adjust their stock market expectations based on the content of the announcements [4]. Company announcements play a key role in shaping investor expectations. For example, the delivery and accuracy of information during the IPO process and the pricing mechanism of the IPO have an impact on investors' expectations. Investors use these announcements to assess the value of the firm and the market opportunity and form their expectations for the future [5]. Positive and negative announcements have different impacts on investors' expectations. Positive announcements usually enhance the market's confidence in the firm, while negative announcements may lead to a decline in confidence. For example, executives' share reductions are often seen as a signal of less optimism about the company's future, which may lead to a decline in investor expectations [6]. Notably, even small announcements may generate disproportionately large reactions in the market, reflecting the market's sensitivity to information [7].

3 Seasonality

Seasonality is a prominent phenomenon in financial markets and refers to regular changes in market performance over a specific period of time. These changes involve not only stock price volatility and trading volumes, but also seasonal patterns in investor sentiment and expectations. For example, as described by Stephen J. Ciccone, the January effect reveals an increase in investor optimism at the beginning of each year, which typically leads to an increase in investment in stocks of high uncertainty companies [7]. This seasonal fluctuation in optimism reflects the expectations and hopes of market participants for the new year. Seasonal effects can also be observed around specific holidays or vacations, such as the Christmas effect noted by Todd Feldman and Alan Jung. It was found that around Christmas, the market volatility index (VIX) usually decreases, showing the stability of the market during this period [8]. Understanding seasonality is crucial for investors as it helps them to predict and explain the performance of the market at different times. Awareness of seasonal patterns allows investors to better tailor their investment strategies and use these patterns to optimize investment decisions. In addition, an in-depth understanding of seasonal factors helps investors and market analysts to more accurately assess market risks and opportunities. However, seasonal effects are not always predictable and their impact may vary depending on other market dynamics. Therefore, when utilizing seasonal patterns in making investment decisions, investors also need to consider other factors affecting the market, such as macroeconomic conditions and company-specific events.

Seasonal variation in financial markets is more than a simple repetition of patterns; it profoundly reflects the complex interplay of market dynamics and investor psychology. Specific holiday effects and tax policy changes provide a unique perspective to understand this complexity. Changes in consumer behavior triggered by holidays such as Christmas and Black Friday not only alter the short-term financial performance of the retail and consumer goods industry, but also influence the sentiment and expectations of the market as a whole. Such changes go beyond mere sales figures; they reflect the far-reaching impact of cultural and social factors on economic activity. For example, the reduction in market volatility over the Christmas period may be related to investors' reduced trading behavior during the holiday season, but just as importantly this period is usually accompanied by increased optimism and consumer confidence. This seasonal trend is not only a numerical change, but also a sign of the psychological state of the market [8]. During major retail events such as Black Friday, it can observe how investors react quickly to market information. Short-term fluctuations in the stock market are not only a reaction to actual sales data, but also a reflection of consumer behavior and expectations of market trends. This situation shows how seasonal events can be a catalyst for investor sentiment and expectations, which in turn influence their investment decisions [2]. Seasonal changes in tax policy, on the other hand, reveal how investors find a balance between macroeconomic policies and micro personal finances. The year-end phenomenon of tax-loss harvesting not only affects the performance of individual stocks, but also reflects how investors make trade-offs between tax optimization and market performance expectations. This pattern of behavior reflects the market's adaptability and flexibility in the face of structural economic incentives.

It is important to note that in financial markets, investor reaction to seasonal information is often complex and variable, and investors may underreact to predictable seasonal information. This is particularly true for seasonal events that have historically had high returns. For example, during China's Double Eleven shopping festival, investors often fail to adequately predict the potential impact of this seasonal event, despite the fact that the historical performance of the retail industry has typically shown significant earnings growth [9]. This underreaction may stem from investors focusing too much on recent data and ignoring long-term seasonal trends. In addition, investors may fail to accurately capitalize on investment opportunities arising from seasonal events due to misinterpretation of market information. Despite the relatively obvious seasonal patterns, many investors still start adjusting their portfolios only after the events have occurred, missing out on the expected peaks in returns. This phenomenon suggests that even in the face of predictable seasonal events, investors' behavior remains limited by their ability to process and interpret patterns of market information. Moreover, this lack of response reflects a general market misunderstanding of seasonal effects. In many cases, investors may incorrectly believe that the effects of seasonal events have been fully absorbed by the market, thereby underestimating the actual impact of these events on stock prices and market dynamics.

In financial markets, investors and market analysts develop more effective investment strategies by utilizing an in-depth understanding of seasonality. The use of seasonal analysis is not limited to identifying market trends over a specific period of time, but extends to risk management and optimization of investment decisions. By analyzing phenomena such as the Christmas effect and the "double 11" phenomenon, investors are able to predict market performance over a specific period of time and adjust their portfolios to maximize returns or minimize risk. The use of seasonal analysis in investment decision-making highlights the importance of a thorough understanding of market dynamics. Investors need to focus not only on short-term market fluctuations, but also consider long-term trends and cyclical patterns. For example, an investor may buy stocks that are expected to perform well during a particular holiday or event in advance, with a view to profiting from the anticipated price increase. Similarly, understanding seasonal changes in tax policy can help investors plan their trades to optimize tax implications. In addition, the impact of seasonality on investor expectations and market performance highlights the importance of understanding market cycles and investor behavior patterns. By tapping into seasonal patterns, market analysts are able to provide more accurate market forecasts and investment recommendations. This deeper understanding provides investors with the foundation to make informed decisions in a complex market environment. Understanding and applying seasonal knowledge is not only a key component of effective market analysis, but also an important tool in developing investment strategies. As the market environment continues to change, adapting to and utilizing these seasonal patterns will be a key factor in investment success.

4 Environmental, social and corporate governance (ESG)

ESG has become an important topic in the contemporary investment world, addressing a company's performance and practices in terms of environmental protection, social responsibility and internal governance. The concept of ESG goes beyond traditional financial metrics to incorporate a company's long-term sustainability and ethical responsibility into its assessment criteria. ESG is critical for investors, companies and the market as a whole. For investors, ESG provides a more comprehensive framework for assessing a company's long-term value and risk, especially in the face of global challenges such as climate change and social inequality. At the same time, companies can improve their market competitiveness, attract responsible investment and contribute to long-term financial performance through active ESG practices. For the market as a whole, emphasizing ESG standards encourages more sustainable and ethical business practices and contributes to a more robust and transparent economic system.

Research in recent years has provided insights in the area of ESG investing, particularly on how investor attitudes toward ESG affect expectations about company performance and investment returns. Researchers have found that investors' views on ESG investing depend heavily on their personal beliefs and values, and that their ESG beliefs significantly drive their portfolio allocations. On the one hand, some investors tend to increase the proportion of ESG investments in their portfolios due to a high level of concern about ESG-related issues, such as climate change. On the other hand, those investors who lack specific ESG beliefs may be conservative about the performance of their ESG investments, anticipating that these investments may not achieve market average returns [10]. While companies with high ESG ratings may benefit from a reduced cost of capital and positive investor preferences, these factors may also lead to lower expected returns for investors. This suggests that investors may face a trade-off between financial returns and social responsibility when choosing ESG investments [11]. This reflects the market's uncertain perception of the risks of ESG investments, as well as the lower expected returns that may result from highly rated ESG stocks due to their popularity. Of course, there are also studies that show a rising value assessment of ESG investments by investors. By analyzing investors' valuations of ESG-oriented index funds, the study reveals their preference for both the financial and non-financial benefits of ESG, and investors' willingness to pay higher fees for ESG funds, reflecting their recognition of the long-term value of ESGs and their high expectations of their financial and non-financial benefits. At the same time, this increase in valuation over time shows investors' growing interest in ESG [12]. Laura Starks et al. show that long-term investors prefer companies with high ESG ratings compared to short-term investors, which further emphasizes the fact that long-term investors place particular value on a company's ESG performance. The fact that these investors tend to choose companies with strong ESG ratings suggests that they believe that these companies are able to create more value over the long term [11].

In modern financial markets, ESG factors are having an increasingly significant impact on investor expectations, which directly influences market dynamics. The rise of ESG has changed the way investors assess the value and potential risks of companies, which in turn has had a profound effect on market performance. First, elevated ESG ratings are often viewed as an indicator of a company's long-term sustainability, triggering positive investor expectations about the future performance of these companies. For example, companies with high ESG ratings typically attract more investors who are looking for long-term investments and are socially responsible due to their sustainable and responsible business practices. These investors tend to perceive high ESG-rated companies as delivering stable returns and reduced risk over the long term [12]. However, such positive expectations do not come without a price. High investor expectations for ESG investments may lead to higher market valuations for these stocks, which in turn reduces expected future returns. Investors' enthusiasm for ESG investments may have pushed up the prices of the underlying stocks, but this has also increased the cost of investing in these stocks, which may lead to lower returns in the long run [10]. In addition, investors' willingness to pay higher fees for ESG funds suggests that they expect higher total returns from ESG investments before fees. This phenomenon reflects investors' confidence in the long-term value-creating potential of ESG investments, despite the presence of possible lower returns in the short term [13]. The popularity of ESG investments has also sparked a discussion about overall market trends. Long-term investors are more inclined to invest in companies with high ESG ratings and show more patience in the face of short-term market volatility [11]. This trend suggests that the market is increasingly recognizing ESG as an important factor in assessing the long-term value and risk of a company. ESG factors affect market performance by influencing investor expectations and, in turn, market performance. This impact is reflected not only in share prices and trading volumes, but also in investors' assessment of a company's long-term performance and risk management capabilities. As ESG becomes increasingly important in investment decisions, so does the market's focus on sustainable and responsible business practices.

5 Conclusion

This paper provides a comprehensive analysis of three core factors that influence investor expectations: company announcements, market seasonality and environment, and social and corporate governance (ESG). It finds that these factors play a key role in shaping investor behavior and market performance. Corporate announcements provide key market information, market seasonality reveals expected cyclical changes, and ESG factors reflect investors' concerns about sustainability and ethical responsibility. However, there are limitations to this study, especially in considering other factors that influence investor expectations, such as macroeconomic indicators, political events, and technological innovations. In addition, the analysis in this paper is mainly based on theories and existing literature studies, which may lack an in-depth examination of real-time market data and recent trends.

Future research should focus on exploring a wider range of influencing factors, including changes in the global economic environment, policy adjustments and technological advances. Analytics using big data and artificial intelligence technologies could provide new perspectives for understanding the impact of these factors on the market. In addition, studying how different types of investors react to these factors and how these reactions manifest themselves in different market environments is an important direction for future research. These efforts will contribute to a deeper understanding of the complex mechanisms that influence investor expectations and provide market participants with more precise guidance and strategies in the dynamically changing financial markets.

References

1. N. Karampatsas, S. Malekpour, A. Mason, C. P. Mavis, EFM, 29, 953–986 (2022).
2. R. Ganesh, A. Safeeda, and K. Issac, TBEM, 13, 4573-45382 (2022).
3. D. Hirshleifer, D. Jiang, Y. Meng, JFE, 137, 272–295 (2020).
4. X. Yan, Empirical Study on Factors Influencing Investor Expectations in China's Stock Market, Xi'an University of Technology (2018).
5. M. Zhao, X. Xu, and T. Li, JMSC, 25(10), 57-75, (2022).
6. H. Zhang, Z. Hu, and Y. Wang, SMH, (01), 71-79 (2021).
7. D. F. Vamossy, JBEF, 30, 100474 (2021).
8. T. Feldman, A. Jung, JAI, 20, 65–75 (2017).
9. J. Zhang, The “11.11” phenomenon in China, Massachusetts Institute of Technology (2016).
10. S. Giglio, et al., Four facts about ESG beliefs and investor portfolios, NBER (2023).
11. L. T. Starks, P. Venkat, and Q. Zhu, Corporate ESG Profiles and Investor Horizons, SSRN (2017).
12. B. Cornell, EFM, 27, 12–19 (2020).
13. M. Baker, M. Egan, S. K. Sarkar, How do investors value ESG? NBER (2022).

Efficiency and Stability in Private Equity Investments: A Comprehensive Analysis of Traditional Financial Models and Strategies

Peixuan Lu[1,*]

[1]School of Business, University of Southampton, Southampton, SO17 1BJ, United Kingdom

Abstract. This paper will discuss Dell's challenges following the acquisition, including the large debt it acquired and the need to innovate continuously in the always-evolving world of technology. Research delivers an array of tactical and financial solutions. One aspect of the strategy to tackle Dell's financial stumbling block could incorporate debt restructuring, equity financing, cost cutting, targeted growth initiatives, pro-active innovation and agility strategies such as capital investments in research and development, efforts to diversify products, and the enactment of strategic partnership agreements will result in what it will be the best outcome for growth. According to this research, there are holistic solutions, but it does not deny the restricted value of these proposed solutions based on theoretical notions and industry-wide generalizations. Application of these solutions should consider the market dynamism, relevant internal organizational characteristics, or even unforeseen macroeconomic events that might strike once the solutions are implemented. Thus, it is extremely important that companies use integrated financial management and strategic positioning as a driving force for business. Many of these tech companies face the same challenges, and, as the industry has proved to be highly volatile, there is a certain amount of risk every time strategic decisions are made.

1 Introduction

Due to its immense popularity, private equity has emerged as a critical financial player on a global scale, reaching the monumental $900 billion in total assets under management by the year 2020 – with so much wealth under its awe, private equity is more relevant to the economy than ever. Nowadays, pre-IPOs retain a powerful business draw in society, serving as an attractive funding source for a company that demands the necessary resources to scale and/or innovate adequately in today's most challenging and competitive entrepreneurial climate. The introduction of why people care about private equity is hardly coincidental. Traditional financing models witness their inefficiency and ineffectiveness when imposed on today's dynamic, erratic, and unstable markets – their lack of flexibility and movement capabilities are a severe regulatory burden.

The efficiency and stability of private equity investments and the various debatable facets of the field to traditional financial models and strategies are areas rife for research. By examining conventional wisdom regarding finance as well as the numerous papers that scientists have dedicated to private equity investments, this study can hope to ascertain certain aspects of modern finance never before considered. One noteworthy recent study regarding private equity investments was conducted by Axelson, Jenkinson, Stromberg, and Weisbach titled "Borrow Cheap, Buy High? The Determinants of Leverage and Pricing in Buyouts." The authors analyze how the market environments affect the structuring of leveraged buyouts and find remarkable correlations with credit market conditions, buyout pricing, and debt levels [1].

Kaplan & Stromberg's comprehensive study, "Leveraged Buyouts and Private Equity," offers an insightful examination of how effective boards of companies backed by private equity are. Researchers determined that firms backed by private equity tend to boast more active, efficient boards, which add operational stability [2].

Phalippou & Gottschalg's article "Risk and Return in Private Equity" details the risk-return trade-off of investing in private equity. While such investments may offer higher potential returns than traditional portfolio investments, the risks involved with private equity investment tend to be considerably greater [3].

Harris, Jenkinson & Kaplan's research "Private Equity Performance: What Do We Know?" compares private and public equity performances and concludes that private investments generally outshone public ones in performance terms [4].

Braun, Jenkinson & Stoff's paper entitled "How Persistent is Private Equity Performance: Evidence from Deal-Level Data" extensively examines how long-lasting

* Corresponding author: pl4g22@soton.ac.uk

superior private equity performance tends to remain [5]. They found that top-performing private equity firms tend to repeat strong performance across subsequent deals.

This collection of work establishes a large piece of research and reveals the positive aspects Private Equity investments have in comparison to the traditional financial models or strategies focusing on efficiency and stability by assessing the material recent literature in the past. In the recent literature, the research about Private Equity investments compared to traditional financial models or strategies focuses mainly on comparing the performance between Private Equity investments and public equities. The effectiveness of the boards in PE-backed firms has also been discussed as a consideration of private equity investments. Furthermore, these investments' risk and reward trade-offs have also been known. Works by Axelson et al., Kaplan & Stromberg, Phalippou & Gottschalg et al. are mainly focused on these three areas.

Though extensive research exists, there remains relatively limited academic exploration on how market conditions impact pricing and debt levels for leveraged buyouts - an area only briefly discussed by Axelson et al. - or on what drives superior performance among private equity investments [5]. These topics remain relatively underexplored.

Harris et al. and Braun et al. have attempted to fill these gaps to some extent with studies using quantitative measures; however, such methods do not offer an in-depth examination of what drives private equity's outperformance over public equity or its persistence. Additionally, these analyses primarily employ deal-level data that might not accurately depict private equity performance's sustainability over time.

There remains an obvious lacuna in the literature regarding qualitative aspects of private equity performance and consistency as well as market conditions influencing buyout pricing and debt levels, leading to very few scholars exploring them deeply enough for sufficient understanding to be gained of what motivates and influences these phenomena. These fields need unbiased, established, and objective research to solve the problems and learn more about them. To fill these gaps in the literature, the next research will focus on qualitative-based studies in unknown parts of the field.

The study employs an analytical and systematic method to explore private equity attributes that have not been fully recognized or explored, such as qualitative aspects of performance consistency and how market forces affect buyout pricing and debt levels.

The research starts with the literature review that contemplates the various tasks written by different authors, both local as well as foreign authors such as Axelson et al., Kaplan & Stromberg, Phalippou & Gottschalg, Harris, et al. and Braun et al. in order to bring a comprehensive understanding in the field of private equity investment. Each author brings value to healthcare investors' decision-making and contributes to the research's aim by clearly showing the gap in the literature that must be filled.

Once the literature review has· identified gaps and weaknesses in the existing research that might obscure bias, primary research questions that will frame the qualitative study will be formulated. These will examine the key features that differentiate high-performing private equity firms, the basis on which high returns are obtained and maintained over time, the factors influencing buyout pricing and debt levels in this context, and the impact of the market conditions on investment opportunities and returns.

This study employs primary data from interviews with industry experts, private equity firm managers, and stakeholders for in-depth qualitative analysis to gain valuable insight into research questions and mechanisms driving these phenomena.

Again, findings from qualitative analyses must be evaluated against prior literature for comparison to ensure an in-depth evaluation and to understand whether they align or diverge with prior studies. This helps validate and ascertain how their results align or diverge with prior studies.

At its conclusion, this research summarized its key findings and provided recommendations for future studies that add to existing knowledge bases while encouraging exploration in these under-explored private equity areas.

2 Case description

Section two of this research article explores private equity dynamics with an in-depth case study on Dell's acquisition by Silver Lake Partners private equity firm, an excellent case for investigating private equity performance mechanisms, consistency, and market conditions influences buyout pricing and debt levels, as well as any possible performance implications of acquisition deals.

Once Dell had ruled the global personal computer market with an iron fist, it started a slow decline in profit and market share a little while back - thanks to a series of self-inflicted errors and an increasingly competitive marketplace. There weren't any surprises as Silver Lake Partners, a big but secretive private equity player, made a success of investment portfolio and business turnarounds with some notable buyouts to their name before buying Dell in 2013 in a widely respected leveraged buyout financed with about $24.4bn of debt finance making it one of the pricier technology buyouts the industry has seen.

Silver Lake Partners' acquisition of Dell provides an interesting case to study various qualitative aspects of private equity's performance, consistency, and market conditions on buyout pricing and debt levels of the leveraged buyout. This paper sees its insight into the leveraged buyout, which will be very helpful in answering a portion of this study's research question regarding buyout pricing and debt levels. After the leveraged buyout was finished by Silver Lake Partners, under their control, several evolutions took place that was designed to fuel Dell's revival and repositioning in the contemporary IT market as it sought to galvanize its status renewal while also ensuring to seize opportunities offered by a shifting technology landscape.

Silver Lake Partners took Dell private in 2006, providing much-needed freedom to pursue radical strategic and operational changes without pressure from quarterly public market performance. This decision marked a new era for Dell; they aimed to transform from a PC manufacturer into a full IT solutions provider.

Silver Lake's acquisition of Dell showcases several aspects of private equity dynamics, especially regarding performance and strategy implementation post-buyout. Smith and Swain explain that leveraged buyouts involve high levels of debt that may produce substantial returns but increase financial risks; such a financing structure was found within Silver Lake's deal, characteristic of leveraged buyouts [6].

Jones and Simmons argue that Silver Lake's success can be traced to its ability to identify undervalued companies and implement strategic and operational improvements, evidenced in Dell's post-acquisition reforms implemented by Silver Lake [7]. Furthermore, Clark and Lee suggest adapting to technological shifts is crucial for company survival, suggesting their initiative of pivoting Dell towards cloud computing and data management was their response to trends changing IT industry dynamics [8].

Under Silver Lake Partners' ownership, Dell has increased its research and development (R&D) budget by 50% and reconfigured its product line to include data storage, networking, and cybersecurity options. Silver Lake Partners says it has also streamlined Dell's operations to reduce costs by consolidating supply chains and improving resource allocation. Since Dell became private, it has improved its operating margin from 7% to 9%. The margin improvements have come from a 25% reduction in costs in some areas of the company - achieved through the smart approach by Dell's management team that is streamlining operations, consolidating its supply chain, and optimizing resource allocation.

Silver Lake Partners successfully orchestrated Dell's entry into the cloud computing market by recognizing consumer shifts toward cloud services. This undertaking proved instrumental in diversifying revenue streams while positioning Dell in a high-growth industry segment.

Dell Technologies now ranks among the world's premier technology solutions providers, servicing consumers and large enterprises alike. Silver Lake Partners' turnaround strategy was widely heralded as one of the most recent and successful private equity engagements.

This case study illustrates how private equity firms can utilize their financial and strategic insight to guide companies toward renewed growth and profitability [9]. Dell's post-acquisition provides ample proof that strategic decisions have an effect on private equity performance and how market conditions influence buyout pricing and debt levels [10].

3 Analysis on the problems

At the core of Silver Lake Partners' acquisition of Dell lies debt financing: Dell was left saddled with approximately a billion in debt as part of a 24.4 billion buyout deal and faced serious risks related to financial dependence due to this high level of borrowing. This analysis highlights this significant factor that put Dell into potentially precarious financial circumstances.

Debt financing primarily fuelled Silver Lake Partners' buyout of Dell that put around $10 billion of debt onto the company's books in a complicated deal as part of a $24.4 billion buyout, a very highly leveraged transaction which increased the company's exposure to the significant financial risks associated with a high level of debt.

By the analysis, this study has identified this factor as considerably contributing to Dell's financial vulnerability. In the post-acquisition period, examining the financial data reveals the extent of the problem, with Dell's Debt-to-Equity ratio increasing dramatically. A higher Debt-to-Equity ratio indicates that a large portion of Dell's capital structure is supported by debt financing. Its operations and plans for growth are highly dependent on borrowed money. This situation exposes Dell to interest rate risks as well as loan repayment obligations.

Worries about Dell also manifest as a falling Interest Coverage Ratio, which is a key test of a firm's financial health and measures its capacity to meet expenses on interest. This ratio, which was already worryingly low before the acquisition, took a massive beating post the acquisition and even started to decline heavily. Dell seemed to be under lot of financial stress as its interest expenses started to creep up due to the massive debt that the company had on its books because of this acquisition.

When looking beyond Dell at other similar LBO deals, high amounts of debt financing are a common theme that many of the firms share. Many companies involved in a leveraged buyout take on too much debt, leading to financial distress or bankruptcy. This is how people's lives get threatened when dealing with leveraged buyouts. Leveraged buyout deals are why companies love to acquire another company with a lot of debt. The method that Michael B. Dell and Silver Lake Partners likely used to finance this acquisition was probably taking loans out against assets of the companies that they acquired from. That is how Sliver Lake Partners typically loans money to acquire companies, like Dell, in this particular deal. Companies like Dell should worry about high levels of indebtedness after this is completed.

Sometimes, private equity firms use a large amount of debt finance to bet on the upside and generate the returns necessary to pay off the debt. Additionally, many private equity firms feel a lot of pressure to deliver strong returns to their investors and decide to resort to debt financing to generate sufficient returns to service the debt and some profits before returning the company's control to its original owners. However, the issue with this is that it is very risky due to the condition of the volatile market.

The Dell case study illustrates how financial risk can be significantly increased and thus impact the organization's Finances; the deal involving Dell has led to the company amassing an enormous amount of debt. Silver Lake Partners have to step in to save the day.

The important lesson that can be learned from this particular instance is carefully managing borrowing levels in leveraged buyout transactions and always carrying out deep and strong risk assessments before remotely considering going ahead with any high-profile deals.

Dell-Silver Lake Partners educates its audience on the risks of LBOs and encourages a well-integrated and balanced approach to structuring these deals that can handle the risk and return correctly.

Dell had encountered challenges in maintaining its competitive advantage and relevance amidst a changing technological landscape prior to its acquisition by Silver Lake Partners. The increased popularity of mobile phones and tablets and the use of cloud computing led to a decrease in consumer demand for Dell products, which threatened their standing in the market and profitability. This, of course, increased the discernible competition to Dell.

Dell's acquisition caused a downfall in global PC sales, according to market research firms and statistics provided by Dell. With a great drop in shipments across the planet in the global PC market, which might have been an honor for Dell cause of reduced market shares, this shows a great deal about the industry to which it belongs.

The inspection details that Dell's PC sector showed a decrease in income before being obtained by Silver Lake Partners. According to their financial statements, Dell's PC products have seen a decrease in revenues. This decrease has been consistent throughout financial statements, which show that Dell is having trouble selling these products, and the problem is severe.

It is frequently a taxing endeavor for a large number of firms that experience comparative constraints to achieve as prompt of an acclimation as many adjacent corporations are typically capable of making. Many companies remain stuck in traditional models and have a difficult time reflecting on branching out into new product lines or markets. Dell is a perfect example of this as their company's progress in the smartphone and tablet markets and the advances in cloud computing are fairly limited.

Dell was penalized because it was not going into the PC industry only. Over the years, Dell obtained a reputation for selling PCs directly to consumers. The direct model was largely popular amongst consumers and, if one must note this, succeeded in boosting Dell to the top. However, this strategy was conceived without the foreknowledge of the transformation in technology, the internet, and the so wide and new wave of online purchasing/selling. The direct model did not serve Dell when the consumers/market moved towards the internet. The primary sticking point is that Dell's market sector was just the industry being hit hardest by this problem, encouraging the turning key.

Something pleasant will not be halted, which is what Apple and Samsung did when they needed to expand their business market to improve their product line, and they have accomplished that. Apple has offered them access to smartphones and tablets, and that preferred standpoint has given them openings. Dell is concerned that they don't have that sort of product to offer.

The failure of Dell in the diversification strategy due to its limited product portfolio was one of the disadvantages that had a big repercussion on its business performance in 2006. Silver Lake Partners then undertook initiatives to expand the range of products that Dell Inc. offered following the takeover. In order to improve their line of products, investment was given into the company's research and development department. Seagate has pushed into the fast-growing areas of data storage, networking, and cybersecurity solutions and positioned itself as a comprehensive IT solution-based provider to enhance its market relevance.

In conclusion, Dell's pre-acquisition pointed out the need to have innovation in order to fulfill the changes in the market rapidly. Companies should try to launch as many products as possible to avoid themselves so that they become reliant on any one segment for business creation and try to be relevant to the market using Dell's experience since IT is rapidly evolving.

4 Suggested solutions to the problems

As was discovered upon further investigation, the main problem revolved around the debt resulting from leveraged buyouts.

There are many ways that Dell can overcome this tough challenge. They can lower some debts and bring in currency, allowing them to be in a better financial condition and a position to remain profitable.

One idea first to be considered is putting in place a debt restructuring for Dell. This process would be modifying existing loan agreements to acquire more practical repayment terms, which cater to extending the repayment schedules, diminishing the interest rate, and, in some cases, even reducing the principal.

The debt restructuring solution in Dell's case will decrease financial pressure in the short run (making payments more manageable), ultimately having a dual impact on the firm: having lesser debt and, on the creditor side, easier to pay.

Another possible resolution would be using equity financing. This would provide Dell with a different way to gain capital. With equity financing, the company can put up shares of the company for sale, resulting in the dilution of current ownership. Afterward, Dell can use the money to pay off debt and reduce its debt-to-equity ratio. With this consequence, potential investors may lean more towards investing in the company due to the fact that the company has less financial risk because of the lower debt-to-equity ratio.

Implementing pricing of the solutions by effects, and operationalities aspects can also be used by Dell. Hence, by eliminating inefficiency, wastage areas and taking the necessary action to eliminate these areas, Dell can reduce operational costs. Ultimately, the profits will be grown and help strengthen the financial standing, hence less dependency on debt financing.

An optimized financial strategy could involve Dell prioritizing its strategic growth initiatives to generate the optimal financial strategies, eliminating inefficiency and wastage areas, and taking the necessary action to eliminate these, which will help Dell reduce operational costs. Hence, the company's ultimate result will be to grow its profitability and help Dell strengthen its financial standing. Also, the company can maintain the debt financing, as reducing debt financing needs to help maintain its financial capability.

Developing an optimized financial strategy would include prioritizing Dell's strategic growth initiatives so as to achieve optimal financial strategies. For example, Dell can reduce operational costs by eliminating inefficiency and waste areas by taking the necessary action; hence, the company's ultimate result will be growth in profitability and help Dell strengthen its financial standing. Also, the company can maintain the debt financing; reducing debt financing needs to help maintain the financial capability.

Complex solutions to the dilemma tend to be impeded by potential barriers and limitations. The accomplishment of debt restructuring is prone to the willingness of Dell's hostile creditors to negotiate new terms. Problematic equity financing to serve as an appropriate fundraising method can subsequently decrease existing shareholders' ownership and potentially lower the share price. Careless management for cost-cutting methods may adversely influence staff morale and efficiency; likewise, emphasizing growth initiatives can blur Dell's primary business if not properly managed.

In order for Dell's strategies to be implemented correctly to reduce the debt, alternatives, and advantages must be planned and executed proficiently to make them more feasible and minimize the risk.

For Dell to effectively manage its high level of debt following its acquisition, it becomes important to implement an effective and thorough strategy, ensuring its long-term growth and sustainability. Dell could consider several alternatives as a part of their comprehensive strategy, which includes utilization of its high level of debt restructuring, sources of equity financing, and cost-cutting measures, along with strategic growth initiatives designed to help mitigate Dell's financial pressure and debt burden, as well as providing Dell the means for future growth.

Dell faces a critical scenario involving two major issues in sustaining its marketability. The rapid technological advancement and intense competition leave Dell with a highly important decision on having the right strategies to react quickly to market trends to build their products and services around it and maintain their competitive edge.

A possible solution in Dell's responses might be increasing the expenditures on research and development (R&D) since it is fundamental to innovation operation. If Dell increases its R&D budget, it can choose different product or service measures to meet its customers' demands. Recruiting more R&D personnel might enable IBM to develop breakthrough technologies and maintain a competitive advantage.

By investing in R&D, Dell has the ability to stimulate its inventiveness in the emerging technology fields of AI, IoT, and cloud computing, giving Dell the ability to yield new profits and gradually escape from the PC market.

Dell uses diversification in a middle amount, therefore decreasing risk. They diversify by putting their products into other markets, such as Data storage, cyber security, and networking solutions. They also diversify by creating a place or product for more people.

Dell needs to utilize its resources better to gain full use of its diversification strategy. This means that Dell needs to use its customer base, market know-how, and experience or knowledge of technology to help the company create new products or services.

Strategic partnerships and collaborations may be attractive to companies such as Dell. For one, it allows them to gain access to particular cutting-edge technologies and/or new geographic markets. Furthermore, the risk and cost of developing new products, processes and/or businesses can be distributed and/or reduced through such a mode of entry by partnering with several different enterprises.

By engaging in strategic partnerships, Dell can gain new insights that will help improve and drive the company forward. Dell's strategic initiatives to assert their wide-ranging impact will require thoughtful and thorough consideration and integration.

Increasing the amount of money that is spent on research and development (R&D) would put Dell in an even greater place as an innovative leader within the technology market, causing it to become further differentiated from its rivals and allowing for the development of new technologies such as disaster recovery/backup or even advanced space-saving compact designs securing Dell as the technology brand to use through increase market share and brand value.

When Dell decides to revise its sources of revenue, it does two main things. First, it is going to reduce its market volatility. It does this by selling more things to its current customer base in addition to its current products. Cross-selling these new products increases sales and also raises its revenue. However, it could not increase its profitability even though it was able to increase revenue.

By cultivating supportive partnerships, Dell can expand its footprint immeasurably in terms of physical global markets and reach new technological footholds. This continuous expansion propels Dell into the enviable position of consistently leading market trends, keeping the company propelled past its foes that continually try to negate its success.

Please be aware that there will be risks to any of these strategies. Increasing R&D expenses may lead to higher costs. Furthermore, Dell has lost time and money if new products do not strike a chord with Dell's customers. By diversifying Dell's product line, its resources may be stretched too thin, causing it to lose focus on its core competencies. Strategic partnerships may lead to a conflict of interest or even cause Dell to rely too heavily on its partner(s).

Though these strategies might help Dell find solutions to its relevant issues in the market, Dell has to plan its implementation strategically. Dell has to balance its R&D efforts along with its cost concerns to execute its diversification without diluting focus or increasing cost, and strategic partnerships should scope because if not planned well ahead, this may lead to complications in the future. By focusing on R & D, Dell can react rapidly to changing market modes, and it also enables them to innovate the offers better than its competitors. By focusing on this, they are addressing the existing issues and positioning Dell better from a sustainable growth point of view. Now, the question is how Dell plans to deploy these approaches to overcome the issues and remain an incumbent in the industry.

5 Conclusion

In conclusion, the above in-depth exploration has illustrated that the complex interactions among financial management and strategic position for Dell in a changing technology environment have posed two major challenges: dealing with a high debt burden and remaining in the increasingly changing technology environment. The findings suggest multiple financial strategies can be implemented to address Dell's first problem simultaneously, e.g., debt restructuring, equity financing and cost-cutting initiatives, and target growth strategy, which can release Dell's financial stress and achieve stability and sustainability, hence decreasing distress chances. Simultaneously, for Dell's second problem, innovation and adaptability are key. Increased R&D investments, product/service diversification, and strategic partnerships with other players worldwide can help Dell follow the market trend and enhance its competitive advantage.

The research differs from previous studies in terms of how much it covers the areas and factors affecting the amount of water being used.

The results of this study indicated a need for an integrated response to these core issues that was not piecemeal. The finding should interest Dell and other technology companies facing similar challenges.

The significance of finding the middle ground of being financially stable but also being strategically flexible in the technology industry has been underscored through this research study.

To thrive in today's quickly advancing technological landscape, it is essential that firms retain healthy budgets within their financial resources. This assessment illustrates how these two seemingly conflicting goals integrate and make businesses perform significantly better.

Although the given article cannot be analyzed deeply overall, the post-acquisition issues, solutions, and limitations are not supported effectively.

These suggestions are based on the principles found in various theories and general industry trends. It is possible, even likely, that the dynamics of the specific market, internal organizational dynamics, or macroeconomic events could make these recommendations useless or counterproductive.

In addition, suggested strategies will need the forethought of implementation and strategic management for the best desirable effect. Debt restructuring might alleviate financial problems. However, it can only be feasible if all debtors agree to negotiate on a new definition when speculations claim the company is in distress. The implementation of R&D/diversification programs can drive creative management and corporate growth but are often costly and risky and need to be carefully managed. In general, this research paper may assist and help guide other high-tech firms encountering post-acquisition problems similar to Dell's. They support the view that effective financial management and strategic positioning approaches should be followed in tackling or avoiding subsequent challenges. Company Strategy plus experiences will always face pros and cons and some uncertainties.

References

1. U. Axelson, T. Jenkinson, P. Strömberg & M. S. Weisbach. The Journal of Finance, **68**(6), 2223-2267 (2013)
2. S. N. Kaplan & P. Strömberg. Journal of Economic Perspectives, **23**(1), 121-146 (2009)
3. L. Phalippou & O. Gottschalg. The Review of Financial Studies, **22**(4), 1747-1776 (2009)
4. R. S. Harris, T. Jenkinson & S. N. Kaplan. The Journal of Finance, **69**(5), 1851-1882 (2014)
5. R. Braun, T. Jenkinson & I. Stoff. Journal of Financial Economics, **123**(2), 273-291 (2017)
6. T. Smith & P. Swain. Journal of Business Finance & Accounting, **43**(5-6), 758-786 (2016)
7. R. A. Jones & L. C. Simmons. Finance Research Letters, 26, 1-8 (2018)
8. J. Clark & H. Lee. Journal of Information Technology, **32**(4), 349-361 (2017)
9. D. T. Robinson. Review of Financial Studies, 21(2), 649-681 (2008)
10. S. N. Kaplan. Journal of Financial Economics, **24**(2), 217-254 (1989)

https://doi.org/10.1051/shsconf/202418801022

A Study on the Inhibitory Effect of Inquiry Letters on the Hollowing out of Shareholders in Non-Punitive Supervision: Taking Nanjing Xinbai Company as an Example

Jingwei Cai[1,*] and *Hanjun* Qiu[2]

[1]Business School, Chengdu University of Technology, Chengdu, 610059, China
[2]International Business Management Department, Fujian Hwa Nan Women's College, Fuzhou, 350108, China

Abstract. The continuous evolution of regulatory methods in the capital market underscores the significance of regulatory inquiries as a primary tool for exchanges. Over the years, the frequency of inquiry letters has risen, demonstrating a growing level of professionalism and detail in questioning. This trend has garnered considerable attention from scholars globally. Recent incidents, particularly involving listed companies facing financial crises, highlight the serious disruption caused by major shareholders hollowing out these firms. Therefore, understanding how regulatory inquiries govern the phenomenon of shareholder hollowing is crucial for enhancing market order and refining regulatory mechanisms. This study focuses on the case of Nanjing Xinbai, analyzing the hollowing-out process of its major shareholders. It investigates the governance mechanisms, inhibitory effects, and economic consequences of regulatory inquiries on such hollowing-out incidents. The case analysis reveals that inquiry letters, by posing questions, alleviate regulatory and public opinion pressure, leveraging intermediary agencies' synergies to deter inappropriate behavior by listed companies. Simultaneously, regulatory inquiries encourage companies to enhance internal controls, safeguarding the interests of small and medium-sized shareholders in the face of potential major shareholder misconduct. The findings underscore the dual role of regulatory inquiries in releasing pressure and prompting positive corporate behavior, while also addressing shortcomings in the inquiry letter mechanism for the benefit of policymakers, investors, and listed companies.

1 Introduction

This article mainly studies how to inhibit the hollowing out behavior of major shareholders of listed companies in corporate governance. In fact, as early as 2001, many exchanges had begun to use annual inquiry letters to assist in the supervision of major listed companies. In 2013, the exchange expanded the scope of inquiry letters and more standardized the application of inquiry letters, increasing the number of questions asked by the inquiry letters on listed companies. At the end of 2014, the Shanghai Stock Exchange began to disclose the status of inquiry letters to listed companies. Therefore, the supervision of inquiry letters was adopted by the Shanghai Stock Exchange as a first-line supervision method. Therefore, when a listed company is suspected of predatory capital operations, capital occupation and other hollowing out situations, the exchange often issues inquiry letters for supervision and monitors and supervises the information disclosure of listed companies. So, does the exchange's hollowing out of major shareholders have a governance effect, and can it inhibit the hollowing out of major shareholders? If supervision is effective, it is worth studying the governance mechanism and economic consequences of exchange inquiry supervision as a front-line supervision method for regulatory authorities.

This article studies the governance of inquiry letter supervision on the hollowing-out behaviour of major shareholders, analyses the regulatory mechanism and economic consequences, discovers the shortcomings of the current inquiry mechanism during the research process, and puts forward suggestions for improvement of exchanges to further improve the supervision of exchange inquiries. Effectiveness is conducive to strengthening the external governance of the hollowing out behaviour of major shareholders of listed companies. At the same time, the case study can present the entire process of inquiry and supervision of the hollowing out of major shareholders, provide rectification reference for listed companies that have received relevant inquiries, and warn listed companies that have not yet experienced problems, so that they can improve the quality of the company's internal control and reduce the risk of being questioned. Hole-out risks and prevent regulatory inquiries due to hollow-out events [1].

2 Related concepts and theoretical basis

* Corresponding author: cai.jingwei@student.zy.cdut.edu.cn

2.1 Related concepts

In corporate governance, the large proportion of company shares held by major shareholders gives them significant influence in the company's decision-making. Major shareholders can both improve corporate governance and may also damage corporate governance. First of all, the interests of major shareholders are closely connected with the interests of the company. They usually do not stand by and just passively enjoy the improvement of the company's performance like some small and medium-sized shareholders. First of all, the interests of major shareholders are closely connected with the interests of the company. They usually do not stand by and just passively enjoy the improvement of the company's performance like some small and medium-sized shareholders. On the contrary, large shareholders are more inclined to actively participate in corporate governance to ensure the healthy development of the company, because this is also crucial to their own interests. Major shareholders usually cannot control the company and have direct cash flow rights at the same time, so they may transfer the company's profits, assets or resources to themselves or related entities by abusing the company's internal resources and related transactions, and may ignore the interests of other shareholders [2].

Some reports pointed out that my country's listed companies have a high degree of equity concentration and imperfect corporate governance mechanisms [3]. The means of hollowing out major shareholders include related transactions, asset transfers, financial engineering, etc., especially parallel transactions implemented through abuse of influence, to transfer company resources to themselves or related parties, and to seek illegal or improper economic benefits. In addition, abnormal dividend distribution methods such as abnormal cash dividends are also one of its methods of hollowing out. Major shareholders usually adopt a variety of means, such as related transactions, false statements and illegal asset transfers, to comprehensively weaken the company's financial strength [4]. The key to studying the complexity of major shareholder hollowing out behaviour lies in a deep understanding, which requires a comprehensive investigation of the company's financial statements, transaction records, related party relationships and other information to grasp the essence [5]. Regulators, investors, and researchers need to work together to detect and respond to this complex hollowing out behaviour.

The risk of major shareholder hollowing out has a profound impact on a company's economic performance, shareholder value and governance. First, by abusing company resources, major shareholders may cause the financial situation to deteriorate and affect the company's economic operations. Secondly, this behaviour directly harms the rights and interests of small shareholders and affects the company's stock price and market value [6]. The hollowing out of major shareholders reveals problems with corporate governance mechanisms, including imperfect supervision mechanisms and opaque information disclosure. In order to mitigate risks, companies need to strengthen internal supervision and ensure the independence and transparency of the governance structure to prevent the hollowing out of major shareholders and improve the level of corporate governance.

Non-punitive supervision is a regulatory method in which regulatory agencies guide and regulate market entities and use preventive means such as information disclosure, self-regulatory organizations, training, etc. to reduce market risks, improve transparency, maintain market order and protect the rights and interests of investors [7]. Compared with traditional punitive regulation, non-punitive regulation emphasizes long-term mechanism construction and provides more flexible and effective regulatory means for the healthy development of the market by stimulating compliance, emphasizing education and win-win cooperation.

Non-punitive regulatory mechanisms include various tools such as inquiry letters, guidance letters and self-regulatory rules. Inquiry letters directly ask questions of listed companies, prompting companies to more proactively disclose information, enhance transparency, and strengthen market supervision. Guidance letters are specific guidance documents issued by regulatory agencies, explaining the details and implementation requirements of regulations and policies, and providing clear guidance to market entities. Self-regulatory rules are formulated independently by industry associations or organizations to standardize industry behaviour, improve governance levels, and strengthen market self-discipline.

These non-punitive regulatory tools work together to build a comprehensive and diverse regulatory system. Among them, the inquiry letter directly interacts with the company, promotes compliance operations and standardizes industry behaviour, and plays a unique and important role.

2.2 The role of inquiry supervision as non-punitive supervision

Inquiry letter supervision is a non-punitive regulatory tool that raises concerns to listed companies through regulatory agencies, prompting companies to proactively disclose information, enhance market transparency, and protect the rights and interests of investors. Its definition and purpose are to guide information disclosure, risk identification, corporate governance supervision and regulatory interaction [8]. Through inquiry letters, regulatory agencies can understand the company's true operating conditions on the basis of prior guidance and prevention, promote active rectification, reduce potential violation risks, achieve positive interaction between supervision and enterprises, and provide a powerful tool for maintaining market order and reducing risks.

Inquiry letter supervision is based on the regulatory agency's ongoing assessment of the operating conditions of listed companies. Once potential violations, opacity, or high-risk situations are discovered, detailed questions will be raised through written inquiry letters. This process includes steps such as identifying issues of concern, asking questions to the company, and the company responding. It emphasizes the interaction and cooperation between supervision and enterprises, prompting companies to actively respond to regulatory concerns, and maintain market transparency and compliance operations [9]. With the gradual advancement of the information disclosure express train of the Shanghai and Shenzhen Stock Exchanges, in addition to disclosing public information such as annual reports and announcements of listed companies, at the end of 2014, the Shenzhen Stock Exchange and the Shanghai Stock Exchange also began to publicly disclose inquiry letters and replies from listed companies to the public. Various inquiry letters from the exchanges differ in terms of letter names, letter characteristics, inquiry matters and inquiry reasons, and the types of inquiry letters from the two major securities exchanges in Shanghai and Shenzhen are also different.

By collecting and sorting the inquiry letters disclosed by the Shanghai and Shenzhen Stock Exchanges, as shown in Table 1, it is found that the inquiry letters issued by the Shanghai Stock Exchange are divided into inquiry letters, major asset restructuring plan review opinion letters, and periodic report information disclosure regulatory inquiry letters. Three categories; the inquiry letters issued by the Shenzhen Stock Exchange are subdivided into seven categories: letters of concern, annual reports/semi-annual reports/non-licensed restructuring, and inquiry letters [10].

Among them, the number of company department letters and regulatory functions is small (only 4), and the number of attention functions is the largest (4628). Once the exchange discovers signs of hollowing out of listed companies when conducting various information reviews, it will initiate inquiries in the corresponding inquiry letters. Therefore, various inquiry letters can be used to supervise the hollowing out behaviour of major shareholders of listed companies.

Table 1. Issuance of inquiry letters from the Shanghai and Shenzhen Stock Exchanges from 2014 to 2020.

	Type	2014	2015	2016	2017	2018	2019	2020	2021	2022
Shenzhen Stock Exchange	letter of concern	0	88	448	388	793	710	1118	1083	748
	Annual report inquiry letter	0	114	188	206	311	447	562	469	179
	Third quarter report inquiry letter	0	0	1	0	0	1	2	7	16
	Semi-annual report inquiry letter	0	25	4	14	55	62	55	74	43
	Licensing Reorganization Inquiry Letter	0	181	297	170	138	100	86	44	30
	Non-licensed restructuring inquiry letter	3	64	67	77	61	46	53	44	29
	Inquiry letter	0	13	34	38	116	155	132	15	7
	Subtotal	3	485	1040	896	1474	1521	2008	1736	1052
Shanghai Stock Exchange	Inquiry letter	0	0	6	195	145	251	148	158	147
	Periodic report post-audit opinion letter	0	0	0	142	145	201	30	38	33
	Review opinion letter for major asset restructuring plan	0	0	0	113	113	94	99	58	55
	Subtotal	0	0	6	450	403	546	277	254	235

Data source: Shanghai and Shenzhen Stock Exchanges

3 Case analysis

Nanjing Xinbai Co., Ltd., founded in 1952, originated from the Nanjing Xinjiekou store of China Department Store Jiangsu Branch. It is the first state-owned department store in Nanjing. It was successfully listed on the Shanghai Stock Exchange in 1993 with stock code 600682. Focusing on the human life cycle, it has developed four core businesses: health care, biomedicine, cord blood stem cell storage and application, and modern business. While maintaining the traditional department store retail business, it will expand diversified businesses.

Nanjing Xinbai's main business income has declined year by year since 2018, and has rebounded slightly in 2021. The operating income in 2020 has dropped by 40.47% compared with 2019. The reason is that, on the one hand, due to the transformation of the traditional retail industry into the large health sector with low turnover and high profits, Nanjing Xinbai's sales profit margin has increased and the overall operating income has decreased year by year. On the other hand, the subsidiary HOFUKI entered bankruptcy proceedings due to poor management and was no longer included in the consolidation scope of financial statements, resulting in a significant decline in operating income. At the same time, the company's net profit has fluctuated greatly in the past six years, reflecting the company's instability in the process of strategic change. Nanjing Xinbai's operating income and profits from 2017 to 2022 are shown in Figure 1.

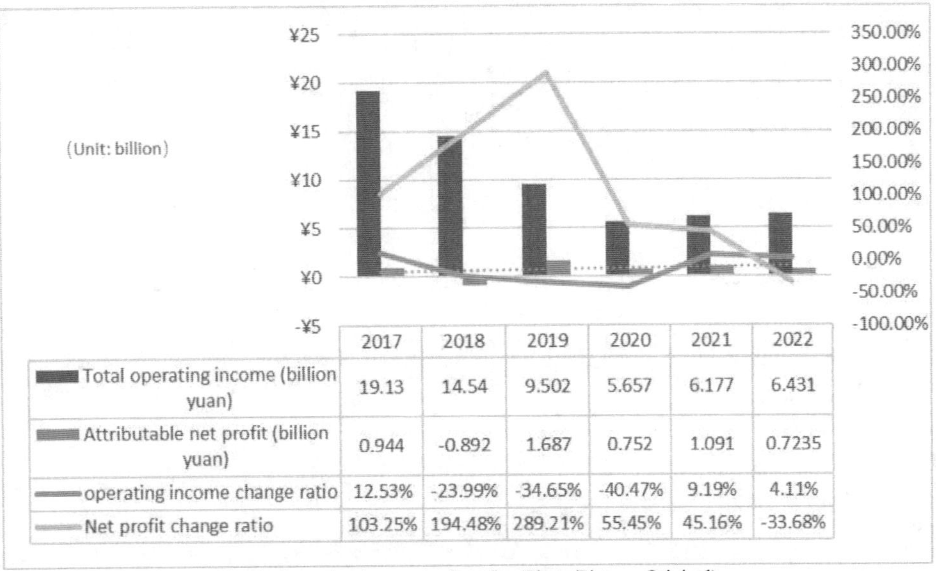

Fig. 1. Operating income and profits (Photo/Picture: Original).

The 2017 annual report of Nanjing Xinjiekou Department Store Co., Ltd. disclosed the non-operating capital occupation by major shareholders. As of December 31, 2017, major shareholders had occupied the funds of the listed company through borrowings and payment of fees. The balances of the occupied funds were RMB 730,000 at the beginning, RMB 335,800 newly incurred, and RMB 21,000 at the end of the period. The highest cumulative occupation during the period was 1.065-million-yuan, accounting for 0.13‰ of net assets. The inquiry letter requires the company to explain whether there are other undisclosed non-operating fund occupations and other related fund transactions, conduct an audit and express opinions.

As of April 29, 2023, the "Special Instructions for Non-operating Fund Occupation of Nanjing Xinbai in 2019" issued by Suya Jincheng Accounting Firm shows that Nanjing Xinbai's non-operating funds occupied by major shareholders in 2019 amounted to 50.2-million-yuan, accounting for 0.38% of the net assets of listed companies. As of December 31, 2022, of the funds raised by Nanjing Xinbai, 226 million yuan was reflected in the book as prepayments, of which 52.99 million yuan of prepayments had been recovered in April 2023. From 2018 to 2022, Nanjing Xinbai Company has been inquired by the exchange many times. The company's annual report involved multiple inquiries, mainly focusing on the occupation of funds by major shareholders, the rationality of the high valuation of the acquisition of Xuzhou Sanpower, and the concealment of related relationships. Capital increase: Whether Hongtu Real Estate will increase funds from major shareholders and the accuracy of information on Nanjing Xinbai Fund Investment Project and other important financial and business matters.

The response to the post-audit inquiry letter of Nanjing Xinbai's 2017 annual report revealed a number of non-operating transactions with Sanpower Group, Mingshan Technology, Hongtu Commercial Management, Hongguo Industrial and other companies, including payment of fees, loans, and lease deposits, warranty deposits, etc., as Table 2 shown.

Table 2. Specific dates, occupation matters and reasons for the occupation of non-operating funds.

Name of the party occupying the funds	The relationship between the occupier and the listed company	Accounting accounts for listed companies	Balance of funds occupied at the beginning of 2017	Cumulative amount of occupation in 2017 (excluding interest)	Cumulative amount of repayment in 2017	Balance of funds occupied at the end of 2017	Causes of occupation	Nature of occupation
Sanpower Group Co., Ltd.	Company controlling shareholder	Other receivables		114,811.20			Payment on behalf of others	Non-business occupation

Jiangsu Mingshan Technology Development Co., Ltd.	Companies controlled by controlling shareholders	Other receivables	730,000.00	3,300.00		3,300.00	Loan and rental deposit 3,300	Non-business occupation
Nanjing Hongtu Business Management Co., Ltd.	Companies controlled by controlling shareholders	Other receivables		200,000.00			loan	Non-business occupation
Hongtusanbao High-tech Co., Ltd.	Companies controlled by controlling shareholders	Other receivables		10,000.00		10,000.00	Warranty deposit	Non-business occupation
Jiangsu Hongtu Property Management Co., Ltd.	Companies controlled by controlling shareholders (transferred in 2017)	Other receivables		7,722.00		7,722.00	Payment on behalf of others	Non-business occupation
Hongguo Industrial Group Co., Ltd.	Companies controlled by relatives of the ultimate controlling party	Other receivables	1,140,000.00	5,847,350.69	6,987,350.69		loan	Non-business transactions
Total			1,870,000.00	6,183,183.89	8,032,161.89	21,022.00		

Data source: Nanjing Xinbai reply letter on June 1, 2018

Nanjing Xinbai Company's response to the inquiry letter for the 2018 annual report pointed out that the company has a major internal control flaw regarding the overseas operating entity HOF. The company should add the following information to the disclosure: (1) Detailed arrangements for borrowings, including time and purpose, amount, repayment situation, exchange rate, etc.; (2) Explain why it is commercially reasonable to continue to provide working capital support after HOF's bankruptcy; (3) What measures the company has taken to address the above major deficiencies.

In the reply to the inquiry letter for Nanjing Xinbai's 2017 annual report, the company detailed the corrective measures taken to address the issues mentioned in the inquiry letter.

(1) The company will solve the problem of small transactions in the next reporting period and ensure timely rectification.

(2) For capital transactions such as lease deposits and warranty deposits, the company promises to promptly recover them after the expiration of the agreement to maintain the normal operation of capital flow.

(3) For the occupation of funds caused by borrowing, the company will implement it in accordance with the agreement, requiring the other party to repay the loan and pay interest on the bank loan in the same period to protect the interests of small and medium-sized investors. The company responded quickly, attached great importance to the problem of non-operating capital occupation, and took practical rectification measures to standardize capital transactions with shareholders and related parties to prevent recurrence.

In the reply to the inquiry letter for Nanjing Xinbai's 2018 annual report, the company has taken a series of corrective measures to deal with the major defects discovered. This includes strengthening the corporate governance layer's understanding of risks, raising the risk prevention awareness of all employees, strengthening information communication between departments, improving internal control systems and management, and adjusting the responsible persons for relevant positions. These measures are designed to effectively solve existing problems and improve the company's overall risk management level. The specific performance of duties is shown in Table 3.

Table 3. Whether the directors appointed by the company can perform their duties normally and their specific performance.

Director	Whether it is appointed by the company	Number of board meetings to attend in 2018	Number of in-person attendance	Communication method participation times	Number of delegated attendances	Start and end date of appointment*
Bu Jiangyong	Yes	4	3	0	0	2018.11.08-present
Xu Fang	Yes	4	4	0	0	2018.11.08-present
Wang Yuzhou	No	4	3	0	1	2017.12.29-present

Wang Tongyan	Yes	1	1	0	0	2018.11.08-present
Zhang Liguo	Yes	0	0	0	0	2019.2.28- present
James Caggiano	Yes	4	4	0	0	2018.11.08-present
Christopher Carr	Yes	4	3	1	0	2018.11.08-present

Data source: Nanjing Xinbai's reply letter on June 26, 2019

During the inquiry letter supervision stage, Nanjing Xinbai Company's performance fluctuated significantly. From 2017 to 2018, the total operating income dropped from 19.13 billion yuan to 14.54 billion yuan, and the attributable net profit dropped from 944 million yuan to -892 million yuan, which may be directly related to the non-operational occupation of funds by the major shareholders revealed in the inquiry letter. During the rectification process, from 2019 to 2020, the total operating income dropped to 5.657 billion yuan, and the attributable net profit fluctuated greatly, ranging from 1.687 billion yuan to 752 million yuan. However, from 2021 to 2022 after the inquiry, total operating income has gradually recovered, reaching 6.177 billion yuan in 2021, an increase of 9.19% over the previous year, and further increased to 6.431 billion yuan in 2022, an increase of 4.11%. In terms of attributable net profit, although there will be a decline in 2022, the overall trend is relatively stable, showing that the company's proactive business adjustment measures are gradually taking effect and performance is gradually stabilizing.

4 Limitations and challenges of supervision of inquiry letters

Although inquiry letter supervision has played a certain role in solving the problem of hollowing out of major shareholders, there are still some limitations and challenges. First, through a case analysis of Nanjing Xinbai Company from 2017 to 2022, it is found that during the inquiry letter supervision stage, the company's performance showed significant fluctuations, especially after the inquiry letter disclosed the non-operating use of funds by major shareholders. This reflects the regulatory role of the inquiry letter. Secondly, during the rectification process of Nanjing Xinbai Company, although the company adopted a series of rectification measures, its performance was still unstable, highlighting the limitations of inquiry letter supervision in guiding the company's long-term standardized operations. Inquiry letters mainly focus on problems that have occurred, and it is difficult to fully predict and prevent risks that may occur in the future, which makes it challenging to govern corporate behavior in the long term.

In order to more effectively prevent the risk of hollowing out by major shareholders, it is recommended to improve supervision methods and the inquiry letter system, including strengthening real-time supervision, introducing advanced technology, improving the transparency of information disclosure, especially related transactions, and clarifying the standards and scope of inquiry letters to ensure comprehensive coverage. Potential risks, promote timely response, improve effectiveness, and streamline regulatory processes to improve effectiveness.

5 Conclusion

Through an in-depth analysis of Nanjing Xinbai Company's performance data from 2017 to 2022, it was found that the company's performance fluctuated significantly during the inquiry letter supervision stage. From 2017 to 2018, the total operating income decreased and the attributable net profit decreased, which may be related to the non-operational occupation of funds by the major shareholders revealed in the inquiry letter. During the rectification process, performance showed instability, but from 2021 to 2022 after the inquiry, total operating income gradually recovered, showing the effectiveness of the company's active business adjustment measures. The conclusion is that the non-operating use of funds by major shareholders has a significant impact on the company's performance, and the supervision of inquiry letters has played a positive role in guiding the company's rectification.

In future research, it can further focus on the improvement of corporate governance mechanisms and innovation of regulatory means, conduct an in-depth exploration of the similarities and differences in the hollowing out of major shareholders in companies of different industries and sizes, and provide specific suggestions. Regarding the restrictions on the supervision of inquiry letters, it is necessary to strengthen supervision standards and the accuracy of inquiry letters to improve the effectiveness of supervision. Future research can also consider cross-national comparisons and study the impact of regulatory systems in different countries on the hollowing out of major shareholders.

Through these prospects, it can be confident that by continuously improving regulatory methods and improving corporate governance levels, it can more effectively prevent the risk of hollowing out by major shareholders and promote the healthy development of the capital market. This will also help provide more research directions and practical experience for future research.

Authors contribution

https://doi.org/10.1051/shsconf/202418801022

All the authors contributed equally and their names were listed in alphabetical order.

References

1. R. Zheng, A governance study on the hollowing out of major shareholders through regulatory inquiries, Chongqing Technology and Business University (2023).
2. S. Lin, Multiple major shareholders, nature of property rights and corporate governance effects, Xiamen University (2021).
3. X. Wang and Z. Zhang, BA(06), 29-32 (2019).
4. J. Jiao, The impact of regulatory inquiries on disguised shareholding reductions by major shareholders, Shanghai University of Finance and Economics (2022).
5. X. Chen and J. Chen, AM, 44(16), 50-56 (2023).
6. Y. Gan and Z. Li, JCUFE(10), 95-110 (2023).
7. Z. Guo and Q. Hu, JSUFE, 35(06), 105-120 (2023).
8. L. Xu, Case Study on the Role of Exchange Inquiries in Supervising Performance Commitment Risks, Jiangxi University of Finance and Economics (2023).
9. K. Wang, Research on the governance and effect of inquiry letter supervision on the hollowing out of major shareholders, Ningxia University (2023).
10. P. Nie and Z. Pan, AER, 34(03), 91-103 (2019).

https://doi.org/10.1051/shsconf/202418801023

A Research on Profit Misappropriation by Controlling Shareholders: Taking ST Zhongzhu as an Example

Yanyi Qiu[1,*], *Qiyue* Yan[2], and *Xinyue* Zhang[3]

[1]Mayfield School, East Sussex, TN20 6PH, United Kingdom
[2]School of Economics and Finance, Jilin University of Finance and Economics, Changchun, 130117, China
[3]College of International Business, Shenyang Normal University, Shenyang, 110034, China

Abstract. This paper selects Zhongzhu Healthcare Holding Co.,Ltd (ST Zhongzhu) as the research object, introduces the means of ST Zhongzhu's controlling shareholders' interest appropriation, studies the factors leading to the behaviour of interest appropriation, and puts forward targeted solution measures. This paper includes the following six parts. The first section is an introduction, combing the related literature and summarizing the background and significance of writing. The third part is the introduction of the case of ST Zhongzhu controlling shareholders encroaching on the interests of listed companies, the controlling shareholders of ST Zhongzhu encroach on the huge interests of listed companies mainly through the appropriation of funds by the related parties and the violation of the provision of guarantees for the related parties, etc., and at the same time elaborates on the negative impacts caused by this behaviour. The fourth part is the reason why the controlling shareholders of ST Zhongzhu's interest encroachment behaviour can be realized. The fifth part is the measures to prevent the controlling shareholders' interest encroachment, and puts forward the countermeasures to solve the encroachment of the company's interests by the controlling shareholders of ST Zhongzhu. The sixth part is the conclusion of this paper. This paper analyses in-depth the current situation of interest encroachment in ST, and puts forward specific measures to solve the problem in view of the contributing factors. Contribute to the corresponding theoretical research.

1 Introduction

The global financial crisis and scandalous events have also highlighted the risk of controlling shareholders' interests being infringed upon, with controlling shareholders' encroachment on the interests of listed companies becoming more and more serious and insidious, with controlling shareholders taking advantage of their controlling position in the company to encroach on the interests of the listed company or other shareholders in an unfair and non-compliant manner, which is usually carried out through the misuse of power and control of resources, resulting in the controlling shareholders gaining illegal economic benefits while the interests of other shareholders are jeopardized. And the emptying means of the major shareholders in the continuous updating, mainly equity pledge, non-fair related transactions, non-operational possession, related guarantees and violation of information disclosure and so on a series of ways [1]. The number of encroachment and the loss of capital market up to the same amount of money, resulting in the lack of stability of China's capital market, the listed company's share price collapse risk is higher, the blow and even destroy the enthusiasm of investors to invest, hindering the healthy development of the capital market, and even induce financial crisis. If the level of corporate governance is low, the controlling shareholders of listed companies use connected transactions to hollow out the company in a very serious situation. It is found through empirical evidence that the proportion of shares held by the first largest shareholder has an inverted U-shaped relationship with the probability of occurrence of connected transactions [2]. This has led to a profound rethinking of corporate governance and regulatory mechanisms. The context of studying this issue requires consideration of multiple factors, such as corporate governance, legal environment, and market mechanism, in order to more comprehensively understand and address the challenge of controlling shareholders' interest infringement. Currently, scholars at home and abroad lack research and analysis of causes and solutions based on typical cases, but mostly focus on empirical analysis of the factors that motivate controlling shareholders to encroach on the interests of the company's behavior.20 On September 12, 2023 ST Zhongzhu Limited announced that the company's de facto controller, Xu Delai, had been arrested on suspicion of the crime of misappropriation of funds. The company and investors suffered significant losses as a result of Xu Delai's violations such as failure to fulfill decision-making procedures and information disclosure obligations in connection with connected transactions, non-operational fund appropriation by

* Corresponding author: yqiu2025@mayfieldgirls.org

controlling shareholders and their affiliates, and significant deficiencies in internal control [3].

The in-depth study of controlling shareholders' interests encroachment problem is to deepen the understanding of corporate governance, market operation and regulations, to study the mechanism of controlling shareholders' interests encroachment problem and the influencing factors, to explore the inherent mechanism as well as the prevention mechanism, to prevent financial statement fraud, to help the financial market healthier and more transparent, to protect the interests of investors, and to improve the quality of listed companies [4]. This paper mainly analyses and researches from the specific analysis of ST Zhongzhu, points out the problems and solutions from all aspects, gives other companies certain inspiration and promotes the long-term development. Internationally, the research on controlling shareholders' interest infringement has made certain progress, covering many aspects from the motivation to the countermeasures. However, there is relatively little research in this field in China, which requires more in-depth excavation and theory construction.

It improves corporate governance, strengthens regulations and systems, warns investors, reveal weaknesses in corporate governance, improves market transparency, promotes sustainable economic development, improves the governance efficiency of listed companies, and maintains the order of the domestic capital market. Based on the research of scholars at home and abroad on this topic, the research in this paper can supplement the relevant theoretical foundation and analyse the research with typical cases. It mainly analyses and researches from the specific analysis of ST Zhongzhu , points out the problems and solutions from all aspects, gives other companies certain inspiration, promotes the long-term development of other companies, and maintains the healthy operation of China's capital market. Internationally, the research on controlling shareholders' interest infringement has made certain progress, covering various aspects from the causes to the countermeasures. However, there is relatively little research in this field in China, which requires more in-depth excavation and theory construction.

2 A case analysis of ST Zhongzhu

2.1 Company description

The basic situation of the company is that the business of ST Zhongzhu Limited mainly involves pharmaceuticals, medical treatment and real estate. Among them, the pharmaceutical aspects of the production and sales of subsidiary Qianjiang Pharmaceutical ophthalmology field of special drugs; medical, medical products are mainly wholly-owned subsidiary of the one medical owned by the field of oncology treatment related products production and sales; real estate business, mainly by the subordinate holding subsidiary for development and sales, mainly residential real estate development. According to ST Zhongzhu disclosed on September 12, the company's actual controller Xu Delai was arrested on August 30 for the crime of misappropriation of funds, approved by Qianjiang City Procuratorate. According to the first financial comb, as of the end of June 2023, the funds occupied by ST Zhongzhu and other related parties of ST Zhongzhu are expected to total 568 million yuan. Among them, 71.09 million yuan of interest, which has been in arrears for five years is still not repaid. And in the first half of this year, the listed company's operating income is only 253 million yuan, net profit loss of 244 million yuan. Xu Delai has almost no shareholding in ST Zhongzhu at present, and the shares of the listed company indirectly held by him through ST Zhongzhu are only 20,000 shares left after several auctions since the beginning of 2020.The shareholding structure of ST Zhongzhu is As of January 2023, the shareholding structure of ST Zhongzhu is as follows: Longland Technology holds 380 million shares of the company, accounting for 19.077% of the total share capital of the company, becoming the largest shareholder of the company. The equity of Longland Technology held by Huang Xinhao and Huang Chao, shareholders of Longland Technology, is entrusted by SZSH on behalf of SZSH.

2.2 Mode of encroachment

There are many ways for controlling shareholders to misappropriated interests, and ST Zhongzhu's irregular misappropriation behaviours are mainly the following three.

The first one is the violation of guarantee, during 2017-2018, ST Zhongzhu provided continuous guarantee for the related parties such as participating shareholders, subsidiaries of participating shareholders and the parent company etc. In April 2018, ST Zhongzhu transgressed the approval procedure and deposited RMB50 million into the designated bank account to provide performance guarantee and deposit for the gap make-up agreement between ST Zhongzhu and Zheshang Bank specifically for the capital management plan. This guarantee remained unreleased and without a predetermined term until the end of 2019, resulting in ST Zhongzhu's 50 mln funds always being restricted.

Table 1. 2018-2019 Statement of Violation of Guarantees for Related Parties by ST Zhongzhu .

*The following data content is taken from the 2019 Annual Report of Central Pearl Healthcare.

Year of disclosure	related party	actual controller	Amount of guarantee (in millions of RMB)	Whether the guarantee was fulfilled during the year
2018	investing as one	Liu Danning	185.9	clogged

2018	Hengqin Zhongzhu Astronergy Medical	Xu Delai	50	clogged
2018	Zhongzhu Group	Xu Delai	50	clogged
2019	One Group, One Jungrun	Liu Danning	20	clogged
2019	investment in a picture frame (e.g. bank)	Liu Yiqing	190	clogged

During the period from January to June 2018, Zhongzhu Medical guaranteed a loan to Qianjiang Zhongzhu, which was guaranteed by Zhongzhu Group, Xu Delai personally and Zhongzhu Medical, and up to 2019, there is still an outstanding loan of RMB 110 million. As the second shareholder of Zhongzhu Medical, One Medical, a subsidiary of One Medical, has also made illegal guarantees for its related parties. During this period, One Medical transferred a total of RMB 185.9 million to the Ping An Bank margin account, which was used as a pledge guarantee for the RMB 175 million loan of One Medical, and it was only until January 23, 2019, that the margin account was formally released from the restricted status (see Table 1). The private use of the RMB 185.9 million was not approved by the company, but was merely the personal behavior of Liu Danning, the majority shareholder of One Group and former legal representative of One Medical [5].

The second is the transfer of illegal related transactions, compared to the direct related party transactions to encroach on the funds of listed companies, Zhongzhu Group's encroachment method is more dazzling, multiple transactions before and after the encroachment of up to 1.258 billion yuan RMB. from January 2019 to May 2019, three grandchildren of Zhongzhu Medical subordinate companies, Spring Dawn Real Estate, Bridgestone Trading, and Chak Hung Co., acquired Henghong Investment in three separate transactions, Zhongzhu Commerce and Trade and Qianhai Shunyaoxiang, whose assets totaled a total of RMB125.8 billion (see Table 2).

Table 2. Zhongzhu Medical Acquisition.

*The following data content is taken from the 2019 Annual Report of Central Pearl Healthcare.

Acquirer	Relationship with Zhongzhu	Subject company	Acquisition target	Purchase price
Spring Dawn Real Estate	wholly owned subsidiary	Heng Hong Investment	Heng Hong Layer Mall	398 million RMB
Bridgestone Trading	wholly owned subsidiary	Zhongzhu Trading	Zhongzhu Trade Center, 1st to 3rd floor shopping mall	313 million RMB
Chak Hung Co.	wholly owned subsidiary	Qianhai Shunyaoxiang	30% Zhongzhu Commercial Shares	630 million RMB

Between January 18 and 23, Chunxiao Real Estate had paid RMB 365 million to HHI, with the transaction completed in seven installments. Another transfer of RMB24 million was made on May 29, totaling RMB389 million. Qiaoshi Trading had transferred RMB200 million and RMB39 million to Zhongzhu Trading on two occasions during the same period of the transaction with Henghong Investment. Zehong transferred RMB250 million to Qianhai Shunyaoxiang on May 22, 2019 for the acquisition and paid RMB380 million to Liaoning Zhongzhu in lieu of Qianhai Shunyaoxiang's equity transfer, by which time Zhongzhu Medical's payment had reached RMB630 million. It was only after the money had been transferred that a public announcement was made to publicize the above three transactions. Such behavior ignored the regulation and was subsequently given a warning by the Hubei Securities Regulatory Bureau.

The third is the problem of funds utilization, in 2016 -2019, this ratio of Zhongzhu Medical is 11.55%, 14.71%, 18.82% and 9.22% respectively (see Figure 1), this ratio of Zhongzhu Medical is too much higher than the average value of the same industry, which indicates that Zhongzhu Medical's capital occupation is very serious, especially in 2018, the capital occupation situation has reached the The highest in recent years, and which is mainly reflected in the occupation of the controlling shareholders and their related parties, the initial principal amount of funds owed by the controlling shareholders and related parties of Zhongzhu Medical was RMB989.437 million, and as of December 31, 2018, the total principal amount of the owed funds and the interest amounted to RMB887.7145 million, and from May 16 to May 29, 2019, Zhongzhu Group and its related parties paid RMB380.34 million through cash repayment of RMB 380.34 million, so the ratio has decreased from 2018, nevertheless, the ratio of Zhongzhu Medical is still much higher than the industry average [6].

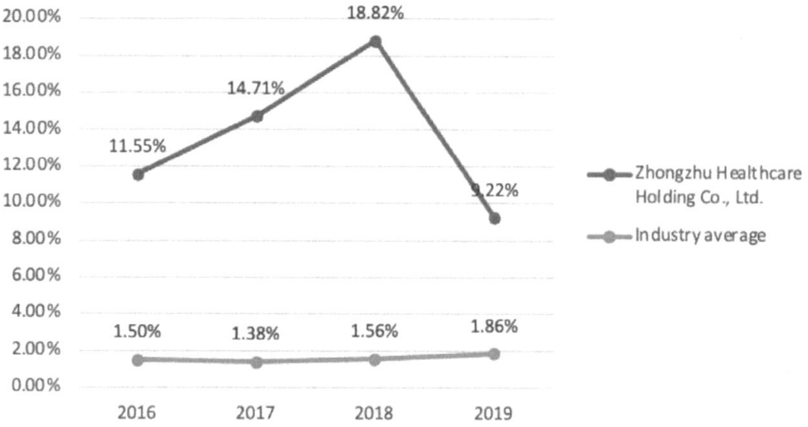

Fig. 1. The Utilization of funds (Photo/Picture credit: Original).

*The above data is from the detailed financial analysis report of Central Pearl Healthcare for 2019.

In February 2018, Zhongzhu Group received RMB50 million of acquisition intention money from Zhongzhu Medical; in addition, Zhongzhu Medical also entrusted a total of RMB300 million of funds to Guangsheng Hengye by way of trust financial management, Tianshui Mechatronics received RMB50 million of commercial promissory notes from Zhongzhu Zhengtai, a wholly-owned subsidiary of Zhongzhu Medical; Zhongzhu Financing, a subsidiary of Zhongzhu Medical, transferred RMB310 million RMB gold to Zhongzhu Building Materials, a subsidiary of the controlling shareholder, by way of finance lease, and ultimately all the funds flowed to Zhongzhu Group. As audited by the accounting firm, at the end of 2017, the net assets of Zhongzhu Medical was RMB614.6 billion, and after the above process of fund borrowing and lending, an additional RMB710 million of occupied funds was added in 2018, accounting for 11.54% of the total assets, which had a serious impact on the normal operation of Zhongzhu Medical's funds (see Table 3).

Table 3. Zhongzhu Healthcare's New Capital Expenditures in 2018.

*The following data content is taken from the 2019 Annual Report of Central Pearl Healthcare.

particular year	occupier	Occupancy pattern	Amount of occupancy (in millions of RMB)	Share of net assets (%)
2018	Guangsheng Hengye, PRC human rights activist	Trust product	300	4.88
	Zhongzhu Building Materials	External financial lease lending	310	5.04
	Tianshui Electromechanical	commercial promissory note	50	0.81
	Zhongzhu Group	Acquisition Deposit	50	0.81
Total			710	11.54

3 Consequences of misappropriation of interests by controlling shareholders

As of the end of June 2023, the funds occupied by Zhongzhu Group and other related parties of ST Zhongzhu are expected to total 568 million yuan. Among them, 71.09 million yuan of interest, which has been in arrears for five years is still not repaid. In the first half of this year, the operating income of the listed company was only 253 million yuan, and the net profit was a loss of 244 million yuan. As the company's audited net profit for the two fiscal years of 2018 and 2019 has been negative for two consecutive years, the total assets of the current period compared with the previous period decreased by 14.93%, and the company's financial situation deteriorated. The Company's shares will be subject to the special treatment of delisting risk warning after the disclosure of the 2019 annual report, as detailed in the Company's annual report disclosed on January 18, 2020, and the Company's financial condition has deteriorated. Announcement of Zhongzhu Medical Holding Company Limited on the Possible Implementation of Delisting Risk Alert on the Company's Shares disclosed on January 18, 2020 The behavior of the Controlling Shareholders may result in the Company being unable to operate and develop normally. As a result of the encroachment of resources, the Company may lack funds for business expansion, research and development of new products or marketing, which may affect its long-term development strategy.

Benefit encroachment may put the Company in financial difficulties and increase operational risks. After suffering from interest encroachment, the Company may adopt short-term operational means to maintain its business, which tends to exacerbate operational instability and increase the Company's operational risk.In 2018, Zhongzhu Medical realized operating revenues of 573 million yuan, a year-on-year decrease of 41.61%, and net profit of approximately -1.894 billion yuan, a year-on-year decrease of 1,219%.

Benefit misappropriation may lead to dilution and impairment of the interests of ordinary shareholders, making the financial position and performance of the company constantly jeopardized. This is a deprivation of legitimate rights and interests for the majority of minority shareholders. Xu Delai has left the position of chairman and president of CZM, but is still the real controller of CZM and its parent company, CZG, making it difficult for small and medium-sized shareholders to play a role in supervision. Xu Delai, as a party acting in concert with shareholders holding more than 5% of the shares, passively reduced his shareholding due to judicial enforcement, failed to fulfill the obligation of pre-disclosure of the reduction of shareholding 15 trading days in advance according to the regulations after receiving notification from the relevant parties, and failed to disclose the reduction of shareholding in a timely manner after it was completed, which was in violation of the relevant regulations. Small and medium-sized shareholders are unable to supervise the forged business because of information asymmetry. Secondly, as the major shareholder has absolute control and the supervisory board has limited supervision over the company's strategic decisions, it will breed the behavior of controlling shareholders' interest appropriation, thus harming the interests of small and medium-sized shareholders. After the investigation issued by the SFC, the share price of Zhongzhu Medical was on a sharp downward trend. According to the disclosure, in April last year, 119 million shares of ST Zhongzhu held by Zhongzhu Group were auctioned by the court at a price of RMB 1.92/share and RMB 230 million. After the auction was completed, Zhongzhu Group's shareholding dropped from 6.009% to 0.001%. After the share price fluctuation, the market value of Zhongzhu Medical has evaporated substantially, which has seriously damaged the interests of small and medium shareholders and investors.

4 Implementation

Through the above research on ST Zhongzhu appropriation means and analysis of financial data, SY Zhongzhu can be through the violation of the guarantee, illegal related transactions transfer and other ways to appropriation of the interests of shareholders, can be from the company's governance structure, improper supervision to analyze the reasons for the realization.

Small and medium-sized shareholders often occupy a very important role in the capital market, and the interests of large and medium-sized shareholders are seriously divergent. In addition to obtaining the legitimate common income, large shareholders are able to manipulate listed companies to transfer the resources of the enterprise to their own enterprises with absolute dominance, thus infringing on the interests of the listed enterprises, while other small-scale investors can only obtain a small portion of the benefits through the value-addedness of the shares or the sale and purchase of shares. Benefits [7]. According to Tonglian Data Datayes, ST Zhongzhu's net attributable profit reached a record level in 2016. However, subsequent data showed that the cumulative balance of funds occupied by the company by the majority shareholder Zhongzhu Group and its related parties reached 500 million in the 2019 annual report. This fund appropriation behavior directly harms the interests of small and medium-sized shareholders.

ST Zhongzhu and its controlling shares have been concerned and penalized by the regulatory authorities for violations of information and disclosure, capital appropriation and other violations. For example, on November 7, 2023, the Hubei Securities Regulatory Bureau announced that on March 9, 2020, the SSE issued the "Disciplinary Decision" showing that, due to the company and its controlling shareholder Zhongzhu Group, the actual controller and the then chairman and general manager of the company Xu Delai, in the areas of information disclosure, standardized operation and other aspects of the duties of the responsible persons in the performance of irregularities in the duties of the company, in accordance with the relevant provisions of Zhongzhu Medical and its controlling shareholder Zhongzhu Group, the actual controller and then chairman of the board of directors and general manager Xu Delai shall be publicly condemned, and publicly determined that the company's actual controller and then chairman of the board of directors and general manager Xu Delai is not suitable to serve as a listed company's directors, supervisors and senior management personnel within 10 years; and the relevant responsible persons shall be notified of the criticism.

On November 16, 2020, because the Company, the controlling shareholder Zhongzhu Group, the actual controller Xu Delai also existed related transactions did not fulfill the decision-making procedures and information disclosure obligations, the controlling shareholder and its related parties non-operational funds occupation, the existence of significant deficiencies in internal control and other irregularities, the relevant responsible persons for the above additional violations of the responsibility of the actual controller, the then chairman and general manager Xu Delai was again to be Public condemnation.

On June 21, 2021, due to untimely information disclosure, the Hubei Supervision Bureau of the SFC decided to take the administrative supervisory measures of issuing warning letters to Zhongzhu Group and its chairman Xu Delai.2021 On September 15, 2021, due to the irregularities in information disclosure and standardized operation, according to the relevant regulations, the SSE issued a public condemnation to ST Zhongzhu, the company's controlling shareholder Zhongzhu Group, the company's de facto controller and then chairman and General Manager Xu Delai, were publicly condemned.

On October 27, 2022, the SSE issued the Decision on Supervisory Warning on Xu Delai.ST Zhongzhu's shareholder Xu Delai, as a party acting in concert with shareholders holding more than 5% of the shares, was given a supervisory warning due to irregularities in information disclosure.ST Zhongzhu and the chairman of the company, among other things, received a warning letter. These irregularities may have provided opportunities for the major shareholders to encroach on the interests of the company and the small and medium-sized shareholders.

The reasons for the realization of the interests of shareholders misappropriated by the majority shareholders of ST Zhongzhu relate to the internal management of the company and the regulatory environment. In order to protect the rights and interests of small and medium-sized shareholders, it is crucial to strengthen the company's internal management and improve the level of corporate governance. At the same time, the regulator should also strengthen the supervision of listed companies to ensure their compliance and maintain the fairness and transparency of the market.

5 Measures to prevent the misappropriation of the interests of controlling shareholders

The problem of controlling shareholders' interests encroachment is a "persistent problem" in China's securities market, in recent years, the Securities and Futures Commission (SFC) has taken a series of supervisory measures, but it still has little effect [8]. The problem of major shareholders encroaching on the interests of minority shareholders needs to be solved both internally and externally. Improving corporate governance is an important part, which involves improving the level of business management and standardized operation of listed companies, and gradually strengthening their internal oversight checks and balances mechanism. Strict implementation of the corporate governance structure and standardization of corporate management practices.

ST Zhongzhu can establish a sound internal control system to ensure standardized and transparent management of the company and reduce management risks and losses. Corporate governance should be sound and the shareholding structure clear. Internal control is an effective means of corporate governance and an important safeguard. It can enhance the level of corporate management, ensure the implementation of corporate management policy, and also help to realize the business objectives [9]. ST Zhongzhu needs to increase the proportion of shares held by major shareholders, optimize the shareholding structure, and prevent minority shareholders from encroaching on interests. At the level of institutional regulation, some specific measures can be taken, such as rationally optimizing the shareholding structure to avoid excessive concentration of shareholding leading to excessive control of the company by the majority shareholders. Reasonably control the power of shareholders and maintain the balance between the interests of the company and the interests of shareholders. ST Zhongzhu Medical can prevent shareholders from misappropriating interests by formulating the articles of association, clarifying the decision-making procedures of the shareholders' meetings, and ensuring that the shareholders' meetings are lawful, just, fair and independent. Enhance the transparency of shareholders' participation and communication, and strengthen the intensity of shareholders' supervision. ST Zhongzhu Medical can enhance shareholders' trust and participation in the company and jointly safeguard the interests of the company by regularly announcing the operating status of the enterprise and relevant information, and maintaining active communication and exchange.

Through enhanced legislative efforts, the Company Law and the Securities Law should be amended to add special provisions restricting the relevant rights of large shareholders and protecting the rights and interests of small and medium-sized shareholders. Finally, the use of economic, legal and administrative means to strengthen external supervision of the behaviour of large shareholders can also be considered.

For the major shareholders themselves, they can also take active action to prevent conflicts of interest from occurring. For example, they can try to control their profit distribution behaviour so that it meets the needs of the company's development while taking care of the interests of minority shareholders.

In general, preventing major shareholders from encroaching on the interests of minority shareholders requires multifaceted efforts, including improvement of corporate governance, optimization of the shareholding structure, enhancement of legislative efforts and self-restraint on the part of major shareholders themselves [10].

6 Conclusion

In recent years, controlling shareholders encroach on the interests of small and medium-sized shareholders of the case occurred frequently, to a certain extent, hindered the sustained and healthy development of the capital market, and harm to investors controlling shareholders encroach on the interests of shareholders mainly through equity pledges, non-fair related transactions, non-operational possession, related guarantees and violation of information disclosure and other ways. Benefit appropriation behaviour will cause bad negative effects, light is to affect the performance and development of enterprises, heavy may directly lead to corporate bankruptcy, stock delisting, at the same time will inevitably increase the risk of the majority of investors will even seriously damage the legitimate rights and interests of enterprises and small and medium-sized investors. This paper takes ST Zhongzhu as an example to carry out the research, for the reasons that ST Zhongzhu's shareholders' interests encroachment can be realized, and puts forward the following suggestions as the company's preventive and improvement measures. Strengthening the role of small and medium-sized shareholders' constraints. Improve the shareholding structure of one-share dominance and limit the over-inflated control rights of Kangde Group and its interference in the allocation of company resources: at the same time, the independence of the company's cash flow rights should be improved. Secondly, improve the awareness of participation of small and medium-sized shareholders. Improve the governance structure of the company. This is done by establishing a mechanism for reviewing and monitoring related-party transactions, improving the screening system for board members, increasing the number of independent directors, improving the composition of the general meeting of shareholders, and improving internal controls. Strengthening external supervision. Measures can be taken to create a transparent, open and accurate information disclosure system to regulate corporate behavior; to strengthen supervision and improve laws and regulations; and to strengthen the supervisory role of external auditing.

Authors contribution

All the authors contributed equally and their names were listed in alphabetical order.

References

1. N. N. Zhang, Research on the Benefit Misappropriation Behavior of Major Shareholders Based on the Protection of Small and Medium-sized Investors, Northeast Agricultural University (2023).
2. G. Lei and S. Shunlin, Zhongnan Univ. Econ. Law, 07 (2007).
3. X. Yang, Property Rights Nature, Equity Structure and Controlling Shareholders' Motivation for Equity Pledge in Listed Companies, Xi'an University of Technology (2023).
4. J. Wang, China Int. Trade, 08, 83-87 (2012).
5. Kingland, Research on Major Shareholders' Hollowing Out Behavior Based on Internal Control, Shanxi University of Finance and Economics (2023).
6. L. Ren and R. Zhang, Business Res., 05, 124-132 (2018).
7. Y. Gan and Z. Li, Fin. Res., 11, 80-94 (2023).
8. L. Li, Research on the problem of interest appropriation by controlling shareholders, Northeast University of Finance and Economics (2020).
9. Y. Qiu, Research on controlling shareholders' interest misappropriation problem and preventive mechanism, Guangzhou University (2023).
10. M. Cha, A case study of interest appropriation by controlling shareholders of Mingli shares, Jilin University (2021).

SHS Web of Conferences **188**, 01024 (2024)
ICDDE 2024
https://doi.org/10.1051/shsconf/202418801024

A Study on the Effectiveness of the Independent Director System on the Governance of Financial Fraud Phenomenon: Taking Kangmei Pharmaceutical as an Example

Yang Xu[1,*]

[1]Business School, Zhejiang Wanli University, Ningbo, 315100, China

Abstract. This paper explores the pervasive challenge of financial fraud in listed companies, emphasizing the vital role of the independent director system in corporate governance and fraud prevention. Beginning with a background overview and theoretical foundation, it assesses the status and significance of independent directors, analyzing factors influencing their involvement in preventing financial fraud. Using Kangmei Pharmaceuticals as a case study, the paper examines the corporate financial fraud methods and relevant risks, focusing on internal governance issues. Emphasis is placed on the independence of independent directors, their relationships with the board and supervisory board, and their impact on Kangmei Pharmaceuticals' governance in the financial fraud context. The study uncovers reasons for perceived failures, concluding with recommendations to enhance independent directors' engagement in corporate governance. This research contributes to understanding financial fraud governance mechanisms, enriching the theory of independent directors, and proposing suggestions to improve the effectiveness of the independent director system.

1 Introduction

With the development of socialism in the new era and the growing maturity of the reform and opening-up policy, China's economic situation is changing day by day, and at the same time, it has also given rise to China's capital market. As the hub of finance, the capital market plays an important role in China's economic development. However, with the further development and expansion of the capital market, a series of problems have arisen. Corporate financial fraud as a capital market "tumour", has been widely concerned by all sectors of society, inflated funds, false disclosure of accounting information and other financial fraud phenomena also come one after another, in order to alleviate or even eliminate financial fraud phenomenon on the financial and economic market harm, has produced a number of new systems and policies, the independent directorship is one of them. The independent director system emerges as a pivotal element among various mechanisms in corporate governance. It assumes a crucial role, serving as a significant strategy to combat corporate financial fraud. The active participation of independent directors in corporate governance is a key means to thwart fraudulent practices within organizations. Therefore, studying the influence of independent directors on the governance of corporate financial fraud holds substantial theoretical and practical significance. This research seeks to unravel the nuanced dynamics surrounding the role of independent directors, acknowledging their importance as a potent force in upholding corporate integrity and preventing financial misconduct. Exploring the involvement of independent directors not only carries profound theoretical implications but also holds practical importance, providing insights that can significantly contribute to enhancing corporate governance practices and fortifying defenses against financial fraud.

Drawing on principles of corporate governance, this paper employs a diverse set of research methodologies, encompassing case studies, literature reviews, and comprehensive analyses, to thoroughly examine the influence of the independent director system on financial fraud within Kangmei Pharmaceutical Co. Initially, the article introduces the research background and significance, organizing relevant literature on the involvement of independent directors in corporate governance. It then elucidates the position and role of independent directors in corporate governance, dissecting their impact on the company's financial misconduct governance. Utilizing Kangmei Pharmaceutical's financial malpractice case as a focal point, the paper meticulously analyzes the methods employed in financial malpractice and the specific influence of Kangmei Pharmaceutical's independent directors on such malpractice.

Subsequently, the study delves into the means and impact of financial fraud, ultimately concluding that independent directors alone cannot resolve the issue of financial fraud within the company. The paper concludes by proposing recommendations to enhance the

* Corresponding author: amy20040323@hhu.edu.cn

independent director system's effectiveness in governing financial fraud. Despite the widespread adoption of the independent director system globally, recent years have witnessed its failure to meet expectations in averting the risk of financial fraud, with such incidents persisting. The opacity of listed companies poses a significant challenge for investors, prompting an exploration of the ultimate impact of the independent director system on financial fraud. This paper concentrates on addressing these issues, examining the role of independent directors and identifying shortcomings in CombiPharma's financial fraud. It concludes by offering judicious enhancements to the independent director system for more effective governance.

2 Literature review and theoretical basis

The integral role of the independent director system in corporate governance is underscored by its significance. In 2022, the Securities and Futures Commission (SFC) issued the Rules for Independent Directors of Listed Companies, followed by the issuance of the Opinions on the Reform of the Independent Director System of Listed Companies by the General Office of the State Council (GOSC) in the subsequent year. These initiatives aimed to bolster the effectiveness of independent directors, enabling them to fulfill their duties and leverage their role to the fullest extent. Despite the introduction of independent directors in China, the existing legal protection framework is deemed insufficient. This deficiency raises concerns about the independence of these directors, sometimes leading them to be labeled as mere figureheads ("vase directors"), posing a significant threat to the rights and interests of small and medium-sized shareholders [1]. The fundamental distinction between independent directors and their counterparts lies in their independence, encompassing functional, legal status, and conceptual independence. Independent directors maintain no business or material affiliations with the company beyond their role as independent directors, and they operate independently of the company's management. Within their designated responsibilities, independent directors possess the authority and obligation to express unbiased opinions that prioritize the company's interests to the fullest extent [2]. Independent directors also use their professional knowledge and social reputations to independently review and make independent judgements on major issues of the company's decision-making and management [3]. In order to eliminate financial fraud scandals in Chinese listed companies, controlling shareholders must be effectively monitored, the independent director system must be improved, and mandatory rules must be enacted through the legislature or regulatory bodies. Through the formulation of regulatory rules and regulations, it is mandatory to increase the number of independent director seats until controlling shareholders or insider managers cannot control the board of directors by any means. The independent director system is an effective system for restraining controlling shareholders from using their control position to make unfavourable behaviours, so it is necessary to supplement and amend the relevant regulations at the legal level, and to enhance the operability of the regulations according to the operation of the independent director system, so that the independent director becomes a clear statutory system, which is able to govern the financial fraud phenomenon in a more effective way [4].

3 The position and role of independent directors in corporate governance

3.1 History of the development of the independent director system in China

With the footsteps of reform and opening up, China's capital market has gradually developed, and in order to meet the needs of modern companies and economic development, corporate governance structure has been mentioned at an academic level, which helps the mutual coordination and unification of company's ownership and operation rights. Financial fraud, as a persistent problem in the capital market, has been regulated by different countries to different degrees, but this has also made the means of financial fraud more covert and changeable, increasing the difficulty of state supervision, while the number of proliferation of the same time remains high. To mitigate the risk of "one-share dominance," the state introduced the independent director system, aiming to prevent the encroachment of small shareholders' rights and interests by dominant large shareholders. Originating in the West, the independent director system holds a crucial role in advancing the governance of listed companies, constituting a vital component of the corporate governance framework. Upon establishment, independent directors were anticipated to play a pivotal role in scrutinizing internal management, curbing corporate misconduct, overseeing equity disputes, and offering professional counsel. Notably, in countries like the United States, Germany, Japan, and Italy, this system not only fosters the growth of local companies but also contributes to the broader economic development. However, while foreign countries have had extensive experience with the independent director system, along with a wealth of practical literature, China's adoption is still in an adaptive phase. Many theories and practices are yet to be perfected, requiring time to align with China's unique national conditions. The ongoing exploration aims to develop an independent director system tailored to the specific needs of China.

3.2 Status and role of independent directors

In 1993, Tsingtao Brewery Co., Ltd. set a precedent for Chinese listed companies by appointing two independent directors when it went public on the Hong Kong Stock Exchange. The status and role of independent directors have become a focal point across various market sectors. Within the capital market, independent directors have effectively addressed gaps in corporate governance, enhancing operational efficiency, and concurrently safeguarding the interests of small and medium-sized investors in corporate governance participation. The introduction of the independent director system has notably ameliorated the internal governance structure of companies.

Examining the Chinese listed companies' independent director system reveals its three main components: legal provisions, departmental rules and regulations, and industry self-regulatory norms. Primarily, the independent director system plays a pivotal role in safeguarding the interests of small and medium-sized investors. It acts as a check and balance on controlling shareholders, overseeing company management, and maintaining the board of directors' independence. This helps limit the powers of major shareholders, protect the interests of smaller shareholders, and enhance overall shareholder value. Independent directors, devoid of ties to the company or specific interest groups, exhibit strong fairness and impartiality, ensuring collective decision-making on the board and mitigating potential "internal control" issues. Furthermore, the independent director system introduces expert independent judgment, with many independent directors possessing extensive knowledge of the financial market. Their multifaceted expertise aids decision-making by providing crucial insights for the company's development. Independent directors contribute valuable suggestions, enabling the board to make informed decisions, expand into new business areas, and formulate long-term plans. Additionally, they collaborate with the company's management to propel business activities forward, elevate the company's reputation, and augment its overall value.

Independent directors can also create tangible value through the use of intangible resources, creating substantial tangible value for the company in terms of general management, trade relations, and industry influence. The ability of the board to fulfil its fiduciary obligations is inextricably linked to a core group of professional and widely regarded independent directors. A company can build up its corporate image by virtue of the reputation of its independent directors, expand its communication channels with other companies by making use of the network of relationships behind the independent directors, and enter into co-operation with companies that can be of mutual benefit and win-win situation, which is of far-reaching significance for the long-term development of the company. Finally, independent directors also contribute a lot in enhancing the professional operation level of listed companies. Enterprises can make scientific decisions without professional knowledge involving the enterprise, relevant policies, laws and other expertise. Independent directors can provide consulting services, use the professional knowledge and independent judgement of independent directors to provide constructive opinions for the development of the company, increase the quality of information obtained by the management, and enhance the scientificity of decision-making while improving the quality of the company's operation.

4 Financial fraud case analysis in Kangmei Pharmaceuticals

4.1 Overview

Established in 1997 by private entrepreneur Ma Xingtian, Kangmei Pharmaceuticals stands as a prominent pharmaceutical enterprise with a primary focus on medicine sales and the integration of traditional Chinese medicinal drinks and medical devices within the private sector. The company boasts a contemporary production base for both Chinese medicine drinks and chemical drugs, contributing significantly to the production of numerous national new drugs, spanning thousands of Chinese medicine drinks and medicines. With offices strategically located across various provinces and cities nationwide, Kangmei Pharmaceuticals has cultivated an extensive marketing network. The company actively collaborates with multiple colleges and universities, playing a key role in spearheading the research and development projects for Chinese medicine drinks in Guangdong Province. This collaborative approach underscores Kangmei Pharmaceuticals' commitment to innovation and its integral role in advancing the pharmaceutical landscape.

Kangmei Pharmaceutical listed on the A-share market, with a wide range of sales business areas and attentive service level, the company's operating income once soared. 2008 quarterly sales revenue of Kangmei Pharmaceuticals increased by 43% year-on-year, earnings per share of 0.08 yuan, the formal implementation of the company's industrial integration. In 2007, the company continued to sales of traditional Chinese medicine tablets as the core business, and gradually to the upstream and downstream of the industrial chain, control of raw materials, Chinese medicine large area resources, the establishment of raw materials, and the development and development of the company's business. Chinese herbal medicine large area resources, the establishment of Chinese medicine logistics port and herbal medicine processing base. 2014 and 2015 Kangmei Pharmaceutical Co., Ltd.'s operating income reached about 16 billion, 18 billion, respectively, and net profit attributable to shareholders of listed companies increased by more than 20% year-on-year, and once in 2018 the market capitalisation exceeded 100 billion, which was favoured and recognised by countless funds. As a benchmark enterprise in China's pharmaceutical industry, its flourishing development trend has also received the attention of the general public, Kangmei's stock as the "white horse stock" in the pharmaceutical industry is sought after by investors from all sides. Until 2019, the Securities and Futures Commission announced the disclosure of the 2016-2018 financial report on the Kangmei Pharmaceuticals there are significant false and other circumstances, and then suspected of accounting information disclosure fraud by the Securities and Futures Commission investigation, the news, the market uproar, the company's share price plummeted.

Next recounts the specific development of the whole incident. On 16 October 2018, Kangmei Pharmaceuticals was exposed as a financial fraud, and the share price of Kangmei Corporation Limited plummeted from 22 yuan to 12 yuan in 10 trading days, with heavy losses.On 28 December, Kangmei Pharmaceuticals Corporation Limited formally received a notification of filing an investigation letter from the China Securities Regulatory Commission (CSRC), and this matter caused an uproar as soon as it came out, and the share price fell from 12 yuan to less than 6 yuan. 30 April 2019, Ma Xingtian director denied financial fraud, claiming that there are 3 billion funds of accounting errors, but the relevant accounting firm Zhengzhong Pearl River held a qualified opinion. After the Securities and Futures Commission (SFC) opened a case for investigation, it found that Kangmei Pharmaceuticals had falsely inflated bank deposits, falsified income, and bought and sold the Company's shares, among other irregularities. The results of the investigation showed that Kangmei Pharmaceuticals has been commencing financial falsification since 2016, and currency fund income falsification, which involves a huge amount of money and is in a bad situation. After a day of suspension, on 21 May, Kangmei applied for a cap, "ST Kangmei" up and down decline, three days later fell below three yuan. 16 August, the SFC issued a penalty notice, found that Kangmei Co., Ltd. and 2016 began financial fraud, money funds and income counterfeiting amount is huge, the situation is bad. 13 May 2020, the Securities and Futures Commission announced a fine of 600,000 yuan on Kangmei Pharmaceuticals, the main responsible persons were also fined and securities market banned and other penalties. and penalties such as securities market debarment; on 12 November of the same year, Guangzhou Intermediate People's Court made a first-instance judgement on the Kangmei Pharmaceutical Special Representative Litigation case, which showed that ST Kangmei assumed a liability of 2.459 billion in damages, four former executives such as Mr. and Mrs. Ma Xingtian assumed a 100% joint and several liability, and thirteen senior executives assumed a joint and several liability, which included five of Kangmei Pharmaceutical's then independent directors.

4.2 Measures of financial fraud of Kangmei Pharmaceuticals

First of all, Kangmei achieved the purpose of financial fraud by inflated monetary funds. since 2010, Kangmei's investment scope has been expanding, on the basis of traditional Chinese medicine segment, expanded to real estate and warehousing logistics and other fields, and has not stopped expanding, which has brought great risks to the cash flow of Kangmei. Kangmei Pharmaceuticals has taken the means of inflating currency funds and bank deposits to whitewash its financial statements and inflate its share price, so as to achieve the purpose of financing. Inflated money funds through bill forgery, financial non-record keeping, false bookkeeping, forgery, falsification of large amount of time deposit certificates or bank statements, with operating income forgery falsification of sales returns and so on.

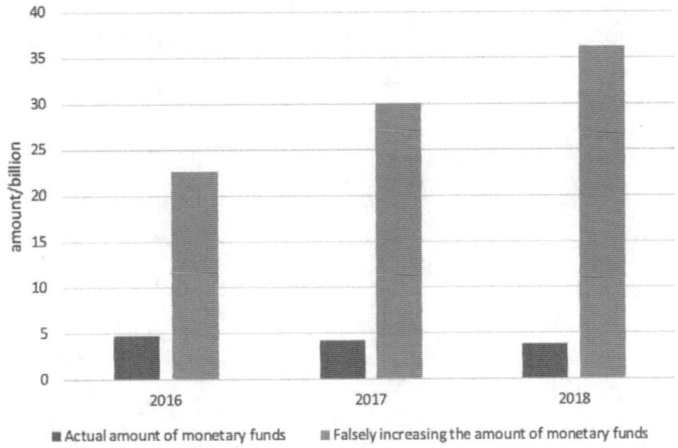

Fig. 1. Comparsion of Kangmei Pharmaceutical's monetary fund correction from 2016-2018 (Picture/Photo Credit: Original).

From Figure 1, the money funds were overstated by 29.944 billion in 2017, the inventory was understated by 19.546 billion, the operating income was overstated by 8.898 billion, the operating cost was overstated by 7.662 billion, the selling expenses were understated by 0.497 billion, and the management expenses were understated by .228 billion , the amount of correction is staggering. At the end of the first half of 2018, the total amount of inflated Kangmei Pharmaceuticals was more than 36 billion, and its inflated amount even reached half of the total assets, far more than the net assets of the company. Secondly, the purpose of cost reduction is falsified by inflating operating income. Kangmei Pharmaceuticals has taken relevant means in operating income by falsifying the data related to the main revenue and cost, i.e., pre-determining the amount of revenue items and delaying the review time of the amount spent, so as to achieve the purpose of inflating revenue and reducing cost.

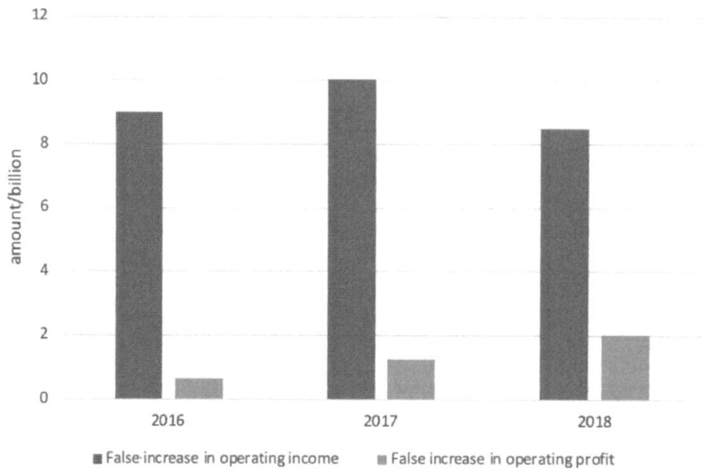

Fig. 2. Kangmei Pharmaceutical Industry's Increase in Operating Revenue after correction (Picture/Photo Credit: Original).

From Figure 2, it can be seen through the icon that Kangmei Pharmaceuticals allegedly inflated its operating income by nearly 29.1 billion, and during the three years from 2016 to 2018, it inflated its profit by about 9, 10 and 8.5 billion respectively, with the inflated profit being higher than 0.1 billion in all cases. furthermore, by using information disclosure falsification, Kangmei Pharmaceuticals failed to disclose the transactions of non-operating funds occupied by shareholders and their related parties in accordance with the regulations. It provided non-operational funds of about 11.6 billion to the controlling party and related parties for speculation, repayment of financing principal and interest, etc. Kangmei Pharmaceuticals also made use of the means of property forgery to deceive records of the company's private inflated fixed assets and investment properties, etc. The incident leads not only to the company itself, but also because of the consequences of the influence of the company, investors may lose trust in the accounting information of other listed companies, which will hinder the good development of the domestic securities market. Various studies have marked that financial fraud incidents have a significant impact on the reputation of the company as well as the reputation of the independent directors and have an impact on the valuation of other companies that are connected to the indicted company through cross-director appointments [5]. Therefore, the financial malpractice case of Kangmei Pharmaceuticals not only damaged the reputation of the company itself, but also disrupted the normal market trading order.

5 Governance mechanism of independent directors on financial fraud of Kangmei Pharmaceuticals

5.1 Independent directors

Table 1. Profile of the Company's Independent Directors.

Gender	Name	Title	Employment period	Professional background	Academic background	Social background
Male	Li Ding'an	Professor	2003-2005 2012-2018	Master of Economics (MSc degree)	School of Business Administration, South China University of Technology	Director, Sino-Swiss CPAs
Male	Zhang Hong	Associate Professor	2006-2012 2014-2018	Post-doctoral fellowship in human resources management	School of Management, Southwest University of Political Science and Law	
Male	Jiang Zhenping		2006-2012 2015-2021			
Male	Guo Chonghui	Professor	2018-2021		PhD in Management Science and Engineering	

https://doi.org/10.1051/shsconf/202418801024

Zhang Ping	male	Associate Professor	2018-2019		School of Business Administration, South China University of Technology	

As can be seen from Table 1, the size of the board of directors before the disclosure of the financial fraud of Kangmei Pharmaceuticals has been maintained at about 9 people all year round, and the independent directors are constant 3 people, the ratio is 1/3. Between 2016 and 2018, five people, namely, Li Ding'an, Zhang Hong, Jiang Zhenping, Guo Chonghui, and Zhang Ping, held the position of independent director of Kangmei Pharmaceuticals.

5.2 Effectiveness of independent directorship on financial fraud governance

According to the independent directors' debriefing report of Kangmei Pharmaceuticals in each year, each independent director has shown that he has fully utilised his experience and knowledge to participate in corporate governance and play a role in scientific decision-making [6]. However, it is worth noting that in the 2016-2018 annual independent director debriefing report shows that no problems have arisen in various matters, while the exposure of financial fraud in 2018, in particular, indicates that the failure to meet the requirements of the "Basic Norms for Internal Control of Enterprises" and related regulations, and the failure to form an effective governance of important financial aspects of the financial report. Kangmei Pharmaceutical's 2018 annual independent director's duty report was signed on 30 April 2019, and at the same time, an announcement on the correction of accounting errors in the previous period was released, and the independent directors also expressed their opinion that the whole process was legal and compliant, and agreed with the correction of accounting errors [7]. However, the investigation results notified by the Securities and Futures Commission (SFC) shortly after on 17 May illustrated the existence of financial fraud in CombiPharma from 2016 to 2018, and these could indicate that the independent directors conferred too much confidence in the implementation of CombiPharma's internal control, and failed to make timely disclosure of the risk of financial fraud. Many studies have found a significant negative correlation between financial fraud and independent directors [8].

The independent directors have also failed to take any action in order to be able to identify financial fraud, which is usually possible by identifying, for example, financial information and business motives, supplemented by big data from the industry, to identify the company's propensity to commit financial fraud.

6 Problems of the independent director system of Kangmei Pharmaceutical

The first is that the independent of independent directors is not complete enough. Kangmei's shareholding structure has an obvious trend of centralisation, and the major shareholders have absolute controlling power, which makes the company's independent director system questioned and unable to play its due role. After investigation, it is found that independent directors of Kangmei are mainly selected by the company's shareholders and management personnel. Only a very few independent directors are elected by other shareholders. This practice not only fails to ensure the independence of the shares of Kangmei Pharmaceuticals, but also fails to meet the needs of the company's long-term development. Therefore, the independent director system of Kangmei is regarded as an empty name by all circles. Despite having the status of independent director, the actual influence is limited and cannot really promote the implementation of the company's management mechanism. Studies have shown that independent directors provide a valuable service to shareholders and that the value of their contribution depends on their independence and may be influenced by the actions of a powerful CEO [9].

Independent directors have only few proposals and voting rights in corporate development matters. Due to the lack of truly independent directors, they are unable to fully perform their monitoring and building functions and do not have a positive impact on the development of the company. Since most independent directors are experts from academia or industry sectors, they value their reputation and social influence more, which may also affect their independence in making decisions and recommendations. Secondly, the risk of execution is not compatible with the remuneration. Independent directors face many challenges in performing their duties, but boards do not give them adequate protection. There are many scruples when independent directors exercise their duties, which makes it difficult for them to perform decision-making and monitoring tasks from an objective perspective [10]. There is no direct link between independent directors and the financial interests of the company, but in order for them to do their job better, the company will link the compensation of independent directors to their performance in order to motivate independent directors from providing developmental advice and monitoring. Despite their heavy responsibilities, independent directors must also face great risks, so their rewards are often not proportional to the risks they take. Only by resolving the interrelationship between risk and remuneration that exists in the execution of independent directors in Kangmei Pharmaceutical Co. can independent directors better provide quality services to the company. Furthermore, the delineation of responsibilities between independent directors and the supervisory board remains

https://doi.org/10.1051/shsconf/202418801024

ambiguous. The supervisory board system and the independent director system emerge from distinct legal frameworks, shaped by diverse economic, political, and cultural environments. China's adoption of the independent director system without concurrent adjustments to the existing supervisory board system has resulted in a lack of clarity regarding the respective functions of the two entities in the operational dynamics of listed companies. This absence of alignment between the two systems has contributed to challenges in defining their roles and responsibilities within the corporate governance framework.

7 Conclusion

Along with the introduction of the independent director system, the research on the participation of independent directors in corporate governance has been ongoing. The independent director of Kangmei Pharmaceuticals was sentenced to huge joint and several compensations for financial malpractice and triggered the trend of the departure of the independent director as a typical case of the association between independent directors and financial malpractice in recent years has aroused people's heated discussion again and again. Through the case study, this paper draws the following conclusions: firstly, the independent director system can effectively govern the financial fraud phenomenon to a certain extent. However, in the case of Kangmei Pharmaceutical Company, there are problems such as over-concentration of shareholding, failure of the board of directors to supervise the management, and lack of independence of the audit department. These problems have led to the low functionality and lack of independence of the independent director system of CombiPharma, which in turn affects the effectiveness of the governance of financial fraud.

Through the case study, this paper draws the following conclusions: firstly, the independence of independent directors should be improved and a series of measures can be taken. For example, the selection and appointment procedures of independent directors should be strengthened to ensure their independence and professionalism; effective communication channels between independent directors and the company's management should be established to enable them to exercise their supervisory duties independently; and clear exit regulations should be formulated to prevent independent directors from being interfered with or manipulated. Secondly, to improve and perfect the incentive and restraint mechanism, we can consider introducing equity incentive plans to make independent directors conform to the interests of the company. Independent directors manipulate their option grants like company executives, who use backdating pricing, early announcement and circumvention techniques to increase the value of their options. Techniques such as backdating pricing have resulted in significant profits for independent directors. In a typical year, approximately 20% of independent directors exhibit significant distractions, manifesting in reduced meeting attendance, decreased stock trading activity, and a higher frequency of board resignations. These signs indicate diminished firm-specific knowledge and a lower level of commitment to board responsibilities. Companies with a higher proportion of distracted independent directors tend to experience lower valuation and operating performance, coupled with weaknesses in M&A profitability and accounting quality. To enhance the effectiveness of the independent director system, it is recommended to bolster the reputation incentive mechanism. This involves implementing a reputation assessment mechanism and a preferential recommendation system for independent directors, aligning their personal reputation with their professional status to strengthen their supervisory role in operating management.

Furthermore, establishing a regular performance evaluation system for independent directors can stimulate motivation and accountability. Lastly, a crucial aspect involves reinforcing a clear functional orientation. This entails delineating the duties and power boundaries of independent directors to ensure their effective performance in monitoring and providing advice. In summary, enhancing the independence of independent directors, refining incentive and restraint mechanisms, and reinforcing clear functional orientation can collectively elevate the effectiveness of the independent director system, contributing to better management of financial fraud occurrences.

References

1. X. Cao and S. Huang, JA (24), 3-4 (2013).
2. X. Cao, CNCNS (01), 45-47 (2008).
3. C. Wu, MB (08), 254-255 (2013).
4. D. Pang, LR (05), 98-106 (2007).
5. J. Sun, On the Protection of Small and Medium Shareholders' Rights and Interests under the Introduction of Independent Director System in Listed Companies in China, Ningxia University (2018).
6. B. D. Nguyen and K. M. Nielsen, JFE, 98(3), 550-567 (2010).
7. R. W. Masulis and E. J. Zhang, JFE, 132(3), 226-256 (2019).
8. J. N. Gordon, SLR (59), 1465 (2006).
9. S. B. Avci, C. A. Schipani, and H. N. Seyhun, ILJ (93), 757 (2018).
10. E. M. Fich and A. Shivdasani, JFE, 86(2), 306-336 (2007).

An Analysis of IPO Motivation and Effects of New Chinese Tea Brands: Taking NAYUKI Tea as an Example

Mingzhen Shi[1,*]

[1]Western Michigan Institute, Guizhou University of Finance and Economics, Guiyang, 550004, China

Abstract. The Initial Public Offering (IPO) listing of emerging Chinese tea brands in Hong Kong has captured widespread attention in current social discourse. Amidst the swift evolution of the tea brand industry and the advent of innovative Chinese tea offerings, the competitive landscape is witnessing a surge, prompting numerous brands to opt for Hong Kong IPOs as a strategic move to "breakthrough the siege." Focusing on NAYUKI Tea as the subject of investigation, this paper delves into the rationale behind NAYUKI Tea's IPO within the context of the tea brand market. It meticulously examines the financial and non-financial transformations both preceding and succeeding its IPO. The analysis reveals an enhancement in NAYUKI Tea's financial operations post-IPO, although formidable challenges persist in the capital market. Building on these findings, the paper consolidates insights into NAYUKI Tea's IPO journey, offering a comprehensive overview of its experiences, coupled with anticipations and prospects for the future of the tea industry.

1 Introduction

Since 2018, the Hong Kong Stock Exchange announced new rules to make Hong Kong Initial Public Offering (IPO) a boom, and many company founders have chosen to IPO in Hong Kong. At the same time, IPO in Hong Kong can also connect the mainland market with foreign markets, and promote enterprises to expand international business so as to better develop [1]. At the same time, the company under the IPO registration system has better performance in financial performance, corporate governance, information disclosure and other aspects than that under the approval system. Meanwhile, the higher reputation of the investment bank in the aspects of financial performance and investment before the listing of the company, the higher the IPO efficiency [2]. In terms of registration system regulation, after the regulatory reform survey found under the registration system regulators penalties for listed companies, especially in the disclosure of violations [3]. It illustrates the through strengthening supervision IPO violations number decline, improve the efficiency of the registration system of market regulation [4]. To a certain extent, standardize the market order, so as to promote the enterprise under the high regulation strictly regulate their own development, but also for unlisted companies IPO to build a good environment [2].

With the rapid development of the new Chinese tea beverage, Emphasizing the integration of Chinese tea with fresh fruit and milk, Loved by young people today, China's new Chinese style tea industry consumption is in a period of rapid development, Various new Chinese tea brands emerge in endlessly, Make the "inner roll" situation of tea brands increasingly intensified, Various brands not only innovate in their products, also jointly cooperate with the cross-border well-known brand like Anime and movie accessories to attract more people to buy their milk tea so that improve the market competitiveness of the products, Strengthening the market competition in the tea brand industry, select an IPO to "break through", by using the IPO listing in Hong Kong to better help companies raise funds to improve their development goals and plans, to enhance the competitiveness of the brand itself, stand out in the new Chinese tea market with serious homogenization competition [1, 3].

This paper mainly focuses on the case analysis of NAYUKI Tea. As the "first" new tea, and the first IPO of a new Chinese tea brand, the paper analyzes the early stage and later stage of IPO, and further clarifies the IPO strategy of NAYUKI Tea [5]. These strategies can also provide reference for other new Chinese tea brands. The main purpose is to explore the significance of capital entering the new Chinese tea market for tea brands, as well as suggestions for other new Chinese tea brands to go to Hong Kong IPO and future development expectations [3, 6].

2 Analysis of the brand development status of NAYUKI Tea before IPO

2.1 NAYUKI Tea

NAYUKI Tea was founded in 2015 by Peng Xin and Zhao Lin couple. "NAYUKI" is Peng Xin's online name,

* Corresponding author: mtz2766@wmich.edu

so it is named NAYUKI Tea. Before the IPO, Peng Xin and Zhao Lin held 67.04% of the shares through Lin Xin Holdings. From the shareholding structure chart,NAYUKI Tea is a "husband and wife" enterprise. Among them, Tiantu Capital holds 13.04%, SGC Capital with ShenZhen SASAC 3.32%, Honghui Capital 0.85%, PAG 6.22%, and Yongle Gao 0.87% [4].

Founded in 2021 in the form of "tea + soft bread", with young people aged 20-35 as the main customer group, it insists on changing the tea base for 4 hours, and the soft bread does not stay overnight. As of May 11,2023, the number of tea stores in China has reached 1158, all of which are directly operated stores and franchise is not accepted.

2.2 Financial analysis of NAYUKI Tea before IPO

Before the IPO of NAYUKI Tea, it raised funds for four times. The first time was in February 2017, when NAYUKI Tea opened its first round of financing, with Tiantu investing 70 million RMB. In March 2018, Tiantu Investment added NAYUKI Tea A + round of 22 million RMB. After this financing, the valuation of NAYUKI Tea reached 6 billion RMB. In June 2020, it obtained nearly $0.1billion round financing from Shenzhen Venture Capital. After the C round of $0.1billion financing in January 2021, the valuation of NAYUKI Tea was close to $2billion (about 13billionRMB) [6].

According to the study of its IPO financial status and the number of tea stores, NAYUKI Tea launched the "National Urban Development Plan" in December 2017, and expanded its stores to South China, Central China, East China, North China, Southwest China, Southwest China, Northwest China and other regions, with more than 200 direct stores. As of September 30,2020, the number of direct tea stores nationwide has expanded from 200 in 2017 to 422, covering 61 cities in mainland China, as well as the Hong Kong Special Administrative Region and Japan [4]. As of 2017,2018,2019 and the first three quarters of 2020, the number of tea stores in NAYUKI is shown in Figure 1, which in 2019 and the first three quarters of 2020 increased by 172 and 95 stores respectively compared with the previous reporting period. It can be seen that the number of teas in the store is increasing, and the market size is also gradually expanding.

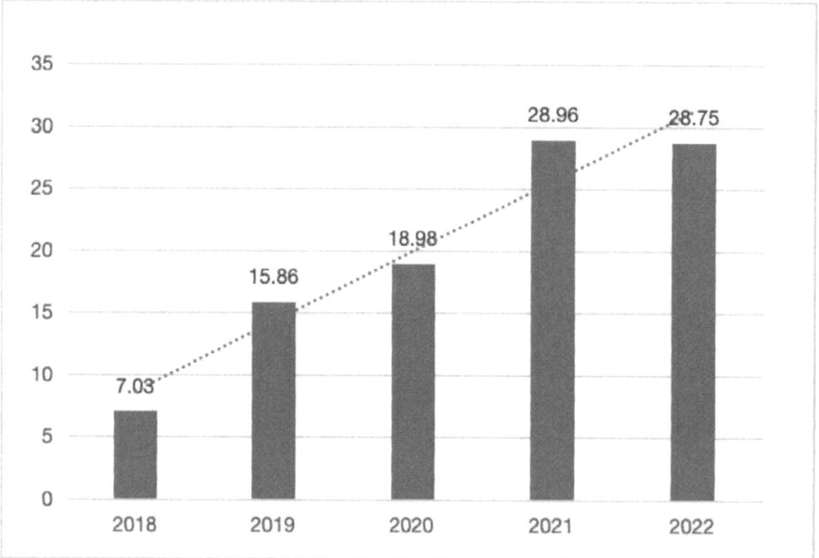

Fig. 1. The number of directly operated stores of NAYUKI Tea in the first three quarters of 2017-2021 (Photo/Picture: Original).

3 Analysis of IPO factors

The main goal of NAYUKI Tea IPO is to raise funds for listing, help enterprises develop better and enhance the market competitiveness of the brand. With the gradual development of tea brands, different new Chinese tea brands and different new Chinese tea products emerge in an endless stream, and the market competitiveness of tea brands is becoming increasingly strong, which makes the development of tea brands extremely unstable. NAYUKI Tea because of its choice stores model, in the market with other tea brand to expand stores, lead to the high investment cost in operating stores, pure straight business mode of operation and joining profit, retail mode store expansion to bring more revenue, but the human cost, raw materials and a series of costs also increase, and join mode can improve profitability with the expansion of stores, human costs will not increase, this lead to NAYUKI Tea debt increased, unable to complete the scheduled shop plan, cash flow is difficult to solve the problem of debt [7]. Before IPO, the tea asset-liability ratio of NAYUKI Tea is compared with the normal asset-liability ratio of enterprises of 30% - 50%, and the tea asset-liability ratio of NAYUKI Tea is high from 2018 to 2020 (see Figure 2).

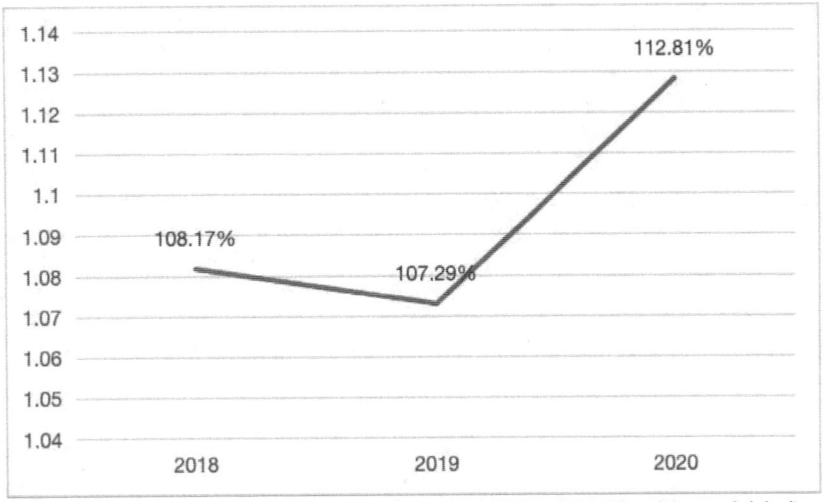

Fig. 2. The tea asset-liability ratio of NAYUKI Tea from 2018 to 2020 (Photo/Picture: Original).

From 2018 to 2020, NAYUKI Tea achieved revenue of 0.91billion RMB, 2.292billionRMB and 2.871billion RMB, respectively, with net losses of 66 million RMB, 39million RMB and 202million RMB, respectively (see Figure 3). This makes NAYUKI Tea to choose the IPO listing to ease its financial debt problems.

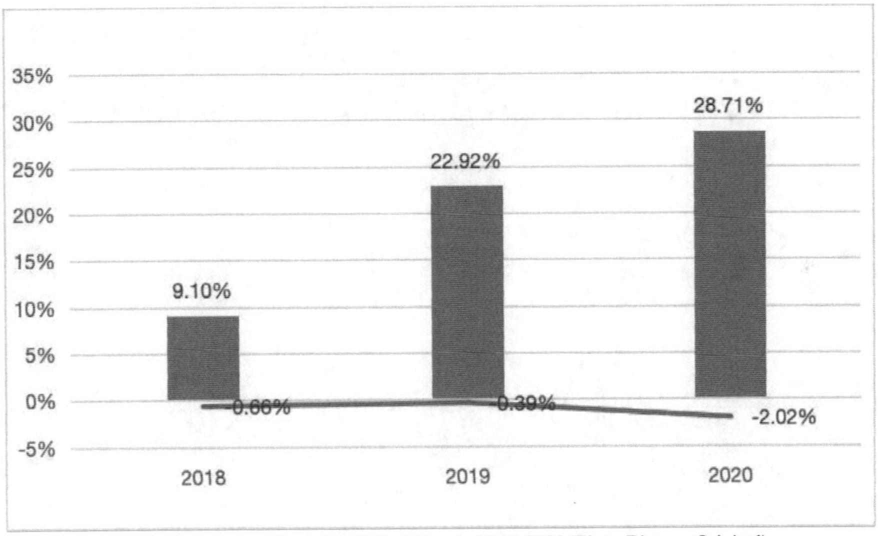

Fig. 3. Revenue and loss of NAYUKI Tea in 2018-2022 (Photo/Picture: Original).

4 Post-IPO performance analysis

4.1 Financial performance analysis

On February 11,2021, NAYUKI Tea formally submitted the listing A1 form to the Hong Kong Stock Exchange and started the listing process, with JPMorgan Chase, China Merchants International and Huatai International as the sponsors. On June 30,2021, NAYUKI Tea, known as "the first" global tea drink ", NAYUKI Tea Holding Co., Ltd. was officially listed on the Hong Kong Stock Exchange. Public offering of 25,726,900 shares, each 500 shares, the total number of public offerings: 51,454 lots, group A group B 25,727 lots. Total IPO net proceeds H K $4.842.4 billion [6].

After the successful IPO of NAYUKI Tea, it did not achieve the expected results. NAYUKI Tea had high hopes before the listing, but the stock price performance after the listing has not been satisfactory. Breaking at the opening, the share price fell in 2022, after which its share price has fluctuated around HK $4-6, well below HK $19.8/share issue price [2, 8]. It shows that the market lacks interest in the new Chinese tea brands, which leads to a serious decline in the stock price and also reflects the challenges in the future development prospects of NAYUKI Tea.

But, from Figure 4, it is possible to intuitively understand the change of the asset-liability ratio before and after the IPO, and the asset-liability ratio of NAYUKI Tea has recovered to the normal level of the enterprise through the IPO. Through the IPO listing, NAYUKI Tea raised a large amount of funds for store expansion and creating new marketing models to enhance product competitiveness, which greatly reduced the asset-liability ratio of NAYUKI Tea after the IPO in 2021.

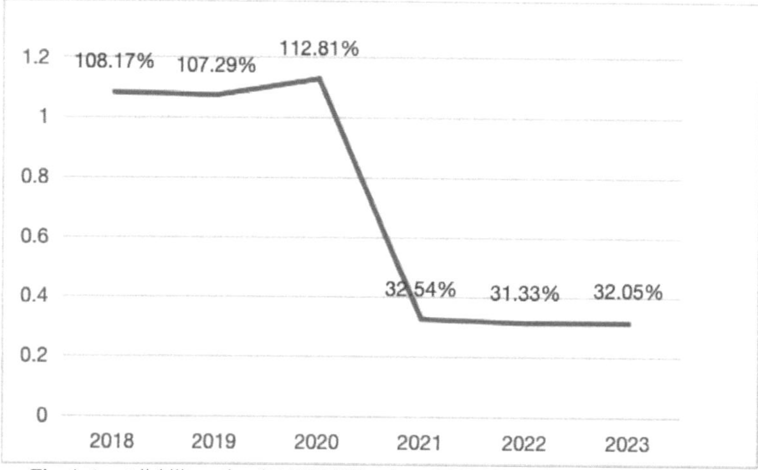

Fig. 4. Asset-liability ratio of NAYUKI Tea from 2020-2023 (Photo/Picture: Original).

It can be seen from Figure 5 that the ROE of NAYUKI Tea at a high level in 2020. Affected by the COVID-19 in 2021, the overall asset liability ratio of enterprise production and consumption at a low level in 2021. However, after the announcement of financing in 2021, and with the improvement of the COVID-19 situation, NAYUKI Tea has developed a new business strategy to create new marketing methods by taking advantage of the upsurge of online goods, so that ROE gradually return to the normal level between 2022 and 2023.

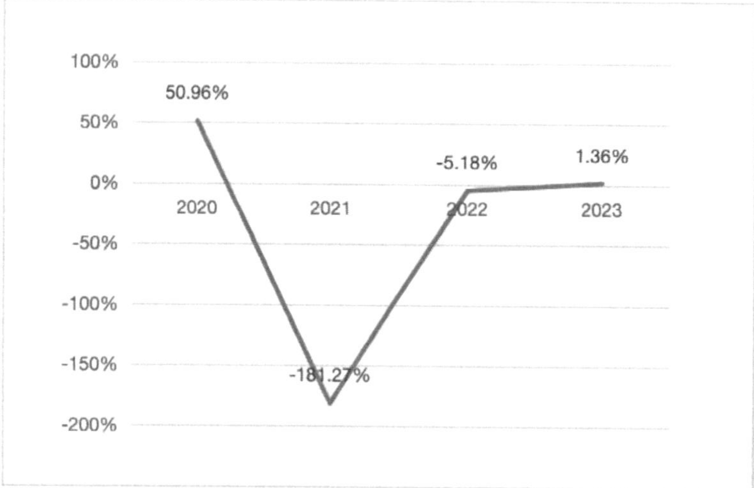

Fig. 5. ROE of NAYUKI Tea from 2020 to 2023 (Photo/Picture: Original).

4.2 Non-financial performance analysis

After the analysis of its post-IPO financial performance, the non-financial analysis was conducted. According to the comparison, there were 155 tea stores in 2018,327 stores in 2019,327 stores in 2020,491 stores, and the number of stores in 2021 and 871 stores in 2022. Figure 6 shows the in 2021 NAYUKI Tea affected by the outbreak, NAYUKI Tea after the listed store expansion number is still on the rise, shows the successful NAYUKI Tea IPO after its financing ability to strengthen, brand awareness, attract more customers, demand, at the same time using capital marketing ideas change, change before shop idea, to reduce costs to open pro store (namely cut store area, etc.) [9].

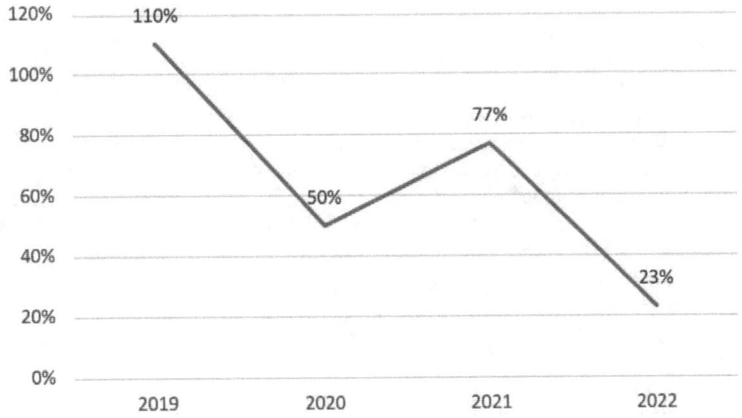

Fig. 6. Store expansion rate of NAYUKI Tea from 2019 to 2022 (Photo/Picture: Original).

Since the tea IPO, NAYUKI Tea reputation and brand influence expanded. For the new Chinese style tea brand, reflecting Chinese characteristics has become another important means to enhance the brand. In 2022, NAYUKI Tea will change its Chinese signature and LOGO from Japanese "NAYUKI" to pinyin "NAYUKI" , change the Japanese elements in the original brand to the "China-fashion label" in line with their own image, NAYUKI Tea follows stricter financial reporting and corporate governance requirements after its IPO, brand awareness in the market, to develop more diversified strategic goals through IPO financing, make NAYUKI Tea won the 2023 China Catering Golden Gourmet Award top 10 most popular tea brands, top row with 82.51 points.

5 Discussion

5.1 Future IPO analysis of other new Chinese tea brands

The tea industry is becoming more and more serious, with the first shot of the tea IPO listing, xi tea, tea hundred, Shanghai aunt, ancient Ming, new brew, Charming Tea and other popular tea brands are also competing to submit applications, ready to market [2]. However, with the slowing down of the growth rate of the scale of tea, the competition pressure of tea has increased. However, only a small number of tea brands such as ChaPanda Tea and Good Me Tea have completed the financing of IPO listing. In order to improve the competitiveness of their products, tea brands have chosen to market [3]. For tea brands, listing can attract more capital, attract more talents, so that enterprises can better develop, improve the competitiveness of enterprises, so as to cope with the increasing competitive pressure of the tea market, but the IPO of tea brands still has a long way to go.

5.2 The future development expectations of the tea industry

As for its future plan, NAYUKI Tea said it plans to open 300 new stores in 2021,2022 and 2022 and 350 stores in 2023. Among them, about 70% of the new stores are NAYUKI Tea PRO store [8]. From this calculation, in three years, NAYUKI Tea stores will reach 1500. In the first half of this year, the revenue of NAYUKI Tea shop was 2.354 billion yuan, up 25.35% year on year.

With the increasingly severe "inner volume" in the tea industry, it is a "big reshuffle" of survival of the fittest to enhance the product competitiveness of tea enterprises, and keeping upright and honest innovation has become a key point in the tea industry [2].

5.3 Suggestions for the development of the tea industry

In terms of tea industry and tea brands, tea brands need to formulate their own enterprise development mode according to their own development mode. NAYUKI Tea belongs to the direct-sale store model, which makes the capital consumed in store expansion far exceed the capital expenditure under the store expansion mode of other brands joining [7]. Second, NAYUKI Tea brand positioning for high-end tea brand, its product raw material cost is relatively high, it also makes its product pricing relative to other tea brand price is higher, so for NAYUKI Tea money plays a vital role for enterprise development, using listed to raise funds can make its brand better development.

Capital intervention in new Chinese style tea brand market will play a role in promoting the development of tea industry, but in the long run, tea brand development or should pay attention to their own enterprise development, carefully choose development path, pay attention to the product itself, reasonable pricing, standardize production, use more healthy raw materials, supply chain resources integration ability. All kinds of tea enterprises can formulate appropriate development strategies according to the development situation of their own enterprises, rather than just choose the road of listing. In the future, tea brands may move towards a more diversified, healthy, green, and enhanced user experience model [10].

https://doi.org/10.1051/shsconf/202418801025

6 Conclusion

From the new tea beverage brand to the Hong Kong IPO and then to the NAYUKI Tea, on the one hand, for new Chinese tea beverage enterprises, from the perspective of financial performance analysis, it is found that using IPO listing can help new Chinese tea beverage brands successfully raise funds, which has a certain promoting effect on breaking through the competition in the tea beverage industry. At the same time, it can also enable enterprises to achieve development goals, innovate development, and help brands find new development models and paths. It can also better enhance the brand effect of the enterprise itself and help the enterprise develop more standardized. However, for the IPO of the tea industry in Hong Kong, the challenge in the capital market is also huge. The homogenization of the tea industry is serious, leading to the lack of motivation for investors and consumers to invest in the new Chinese tea. Tea enterprises also need to choose whether to IPO in Hong Kong according to their own enterprise model. Listing in Hong Kong is not plain sailing, and it also means that enterprises need to face huge listing challenges. With the enhancement of market supervision efficiency of IPO in Hong Kong, the pressure of new Chinese tea industry to IPO in Hong Kong is also greater.

Second, for the tea industry and tea brands, tea brands need to clarify their own development path and formulate their own development model. NAYUKI Tea belongs to the direct store model, which means that the funds required for store expansion and other aspects are much higher than those for other brand franchise store expansion methods [7]. Furthermore, NAYUKI Tea brand is positioned as a high-end tea beverage brand, and its product raw material costs are relatively high, which makes its product pricing relatively high compared to other tea beverage brands. Therefore, for NAYUKI Tea, funds play a crucial role in the development of the enterprise, and using listing to raise funds can help its brand develop better. It shows that different ways of store expansion have both advantages and disadvantages for new Chinese tea brands. On the one hand, enterprises are required to pay attention to market share and revenue rate, and on the other hand, enterprises are required to pay attention to food safety and business environment.

The IPO development of new Chinese tea brands in Hong Kong is facing great challenges, and it is particularly critical to choose a development path suitable for themselves. Chinese modern tea beverage enterprises need to develop in a more standardized manner, pay more attention to the development of the brand itself. Moreover, innovative products, balance market share, revenue, product safety and health issues. Especially pay attention to improving the quality of products, in order to enhance market competitiveness, and striving to build a new type of Chinese tea industry enterprise that is deeper, healthier, more environmentally friendly, and more innovative.

References

1. J. Zhou, Hong Kong stock IPO boom and break, Financial Expo (2023).
2. X. Zhang, JSBS, 24(05), (2023).
3. L. Ren and C. Wu, BWF, (7), (2023).
4. Sina Finance. Cross-strait Tea Industry Exchange Association, NAYUKI Tea went to IPO in Hong Kong, planning to sprint for 'the first share of new tea drinks (2023).
5. J. Zhang, New tea lifts the IPO boom: stores and supply chain 'grasp both hands,' but the crowded track has become a red sea, Blue Whale Finance (2023).
6. Sina Finance. NAYUKI Tea IPO analysis + purchase strategy, this cup of tea, you dare to drink (2021).
7. Node Finance. Behind the IPO of all tea products, the prosperity and bubble of new tea drinks (2023).
8. X. Yi, C. Lu, NAYUKI Tea listed for two years, the market value evaporated 20 billion yuan, Blue Whale Finance (2023).
9. E. Yong, NAYUKI Tea IPO mystery: Why Never Become Starbucks, The Paper (2021).
10. X. Du, S. Lai, J. Weng, and L. Xiao, AM, 44(23), (2023).

SHS Web of Conferences **188**, 01026 (2024) https://doi.org/10.1051/shsconf/202418801026
ICDDE 2024

A Research on Identification and Prevention of Corporate Financial Fraud Behaviour in the Context of High-Performance Commitment: Taking Aerospace Communications' Merger and Acquisition of HiPAD Intelligent as an Example

Yuhan Wang[1,*]

[1]Business School, East China University of Political Science and Law, Shanghai, 201620, China

Abstract. In recent years, there are often high premium acquisitions based on high-performance commitment in corporate mergers and acquisitions. The performance commitment is intended to alleviate the information asymmetry between the two parties of mergers and acquisitions, but the pressure brought by the high-performance commitment often triggers the company's financial fraud behaviour. This paper will use the case study method to select the classic case of Aerospace Communications merger and acquisition of the HiPAD, in-depth analysis of the merged party HiPAD of the financial counterfeiting means, and corresponding to the identification of signs of financial fraud research. This paper analyses the abnormal signs in the public disclosure information of HiPAD from the unique perspectives of financial information identification and non-financial information identification, parent company and subsidiaries, providing a reference direction for the financial fraud identification path. Finally, it puts forward a universal proposal for the prevention of corporate financial fraud in the context of the pressure of the performance commitment, which provides a feasible method for the similar mergers and acquisitions and high-performance commitment cases.

1 Introduction

In the process of mergers and acquisitions (M&A), companies mostly adopt performance commitments to reduce their own losses to avoid valuation differences and agency cost problems caused by information asymmetry between the two parties to the transaction, and to reduce the risk of merger and acquisition premiums and merger and acquisition integration failures [1-3]. However, high premium acquisition is often accompanied by high-performance commitment. In the performance commitment stage, the merged party often implement financial fraud to achieve high-performance commitment to achieve their own interests.

In the merger and acquisition performance bet, if the target company's performance fails to meet the target, the management needs to compensate the merger and acquisition party [4, 5]. The high-performance promise can effectively reduce the risk of information asymmetry, and provide the market with good performance expectations, which helps to enhance the secondary market share price to achieve high cash [6, 7]. Subsequently, due to the short-sighted behavior of the management, the M&A parties may disguise their "high" performance commitments through "financial fraud" [7]. Possible reasons for financial fraud include preventing goodwill impairment of the parent company and share price collapse, in addition to the management's desire to benefit from the achievement of performance targets. If the acquired party fails to meet its performance commitments, it will lead to a significant impairment of the acquirer 's goodwill, which will significantly increase the risk of a share price crash [8]. Financial fraud potential will bring certain financial risk and goodwill impairment risk.

Based on the above theory, this paper will select the classic case, a large state-owned enterprise Aerospace Communications mergers and acquisitions of famous ODM manufacturers, HiPAD Intelligent (HiPAD). In order to achieve the high-performance commitment, HiPAD committed the implementation of financial fraud. Then, the financial fraud scandal led to the parent company of Aerospace Communications into serious financial difficulties and the full amount of its goodwill impairment provision. Although this financial fraud occurred in 2016-2018, this case still has a strong typical reference role, which will be the subject of fraud transferred to its merged and acquired subsidiaries, so as to fictional revenue and profit, the implementation of financial fraud [9].

This paper adopts the case study method to analyse and study the financial fraud of HiPAD under the background of high-performance commitment, and then analyze and study the identification of signs of financial fraud from financial and non-financial information, parent company and subsidiaries, and then put forward

* Corresponding author: 210514010086@ecupl.edu.cn

https://doi.org/10.1051/shsconf/202418801026

the universal financial fraud prevention measures based on the pressure of high-performance commitment. The unique perspective of this case has a revealing effect on the identification of signs of financial fraud in the capital market, especially in the case of mergers and acquisitions under the background of high-performance commitment. When performance is not affected, effective identification and prevention of corporate financial fraud can help to protect the rights and interests of investors and safeguard the healthy development of the market economy.

2 Background of the case

The acquirer, Aerospace Communication Holding Group Company Limited, is a large state-owned enterprise, which was listed and traded on the SSE in 1993. Prior to this case, it had committed financial fraud on three occasions through the fraudulent behaviour of its subsidiaries for the purpose of whitewashing the financial statements of its parent company. The acquired party, HiPAD Intelligent, registered in July 2014, is a high-tech enterprise focusing on the design and manufacture of intelligent terminals.

As shown in Figure 1, Aerospace Communication's non-deductible net profit was negative from 2013 to 2015, and the loss in 2014 and 2015 exceeded 300 million yuan, thus Aerospace Communications planned to merge and acquire HiPAD to reverse the situation of consecutive losses. In December 2015, Aerospace Communications acquired 51% of HiPAD's equity at a high premium. And at the same time, both parties entered into a high-performance wagering agreement, with the subsidiary HiPAD committing to annual earnings need to reach 250 million yuan, 300 million yuan and 320 million yuan respectively. As shown in Figure 2, HiPAD's 2016-2018 annual fake completion number is slightly higher than the number of performance commitments, all accurately implementing the performance commitment. And the completion rate was 116.54%, 103.74% and 109.61%, respectively.

In October 2019, due to Aerospace Communications' largest profitable subsidiary, HiPAD's capital chain broke, and a number of bank loans appeared in early warning, thus self-revealing that its subsidiary, HiPAD, had false performance and other major risk matters. Later, Lixin was hired to re-verify and restate the performance of HiPAD from 2016-2018. As shown in Figure 2, it approved that the actual completion rate of its annual performance was -278.78%, -344.31%, and -780.17%. In the market was depressed and HiPAD's major customers were in crisis, HiPAD's management realized financial falsification to protect its own interests. Subsequently, Aerospace Communications chose to voluntarily delist in January 2021 due to its own mismanagement and disclosure of illegal and illicit information.

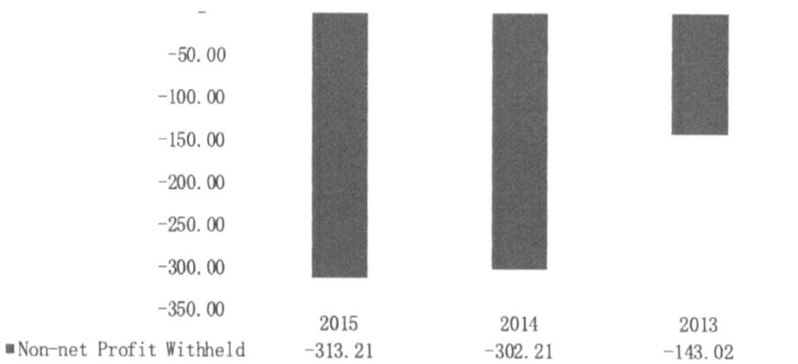

Fig. 1. Aerospace Communication's Non-Deductible Net Profit, 2013-2015 (in millions) (Photo/Picture Credit: Original).

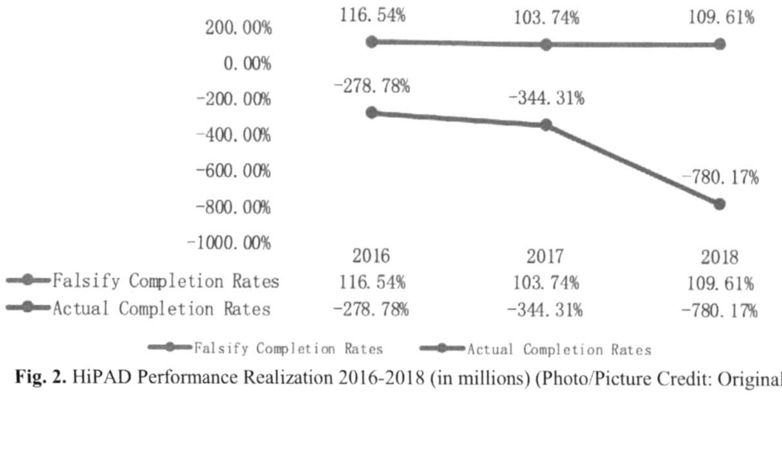

Fig. 2. HiPAD Performance Realization 2016-2018 (in millions) (Photo/Picture Credit: Original).

3 Analysis of financial fraudulent means of the subsidiary HiPAD

HiPAD implemented financial fraud in 2016-2018 mainly through upstream and downstream shell companies to carry out specific business process fictitious business, inflate revenue, cost and profit, and fictitious R&D contracts and R&D income. The following is a specific analysis of HiPAD's financial fraud means:

3.1 Fictitious business cycle using related party transactions

HiPAD formed a cumulative false revenue of 6,902 million yuan and a false profit of 2,574 million yuan from 2016 to 2018 by means of fictitious business cycles through related parties. There are two ways to conduct related party transactions as follows:

First, fictitious R&D business. HiPAD is a well-known ODM manufacturer. In fact, according to the analysis, its R&D capacity is weak, and it does not need such a huge amount of R&D investment (see Table 1). In order to achieve the performance commitment target, HiPAD and its related parties fictitious R&D contracts and fictitious huge R & D expenses, thus inflating R&D revenue and profit by 328 million yuan.

Table 1. Aerospace Communications R&D Investment Table, 2015-2018 (in millions).

	2015	2016	2017	2018
Expensed Research and Development Investment for the Period	162.82	385.39	351.13	368.50
Capitalised Research and Development Investment for the Period	0.54	0.70	18.15	12.73
Total R&D Investment	163.37	386.10	369.28	381.23
Total R&D Investment as a Percentage of Operating Revenue	2.71%	3.27%	3.62%	3.05%

Second, fictitious purchase and sale business, that is, pure fictitious business. HiPAD creates fictional procurement and sales business through the upstream and downstream related parties, forming a fake "assembly line" of C single business. As shown in Table 2, HiPAD had a fictitious income of 6.574 billion yuan from 2016 to 2018, forming a false profit of 2.246 billion yuan.

According to statistics, The number of main customers of the HiPAD fictional purchase and sales business has reached 39, involving Shenzhen, Hunan, Hong Kong and other places. It involved a large number of customers and a wide range of areas. And it built a perfect fictitious business chain, in order to improve its business "authenticity". Among the top five customers of HiPAD, Jiangxi Hongpai Technology, Shanghai Woluo Technology and Jiangxi Haihang are all related parties after analysis. In the following part, the identification of signs of financial fraud will focus on analyzing the anomalies of customer information and data in the annual report, to identify its hidden affiliation with the HiPAD.

Table 2. Revenue and Profit from Fictitious Sales of HiPAD, 2016-2018 (in millions).

	2016	2017	2018
Fictitious Sales Revenue	2120.84	2043.61	2409.98
Imaginary Profit	713.15	741.13	791.78

3.2 Inflated export revenues and profits

Firstly, inflate BS business revenue and profit. From 2017 to 2018, HiPAD purchased materials and exported them to Hong Kong United Kingdom Group Limited and other affiliated companies, and inflated the export amount by overstating the price to achieve the purpose of inflated sales revenue. From 2017 to 2018, the inflated revenue and profit was 404 million yuan, of which 181 million yuan was inflated in 2017, and 223 million yuan was inflated in 2018.

In this process, HiPAD fictionalized a large number of accounts receivable through Hong Kong related parties. Up to now, most of the customers with overdue accounts receivable of HiPAD are overseas customers, and 2.999 billion yuan of overseas customers are overdue. Meanwhile, check the top five accounts receivable of HiPAD in 2017-2019, and find that most of them are Hong Kong companies.

Second, export tax rebate for inflated business. HiPAD obtained an export tax refund of 335 million yuan by falsely increasing its export business. After receiving the notification of relevant tax matters in the later period, the HiPAD needs to pay a total of 335 million yuan of tax deduction and pay the corresponding late fee.

3.3 Transfer of benefits from upstream related supplier transactions

As Table 3 shown, in advance payment top five suppliers list of 2016, the three major suppliers of Shengbao Long, Ying Jucheng and Hongda Innovation are all affiliated enterprises of the HiPAD. The three of them cooperate with the HiPAD to increase the advance payment of the HiPAD, which can complete the transfer of related party interests. In 2016, the virtual advance payment of the HiPAD through these three companies has reached 520 million yuan.

Table 3. Top Five Prepayments by Prepayment Recipients with Closing Balances at the End of 2016 (in millions).

Company Identification	Sum of Money	Affiliated or not (Self-Check)	Whether or not Associated (Actual)
Shenzhen Shengbao Long Technology Co.	240.19	clogged	be
Shenzhen Zhongxing Supply Chain Co.	190.16	clogged	clogged
Shenzhen Yingjucheng Technology Co.	177.43	clogged	be
Guangzhou Chengxing Marketing Management Co.	100.46	clogged	clogged
Shenzhen Hongda Innovation Technology Co.	97.21	clogged	be
Add up the Total	805.40		

4 Identification of financial fraud

4.1 Identification on financial information

Firstly, HiPAD precisely fulfills the performance commitment. According to the foregoing, HiPAD accurately fulfilled the high-performance commitment, and the three-year performance completion rate was 116.54%, 103.74% and 109.61% respectively. The actual operating performance is affected by the market macro-environment, and it may be different from the performance of the amount of betting. So accurate performance commitment completion rate inevitably attracts suspicion.

Secondly, by analyzing the gap between HiPAD's gross profit margin and the industry average, it is found that its business growth and profitability are deviating from the market characteristics and industry trends. The distribution of ODM shipment rankings after HiPAD was merged and acquired was 4th in 2016, 5th in 2017, and not even in the top 5 in 2018, gradually showing a downward trend. In these three years, Wingtech Technology and Huaqin Communication are ranked 1st and 2nd, and the gap between their shipments and HiPAD is large.

From Figure 3 and Figure 4, it can be seen that the sales revenue and cost of HiPAD is much lower than that of Wentai Technology, while the gross profit margin is much higher than that of Wingtech Technology, which is not in line with the laws of market logic. At the same time, the revenue growth rate of HiPAD in 2016-2018 is 46.53%, which is also higher than the 31.98% of Wingtech Technology, and is not in line with the change of its shipment ranking.

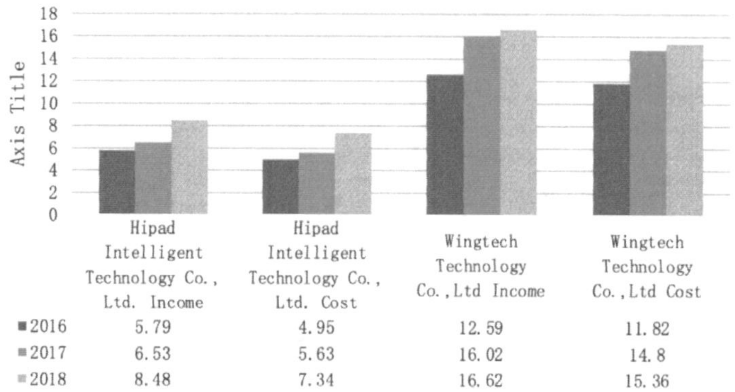

Fig. 3. Cost of Revenue Comparison between HiPAD and Wingtech Technology, 2016-2018 (in billions) (Photo/Picture Credit: Original).

Fig. 4. Gross Profit Margin Comparison between HiPAD and Wingtech Technology, 2016-2018 (Photo/Picture Credit: Original).

Thirdly, analyze the anomalies of its relationship between operating income and accounts receivable. As shown in Table 4, after Aerospace Communications 's merger and acquisition of HiPAD, HiPAD's operating income has a huge increase, but the proportion of accounts receivable to operating income is also getting higher and higher, and even as high as 73.14% in 2018. And such a huge abnormal accounts receivable proportion can be seen in the end of its financial fraud. This corresponds to the financial fraud tactics in the previous article, HiPAD fictionalized a large number of accounts receivable through overseas related parties, and most of the overdue accounts receivable are from overseas companies.

Table 4. Analysis of the Relationship between Operating Income and Accounts Receivable (in billions).

Year	2015	2016	2017	2018
Revenues	6.02	10.54	10.20	12.51
Accounts Receivable	1.08	3.46	4.35	9.15
Revenue Growth Rate	-	74.99%	21.17%	59.81%
Accounts Receivable Growth Rate	-	200.58%	100.40%	251.23%
Accounts Receivable/Operating Income	17.93%	32.82%	42.70%	73.14%

Aerospace Communications 's overseas sales accounted for 53.2% in 2018, and this proportion was 8.6%, 5.4%, and 29.5% in 2015-2017, respectively. And the company's overseas sales scale has expanded tremendously, and this extremely abnormal customer change can be seen as an indication of its financial fraud. This sign of financial fraud can correspond to the previously mentioned fraudulent means of HiPAD to inflate operating income by colluding with overseas related parties and fictitious price increase BS business.

Fourthly, analyze the anomalies in the relationship between cash flow and net profit. As shown in Figure 5, in 2015, which is before the consolidation of HiPAD, the gap between net cash flow and net profit was not large. But in 2016-2018, the amount of Aerospace Communication's cash flow was much smaller than its net profit. This is associated with HiPAD's fraudulent means of fictitious accounts receivable to complete financial fraud. As mentioned in the previous section, HiPAD's accounts receivable increased tremendously, which led to an abnormal relationship between Aerospace Communication's net cash flow amount and net profit.

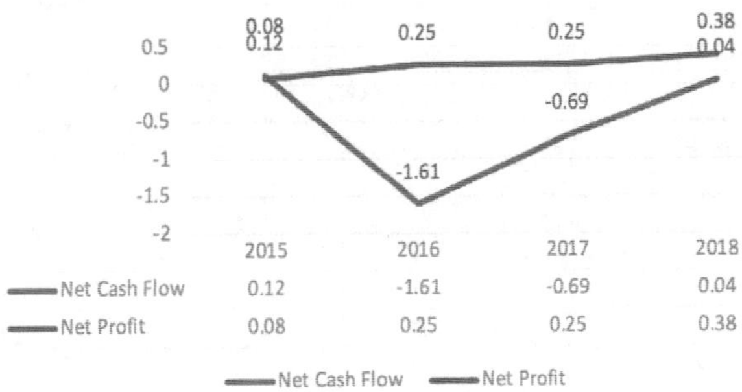

Fig. 5. Relationship between Net Cash Flow and Net Profit of Aerospace Communications, 2015-2018 (in billions) (Photo/Picture credit: Original).

Fifth, this paper analyzes its abnormal customer information anomalies. From the above analysis, it can be seen that HiPAD carries out purely fictitious business through affiliates. And at the same time, it increases export revenues and profits through the fictitious price-raising BS business. Behind the transaction fraud type of financial fraud is often accompanied by upstream and downstream transactions with the collusion and complicity of fraud [10]. HiPAD and important trading objects have implicit affiliation. Its corresponding upstream and downstream suppliers and customers have abnormal characteristics, the enterprise and suppliers and customers conspire with the fictitious business flow, physical flow to inflate the performance. In this way, it cooperates with the enterprise to complete the closed loop of the flow of funds to cover the fraud.

This paper starts from the annual report disclosure of the top five customers of the HiPAD faction in 2016 information, analyzes the large customers and the HiPAD faction of the invisible relationship, and fully analyzes the customer's own business situation, and also the customer in the subsequent disclosure of the annual report and the macro-industry background of the anomalies. This process can help to effectively discover the signs of corporate financial fraud. Large customer, Hongpai Technology was established in 2014. According to the 2016 annual report, the first year of its emergence is 2016. But it became the first major customer of the HiPAD in that year, contributing up to 1.099 billion yuan of sales revenue, accounting for 16% of the total sales of the current period. And in 2017, it became the first place in the half-yearly report of the Aerospace Communications 's accounts receivable. However, Hongpai Technology only has 12 participants and has no reputation in the industry, which can be regarded as an anomaly. At the same time, it can be found that Hongpai Technology is associated with HiPAD through the relationship of two other companies.

Sixth, this paper analyzes the supplier information anomalies. The HiPAD inflated a huge amount of advance payments through affiliated suppliers. This paper fully analyzes the top five advances company information, and their affiliation. And by this way, it can be seen that, the HiPAD's upstream suppliers, the Sheng Baolong, Ying Jufeng and Hongda Innovation are its affiliates to the HiPAD, which transport the interests to HiPAD to help it to commit financial fraud financial counterfeiting behaviour. Taking Shenzhen Shengbao Long as an example, it is actually associated with HTC Innovation and HiPAD through Blue Boxing Communication. The directors and senior affiliation can be used as the abnormal information point of suppliers, which is a basis for financial fraud identification. As a result, starting from the large prepayment company, analyzing its affiliation with the subject, abnormal supplier information can be found.

4.2 Identification on non-financial information of the parent company Aerospace Communications

First, the corporate governance structure is defective. Based on the annual reports of Aerospace Communication from 2015-2018, analyzing the corporate governance structure of the parent company Aerospace Communication, and found that it have serious defects. As shown in Table 5, most of the members of the board of directors of Aerospace Communication are related to Aerospace Science and Industry Group (Aisino), the largest shareholder. And there are serious defects in the internal control system of Aerospace Communications, which can be regarded as a sign of its financial malpractice. Meanwhile, Wang Jiansheng, the chairman of the supervisory board, and the three incumbent vice presidents, the secretary of the board of directors and the chief financial officer are all from Aerospace Science and Industry Group. In addition, the corporate governance system has undergone large-scale changes. The CFO and secretary of the board of directors, Chen Jiawu, left in 2016. A large number of directors and supervisors left in 2016-2018, and the former chairman of the board of directors also left in 2018. The concentrated departure of executives of listed companies indicates that there is a greater risk in their own performance of duties, which indicates that there may be certain problems in the financial situation of Aerospace Communications.

Table 5. Composition of Key Members of Aerospace Communications' Board of Directors in 2015.

Name and Surname	Duties	Relationship of Interest with the Aerospace Science and Industry Group
Ao Kong	chairman of the board	Chairman of Beijing Aerospace Changfeng Co., Ltd, one of the nine listed companies under China Aerospace Science and Industry Corporation (CASIC).
Guo Zhaohai	director president	He was the Deputy General Manager, Secretary of the Party Committee, Secretary of the Discipline Inspection Committee and Secretary of the Party Committee of Aisino Chenguang Company Limited, which is a grandson company of Aisino Science and Industry Group.
Wang Yao Guo Ding Zuozheng Zhao Jiangbin Li Tieyi	board member	All work for China Aerospace Science and Industry Corporation and received zero total pre-tax remuneration from the Company during the reporting period, and all received remuneration from Aerospace Communication related parties.
Chen Huaigu	independent director	Ltd., of which the main source of business of Shanghai Zhong Caixin Accounting Firm is Aisino Corporation and its subsidiaries.

Second, Change accounting firms frequently. Since 2015, Aerospace Communications has begun to change the accounting firm frequently, which can be seen that it wants to cover up the fact of its own financial fraud. In 2015, after a disagreement between Lixin and Aerospace Communications in 2015, it was replaced by Baker Tilly International in 2016, and then replaced by Ruihua in 2017-2018. And the completion rate of 2016 performance of the HiPAD announced by Tianzhi is 85.66%, while the completion rate announced by Ruihua is 116.54%, and there is a big difference between the two.

Third, there are deficiencies in Aerospace Communication's internal control. As shown in Table 6, before 2017, the Lixin and Baker Tilly International both issued a negative opinion on its internal control system, but Aerospace Communications did not pay attention to the rectification of the internal control system. Later in 2019, it was exposed to the incident of financial fraud of its subsidiary, and after questioning by the SFC, it was requested to change the accounting firm to Lixin. And Lixin still issued a negative internal control audit opinion. Aerospace Communications lacks effective supervision and internal control system. Its top management is only concerned about performance expansion and profit growth, but lack of supervision of subsidiary executives internal control management system. It only assigns some executives to participate in the operation and management of the subsidiary HiPAD. It even acquiesces in the financial malpractices of subsidiaries in pursuit of its own interests.

From the first two negative internal control audit opinions in 2019, it can be seen that there is a failure of the internal control system of Aerospace Communications, which can help investors to identify the risk of their investment. And it also laid a certain foreshadowed for the subsequent HiPAD financial fraud incident.

Table 6. Aerospace Communications Group, Inc. Internal Control Audit Report, 2012-2019.

Vintages	Internal Control Audit Opinion	Accounting Firm
2012	unqualified opinion	Lixin
2013	unqualified opinion	Lixin
2014	negative opinion	Lixin
2015	unqualified opinion	Lixin
2016	negative opinion	Baker Tilly International
2017	unqualified opinion	Ruihua
2018	unqualified opinion	Ruihua
2019	negative opinion	Lixin

4.3 Identification of non-financial information of the subsidiary HiPAD

First, "the independent research and development capabilities" of HiPAD is doubtful. Application materials of HiPAD show that since its establishment, it has been focusing on intelligent terminal ODM business, and ODM mobile phone products all use their own R&D mode. In fact, the expression of its business model is different from the reality, which means independent research and development business is less. This can correspond to the financial fraudulent means of fictitious R&D business of HiPAD mentioned above. HiPAD dose not have high independent R&D capabilities. However, there are huge R&D investment and profits that do not correspond to the logic of facts, which can be seen as the clues of financial fraud. The following is a specific analysis of the weak independent research and development ability of HiPAD:

First, what it sells to its major customers are mobile phones with no technical content. As shown in Table 7, Motorola is the first major customer of HiPAD from January to May in 2015, and Dongguan Yulong is the first major customer of HiPAD from 2013 to 2014. HiPAD sold with the two are mobile phone machine. In fact, most of its main business is mobile phone processing, which is difficult to relate to the "own R&D model". And the intangible assets of HiPAD are small. From the notes to its financial statements, it can be learned that its intangible assets account value of removing land ownership on May 31, 2015 is only 5.58 million yuan, and it is difficult to reflect its independent research and development capability here.

Second, analyze the huge change of its customers and huge accounts receivable. This study focuses on the hidden problems that existed before the acquisition of HiPAD in 2016. It aims to explain the problems that have always existed in HiPAD, which provides the basis for identifying the signs of financial malpractice that were implemented after the subsequent acquisition of HiPAD.

Table 7. HiPAD's Business Contribution from Large Customers in Operating Revenues, 2013-2015 (in millions).

Client Name	January-May 2015		Annual 2014		2013 Annual		Product Category
	Sum of Money	Percentage of Main Operating Income (%)	Sum of Money	Percentage of Main Operating Income (%)	Sum of Money	Percentage of Main Operating Income (%)	
Dongguan Yulong Communication Technology Co.	261.72	14.75	1776.93	56.94	746.78	64.45	mobile phones
Motorola (Wuhan) Mobile Technology & Communications Co.	792.12	44.63	306.66	9.83			mobile phones

In 2013 and 2014, Dongguan Yulong, the largest customer of HiPAD, was in crisis, so the main business contribution rate plummeted to 14.75%. While Motorola, a newly developed customer in 2014, soared to 44.63% in the first half of 2015, becoming the largest client. However, Motorola is the first place in the closing balance of accounts receivable, as high as 52.66%, and this huge amount of accounts receivable forms the assets of the HiPAD. But at the same time, this phenomenon shows that in fact, it is not reasonable that HiPAD is still willing to sell a huge amount of inventory to Motorola. From 2013 to 2015, the receivables of HiPAD increased rapidly, and the inventory also increased greatly. It contradicts the fact that electronic products are rapidly being replaced. Such huge changes of large customers, huge increase in accounts receivable and extremely unstable appearances can be regarded as the problems that existed before the merger and acquisition, and also laid hidden dangers for its continued financial fraud in the future.

5 Conclusion

This paper focuses on the analysis of financial fraud and the study of signs of fraud, analyzing the anomalies in public disclosure information such as annual reports from the perspective of uniqueness, including analyzing the traces of financial fraud in terms of financial and non-financial information, and in terms of parent companies and subsidiaries. The identification of performance commitment fraud can be carried out in this direction: it can start from the parent company and subsidiaries to identify the characteristics of financial information fraud, and analyze non-financial information. It can compare the gross profit margin with the same industry of the acquired company, pay attention to the abnormal related party information, and analyze whether there are signs of financial fraud in combination with accounts receivable and cash flow.

Finally, based on the pressure of performance commitment, this paper proposes universal financial fraud prevention measures, including: first, listed companies should improve the internal control system to monitor their subsidiaries, improve the shareholding structure, optimize the governance system, strengthen the management's ethical awareness, and set reasonable performance commitment targets; second, small and medium-sized shareholders need to improve their own awareness of risk prevention, and observe whether there is any sign of financial fraud; third, the regulatory authorities should strengthen the supervision of the company's performance commitment; and third, the regulatory authorities should strengthen the supervision of the company's performance commitment and the supervision of external auditors.

The shortcoming of this paper is that due to the lack of professional knowledge, it is not possible to put forward verifiable, real and feasible financial fraud prevention measures. And future research will use empirical studies to explore the feasibility of specific preventive measures.

References

1. J. Qiu, X. Li, X. G. Zhang, STPC, 40(20), 99-109 (2023).
2. Y. Wang, X. Fang, and D. Hou, FTR, 34(08), 87-98 (2023).
3. C. Yang, Z. Xie, and D. Song, NMR, 21(06), 198-209 (2018).
4. C. Wu and J. Jiang, MW, 39(06), 139-159 (2023).
5. A. Pan, Q. Jinlong, and Y. Yang, AR (03), 46-52+95 (2017).
6. K. Feng, X. Xing, and L. He, FR (01), 188-206 (2023).
7. J. Wang, Q. Fan, AR (10), 71-77+97 (2017).
8. M. Deng and C. Mei, RFE, 34(06), 56-69 (2019).
9. Q. Ye and S. Huang, China CPA (02), 39-43+3 (2023).
10. Q. Ye, F. Ye, and S. Huang, FA (23), 35-40 (2021).

A Study on the Collaborative Development Path of Technological and Financial Innovation in Guangdong-Hong Kong-Macao Greater Bay Area

Chengcheng Liu[1,*]

[1]Faculty of Business and Management, Beijing Normal University-Hong Kong Baptist University United International College, Zhuhai, 519087, China

Abstract. Strengthening the synergistic development of science and technology finance in the Guangdong-Hong Kong-Macao Greater Bay Area (GBA) is of great significance in further promoting financial liberalization and innovation, and deepening the financial co-operation and development between the Mainland, Hong Kong and Macao. In view of the positioning and mission of the GBA, there are still a lot of areas that need to be strengthened in the synergistic development of science and technology finance among the three places. For example, there is no synergy in regional science and technology co-operation and innovation, such as differences in institutional systems, lack of science and technology and financial talents, lack of mechanisms for circulation and sharing of innovative resources, and uneven distribution of innovative advantages. Based on this, GBA needs to build a unified and efficient platform for collaborative innovation and vigorously promote the circulation of resources; strengthen innovation cooperation and cultivate a strategic engine to lead industrial development; and focus on industrial upgrading and promote institutional innovation to form a new pattern of science and technology financial cooperation.

1 Introduction

At present, China finds itself in a phase marked by swift adjustments in its economic structure, a shift in industries, and active strides in scientific and technological innovation. Within this context, it is imperative for the financial sector to assume a more significant role in propelling high-quality economic development [1]. The Greater Bay Area (GBA) Development Plan Outline underscores the importance of supporting Shenzhen in implementing pioneering initiatives in science and technology finance. It advocates for the robust growth of financial sectors with distinct characteristics within the GBA, the reinforcement of financial and technological frameworks, and the facilitation of collaborative advancements in science, technology, and financial innovation across Guangdong, Hong Kong, and Macao. The ultimate goal is to establish an international hub for science, technology, and innovation in the GBA [2].

Meeting the capital demands essential for scientific and technological innovation proves challenging for the innovation entity solely through internal capital accumulation. This underscores the need for establishing an efficient financial system dedicated to supporting such innovation. The strategic challenge then becomes how to guide the rational allocation of science and technology resources through financial development, enhance the regional innovation system, and boost the innovation capabilities of relevant entities within the GBA construction efforts. Consequently, at this juncture, recognizing science and technology finance as a pivotal point becomes highly significant for Guangdong, Hong Kong, and Macao. It serves as a strategic breakthrough to open avenues for factor flow, optimize the distribution of resources like talent, technology, and capital, and maximize synergistic effects for achieving cohesive development in the construction of a world-class city cluster within the GBA. Building upon this premise, this paper examines the underpinnings of science and technology finance development in the GBA, scrutinizes existing issues and hindrances, and proposes conceptual frameworks and pathways for the integrated development of science and technology alongside financial innovation.

2 Basis for collaborative development of technology and finance in GBA

The GBA has a solid foundation in the financial industry and advantages in science and technology innovation. Financial co-operation among the three places has gradually deepened, with smooth channels for capital flow and technology docking, and a synergistic development of science, technology and finance has initially taken shape.

* Corresponding author: p930006116@alumni.uic.edu.cn

2.1 Solid foundation for the development of the financial sector

The financial industry of the GBA has outstanding advantages and distinctive features, and the financial co-operation among Guangdong, Hong Kong and Macao has gradually deepened, and the development of the financial industry has a solid foundation. It is specifically manifested in the significant advantages of the financial industry in Hong Kong, Shenzhen and Guangzhou within the GBA have obvious advantages in the development of the financial industry, with two major stock exchanges, the Hong Kong Stock Exchange (HKSE) and the Shenzhen Stock Exchange (SZSE), and numerous banking, insurance, securities, and venture capital fund institutions clustered in the Bay Area. In 2022, the total economic output of the GBA will be more than 13 trillion RMB, with less than 1 per cent of the country's land area, 5 per cent of the country's total population, and Creating 11% of the country's total economic output, it is becoming an important powerhouse leading China's high-quality development. In 2021, the value added of the financial industry in the GBA will exceed RMB 1.5 trillion, an increase of nearly 35% from 2018, and accounting for over 10% of GDP. According to the 34th Global Financial Centres Index (GFCI) ranking published by GFCI in September 2023, a total of three cities in the GBA are among the top 30 global financial centres, with Hong Kong ranked No. 4, Shenzhen ranked No. 12, and Guangzhou ranked No. 29, demonstrating the strong financial strength of the GBA.

In addition, from a regional perspective, the 11 cities in the GBA are distributed in four echelons: Hong Kong, Shenzhen and Guangzhou are in the first echelon, with a total GDP of more than RMB 2 trillion and an added value of the financial industry of more than RMB 200 billion, with the added value of the financial industry in the three cities accounting for more than 80 per cent of the total added value of the financial industry in the GBA; Foshan and Dongguan are in the second echelon, with the value added of the financial sector in the range of RMB 50 billion to RMB 60 billion; Huizhou, Zhuhai, Macao and Zhongshan belong to the third echelon, with the value added of the financial sector ranging from RMB 30 billion to RMB 50 billion; and the fourth echelon consists of Jiangmen and Zhaoqing, with the value added of the financial sector below RMB 25 billion.

On top of that, the financial markets in the GBA have vibrant capital flows. By 2022, Hong Kong's assets under management will be as high as HK$30.5 trillion. As at the end of June 2023, the consolidated total capital adequacy ratio of Hong Kong's local banks was 21%, which was much higher than the international minimum requirement of 8%. As the world's largest offshore Renminbi market, Hong Kong's Renminbi capital pool is close to RMB 900 billion yuan, and more than 70% of offshore Renminbi transactions are completed in Hong Kong. As for the securities industry, Hong Kong has ranked first in the world for the second consecutive year in terms of the total amount of funds raised through initial public offerings, further consolidating the HKSE's leading position in the global IPO market.

In addition to this, the development cities in the GBA have unique location advantages. The developed level of economic development and strong level of technological development of the Bay Area provides a good foundation for the development of fintech in GBA, and the inclusion of Hong Kong and Macao such as the window of the intersection of China and the West, with the convenience of international and domestic exchanges, provides a good condition of location advantage for the development of financial innovation, especially the development of fintech.

This unique advantage provides fertile ground for the development of financial innovation such as fintech and digital finance in the Bay Area. The four echelons of the GBA also create favourable conditions for regional fintech to promote technological innovation, as well as joint regional development [3].

Additionally, financial co-operation in the GBA has gradually deepened. In terms of direct investment, direct investment from Hong Kong and Macao accounts for about 90% of the investment capital flowing into the nine PRD cities. In terms of co-operation in mutual establishment of financial institutions, more than 10 Shenzhen securities, funds and futures companies have set up subsidiaries in Hong Kong; nine Hong Kong securities and futures operators have set up representative offices in Shenzhen, and a number of innovative institutions such as HSBC Qianhai Securities and East Asia Qianhai Securities have set up their offices one after another [4]. In terms of cross-border financial business, the Mainland and Qualified Foreign Institutional Investors (QFII), Qualified Foreign Limited Partner (QFLP), Qualified Domestic Institutional Investor (QDII), Qualified Domestic Limited Partner (QDLP) have been piloted or launched, enriching the categories of investment products and investment channels for domestic and foreign investors.

2.2 The advantages of science, technology and innovation

There is a continuous emergence of financial and technological enterprises, showcasing a robust allure for innovation factors. The GBA stands out with formidable innovation capabilities, a well-rounded innovation system, and abundant innovation vitality. Notably, Guangzhou and Shenzhen take the lead in driving Guangdong's innovation-oriented development, fostering numerous national high-tech enterprises and "unicorn" companies, alongside a plethora of small and medium-sized high-tech firms. In 2022, CB Insights, a US-based venture capital research organization, unveiled the Global FinTech 250, where fintech enterprises in the GBA demonstrated noteworthy performance. According to the Hong Kong Monetary Authority, the swift expansion of fintech companies in Hong Kong, coupled with the issuance of relevant licenses, surged, exceeding 600 in 2021, with over 30 enterprises originating from the Mainland [5].

Furthermore, Guangdong, Hong Kong, and Macao house a multitude of universities, research institutes, high-tech enterprises, and nationally significant scientific projects, wielding substantial influence nationally and globally. This robust presence of innovation factors lays a solid foundation for establishing an international science, technology, and innovation hub, as detailed in Table 1.

Table 1. Comparison of data on innovation entities and innovation outcomes in the four major bay areas.

Indicator name	unit (of measure)	GBA	Bay Area, New York	Tokyo Bay Area	San Francisco Bay Area
Fortune Releases Fortune 500 Companies	classifier for families or businesses e.g. shops, companies	25	24	40	10
universities and colleges	classifier for houses, small buildings, hospitals and institutions	180	227	120	73
Top 100 Universities in the World	classifier for houses, small buildings, hospitals and institutions	5	2	2	3
Patent disclosure of inventions	ten thousand pieces	176.9045	21.9394	72.616	29.9919

Secondly, the innovation system is well developed and has strong complementarity. The GBA has developed a complete science and technology innovation system with the help of a good innovation foundation and huge innovation investment in the GBA. There are a large number of scientific research structures and innovation platforms in the GBA. Including 39 universities in Hong Kong and 12 in Macao, the GBA has as many as 172 institutions of higher education of various types, among which five universities, are ranked among the top 100 universities in the world. South China University of Technology (SCUT) and Beijing Normal University - Hong Kong Baptist University United International College (UIC) are all well-known universities in China. SCUT has a strong engineering focus and has nurtured a large number of innovative talents. As early as in the 1980s, it produced the three giants of China's television industry, which was a high-tech industry at that time. Nowadays, SCUT has nurtured the founder of Xiaopeng Automobile, leading the development of new energy vehicles in China. UIC, as a cooperative university between Mainland China, Hong Kong, Macao and Taiwan within the city of Zhuhai, Guangdong Province, China, is in line with the international standards and provides students with high-quality academic resources and advanced teaching methods.

There are also a large number of autonomous innovative enterprises in the GBA. Huawei in Shenzhen, Tencent and BYD are leaders in independent innovation across the country and the world, and have achieved fruitful results. In addition, the GBA has a large number of co-operative innovation platforms, making the innovation system more complete. Four national key laboratories, including the University of Macau, have set up branches in the special area of Hengqin. 2022-2023 will see more than 20 joint Guangdong-Hong Kong science, technology and innovation funding programmes, with substantial financial support from Guangdong's provincial coffers.

In addition, there exists a strong mutual complementarity in the innovation systems. Hong Kong plays a pivotal role as an "international bridge" in constructing technology and financial ecosystems within the GBA. On the western coast of the PRD, encompassing cities like Guangzhou, Foshan, Zhuhai, and Zhongshan, there is a robust foundation in household electrical appliances, equipment manufacturing, and scientific research support. Meanwhile, the east coast cities, primarily Shenzhen and Dongguan, excel in strategic emerging industries such as communications, internet, and electronic equipment manufacturing. Particularly in Shenzhen, the added value of advanced manufacturing industries contributes to over 70% of the added value of industries above designated size. In Guangzhou, the advanced manufacturing sector represents 58.4% of the total industrial output value, with the number of national high-tech enterprises experiencing rapid growth at an average annual rate of around 89% for three consecutive years.

Thirdly, the GBA has invested heavily in R&D. The GBA has invested heavily in research and development (R&D). According to the Statistical Yearbook of Guangdong Province and the statistical yearbooks of Hong Kong and Macao, in the past two years, R&D investment in the GBA accounted for about 3.72% of the GDP, and the R&D expenditure exceeded RMB 360 billion yuan, which is far more than the national R&D expenditure as a percentage of the GDP of 2.4%, and far more than the average level of the United States of America of 2.8%. This achievement is itself achieved with a relatively large share of GDP. The proportion of R&D investment in GDP is an important indicator of the region's commitment to science and technology innovation, and shows a strong correlation between real money and investment and again, not only does it perform better domestically, but internationally, it is also stronger when compared to developed countries such as the United States.

The GBA also performs well in terms of the growth rate of R&D personnel and R&D investment, with the GBA experiencing a good growth rate in both R&D activity personnel (persons) and internal expenditure on R&D funding (billion) in 2019-2020, as Table 2 shown.

Table 2. R&D activities and expenditures of industrial enterprises above designated size by sub-city.

		Number of R&D Personnel(Person)		Internal Expenditure on R&D (100 Per Cent; Million Yuan)	
		2019	2020	2019	2020
	Guangzhou	99979	105364	286.24	315.11
	Shenzhen	302042	345344	1049.92	1157.31
Guangdong	Zhuhai	34234	34522	93.33	93.94
	Foshan	92022	98761	259.71	238.86
	Huizhou	56291	57344	99.78	115.26
	Dongguan	124459	135841	260.57	308.42
	Zhongshan	31176	32129	59.66	68.03
	Jiangmen	33170	37269	65.07	70.13
	Zhaoqing	10640	10340	23.35	21.19
Hongkong		35416	36106	263.32	265.53
Macao		1720	1735	30.35	30.33
GBA		784013	856914	2197.63	2388.24

Furthermore, GBA is rich in innovation policies and strong in innovation service support. And the types and perspectives of Science and Technology Innovation (STI) policy support are also diverse, basically covering the policy support needed for STI development. The policies and measures provide a solid foundation for the development of science and technology innovation in the GBA. In addition, the GBA has a strong support capacity for innovation services. Efforts have been made to give full play to the role of policy funds in demonstrating guidance and capital amplification, and to address issues such as fund positioning, operation modes and incentive mechanisms. The government participates in VC, science and technology innovation through various modes such as direct investment, equity participation in the establishment of new funds for investment, and follow-up investment.

Since 2022, Guangdong Province has set up 13 cities in Guangzhou, Shenzhen, Zhuhai, Shantou and other cities to establish Guangdong Free Trade Zone (FTZ) linked development zones, and the FTZ linkage test, synergistic innovation, resource sharing [6]. At the same time, Zhuhai actively linked with Macao, Hengqin to build the "Cross Gate Financial Zone" [6]. At the same time, Zhuhai actively linked to Macao, Hengqin construction of the "Cross Gate Financial District", planning to use 5-10 years to create Guangdong's financial development "third pole". On this basis, the future can further promote the Guangdong Pilot Free Trade Zone Guangzhou Nansha, Shenzhen Qianhai, Zhuhai Hengqin three large areas of complementary advantages and linkage development, promote the construction and sharing of resources, and enhance the overall competitiveness; to strengthen the Pearl River Delta and Hong Kong's financial industry division of labour and the pattern of collaboration, in the international financial hub in the construction of the consolidation and enhancement of Hong Kong's position as an international financial centre [7].

2.3 Initial formation of synergistic dynamics in science, technology and finance

In recent years, Guangdong Province has placed significant emphasis on the convergence of science and technology with finance. In 2023, a substantial investment of 0.93 billion yuan was allocated to the realm of science and technology finance. This investment facilitated 427 instances of venture capital injections and 169 cases of intellectual property pledge financing. The integrated network of science and technology finance, established and solidified during this period, essentially blankets the entirety of Guangdong Province. Additionally, within the GBA, Hong Kong has already secured its position as one of the world's top three financial centers. Simultaneously, Shenzhen has established a comprehensive market structure, encompassing the main board, small and medium-sized board, and venture board markets, leveraging the Shenzhen Stock Exchange. Furthermore, the region boasts Guangdong's three major regional equity trading markets, collectively providing a diverse array of financial resources and multi-tiered channels for capital inflow and exit strategies, thus fortifying support for the development of science and technology innovative enterprises in the GBA [8].

The specific performance is as follows: the co-operative service system has basically been completed and The double-wheel drive of science and technology + finance is in a good situation. In the area of financial technology, Shenzhen and Hong Kong have signed a Memorandum of Understanding (MOU) to jointly launch the Financial Innovation Award and the Special Award for Financial Technology, jointly organise a series of activities such as the "China-Shenzhen FinTech Global Summit", and take the lead in launching the "Shenzhen-Hong Kong-Macao Financial Technologist Talent Scheme" to lay a solid foundation for the innovative development of financial technology in the GBA. At the same time, it also took the lead in launching the "Shenzhen-Hong Kong-Macao Financial Technologist Programme", laying a solid foundation for the innovative development of financial technology in the GBA.

The GBA endeavours to promote the clustering of innovation resources and create an innovation capital system based on the Bay Area and radiating to Southeast Asia and South Asia. The number and scale of VC/PE in Guangdong is expanding rapidly. As at the end of August 2023, the number of private equity fund managers in Guangdong Province (excluding Shenzhen) was 1,704 private equity fund managers in Guangdong Province (excluding Shenzhen), with a fund size of 1,300.430 billion yuan under management, while the number and size of private equity fund managers in Shenzhen reached 3,472 and 2,199.666 billion yuan respectively, which is at the forefront of the country. Hong Kong is the second largest private equity fund investment centre in Asia, with its funds accounting for about 15% of Asian private equity fund investment, and it has obvious advantages in the field of international VC/PE funding. Macao and Zhuhai have more obvious characteristics in the bond market, financial leasing, wealth management and other business areas. Zhuhai has accelerated the development of equity and venture capital industry in recent years, and has become one of the three major private equity fund clusters in the province.

3 Constraints affecting the integration of technology and finance in the GBA

Confronted with the challenge of coordinating the nine prefecture-level cities in the GBA along with the two Special Administrative Regions of Hong Kong and Macao, the primary objective is to enhance the integration and development of city clusters in the GBA, particularly in the realms of science, technology, and finance. This constitutes the foremost task in propelling the synergistic development of innovation across science, technology, and finance. Several constraints hinder the integrated development of science, technology, and finance in the GBA:

Firstly, obstacles arise from institutional system differentiation. Guangdong, Hong Kong, and Macao grapple with the complex "one country, two systems, and three sets of legal systems" framework. Notably, substantial variations exist in institutional policies pertaining to science and technology, finance, economy, and international exchange and cooperation. Additionally, specific cooperative policies necessitate approval from relevant state departments, amplifying the cost of communication and negotiation among the three regions. These factors stand as foundational constraints impacting the harmonized development of science, technology, and financial innovation in the GBA.

Secondly, discernible differences persist in the level of science and technology finance across the GBA. Despite being in close proximity, Guangdong, Hong Kong, and Macao have yet to achieve differentiated and complementary development. Notably, there is a considerable internal development gap, with non-core cities engaging in homogeneous competition for financial resources. This results in suboptimal efficiency of financial cooperation, lacking the desired synergy and inclusiveness.

Thirdly, challenges emerge from the uneven distribution of innovation resources and the absence of a resource circulation and sharing mechanism. Hong Kong, Macao, and the nine cities in the Pearl River Delta possess distinct innovation advantages. The specific challenge lies in realizing interoperability and complementarity concerning policy planning, the flow of innovation resources, and industrial undertakings. Addressing this challenge is crucial for achieving the desired synergy in science, technology, and financial innovation in the GBA.

To achieve interoperability and complementarity within the GBA, it is crucial to establish a long-term mechanism for the circulation and sharing of innovation resources. In addition, there is administrative fragmentation and exclusivity in the sharing of science and technology innovation factors among the nine cities in Guangdong. How to establish and improve the relevant systems and incentives regarding the circulation of innovation resources among cities in different institutional contexts is the key to promoting the synergistic development of science and technology and financial innovation in the GBA.

4 Development path of technology and financial innovation co-innovation in GBA

GBA needs to continuously improve and perfect the system of scientific and technological innovation, and form a market-oriented and enterprise-oriented scientific and technological innovation system. In the process of constructing a collaborative innovation platform, the participation of relevant departments as well as colleges and universities should be encouraged more, and their active role should be given full play to, so that better scientific and technological achievements can be achieved [9]. For example, the Pearl River Delta should learn from the advanced institutional mechanisms of Hong Kong and Macao's free ports, and explore more flexible policy systems, regulatory models, and management systems in the areas of trade, investment and financing, fiscal and financial services, and customs clearance and facilitation, so as to build a pioneer zone for a new open economy system and further enhance the internationalization of the business environment in the Bay Area. Hong Kong, Guangzhou, Shenzhen and Zhuhai will be regarded as the core area for the concentration of scientific and technological financial resources and an important platform for financial innovation and development in the Bay Area, so as to build a demonstration zone for the innovation of the institutional mechanism for in-depth regional cooperation among Guangdong, Hong Kong and Macao, and thus trigger the "chemical reaction" of the complementarity of the two systems. In addition, the GBA should accelerate the interconnection of financial factors and establish collaborative innovation bases and alliances, etc. In particular, the establishment of the "Bay Area Science and Technology Finance Co-ordination and Innovation Alliance" will play a pivotal role in instituting a systematic coordination mechanism for the financial industry within the GBA. This initiative aims to deepen collaboration across various dimensions, including the financial market, institutions, talent pool, legal frameworks, and other critical areas. It also seeks to advance the development of science and technology financial operational rules and systems characterized by both Chinese uniqueness and alignment with international practices [10]. Proactively advocating for the relaxation or elimination of restrictions on the foreign shareholding ratio in securities and financial asset management companies, the initiative aims to reduce the barriers for entry for financial institutions from Hong Kong and Macao. Furthermore, concerted efforts will be made to establish channels for mutual establishment with financial enterprises in Hong Kong and Macao. Another strategic move involves intensifying efforts to expand cross-border RMB businesses, such as two-way financing and capital pooling, along with the issuance of RMB bonds in Hong Kong. Simultaneously, there will be a deliberate exploration of initiatives to enhance account innovation and facilitate cross-border trading of financial assets within the FTZ.

According to the differences in the level of economic development of various places, the GBA should optimise the layout of finance, industry, science and technology research and development, so as to achieve positive interaction and coordinated development of modern finance in the Bay Area. Vigorous efforts should be made to develop innovative finance, including venture capital, risk investment, and the SME and GEM boards. The region should focus on optimising the pattern of synergistic development; and accelerate the promotion of the flow of scientific and technological talents in cross-border cooperation. For the GBA, the "Talent Green Card" system can be constructed to continuously improve and perfect the mechanism for introducing scientific talents, so as to make it more attractive to professional talents. In addition, universities can be promoted in the GBA to carry out multi-level and multi-disciplinary exchanges, and actively explore the mechanism of joint cultivation of talents and mutual recognition of credits; introduce foreign high-quality educational resources, build a cross-regional platform for the exchange of talents, and cultivate composite international scientific and technological innovation talents. In addition, it should build a cooperation carrier for science and technology finance, and promote the construction of national independent innovation demonstration zones and national dual-innovation demonstration bases and crowds creation spaces. Based on the relevant financial reform and innovation experimental work, such as the Pearl River Delta Financial Reform and Innovation Comprehensive Experimental Zone and the "Internet Plus" Crowd Creative Financial Demonstration Zone. The Hong Kong Government has invested more than HK$18 billion, mainly for cooperation with Mainland institutions, to support more Hong Kong universities to build their branch campuses, industrialization bases and research centres in the GBA. In addition, it will build financial industrial parks with special characteristics in Hong Kong and Macao, and actively explore new modes of co-operation in the operation of enclave cities, so as to provide high-quality office environments and ancillary facilities for financial institutions with special characteristics, such as financial leasing, wealth management, and so on.

To facilitate industrial transformation and upgrading, elevate the regional level of scientific and technological innovation, and enhance the core competitiveness of industrial development, a synergistic model for integrating science, technology, finance, and industry is envisioned. Firstly, the emphasis lies in establishing a financial chain closely aligned with the industrial chain. This involves encouraging insurance companies to fortify specialized branches dedicated to science and technology insurance. Simultaneously, support is extended to banks and insurance institutions to craft financial products tailored to the characteristics of technology trade. The initiative includes establishing investment and financing docking platforms to provide financial services for both the industrial and innovation chains. In key areas such as Zhuhai, Foshan, Jiangmen, and Zhaoqing, there is a strategic focus on constructing and shaping the advanced equipment manufacturing industry belt on the west bank of the Pearl River Estuary. The objective is to facilitate the integration of industrial and financial capital by actively developing new business forms, including financial leasing.

Secondly, the central focus of the integrated development of science and technology and finance in the GBA aims to serve the transformation and upgrading of the industrial structure across the three regions, augmenting the core competitiveness of regional industries. Future collaboration among Guangdong, Hong Kong, and Macao should be geared towards joint advancements in science, technology, industry, and finance, fostering the creation of additional key industrial zones. Accelerating the development of industries such as information consumption and high-tech services is a specific goal. Moreover, in the GBA's industrial integration and development process, careful attention must be given to optimizing industrial spatial distribution. This involves expediting the outward relocation of traditional manufacturing while actively promoting the concentration of advanced manufacturing and modern service industries in the central city. The ultimate aim is to gradually shape a world-class science and technology innovation corridor, with Hong Kong, Shenzhen, and Guangzhou serving as the primary axis of development.

5 Conclusion

In the current phase of development, the GBA has strategically positioned itself to leverage technology and finance as key drivers for breakthroughs. Recognizing the imperative to establish seamless channels for the flow of essential elements, the region aims to optimize the allocation of resources such as talent, technology, and capital. This optimization is envisioned to enhance synergies, fostering collaborative effects for the realization of integrated development. The implications of such collaborative efforts extend to the construction of a world-class city cluster within the GBA, thereby underlining the pivotal significance of this approach.

This article systematically reviews the foundational elements of the development of science and technology in the financial sector within the GBA. It delves into an insightful analysis, identifying prevailing challenges and obstacles that impede the seamless integration of technology and finance. In response to these challenges, the paper proposes a comprehensive strategy aimed at fostering synergies between technological and financial innovation. The outlined approach seeks to address the identified issues and unlock the full potential of collaborative development.

Central to the proposed strategy is the optimization of the interconnectivity between the technological and financial sectors, with an emphasis on streamlining the flow of resources. The article underscores the need for strategic interventions to overcome existing barriers, paving the way for a harmonious and mutually reinforcing relationship between science, technology, and finance. By charting a course for collaborative development, the paper contributes to the ongoing discourse on positioning the GBA as a global exemplar of integrated urban development.

References

1. T. Zhou, SF (05), (2020).
2. People's Daily, Outline of the development plan for the Guangdong-Hong Kong-Macao Greater Bay Area. http://politics.people.com.cn/n1/2019/0219/c1001-30803984.html.
3. Guangdong South China Science and Technology Capital Research Institute. 2017 Research Report on Science and Technology Financial Development in Guangdong Province (2017).
4. L. Peng, N. Meng, L. Ma, Y. Ma. SF (1), (2019).
5. J. Xie, J. Xu. WF- (8), (2013).
6. Guangzhou Daily Data and Digitalisation Institute. Guangdong, Hong Kong and Macao Greater Bay Area Collaborative Innovation Development Report. http://gd.people.com.cn/GB/n2/2018/0921/c123932-32085048.html
7. F. Li, Innovation of Guangdong-Hong Kong-Macao Greater Bay Area Co-operation Mechanism to Build a World-Class City Cluster in Proceedings of China Think Tank Economic Watch Conference (CTTEWC) (2018).
8. W. Xu, Z. Fu. JSCUT (4), (2019).
9. J. Long. GE (2), 62-65 (2018).
10. Y. Zhong, X. Hu, Econ. (12), 27-35 (2017).

A Research on IPO Pricing Efficiency under the Approval System and Registration System

Zhelin Chen[1,*] and *Yidan* Wang[2]

[1]Bryant University-BITZH, Beijing Institute of Technology, Zhuhai, Zhuhai, 519088, China
[2]Business School, Northwest University of Political Science and Law, Xi'An, 710122, China

Abstract. This article examines China's evolving stock issuance system within its market-oriented economy, particularly focusing on the transition from the approval system to the registration system. The study evaluates the efficiency of Initial Public Offering (IPO) pricing under incomplete games, identifying high risks and uncertainties in the process. By analyzing 31 selected articles, the research categorizes IPO pricing efficiency based on the timeline of system transformation and explores three key influencing factors: macro-environmental factors, information factors, and role behavioral factors. The findings reveal minimal differences in the study of IPO pricing efficiency under different time intervals in the Chinese capital market. Moreover, the shift from the approval system to the registration system has positively impacted information disclosure, transmission speed, freedom, and individual responsibility in China's capital market. The article concludes with a summary of the organized content and suggests future research directions, emphasizing the importance of continuous guidance and optimization for resource allocation in China's capital market to foster healthy and stable development.

1 Introduction

The pricing of new shares is a core part of the stock issuance market, and whether it is reasonable or not directly affects the resource allocation efficiency of the stock market. However, in China, which has experienced many changes in the issuance system, its political factors often have a certain impact on the financial market, and also impact the relevant content of new stock issuance pricing to a certain extent. IPO pricing, an ex-ante judgment on the value of the stock, has Strong risks and uncertainties. Under different issuance systems, few scholars have paid attention to the differences and trend characteristics of the research results under the research topic "IPO pricing efficiency". Therefore, this article is based on the relevant issues under the approval system and registration system in China's stock issuance system. The research on IPO pricing efficiency was sorted out and compared, and the differences and trend characteristics of the research results under the two institutional backgrounds were explored. Through comparison, the reasons for its occurrence were deepened and corresponding suggestions were put forward.

In terms of literature screening, the author first searched important financial journals and important economic journals in Chinese and foreign databases one by one, and checked the titles or abstracts containing ipo pricing efficiency, market efficiency, arrival-based system, registration system, and based on the approval system and registration Divide the time when the system was implemented in China, and the time is limited to "January 1, 2004 to January 31, 2020" and "January 1, 2021 to September 30, 2023", and the filtering condition is "relative" "Strong theoretical foundation" or "empirical research", and were screened according to the number of citations of the papers, and 20 and 11 papers were determined respectively.

2 Overview of research on IPO pricing efficiency under the approval system

2.1 Research basis related to approval system

China's approval system was implemented from 1999 to 2019. Among them, before 2001, it was stipulated that allocation should be carried out by administrative methods, with strong planning intervention and lack of market autonomy and regulation. In 2001, it was changed to be recommended by the lead underwriter, independently voted by the issuance review committee and approved by the China Securities Regulatory Commission in accordance with market principles. method, the degree of marketization has improved. In 2004, China introduced the sponsor representative system, changing "gateway supervision" to "channel supervision", starting from the sponsor's own interests, through its relevant information on the issuer Disclosure and regulatory constraints, strengthening external supervision and self-discipline of issuers to better enter the market [1]. In the time span of the implementation of

* Corresponding author: Zhelin.chen@zhuhai.bryant.edu

the system, it is not difficult to see that the period of the sponsorship system under the approval system had a more profound impact on China's capital market and accounted for a larger number of studies.

The foundation of China's approval system can be encapsulated as follows: Initially, the securities regulatory bodies possess the authority to reject applications for stock issuance. These regulatory entities conduct thorough assessments of the declaration documents, scrutinizing their comprehensiveness, accuracy, authenticity, and timeliness. The second aspect involves the pricing determination carried out by the lead underwriter. Collaboratively, the issuing company and the lead underwriter are tasked with defining the scale, method, and price of the issuance. Before preparing issuance application materials, the lead underwriter must provide one-year pre-issuance guidance to the issuing company; the third is the sponsor system. The sponsor must verify the issuance documents in accordance with the law, issue recommendation opinions to the China Securities Regulatory Commission, and conduct continuous supervision after listing. The sponsor is dedicated to protecting the interests of investors and helping to reduce market risks; the fourth is the inquiry system. That is, the issuing company and the lead underwriter can set an issuance price range, and then inquire with legal investors online first, and finally determine the issuance price based on the inquiry information.

The introduction of China's approval system has increased the rights and responsibilities of the lead underwriter, and the third-party perspective can more comprehensively measure the company's value and evaluate its development; secondly, companies determine the issuance scale based on capital operations, which has greatly improved Feedback and supplementation of corporate financial information; and the gradual shift from issuance review to mandatory information disclosure and compliance review, improving the degree of marketization. The implementation of the approval system is conducive to clarifying the rights and responsibilities of market regulatory entities and market participants, determining market mechanisms and improving resource allocation efficiency; the securities regulatory authorities encourage independent choice and innovation, establish and maximize the use of advantages, and ensure that securities issuers and underwriters A risk-taking mechanism.

2.2 Research on pricing efficiency under the approval system

Under the approval system, most studies analyze the factors of the issuance system, as Table 1 below shown. Wang Jin proposed that government intervention will restrict the operation of the market mechanism and reduce market efficiency and market liquidity [2]. Ni Xin further pointed out that the functional positioning of China's stock market is unclear, the separation of shares and the degree of administrative supervision of the stock market [3]. It has high characteristics and proposed that the boundary between the government and the market should be redefined; Weng Shichun found through differential comparative analysis that there is institutional ineffective supply in the changes in China's new stock issuance system, and proposed that the role of the system subject should be changed to realign the supply and demand relationship [4]. Yu Zengbiao and others compared the initial returns on the first day of listing of A-shares under different conditions and found that the market inquiry process under the approval system lacked substance and the degree of marketization has not improved [5]. Since then, Huang Yuncheng and others supported the adoption of the sponsor system [6]. The joint liability mechanism links the quality of the issuer and the interests of the sponsor, effectively improving the quality of information disclosure. Zhang Sining found for the first time through empirical comparison that the superiority of the approval system was not reflected in the market value of listed companies, and the reason was attributed to the path dependence in institutional changes [7]. Under the same conditions, Gu Xiujuan et al. starting from the PO premium rate, it supplemented and refined the results of Yu Zengbiao et al. [5, 8]. Zhang jian found through the stochastic frontier model that the behavior of lowering prices still exists in the current market, and the "window guidance" to strengthen the supervision of new stock issuance has actually led to Market imperfection once again reflects the reverse effect of government intervention on market efficiency [9].

Luo yang concluded for the first time that there is a negative correlation between the issuance system, issuance costs and IPO underpricing, affirming that the sponsor approval system is conducive to improving pricing efficiency [10]. Wen Yuchun systematically considered the issuance efficiency of new stock issuance prices on various types of information [11]. Once again recognized the improvement and optimization of the information content of the approval system: intrinsic value factors, market environment factors, and issuance factors have an increasing explanation rate for the impact on pricing trend, but the explanation rate of issuance factors is low and has no significant impact, and information asymmetry still exist. Wang Bing and others first focused on auditor reputation as an indirect external information factor, and found through multiple regression that auditor reputation significantly affects IPO depression [1]. Price rate, answered that audit fees are an important factor in issuance fees. Later, Chu Kejia expanded the scope of data and found that with the reform of China 's issuance system, the IPO underpricing rate gradually decreased, improving pricing efficiency [12]. At the same time, the conclusion that the degree of government intervention leads to higher levels of underpricing is further refined.

Table 1. Research on pricing efficiency under the approval system.

Literature index	Issuing time	Main research conclusions and contributions
Wang Jin	2002	Government intervention will affect market efficiency
Weng Shichun	2004	China's stock issuance system has ineffective supply
Yu Zengbiao, Liang Wentao	2004	The approval system has not alleviated the low price of A-share issuance
Ni Xin	2005	The functional positioning of China' s stock market is unclear and the market and government boundaries should be redefined
Zhang Sining	2006	Path dependence in institutional changes makes it difficult to exert the superiority of the institution
Gu Xiujuan, Men Yanshun	2010	The IPO pricing mechanism is a combination of legal person placement and secondary market investors; the underwriting method of full reimbursement is more efficient
Zhang Jian	2014	The inquiry system, there is still behavior of lowering the issuance price; the "window guidance" method reduces pricing efficiency.
Luo Yang	2014	Both the issuance system and issuance fees can significantly reduce the underpricing rate
Wen Yuchun	2009	The company's intrinsic value and market information factors largely affect and reflect pricing efficiency.
Wang Bing et al.	2009	Auditor reputation affects stock pricing efficiency
Chu Kejia, Zhang Haoyu	2019	Pricing controls have led to high levels of underpricing; capital raised, corporate bargaining power, positive market sentiment, and the company's own financial quality are positively related to the IPO underpricing rate

2.3 Research on factors affecting pricing efficiency under the approval system

The relevant literatures are summarized in Table 2 below. Duan Jindong and other information factors such as the issuance volume of new shares and the pre-issuance market sentiment reflected in the issuance price of new shares have confirmed that the pricing of new shares issuance has a certain information efficiency [13]. They used larger variables to supplement the conclusion of Zhang Renji and comprehensively reflected the stock issuance price has systematic and non-systematic information efficiency, and pointed out that the issuance price has limitations in reflecting factors related to the issuing company [14]. Chen Shenglan found for the first time that "manipulative accruals" in corporate financial accounting information have a significant negative impact on IPO underpricing [15]. It further explains the guiding role of issuing company information in the pricing of new shares. In terms of risk capital factors, Sun Jianhua based on the GEM, studied the Chinese market risk capital has no significant impact on IPO underpricing, denying Liu Yuanyuan's conclusion [16, 17]. Monica et al. found that the differences in driving factors of initial returns, fair value and overreaction in different periods are due to regulatory changes [18]. Institutional changes change demand-driven to value-driven, so the increase in marketization will increase the influence of value information. Huang Yuqin and others found that under the conditions of excessive underwriting fee incentives and reputational risk constraints, the lack of incentives will lead to institutional investors taking more emotional behaviors [19]. The approval system increases the information supply to individual investors, increases the degree of inquiry and information asymmetry, and leads to low efficiency. Based on inquiry information, Tian Yejun and Zhang Yonglin believe that the inquiry process has the ability to reveal information, which helps in predicting the realization of new shares [20]. Zheng Kai and other studies confirmed that pricing efficiency is reflected in the degree to which the issue price reflects the company's intrinsic value, supporting the conclusion of Wen Yuchun, but at the same time found that this information is difficult to reveal at the risk level [11, 21]. Zhou Yaling combined the research on the Science and Technology Innovation Board and found that the financial indicators that reflect the company's intrinsic value have little correlation with the issuance price, and the level of market atmosphere will affect investor sentiment in the same direction [22]. The preparation period for the approval system is too long, supply exceeds demand. From the perspective of market role factors, Ba Shusong and others concluded that analysts improved the pricing efficiency of accrual profit information and conveyed pricing signals to company growth potential predictions, but the information response speed was too slow and efficient information transmission was difficult [23, 24]. Three years later, they added again: Analysts' adjustment of the proportion of earnings behavior significantly reduced the deviation between expectations and actual performance, and timely supplemented the information content of listed companies. However, there was still a lack of rational pricing mechanism, and investor sentiment factors still existed.

Table 2. Research on factors affecting pricing efficiency under the approval system.

Duan Jindong, Chen Haiming	2004	The issuance price of new shares has information efficiency; the information reflects relatively limited factors related to the issuing company.
Chen Shenglan	2010	The new stock pricing market makes full use of available financial accounting information: small and medium-sized investors can identify, to a certain extent, the issuing company's use of accounting control rights.
Sun Jianhua	2013	Venture capital has no significant impact on IPO underpricing in the Chinese market; factors that significantly impact pricing efficiency: first-day turnover rate, total asset size one year before issuance and earnings per share
Monica et al.	2021	Marketization of the issuance system can enhance information spillover effects
Huang Yuqin et al.	2013	The lower the degree of information reflected in the quotation behavior of institutional investors, the higher the degree to which the new stock pricing exceeds the company's reasonable value expectations under the underwriter's optimal choice; the worse the performance of the new stock after listing, the greater the possibility that investors will suffer from the "winner's curse"
Tian Yejun, Zhang Yonglin	2013	The hard constraints of the price range on the issuance price and the allotment policy limit the ability to reveal inquiry information.
Zheng Kai et al.	2014	Pricing efficiency is reflected in the degree to which the issue price reflects the company's intrinsic value; inquiry targets are more sensitive to the potential growth information of the issuing company and are less sensitive to market investor sentiment.
Zhou Yaling	2014	The level of market atmosphere will affect investor sentiment in the same direction.
Ba Shusong et al.	2015; 2018	Analysts have improved the market's pricing efficiency for accrual profit information, but the information response speed is slower; analysts' earnings adjustment behavior has significantly reduced the deviation between expectations and actual performance, and improved the information content

3 A review of research on IPO pricing efficiency under the registration system

3.1 Research basis related to registration system

The fundamental idea behind the reform based on registration is to entrust the market with the power of choice and restore pricing authority to investors. Unlike the approval system, this reform not only brings about changes in the review process but, more significantly, embodies the core principle of information disclosure. The entire process of issuing and listing stocks becomes more standardized, transparent, and predictable, emphasizing the empowerment of the market. Concurrently, the registration system places a strong emphasis on information disclosure, ensuring that the overall procedure for stock issuance and listing adheres to high standards of standardization, transparency, and predictability.

The important aspect of the registration-based reform lies in its emphasis on information disclosure, granting greater flexibility to the market, optimizing the resource allocation role of the capital market, and enhancing the pricing mechanism for market issuances. Under the registration system, the securities issuance review body merely performs a formal examination of the registration documents without making substantive judgments. If the disclosure approach is deemed appropriate, the securities regulatory body refrains from unfairly influencing the price or imposing other conditions on the securities issuance, unless there are valid reasons to reject registration, such as unconvincing prospects presented by the issuer.

3.2 Exploration of IPO pricing efficiency and its influencing factors under the registration system

Among the existing studies, for the convenience of data search and comparison, some studies focus on companies listed on the Science and Technology Innovation Board. Therefore, it can subdivide the selected literature according to whether it is based on data from companies listed on the Science and Technology Innovation Board (see Table 3 and Table 4). The study by Dong Xiuliang et al. compared the Science and Technology Innovation Board with the GEM whose positioning is similar to it, thus leading to the current problems of low IPO pricing efficiency and weak supervision [25]. This study proposed a model for testing the pricing efficiency of IPOs and used it to conduct data analysis, and finally concluded that although IPO pricing efficiency has not been very effectively improved in a short period of time, it has still increased. In particular, in the research of Zuo Xuan and others, they first defined the behavior of companies to improve the IPO approval rate by manipulating financials, beautifying book information and other behaviors as whitewashing behavior, and then explored the role of this behavior in the IPO pricing process [26]. By establishing a regression model to compare the data, it finally came to the conclusion that whitewashing behavior reduces the efficiency of IPO pricing. In the study of Zhang Mengyuan, a comparative study was conducted using company data on both the Science and Technology Innovation Board and the GEM [27]. The IPO pricing efficiency was measured by calculating the IPO underpricing rate, from the registration system itself and stock issuance. The possible impact was discussed from two major aspects: the role of scale and winning rate, and it was concluded that the increase in investor enthusiasm and corporate R&D intensity led to an increase in the IPO underpricing rate, while the increase in supply and demand levels led to an increase in the underpricing rate. Yin Jinwei analyzed data through the establishment of a stochastic frontier model, also compared the Science and Technology Innovation Board with the GEM, and concluded that the IPO pricing efficiency of the Science and Technology Innovation Board is lower than that of the GEM [28].

Table 3. Research based on data from companies on the Science and Technology Innovation Board.

Literature index	Research methods	Main research conclusions/contributions
Dong Xiuliang et al.	Empirical Research	The rise in underwriting fees has led to a decline in IPO pricing efficiency, and rising investor sentiment has led to an increase in IPO pricing efficiency, while company quality has played a smaller role; after the implementation of the registration system, the overall efficiency of IPOs has not been effectively increased.
Zuo Xuan et al.	Empirical Research	There is a phenomenon of whitewashing in the current market, which reduces the efficiency of IPO pricing.
Zhang Mengyuan	Empirical Research	The registration system as a whole and through different paths have an impact on the IPO underpricing rate and increase the IPO underpricing rate.
Yinjinwei	Empirical Research	In the Science and Technology Innovation Board market, due to the scarcity of companies that can be used for pricing comparisons, the low-income characteristics of technology-based companies engaged in R&D in the early stages, and the limited pricing capabilities and lack of moral restraint of various market participants, the IPO pricing efficiency is lower than that of the GEM., the overall pricing efficiency is low.

The rest of the literature does not only focus on the Science and Technology Innovation Board, but expands the scope of research sample selection to other boards and even the entire market. Zhang Yuxin and others focused on the GEM and mainly studied the impact of the level of information disclosure on IPO pricing efficiency [29]. Through modeling research, they concluded that while the IPO pricing efficiency improves, the level of information disclosure is related to intermediaries. The pricing effect of these two factors in the IPO pricing process has also been enhanced. In the research of Chen Shuai, by establishing a stochastic frontier model and a double difference model for data analysis, he concluded that the IPO pricing efficiency in the GEM market has not improved as expected, but it has considerable development potential [30].

Table 4. Research not based on data from companies on the Science and Technology Innovation Board.

Literature index	Research methods	Main research conclusions/contributions
Zhang Yuxin et al.	Empirical Research	The efficiency of IPO pricing has been improved, while the level of information disclosure and the role of the pricing effect of intermediaries have also been improved.
Chen Shuai	Empirical Research	Since the industry scope of the Science and Technology Innovation Board is significantly smaller than that of the GEM and the registration system of the GEM is later than that of the Science and Technology Innovation Board, the IPO pricing efficiency has shown a slight decrease on the GEM; however, with the economic recovery, it has gradually improved and formed a virtuous cycle. the trend of.

By reading and extracting keywords that appear repeatedly in the literature, it can find that although there are differences in specific choices, the three factors of underwriter selection, investor sentiment, and company quality are actually relatively widely used. Among them, the quality of the company plays a smaller role while the underwriter plays a more important role and has a relatively large impact.

In addition, during the literature search process, it is not difficult to find that a considerable number of researchers have focused their main research scope on the Science and Technology Innovation Board. In the current lack of relevant literature research, it cannot conclude that there is some inevitable relationship between the two.

4 Conclusion

In short, the IPO underpricing rate is a relative indicator commonly used to measure the efficiency of IPO pricing . Various factors in market operations will affect the trend of this difference to a certain extent - a high underpricing rate means a large deviation between the issue price and the company's actual value, and the IPO pricing efficiency is low, and vice versa.

Using the basic classification logic of factor analysis, it divides influencing factors into three categories: information factor level, behavioral factor level and macro-environmental level. Because of the inherent flaws of the approval system, early research mainly focused on this and was more inclined to point out some of the negative impacts of the approval system on the market. The degree of attention paid to external factors under the registration system is much greater than that under the approval system - which solves some of the inherent information problems of the approval system - and the more transparent information of listed companies increases the focus on external factors. Overall, there is a consistent conclusion on institutional reform: too much government intervention will reduce IPO pricing efficiency, that is, the registration system can improve IPO pricing efficiency, affirming the promotion effect of increased marketization on the Chinese market; simplification of listing procedures and Enhanced information disclosure improves the freedom and speed of information in the market, strengthens the responsibilities of underwriting institutions, and promotes the improvement of investor capabilities. Therefore, it can be concluded that the registration system has improved the quality of information disclosure due to the "checking" of multiple parties and changes in the degree of attention to external factors. However, an honest and law-abiding market environment has not yet been fully formed, perhaps because the weakening degree of government intervention and the interweaving of multiple relationship chains of interests have allowed the growth of some "opportunistic" behaviors.

By comparing the factors that appear repeatedly under the study of the two systems, explore the reasons why they can always affect the market. Even in studies of different years and topics, the same variables still exist. However, there is still a lack of research on how these variables themselves affect IPO pricing efficiency under different systems. Driven by interests, how can the objective fairness of the market be further improved? Compared with the approval system, the registration system has become more market-oriented and information disclosure has expanded horizontally and vertically. Does it mean that supervision can be appropriately relaxed for the Chinese market? Further strengthening and stimulating the allocation role of the market deserves further study. Whether the information efficiency of information disclosure itself is efficient, whether there are certain types of information tendencies and avoidances in the information content in the market, whether the reform of the registration system can completely get rid of the path dependence of the approval system, and the impact of different information on different systems under different systems. The impact of new stock pricing still deserves further discussion.

Authors Contribution

All the authors contributed equally and their names were listed in alphabetical order.

References

1. B. Wang, Q. Xin, and D. Yang, AR (11), 73-81+96 (2009).
2. J. Wang, FTP (09), 52-53 (2002).
3. X. Ni, FF (10), 57-61+63 (2005).
4. S. Weng, SF (11), 36-39+46 (2004).
5. Z. Yu and W. Liang, FR (08), 51-58 (2004).
6. Y. Huang and R. Ge, IFR (02), 74-78 (2005).
7. S. Zhang, FTP (07), 60-62 (2006).
8. X. Gu and Y. Men, FTP (08), 40-44 (2010).
9. J. Zhang, FER (02), 53-61+118 (2014).
10. Y. Luo, SF (07), 12-14 (2014).
11. Y. Wen, FTP (10), 39-45 (2009).
12. K. Chu and H. Zhang, FER (01), 83-93 (2019).
13. J. Duan and H. Chen, FR (02), 87-94 (2004).
14. R. Zhang, H. Zhu, W. Wang, and X. Han, ES (04), 65-71 (1999).
15. S. Chen, FR (05), 152-165 (2010).
16. J. Sun, FTP (09), 82-86 (2013).
17. Y. Liu, Z. Huang, and X. He, CES (02), 64-70+126 (2012).
18. M. Hussein, Z. Zhou, and Q. Deng, ChiNext IPOs' initial returns before and after the 2013 stock market reform: What can we learn?, Emerging Markets Review (2021).
19. Y. Huang, L. Li, and L. Tao, FR (07), 180-193 (2013).
20. Y. Tian and Y. Zhang, SF (04), 74-79+118 (2013).
21. K. Zheng, G. Hua, and Z. Liu, SF (07), 80-85 (2014).
22. Y. Zhou, FTP(07), 78 (2014).
23. B. Shusong, W. Chao, and Y. Sile, FSR (04), 15-35 (2015).
24. B. Shusong and W. Chao, FF (10), 3-17+53 (2018).
25. X. Dong, J. Liu, and S. Xu, MSM, 40(03), 526-543 (2021).
26. X. Zuo and W. Zhang, CFE (09), 135-146 (2023).
27. M. Zhang, Research on the impact of registration system reform on IPO underpricing on the Science and Technology Innovation Board, Xi'an University of Technology (2022).
28. J. Yin, Empirical study on IPO pricing efficiency under the science and technology innovation board registration system, East China Normal University (2023).
29. C. Zhang and Z. Zhu, JLUFE, 39(03), 90-97 (2023).
30. S. Chen, The impact of the implementation of the registration system on the pricing efficiency of GEM IPOs, Yunnan Normal University (2023).

https://doi.org/10.1051/shsconf/202418801029

An Analysis on Multiple Rounds of Questioning Under the Registration System: Taking Hitake as an Example

Keyu Chen[1,*]

[1]Keuka College, New York, NY 14478, United States

Abstract. The traditional approval system has in the past suffered from low approval efficiency and inadequate information disclosure, and was prone to market speculation and information asymmetry. In order to improve market transparency and standardization, the China Securities Regulatory Commission (CSRC) formally implemented a registration system for stock issuance in 2019 and is gradually promoting related reforms. Under the registration system, if the regulator still has questions about a company's response or needs further information, it may ask additional questions and request more information and explanations from the company. At this point, the company will face multiple rounds of questioning. Through the multiple rounds of questioning procedures, the regulator can gain an in-depth understanding of the situation of the proposed listed company, ask questions and request additional information, so as to better protect the rights and interests of investors and the stable operation of the market. This paper analyzes Hitake as an example of a company, and studies the reasons why Hitake experienced multiple rounds of questioning as well as the economic results of multiple rounds of questioning from both financial and non-financial perspectives. The significance of this paper is that by analyzing the multiple rounds of inquiries under the registration system of Hitake, it reflects the impact of the multiple rounds of inquiries, thus reflecting the far-reaching role of the registration system in today's market as well as the revelation.

1 Introduction

The traditional approval-based issuance system suffered from long approval cycles and cumbersome procedures, which limited market development and innovation. On February 1, 2023, the reform of the full implementation of the registration system for issuance of shares was officially launched. On February 17, 2023, the improve market transparency and standardization, the China Securities Regulatory Commission (CSRC) issued the rules of the system related to the full implementation of the registration system for issuance of shares, which came into effect on the date of its announcement. The CSRC also issued the rules of the system related to the registration system for issuance of shares, which came into effect on the date of its announcement. The introduction of the registration system simplifies the issuance process, improves market efficiency, and promotes the development and activation of the market [1]. The implementation of the registration system can enhance corporate governance and protect the legitimate rights and interests of investors through information disclosure and market supervision [2]. The implementation of the registration system can provide more convenient and flexible financing opportunities for innovative and growth-oriented enterprises, promote economic transformation and upgrading, and cultivate new economic growth points. It also shows that China's capital market is becoming more and more mature. In addition, the example of Hitake provided in this paper is one of the Growth Enterprises Market(GEM). GEM is a stock exchange market established to support the development of innovative and growth-oriented enterprises. The main aspects of GEM companies applying for listing include the following: first, government support. Secondly, the demand of the capital market. GEM provides a platform specialized in providing financing and growth opportunities for such enterprises. Next, innovation ability and growth potential. GEM companies usually have strong innovation ability and growth potential, possess independent intellectual property rights and core technologies, and have market competitiveness and sustainable development ability. Further, financing needs: GEM provides more convenient and flexible financing opportunities. Finally, market opportunity, after listing, it is expected to gain more market attention and investment opportunities.

The research methods adopted in this paper are mainly literature review and case study. By collecting and analyzing relevant literature, it explores the reasons for multiple rounds of inquiries under the registration system as well as the economic results. At the same time, the conclusions and insights brought by the case of this paper are explored through logical analysis. This paper will explore the reasons and results from the case study, with relevant illustrations to assist the analysis. The significance of this paper lies in the in-depth exploration of the causes and results of multiple rounds of

* Corresponding author: 312948802@keuka.edu

questioning under the registration system, with the aim of analyzing the economic results brought about by multiple rounds of questioning.

2 Related concepts

2.1 Conceptual basis of the registration system

The registration system for the issuance of shares mainly means that when an issuer applies for the issuance of shares, it must, in accordance with the law, completely and accurately declare all kinds of publicly available information to the securities regulator. The role of the securities regulator is to conduct a formal review of the comprehensiveness, accuracy, truthfulness and timeliness of the filings, and to leave it to the market to decide whether the issuer's stock is good or bad, without conducting a substantive review of the issuer's qualifications or making value judgments. Under the registration system, companies are required to submit detailed disclosure materials and are subject to multiple rounds of inquiries and audits by regulators. The overall goal of the registration system is to create a capital market that is standardized, transparent, open, dynamic and resilient. "Generally speaking, international mature capital market markets tend to implement the registration system [3]. The essence of the reform gives the choice to the market, strengthens market constraints and rule of law constraints, and adjusts the relationship between the government and the market.

2.2 Registration system audit process

After this registration system reform, the main body of the audit is transferred from the Securities and Futures Commission to the Exchange, which then conducts the audit [4]. The audit process of the registration system begins with the company submitting the listing application to the regulator, including the company's registration documents, prospectus, financial statements and other related materials (corrective materials need to be submitted within 30 days). The application will be accepted by the regulator within five working days. The regulator will conduct a preliminary review of the submitted application materials, including the completeness and compliance of the materials. Within the next twenty business days, the company will have its first round of inquiries. Based on the results of the initial review, the regulator sends a letter of inquiry to the company requesting further information and explanations. The letter of inquiry usually includes questions about the company's basic situation, financial condition, risk disclosure, governance structure, and so on [5]. When a company receives an inquiry letter, it is required to respond to the inquiry: the company responds to the inquiry letter in a timely manner and provides detailed information and explanations as required by the regulator. The materials for the response usually include supplementary materials, statements, legal opinions and so on. The regulator reviews and evaluates the company's response and materials provided, including a comprehensive assessment of the company's financial position, risk disclosure, and governance structure. Some companies need to ask additional questions: If the regulator still has questions about the company's response or needs further information, it may ask additional questions and request more information and explanations from the company. Finally, based on the results of the review, the regulator decides whether to approve the company for listing. If the audit is passed, the regulator will issue an announcement approving the listing. If the audit is not passed, the regulator will issue a notice of non-approval to the company with reasons. If the company is approved for listing, the company needs to complete pre-listing preparations, including signing a listing agreement with the stock exchange, conducting share registration, and conducting investor education. After the company completes the preparation for listing, it begins to be listed and traded on the stock exchange, and the company's shares are officially traded to the public.

3 Case analysis using Hitake as an example

Founded in 2003, Qingdao Hitake Mould & Plastic Technology Co., Ltd. has long been committed to the research and development, design, manufacture, sales and project management services of automotive injection molds and plastic parts [6]. The company continuously improves the automation and intelligence level of mold manufacturing, contributing to the modern manufacturing industry. Hitake currently has two subsidiaries, Hitake Mould was established on January 7, 2004, and is mainly engaged in the research and development, design, manufacturing and sales of injection molds and plastic parts. Hitake Thailand was established on July 8, 2019, and mainly undertakes the Company's production and operation business in Thailand, with the main production products being plastic parts and mold repair services. Hitake applied for listing on the GEM in July 2020 and the registration became effective on June 2, 2021. In close to a year's time, Hitake has gone through four questioning sessions. In the first round of questioning, Hitake was asked a total of thirty questions. The questions covered the issuer's basic information, corporate governance, business and technology, financial and accounting information and management information. In the second round of questioning, Hitake was asked seven questions. This time the questions were more targeted, covering both financial accounting information and management information as well as business and technology. These were additional disclosures to the first round of questioning. In the third round of questioning, Hitake was asked five questions, including financial and management information and corporate governance. In the last round of questioning, Hitake was asked seven questions. The questions were about financial and management information, corporate governance and basic information about the issuer. As shown in Figure 1 below, Hitake was asked a total of 49 questions, of which thirty were about financial accounting and management information. This shows that there are still some problems with Hitake's financial accounting and management.

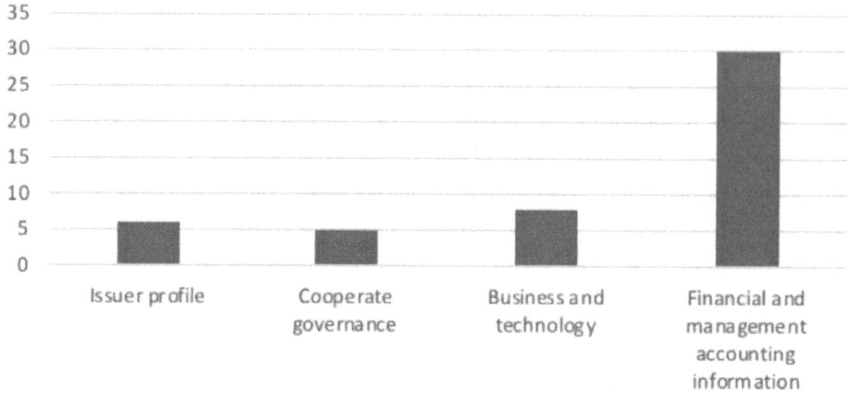

Fig. 1. The number of questions in the four rounds of Hitake's inquiries (Photo/Picture credit: Original).

4 Analysis of the reasons why Hitake experienced multiple rounds of questioning

4.1 Inadequate disclosure of information

A quantitative analysis of the Corporate social responsibility disclosure level of three hundred enterprises in 2011 showed that with a full score of 100, the average score of the enterprises was 19.7 points. This shows the low level of overall disclosure. For example, in the prospectus, on the issue of financial internal control irregularities, it was pointed out that the issuer was requested to make additional disclosure on the background reasons for Qingdao New Material's disbursement of funds to Hitake Mould. Subsequently, the issuer has made additional disclosure. Qingdao New Material, as a municipal-level business incubator in Qingdao, provides entrepreneurial services to technology-based enterprises, and therefore endorsed its outstanding notes receivable to Hitake and provided guarantees in order to provide corresponding financial support to Hitake.

In the comments of the issuer and the sponsor of Hitake in response to the fourth round of audit inquiries, it was pointed out that the issuer's responses to the third round of audit inquiries were insufficient and incomplete, and it was requested that the issuer provide a complete response to the question of "the periodical expense ratio and the net profit margin". According to this request, Hitake revised and supplemented the relevant questions. First of all, Hitake has supplemented the analysis of the reasons why the period expense rate is lower than the comparable companies in the same industry, secondly, it has supplemented the sales profit margin, return on net assets with the comparable companies in the same industry, then it has supplemented the fluctuation of the detailed costs of management expenses, the reasons for it and the comparison with the same industry, and then it has supplemented the reasons for the reason and the reasonableness of the financial expense rate being lower than the same companies in the same industry, and finally, it has supplemented the verification opinions of intermediary institutions. Supplementary disclosure of the issuer's organizational structure, management system, number of subsidiaries of the issuer, etc., the composition of staff remuneration included in management expenses and their respective numbers and average remuneration, analysis of the reasons for and reasonableness of the staff remuneration in management expenses being lower than that of the comparable companies in the same industry, the specific accrual criteria and changes in management expenses such as depreciation and amortization expenses, office expenses and business hospitality, etc., and in connection with the aforesaid matters Further analyze and disclose the reasons for and reasonableness of the management expense ratio being lower than that of comparable companies in the same industry, whether there is any compression of fee parks or advancement of costs and expenses outside the Company, and whether the lower expense ratio is sustainable.

4.2 Information asymmetry

Information asymmetry is a phenomenon due to the theory of information asymmetry [7]. In the market, everyone seeks information symmetry, but in fact, information is always asymmetric. For example, fees, costs, etc. In Hitake's fourth round of audit inquiry reply comments, it is proposed to re-verify the authenticity and completeness of the issuer's operating costs. According to this requirement, Hitake firstly gave the production process, costing methods; and extracted the company's product costing table, checking the accuracy and reasonableness of the company's costing; then obtained a series of further proofs such as details of raw materials in and out of storage to ensure the authenticity and completeness of the operating costs; and then obtained the project budgets and bill of materials lists, and finally gave the main business cost schedule, personnel change table, etc. to verify the authenticity and completeness of the operating costs. Finally, it also gives the detailed list of main business cost, personnel change table, etc. to make additional disclosure on the existence of doubts.

In the third round of Hitake audit in response to the letter of inquiry, on the fifth question "overlapping suppliers" in the reporting period, the issuer pointed out that the issuer and the related party Qingdao Changxinyuan, Hitake mold within the Sea Meijia mold, Qingdao Chang Yong solid there are overlapping customers and suppliers. The purchase amount of the suppliers were 5.6374 million yuan, 9.6515 million yuan, 15.7923 million yuan and 9.753 million yuan, accounting for 4.21%, 4.79%, 7.12% and 7.97% of the total purchase amount of the issuer in the respective period; the sales amount of the issuer to the above overlapping customers were 7.270 million yuan, 909,900 yuan, 4.630 million yuan and 51,600 yuan, accounting for 5.6% of the total sales of the issuer in the respective period. The amount of sales made by the Issuer to the above overlapping customers was RMB7.2770 million, RMB909 million, RMB4.6030 million and RMB5.16 million respectively, which accounted for 3.28%, 0.03%, 1.35% and 0.03% of the Issuer's operating revenue in each of the periods. In light of this, the issuer was requested to continue to make additional disclosures. In accordance with this request, the Issuer made additional disclosure on whether there are more differences between the overlapping and non-overlapping with the abovementioned related parties in various aspects and the reasons for such differences. The explanations were made in the form of a table, which was very convincing.

5 Economic results of multiple rounds of questioning

5.1 Financial perspective

Through the Hitake initial public offering prospectus can be seen in the company there are still many problems. Through the Hitake initial public offering prospectus can be seen in the company also has a lot of problems. (1) The enterprise scale is generally small, the vast majority of mold enterprises with annual revenues of less than 100 million yuan, mold industry competitiveness is small. (2) New energy automobile market changes, the company will face the risk of declining market share. (3) The U.S.-China trade friction on the company's business development and profitability growth adversely affected. (4) Raw material price fluctuations affect profitability levels. (5) Rising human resource costs affect profitability. (6) There are many uncertainties affecting the international, and there are operational risks in the Thai subsidiaries. (7) The company's technology needs to be further upgraded. (8) There is a lack of perfection in the introduction of talent, cultivation, and incentive system. (9) The company's outsourcing suppliers are relatively more dispersed, and there are many processing projects and processes. (10) The company's current fund-raising There is a risk that the company's fund-raising investment projects will not realize the expected returns. (11) There is a risk that the company's return on net assets will decline after issuance. For example, in the response to the first inquiry, the issuer was asked to make additional disclosure on the specific impact of the trade friction between China and the United States on its production and operation as well as the reasons for the change in sales revenue to U.S. customers. The company then responded to the question by listing the products on the tariff increase list and related measurements, etc. After verification, it was considered reasonable. Thereafter, in the third inquiry response showed the specific data given in the previous period, this time the issuer was asked to continue to disclose the specific types of tariff increases, revenue share and actual impact, and further disclosure of friction risk. According to this request, the issuer has further analyzed the financial statements, orders and other explanations. The relevant data in the financial statements belong to the basic data for the implementation of the financial management of the enterprise [8, 9]. For this time disclosure, it is considered that the issuer has taken active measures to minimize its impact. Its overseas sales revenue continues to grow steadily. It can be seen that after many rounds of questioning, Hitake has solved some of the initial problems of the company, thus optimizing its corporate financial performance. And it can be seen that the traditional financial performance system is more and more difficult to meet the demand in the development, and it is necessary to carry out the digital strategic transformation of the enterprise to adapt to the changing market environment [10].

In addition, through the multi-theory questioning, Hitake is gradually making relevant improvements for the problems, so as to successfully pass the audit and successfully go public. As shown in Table 1 and Table 2, firstly, it can be clearly seen that Hitake's net assets per share have increased significantly after the issuance, indicating that the company's economic strength is increasing. Secondly, the gearing ratio of Hitake after the issuance is also significantly reduced, indicating that the solvency of Hitake is getting stronger and stronger.

Table 1. Comparison of net assets per share before and after Hitake's IPO.

Net assets per share before issue (Yuan)	7.26	Net assets per share after issue(Yuan)	12.52

Table 2. Comparison of Hitake's gearing ratio before and after issuance.

particular year	Pre-issue gearing ratio (%)	particular year	Pre-issue gearing ratio (%)
2017	74.11	2022	32.28
2018	57.68	2023 . 3.31	35.43
2019	53.87	2023.6.30	36.38
2020	53.53	2023.9.30	43.71

5.2 Non-financial perspective

The above tells us that although the first prospectus raised problems, the transparency, accuracy and truthfulness of the information disclosure were improved through repeated inquiries and additional disclosures, which greatly improved the quality of the information disclosure. What it should know is that information disclosure is the main way for listed companies to transmit effective information to the outside world, and it is also the main factor determining the stock price and market value of listed companies. For example, the issue of interest rate was mentioned in the prospectus. In the first reply to the comments, the issuer was requested to make additional disclosure on the nature of after-sales service fees, the ratio of the amount of expenses incurred to the size of revenue, etc. In turn, in the third reply to the comments, the issuer was requested to continue to disclose the gross profit margin in comparison with companies in the same industry and other contents. In the last round of questioning, the third round of inadequate and incomplete responses were requested to continue to make additional disclosures. Hitake, after four rounds of layers of supplementation and disclosure, after verification, that the issuer's management expense ratio is lower than the average level of comparable companies in the industry, in line with the issuer's products and organizational structure characteristics, with reasonableness. It can be seen that the following conclusions can be drawn from the multiple rounds of questioning: 1. Securities regulators may be concerned about the governance structure and operation of the company, and they may ask whether the company has sufficient independent directors and an independent audit committee, as well as whether there is any risk of potential conflict of interest or misconduct on the part of the company. 2. Securities regulators may be concerned about the risk management capabilities and measures of the company, and they may ask whether the company has a sound risk management system and process, and whether the company is able to identify and respond to potential risks in a timely manner. 3. Securities regulators may inquire about the company's strategic planning and competitive advantages in order to understand the company's positioning in the marketplace and its prospects for development. 4. Securities regulators may pay attention to a company's intellectual property rights (IPR) protection, including patents, trademarks, copyrights, and other aspects of IPR protection. For example, they may ask whether the company has effective IP protection strategies and measures, and whether the company is at risk of IP disputes or infringement. 5. Securities regulators may also pay attention to the company's sustainability strategy and environmental, social, and governance (ESG) performance. They may ask about the company's practices and achievements in environmental protection, social responsibility, and employee welfare in order to assess the company's sustainability and social responsibility. Institutional inquiries about corporate governance, risk management, strategy and competitive advantage, intellectual property protection, and sustainable development can ameliorate the risk of potential conflicts of interest or misconduct in Hitake, and can protect the interests of investors and the stable operation of the market. Hitake has proved the reasonableness of its explanation during the questioning process. At the same time, through multiple rounds of questioning also see the development of Hitake still has a large range of room for improvement.

6 Conclusion

Some conclusions and recommendations can be drawn based on Hitake's registration inquiry. The company disclosed the first quarterly report shows: 2023Q1 realized revenue of 104 million yuan, +15.60% year-on-year; net operating cash flow +72.95% year-on-year. As a segment with strong competitive advantage, high brand awareness of listed companies, Hitake's medium- and long-term development is worth paying attention to, the company is expected to 2023, 2024, 2025 EPS were 1.02, 1.21, 1.44 yuan, corresponding to the PE were 29.98, 25.20, 21.17 times, give recommended rating. From the perspective of the secondary market investment transactions, taking into account the current macro situation at home and abroad, in the low valuation of the position or more medium-term margin of safety. This is all thanks to Hitake in the process of registration system inquiries, according to the questions raised by the continuous supplemental disclosure and improvement. Hitake in the questioning process to supplement the disclosure of information and issues related to financial accounting, so as to more accurately understand its true financial position, operating conditions and risk profile. This shows that the company should be fully prepared: the company should be fully prepared to answer all kinds of questions in the inquiry, including financial status, business model, market competition and other aspects. Adequate preparation by the company can improve the accuracy and professionalism of answering questions and increase investors' confidence. The company should ensure the transparency and accuracy of information disclosure. During the questioning process, the company should provide sufficient information, including financial statements, operating conditions, risk factors, etc., so that investors can make informed investment decisions. The questioning process may involve the internal control of the company. At this time, the company should strengthen the internal control system to ensure the accuracy and compliance of the financial statements. The company should maintain good communication with the regulator and respond to inquiries and answer questions in a timely manner. Positive interaction with regulators can enhance the company's reputation and trust. The inquiry process may involve the company's business model, market competition and other issues. GEM companies should improve their business capabilities and enhance their market analysis and competitiveness analysis in order to better answer these questions.

References

1. X. Han and X. Wu, FAC (12), 107-112 (2023).
2. Q. Li, Reflections on the Current Status of Social Responsibility Information Disclosure of Listed Companies and Ways to Improve It, China University of Political Science and Law (2022).
3. X. Du, S. Lai, J. Weng, et al., "FM 44 (23), 10-15 (2023).
4. Q. Ling, CER (11), (2023).
5. W. Zhao, Disclosure of Listed Companies and the Risk of Stock Price Crash, School of Finance, University of International Business and Economics (2021).
6. Q. Yu, Review Report: Automotive Injection Molds Leading Supplier Expected to Grow Steadily, AJ Securities (2023).
7. X. Liu, Information Asymmetry and the Platform Economy, Institute of Digital Finance, Peking University, 2021.
8. T. Shi, CER (14), (2023).
9. X. Li, RO (23), (2018).
10. J. Li, IJAF 12(2), 184-194 (2023.

An Analysis of the Causes of Evergrande Debt Crisis

Jiahua Li[1], and *Yangchunwang* Qin[2,*]

[1]Springboard International Bilingual School, Beijing, 101318, China
[2]Aquinas International Academy, Garden Grove, CA 92845, United States

Abstract. Since August 2020, new regulations on real estate financing have been issued, emphasizing "the need to improve the marketization, standardization, and transparency of financing". Subsequently, the capital liquidity crisis caused by Evergrande's high debt and high turnover mode has become the focus of public attention in the market and has triggered the credit crisis of the real estate industry to a certain extent. This study is based on the public information such as the financial statements. To analyze and study the causes of the crisis, this paper will analyze the causes of the Evergrande Group crisis by comparing the previous financial statements of the company, using the balance sheet and comparing the profitability, and putting forward suggestions on the future liquidity and long-term development of Evergrande Group. The suggestions give inspiration to the same industry or enterprises in the same model. Warning the existing housing enterprises, Evergrande Group serves as the most negative example in textbooks, playing a warning role to prevent such a serious crisis from happening again.

1 Introduction

Since the reform and opening up, the rise of real estate has greatly increased the housing demand of the people. In just 30 years, nearly 10,000 real estate companies have been established. While raising the people's housing demand, there are also many problems. For example, Evergrande Group, a company that has borrowed money to develop, has caused great chaos to the country and its people. China Evergrande Group, a Hong Kong-listed company, founded in 1996, has more than 100,000 employees. The company originally owned four core companies, including China Evergrande New Energy Automobile Group Co., LTD., Evergrande Real Estate Group Co., LTD., Hengteng Network Group Co., LTD., and Evergrande Real Estate Group Co., LTD. Evergrande Wealth has suspended payments of all wealth management products since September 2021, when Evergrande notified the two banks to suspend interest payments on loans due on September 21. From the perspective of macro shareholding structure, Evergrande shareholding structure is very centralized. Being too centralized can lead to a brain drain, which means that a large number of brands and buildings cannot be highly regulated. Excessive debt and leverage diversification already led the vulnerable Evergrande Group step by step to the crisis. Evergrande Wealth has announced three solutions: cash installment payment, housing payment, and physical asset payment. The move has sparked a heated discussion in both the market and among the public. Since then, a large number of Evergrande Group business tickets have stopped the default payments. Therefore, Evergrande's capital liquidity crisis has further turned into the market trust crisis and further spread in various industries. For example, the Sankeshu Group, as well as the famous decoration company Gold Mantis, fell into a liquidity crisis involving up to 40 billion yuan. At the same time, Evergrande's liquidity crisis has also led to a large number of real estate "rotten housing" that cannot be delivered in time. Since 2021, Evergrande Group has incurred contractual liabilities of about 215.8 billion yuan since making a profit. The average floor price in 2021 was about 9,000 yuan per square meter. For every 100 square meters, it was calculated four times. Approximately 1 million people are waiting for Evergrande to hand over the properties. This paper will review the timeline of Evergrande's "debt crisis," analyze the causes of Evergrande Group's crisis during the same period in the same industry, and propose suggestions and thoughts on Evergrande Group's crisis.

2 The beginning of the debt crisis

2.1 Capital structure

The shareholding structure of Evergrande Group is very rigorous and complex. It uses a multi-layer structure and double-tier overseas holding, so that enterprises can better finance overseas, hide information and reasonably avoid tax. Xu Jiaying first established Xinxin (BVI) Limited, controlling 59.84% of Evergrande Group's shares, while his wife Ding Yumei established Junrong Holdings Limited, controlling 5.05% of Evergrande Group's shares. The remaining shares are held by the public and investors. By using a Cayman Islands company to control Angi BVI, domestic commercial

* Corresponding author: 21311120100020@bwu.edu.cn

entities are controlled. Evergrande Group utilized hidden shareholding and shareholder names through British Virgin Islands companies. Evergrande Group used Cayman Islands registered companies approved by the stock exchange. By adopting the Xiao Hong Chou structure, corporate tax costs are reduced. By using this structure, Xu Jiayin has full control of Evergrande Group. In addition, Evergrande Real Estate Group Co., Ltd. (registered in the Cayman Islands) may carry out business restructuring before and after listing, which is also convenient for enterprises to adjust their business through the use of structure, and listing financing. It expands the company's business scope, further leading to the formation of a giant enterprise internal crisis so that the crisis of Evergrande gradually formed step by step [1].

Evergrande Group's financing is fast-paced. Financing methods include war, IPO, rights issue, and additional issuance channels, such as China Evergrande's financing. In addition to the first two rounds totaling $830 million and personal investment structures, a large amount of market financing is approximately 108.7 billion yuan, with a significant portion of investments concentrated in real estate, property, automotive, food, and other e-commerce platforms through war and stock market financing [2]. Raising and other funds did not enter the actual operation, more to expand new products, so that new products quickly raise funds in the market, resulting in a very tight use of funds.

2.2 The changes in regulation

Early on, Evergrande Group accumulated a large amount of land reserves and obtained bank loans. However, due to policy constraints (the "three red lines"), high debt levels prevented Evergrande Group from further expansion. In the early stages, the inability to fulfill bank loans led to a liquidity crisis caused by the company's high turnover and high debt. This crisis was exacerbated by the inability of numerous suppliers, construction contractors, and related industries to receive payments, leading to further crisis escalation. According to the 2021 data (see Table 1), Evergrande Group's financing costs increased from 8.63 to 9.64 and then to 9.02. Combined with policy impacts, Evergrande Group had crossed the third line, depleting liquidity and rendering it unable to redeem bank loans or issue timely financing instruments upstream and downstream. The "three red lines" refer to the committee's assessment of high debt, high leverage, and high turnover in Evergrande Group's business model. Given Evergrande Group's diversification and sudden transition to other industries, it became virtually impossible, resulting in difficulties in fund withdrawal and directly causing a liquidity crisis for Evergrande.

Table 1. Evergrande capital structure (¥billion).

Year	2013	2014	2015	2016	2017	2018	2019	2020	2021H1
Total assets	3181	4745	7570	1350.9	1761.8	1880.0	2206.6	2301.1	2377.6
Actual total liabilities	2938	4149	6906	1301.3	1649.5	1701.4	1987.0	1950.7	1966.5
Total nominal liabilities	268.8	362.1	614.9	1158.3	1519.5	1571.4	1848.0	1950.7	1966.5
Nominal total asset-liability ratio (%)	77.22	76.31	81.23	85.74	86.25	83.59	83.75	84.77	82.71
Real total asset-liability ratio (%)	84.40	87.44	91.23	96.33	93.63	90.50	89.64	84.77	82.71
Average financing cost (%)	9.52	9.74	9.59	8.27	8.09	8.18	8.63	9.46	9.02

Data source: Evergrande 2021 financial report.

2.3 Evergrande diversified operation

Evergrande's business scope is mostly extensive, covering a wide range, including mineral water, grains and oils, automobiles, and finance. Despite having numerous successful brands, they have not achieved substantial profits. For instance, Evergrande Mineral Water initially gained some success in sales through extensive advertising efforts. However, due to issues with product quality, distribution channels, and pricing strategies, Evergrande Mineral Water faced challenges. Pricing inconsistencies and significant fluctuations in distributor prices led to losses for some distributors, diminishing trust in Evergrande. As a result, sales were affected, and in some cases, failed to cover marketing costs, ultimately resulting in financial deficits. Because

https://doi.org/10.1051/shsconf/202418801030

the whole department except for the real estate products have economic profits, the rest of the products and brands are basically in a loss state. In the long run, Evergrande Group's diversification is a failure, in terms of debt repayment and profitability. The working capital ratio of Evergrande (see Figure 1) decreased from 1.52 to 1.26 after 2016, and the quick ratio decreased from 0.62 to 0.33, significantly higher than the market level. The asset-liability ratio of Evergrande has been growing continuously since 2016. However, Evergrande's debt repayment ability is not clear (see Figure 2). Since 2017, the debt repayment index has plummeted from a peak of 30% to 5%. Since the three red lines, a large number of enterprises in the same industry have generally reduced their debts to protect themselves, but Evergrande continues to adhere to diversified development. In terms of profitability. According to the profitability analysis, after the diversified investment strategy, its profitability did not show an upward trend, especially after 2018, all the profit data declined significantly, and the payback up of Evergrande BBB 1 products is not optimistic. After Evergrande sold some of its lower profitability assets in 2017, its profitability rebounded significantly, indicating that Evergrande's blind diversified investment did not improve its profitability [6].

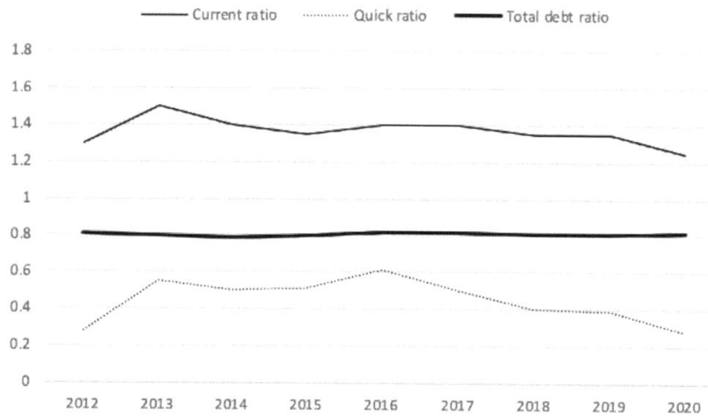

Fig. 1. Liquidity ratios of Evergrande (Photo/Picture credit: Original).

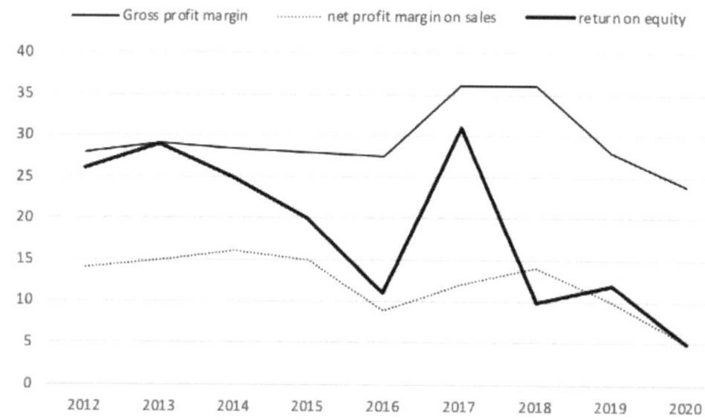

Fig. 2. Profitability ratios of Evergrande (Photo/Picture credit: Original).

3 Consequences

3.1 Company comparison during the same period

Compared to high-debt and low-debt models, real estate companies should anticipate market trends and reduce their debt levels. Within the same real estate company, Evergrande encountered the three red lines in 2021, signalling the onset of a liquidity crisis. Compared with the same period of Jinmao Group, the outcome is not ideal.

Jinmao Group predicted the market in advance and sold some assets to trust companies to let Jinmao set. From 2021 to 2023, the debt is just over 75%, which belongs to a healthy housing enterprise, and the three red lines are all passed (see Figure 3). Even if Jinmao Group is a healthy enterprise, the profitability of Jinmao Group is also in a downward trend due to the market and policy relationship, according to Figure 4.

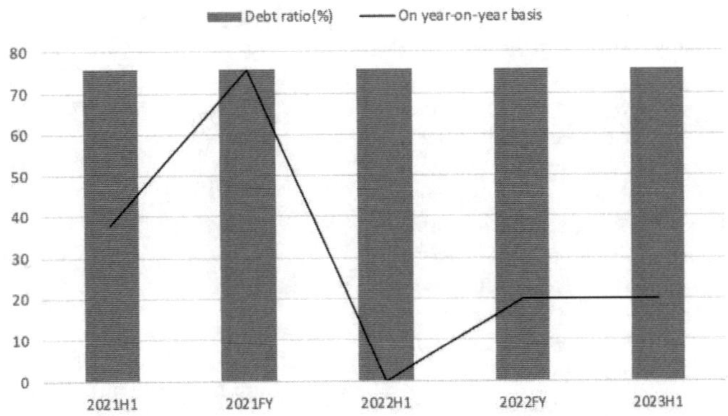

Fig. 3. Solvency ratios of Jinmao Group (Photo/Picture credit: Original).

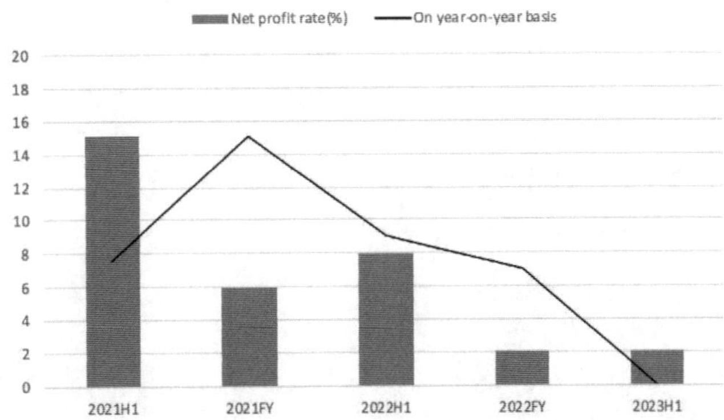

Fig. 4. Profitability ratios of Jinmao Group (Photo/Picture credit: Original).

However, due to the healthy debt ratio and the advance prediction of the policy, Jinmao Group has been operating normally, and there has been no large number of commercial bills to stop the payment, or stop the payment of bank loans.

Compared with Evergrande Group, the current situation of Jinmao Group is very ideal [7]. In the process of operation, enterprises should pay great attention to the policy trend, and pay more attention to the internal operation of the enterprise. For example, for Evergrande Group, the equity is too central and is not effectively allocated [8]. If the equity of the enterprise is not effectively distributed, it will lead to improper project management, difficult project promotion, and high personnel liquidity. Today, a large number of companies make full use of their resources and capital by using equity records and motivating employees at low cost. For example, Huawei Group can use equity incentives to effectively improve the utilization rate of funds and obtain the talents needed for diversified operations [9]. Huawei utilizes an employee union holding system to link employee performance with company performance, effectively enhancing the company's operational and innovation capabilities. By holding 99% of the shares through the union, employees are encouraged to innovate and collaborate. Through legislation, the union enjoys dividends without decision-making responsibilities, ensuring the interests of the decision-making body are safeguarded. If Evergrande Group takes the same measures, it may enable a large number of construction sites and affiliated brands to get a large number of talents, reduce the management cost, reduce the operating cost of enterprises, and reduce the tax burden cost, so that Evergrande can smoothly pass the policy transformation and market trough.

3.2 Consequences of the debt crisis

Under the mode of high debt and high turnover, Evergrande Group led to the capital liquidity crisis due to the three red line policies. Due to the liquidity crisis, a large number of ongoing projects were forced to stop construction. By the end of 2022, Evergrande has contract liabilities of 721 billion yuan [3]. If calculated at 1 million yuan per house, Evergrande and 720,000 houses have been sold, but they have not been delivered yet, which will affect millions of people. The real estate enterprises are unfinished, but the loans of buyers are still in progress, and a large number of buyers have encountered unfinished houses. A large number of unfinished buildings reduce the confidence of residents in buying property, but also reduce the confidence of the market and consumers, greatly accelerating the desolation of the real estate market. If Evergrande Group goes bankrupt, it will have a huge impact. For example, a large number of employees are laid off, a large number of non-performing assets are difficult to dispose of, and a large number of investors lose all their money [10].

Evergrande Group has up to 123,000 employees. Most of these employees have housing loans. If they lose their jobs, they will face the risk of a housing shortage, which will hit the market again, and increasing bank losses may lead to the birth of a huge financial crisis [11]. A large number of overdue bank loans will lead to the bank stock price decline, such as the double blow is likely to make banks have a liquidity crisis. If there is a liquidity crisis, there will be a subprime crisis as in the United States in 2008. If a giant group falls, it is very likely to lead to a series of industry thunderstorms, leaving the market in a chaotic state and reducing consumer confidence. Under high leverage, bankruptcy is not only the interruption of supply but also a large number of non-performing assets in the market. Enterprises such as Evergrande Bank will fall into a cash flow liquidity crisis. It leads to a large number of real estate-related industry closures tide.

4 Conclusion

In recent years, with the rise of housing prices, the state has constantly adjusted its real estate policies. In recent five years, Evergrande has maintained a debt ratio of 60%. It reflects that Evergrande BBB 1 itself is a business model with high debt and high leverage. There are also differences in the internal governance of the company. It can be seen from the equity structure of Evergrande. 76% of the equity makes Xu Jiayin have absolute control over Evergrande, which limits its diversified development to a large extent. From this, one is that entrepreneurs should constantly improve their quality. To be able to accurately predict the future development form and respond in advance. Second, it pays attention to the cash flow situation of enterprises. It depends on the needs of the investment, construction, or production, builds an effective fund operation and management mechanism, scientific and reasonable pre-management of funds, avoids short loans and long use, and the rupture of the capital chain. To focus on the core business, it avoids blind diversification. In the process of business diversification, it tries to choose the industry with strategic synergistic development characteristics with the original business. Fourth, in line with the direction of national policy regulation, it is important to correctly understand the advantages and disadvantages of various financing methods. By effectively combining these methods, diversified financing channels can be achieved, optimizing the capital structure and avoiding the rupture caused by excessive borrowing risks in the financial chain. Fifth, enterprises should focus on their core business, which will enhance their core competitiveness. Enterprises should avoid excessive reliance on financial innovation tools, adjust accounting items to lower the enterprise's asset-liability ratio, and prevent over-expansion.

Authors Contribution

All the authors contributed equally and their names were listed in alphabetical order.

References

1. D. Shi, WE, 23(12), 37-44 (2000).
2. W. Liu and T. Wu, TF(5), 154-156 (2018).
3. W. Hu, W. Chen, and Z. Hu, AC(2), 115-119 (2023).
4. X. Ni, IE, 34(7), 118-120 (2023).
5. P. Ding, ME(6), 167-168 (2022).
6. Z. Ji, CEE(2), 95-97 (2023).
7. G. Lin, The impact of the real estate trust issuance on the financial situation of commercial real estate enterprises-Take 'China Jinmao' Group as an example, Jinan University (2023).
8. Y. Chen, J. Li, H. Hao, and L. Xu, JHUT, 37(4), 97-104 (2023).
9. P. Wu and Q. Hu, CET(13), 116-117 (2020).
10. W. Zhang, HF(5), 25-26 (1997).
11. B. Wang, CWTI(4), 48-50 (2023).

Research on Option Pricing Strategies for Forestry Carbon Sinks Based on Black-Scholes Modeling-Take Sanming City as an Example

Zichen Wang[1,*]

[1]School of Economics and Management, Beijing Forestry University, Beijing, 10000, China

Abstract. Sanming City, Fujian Province, is known as the green capital of China. This paper focuses on the local forestry carbon sink projects in Sanming City and analyzes their carbon trading prices based on the real option pricing theory and the Black-Scholes model and concludes that the value of the forestry carbon sink projects in Sanming City has been underestimated. This paper seizes the undervalued situation and puts forward certain suggestions for working on projects to develop forestry carbon sink in Sanming, such as increasing the well-being of residents by utilizing forestry carbon sink projects, increasing the number of trading entities in the carbon market, and perfecting the carbon trading market, etc. It also points out that the rationalization of forestry carbon sink products should be carried out reasonably. At the same time, it also points out the significance of reasonable pricing of forestry carbon sink products for the local carbon trading market, which leads to the significance of the rational development of forestry carbon sinks for China's green development.

1 Introduction

1.1 Research background

Global climate change has become one of the world's most important ecological and environmental issues today, and China has made great contributions to global environmental governance to cope with the worsening climate problems. At the 75th session of the United Nations General Assembly, China formally put forward the "dual carbon" goal of carbon peaking and neutrality. To realize the "dual-carbon" goal, China has been promoting the development of forestry carbon sinks in combination with the theory of a low-carbon economy. Forestry carbon sinks can give full play to the carbon sequestration function of forests, reduce the concentration of greenhouse gases in the atmosphere, slow down global warming, and directly improve the ecological environment. As of 2022, China has set up 18 key forestry carbon sink cities and 21 state-owned forest farms to pilot forestry carbon sinks nationwide and has carried out several forestry carbon sink projects. The rapid development of forestry carbon sinks has a direct effect on mitigating the harm of global climate change, and while improving the global environment, it can obtain green economic gains, facilitating the development of the forestry economy, and contribute to the progress of the forestry industry.

1.2 Literature review

Forestry carbon sinks are an innovative combination of forestry and finance, linking forest carbon sequestration to financial products with multiple benefits. Since the option value of forestry carbon sinks is prosperous, option pricing is assessed for forestry carbon sinks. The trading process of forestry carbon sinks belongs to a kind of carbon trading, and the pricing and optimization of such carbon trading can better promote environmental protection and the social welfare process [1]. Regarding the pricing of forestry projects, scholars earlier evaluated forestry projects based on the traditional Faustmann model and pricing by real option method [2]. Gao Yongqi Pan et al. improved the above method and assessed the value of forestry carbon sinks by binomial tree real options based on the Hartman model [3]. Zhang Kaixuan et al. selected the Black-Scholes option model to evaluate the value characteristics of real options [4]. Anqi Chen et al. analyzed the option characteristics of forest resources [5]. They thought it was necessary to use real options for the value evaluation of forest resources. The Black-Scholes option model also provides a good basis for pricing forestry options, which is a great inspiration for this paper.

1.3 Research framework

In summary, this paper first determines the research method, based on Black-Scholes Modeling, to evaluate the pricing of forestry carbon sink projects through the real options method. Secondly, the research object is selected. Analyze the specific research object with the

* Corresponding author: ym2121@bjfu.edu.cn

selected method. Summarize the experience according to the results obtained from the analysis, and finally put forward relevant suggestions for developing forestry carbon sinks.

2. Case description

Carbon financial derivatives such as futures and options have played a dominant role in the European carbon market. They have significantly increased the liquidity and marketization of the market, and have contributed greatly to the discovery of the true price of carbon. Forestry carbon is a form of carbon emissions trading that integrates ecological, economic, and social benefits , it is an effective tool for ecological compensation and the realization of ecological product value [6]. By freeing up space at the national level, carbon emissions can be reduced.

China has proposed to develop forestry carbon sinks utilizing the Chinese Certified Emission Reduction (CCER) program. CCER is a voluntary certification which is registered with carbon exchanges. The proposal demonstrates China's commitment to reducing carbon emissions by incentivizing the development of carbon sinks.

By utilizing CCER, China aims to facilitate and promote implementation of low-carbon technologies and practices while promoting sustainable development. The forestry carbon sinks proposed under this initiative have the potential to play a vital role in reducing carbon emissions while providing numerous co-benefits such as biodiversity conservation, soil conservation, and improved ecosystem services. Chinese Certified Emission Reduction is not the only option for some pilots, and the Fujian carbon market can use the Fujian forestry carbon sink [7]. At the end of 2016, the Fujian carbon market included forestry carbon sink trading, pioneering the FFCER. The carbon sink afforestation project in Youxi County, Sanming City, Fujian Province, passed the FFCER project filing in 2018, and this paper selects the project as an example for empirical analysis. Youxi County Forestry Construction and Investment Company operates the Youxi County Carbon Sink Afforestation Project to increase forest carbon sinks, which utilizes the carbon sink function of forests and reforest trees to increase forest carbon sinks, reduce the overall CO2 content in the atmosphere, and achieve the purpose of slowing down the trend of climate warming. The project is in Youxi County, Sanming City, and was developed using a methodology documented by the National Development and Reform Commission (NDRC), with an operating area of 2,283 hm2. The afforestation activities of the proposed project commenced on March 31, 2005, and the first crediting period is from May 01, 2005, to April 30, 2025 (inclusive of the first and last days). During the first 20-year crediting period, the proposed project is expected to generate 561,529t CO2e of GHGs, which will be used as a carbon sink. During the first 20-year crediting period, the proposed project is expected to generate a total of 561,529 tCO2e of GHG emission reductions, with an average annual emission reduction of about 28,076t CO2e.

3. Analysis of the problems

3.1 Data description

The selected site of the Youxi County Carbon Sink Forestation Project is Youxi County, located on the southwest side of the Minjiang River in the middle of Fujian Province. The project's boundary is sketched on-site using a 1:10,000 topographic map and GPS for accuracy control. Then, the plot boundary is determined with the assistance of GIS software (ArcGIS), and the boundary coordinates of the project plot are read to determine the plot boundary.

3.2 Project income

In September 2020, the first phase of monitoring emission reductions of 131,600 tons of CO_2e through the provincial Department of Ecology and Environment for the record and issued in October to enter the Straits Equity Exchange listed on the market, and now complete the transaction of 88,600 tons of CO_2e, the turnover of 14,966,681 yuan.

3.3 Project costs

Forestry carbon sink projects incur costs such as land use fees, afforestation inputs, baseline measurements, monitoring, and carbon sink forest operating costs, along with other inputs.

The silvicultural model involves planting an average of 200 seedlings per mu per year in pure pinyon pine, pure fir, and mixed pinyon pine-fir forests. This is done every year from 2005 to 2012, resulting in annual silvicultural inputs.

3.4 Estimated value of carbon sinks

The project owner, Youxi County Forestry Construction Investment Company, organized the implementation of carbon sink afforestation from 2005 to 2012, with a total afforestation scale of 35,133 mu (2,343 ha), of which 241 mu were afforested in 2005, 447 mu in 2006,1,266 mu in 2007, 575 mu in 2008 and 575 mu in 2009.

Of these, 241 mu were afforested in 2005, 447 mu in 2006, 1,266 mu in 2007, 575 mu in 2008, 3,199 mu in 2009, 21,438 mu in 2010, 7,644 mu in 2011, and 323 mu in 2012. The afforestation tree species are mainly ponytail pine and fir, of which 16,001 mu are fir, 15,927 mu are ponytail pine, and 3,205 mu are mixed fir-horse forests, as shown in Table 1.

Table 1. Sink benefits (Unit: tCO2e·a- 1)

Timing	Project carbon sinks	Cumulative carbon sinks
May 01, 2005-December 31, 2005	13.87	1

https://doi.org/10.1051/shsconf/202418801031

January 01, 2006-December 31, 2006	9	10
January 01, 2007-December 31, 2007	50	59
January 01, 2008-December 31, 2008	172	232
January 01, 2009-December 31, 2009	447	679
January 01, 2010-December 31, 2010	1096	1775
January 01, 2011-December 31, 2011	2623	4398
January 01, 2012-December 31, 2012	5617	10014
January 01, 2013-December 31, 2013	10349	20363
January 01, 2014-December 31, 2014	16660	37032
January 01, 2015-December 31, 2015	24059	61082
January 01, 2016-December 31, 2016	31917	92999
January 01, 2017-December 31, 2017	39615	132614
January 01, 2018-December 31, 2018	46640	179254
January 01, 2019-December 31, 2019	52630	231884
January 01, 2020-December 31, 2020	57373	289257
January 01, 2021-December 31, 2021	60790	350047
January 01, 2022-December 31, 2022	62902	412949
January 01, 2023-December 31, 2023	63807	476755
January 01, 2024-December 31, 2024	63645	540400
January 01, 2024-December 31, 2025	21129	561529
Total	561529	

3.5 Estimating the price of carbon sinks

Based on historical data on carbon market transaction prices in Fujian Province from 2017-2022, the gray prediction model is used to determine the transaction prices. The results of the calculations are shown in Table 2.

Table 2. Gray prediction model prediction results (Unit: yuan per ton)

Time	Real value	Predicted value
2017	13.03	13.03
2018	8.90	5.20
2019	9.11	8.25
2020	10.82	13.10
2021	22.64	20.81
2022	37.80	33.04

3.6 Construction of the black-scholes model

The value of forestry carbon sinks consists of two aspects: one is to utilize their inherent capital value, and the other is based on the investor's optionality, i.e., the price of real options. The Black-Scholes model has been used in the study of real options on financial products, and the main feature of the model is reflected in the fact that when investors are faced with the decision of future uncertainty, they can relate the expiration price of the option to the pricing of stocks, thus achieving the accurate pricing of stocks.

The Black-Scholes option pricing model is based on the following assumptions. Firstly, it presumes that the stock price conforms to a normal distribution within a standardized interval. Secondly, it assumes that the financial asset in question will not receive any dividends or other income during the option's lifespan. Lastly, it presupposes that the option is of a European-style breed, i.e., it can only be exercised upon expiry.

Therefore, in this paper, the Black-Scholes model is used to value the real options of forestry carbon sink afforestation projects in Fujian Province and provide a reference for the pricing of forestry carbon sink financial products. According to the forecast data, the gray forecast model was used to derive the volatility of China's treasury bond market c = 0.59, option price sensitivity d1=0.94, the possibility of option implementation d2=0.12, and the interest rate of risk-free treasury bonds r=8%. The value of forestry project is calculated as follows: S_0=267.4 ten thousand yuan； K=868.4 ten thousand yuan

$$c=S_0 N(d_1)-Ke^{-rT} N(d_2) \tag{1}$$

$$d_1 = \frac{\ln(S_0/K)+(r+\sigma^2/2)T}{\sigma T} \tag{2}$$

$$d_2=d_1-c\ T \tag{3}$$

4. Suggestions

4.1 Selection of tree species

The Carbon Sink Forestation Project in Youxi County is a remarkable initiative to combat climate change by promoting afforestation. The project comprises a vast expanse of land, spanning over 35,133 mu, primarily covered by ponytail pine and fir trees. The project has been meticulously planned, with 16,001 mu dedicated to fir trees, 15,927 mu to ponytail pine, and 3,205 mu to mixed fir-horse forests. The region of Sanming City is known for its abundance of fir and ponytail pine trees, but the project's organizers understand the importance of biodiversity in carbon sequestration. Thus, they have incorporated diverse tree species into the project to enhance its effectiveness.

This approach will reduce the number of carbon sinks that fall short of the expected yield due to targeted disasters and promote rational timber forest replanting. Ultimately, the Carbon Sink Forestation Project will maximize Sanming's forestry strengths, contributing significantly to the region's economic and environmental sustainability.

4.2 Increased well-being of local populations

Increase the income of residents through forestry carbon sink projects. Forestry carbon sink projects increase local forest resources and should focus on increasing the income of forest farmers. Carbon credits afforestation and forest conservation activities provide more employment opportunities for residents and solve the problem of employment of local surplus labor. It is recommended to carry out forestry production work such as afforestation, planting, fostering, care, and fertilization during the project period to improve the quality of life of the local people, thus mobilizing the enthusiasm of the people and promoting the development of forestry carbon sink projects, which is conducive to the improvement of the value of carbon sink options.

The process of creating forestry carbon sink projects should reduce the pressure on the protection of existing forest resources, especially natural forest resources, promote the structural adjustment of agricultural industries, strengthen the local forestry economy, increase forestry income, and is also an important measure to solve the "three rural" problem [8].

4.3 Improve the carbon trading market and increase the number of trading entities

To accelerate the scale of the carbon trading market, the Sanming government should primarily focus on increasing the number of entities engaged in forestry carbon trading while encouraging the circulation and trading of carbon options. The government should provide additional policy and financial support for forestry carbon sink projects to attract more trading subjects, such as enterprises, to the market. It is important to continuously refine the carbon sink trading mechanism so that a variety of trading subjects can be introduced effectively, which will facilitate the market's growth.

As the carbon trading market advances, carbon sink trading can more efficiently reduce the cost of carbon emission reduction while also generating economic benefits for underdeveloped regions with abundant forest resources [9-11]. Consequently, the value of forestry carbon sinks will be further enhanced, leading to a more sustainable future for the region.

5. Conclusion

5.1 Key findings

This paper analyzes the difficulty of option pricing for forestry carbon sinks and evaluates the investment value of the forestry carbon sink project in Youxi County, Sanming City, Fujian Province, using the gray model and the Black-Scholes model. It is found that the real option value of the forestry carbon sink is too low, and if the real options method is used to price the forestry carbon sink project reasonably and combined with the proposed suggestions to increase the reasonableness of tree species of the forestry carbon sink project, mobilize the enthusiasm of residents to participate in the forestry carbon sink project, improve the carbon financial trading market, and increase the main participants of the carbon trading market, the forestry carbon sink project can be greatly promoted, and the "dual-carbon" project can be facilitated.

5.2 Research significance

It also points out that the rationalization of forestry carbon sink products should be carried out reasonably. At the same time, it also points out the significance of reasonable pricing of forestry carbon sink products for the local carbon trading market, which leads to the significance of the rational development of forestry carbon sinks for China's green development. This can greatly promote the development of forestry carbon sink projects and facilitate the realization of the "double carbon" goal, which is of great significance to the green development of China.

5.3 Limitations and future study

This paper has some limitations in terms of data. Only the data of a forestry carbon sink project in Youxi County of Sanming City is selected, which does not completely cover the pricing problem of forestry carbon sink projects in the whole of Sanming. It may have a large deviation from the actual carbon trading market situation in Sanming. At the same time, the model also has certain limitations. The research on pricing using the real options method needs to be more in-depth, and only by continuously improving the model can we get more accurate prediction results.

References

1. P. A. Sauter, O. Mußhoff, B. Möhring, et al. Journal of Forest Economics, **24**: 1-20 (2016)
2. G. Galdi, S. F. Verde, S. Borghesi et al. European University Institute (2022)
3. Pan at al. Issues of Forestry Economics, **43**(2) (2023)
4. Zhang at al. Forestry Economic Issues, **37**(1): 87-92, 111 (2017)
5. Chen at al. Forestry Economy, **39**(11): 70-75+92 (2017)
6. Niu Ling. Path to Marketization of Carbon Sink Ecological Product Value[J]. Macroeconomic Management,2020(12):37-42,62
7. L. Jindi. Agricultural Disaster Research, **13**(07): 263-265 (2019)
8. W. Xianming. Theory and Modernization, 1-11 (2023)
9. Lin at al. Journal of cleaner production, **224**: 455-464 (2019).
10. Chen at al. Fujian Forestry, (04):10-12 (2021)
11. G. Li. China Economic and Trade Guide, (06):61-63 (2022)

A Systematic Analysis of the Quality of Profit Growth in Chinese Construction Firms

Xiaoyang Du[1,*]

[1]Economics and Finance, University of Southampton, SO17 1BJ, United Kingdom

Abstract. China is a country with a large land area and a large population, but the infrastructure is relatively poor. After decades of hard work by the Chinese people, they increased dramatically, and the infrastructure has improved significantly. China now has the world's largest range of motorways and high-speed railways. At the same time, thirty years ago, China's per capita residential space was relatively small. Study the quality of profitability of China's construction companies in the golden period through the most representative listed construction companies in China in the last 10 years, and it hopes to study the characteristics of the construction industry and hope to understand some deeper issues through this. The research subjects selected for this report are all public companies listed on the Shanghai Stock Exchange or the Hong Kong Stock Exchange in China. The following three factors have contributed to this improvement: the massive construction of speed railway companies and the construction of high-speed railways. Vigorous development of the real estate industry formed the golden period of China's first three decades of rapid development of construction companies.

1 Introduction

Study the quality of profitability of China's construction companies in the golden period through the most representative listed construction companies in China in the last 10 years, and it hopes to study the characteristics of the construction industry and hope to understand some deeper issues through this. The research subjects selected for this report are all public companies listed on the Shanghai Stock Exchange or the Hong Kong Stock Exchange in China. They are also Fortune 500 companies: China Railway Construction (601186), China Railway (601390), China Communications Construction (601800), and China Construction (601688) [1].

2. Description of Chinese Construction Firms

China Railway Construction (601186, 01186) Introduction: The company is the world's most powerful scale of the mega integrated construction group, ranked 43rd in the world's top 500 in 2023. The main business includes engineering contracting business, accounting for 83.88%; material logistics and other business, accounting for 8.36%; real estate development business, accounting for 3.96%; industrial manufacturing business, accounting for 2.25%; planning and design consulting business, accounting for 1.55%;

China Railway (601390, 00390) Profile: The company is one of the world's largest multi-functional and integrated construction groups and ranked 39th among the world's top 500 companies in 2023. It is able to provide customers with a full range of engineering and industrial products and related services. The company is an industry leader in infrastructure construction, investigation, design and consulting services, and engineering equipment and parts manufacturing. Major businesses include infrastructure construction, 85.88%; other businesses, 6.75%; property development, 3.54%; equipment manufacturing, 2.25%; and design and consulting services, 1.58%.

The research methodology of this report: mainly through the analysis of these listed companies, the level of income from the main business in the past ten years, accounts receivable, the number of bad and doubtful debts, changes in the level of gross profit margins, changes in the level of net profit, rate changes in the level of total profit size, etc., in order to comprehensively analyze China's representative architectural companies, in the last 10 years of rapid development of the period of changes in the corporate profitability, and the quality of the effective winnings.

There are a lot of financial data of listed companies, and focus on choosing to analyse these indicators for the following reasons: Firstly, to analyse the size of the market space of the overall industry and the overall market space through the growth of the main business income of the leading listed companies [2]. Second, to analyse the strong and weak position of listed companies in the whole industry chain through the changes in the amount and size of accounts receivable, and to analyse the management level of listed companies through the

*Corresponding author: xd8n22@soton.ac.uk

changes in the number of accounts receivable. Third: to analyse the average level of the industry, as well as the quality of profitability and the management level of the enterprise through the changes in the number and size of bad and doubtful debts. Fourth: Through the gross profit margin of how many changes are needed to analyse the ease of entry into the industry, the relative monopoly, and the industry boom index? It is five: through the net interest rate of the size of the changes to analyse the ease of profitability of enterprises and the level of corporate management, but also according to the law of change to analyse the industry's boom index. Sixth: the total profit can analyse the overall profitability of enterprises, but also, according to the law of change, to analyse the industry boom index, the total amount of change can analyse the industry's market space size. In short, through the above key indicators, we can comprehensively analyse: the listed companies in the industry's strengths and weaknesses, the industry boom index, the management level of enterprises, the development of the industry space, the intensity of competition in the market, the net profit of enterprises, such as the gold content [3]. These key indicators are also enough for us to see an industry and a listed company, which is also why we choose these indicators among many financial data.

The main business of China Railway Construction and China Railway are highly similar, so let's compare and analyse these two companies first.

China Railway Construction (601186) The company is one of the world's most powerful, large-scale, integrated construction groups. The main business includes engineering: data from the Shanghai Stock Exchange Company annual report (Table 1) and China Railway (601390) Data from the annual report of the Shanghai Stock Exchange Company (Table 2).

Table 1. The Shanghai Stock Exchange company annual report Unit: billion yuan

	2013	2014	2015	2016	2017	2018	2019	2020	2021	2022
Revenue	5867.7	5933.03	6005.39	6293.27	6809.81	7301.23	8304.52	9103.25	10200	11000
Receivable	877.98	1155.29	1280.28	1334.28	1465.04	993.82	1121.39	1256.96	1556.77	1412.3
Bad debt	14.31	15.83	35.65	6	44.7	44.72	50.11	37.25	98.66	79.39
Gross profit rate	10.15%	10.85%	11.45%	9.21%	9.24%	9.78%	9.64%	9.26%	9.6%	10.09%
Net profit ratio	1.78%	1.95%	2.23%	2.36%	2.48%	2.72%	2.72%	2.82%	2.87%	2.9%
Net margin	103.45	117.35	126.45	140	160.57	179.35	201.97	223.93	246.91	266.42

Table 2. China Railway Data from the annual report of the Shanghai Stock Exchange Company Unit: 100 million yuan

	2013	2014	2015	2016	2017	2018	2019	2020	2021	2022
Sales eevenue	5604.44	6125.59	6241 . 04	6433.57	6933.67	7404.36	8508.84	9747.49	10700	11500
Receivables	1230.9	1458.31	1316.6	1405.32	1111.27	1059.09	1037.12	1078.77	1221.2	1223.38
Bad debt	6.88	25.74	34.69	38.79	92.44	82.01	60.34	80.54	79.70	61.28
Gross profit rate	10.82%	10.49%	9.39%	8.91%	10.34%	8.97%	10.69%	9.86%	10.03%	10.38%
Net profit ratio	1.8%	1.75%	1.9%	1.99%	2.06%	2.36%	2.99%	2.81%	2.85%	3.04%
Net margin	93.75	103.6	122.58	125.09	160.67	171.98	236.78	251.88	276.18	312.76

3 Research and analysis: China Railway Construction and China Railway

The main revenue grew in 10 years: 87.46 percent and 105.19 percent, respectively. The company's net profit increased by 157.53% and 233.61%, respectively, in 10 years.

From China Railway Construction and China Railway's main revenue and proportion of analysis: The two companies' main business and industry similarities are relatively close, but China Railway Construction's main business revenue and total net profit growth are weaker than China Railway's.

3.1 Analyzes the reasons for the difference

After analyzing the reasons for the above differences, we can see that the receivables of China Railway Construction with increased business are higher than the magnitude of China Railway. Secondly, the growth rate of the main revenue of China Railway Construction is lower than that of China Railway. Thirdly, the net interest rate of China Railway Construction is slightly lower than that of China Railway for a long time.

After research and analysis, the accounts receivable with the company's business growth and growth may be a relatively normal phenomenon in this industry, but too high accounts receivable will give the company a greater risk of bad debts and greater financial costs, which will give the company's net profit will bring greater losses and potential risks. Although both companies are Chinese state-owned enterprises and are the world's top 500 enterprises, from these three financial indicators, China Railway's management efficiency and profitability are significantly stronger than China Railway Construction.

At the same time, analyse the two companies, hoping to better understand the industry according to 10 years of long-term gross profit margins. Find that the long-term gross margins of both companies are around or below 10% over the 10-year period. Let's look at the long-term net margins of the two companies over a 10-year period. The long-term net margins of both companies over a 10-year period are only around 2%. It is relatively reasonable for a great company to maintain a gross margin of around 30% if it is to remain competitive over the long term. But these two companies 10 years are very low gross margins and analyse the industry and the company's conclusions, mainly the following two points: First, the overall competition in this industry is still very fierce, and the two companies' competitive advantage may come mainly from the Chinese people's hard work and demographic advantages, as well as the spirit and tradition of selling more for less. Second, at the same time, check the China Railway and China Railway Construction website lists some of the best projects, such as the Qinghai-Tibet Railway. The construction of these projects is still quite difficult, and there is also quite high technical content [3]. The gross profit margin of China Railway Construction is still only about 10%, and Europe, the United States, and other large enterprises with higher gross profit margins often more than 50%) and net interest rate levels often more than 20% gap is still large. Chinese enterprises are still in the world's industrial chain division of labor in the middle and lower reaches. Third: for companies with considerable technical difficulties, up to 10 years of gross profit margin of only about 10%, net profit of only about 2%, and there may also be a huge risk of bad and doubtful debts and other companies, with the passage of time, the company itself will also form a competitive barrier. Fourth, construction is not a particularly good industry; it is difficult to make money, is high risk, and has strong technical requirements [4,5]. Fifth, some construction jobs in the construction industry may require a very high level of skill. But at the same time, most building construction companies do not have particularly high requirements, too low barriers to entry, in general, pulled down the construction of gross profit margins and net interest rate levels.

This study analyses two other Fortune 500 construction companies in China.

China Jiaotongjian (601800, 01800) Profile: The company is China's leading transport infrastructure enterprise, the world's largest port, highway, and bridge design and construction company; the world's largest dredging company; China's largest international engineering contracting company; China's largest highway investor with the world's largest fleet of construction vessels, ranked 63rd of the world's top 500 in 2023. Major businesses include infrastructure construction business, accounting for 84.55%; dredging business, accounting for 7.12%; infrastructure design business, accounting for 5.06%; and other businesses, accounting for 3.27%.

China Construction (601668) Profile: The company is one of the investment and construction groups with the most recent professional development, the earliest market-oriented operation, the highest degree of integration, and the largest global scale in China, and is one of the most powerful investors in China, and ranked 13th among the world's top 500 enterprises in 2023. Its main investment directions are in the fields of property development, financing and construction, and comprehensive urban construction. China Construction is the world's largest engineering contractor. Its main businesses include building construction, accounting for 65.17 percent; infrastructure construction and investment, accounting for 20.98 percent; real estate development and investment, accounting for 11.46 percent; survey and design, accounting for 0.47 percent; and other businesses, accounting for 1.92 percent. China Communications Construction (601800) Data from the annual report of the Shanghai Stock Exchange Company is shown in Table 3, and Table 4 shows China Construction (601668) data from the annual report of the company on the Shanghai Stock Exchange.

Table 3. China Communications Construction Data from the annual report of the Shanghai Stock Exchange Company Unit: 100 million yuan

	2013	2014	2015	2016	2017	2018	2019	2020	2021	2022
Revenue	3324.87	3666.73	4044.2	4317.43	4828.04	4908.72	5554.46	6272.86	6858.31	7202.75
Receivable	587.37	599.54	638.46	834.37	680.45	834.55	961.14	1024.21 .	975. 6 4	1038.86
Bad debt	18.71	13.01	43.09	44.47	56.93	27.93	44.51	56.50	74.48	99.76
Gross profit rate	13.03%	13. 61 %	15.2%	14.9%	13.97%	13.49%	12.76%	13.02%	12.52%	11.65%
Net profit ratio	3.57%	3.75%	3.9%	3.99%	4.42%	4.13%	3.9%	3.08%	3.43%	3.44%
Net margin	121.39	138.87	156.96	167.43	205.81	196.8	200.13	162.06	179.95	191.04

Table 4. China Construction data from the company's annual report on the Shanghai Stock Exchange. Unit: 100 million yuan

	2013	2014	2015	2016	2017	2018	2019	2020	2021	2022
revenue	6817.92	8000.29	8805.77	9597.65	10500	12000	14200	16200	18900	20600
receivable	836.82	1184.3	1155.57	1386.49	1377.14	1675.53	1539.62	1604.98	1805.99	2104.32
Bad debt	16.66	45.24	37.56	53.65	70.49	104.66	35.38	36.70	126.33	138.48
Gross	17.28%	16.24%	15.52%	15.68%	15.34%	15.68%	15.11%	14.96%	14.95%	13.26%

Profit rate										
Net Profit ratio	4.31%	4.15%	4.08%	4.29%	4.43%	4.62%	4.45%	4.39%	4.11%	3.37%
Net margin	203.99	225.7	260.62	298.7	329. 42	382.41	418.81	449.25	515.49	509.5

3.2 Comparative analysis of two companies

China Communications Construction and China Construction's main revenue growth in 10 years were 116.32% and 202.14%, respectively. The company's net profit increased by 57.37% and 142.73% in 10 years. The main businesses of China Communications Construction and China Construction have some similarities but are not exactly the same. This study analyses the development of the two similar but somewhat different industry leaders, industry changes, the quality of corporate profits, and the investment value of the two companies.

Analyzing the main revenue growth of the two leading companies, China Construction is significantly faster than China Communications Construction. The main reason for this is related to China's real estate policy in the last 10 years, including the active demand for improved housing, the Chinese government's land finance policy, and the fact that housing is the most important financial investment tool for the Chinese people. In the last 10 years, China Construction's Industry Prosperity Index has been significantly better than China Communications Construction's.

4 Suggestion

In the last 10 years, China Construction's net profit growth rate is also significantly faster than China Communications Construction's. As we can see from the chart, the main reasons are as follows: one is that the main revenue of China Construction has grown much faster than China Communications Construction. The second is that the net profit margin of China Construction is higher than that of China Communications Construction in most periods [5,6]. Thirdly, the gross profit margin of China Construction is higher than that of China Communications Construction in most periods. It shows that in the past 10 years, China Construction's industry boom index profitability has been significantly better than China Communications Construction's.

The overall earning capacity of China Construction is stronger than that of China Communications Construction in the first 10 years, but the following problems need to be paid attention to: firstly, the gross profit margin of China Construction has been in decline since 2018. At the same time, in 2018, China Construction's net profit margin has been moving downward. From 2018, China Construction's receivables have started to increase, and there has been an acceleration in the last two years. Thankfully, China Construction's bad and doubtful debts have not formed a trend after 2018, although they have increased in some years. This study can draw two conclusions from these data: one: China's real estate industry has basically hit a high point since 2018, the industry boom index has declined, the industry's gross and net profit margins have declined, and receivables have begun to increase, which is bad news for stock investors, especially bond investors. Second, the leading company in China's construction management efficiency is still very high and did not appear to systematically increase in bad debts, indicating that a leading company in the industry downturn to come, on the one hand, will be affected by the industry downturn, but at the same time, also has a stronger anti-risk ability [7,8]. As an investment institution, the choice of large companies will have a greater ability to resist risk. For bond investors to choose a large leading company, the company's management efficiency is very important.

Analysing China Communications Construction from the chart, from 2015, China Communications Construction's gross margin slowed from 15.2% to 11.65% in 2022. However, the company's net profit margin did not trend down from 3.9%, indicating that China Communications Construction's management efficiency is still very high. The company's receivables and bad and doubtful accounts growth rate, main business growth rate, and net profit increase rate are similar with the same convergence. It shows that the transport construction industry, on the whole, is still relatively stable, and the market space is still increasing. The gross profit margin declined slowly, but the company's net profit did not fall at the same time, indicating that the company's management efficiency, cost control, technological advances, and other aspects have been improved [9, 10].

5 Conclusion

First, the four companies are the world's top 500 companies in the construction industry, but in terms of investment value, the overall China Railway in the four companies have more investment value and growth. Management level is also more excellent, and whether it is the stock of institutional investors or bond institutional investors, it is recommended to choose China Railway in the case of the same or similar market valuation level. Second, the gross and net profit margins of the four companies are very low, indicating that the world's top 500 important Chinese enterprises are still in the small and medium-sized parts of the world's industrial division of labor. With small gross and net margins, it will take a long time and continuous improvement for Chinese companies to compete with the world's best. Third, China's real estate industry has begun to show a downward trend after the industry's high point starting in 2018, and there has been no obvious improvement so far. Fourth, China's construction enterprises are slowly improving their market scale, operating experience, and efficiency after a long development period. Due to the low gross profit margin and net interest rate, enterprises that want technological progress must maintain relatively low wages. Otherwise, it won't be easy to accumulate the financial strength to achieve sustained technological progress and attract the world's best talent to continue to join. Finally, the construction industry has a low gross profit margin, low net profit margin, more receivables, more bad and doubtful debts, and inevitably, at the same time, the technical requirements are high, and there are many bad debts, so it is difficult to make money. It is also difficult to make money because of the high technical requirements and bad debts. It is also quite risky and difficult for other big companies to enter this industry and form an advantage.

References

1. G. Ballard. Eng, Constr, Archit. Manage, **9**(3), 284-291 (2022).
2. J. Bennett. Seminar on Strategic Planning in Construction Companies, 288-303 (1994)
3. H. Guizhen, et al. Environmental Management, **44** (3), 579–89 (2009)
4. G. Ofori. Constr. Manage. Econom., **18**, 257-262 (2000)
5. R. Yin. Case study research: Design and methods, Sage Publishing, Beverly Hills, Calif (1984)
6. S. B. Zhang and M. A. Liu. Constr. Manage. Econom., **24**, 817-828 (2006)
7. C. Honghan. Research on Financial Risk Management of China Railway Construction Corporation Limited]. Jinan university (2023)
8. Y. Yang. Rural Economics and Science and Technology, **30**(16):85-86 (2019)
9. Z. Xiao. Financial Statement Analysis of China Railway Construction under the framework of Harvard Analysis. Jilin University (2019)
10. 2013-2022 Annual Report of China Railway Construction Co., LTD. China Railway Construction News, 2019-04-04 (002).

The comparison of macroeconomic development between the united states and japan in recent in recent years is analyzed from nasdaq and nikkei index

Rongzhan Deng*

Faculty of Business, Economics & Law, The University of Queensland, St Lucia, Brisbane QLD, 4072, Australia

Abstract. The changes in the Nasdaq and Nikkei over the past in recent years offer valuable insights for evaluating macroeconomic developments in the United States and Japan. Through an analysis of these two indicators, this paper can initially draw conclusions about the state of both countries' economies. Over the past three years, the Nasdaq index has exhibited a relatively stable growth trend, maintaining strong overall growth despite fluctuations caused by global uncertainties. This may reflect advancements in areas such as technological innovation and the Internet sector, as well as investors' optimism regarding future prospects. In contrast, the Nikkei index has displayed a more intricate and volatile pattern during this same period. While there have been some gains, it has experienced an overall decline marked by shocks. This could be attributed to various challenges faced by Japan including an aging population, low growth rate, and declining corporate competitiveness. The objective of this paper is to explore a similar model that explains stock markets in both the US and Japan. Many long-term investors base their stock decisions on the assumption that corporate cash flows should grow alongside economic performance while considering a constant or slow-moving discount rate. Therefore, it is expected that stock returns may exhibit correlation with future economic performance. Another concern worth addressing is how deflation might impact real stock returns.

1 Introduction

The primary motivations of the Federal Reserve for raising interest rates include inflation control, economic stability maintenance, and employment boost. By increasing interest rates, the Fed can effectively curb inflation, prevent overheating of the economy, and maintain a stable value of money [1]. Moreover, higher interest rates can impact consumption and investment behavior, thereby influencing various aspects of the economy such as stock market performance, bond market dynamics, currency exchange rates in global markets as well as affecting enterprises' and individuals' financial situations [2]. This paper aims to explore the potential impact of the Federal Reserve's policy on raising interest rates specifically on the stock market. It does so by constructing an ARIMA model to forecast stock index trends while considering both policy effects on the market and non-white noise components within the forecasting model. Additionally, this paper proposes a method for identifying significant influencing factors and analyzes time characteristics related to policy implementation in financial markets [3].

The subsequent sections are organized as follows: Part 2 introduces data sources and unit root testing; Part 3 employs an ARIMA model to forecast stock index trends; Section 4 discusses findings including analysis of policy implications and non-white noise components; Finally, Section 5 summarizes research findings while providing suggestions for policymakers and investors [4].

2 Research design

2.1 Source of data

According to the demand, the analysis involves downloading and examining the closing price data of the Nasdaq Index and Nikkei Index from investing [1] for the period spanning from March 2021 to March 2023. These two indexes hold significant importance as representative indicators in the global financial market and possess substantial reference value for investors. Being one of the most prominent technology stock indexes in the US stock market, the Nasdaq index encompasses numerous renowned technology companies such as Apple, Microsoft, Amazon, among others.

By analyzing the closing price data of the Nasdaq index, valuable insights can be gained into the trajectory of economic development. The Nikkei index serves as a pivotal and extensively monitored composite average of stock prices in the Japanese stock market, encompassing companies from diverse industries and reflecting the overall performance of Japan's economic system.

* Corresponding author: rongzhan.deng@uqconnect.edu.au

Through acquiring and scrutinizing daily and weekly closing price data, profound understanding can be acquired regarding the challenges and opportunities encountered by companies listed on the Tokyo Stock Exchange, as well as comprehending Japan's economy holistically in recent years. To ensure utmost accuracy and comprehensiveness, it is imperative to exercise caution while selecting reliable sources and employing professional tools for data extraction and processing. Additionally, attention should be paid to whether both daily and weekly closing price information is included since these different frequency types of data offer a more comprehensive and detailed perspective on asset movement. In summary, upon obtaining and analyzing the closing price data of both Nasdaq index and Nikkei index within a specific time frame, more intricate yet precise conclusions pertaining to global financial market dynamics, Tokyo Stock Exchange-listed companies' status quo, as well as Japan's overall economic situation can be drawn; thereby providing robust support and reference for investors [5].

2.2 Unit root test.

The test statistics and corresponding p-values for different conditions are presented in Table 1. Unit root tests are employed to examine the presence of unit root characteristics, indicating non-stationarity, in the time series data. Generally, if the p-value is less than the significance level (usually set at 0.05), he null hypothesis can be rejected, indicating that the time series is stationary. Based on the data presented in the table, this part are able to provide the following explanations:

The provided daily frequency data shows that all p-values of the original series are greater than 0.05, indicating that there is insufficient evidence to reject the null hypothesis of a unit root presence.; thus, confirming non-stationarity of the original series. However, after applying first and second differencing techniques, all resulting p-values fall below 0.05, indicating stationarity of these differenced series.

For weekly frequency data from US and daily frequency data from Japan, similar observations hold true: initial p-values for both original series surpass 0.05 denoting non-stationarity; however, after employing first difference technique on each dataset separately, resulting p-values become lower than 0.05 signifying stationarity.

Regarding weekly frequency data from Japan alone: just like previous cases mentioned above, the initial p-value exceeds 0.05 implying non-stationarity; nevertheless-value drops below 0.05 upon implementing first difference technique which indicates stationarity. Therefore, based on outcomes derived from unit root tests, it can be concluded that in these scenarios, the application of first differences renders stationary time series suitable for subsequent analysis and modeling.

Table 1 Weak stationarity test

	t	p
	US, daily	
Ln index	-1.021	0.9412
1st order difference	-12.010	0
2nd order difference	-17.991	0
	US, weekly	
Ln index	-1.435	0.8505
1st order difference	-5.433	0
	Japan, Daily	
Ln index	-2.330	0.4176
1st order difference	-11.033	0
2nd order difference	-18.092	0
	Japan, weekly	
Ln index	-3.162	0.0922
1st order difference	-5.796	0

2.3 Model specification

The autoregressive component in the ARMA model establishes a linear relationship between the current observation and past observations, while the moving average component represents a linear relationship between the current observation and previous error terms. By fitting historical data and incorporating known parameters for prediction, valuable insights can be gained into patterns and characteristics underlying time series data. The fundamental structure of this article utilizing the ARMA model is as follows:

$$X_t = \phi_0 + \sum_{i=1}^{p} \phi_i x_{t-i} + a_t - \sum_{i=1}^{q} \theta_i a_{t-i} \quad (1)$$

Where $\{a_t\}$ is a white noise sequence, p and q are non-negative integers. Both AR model and MA model are special cases of ARMA(p,q), and using the delay operator, the above model can be written as:

$$(1-\phi_1 B - \cdots - \phi_p B^p)X_t = \phi_0 + (1-\theta_1 B - \cdots - \theta_q B^q)a_t \quad (2)$$

Among them $1-\phi_1 B - \cdots - \phi_p B^p$ is the AR polynomial model, similarly, $1-\theta_1 B - \cdots - \theta_q B^q$ for MA polynomial model. The AR and MA polynomials are required to be different from each other to ensure that the order (p, q) of the model is the same as that of the AR model. The AR polynomial introduces the characteristic equation of the ARMA model, and if the absolute value of all the solutions of the characteristic equation is less than 1, the ARMA model has the weakly stationary property. At this point, the unconditional mean of the model is:

$$E(x_t) = \phi_0/(1-\phi_1 - \cdots - \phi_p) \quad (3)$$

The date data from the four dta documents should be imported separately before importing the STATA software. To facilitate subsequent modeling analysis, March 16, 2022 should be designated. as T_0, representing the first interest rate hike time by the Federal Reserve. Once data import is completed, the next step involves generating a logarithmic series of the stock index and its corresponding logarithmic return series. By applying a log transformation, Enables more accurate observation of the trend in stock price changes and calculation of the logarithmic return rate between consecutive days. Subsequently, a stationarity test is required to verify whether these resulting four log series and log return series exhibit stationarity characteristics. Stationarity serves as one of the prerequisites for establishing various time series models; hence appropriate statistical methods are employed in this step for testing purposes. Upon confirming stationarity, partial autocorrelation function plots (PACF) and autocorrelation function plots (ACF) can be generated for analyzing log return series. These graphs aid in determining suitable order parameters for AR (autoregressive) and MA (moving average) models. Finally, after selecting appropriate AR and MA order parameters, an ARIMA (p, d, q) model can be constructed to predict stock price trends beyond T_0.

3. Empirical results and analysis

3.1. Order of order

The order in the first difference of the daily data cannot be determined, indicating either an excessively large order or indeterminacy. Consequently, a second-order model is employed for the daily data while a first-order model is utilized for the weekly data. This holds true for Japan as well. Although the original series is non-stationary, its difference series exhibits stationarity; hence, modeling should be based on the difference series. Notably, in daily and weekly data analysis, first differences are used in one case while second differences are used in another case. Subsequently, PACF and ACF are employed to determine parameters of the ARIMA model which comprises three components: p, d, q; where p represents the parameter of AR part and q denotes that of MA part; meanwhile d signifies the number of differencing operations applied [6]

The value of d is set to 2 for daily data and 1 for weekly data. Therefore, the parameters p, sf, and sf are utilized to determine the order of p, i.e., its specific value. Let us ascertain the order or specific value of q through sf. The determination of PD has already been made. Now it is necessary to establish the orders or values of both p and q corresponding to the daily data us while generally disregarding cases exceeding a magnitude of 10 [7]. Since the MLE method often fails to converge, an evaluation standard typically selects levels less than or equal to 10. If the significant interval lies outside this range, a level (ranging from 1 to 10) is chosen instead. The temporal correlation is selected based on whether time exhibits significance or not; if it exceeds a certain threshold, then it is considered significant and corresponding values for p and q are chosen (e.g., selecting "1021" for the first model). Similarly, The respective orders for all four models will be determined (US daily, US weekly, Japan daily, Japan weekly) as (10.2,1) (4,1,4) (10,2,1) (4,1,0) (please see Fig. 1).

The value of d is set to 2 for daily data and 1 for weekly data. Therefore, The parameters p, sf, and sf are utilized to determine the order of p, i.e., its specific value. Let us ascertain the order or specific value of q through sf. The determination of PD has already been made. Now it is necessary to establish the orders or values of both p and q corresponding to the daily data us while generally disregarding cases exceeding a magnitude of 10 [7]. Since the MLE method often fails to converge, an evaluation standard typically selects levels less than or equal to 10. If the significant interval lies outside this range, a level (ranging from 1 to 10) is chosen instead. The temporal correlation is selected based on whether time exhibits significance or not; if it exceeds a certain threshold, then it is considered significant and corresponding values for p and q are chosen (e.g., selecting "1021" for the first model). Similarly, The respective orders for all four models will be determined (US daily, US weekly, Japan daily, Japan weekly) as (10.2,1) (4,1,4) (10,2,1) (4,1,0).

PACF ACF

US, daily

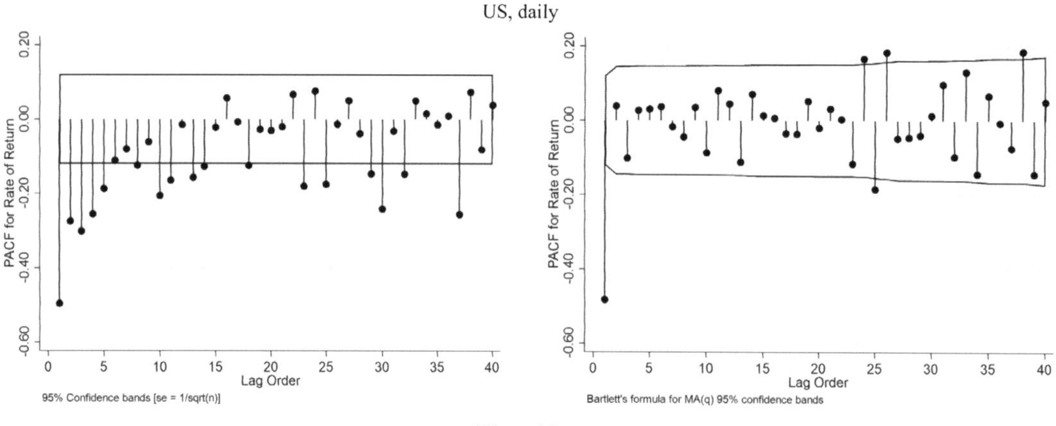

US, weekly

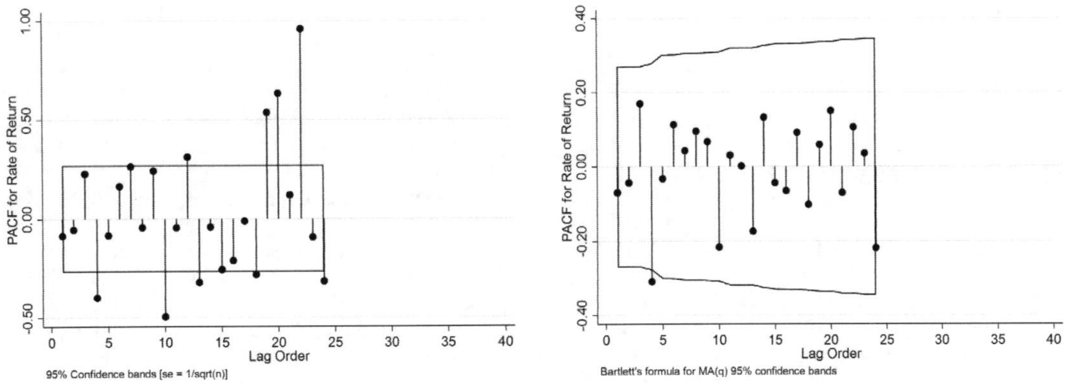

Japan, Daily

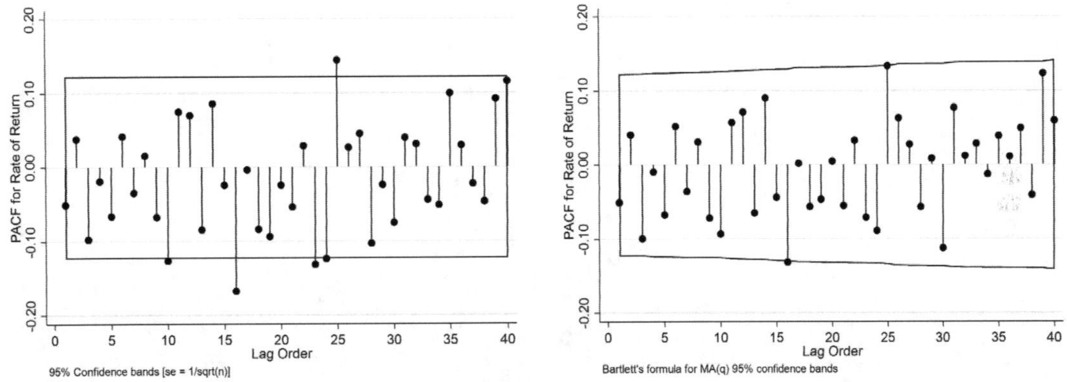

Japan, weekly

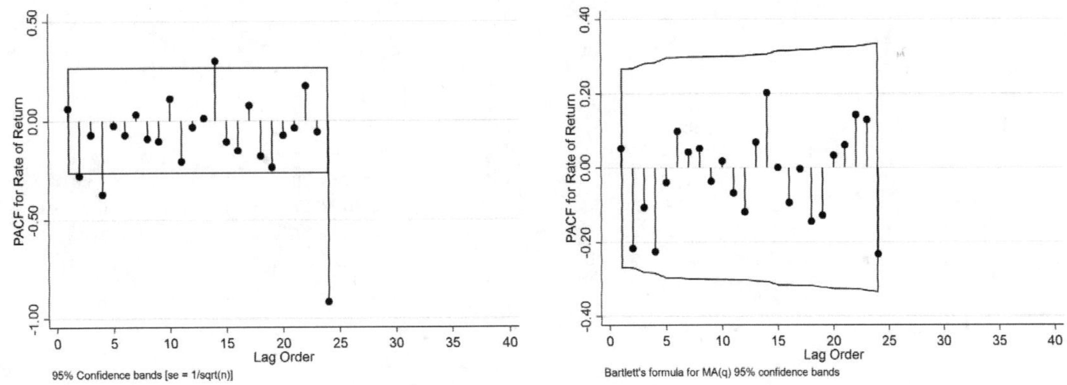

Fig. 1. ARMA (p, q) identification

Photo credit: Original

For the two models with d=2, a residual test is conducted, and Table 2 presents the results indicating that the residuals adhere to the white noise property. However, for the two models with d=1, they fail to meet the condition of white noise. In a model Y=xbeta+epsilon, where epsilon represents the residual and should conform to the characteristics of a white noise distribution. Although there are two non-white noise components present in our current scenario, they do not pose significant concerns for those who are not engaged in quantitative trading and only seek marginal gains of 1% or 2% at most. Hence, even if it deviates from white noise characteristics, it holds no substantial consequences nor leads to model failure. The developed models primarily serve for predicting overall trends of Y; thus minor deviations within a few percentage points do not require excessive attention. Despite some non-white noise components present in these two models, their impact remains acceptable.

Table 2 Residual test

Model	Portmanteau (Q) statistic	Prob > chi2
US, daily - ARIMA(10,2,1)	43.1163	0.3395
US, weekly -	70.6821	0.0020

ARIMA(4,1,4)		
Japan, Daily-ARIMA(10,2,1)	*47.6192*	0.1904
Japan, weekly-ARIMA(4,1,0)	91.3388	0.0000

3.2. Forecast results and interpretation

Making forecasts is akin to our previous objective of utilizing historical data for future prediction. If a certain event had not occurred, what would have been the performance of the index? The predicted values from the orange line and the actual values from the blue line are presented below. In case the Fed had not raised rates, which stock index would you have chosen - Nasdaq 100 or CSI 500? Contrary to expectations, in absence of a rate increase by the Fed, it should have declined but instead showed an upward trend. Reflecting on our earlier narrative, how should the stock market respond following a rate hike by the Fed? Shouldn't there be a decline in stock market indices? According to theory, this should be true as an increase in risk-free rate prompts individuals to prefer holding risk-free assets over risky ones [8]. However, this example contradicts that notion since even though the blue line remains above the orange line, it is crucial to note that this observation is only applicable in short-term scenarios [9]. The interest rates were increased on March 16 and projected backwards for only a period of 10 days, which is the longest time frame considered. Therefore, during this subsequent 10-day period (i.e., from March 16th to March 28th), no significant downward trend can be observed; thus, it cannot be concluded that its impact is absent in short-term durations.

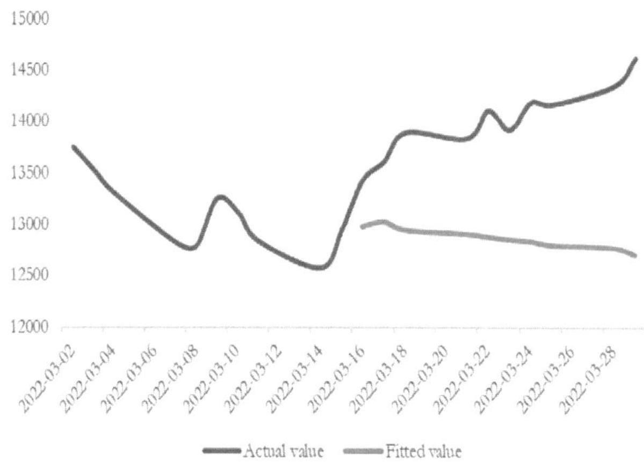

Fig. 2. Actual value and fitted value, US-daily

Photo credit: Original

Figure 2: The graph depicts the correlation between the actual values (blue line) and model-fitted values (orange line) of daily frequency data for the United States. By computing the root mean square error (RMSE), it can be inferred that the model's prediction error is 0.012, indicating high accuracy in its predictions. As illustrated in the figure, variations may occur in differences between model-fitted and actual values across different time periods; for instance, during early 2019, there was a significant difference between these two values which gradually decreased after mid-2019.

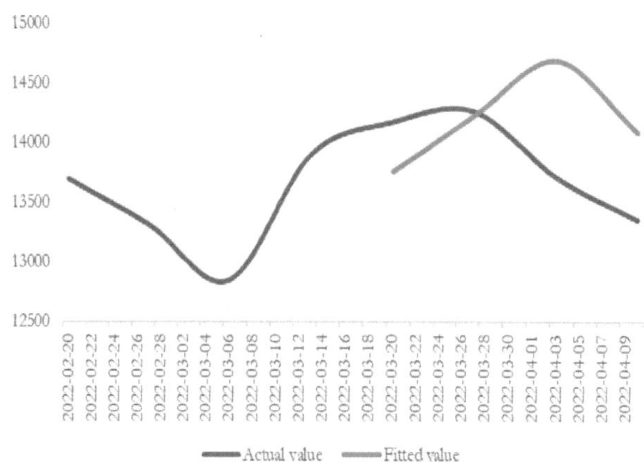

Fig. 3. Actual value and fitted value, US-weekly

Photo credit: Original

Figure 3: The graph illustrates the correlation between the actual weekly frequency data for the United States (blue line) and the model-fitted values (orange line). -By computing the RMSE, it can be inferred that the model's prediction error is 0.008, indicating a high level of accuracy in its predictions. -As depicted in the figure, there are fluctuations in the difference between actual and fitted values over different time periods. For instance, at the beginning of 2022, there was a significant gap between these two values; however, after mid-2022, this difference gradually decreased.

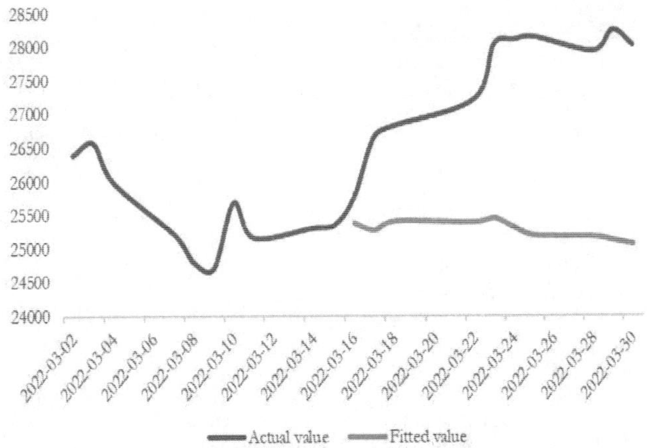

Fig. 4. Actual value and fitted value, Japan-Daily

Photo credit: Original

Figure 4: The graph depicts the correlation between Japan's daily frequency data, represented by the blue line, and the model-fitted values, depicted by the orange line. By calculating the RMSE, The model's prediction error can be determined to be 0.011, indicating a high level of accuracy in its forecasts. As illustrated in the figure, there are temporal variations in the disparity between the model-fitted and observed values. For instance, during early 2019, there was a notable discrepancy between these two sets of values; however, this difference gradually diminished after mid-2019.

Therefore, a weekly data model, 4,1,4, is utilized to conduct an in-depth analysis of short-term movements in financial markets. Through this model, can provide precise predictions for the future state of the financial market in the upcoming month. From this perspective, it becomes evident that financial markets are undergoing a reversal and gradually experiencing the impact of interest rate hike policies. However, it should be noted that policy implementations in financial markets typically do not yield immediate and conspicuous effects; rather they require a certain period of time to manifest fully[10]. This implies that investors and participants need to exercise patience and consider long-term trends comprehensively when making decisions. Furthermore, with regard to the Japanese market specifically, neither daily nor weekly data indicate any discernible impact as evidenced by the consistent positioning of the orange line below the blue line; thus suggesting relative stability at present which may be attributed to unique economic circumstances and policy measures within the country. In summary, through understanding and analyzing various data models meticulously, The future trend of financial markets can be predicted more accurately by adjusting the strategy, taking into account the specific characteristics exhibited by different countries or regions. Simultaneously acknowledging both implementation timelines for policies and variations in economic environments across nations is crucial for maintaining rational thinking throughout investment processes while conducting comprehensive assessments of risks and benefits [7].

4. Discussion

Compared to the existing literature, the conclusions of this paper are partially consistent with other studies [4, 5, 11]. For instance, numerous studies utilize ARIMA models for forecasting stock index trends and focus on policy impacts on the market. However, this paper delves further into examining the influence of non-white noise components on prediction results and proposes a method for establishing acceptable influencing factors. These aspects are relatively scarce in current literature.

The implication of this study is that when constructing forecasting models, various factors should be comprehensively considered, including policy impacts on the market and non-white noise within the model. Simultaneously, attention must also be given to parameter selection and residual testing to ensure model accuracy and reliability. Additionally, the results indicate that policy implementation effects in financial markets typically do not occur immediately but take some time to materialize. This has significant implications for policymakers and investors.

According to the findings of this study, policymakers should recognize that policy implementation usually requires a certain amount of time before producing effects. Therefore, it is necessary to fully predict and analyze market reactions when formulating policies while considering the impact of non-white noise components in forecast models.

Investors can learn from this research that employing an ARIMA model can effectively predict stock index trends while considering policy impacts on the market. Furthermore, investors should also pay attention to how non-white noise components within their models affect prediction results and determine their acceptability level accordingly. When making investment decisions, investors can adjust their strategies based on forecasted outcomes in order to achieve better returns.

5 Conclusion

This study focuses on the issue of stock index forecasting. Through in-depth analysis of daily and weekly data, The ARIMA model for trend forecasting was successfully constructed by employing differencing series and utilizing the PACF and ACF to determine the parameters during the model building process. The results of residual tests indicate that in both models with d=2, the residuals conform to white noise characteristics. However, this white noise condition is not satisfied in the two models with d=1. Although there are some non-white noise components present, their impact is deemed acceptable. In terms of forecasting, By constructing a weekly data model, It is possible to anticipate the potential impact of policy measures, such as a Federal Reserve interest rate hike, on the stock market through forecasting. Our analysis indicates that financial markets have initiated a reversal trend, observed one month in advance, indicating that the effects of interest rate hikes are gradually becoming apparent. This also demonstrates that policy implementation within financial markets typically requires time to yield results. Additionally, neither daily nor weekly data is affected in Japanese markets where consistently throughout observation periods, represented by orange lines always being below blue lines. In summary, this study's findings highlight that ARIMA models can effectively forecast stock index trends while emphasizing consideration for market impacts resulting from policies and attention towards non-white noise components when determining acceptable factors.

References

1. S. Choi. Analysis of stock market efficiency during crisis periods in the US stock market: Differences between the global financial crisis and COVID-19 pandemic. SMIA, 574, 125988 (2021).
2. M. Goldstein, A. Shkilko, B. Van Ness, & R. Van Ness. Competition in the market for NASDAQ securities. JFM, 11(2), 113–143 (2008).
3. Investing. https://cn.investing.com
4. A. Serletis, & A. Rosenberg. Mean reversion in the US stock market. CSF, 40(4), 2007–2015 (2009).
5. Masaryk University. Proceedings of the 14th International Scientific Conference European Financial Systems 2017. In J. Nešleha, K. Urbanovský, & T. Plíhal (Eds.), Proceedings of the 14th International Scientific Conference European Financial Systems 2017 (1st ed.). Brno: Masaryk University. ISBN 978-80-210-8609-8 (2017).
6. P. Pasquariello, & C. Vega. Strategic Cross-Trading in the U.S. stock market. EFR, 19(1), 229–282 (2013).
7. Y. Hsing. (2013). The Stock Market and Macroeconomic Factors in Japan and Policy Implications. ISJFA, 1(1), 20-31 (2013).
8. A. Humpe. Macroeconomic variables and the stock market: An empirical comparison of the US and Japan (Doctoral dissertation, University of St Andrews) (2007).
9. A. Humpe & P. Macmillan. Non-linear predictability of stock market returns: comparative evidence from Japan and the US. IMFI, 11(4): 36-47 (2014).
10. A. Humpe, P. Macmillan. Can macroeconomic variables explain long-term stock market movements? A comparison of the US and Japan. AFE, 19(2): 111–119 (2009).
11. M. Naseem, M. Mohsin, L. Hui, Z. Liyan, & K. Penglai. Investor Psychology and Stock Market Behavior During the Initial Era of COVID-19: A Study of China, Japan, and the United States. FP, 12, 626934 (2021).

The Impact of China's Tax Policy Reform on the Gap between Rich and Poor

Lin Liu[1,*]

[1] School of International Economics and International Relations, Liaoning University, Dalian, China.

Abstract. Common prosperity is the goal that the Chinese government is constantly striving for, and the reform of the tax system is the only way to achieve this goal. In the past ten years, China has continuously carried out tax reform and achieved good results. Previous scholars have conducted in-depth research on China's tax reform from multiple perspectives. Previous research has focused on the impact of tax policy on China's economic growth, exploring how taxes stimulate or constrain the development of different industries and regions. And early research focused on social equity issues, examining the impact of tax policies on income distribution, and how to reduce the social gap between rich and poor through taxation. These studies provide lessons and theoretical support for current tax reforms and provide a basis for future research. This article will start from two aspects: personal income tax reform and value-added tax reform, and analyze the impact of personal income tax and value-added tax reforms on the gap between the rich and the poor.

1. Introduction

Taxation is the backbone of national finances, providing funds for the government to provide public services and infrastructure. Regulation of the economy through taxation to promote growth and stability. The tax system can also be used to achieve social equality and reduce the gap between rich and poor. This is vital to maintaining the functioning of the country and promoting economic prosperity and social justice. However, the so-called equality is not egalitarianism. Egalitarianism has great negative effects and seriously affects efficiency. Tax reform can only make a trade-off between efficiency and equality [1]. In the past ten years, China has continuously carried out tax reform and achieved a series of achievements. One focus is the reform of the personal income tax system, including adjustments to the tax rate structure and thresholds. Regarding whether personal income tax can alleviate the inequality of income distribution, some relevant scholars have studied the equal opportunity effect of personal income tax in my country based on the empirical paradigm of equal opportunities in income distribution, and believe that reducing personal income tax can reduce the inequality Gini coefficient [2]. On the other hand, value-added tax reform has also attracted much attention. While ensuring that fiscal revenue remains unchanged, using value-added tax to replace social security payments for financing can improve income distribution and promote fairness to a certain extent [3]. In addition, the relationship between local finance and central finance and the reform of the tax collection and management system are also topics that have attracted widespread attention and discussion [4]. China's tax reform faces some potential gaps and challenges. One of them is that local governments are highly dependent on finance, and reform needs to balance the relationship between local and central finances to ensure sustainable development of the local economy [5]. On the other hand, tax system complexity and opacity are also an issue, requiring clearer and simplified tax policies [6]. In addition, the development of emerging industries such as the digital economy may also cause the tax system to lag, requiring corresponding adjustments to adapt to the new economic form. These gaps require finding a balance in tax reform to ensure that the reform can promote economic development and maintain fiscal sustainability. Studying the impact of taxation on the gap between rich and poor is crucial because tax policy directly affects the distribution of wealth and social equity.

2. The impact of tax reform on inequality

2.1 China continues to deepen the value-added tax reform.

In 2012, the "business tax to value-added tax" pilot was implemented, and in 2016 the pilot was fully launched. In 2017, the 13% tax rate was canceled, and the four tax rates were simplified into three. In 2018 and 2019, the value-added tax rate was continuously reduced, starting from the "13th Five-Year Plan" During the period, the scale of domestic tax cuts and fee reductions exceeded 7.6 trillion yuan. By 2022, the new tax cuts fee

* Corresponding author: yangxu@lnu.edu.cn

reductions tax rebates, and tax deferrals will exceed 4.2 trillion yuan. This shows that the structural tax cuts policy has effectively alleviated the burden on residents. and the burden on enterprises [7].

At the same time, the scope of input tax deductions has been expanded, and a system for refunding retained tax at the end of the period has been established. While establishing a modern value-added tax system, the tax burden of all industries has been "only reduced but not increased", significantly reducing the tax burden of taxpayers [8].

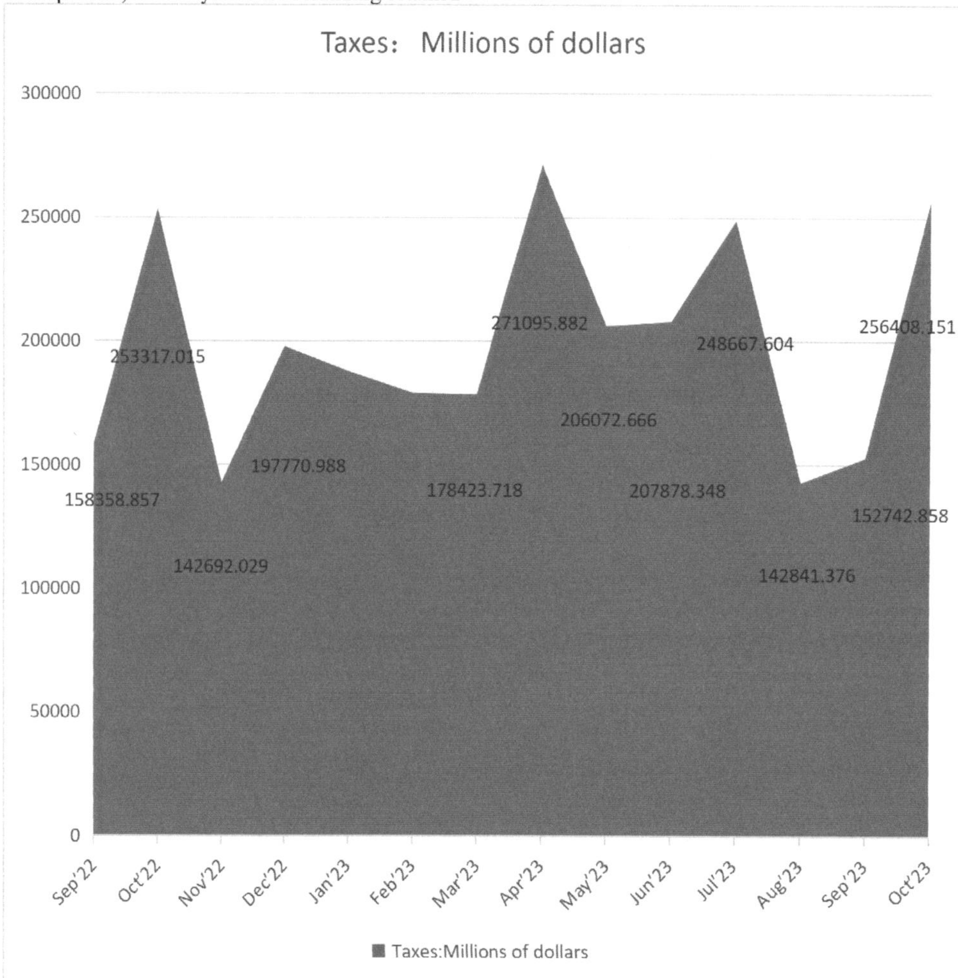

Fig. 1. China's taxes from 2022 to 2023 (Picture credit :Original)

As shown in Figure 1, it can be seen that taxes will be the highest in April 2023, and will be lowest in November 2022. The tax rate was the lowest in March. In the tax range from September 2022 to October 2023, the tax change has been rising to around 140,000 million dollars and then rising and has always been stable in the range of 140,000 million dollars to 250,000 million dollars float. Figure 2 can be analyzed in the same way. It can be seen that China's tax flexibility is relatively large and has good stability. As can be seen from the table data above, the Chinese government is implementing a cyclical tax reduction policy. This paper believes that tax and fee reductions will have a positive impact on promoting social equity and narrowing the gap between rich and poor. Of course, there are also disadvantages. Please see the analysis below.

1. Promote consumption: Lowering the value-added tax may lead to lower prices for goods and services and encourage people to increase consumption. This could be good news for those at the bottom, whose living expenses are relatively high. After the country lowered the value-added tax, commodity prices fell, making it easier for lower-class families to purchase necessities, thus improving their living standards.

2. Stimulate small and micro enterprises: Reducing value-added tax may reduce the tax burden of small and micro enterprises, encourage their development and growth, and promote employment.

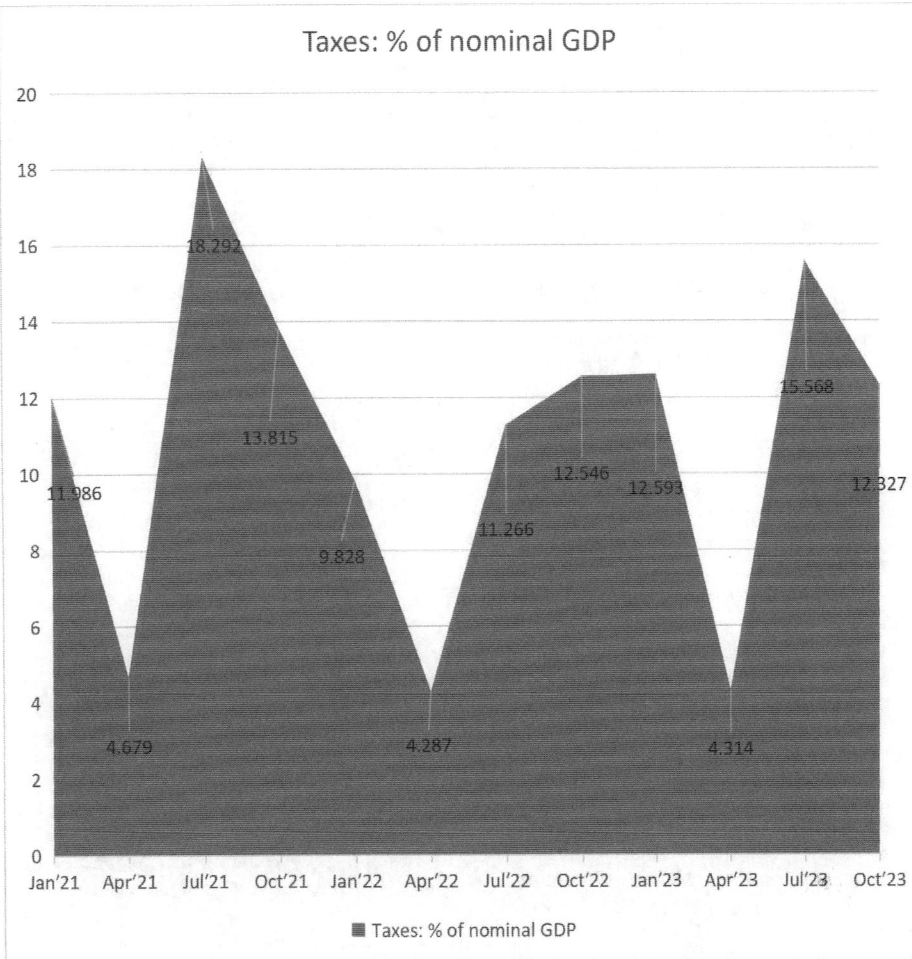

Fig. 2. Nominal GDP (Taxes:%) (Picture credit :Original)

If a country implements a differentiated value-added tax policy and provides larger tax reductions to small and micro enterprises, it will help these enterprises obtain more funds to expand their business and provide more employment opportunities. However

1. Benefits favor the rich: If the benefits of reducing the value-added tax mainly flow to high-income groups, it may widen the gap between the rich and the poor.

If the effects of falling commodity prices are felt more by wealthier households, while lower-income households fail to fully enjoy them due to other factors, the gap between rich and poor may further widen.

Overall, lowering VAT may have a positive impact on reducing the gap between rich and poor, but there is a need to ensure that its benefits reach more of those at the bottom, while balancing fiscal sustainability.

2.2 China has implemented personal income tax reform to reduce the tax burden on low- and middle-income groups.

The threshold for personal income tax has been raised, the scope of comprehensive income taxation has been clarified, special additional deductions have been established, the tax rate structure has been optimized and adjusted, and a personal income tax system that combines comprehensive and classified income has been initially established [5].

Table 1. Personal income tax rate table

Level	Annual taxable income	tax rate （%）	quick calculation deductions
1	Not exceeding 36,000 yuan	3	0
2	More than 36,000 yuan to 144,000 yuan	10	2520
3	More than 144000 yuan to 300000 yuan	20	16920
4	More than 300000 yuan to 420000 yuan	25	31920
5	More than 420000 yuan to 660000 yuan	30	52920
6	More than 660000 yuan to 960000 yuan	35	85920
7	More than 960,000 yuan	45	181920

As an important part of tax reduction and fee reduction, personal income tax reform is a key measure to adjust the gap between the rich and the poor. Raising the personal income tax threshold will have a positive impact on reducing the gap between rich and poor.

1. Reduce the tax burden on the bottom group: Raising the threshold can reduce the tax burden on the bottom group, allowing them to retain more income for living expenses. Raise the threshold for personal income tax. As shown in Table 1, the quick deduction number for annual income not exceeding 36,000 yuan is 0, allowing more low-income people to be exempted from personal income tax, which can increase their disposable income and improve their living standards.

2. Promote consumption: After the people at the bottom gain more disposable income, they may increase consumer spending, thus stimulating economic growth. Due to the increase in the personal income tax threshold, lower-income families have more funds available to purchase goods and services, which helps promote market activity. However, this behavior has a drawback, which is that it will affect fiscal revenue and thus the funding sources for public services and social welfare projects.

3. Conclusion

China's reforms to value-added tax and personal income tax have complex effects on the gap between rich and poor. VAT reform may help improve the living standards of people at the bottom by reducing the burden on businesses and promoting economic growth. However, care needs to be taken to ensure that the benefits of the reforms are more equally distributed and to avoid benefits flowing primarily to the wealthy.

Reform of personal income tax, especially raising the threshold, will help reduce the tax burden on low-income groups and encourage more people to share the fruits of economic growth. This is positive for narrowing the gap between rich and poor. However, policy implementation needs to be cautious to avoid benefits mainly benefiting high-income groups, thereby widening the gap between rich and poor.

Generally speaking, the impact of tax reform on the gap between rich and poor is related to specific policy design and implementation. If we can ensure that reform measures benefit more people at the bottom, it will help reduce the gap between rich and poor by promoting economic growth and increasing the disposable income of low-income people. However, reform measures that lead to fiscal imbalances and cuts in social services should be avoided, so as not to negatively impact those at the bottom.

When implementing tax reform, social equity, economic growth, and fiscal sustainability need to be comprehensively considered to ensure that the reform effect is consistent with the overall economic and social development goals. Different tax reforms should be coordinated and coordinated to form a comprehensive tax policy to promote fair, inclusive, and sustainable economic growth, and ultimately reduce the gap between rich and poor.

Generally speaking, tax and fee reductions have a profound impact on the distribution of rich and poor in China. First, by reducing the tax burden on low- and middle-income earners and lowering corporate tax rates, this policy will help narrow the income gap and promote a more balanced distribution of wealth. As a result, low- and middle-income people can enjoy more real income, improve their living standards, and promote social equity.

Secondly, tax and fee reductions encourage business investment and innovation, creating more opportunities and jobs for the economy. This kind of economic growth will help improve the overall social welfare level, enable more people to share the fruits of development, thereby slowing down the widening trend of the gap between rich and poor.

In addition, tax and fee reductions will also help stimulate market vitality and promote the upgrading of the economic structure. By reducing the burden on enterprises and stimulating innovation and competition, it can not only promote industrial upgrading, but also provide more opportunities for more people and promote the development of poor areas.

Finally, the significance of tax reduction and fee reduction on the distribution of rich and poor in China is to promote social equity and improve the living standards of low- and middle-income people. At the same time, by promoting economic growth, it creates opportunities for a wider range of people and helps achieve the goal of a comprehensively well-off society.

References

1. Z. Y. Yang, International Taxation In China, 3-11, 2020.
2. Z. Yang, Journal of Guizhou University of Finance and Economics, 225 (2023).
3. H. J. Xiong, Z. W. Tian, J. X. Zheng, Collected Essays on Finance and Economics, 10, 303 (2023).
4. W. Y. Xu, Q. S. Mo, J. H. Ma, Academic Journal Electronic Publishing House,2019.
5. Z. X. Dai, H. Y. Gao, B. W. Zhang, X. T. Wang, Tax system and policy, 87, 3 (2023).
6. Y. W. Cui, Tax research, 9 (2023).
7. Y. R. Li, H. Ding, Finance and economics, 2023 .
8. China in the past ten years: tax system reform has achieved a series of results, cctv.com. 2022.
9. D. Y. Chu, S. X. Chi, Research on Economics and Management, 38,10 (2017).
10. J. Yu, Huaqiao University, 2019.

SHS Web of Conferences **188**, 02003 (2024) https://doi.org/10.1051/shsconf/202418802003
ICDDE 2024

Negative Impact of Income Tax on Economic Growth

Wenting Fang*

Seventh College, University of California-San Diego, San Diego, California, 92122, United States

Abstract. In the intricate development of global trends, economic growth is a crucial part shaped by the factors all around from indicators like Gross Domestic Product (GDP), Gross National Income (GNI) to policies for taxation, exportation, social welfare and so on. Among them, taxation is an interesting topic discussed frequently by analysts and economists, which also contributed to wealth redistribution and inequality as important considerations. This article focuses on researching the impact of income tax on economic growth, including individual income tax and corporate income tax. The purpose of this research is to figure out whether cut in tax promotes economic growth in the United States. The results show that income tax rate indeed have a negative relationship with economic growth rate. The research's data specifically shows how GDP shift up or down with the change of consumption, investment, employment rate, and so on. Cut in taxation somewhat promotes the GDP growth, while people are more willing to consume, invest, and governments are more abundant in funding. Finally, this research suggests the policy maker to consider the lagging effect of taxation policy on economic growth and timely adjustment of taxation structure progressivity, and further research and development.

1 Introduction

At the beginning of the era of global economic growth, all nations share a commitment to harness the power of innovation to promote sustainable development and build a more inclusive and interconnected world. In this era, the pursuit of economic progress has become synonymous with a broader vision to not only lift the economy, but also improve the happiness level which indicate how people live and consume all around the world. Economists and researchers are committed to finding opportunities for countries to catch up with global trends and go even further.

Among all economic topics, taxation policy is the most interested one, which is a human reaction toward natural economic fluctuations. For centuries, human devote to perfect strategy in all fields. Similarly, making decision about reforming or creating taxation policy is like a strategic game. To make the research more precise and professional, the topic is to specify two common taxation which are individual income tax and corporate income tax. Therefore, this article explores on the topic of the how does individual income tax and corporate income tax impact on economic growth. One crucial motivation to be committed to this field is that taxation can be used as a tool of redistributing income or wealth [1]. This can help reduce income inequality by creating more opportunities for upward mobility. From another perspective, countries also used taxation to fund government service, correct market imperfection, and stimulate or press certain economic behaviors [1]. By using tax policies to stimulate investments in education, research, and economic development, governments can promote economic growth that benefits a broader segment of the population.

Existing literature investigated the rank of taxation which are the most harmful to economic growth. According to investigation provided, "corporate taxes are found to be most harmful for growth, followed by individual income taxes, and then consumption taxes" [2]. Thus, it is a good opportunity to deeply discussed how these taxation impact on economic growth, in order to give an initial enlightenment for national economists and politicians to publish helpful regulations.

2 Importance of taxation

It is important to figure out the formulation of taxation as a first step. The tax base refers to the economic activities or entities that are subject to taxation. Governments decide which types of income, transactions, or assets will be taxed. The tax structure involves determining the rates and brackets for different types of taxes including income tax, consumption tax, import and export tax and so on. To summarize governments' process, they firstly assess the overall economic conditions, including the growth rate of Gross Domestic Product (GDP), inflation, employment levels, and business cycles. Economic conditions influence the government's decisions on whether to stimulate or restrain economic activity through taxation. Thus, formulation of taxation can be a complex combination of several dilemmas.

Tax systems primarily help government with financing public expenditure [3]. To promote fairness or to address social and economic issues, the tax system

* Corresponding author: wefang@ucsd.edu

plays an indispensable role. Efficient tax systems should be implemented to reduce the burden of compliance on taxpayers and minimize administrative costs for governments. Simultaneously, these systems should serve as deterrents to tax avoidance and evasion. Nonetheless, taxes influences households' choices related to saving, labor participation, and investment in human capital. Similarly, taxes also impact the decisions of businesses, including choices regarding production, job creation, investment, and innovation, as well as influencing investors' decisions regarding savings channels and asset allocation [2,3].

2.1 Importance of income taxation

The United States created a progressive individual income tax. Individuals who have a higher income need to pay federal a higher rate of individual income tax [4]. Figure 1 shows that individuals who have a low income like people who earn less than 50k dollars annually have negative income tax. These data indicate governments might even give low income people subsidies or other social welfare. By contrast, individuals earn a high level of income pay a large portion of individual income tax. For example, a rich person with 1-million-dollar annual pays federal 40% of the income.

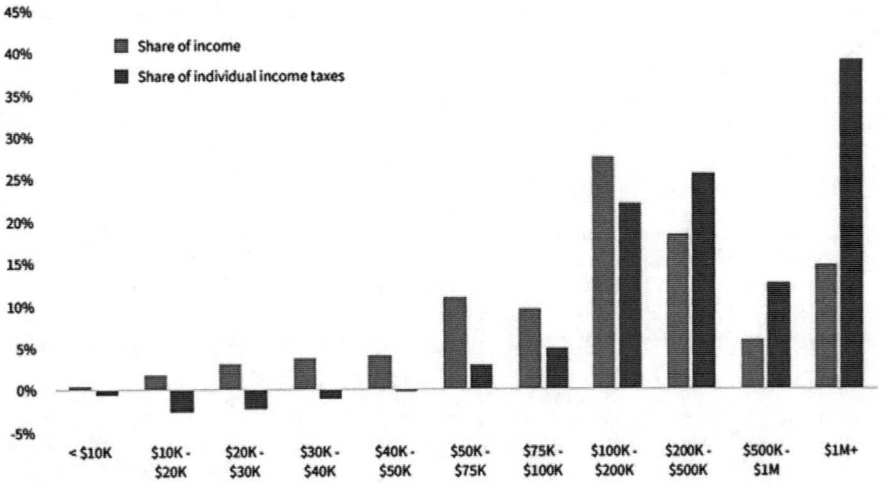

Fig. 1. Share of individual income and in different level and their taxes in 2019 [4].

The importance of income taxation mostly followed its influence on individuals, companies, and governments. Individuals observe how governments reform and adjust income taxation policies, which affect their daily income or expenditure. Then, individuals make their own economic decision on consumption, savings, investment, working, and retirement. At the same time, entrepreneurs, companies, and organizations observe income taxation policies to organize businesses, borrow capitals, invest projects.

The most important contribution of income tax is federal tax revenue. In Figure 2, a total of 57% of federal tax revenue comes from both income tax and corporate income tax. This number indicates the significance of income tax to federal, because a small change in income tax revenue transform a large proportion of the funding used by federal. Federal tax funding is crucial in promoting the investment in education, research and development and other projects.

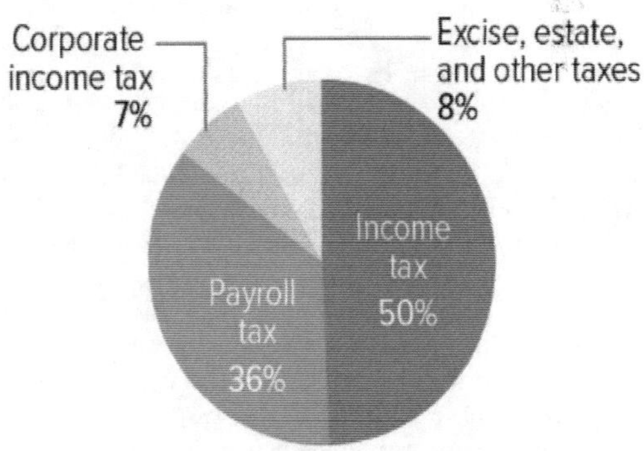

Fig. 2. Structure of federal tax revenue in 2019 [5].

3 Taxation and economic growth

US taxation reforms happened when some acts published by federal government. The Revenue Act of 1964 and the Jobs and Growth Tax Relief Reconciliation Act of 2003 contributed to the change of individual income taxes. These cuts reduced the marginal tax rates on individual income, capital gains and dividends [6]. The alteration of income tax rates influences the actions of both individuals and businesses, primarily through income and substitution effects. Lower tax rates positively impact on the size of the economy comes from the fact that because of lower tax rates higher after-tax returns to work, savings, and investment are realized. Increased after-tax returns act as incentives, prompting greater work effort, savings, and investment, primarily driven by substitution effects. This is the anticipated impact of tax cuts on the overall size of the economy. An additional benefit of a straightforward reduction in tax rates is the diminish of existing tax distortions, leading to an efficiency-enhancing effect. However, pure tax rate cut also has a positive revenue effect, which reduces the need to work, save and invest [7].

Several studies have demonstrated a negative correlation between taxation and economic growth. The study of US federal income tax changes between 1947 and 2006 shows that a 1% of GDP tax increase resulted in an estimated 3% decline in GDP after 3 years [8].

3.1 Effect of individual income tax on GDP

Gross domestic product (GDP) composted with four normal factors, which are consumption, investment, government expenditure, and net export. Individual income tax can have a direct and indirect impact on GDP, depending on how it is implemented and the overall economic environment.

The study of US federal income tax changes between 1947 and 2006 shows that a 1% of GDP tax increase resulted in an estimated 3% decline in GDP after 3 years [8]. The possible reasons are various.

Raising individual income tax reduces disposable individual income. When people have less money after taxes, their tendency to spend less on goods and services may result in a decrease in consumer spending, thereby exerting a negative impact on businesses and subsequently affecting GDP [1].

Some tax policies may facilitate saving and investment by offering deductions or exemptions on certain savings instruments. This can lead to increased capital formation, positively impacting GDP in the long run. With the same tax rate and equal income, an expenditure tax is more conducive to saving than an income tax, because under an expenditure tax, savers can defer paying tax on their savings. The gains came from the opportunity to earn interest on deferred taxes and other benefits of holding wealth. If temporary taxes are compared, or more generally, if tax rates are expected to fall in the future, then spending taxes are particularly beneficial to those who postpone consumption [6]. According to the theory of permanent income, people's consumption patterns reflect not only their current income, but also their expected income in the future. Thus, this is a permanent change. Temporary income taxes encourage people to defer income, but not necessarily to defer consumption [9].

Another reason related to GDP is employment rate. A one percentage point reduction in marginal tax rate increased probability of employed head of household moving to better job by 0.158 percentage points [8]. Better jobs encourage people to work and participate in employment rate. Employment is a significant component of economic activity, which means that more labor with more production. Meanwhile, when GDP is increasing, it often implies that businesses are expanding their operations. As businesses produce more goods and services, they often need to hire more workers to meet demand.

Individual income tax is a part of government revenue. Governments can use these revenues for public spending, which can have a directly positive impact on GDP through investments in infrastructure, education, health care, and other public goods. The efficiency of government spending also plays an indirect role. If government spending is productive and contributes to long-term economic growth, the overall impact on GDP can be positive.

3.2 Effect of corporate income tax on GDP

Corporate income tax affects the factor of investment in GDP. When companies calculate their returns on investment, they take into account the cost of capital. A higher corporate tax rate means a higher cost of capital, potentially reducing the incentive for companies to invest. Corporate income tax also directly affects a company's profitability. After-tax profits determine the amount of cash available for investment. Higher tax rates can reduce after-tax profits, limiting the funds available for investment in new projects, research and development, or expansion.

The burden of corporate income tax also falls on capital owners such as shareholders, which affects investment decisions and thus economic growth. Workers and consumers may share the burden through lower wages and higher prices. That, in turn, limits business expansion and impedes economic growth.

Figure 3 shows the how corporate tax rates change and how real GDP grow from 1982 to 2019. The reduction in corporate income tax might cause GDP to grow. By compiling and analyzing a novel data set consisting of 441 estimates from 42 primary studies, the results indicate that the positive impact of corporate tax cuts on growth is about 2.7 to 3 times greater than the negative results [10].

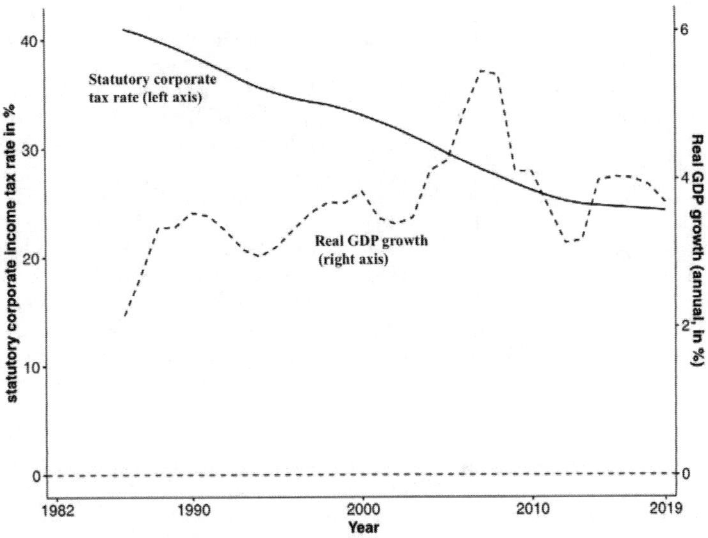

Fig. 3. Five-year world average corporate tax rates and real GDP growth rates from 1982 to 2019 [10].

However, reform corporate tax is not a simple and straight idea, because it cannot be declined too much. As mentioned, corporate income tax is a part of government revenue. It is levied on the profits earned by corporations, and the amount collected depends on the prevailing tax rate and the profitability of businesses within the jurisdiction. The impact of corporate income tax on government revenue is about fiscal policy and public finance. The level of corporate income tax influence governments' investment decisions. Governments rely on corporate income tax revenue to fund various public expenditures, including infrastructure, social programs, and public services. Change in corporate tax revenue affect the ability of governments to achieve their budgetary commitments.

Figure 4 indicates that from 2000 to 2019, governments' revenue from corporate income tax lowered about 200 billion dollars [11]. A reduction in the corporate income tax rate would have a significant impact on government revenues that posts challenges to fiscal sustainability and the ability to fund essential public services. Corporate income tax is a fundamental source of revenue for the government, and any reduction in the tax rate will directly affect the funds available for public spending. In long term, a continued decline in corporate tax rates would undermine the government's fiscal health. This leads to budget constraints that lead to cuts in education, health care and social welfare programs, negatively impacting the overall well-being of the population.

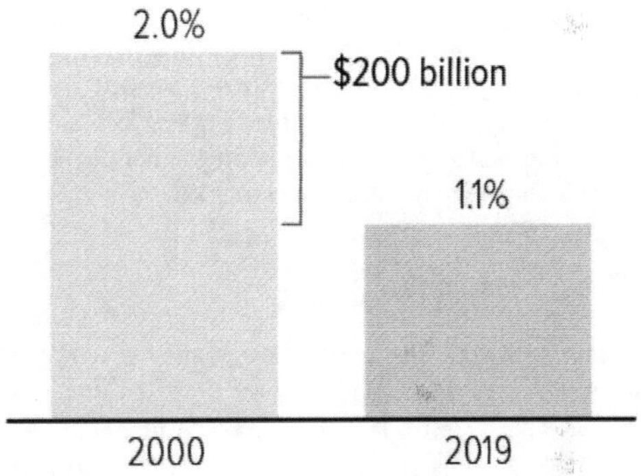

Fig. 4. The proportion of corporate tax revenue in GDP [11].

4 Policy recommendations

Policy making is crucial for a country's economic growth and development. Government should Carefully consider the implementation details to avoid unintended consequences. For example, some researchers can assess the possibility of introducing or adjusting wealth taxes to address wealth inequality. This may involve taxing assets such as property, investments, or other forms of wealth. Before making major changes to income tax policy, a comprehensive economic impact assessment is necessary. Analysts examine how changes affect economic growth, investment, and job creation, ensuring a balanced approach that benefits both individuals and the economy as a whole.

By researching the data, it is understandable that the effects of tax policy changes are not immediate. It takes time for businesses, investors, and consumers to fully comprehend the implications of new tax regulations and to adjust their decisions accordingly. Thus, there are some suggestion for reducing the lagging effect of tax policy on economic growth. Related institutions and organizations should regularly monitor economic indicators to assess the effects of tax policy changes. If the expected outcomes are not materializing, policymakers may need to consider adjustments or additional measures. Meanwhile, businesses often plan their investments and spending over the medium to long term.

With the impact of employment rate on GDP, one of the most important suggestion for making taxation policy is to consider the tax structure progressivity. Current study shows each percentage point decrease in measure of tax structure progressivity increased probability of moving to a better job by 0.277 percentage points [12]. People's willingness to find a job creates more labor participation. Besides, those who find a better job increase a country's productivity, which is also helpful to the economy.

Ultimately, it is advisable for governments to promote increased corporate research and development endeavors along with encouraging venture capital investment within the state. One strategy to stimulate research and development involves augmenting tax credits for businesses. Perhaps the most helpful approach would be to decrease or eliminate the prevailing capital gains tax rate, which effectively serves as a tax on initiating business ventures. Moreover, state policymakers might contemplate permitting state governments to invest in venture capital firms located outside the state, with the stipulation that these firms establish a presence within the state [12].

5 Conclusion

By combining all the current researches and data, the question of how income tax impact on economic growth should be answered. The results show that income tax cut brings more help to economic growth rather than harms the economy, by encouraging consumption, investment, participation in employment rate, government expenditure and so on. Although decrease in corporate tax might bring some negative influence on government revenue, the corporate tax counted as only 7% of government revenue. Therefore, the positive consequences are still greater than negative ones. The Then, there are some suggestions provided in this article. Firstly, government need to be cautious when making decision on reforming income taxation policies. Secondly, the lagging effect of policy on country's economy is an indispensable consideration. Then, income taxation will change the tax structure progressivity. Finally, investment as a large portion of economic growth greatly affect by income tax change. Thus, government should care about and promote nation investment. Researching on taxation is an important thing to do with the global trend of paying more attention on economic development of every country. Making decision on income tax should consider from all aspects from wealth distribution, inequality to consumption, investment, and government expenditure.

This research is limited from the perspective of time and methodology. Observing economic development takes time from month-long to year-long, which is not available for current writing situation. From the perspective of methodology, more up-to-date and valid data and resources should be gathered from national statistic or economic organization. Besides, analyzing in this research paper is relatively simple by comparing the income tax rate and economic growth rate. A more advanced research should use model like regression, empirical, or other complex models which take various factors into consideration and control the interaction between each other to reduce the errors and deviations. Moreover, it seems that the relationship between corporate income tax and economic growth is more complicated than the obvious negative relationship between individual income tax and economic growth. Corporate income tax brings negative influence on government revenue, but increase the investment in businesses. Thus, this article's conclusion is draw under the condition of comparing both positive and negative influence rather than absolute results. Therefore, further studies might suggest to conduct a more deeply research on the negative or positive relationship between corporate income tax and economic growth. Meanwhile, another perspective is to research on how to design a helpful taxation policy for a country's economy.

References

1. R. Bird, E. Zolt, UCLA L. Rev., **52**(6), 1627-1695, (2005)
2. A. Johansson, C. Heady, J. M. Arnold, B. Brys, L. Vartia, ECO/WKP, **28**, (2008)
3. R. Macek, REP, **14**(4), 309-328, (2014)
4. J. L. Streeter, How Do Tax Policies Affect Individuals and Businesses?, https://siepr.stanford.edu/publications/policy-brief/how-do-tax-policies-affect-individuals-and-businesses#3
5. Center on Budget and Policy Priorities, Policy Basics: Where Do Federal Tax Revenues Come From?, https://www.cbpp.org/research/policy-basics-where-do-federal-tax-revenues-come-from
6. K. Mertens, M. O. Ravn, Am Econ Rev, **109**(7), 2679-91, (2019)
7. W. Gale, W. G., A. Samwick, The Economics of Tax Policy, 13-39, (2017)
8. C. D. Romer, D. H. Romer, Am Econ Rev, **100**(3), 763-801, (2010)
9. R. Goode, Am Econ, Rev, 327-334, (1962)
10. S. Gechert, P. Heimberger, Eur. Econ. Rev., **147**, (2022)
11. C. Marr, S. Jacoby, G. Fenton, S. Washington, Corporate Rate Increase Would Make Taxes Fairer, Help Fund Equitable Recovery, https://www.cbpp.org/research/federal-tax/corporate-rate-increase-would-make-taxes-fairer-help-fund-equitable-recovery
12. W. M. Gentry, R. G. Hubbard, J. Public Econ., **88**(9), 2301-2322, (2002)

SHS Web of Conferences **188**, 02004 (2024) https://doi.org/10.1051/shsconf/202418802004
ICDDE 2024

Comparison and Analysis of Sustainable Development between China and America

Rui Huang[1,*]

[1]College of Arts and Science, Miami University, Oxford, United States of American.

Abstract. In recent years, sustainable development has been widely discussed. This article primarily explores the reasons behind the necessity for sustainable development. The inevitable environmental degradation resulting from rapid economic development is a crucial factor. Economic development is closely tied to the demand for energy, and sustainable development reduces environmental pollution and alleviates energy shortages. The environmental benefits brought about by sustainable development, in turn, positively impact economic growth. Therefore, sustainable development is indispensable. The strategic approaches to sustainable development in China and the United States differ due to their respective national conditions. This article also delves into the disparities in the sustainable development strategies between China and the U.S. China's sustainable development leans towards technological advancement, energy conservation, and environmental protection, while the U.S. prioritizes addressing social inequality. Post-COVID-19 pandemic, the sustainable development strategies of China and the U.S. have become increasingly apparent. The article explores what sustainable development strategies China and the U.S. have chosen post-pandemic to swiftly recover their economies. It also analyzes the characteristics of social inequality in China and the U.S., noting that China's economic inequality is regional, whereas the economic inequality in the U.S. stems from differences in educational attainment. The article further proposes solutions for these economic inequalities. In sustainable development strategies, despite differing national conditions, addressing economic inequality is a crucial component. China requires balancing the allocation of resources across its regions, while the U.S. needs to alleviate wealth disparities resulting from educational differences and address the issue of higher education accessibility.

1. Introduction

Sustainable development, as a widely discussed topic in recent years, is familiar to many. This article further delves into what sustainable development is and why nations need to implement sustainable development strategies. The environment and economic development are interconnected, as economic progress relies on environmental resources. Many factories emit wastewater and generate waste, while the environment also drives the development of tourism and other economic industries. Sustainable development aims to ensure a balanced development that integrates economic growth with the preservation of natural resources.

Post-COVID-19, there have been changes in the sustainable development strategies of China and the United States, two typical nations worth studying. China, with a weaker economic foundation, experiences rapid economic growth. The United States, possessing a stronger economic base, undergoes slower economic development.

The environmental challenges brought about by swift economic development are severe, and China's issues with environmental pollution cannot be overlooked. In contrast, the U.S. needs to give more consideration to problems related to economic inequality. China, with its status as the world's most populous country, also faces significant economic inequality. Addressing economic inequality is thus the most urgent need for both nations. China can alleviate economic inequality through technological development, while the U.S. needs to address the relationship between education levels and income. Both governments require substantial efforts to formulate policies suitable for their respective countries.

Simultaneously, effective communication of sustainable development strategies is essential. Everyone needs to stay informed and collaborate on sustainable development to ensure its successful implementation.

2. Comparison and analysis of sustainable development between China and America

2.1 The problem of sustainable development caused by rapid economic development

Sustainable development has become a frequently discussed topic among people. Moreover, given the current international economic environment, sustainable development will continue to be a subject of discussion [1]. So, what is sustainable development, and why is it necessary? Sustainable development ensures the sustained and stable growth of the economy by increasing energy efficiency and protecting the environment. Without the presence of

* Corresponding author: huangr22@miamioh.edu

sustainable development, although the economy may experience rapid growth in the short term, there is a risk of slowed or reduced economic growth in the future due to issues such as energy shortages and environmental pollution.

From the perspective of the growth rates of energy consumption and economic expansion, there is a positive correlation between the pace of economic growth and the rate of energy usage [2].

Since the beginning of the 21st century, China's economic growth has been remarkably rapid. China's economic development benefits from its large population, and as the population increases, the consumption of resources also rises. The economic growth of the United States, on the other hand, is attributed to technological advantages and a strong economic foundation. Due to technological reasons, the energy efficiency in the United States is slightly higher compared to China. Although the energy issue is smaller compared to China, the United States still faces energy challenges. Unlike China, the energy shortage problem in the United States is reflected in the issue of income proportion and energy expenditure, with some households unable to afford the costs associated with energy [3].

If people only care about economic growth and ignore environmental issues, the rate of economic growth would be much higher than it is now. However, we cannot do that. In the past few decades in China, the country sacrificed the environment for rapid economic development. Air pollution and water pollution are the most relevant environmental issues in China.

The cost of economic development is the increase in energy consumption. China's demand for coal has resulted in a significant amount of carbon dioxide emissions. Industrial emissions contribute to water pollution as factories, in pursuit of higher profits, choose to directly discharge wastewater. These environmental pollutants not only have a direct impact on people's lives but also have indirect effects on future economic development [4].

Similar to China, the United States also faces environmental pollution issues, but because the United States identified these problems earlier and is already in a period of stable economic development, the U.S. government, businesses, and social groups have been working hard to take measures to mitigate these environmental problems. Environmental protection regulations, the promotion of renewable energy sources, and the application of innovative technologies are some of the efforts to address these issues [5]. In general, the difference between the economic development of the United States and China lies in the fact that the United States has already passed through a period of rapid development and entered a phase of stable growth, while China is currently in a period of rapid development. Economic development inevitably brings about environmental pollution. In the case of the United States, which is in a phase of stable development, attention has been drawn to environmental issues, and efforts are being made to address them. China is also gradually becoming aware of these problems.

The impact between economic activities and natural resources is bidirectional, and thus environmental pollution can have a significant effect on the economy. This is precisely why sustainable development is essential. Resource scarcity can lead to disruptions in the production chain, forcing factories to purchase more expensive raw materials from other countries at higher prices. Environmental pollution can trigger climate change, and droughts may affect agricultural output, thereby influencing the stability of the economy. Environmental pollution has a direct impact on people's health. Simultaneously, it can result in significant losses for the tourism industry. The relationship between these natural resources and economic development is interconnected. The goal of sustainable development is to ensure that the economy can develop with a long-term and stable trajectory.

Sustainable development is not only closely related to environmental issues but also has a certain connection with social equity. The stability of society is a crucial part of sustainable development. The economic development of a country often relies on the stability of society, and in turn, societal stability can propel economic development. In the rapid pace of economic development, various economic inequality issues may arise, such as unequal distribution of medical resources and regional economic disparities.

The stability of society can be influenced by economic inequality. If society is not stable enough, economic development will inevitably suffer. One of the goals of sustainable development is to eliminate poverty and reduce inequality. The equitable distribution of resources can help promote more stable economic development. The purpose of sustainable development is to enable a country to achieve economic growth in a more stable manner, and societal harmony is inevitably one of the key components.

Education resources are also crucial. The education system continuously provides talent for the country. If there are significant disparities in education, the wealth gap will widen, subsequently affecting the stability of the country and hindering sustainable development.

In the pursuit of sustainable development, it is essential to address economic inequalities, ensure the equitable distribution of resources, and promote social harmony. A stable and harmonious society contributes significantly to achieving sustainable development goals.

2.2 Differences in sustainable development strategies between China and the United States

Covid-19 has had a significant impact on the global economy, and the differences in sustainable development strategies between China and the United States have been reflected in the aftermath of Covid-19.

After COVID-19, the primary task for countries is the same – the pandemic has caused a setback in the world economy, and economic recovery has become a common goal for global development [6]. However, the speed of economic growth is closely tied to resource consumption [2]. Therefore, rapid economic recovery has become a crucial issue for sustainable development in both China and the United States. Due to pollution issues, China places a high emphasis on carbon emissions and environmental protection in the process of economic development. The more energy-rich a province is the higher China's requirements for energy conservation and environmental protection become [6]. China has enacted numerous laws to promote green development, aiming to protect the environment and ecosystems during the process of economic development [6]. Having experienced rapid economic growth and economic challenges posed by COVID-19, China has realized that economic development alone cannot address the issues of development. China is comprehensively implementing strategic goals for sustainable development, aiming for high resource utilization rates and protecting ecosystems to facilitate ecological forces driving economic development.

China is also changing its energy usage structure, reducing the consumption of carbon and petroleum, and promoting the utilization of renewable resources. The use of renewable resources is primarily costlier than traditional resources, and the efficiency of their utilization is not as high as that of traditional resources. China needs to explore technological advancements in this field to enhance the efficiency of using renewable resources. China has also participated in numerous international agreements, collaborating with other countries for sustainable development [6]. Therefore, China has actively responded to sustainable development after the pandemic. China recognizes the relationship between economic growth and social stability. The Chinese government is attempting to increase the use of new energy sources to reduce carbon emissions. China is also promoting the importance of environmental protection among its people. The government is prioritizing policies to elevate the significance of addressing poverty in various regions. As a densely populated and vast country, China places significant emphasis on addressing economic inequality. The country is strengthening the education system in impoverished areas to ensure that educational disparities are not excessively large across different regions.

The pandemic has indeed caused considerable economic losses for China. However, the Chinese government continues to find the right direction for precise development of sustainable development strategies. Despite being a major global player, these efforts may have limited impact, and economic inequality in China remains substantial.

Covid-19 has posed significant challenges to sustainable development in the United States. The pandemic has not only reversed the progress made in sustainable development but also exposed underlying economic issues. Low-income areas in the U.S. have been particularly affected by the impacts of Covid-19 [7]. The long-standing stability of the U.S. development has sometimes overshadowed existing problems. In the wake of the COVID-19 crisis, the U.S. must address the issue of economic inequality about sustainable development. People in impoverished areas have struggled to access necessary treatments due to insufficient medical resources, amplifying the impact of COVID-19 on their lives [8].

Post-COVID-19, the U.S. sustainable development strategy needs to focus more on addressing developmental inequalities. Moreover, given the advanced technological capabilities of the U.S. compared to China, the country has the opportunity to delve deeper into environmental sustainability research in the aftermath of Covid-19. The U.S. post-Covid-19 sustainable development strategy emphasizes social equity and technological advancements. Technological growth can enhance energy efficiency, reduce energy consumption, and mitigate environmental pollution. Social equity ensures fair access to resources and contributes to the stability of society, an essential goal in sustainable development.

Addressing economic inequality is crucial for ensuring sustainable development, often accompanied by disparities in educational opportunities. The wealthy are more likely to access better education, while the poor may face limitations in educational opportunities, exacerbating difficulties in social mobility. Excessive economic inequality can impede overall economic growth. Larger wealth gaps may result in a smaller middle class, diminishing the purchasing power of the majority and restricting market demand. China, currently the most populous country globally, grapples with severe economic inequality issues. Assisting impoverished groups is a top priority in China. Despite some regions in China surpassing many others globally in economic terms, the per capita income in these areas remains relatively low [9]. Therefore, China's current objective should continue to prioritize balancing economic levels across different regions.

If one of China and the United States gives up its sustainable development strategy, will it affect the other countries?

If either China or the United States were to abandon the strategy of sustainable development, it would undoubtedly impact both countries and even the entire world. A country relinquishing the strategy of sustainable development may, in the short term, produce goods with extremely low costs and high environmental impacts for export, leading to social dumping. This could devastate the markets of trading partners. However, over time, a country abandoning the strategy of sustainable development would excessively exploit resources, potentially leading to resource depletion. The ecological environment would also suffer damage, amplifying issues of economic instability and inequity. The nation's reputation would be tarnished. Therefore, to ensure sustained prosperity, sustainable development is a meaningful and imperative strategy that must be implemented.

Sustainable development relies heavily on technological innovation, and both China and the United States have not abandoned innovation due to the high costs associated with it. In sustainable development, technological innovation brings numerous benefits. New energy sources are products of technological innovation, and many clean energy sources, such as solar and wind energy, depend on technological innovations. Technological advancements significantly increase the utilization of clean energy, reducing reliance on traditional resources. Additionally, technological innovation enhances the efficiency of traditional resources, allowing fewer non-renewable resources to generate more energy. Technological innovation also contributes to improvements in recycling. Many recyclable materials help reduce waste production.

Furthermore, technology introduces new educational models. Online libraries are often more convenient and easier to manage than physical ones. In terms of educational resources, many regions with a scarcity of resources can gain more knowledge through online learning. Moreover, during the Covid-19 period, online courses have been widely utilized. Technology provides a more convenient means of education for an increasing number of people.

Technology has also brought about more convenient modes of transportation, enhancing global cooperation. For sustainable development, the world is interconnected, and achieving sustainability is not confined to a single country. Globalization has deepened the connections among various economic entities worldwide. The economic collapse of one country often impacts the economies of other nations. Therefore, international cooperation is a crucial component of sustainable development.

Both China and the United States have made significant efforts in technological innovation. Technology provides essential tools and means for sustainable development. Through technological innovation, societies can develop in a more stable manner.

Economic inequality in the United States is evident in the significant imbalance between the labor costs and capital proportions of high-income individuals, a phenomenon closely tied to education [10]. Despite the economic prosperity of the United States, there is a substantial education gap between the poor and the wealthy. As the share of income allocated to education gradually increases, the impoverished still struggle to access quality education, perpetuating a cycle of deepening poverty for the less affluent and increased wealth for the affluent. This is a highly challenging issue that has plagued many countries for years.

The United States now requires bold innovation to mitigate the impact of economic inequality. This problem cannot be entirely eradicated at its root. Therefore, the U.S. needs to diminish the influence of this factor. Initiatives such as raising the minimum wage and increasing taxes on the wealthy, while offering temporary relief, do not address the fundamental issue of economic inequality. Strengthening educational infrastructure and promoting higher education accessibility are the fundamental approaches to resolving this problem. Therefore, the future sustainable development strategy of the United States needs to emphasize strengthening educational policies.

3. Conclusion

For China, the strategic focus on sustainable development leans towards technological advancement. However, being a unique country with a massive population, addressing economic inequality is also a crucial consideration. The government needs to balance resources among different regions, strive to equalize the pace of economic development, and encourage technological advancements and exploration of new energy sources. As for the United States, resolving economic inequality is the most critical issue.

With a stable and growing economy and a high baseline, the U.S. needs to address the severe problem of economic inequality stemming from educational disparities. Leveraging its technological advantages, the U.S. can alleviate issues arising from economic inequality, and revising legislation related to higher education can be attempted to tackle this problem.

Sustainable development is a global endeavor; it is not sufficient for a single country to maintain sustainable development on its own. The Earth's ecosystems are interdependent, so the failure of one country to protect the environment can have repercussions on other nations. The fluidity of various resources is also high, and with the development of globalization, the economic activities of one country can rapidly impact another. Certain environmental issues, such as those related to the oceans and climate, transcend national borders.

The purpose of sustainable development is to ensure the enduring and stable growth of economies. Therefore, achieving sustainable development requires collective efforts from all countries worldwide.

The benefits of sustainable development may not be immediately apparent, so as the institution makes decisions on behalf of the people, the government needs to consider sustainable development for the well-being of its citizens. It is essential to actively promote the benefits of sustainable development. The path to sustainable development may be challenging, but commitment to it is imperative.

References

1. J. Mensah, Cogent Social Sciences, 5(1), (2019).
2. R. Waheed, S. Sarwar, W. Chen, Energy Reports, 5, 1103–1115, (2019).
3. Q. Wang, M. Kwan, J. Fan, J, Lin, Renewable & Sustainable Energy Reviews, 137, 110620, (2021).
4. W. Liang, M. Yang, Sustainable Computing: Informatics and Systems, 21, 1–9, (2019).
5. S. Umer, F. Zeeshan, S. Farrukh, S. Khurram, Journal of Cleaner Production, 279, 123806, (2021)
6. X. Zhang, J. Wen, X. Zou, Q. Wang, C. Chang, Sustainable Development, 31(1), 426–438, (2022).
7. R. Mejia, P. J. Hotez, M. E. Bottazzi, Current Tropical Medicine Reports, 7(4), 99–103, (2020).
8. Q. Wang, R. Huang, Environmental Research, 202, 111637, (2021).
9. C. Lee, R. Lou, F. Wang, Economic Analysis and Policy, 77, 418–434, (2023)
10. F. Hoffmann, D. S.Lee, T. Lemieux, Journal of Economic Perspectives, 34(4), 52–78, (2020).

The Analysis of the US's Technology Policy toward China

Yiyi Wang*

A. B. Freeman School of Business, Tulane University, New Orleans, Louisiana, 70118, United States

Abstract. Since the late period of the US Obama administration, the US and China's competitions have spread from military diplomacy to trade and science and technology. As the brain of modern electronic devices, the semiconductors have a wide range of applications in various industries. So far, the US semiconductor technology issue against China has become the key axis of the current Biden administration's anti-China policy. Under the policy line of technology resistance against China, the United States and the global semiconductor industry are facing both opportunities and challenges under the strategy of "building high walls" and "multilateral alliances". To maintain its significant leading position in semiconductor key technologies, the United States should support the development of independent core technologies and standards through national policies in the semiconductor industry, while looking for major domestic and foreign semiconductor allies, industry, academia, and research and development stakeholders. It is also important for the US to observe the continuous innovation of Chinese private technology enterprises, the development of truly independent core technologies of China, the development of digital economic industry of China, as well as the Chinese government policies towards international restrictions in the face of suppression from US.

1 Introduction

Semiconductors are the core of modern electronic industry technological progress and are known as the brain of electronic devices. Due to its wide range of applications, the research and development, production, and manufacturing of semiconductors have gradually become one of the key strategic issues and materials that countries attach importance to, especially in the current situation where technology products and applications are closely related to military, economic, technological, safety, and consumer needs in various countries.

Since the late period of the Obama Administration, after the Trump Administration and even the current Biden Administration took office, the fields of competition between the United States and China have spread from traditional military diplomacy to trade and even science and technology. Among them, the issue of semiconductor technology from the United States to China has become the key axis of the current Biden Administration's anti-China policy. Its impact on global technology, economy, and security is quite profound and worth exploring.

In this article, this study aims to explore the recent formation, transformation, and main possible impacts of the US technology policy towards China, with a particular focus on the semiconductor industry as an example for analysis. Firstly, this paper explores the development overview of the global semiconductor technology industry. Secondly, the paper explains the semiconductor policy towards China during the Obama administration and the Trump administration. Furthermore, this paper analyzes the formation, transformation, and possible main impacts of the current Biden administration's semiconductor policy towards China. Finally, this paper summarizes the key points of this article, and explain the future observation focus of the United States on semiconductor technology policy issues.

2 Development overview of global semiconductor technology industry

With the high development of technology, the research and development, manufacturing, and application of semiconductors have become the core of modern global electronic industry development. The so-called semiconductor system is composed of materials (such as silicon) with resistance between conductors and insulators, and its main products include discrete components and integrated circuits (ICs). Among them, ICs with a high proportion of production refer to the integration of components such as transistors, diodes, resistors, capacitors, etc. into a single chip through precise manufacturing technology by semiconductor manufacturers. The complete logic circuit formed by this chip can be applied in various electronic products due to its functions of control, calculation, or memory, becoming the basic component on which various electronic devices rely for operation.

In the current era of electronic technology, semiconductors have a wide range of applications. Equipment such as data processing electronics,

* Corresponding author: ywang143@tulane.edu

military/civil aviation electronics, communication electronics, consumer electronics, automotive electronics, and industrial electronics all rely on the supply side of semiconductors for normal manufacturing and operation. In the future, emerging technological applications, such as unmanned driving, quantum computing, artificial intelligence (AI), robotics, energy-saving sensing, 5G and the Internet of Things (IoT), rely more on the production and manufacturing of the new generation of advanced semiconductors to seize the development opportunities. Thus, in the current trend of technology becoming an indispensable "hard power" for countries around the world, the research and development, production, and manufacturing of semiconductors have also become key strategic issues and materials valued by major advanced countries.

Due to the continuous innovation of global technology applications in the past decade, the size of the semiconductor market has shown a continuous upward trend. According to the World Semiconductor Trade Statistics (WSTS), the global semiconductor industry's sales in 2012 were about 291.6 billion US dollars. In 2013, it exceeded 300 billion US dollars for the first time, and in 2017, it further exceeded 400 billion US dollars. As of 2020, it remained at the level of $440.4 billion. In 2022, driven by the double-digit growth demand for global memory, the global semiconductor industry's sales amount exceeded the new high level of $600 billion.

3 The formation and transformation of the US semiconductor policy towards China

3.1 Industrial policies and trade interests

Compared with the Trump government's desire to comprehensively improve the US trade deficit with China, and to raise tariffs and exert pressure, the Biden government adopted the strategy of "small yard, high fence" and "multilateral alliance" to deal with China's security threats at the beginning of taking office [1]. Although the Biden administration has so far maintained some restrictive measures and tariffs on China's trade during the Trump administration, it has focused on science and technology as the main axis, targeted China in key areas, clarified and identified specific technologies and fields directly related to the national security of the United States (the so-called courtyard), and established appropriate strategic boundaries (the so-called high wall). The approach of increasing countermeasures and blockades within specific technologies and fields, but considering reopening or maintaining the status quo outside specific technologies and fields, has become a new strategy for the United States in its science and technology policy towards China. In addition, the Biden government adopted the strategy of "multilateral alliance", including inviting 19 major international technology enterprises, including Taiwan Semiconductor Manufacturing Company Limited, Samsung, and Intel, to hold the "Semiconductor and Supply Chain Resilience Summit", and held summits with leaders of Japan, South Korea and the European Union, and promised to strengthen the strategic cooperation relationship between the two sides in semiconductor industry [2]. All these are the Biden government's bilateral ways to change the past of the Trump government and actively establish a multilateral anti-China technology alliance.

3.2 Technology regulation

In terms of science and technology control, the Biden government's policy towards China roughly follows the legal basis and policy direction of the Trump government's Export Control Reform Act (ECRA) and the 2018 Foreign Investment Risk Review and Modernization Act (FIRRMA) for science and technology control over China. In the near future, the Biden government will also follow the path of strengthening science and technology control over China. After the Trump government's ban on Semiconductor Manufacturing International Corporation (SMIC) and Huawei, the United States first identified seven Chinese institutions in April 2021 involved in assisting China's military modernization and developing weapons of mass destruction, and American enterprises are restricted from doing business with them. At the beginning of June 2021, President Biden signed an order to modify the Trump government's investment ban on Chinese enterprises, listing 59 Chinese enterprises related to the Chinese military or belonging to the monitoring industry. Besides Huawei, the three major telecommunications companies (China Unicom, China Mobile and China Telecom) in China were also in the list. The ban came into effect in August 2021, stipulating that American investors must withdraw their investment within one year after it came into effect [3].

3.3 Future technological dominance

Among the major priority governance projects unveiled by the Biden administration, one of its major governance goals is to revive the economy and ensure the US position in the world. The Biden administration's recently released "100 Day Key Supply Chain Survey Report", suggesting that if the United States wants to enhance its leadership and resilience in the semiconductor industry, it must provide at least $50 billion in funds to implement the Chip Act (CHIPS), as support measures for advanced chip manufacturing production, ensuring the safety of mature node chip production supply chains, and the production safety of domestic and foreign allies and business partners. In addition, the United States should also focus on supporting manufacturing, research and development, and establishing a multilateral fund for semiconductors. Lastly, the United States should find international allies to jointly implement export control, foreign direct investment review, supply chain security, intellectual property protection, and subsidy transparency requirements for semiconductor technology, ensuring the dominant position of the United States in future technology [4].

4 The impacts of the US semiconductor technology policy

In recent years, there have been significant changes in the US semiconductor technology policy towards China since the late Obama administration. China has been promoting two consecutive "National Integrated Circuit Industry Investment Funds" since 2014, attempting to support the domestic semiconductor industry. In 2015, the "Made in China 2025 Plan" was proposed, aiming to achieve a 70% chip production rate by 2025. In recent years, China has actively invested in and acquired American semiconductor companies, gradually arousing the US government's vigilance towards China's technology strategy. Up to the time of the Trump administration, the United States and China have conducted a relatively comprehensive competition from trade war, science and technology war, diplomatic war and military strength display. Until the Biden administration took office, although the intensification of strategic competition between the United States and China has not fundamentally changed, under the Biden administration's policy of focusing on the technology sector and adopting a strategy of "small courtyards and high walls" and "multilateral alliances" to resist China, it may bring the following opportunities and challenges to the United States and the global semiconductor industry, which may have the main potential impact.

4.1 Opportunity

The United States and China are the top two major consumer markets of semiconductors in the world, including communication, computers, consumer electronics, automobiles, as well as emerging technological needs such as artificial intelligence, quantum computing, 5G, Internet of Things, electronic game equipment, medical equipment, aviation, 3D printing, auto drive system, virtual/augmented reality. In the semiconductor industry, the United States and China's own preferred semiconductor industry and supply chain manufacturers may have new development opportunities arising from the technological confrontation [5].

The recent support policies promoted by the US government for the semiconductor industry have led major international semiconductor companies such as Taiwan Semiconductor Manufacturing Company Limited (TSMC), Samsung, Intel, and Global Foundries to announce their plans to invest in and establish semiconductor wafer fabs in the US, which will help support the development of the local semiconductor supply chain and create employment opportunities in the US. Taking TSMC as an example, it would invest $12 billion to establish a 5-nanometer advanced process wafer factory in Phoenix, Arizona, USA. After production, it is estimated to produce about 20000 wafers per month and hire 1600 employees.

The Biden administration emphasizes "multilateral alliances" in its policy path of technological resistance, and through the issue of semiconductor industry cooperation, the United States can increase strategic cooperation with its allies or like-minded countries or businesses. On the one hand, it can coordinate and solve the problem of international chip supply shortage, and on the other hand, it can enhance the international competitiveness of American semiconductor industry to strengthen its leadership position in semiconductor technology [6].

Due to its anti-China strategy, the United States is re-evaluating and reviewing the supply chain of its key industry sectors, assisting its semiconductor industry and semiconductor end-users in identifying the sole or primary source of various semiconductor key materials. This would help the United States strengthen its semiconductor supply chain resilience in supplier diversification, diversifying supplier geopolitical distribution risks, and establishing demonstration guidelines [7].

4.2 Challenge

The global semiconductor industry, which has been established based on economic comparative advantages over the past 30 years, may face the impact of adjustment or restructuring due to intensified technological competition and confrontation between the United States and China [8].

In the face of technological competition and confrontation between the United States and China, the world would pay more attention to the geopolitical risks of the semiconductor industry, and pay more attention to policy promotion to improve domestic semiconductor production rates under the influence of chip supply shortages. According to a research report released by Boston Consulting Group (BCG) and the American Semiconductor Association (SIA) in April 2021, the global semiconductor industry would need to invest at least $1 trillion in initial capital investment to meet the current semiconductor consumption needs of major regions worldwide and pursue complete self-sufficiency in supply. Due to the significant additional capital expenditures, semiconductor cost may increase by 35% to 65%, ultimately leading to an increase in the cost of electronic devices that rely on semiconductor product supply for manufacturing. This will also increase the consumption costs of global electronic terminal device users and bring unfavorable variables to future global economic growth [9].

In the ongoing intensification of technology competition between the United States and China, it may lead to the risk of losing business opportunities in the Chinese semiconductor consumer market due to the need for American semiconductor manufacturers and foreign companies to rely on the American semiconductor consumer market to make choices between the United States and China. The revenue of the global semiconductor industry may decline as a result, which would undermine the ability of semiconductor manufacturers to maintain a global semiconductor consumer market to support massive research and development, and innovation expenditures [10]. This will also have an adverse impact on innovation in the semiconductor and other related industries.

Promoting positive US-China cooperation stands out as a crucial element in tackling the plethora of opportunities and challenges on the international scene. Through fostering diplomatic relations and creating a climate that is favorable to cooperation, both countries can actively participate in the development of a competitive environment that benefits both parties. Prioritizing common interests in a strategic alignment can open doors for innovation, economic expansion, and improved international stability. Accepting the possibility of cooperation emphasizes a diplomatic stance that looks for points of agreement and promotes communication and comprehension. With the power to overcome antagonistic dynamics, this cooperative framework can create a setting where international interdependence acts as a catalyst for peaceful and sustainable development.

5 Conclusion

The semiconductor system is a modern electronic device brain with a wide range of applications. Due to the fact that current technological products and applications are closely related to the military, economic and trade, science and technology, safety, and people's consumption needs of various countries, the research and development, production, and manufacturing of semiconductors have become a key strategic material that countries attach great importance to. Since the late period of the US Obama administration, the US and China's competitions have also spread from military diplomacy to trade and science and technology. So far, the US semiconductor technology issue against China has become the key axis of the current Biden administration's anti-China policy. Until the Biden administration took office, although the intensified strategic competition between the United States and China has not fundamentally changed, the Biden administration has particularly focused on the technology sector, especially semiconductor industry.

Under the policy line of technology resistance against China, the United States and the global semiconductor industry are facing both opportunities and challenges under the strategy of "building high walls" and "multilateral alliances". Firstly, in terms of industrial policies and trade interests, the relevant semiconductor support policies and anti-China bills promoted by the Biden administration would be formally submitted to President Biden for signing after consultation between the two houses of Congress, along with the actual budget size and implementation level of the bills. It would determine the effectiveness of the Biden administration in promoting technological resistance in the semiconductor industry and strengthening the leadership position of the US semiconductor industry. Secondly, in terms of science and technology regulation, the Biden government continues the Trump government's line of science and technology regulation on China in the past. In the future, if it further develops in the direction of more rigorous and expanded scope, the countermeasures that China would take, the specific impact on the US and other foreign semiconductor companies, and the respond from the US and foreign semiconductor companies would all be questionable. Lastly, in terms of future technological dominance, according to research by the US-China Economic and Security Review Commission (USCC), Chinese semiconductor companies still lag behind major international competitors by one to two generations in technology, and are highly dependent on foreign semiconductor technology for production.

However, the United States is well aware of China's expertise in semiconductor assembly, advanced packaging, and more key raw materials, optical electronics and other fields have gained international competitiveness, while actively supporting the development of independent core technologies and standards through national policies. Therefore, whether the United States continues to maintain its significant leading position in semiconductor key technologies in the future depends on its participation and implementation of current policies that assist and support the development of the US semiconductor industry. The United States would also need major domestic and foreign semiconductor allies, industry, academia, and research and development stakeholders. It is necessary to observe whether the Chinese government could promote the continuous innovation of Chinese private technology enterprises and continue to lead their digital economic industry development, as well as whether Chinese technology industry can break through international restrictions and develop truly independent core technologies in the face of suppression from US.

References

1. M. Kang, Asia Pacific Economy, **3**, 4 (2005)
2. R. Tan, Financial Think Tank, **8**, 22 (2023)
3. L. Tie, China High Tech Zone, **6**, 134 (2021)
4. L. Qin, China Science and Technology Forum, **5**, 172 (2023)
5. G. Song, J. Zhang, World Economy and Politics, **3**, 31 (2023)
6. M. Cui, Y. Cui, Northeast Asian Economic Research, **7**, 29 (2023)
7. K. Qi, Y. Li, International Forum, **24,** 21 (2022)
8. J. Feng, M. Rui, H. Li, Science and Technology China, **9**, 48 (2023)
9. X. Zhang, Chongqing Economy, **5**, 4 (2019)
10. Y. Yao, Frontiers of Social Sciences, **11**, 14 (2022)

SHS Web of Conferences **188**, 02006 (2024) https://doi.org/10.1051/shsconf/202418802006
ICDDE 2024

The Communication Effect of Elevator Multimedia Advertisement Based on the AIDMA Model – Taking a commercial plaza in Shanghai as an example

Ke Tao

College of Literature Art, Shihezi University, the Xinjiang Uyghur Autonomous Region, 832003, China

Abstract. The Attention-Interest-Desire-Memory-Action (AIDMA) model describes the psychological process of consumers from exposure to advertising to final purchase, including five stages: attention, interest, desire, memory, and action. This model has important guiding significance in the early stage of traditional media and the Internet. However, with the development of the Internet, users' behavior patterns changed, and new marketing models such as the Attention-Interest-Search-Action-Share (AISAS) model appeared. However, the AIDMA model still has reference value and application scenarios, especially in elevator multimedia advertising. In a relatively closed and focused environment, elevator multimedia advertising is more likely to attract passengers' attention, stimulate interest and purchase desire, and strengthen brand memory. This form of advertising is suitable for various industries and brands, and it can improve brand awareness and image. In order to evaluate the effect of elevator multimedia advertising, it can be investigated from three aspects: communication effect, psychological effect, and sales effect. Through these investigations, the study provides an understanding of the communication effect of advertising and provide a reference for future advertising planning.

1 Introduction

Under the wave of the digital era, the advertising communication mode is constantly evolving, and elevator multimedia advertising has become an indispensable part of the modern city by virtue of its unique communication advantages.

As a kind of high-quality outdoor advertising form, elevator advertising accurately locks the target audience in various regions. It usually makes and publishes advertisement (AD) on the inner wall of urban buildings elevators, and uses the advantages of high exposure rate and precise positioning to transmit information to different audience groups such as office workers, customers in commercial areas and, owners in residential areas. With the continuous innovation of technology, elevator multimedia advertising uses digital display screens, touch screens, and other equipment to provide diversified advertising content for the audience.

However, under the impact of digital advertising, how to attract and influence the audience more effectively has become the key. AIDMA model, as a classic advertising communication model, provides strong theoretical support for elevator multimedia advertising. This model emphasizes that starting from attracting attention, stimulating interest and desire, strengthening memory, and finally prompting the audience to take purchase action. Elevator multimedia advertising follows this process, starting from attracting attention and stimulating the audience's interest and purchase desire through visual and auditory impact; The characteristics of repeated exposure help to strengthen the memory of the audience and improve the brand recognition and image; At the same time, it directly transmits the purchase information and prompts the audience to take the purchase action.

Through the application of AIDMA model in elevator multimedia advertising, it can promote a deeper understanding of the effect of this advertising form in attracting attention, stimulating interest and desire, strengthening memory and promoting action. This will help advertisers to develop more targeted marketing strategies and achieve more efficient brand communication.

The purpose of this paper is to discuss the application of AIDMA model in elevator multimedia advertising, and how this advertising form can accurately target the audience and achieve efficient brand communication.

2 Literature review

The research on elevator advertising as a whole mainly focuses on three aspects: the study on the media characteristics of elevator advertising. The research on the media characteristics of elevator advertising mainly analyzes the value and existing problems of elevator advertising. Chen Fengqi compared the differences between traditional advertising media and elevator

Corresponding author: 20201004265@ stu.shzu.edu.cn

advertising media from the perspective of the commonality of communication value, and summarized the advantages of elevator advertising such as close contact, high reach rate, strong pertinence, good coercion, strong plasticity and flexible communication combination [1]. Wang Siyi summarized the problems existing in the development of elevator advertising from three aspects. The first aspect is the problem of communication effect. He believed that the communication content of elevator advertising is repeated and the form is single, the replacement frequency cycle of elevator advertising is fast and the delivery time is uncertain, and the one-way communication of elevator advertising cannot form a good interaction with the audience. These factors will largely restrict the communication effect of elevator advertising; The second aspect is moral and ethical issues, including misleading deception, bad vulgar, false information, in the long run, this will make the audience on the perception and attitude of elevator advertising has a negative impact, not conducive to the long-term development of elevator advertising; The third aspect is the problem of laws and regulations, in the operation and income of elevator advertising are lack of corresponding legal norms and regulation [2]. Wang Xuemang analyzed the audience psychology and behavior in the closed scene of elevator media and its influencing factors, studied the exploitation of the audience by ladder media, and put forward the problem of passive labor of the audience in the current ladder media advertising [3].

The next is research on the value of elevator advertising. The value research mainly analyzes the cultural value and economic value of elevator advertising. In his master's thesis, Zhang Yanyan emphasized that elevator advertising is not only a means used by advertisers to promote, nor is it just a renderer presented by designers. It is also a reflection of culture. For example, elevator advertising in residential areas also bears the elevator culture of the whole community and the cultural development of the whole residential area, which is an important part of highlighting urban culture. And as a kind of art and cultural symbol for the development of the city economy also has special significance [4]. Chen Hua explored the value of "waiting economy" in elevator advertising [5]. Elevator advertising can penetrate into consumers' life trajectory, and is targeted, and can put different brands according to the characteristics of different communities, so as to achieve accurate positioning of target groups and the most effective achievement of advertising. This helps to maximize the guarantee of advertisers' input-output benefits, to achieve greater economic value [6].

Thirdly, some research is about elevator advertising communication level. Communication research is also a level that scholars focus on at present, mainly analyzing the factors affecting the communication effect of elevator advertising and the communication strategy of elevator advertising. In terms of the influencing factors of elevator advertising effect, Song Yujie believes that the audience's age, gender, living habits, interests, psychological characteristics and other aspects of the detailed positioning analysis, multi-angle analysis of the audience's preference for advertising types and publicity methods, greatly improve the communication effect of elevator advertising; In addition, based on the perspective of visual communication design, it is proposed that in high-end office buildings, shopping malls, theme industrial parks, amusement parks and other places, the visual communication and design of elevator advertising should match the style of architecture and elevator interior, and the overall effect of advertising in the internal space and the atmosphere of space effect should be integrated [7]. In terms of the communication strategy of elevator advertising, Gu Chunxiao took Focus Media as an example to explore the influence of holographic technology on elevator advertising communication [8]. Han Dong and Wang Siyi emphasized the innovative expression of elevator advertising content [9]. From the perspective of audience, Zhang Jixue emphasized that elevator advertising should realize the linkage between online and offline, and realize the deep interaction between advertising and users, so as to improve the communication power of elevator advertising [10]. Du Lanxuan and Cui Jie briefly analyzed the characteristics and marketing communication of sedan car elevator advertising in China [11].

For the classification of elevator advertising, the research on multimedia advertising, except for some research on multimedia equipment, there is no related communication level research. The above literature review covers multiple research levels of elevator advertising, deeply explores the characteristics and values of elevator advertising, and analyzes the influencing factors and strategies of its communication effect. However, there are still some problems in the existing research, such as the relatively few studies on the communication effect of multimedia advertising in elevators. This article will conduct in-depth research on the communication effect of elevator multimedia advertising based on the AIDMA model, taking Shanghai's commercial square as an example, in order to fill this research gap.

3 AIDMA in the elevator advertising industry

3.1 Overview of AIDMA model

The AIDMA model was proposed by the American advertising scientist E.S. Lewis, which represents the psychological process of a consumer from exposure to an advertisement to the final purchase action. This process is sequentially patterned and dynamic. The specific steps of AIDMA are as follows (shown in Table 1).

Table 1. The specific steps of AIDMA.

Attention	The consumer notices the AD, which is the beginning of the process. At this stage, the goal of the AD is to capture the consumer's attention.
Interest	Consumers are interested in the advertisement and are willing to continue to learn about the product or service in the advertisement.
Desire	After learning about the product or service, the consumer develops a desire to buy it. This is the critical stage at which the effects of advertising begin to translate into actual purchase behavior.
Memory	Consumers remember the brand or product in the AD to consider in future purchase decisions. At this stage, the goal of advertising is to build brand awareness and brand image.
Action	In the end, the consumer takes the purchase action to achieve the ultimate goal of the advertisement.

AIDMA model has been effectively guiding advertising creativity and marketing planning in the early days of traditional media and the Internet, which has the characteristics of a direct and quick effect. This model pays attention to the spread effect, cumulative effect, and resonance effect of marketing effect, and takes "media" as the core and "attracting attention" as the primary task of communication strategy. However, with the development of the Internet, the user behavior pattern has changed, so new marketing models such as the AISAS model have emerged. Nevertheless, the AIDMA model still has certain reference values and application scenarios [12].

At present, all aspects of AIDMA theory are subject to new challenges and opportunities. For example, in the "get attention" stage, information explosion makes it more difficult to get consumers' attention. In the "interest" phase, personalized recommendations and big data analytics enable companies to more accurately capture consumers' interest points. At the same time, the "arousing desire" stage requires more consideration of consumers' emotional needs and values.

The core knowledge in the field of marketing effect and communication effect mainly involves consumer behavior, market segmentation, media strategy, and data analysis. This knowledge helps enterprises to better understand the consumer decision-making process, so as to formulate more effective marketing strategies. The application of AIDMA theory in the field of marketing and communication is mainly reflected in the following aspects (shown in Table 2) [13].

Table 2. The application of AIDMA theory.

Content marketing	By creating valuable content, it attracts consumers' attention and interests, so as to stimulate the desire to buy.
Social media marketing	Use social media platforms to precisely target audiences and increase brand awareness and user engagement.
Data analysis	By analyzing consumer data, it can been seen the consumer behavior and interests, optimize marketing strategies, and improve marketing effectiveness.
Advertising strategy	According to AIDMA theory, formulate advertising strategies from attracting attention, and arousing interest to promoting action.

In data analysis, AIDMA theory mainly analyzes social media and search data to understand what content or products consumers are interested in, as well as their concerns and pain points; By analyzing e-commerce and questionnaire data, the study can understand the conversion rate of consumers in each link of the purchase process, so as to optimize marketing strategies to improve the conversion rate; Analyze the effect data of various marketing activities to evaluate the effectiveness of various strategies, so as to optimize the allocation of resources; Through the big data platform data, understand the market trends and competitors' marketing strategies and effects [14].

The main purpose of using the AIDMA model is to better understand consumer behavior and market trends, so as to develop more effective marketing strategies to improve brand awareness and sales performance. At the same time, through the analysis and mining of data, it can provide a scientific basis and reference for enterprises to make decisions.

3.2 Overview and value of AIDMA model

In the elevator, which is relatively closed and people's attention is more concentrated, multimedia advertising is easier to attract the attention of passengers. This is in line with the "Attention" phase of the AIDMA model because the first task of advertising is to attract the attention of the target audience. Elevator multimedia advertisements usually have a visual and auditory impact, which can stimulate passengers' interest in products or services and purchase desire. This is consistent with the "Interest" and "Desire" phases in the AIDMA model. As elevators are frequently used as a means of transportation in People's Daily lives, multimedia advertisements for elevators are characterized by repeated exposure. This repeated exposure helps to strengthen passengers' memory of the advertisement content, thus improving brand awareness and brand image. This corresponds with the "Memory" phase in the AIDMA model. Elevator multimedia advertisements can directly convey purchase information to the target audience, such as promotional activities and discount offers, so as to prompt passengers to take purchase actions after they leave the elevator. This is consistent with the "Action" stage in the AIDMA model, which achieves the ultimate goal of the advertisement.

Therefore, the AIDMA model has a high degree of fit with the research on the communication effect of elevator multimedia advertising. By utilizing the AIDMA model, a deeper understanding can be gained regarding the effects of elevator multimedia advertising in attracting attention, stimulating interest and desire, strengthening memory, and promoting action. This understanding can then facilitate the provision of more targeted marketing strategies and suggestions for advertisers.

3.3 Overview of the elevator advertising industry and classification

Elevator advertising is a kind of high-quality outdoor advertising. Its specific forms include elevator posters, elevator television, electronic screens and projections, etc. It is mainly made and published on the inner wall of the elevators in urban buildings. The specific forms of elevator advertising include posters inside the elevator, screen advertising, audio advertising, etc., as well as the elevator door directly installed advertising. Elevator advertising has the advantages of accurate delivery, high exposure rate, and target audience positioning, so it is favored by advertisers. The audience of elevator advertising is different because of the area where the elevator is located, mainly including the owners of residential areas, office workers, customers in commercial areas, and so on. With the development of the Internet, the forms and communication channels of elevator advertising are constantly changing and updating.

3.4 Current situation of elevator multimedia advertising

Elevator multimedia advertising, as a form of advertising that has emerged rapidly in recent years, has gradually occupied a place in the city by virtue of its characteristics of strong pertinence, clear audience, and remarkable communication effect. This form of advertising mainly uses the digital display screen, touch screen, and other equipment in the elevator to display a variety of business information, covering office buildings, residential buildings, shopping malls, and other places. With the acceleration of urbanization and the increasing number of high-rise buildings, elevators have become the only way for people to travel daily. The coverage of elevator multimedia advertising has expanded accordingly, becoming an indispensable advertising medium in the city. Elevator multimedia advertising continues to innovate in technology, such as high-definition display, dynamic screen display, and touch screen interaction, providing advertisers with more diversified display methods, but also enhancing the audience's viewing experience. The content of elevator multimedia advertising covers various fields, including catering, entertainment, shopping, education, and so on. Advertisers can customize personalized advertising content according to the characteristics and needs of the target audience. According to market research reports, in recent years, the market size of elevator multimedia advertising has continued to grow, with a compound annual growth rate of more than two digits. From January to May 2023, Shanghai is the city with the highest total amount of intelligent screen advertising for community elevators. More than 70% of urban residents said they would actively pay attention to multimedia advertising content in the elevator. Compared with traditional advertisements, the click-through rate and conversion rate of multimedia advertisements in elevators have increased by more than 30% and 20% respectively.

4 The elevator multimedia advertising communication effect investigation

This study used a non-sampling survey method to collect questionnaires by intercepting interviews at the entrances and exits of elevators. The questionnaire was developed by reviewing relevant literature. The questionnaire mainly consists of three parts: firstly, the sociodemographic characteristics of the respondents, including gender, age, education level, and income; Secondly, the content and form of elevator multimedia advertising. Finally, the evaluation and measurement of communication effect based on the AIDMA model.

In this paper, community A in Shanghai was selected for investigation. Community A is a community with a large scale, complete supporting facilities, a beautiful environment, and excellent property management. It belongs to the middle-class community, and its residents have strong purchasing power. A total of 215 valid questionnaires were collected in this survey. Among the valid questionnaires, 56% of the respondents were female; Most of the respondents were middle-aged; Their occupations are mainly concentrated in corporate company personnel and freelancers. Office workers commute daily and use the elevator at least twice, while students use it between two and six times to get to and from school, and freelancers are exposed to elevator advertisements more often. Therefore, it can be considered that the exposure rate of community elevator multimedia advertisements is relatively high.

5 Analysis of the communication effect

5.1 Draw attention

According to the survey question "Do consumers pay attention to multimedia elevator advertisements?", 58.1% (125 people) selected "occasionally pay attention" to multimedia elevator advertisements, and 27.9% (60) of the respondents chose "often". In the multiple-choice question "How to pass the time and relieve embarrassment by taking the elevator", 40 percent (86) chose "looking at the elevator floor button", 45.7 percent (118) chose multimedia advertisements, 38.6 percent (83) chose mobile phones, and 12.1 percent (26) "didn't look at anything or looked in the mirror". These data reflect that the strong media characteristics and mandatory role of elevator multimedia advertising in the context of interference and blocking by various factors is limited, but in most cases, elevator multimedia advertising can still play a stable role in attracting attention. In the survey, all of them reflected that multimedia advertising will attract their attention the first time because the voice of video advertising will inevitably be heard by the respondents, which reflects that the communication characteristics of multimedia advertising are easy to attract the unintentional attention of the audience.

The survey question "What content do consumers pay more attention to in the advertisement?" Of the respondents, 113 said that interesting language was the most important factor in attracting attention, 81 said that the brand awareness of the advertised product was very important,11 said that the discount rate of the promotion was very important, and the rest of the respondents said that the image of the advertisement was attractive, the celebrity endorsement and the unique marketing method also played a role.

In the field visits, the study found that advertisers will advertise according to product characteristics and market demand. For example, Fast-Moving Consumer Goods (FMCG) products focus on discounts and interactions; While fashion products will focus on the image of the celebrity, and try to establish the psychological hint and association between the celebrity and the product. The advertising content of most advertisers mainly spreads the concept of quality life, which is in line with the trend of community elevator multimedia advertising. For example, the dairy beverage brand "Six Walnuts" invited the famous pianist Lang Lang to endorse it. But most of the audience said it was the funny slogan "Six walnuts, give to a friend" that attracted attention. Friend, 666 ". Audio playback of the tagline also forces users. This shows that although users can avoid visual interference, it is almost impossible to avoid auditory stimulation. Rhyme and repetition of advertising words combined with rhythmic background music have a stronger communication effect.

5.2 Psychological effect

5.2.1 Stimulate Interest

For the multiple-choice question "Interested in advertising in what industries?" The conclusion is food and beverage category, 146 people, 67.9%; 140 people, 48.37%; Internet e-commerce, 99,46.04%. The response rate and penetration rate of these three items were significantly higher than those of other categories. It can be seen that advertising audiences are more interested in elevator ads related to catering, tourism, and fashion content. Audiences prefer products that are more accessible and closely related to life.

5.2.2 Create desire

In order to know whether the elevator multimedia advertisement can effectively stimulate the user's expectation of obtaining product information, the question "I would like to learn more about product information" was designed. The community field survey shows that the vast majority of advertisements have Quick Response (QR) codes in the most prominent position. However, 44.65% of respondents were very reluctant to scan QR codes; Then, 30.69% of them thought that scanning or not scanning was indifferent; Only less than 25% of the respondents had the intention to learn more about the products. This shows that the short exposure time of elevator multimedia advertising produces a short memory.

5.2.3 Forming memory

Whether the audience of community elevator advertisement can effectively recall is an effective means to measure the long-term effect of advertisement. Only when the audience pays attention to the advertisement, understands its theme and selling point, identifies with the brand, and becomes interested in it, will they have the willingness to understand the product, form the memory point, and achieve "advertisement re-recognition" when purchasing goods or services in the future. The questionnaire data show that 60% of the audience said that the memory degree of elevator multimedia advertisements is vague, and it needs to reproduce the advertisement to recall. In addition, 33.02% of the people said they could recall it after reminding them, while 5.58% of the people completely forgot the content, and only 1.39% of the people could completely remember it.

These data suggest that the audience has a relatively shallow degree of memory for elevator advertising. Forty percent remembered the endorser and the image. However, the number of people who remembered the name and brand was relatively small, accounting for 32.55% of the total. These statistics show that endorsers and images are more likely to be remembered.

In general, the reason why audiences are more interested in elevator advertisements related to catering, tourism, and fashion content is mainly because the products or services of these industries are closely related to People's Daily lives. Therefore, advertisements in these industries are more likely to arouse people's attention and interest. The reason why most respondents are reluctant to learn more about product information is that the short exposure time of elevator advertisements is not enough to stimulate users' expectations of obtaining product information. In elevator advertisements, time is very limited, usually only a few seconds to capture the audience's attention. Therefore, in order to create the audience's desire to learn about the product, it is necessary to convey the unique selling point of the product in a short period of time and guide the audience to create the desire to learn about the product through a powerful call to action. In terms of forming memories, advertising spokespersons and images are usually the most prominent and eye-catching elements. In contrast, key messages such as brand names and taglines are overlooked because the location is not prominent enough or it lacks originality. Therefore, when making elevator advertisements, attention should be paid to balancing the relationship between various elements and ensuring that the brand name and key information can be remembered.

5.3 Sales effect

For the question "I have a direct intention to purchase the product presented by the elevator advertisement", a five-point ranging scale was used, with 1-5 indicating "very reluctant" to "very willing". The survey data show that the effect of community elevator advertising on direct consumption intention is not obvious. The data show that most of the advertising themes preferred by the advertising audience are food and beverage, tourism, outdoor, and Internet e-commerce advertising, among which 48.09% of the respondents choose "neutral", that is, they do not care about the attitude of direct purchase intention of the products presented by the advertising. The average value is about 2.5, indicating that the respondents' purchase intention is relatively low. This is related to the higher daily consumption demand for these categories of products, and these advertising themes are more able to attract the audience's attention and stimulate their interest. The data show that this is associated with a very low willingness to "learn more about the product". Although community elevator advertising is effective in attracting attention and stimulating interest, it still needs to be improved indirectly inducing consumption intention. This may require advertisers and advertising agencies to think more deeply and innovate in terms of creativity, positioning, and communication strategies to better meet consumers' needs and stimulate their desire to buy.

6 Analysis of the communication effect

With its wide coverage, accurate audience positioning, diversified display methods, and significant communication effects, elevator multimedia advertising has become a highly concerned form of advertising in the city. With the continuous innovation of technology and the growing market demand, elevator multimedia advertising still has a lot of room for development in the future.

In today's information explosion era, people's attention is more divided. Compared with the multiple forms of information and entertainment on the Internet, advertisements inside elevators may no longer be the focus of passengers' attention. Passengers may be checking their phones, talking to other people, or doing other things while the AD is playing, which greatly reduces the attentional appeal of the AD. Traditional elevator ads tend to be one-way communication and lack interaction with passengers. However, in the digital era, consumers pay more attention to participation and interaction. If advertisements fail to provide interesting and engaging interactive experiences, passengers may not develop interest or memories. Despite its wide coverage, elevator advertising lacks a deep understanding of its audience. Without sufficient user data support, advertisers may not be able to accurately target audiences or develop personalized marketing strategies. This can lead to wasted or ineffective advertising. Due to the special nature of the elevator advertising environment, creativity and content may need to be updated regularly to keep it fresh. However, some advertisers may not update the content in time or lack innovation, leading to the gradual weakening of the advertising effect. Due to the particularity of the elevator advertising environment, creativity and content may need to be updated regularly to maintain freshness. However, some advertisers may not update the content in time or lack innovation, leading to the gradual weakening of the advertising effect.

7 Conclusion

In this study, the communication effect of elevator multimedia advertising based on the AIDMA model was evaluated. The AIDMA model, which includes the stages of attention, interest, desire, memory, and action, has been traditionally used to describe the consumer's psychological process from exposure to advertising to final purchase.

Elevator multimedia advertising, due to its unique environment of a closed and focused setting, is highly effective in capturing passengers' attention and stimulating interest and purchase desire. This form of advertising is suitable for a wide range of industries and brands and can enhance brand awareness and image. To evaluate its effectiveness, this study examined the communication effect, psychological effect, and sales effect of elevator multimedia advertising.

The findings demonstrate that elevator multimedia advertising utilizing the AIDMA model can significantly impact consumers. The attention stage is highly effective, as the captive audience is more likely to notice the advertising. At the interest stage, the ads successfully engage the audience and create a connection between the brand and the consumer. The desire stage is also well-supported, as the ads effectively communicate a call to action and create a strong pull towards a purchase. Memory and action stages are also important factors; elevator multimedia advertising helps to reinforce brand memory and drive actual sales.

With the ever-evolving digital era, elevator multimedia advertising will continue to play a crucial role in reaching target consumers. As technology advances, further innovations in elevator advertising are expected, such as interactive displays and personalized content delivery. Furthermore, as consumer behavior patterns continue to change, understanding the impact of elevator advertising on different age groups and cultural backgrounds will become increasingly important. Therefore, future research should focus on exploring the full potential of elevator multimedia advertising and its adaptability to different marketing models.

References

1. F. Chen, Sound Screen World: Advertisers Z1, 3 (2004)
2. S. Wang, Chinese Media Technology 5, 2 (2013)
3. X. Wang, International Public Relations 12, 3 (2023)
4. Y. Zhang, Harbin residential elevator advertising on and strategy research, Harbin Normal University (2024)
5. H. Chen, The Advertiser 5, 1 (2006)
6. J. Ya, Z. Tan, China Advertising 5, 3 (2006)
7. Y. Song, Popular Arts: Academic Edition 1, 2 (2020)
8. C. Gu, Sound Screen World: Advertisers 11, 2 (2018)
9. D. Han, Journal of Art and Design: Theory 8, 3 (2011)
10. J. Zhang, China's Property Management 6, 5 (2019)
11. L. Du, J. Cui, Journal of Shanghai Business 1, 1 (2021)
12. Y. Zhao, W. Jing, Z. Yan, Journal of Chongqing Institute of Technology (Social Science Edition) (2007)
13. L. Amaly, H. Hudrasyah, Measuring Effectiveness of Marketing communication Using Aisas Arcas Model (2024)
14. B, Bobylev, Modern Communication Studies 4, 6 (2015)

The Dilemmas and Improvement Strategies of China's Informal Economy in the Post Epidemic Era

Mingqin Chen[1], *Xuzhu* Liu[2,*], and *Jianyu* Xiong[3]

[1]Shangyu High School, Shaoxing, 312000, China
[2]New Oriental Education & Technology Group Inc University, Chengdu, 610095, China
[3]Chongqing Yucai Secondary School, Chongqing, 400050, China

Abstract. This research explores the development trend of the informal economy after the Covid-19 pandemic and the ways to avoid the increase informal economy. The paper discusses the development process of the informal economy, the difficulties it faces, and the causes of its emergence. Based on the detailed analysis of the current situation of informal economy and its possible impact on society, this paper points out that solutions should be implemented from the perspectives of government, enterprises and individuals, which prevent the informal economy from growing at an uncontrollable rate. For example, once the government's five insurance policies are formulated and laws and regulations are publicized; And the way enterprises treat new technical talents have affected the informal economy to some extent. The research of this paper will increase the understanding and attention of the society to the informal economy. Providing some substantial improvement strategies for the current informal economic system will help more people benefit from the regulated economic system.

1 Introduction

The first month of the Covid-19 outbreak in late 2019, Incomes of 1.6 billion workers in the informal economy fell by 60%. The economic community takes this as a turning point to implement sustainable development to restore the original economy. This not only guides economic recovery but also promotes more inclusive economic development [1]. The government should strengthen supervision of informal economies and provide supportive policies to transform informal economies into formal economies.

Under the Covid-19, the money supply in the market decreases and interest rates increase, leading to a decline in people's consumption, corporate investment profits decline and unemployment rate increases. While informal workers need employment security, employers need labor resources with continued flexibility. So informal workers may experience greater labor exploitation and accept lower wages.

Due to the Closure policies during the pandemic, informal workers perform "customer-facing" jobs, and they face a high risk of unemployment. The employers may lay off informal workers without any formal procedures and costs. The costs generated by the decline in production and consumption demand of enterprises will also be transferred to informal workers, so informal workers will both lose their income and be unable to seek help from the government.

The informal economy increases the tax pressure on the country because it can provide opportunities for tax evasion through the establishment of informal enterprises, leading to a deficit in the national treasury and huge economic pressure on the country.

From the perspective of values and beliefs, it is reasonable to encourage people to re-evaluate their potential loss and gain of entering and leaving the informal economy. Based on the above facts and background, this study addresses the negative impact of informality on informal economic groups under Covid-19 and provide new policies based on the pandemic's impact. The policies can optimize previous old policies and provide informal economic groups with the best solutions at present. This initiative not only helps informal groups but also helps the country's economic growth because the informal economy has always been an important factor hindering the growth of the state-owned economy.

2 Literature review

Judging from the relationship between offline micro businesses (OMB) activities and sales after Covid-19, researchers from famous domestic universities found that urban OMB is particularly hard-hit, especially the number of OMBs where female merchants are active and the activity of non-local self-employed households have dropped significantly, reaching about 53% to 57%. Using a machine learning method called gradient boosting decision tree (GBDT) and linear regression in a difference in difference specification, researchers explore whether the activity frequency of the economy,

* Corresponding author: siyun@ldy.edu.rs

population, and OMB is linearly related to the frequency of OMB activity after the new crown epidemic [2].

Members of the Fujian University of Technology analytical Institute found that as early development economists said that the informal economy is no longer a gradual outcome of modernization. This study describes and analyzes the future development direction of the informal economy based on the regulations issued by Sichuan Province. In order to encourage the employment of vendors, the government provides support to temporary mobile vendors to restore community vitality [3].

Aiming at the development of small and medium-sized enterprises, some scholars analyze on the relationship between the business environment, economic growth and funding sources of small and medium-sized enterprises in China's informal economy to identify the link between the business environment and technology Small and Medium Enterprises (SMEs). Then the study utilizes information asymmetry as an entry point to describe how it affects small and medium-sized enterprises. Information asymmetries were found to be largely due to lenders' reluctance to lend to businesses it considered risky, apply econometric techniques and core questionnaires are adopted to test these links [4].

Investigating the development of sharing economy in tourism during Covid-19, Ouyang Rihui asserts sharing economy in tourism boosts the economy. Meanwhile, sharing economy in tourism brings some risks, involving management and user rights. So, Ouyang Rihui concludes some suggestions for encouraging the growth of sharing economy in tourism [5]. Exploring the traditional second-hand market in China, Zheng Qian, Zhang Xinyu, Bai Changshan, Tang Min, and Dong Zhengzheng elaborate on the development process of China's secondary market, its current situation, and its transaction model. The study analyzes the potential of second-hand markets in the informal economy [6]. Through literature research and semi-structured interviews with local government officials, entrepreneurs, and small and medium-sized workshops, Weicheng Tang and Jin Zhu clarify some risks generated by the development of e-commerce in rural China. Moreover, this study offers political suggestions for the sustainable growth of e-commerce in China's countryside [7].

In the cause of informal economy, excessive regulation, such as labor market regulation and social security legislation, and increased tax burdens can expand the informal economy. It also discusses the impact of insufficient government regulation or action on the rise of the informal economy, such as bureaucracy, over-regulation and corruption in the government sector, which can contribute to the development of the informal economy, especially now that many informal economy participants in start-ups are increasingly seen as "need" or "opportunity" driven entrepreneurs. Many scholars regard informal entrepreneurs as egoists. When motivated, it contrasts sharply with the liberal alternative. Other factors that influence the informal economy include time distribution, socioeconomic factors, and demographic factors [8].

In conclusion, present researches lack specific analysis of various difficulties of informal economy and universally valid solutions. Thereby, detecting existing difficulties for informal economy, analyzing the difficulties' causes and the influences, and exploring solutions from multiple perspectives for challenges faced by informal economy are the core motivations for the article to research.

3 Analysis and discussion

3.1 The development history and main difficulties of the informal economy

3.1.1 Development history

Between 2000 and 2010, the number of urban informal workers in China increased from 111.5 million to 214.8 million, and the average annual growth rate of informal employment reached 6.8%. Accounting for more than half of the urban employed population. It shows that the employment growth in China's cities and towns during this 10-year period mainly comes from the employment rate in the informal economy [9]. In 2016, statistics show that informal employment accounted for 62.8% of non-agricultural employment in developing Asia-Pacific regions. In 2008, the informal economy accounted for 74% to 91% of the total reported economy. It was observed that a larger proportion (over 73.3% of workers) in the informal sector were employed outside agriculture, in rural areas rather than urban areas. According to the 2008-2009 Labor Force Survey, most of these involve the construction and transport sectors, personal, social and public services, trade manufacturing and finally wholesale and retail businesses. In the Middle East and North African countries. Being self-employed and small and medium-sized employ approximately 70 percent of the population, and this proportion approaches 80% throughout South Asia and Africa.

3.1.2 The situation and characteristics of informal workers

Targeting informal workers in the informal economy rely on manual labor and most of them have low education. Therefore, they do not need to have professional skills, and their opportunities to get regular jobs are very limited.

Most people choose to continue working when they are sick because there is no social security. Therefore, emergencies at work are the biggest threat to them. Construction is one of the most dangerous occupations, according to Safe Work Report 2018. It is also the occupation with the highest incidence of occupational diseases [10]. Under such circumstances, they still receive wages that are lower than equilibrium wages. At present, informal workers face three major problems: dirty, high-risk occupations, and difficult occupations.

With the advent of Covid-19, informal construction workers are engaged in "face-to-face" work. Without a job, your source of income will be completely cut off. However, the contractor will only choose those who want to earn income and take risks to complete the company's requirements. This requirement directly curbs the survival of the informal worker economy. In order to earn income, they can only go to work despite the extremely high risk of infection rate and without any social assistance guarantee.

3.1.3 Main difficulties

The epidemic has dealt a heavy blow to informal workers, especially the street stall economy because they can't work from home. It relies on the liquidity of the external environment to implement operations, and relies on cash flow and loans to survive when savings are limited. The arrival of the epidemic prompted countries to adopt lockdown policies to keep them away from society. As a vulnerable group, their income and even survival have been seriously threatened and they are unable to obtain government relief.

Compared with rural areas, the street stall economy in urban areas has been hit harder, especially female self-employed people in the industry. Activity frequency dropped by more than half and by half the amount in men [2]. The same is true for the non-native population, there is no advantage like local people being protected by the government. Coupled with housing and loan problems, it is even more difficult for them to survive.

The economy has suffered a severe blow after the epidemic, leading to a general increase in unemployment in formal industries. Major companies such as Tencent, Alibaba, and NetEase. Many senior leaders are at risk of being laid off. The reason is that they are older and the number of fresh graduates is increasing, more young talents entering the market. In order to improve economic development, enterprises introduce a large number of new talents. Increasing employment rate is to promote economic development. When most ordinary workers are unemployed, the best thing to do is to join the informal economy as self-employed households.

Due to the epidemic, the right to go out is limited. But people need to buy daily necessities and food, so an industry called e-retail has been born [11]. Direct online ordering and door-to-door delivery bring great convenience to the masses. Even after the epidemic is lifted, this industry is still emerging. As a result, the market for the street stall economy began to shrink because their customer resources are losing. Therefore, the street stall economy has also become a potential laggard in technological development.

Micro-enterprises under the epidemic face massive reverse migration of labor force [12]. Most micro-enterprises still have loans that need to be repaid every month, because many of the bank's corporate customers have gone bankrupt due to the epidemic and cannot repay on time or even fail (accounts receivable become bad debts). Thus, banks will not reduce interest rates. The impact of the epidemic on SMEs can be summarized in the following four points: (1) The production chain is almost directly broken. (2) Market loss and supply chain disruption. (3) The economic impact of companies on the market in an economy [13]. Due to insufficient distribution and manufacturing, 90% of micro and small enterprises had to file for bankruptcy [14]. Moreover, if the staff turnover rate and turnover continue to decline, it will indirectly indicate the vulnerability of enterprises due to the epidemic. They do not have a clear enterprise structure, personnel division, and authorization from superiors to subordinates, so the vulnerability at the enterprise level is very high. The government may introduce some relevant "protection policies". It is precisely because of the "informality under the informal economy" that they can only say that relying on these policies to slow down the rate of bankruptcy still ends in bankruptcy.

3.2 The reasons for its formation and its impact on the economy and society

The first reason is that the heavy tax burden stimulates the emergence of the informal economy. The informal economy for individuals can have the advantages of unregulated industries in evading government taxes and registration activities, which can reduce costs for businesses. In the recent years, as the recession of the national economy, the study detects that the cost to run a business increases and informal economy has exploded. In addition, by using dynamic multi-indicator multi-cause model (DYMIMIC), it can be discovered that the informal economy as a hidden economic system, which can be measured by the power consumption of enterprises, and points out that the vigorous development of this hidden economic system is indeed a response to the heavy tax burden [15].

The second reason lies in the legal and policy constraints. United States is a good example of the government constriction, according to the US Small Business Administration (SBA), registering a small business needs to meet certain requirements, especially the requirements of the business structure. For instance, the company shall hold its first and annual meetings of directors and shareholders and shall be required to record its meetings, and companies will then need to meet filing requirements, for instance, some states set the deadline on the anniversary of the establishment of the business, while other states choose a specific day for all businesses. Costs are usually accompanied by annual reports or biennial statements and can exceed $300. Some states impose franchise taxes on corporations or limited liability companies operating within their borders. Some states require an initial report to be filed and charged shortly after the company is incorporated. If the company makes a significant change - such as an address, name, new shares or membership - report it in the articles of association. Then, there are federal government requirements, including but not limited to licenses, permits, or certificates. These cumbersome procedures make it difficult for many ordinary people to choose the formal economy, and then they choose the informal economy to avoid these legal procedures.

The third reason for the informal economic boost is the lack of jobs due to the economic downturn, especially after the Covid-19 pandemic. For example, during the Covid-19 period, the lockdown in China has led to reduced consumption and production disruptions. Across the globe, the functioning of global supply chains has been affected, as have companies around the world. Millions have lost their jobs. Moreover, every day there are more and more companies shutting down operations, revising forecasts or announcing layoffs, such as the bankruptcy of China HengDa Group. Global financial markets have fallen sharply, with volatility at or above levels seen in the 2008/9 financial crisis. In the midst of all this turmoil, the International Monetary Fund (IMF) has made estimates for growth in 2020. In its revised estimates, the IMF expects China's growth to slow by 0.4 percentage points and global growth to slow by 0.1 percentage points. According to the Organization for Economic Co-operation and Development (OECD), it presents that global growth slow to 2.4 per cent in 2020, compared with 2.9 per cent in 2019. When compared the differences in Gross Domestic Product (GDP) growth across countries, Table 1 shows the economic shocks (and confidence intervals) caused by the Covid-19 crisis, expressed as a percentage of GDP across countries. It can be seen that the growth rate of GDP is declining across the board. According to the Phillips curve, the reduction in aggregate supply will lead to high unemployment, which will significantly stimulate the growth of the informal economy [16].

Table 1. Economic impact.

Argentina	-4.3%
Australia	-4.4%
Austria	-5.5%
Belgium	-4.3%
Brazil	-3.9%
China	-4.3%
Czech Republic	-4.6%
France	-4.3%
Germany	4.8%
Greece	-6.2%
India	-4.0%
Ireland	-4.8%
Italy	-5.0%

3.3 Solution

The government should reinforce five insurances and fund in rural and urban regions. Injury insurance shows it can help informal workers reduce the expense of medical care and release the worries when informal workers are injured during work. Thus, the workers can better focus on production, supporting the growth of general social productivity. The government should make sure five insurances and one fund are in place and offer efficient payment ways. Therefore, informal workers can completely enjoy the basic insurances.

The legislatures should establish perfect laws and policies. For one thing, the legislative department should perfect laws to reduce the occurrence of tax evasion and relevant illegal persons should be punished. Due to enough taxes, the nation can have the money to invest in public utilities, contributing to better welfare and government services. So unofficial economic groups can enhance their living quality. For another, the legislatures should complete laws on informal economy. Many voids and ambiguities exist in the laws of informal economy. Clarifying the scale of informal economy and providing legal support for contracts between informal workers and employers effectively guarantee the rights and interests of both sides.

Platform enterprises should treat formal workers and informal workers equally. Based on labor laws, equal payment for equal effort should be extended to informal laborers. Besides, platform enterprises should create promotion opportunities for informal laborers and realize informal laborers' greatest potential [17].

The government should conduct legal education and allocate technicists to instruct informal workers in skills. Besides, the informal laborers should actively learn. Firstly, the reason why the rights of informal laborers lack assurance is partly because the workers have no contracts or sign illegal contracts. The legal education in informal workers' communities can help them increase legal awareness. Secondly, the technicists assigned to specific regions investigate and utilize local resource advantages. They guide informal laborers on professional techniques, which facilitates lasting and stable employment for informal workers. For informal workers, they should be proactive in learning professional skills and studying how to guard their rightful interests.

4 Conclusion

This study reveals the development process of informal economy: increasing yearly proportion of informal economy, informal economy mostly found in rural regions, a considerable percent of informal workers. The process suggests that informal economy is expanding. From the perspective of the whole, micro and small businesses, and informal workers, the article also reveals the challenges encountered by informal economy during the pandemic. Then, the article discovers tax evasion led by tax burden and excessive limitations on companies are main factors of the challenges. The paper analyzes how the challenges affect national economy and societal development: the decreasing GDP and surge in unemployment. Therefore, the paper offers solutions from the perspective of the government, platform enterprises, and individuals. The government should bolster five insurances and one fund and direct legislation; The platform enterprises should regard informal labor equally; Individuals should learn techniques and laws. This study enables more people to pay attention to informal economy and provides some measures on informal economy, contributing to the growth of informal economy. Thereby, more people could benefit from the progressively ideal informal economy. However, the paper is not supported by thorough figures and lots of data such as the present scale of informal economy. The article would conduct field research so that the article can explore the challenges for informal economy in China more deeply.

Authors contribution

All the authors contributed equally and their names were listed in alphabetical order.

References

1. Q. Wang, R. Huang, Environmental Research 202, 39 (2021)
2. F. Guo, Y. Huang, J. Wang, et al., China Economic Review 71, 8 (2022)
3. K. Kadiriya, Y. Zhang, Bilingual Publishing Group 4, 4 (2021)
4. Y. Liu, D. Azer, K. Xu, et al., Economic Analysis and Policy 76, 4 (2022)
5. R. Ouyang, New Economic Guide 4, 6 (2020)
6. Q. Zheng, X. Zhang, C. Bai, et al., Shopping Mall Modernization 10, 2 (2019)
7. W. Tang, J. Zhu, Journal of Rural Studies 75, 10 (2020)
8. E. Igudia, R. Ackrill, S. Coleman, et al., International Journal of Entrepreneurship & Small Business 28, 2 (2016)
9. G. Hung, D. Xue, B. Wang, et al., Sustainability in Geographic Science 12, 7 (2020)
10. W. Maranatha, L. Kukuh, N. Ellysa, et al., Heliyon 8, e10321 (2022)
11. R. Bandyopadhyay, Borders of an Epidemic 31 (2020)
12. A. Sharma, Vikalpa 47, 1, (2022)
13. R. Rachmawati, S. Sawitri, M. Musdalifah, et al., Research Horizon 2, 13 (2022)
14. S. Windu, K. Indra, International Journal of Social Science and Human Research 6, 16 (2023)
15. C. Deléchat, L. Medina, Finance & Development 57, 4 (2020)
16. N. Fernandes, SSRN Electronic Journal 3557504 (2020).
17. X. Xiong, G. Li, Journal of Modern Management 10, 9 (2020)

 https://doi.org/10.1051/shsconf/202418802008

How can Developing Countries in Asia Achieve Economic Growth? Taking Bangladesh as an example

Hao Wu

Department of Economics, University of Sheffield, 9 Mappin Street, Sheffield, S1 4DT, United Kingdom

Abstract. This study analyzes the key drivers of economic growth in Bangladesh from 1980 to 2018 based on theoretical frameworks and historical data. It takes Bangladesh's development experience as the research object and aims to make three contributions. Firstly, it examines the main contributing factors to Bangladesh's past growth within the analytical framework of the neoclassical growth theory. This allows summarizing the underlying causes of Bangladesh's historical economic growth trajectory. Secondly, it investigates the current contributing factors and obstacles to growth in Bangladesh to understand how countries like Bangladesh, Myanmar and Vietnam can achieve ongoing economic growth. Lastly, the research methodology employs empirical analysis of time series data on factors such as investment, labor force, technology and GDP within the framework of neoclassical growth theory. The findings suggest that capital accumulation, driven by investment, has made the largest contribution to Bangladesh's strong economic performance in recent decades. However, risks remain if over-reliance on the garment industry and uneven regional development are not addressed through continued policy reforms focusing on diversification, balanced development and social inclusion. The study provides preliminary guidance for Bangladesh and similar nations to sustain their growth momentum.

1 Introduction

Developing countries in Asia have experienced rapid economic growth in recent decades through industrialization and export-oriented development. Many adopted an export-led growth strategy focused on labor-intensive manufacturing. This transformed their economies and lifted hundreds of millions out of poverty. Countries like China, India, Indonesia and Vietnam achieved strong growth rates between 6-10% annually from the 1980s through industrial upgrading and participation in global and regional supply chains. Bangladesh is one such success story, achieving over 6% GDP growth annually since 1990 according to World Bank data. Its economy has grown from \$6.2 billion in 1990 to \$305.8 billion in 2021, transitioning from a low-income to lower-middle income country. This rapid growth was driven by ready-made garments manufacturing, which now accounts for over 80% of exports. Garment exports rose from \$0.5 billion in the 1980s to over \$35 billion currently, making Bangladesh the second largest apparel exporter globally. Strong remittance inflows from overseas Bangladeshi workers have also supported domestic consumption and poverty reduction.

However, Bangladesh faces challenges to sustaining this growth trajectory. Firstly, over-reliance on the garment industry leaves the economy vulnerable to external shocks. Secondly, low productivity in other sectors and a lack of economic diversification hampers transition to higher value industries. Thirdly, infrastructure deficits and skills shortages constrain private sector investment and competitiveness. This paper aims to analyze the key drivers of Bangladesh's past economic growth and discuss policy recommendations based on growth theories. Section II will review relevant literature on growth models and Asian developing countries. Section III applies analytical frameworks to Bangladesh's historical growth. Section IV discusses limitations and future outlook. Finally, Section V concludes with policy implications.

2 Literature review

2.1 Economic growth theories

A seminal theoretical framework elucidating the dynamics of macroeconomic progression is the neoclassical accumulation paradigm conceptualized by Solow and Swan, regarded as a foundational piece of scholarship on the sources and sustainability of gains in material well-being at the national scale [1]. The theory proposes that long-term economic expansion is shaped by the accumulation of capital resources, growth of the populace, and advances in applied knowledge. It envisions progressively smaller incremental benefits from additional units of work and investment. Typically, total output is modelled as correlating with capital stock and man-hours in a Cobb-Douglas formulation,

Corresponding author: hwu69@sheffield.ac.uk

quantifying how the economy's aggregate productivity draws from the combined contributions of physical assets and human efforts [2]. According to the Solow-Swan model, economies converge towards a steady-state equilibrium level of per capita output determined by the exogenous rate of technological progress. Population growth and savings rates affect the transition path but not the long-run growth rate. Technological advancement is the only sustained source of long-run growth in per capita GDP. The model predicts that poor countries with lower initial capital stocks will tend to grow faster than rich nations until they approach their own steady states. However, the model has been criticized for treating technological progress as exogenous and for not explaining divergences across countries' growth experiences. Endogenous growth theories later emerged to address these limitations. Models by Romer and Lucas incorporated technological change as endogenous and driven by human capital accumulation and knowledge spillovers. These new growth theories highlight the importance of institutions, economic policies, and other supply-side factors in generating sustained long-run growth. Overall, the neoclassical and new growth paradigms provide useful frameworks for understanding sources and determinants of economic development across countries over time.

2.2 Characteristics of developing countries

Developing countries are typically characterized by low levels of industrialization, income per capita, and human development indicators relative to advanced economies. Common obstacles to economic growth faced by developing nations include low domestic savings rates, lack of skilled labor, underdeveloped physical infrastructure, weak institutions, and over-reliance on primary commodity exports and foreign aid [3, 4]. Specifically, developing Asian countries tend to have large populations engaged in subsistence agriculture with low labor productivity. Manufacturing and modern services sectors remain underdeveloped in most cases. Access to credit, electricity, transportation networks and other basic infrastructure is often limited outside major urban centers as well. Bureaucratic inefficiencies, corruption, unstable macroeconomic policies and conflicts also impede the investment climate and private sector development in many developing nations. Empirical studies have examined the development experiences of countries such as Sri Lanka and Bangladesh. Athukorala and Kelegama analyzed Sri Lanka's trade liberalization and export-oriented industrialization policies of the late 1970s which boosted industrial and overall GDP growth [5]. Mahmud, Devarajan, and Lakshman evaluated Bangladesh's prudent macroeconomic management along with trade, investment and financial sector reforms that supported transition to a more open, market-based economy and higher growth rates in recent decades despite various challenges [6]. Outward-oriented reforms, export promotion, infrastructure investment, institutional improvements and macroeconomic stability have played important roles in accelerating economic growth for developing Asian countries.

2.3 Economic growth in Bangladesh

Bangladesh has experienced relatively steady economic growth in recent decades, substantially reducing the poverty headcount. However, obstacles to even faster and more inclusive development remain. Key challenges include weak infrastructure, governance and institutional deficiencies, and over-dependence on the ready-made garments sector for export earnings and growth [7]. Several studies have analyzed the determinants facilitating Bangladesh's economic progress as well as the sustainability of current growth trends. Rahman and Razzaque assessed the roles of remittances, foreign direct investment, exports and domestic investment in driving GDP expansion from 1990-2013 [8]. Their findings highlight the importance of stable macroeconomic management, open trade policies and growing expatriate worker remittances in supporting growth. Meanwhile, the World Bank evaluated Bangladesh's resilience in the face of external shocks like natural disasters and global financial crises. However, the study also warned that limited economic diversification beyond the garment industry increases vulnerability. Ahmed and Siddique examined cointegration and causality between infrastructure, energy consumption, trade openness and output, concluding that infrastructure bottlenecks constrain growth potential [9]. Ongoing efforts to strengthen physical infrastructure, energy security, governance and private sector development are thus vital for Bangladesh to sustain its growth momentum.

3. Analytical framework and discussion

3.1 Analysis based on Neoclassical Growth Theory

The neoclassical growth theory provides a useful framework for understanding Bangladesh's strong economic performance over recent decades. At the core of the theory is the premise that investment in physical and human capital accumulation leads to long-term growth. Bangladesh has witnessed significant capital deepening since the late 1980s as predicted by the theory. Gross fixed capital formation as a percentage of GDP rose steadily, indicating expanded investment in factories, machinery, infrastructure and other productive assets. Through maintained macroeconomic harmony and an export-focused industrialization strategy, Bangladesh experienced rapid accumulation of physical assets. As the theoretical theory suggests, heightened investment consequently increased production capacity and prosperity standards. Simultaneously improving human capital, an additional key driver of advancement per neoclassical doctrine, Dhaka implemented initiatives to uplift primary education participation, literacy and wellness benchmarks, thereby cultivating a more skilled workforce. As Momen and Marzina highlighted, adult literacy escalated from under 30% in the early 1980s to over 70% in modern times, demonstrating Bangladesh's combined prioritization of physical and human capital development for sustainable growth [10]. Similarly, life expectancy at birth lengthened from around 55 years to over 72 years over this period. Reduced fertility rates from 6 children per woman in 1980 to around 2 currently helped to balance population growth with economic and social development. These human capital augmenting policies and outcomes are thought to have equipped Bangladeshis with stronger skills and productivity to benefit from increasing investment opportunities [10].

While neoclassical theory provides a reasonable framework for Bangladesh's growth trajectory, some aspects require further examination. While physical and human capital deepening have increased substantially, as highlighted in the literature review, productivity growth has been more modest. Additionally, while the development of the ready-made garment sector stimulated investment and output growth, contributing to Bangladesh's strong economic performance as the model anticipates, over-reliance on this single export industry increases vulnerability to external shocks. This concentration of investment in garment manufacturing, rather than a more diversified industrial base, poses risks to sustainability not fully captured by the model. Nonetheless, as Section 3.1 discussed, policies strengthening infrastructure, education and health that augment physical and human resources have significantly supported Bangladesh's capital formation and rising income levels in line with neoclassical theory. Going forward, further examination of how Bangladesh can address these inconsistencies will be important to guide long-term planning and ensure the continued realization of growth potential predicted by the model.

3.2 Historical events shaping growth trajectories

Several historical events have played a role in facilitating or hindering Bangladesh's economic growth trajectory relative to neoclassical predictions. The country's independence from Pakistan in 1971 created conditions conducive for reforms and growth acceleration. Free from colonial rule, Bangladesh gained autonomy over fiscal, monetary and trade policies [10]. This enabled pursuing export-oriented industrialization strategies focused on ready-made garments that stimulated investment and output growth [8]. Average GDP increased from 1.5% in the 1970s to over 6% since 2000, supported by foreign aid inflows and a stable macroeconomic environment. Notwithstanding, the political volatility of the post-independence era diverged from the model's hypothesis of stable governance. The recurrent changes of administration through non-democratic means and military incursions during the 1970s-1980s undermined consistency of policy formulation and discouraged private sector commitment of capital. This instability postponed the deepening of investment and gains in productivity as envisioned by neoclassical economic theory. Moreover, the model failed to accommodate external events that would periodically reset Bangladesh's growth curve. For instance, the catastrophic floods of 1988 devastated infrastructure and agriculture, interrupting output by diminishing the stock of capital and labor efficiency. More recently, the COVID-19 pandemic slowed investment and exports, curbing GDP growth to 3.5% in 2020. Such unforeseen events inhibited realizing the model's full growth potential. Overall, while independence facilitated policy reforms and foreign inflows supporting investment-led growth, political turbulence and natural disasters represented divergences with neoclassical expectations.

3.3 Impact of policy reforms and industry development

Bangladesh embarked on significant policy reforms in the 1980s that helped accelerate economic growth. The country transitioned from import substitution to export promotion strategies through trade liberalization. This facilitated the rapid emergence of the ready-made garments industry as a major export sector. As "Moving Forward: Connectivity and Logistics to Sustain Bangladesh's Success" demonstrates, garment exports now account for over 80% of Bangladesh's total exports, up from just 12% in 1980. The garment industry has since served as the primary driver of growth, stimulating employment, foreign exchange earnings, consumption and investment. However, becoming overly reliant on a single industry carries risks. Over-specialization in clothing leaves the economy vulnerable to macroeconomic instability from external shocks like the ongoing COVID-19 pandemic, which has severely impacted global apparel demand and Bangladesh's export earnings. With limited efforts to diversify production beyond textiles, growth remains exposed to fluctuations in global garment market conditions. To strengthen resilience, Bangladesh must pursue economic transformation by developing new competitive industries aligned with its comparative advantages.

Financial sector deregulation in the 1990s increased credit availability and supported investment and business expansion. But uneven development across regions persists, as rural credit access still lags urban areas [11, 12]. This inhibits inclusive growth and the ability of agricultural sectors and small enterprises to participate in industrialization [11]. Concurrently, diverse public initiatives in education, healthcare and infrastructure implemented through sequential Five-Year Plans have beneficially impacted the development of human capital. However, challenges surrounding equitable admission to high-quality social and economic amenities nationwide remain partially unaddressed. Solving these constraints will be pivotal for Bangladesh to foster skilled workforces harmonized with endeavors to modernize industry. Doing so is indispensable to sustaining the long-term progress anticipated by neoclassical economic theory as the nation strives to attain higher income standing. Continuing reforms must also concentrate on strengthening incorporation in financial systems and further diversifying the economy to construct macroeconomic resilience.

3.4 Investment in physical and human capital

Bangladesh has witnessed significant accumulation of physical capital over the past few decades. According to data from the World Bank, gross fixed capital formation as a percentage of GDP increased from around 15% in the 1980s to over 30% in recent years. This growth in the capital stock has been driven by rising investments from both public and private sources. Total investment, including private consumption of fixed capital, has risen from less than 20% of GDP to over 33% during the same period. The increased investments have supported the development of Bangladesh's industrial and infrastructure sectors. On the industrial front, capital investments have facilitated the expansion of manufacturing industries. According to the Bangladesh Bureau of Statistics, around 85% of manufacturing employment is concentrated in the textiles and clothing industries as of 2021. However, returns to physical capital may have diminished in some labor-intensive industries like ready-made garments due to rising capital intensity [13]. This suggests Bangladesh still has potential to diversify production into new sectors by attracting capital investments. Infrastructure development has also benefited from the rising investments. Key transport and utility projects have helped strengthen connectivity and access to basic services. While capital deepening has contributed to strong GDP growth over the past decades, maintaining high returns on investment will require further structural economic changes. This includes diversifying the industrial base beyond textiles and clothing to take advantage of unused capital. Prudent investments in new sectors can help maximize returns on the accumulated physical assets.

Concurrently, human capital development in Bangladesh has lagged the pace of physical capital accumulation. The labor force participation rate remains relatively low, with female labor force participation below 30%. While primary school enrollment reached near universal levels, secondary school completion rates are only around 50% [14]. These educational outcomes are below the average for countries with Bangladesh's income level. Health indicators have shown progress but remain short of targets. Life expectancy increased from under 60 years in 1990 to over 72 years in 2019 but is still lower than expected given income levels. Under-5 and infant mortality rates have halved from 1990-2019 but are off-track to achieve SDG targets by 2030. Persistent gender gaps also exist across health outcomes. Inconsistencies between Bangladesh's human capital indicators and returns to investment suggest market and government failures. Expanding access to quality education and strengthening health systems will be critical to develop skills, support economic diversification and maximize returns to physical capital. This remains a key policy priority if Bangladesh is to transition to efficiency-driven growth.

4. Limitation and outlook

The study provides valuable insights but has some limitations that future research could address.

As a single-country analysis, the narrow scope limits generalizability of findings to broader contexts. While the Solow growth framework offers a useful lens, the model's restrictive assumptions may not fully capture complex realities in a developing economy like Bangladesh. Additionally, data availability poses challenges for robust empirical analysis. Statistics on key indicators from Bangladesh often have reliability issues common to emerging markets. This constrains validation of quantitative results. Qualitative data to supplement quantitative findings was also not utilized. Methodologically, the study relies primarily on literature review rather than advanced econometric techniques. Endogenizing variables and relaxing structural assumptions could generate more nuanced insights. Incorporating macro-level policy factors beyond capital and labor is needed to impart actionable policy guidance. Broader contextual factors influencing growth, such as institutional quality, geopolitics, and social dynamics, are also not sufficiently explored. Future research could employ mixed methods to address these shortcomings. For example, comparative analyses applying consistent techniques across countries may yield more general conclusions regarding growth determinants. At the firm and household levels, qualitative interviews addressing perspectives of economic agents could complement aggregate data. This may help uncover constraints to productivity and participation not evident in national accounts. Time series or panel data approaches may better capture linkages between human capital, innovation, and long-term growth. Addressing these limitations would strengthen understanding of Bangladesh's development experience and inform evidence-based policymaking.

In addition, focusing exclusively on Bangladesh also narrows the scope for drawing broader insights that could be gained through comparative cross-country analyses applying consistent econometric techniques. Single-country studies are inherently less generalizable due to country-specific economic, social and political factors. This issue is further exacerbated by prevalent data limitations stemming from Bangladesh's standing as a developing nation. Statistics on key macroeconomic indicators may not fully capture realities on the ground owing to challenges with data availability, measurement and accuracy that are common in emerging market contexts. For example, a large informal sector and lack of comprehensive national accounts make GDP estimation difficult. Such data constraints pose obstacles for validating and interpreting the quantitative findings from a Bangladesh-only analysis. Cross-checking results against other comparable developing Asian economies could help address some of these limitations. However, the unavailability of long-run, high-frequency data for all relevant countries prohibits a more robust comparative assessment. Overall, data and generalizability issues constrain the explanatory and predictive power of single-country studies.

Moving forward, incorporating qualitative research methods may help address data limitations while exploring perspectives of economic agents. Longitudinal analyses employing expanded datasets could provide deeper insights into linkages between human capital, innovation, and growth over Bangladesh's development trajectory. Expanding the analytical scope to include policy variables such as education spending, infrastructure, and R&D investment would impart valuable guidance for stakeholders.

5. Conclusion

This study analyzes the key drivers of Bangladesh's strong economic growth over recent decades using the Solow neoclassical growth model framework. The findings suggest that large capital accumulation, as evidenced by rising gross fixed capital formation and total investment levels, has been the primary contributor to output and productivity gains. This accumulation has been driven by increased private and public investments in physical capital, particularly in the manufacturing sector through expansion of the ready-made garments industry. However, the over-reliance on this single export industry leaves Bangladesh vulnerable to external shocks. Meanwhile, human capital development has lagged physical capital accumulation, with inconsistencies in health and education outcomes relative to income levels. To sustain its growth momentum and transition to efficiency-driven growth, Bangladesh must pursue further reforms to strengthen and balance its physical and human resource development. This includes promoting skills training to develop a more productive workforce, expanding access to quality healthcare and education nationwide, diversifying the industrial base through developing new competitive industries, and increasing rural infrastructure investments to foster more inclusive development across regions. Maintaining macroeconomic stability and improving the business environment will also be important to maximize returns on Bangladesh's past and future investments in capital over the coming decades as it aims to achieve upper-middle income status.

References

1. R. Solow, The Quarterly Journal of Economics 1, 65 (1956)
2. C. Charles, P. Douglas, The American Economic Review 18, 27 (1928)
3. P. Romer, Journal of Political Economy 94, 36 (1986)
4. M. Todaro, S. Stephen, Economic Development 1, 20 (2015)
5. P. Athukorala, Journal of Development Studies 36, 16 (2000)
6. S. Devarajan, Journal of African Economies 13, 23 (2004)
7. M. Hussain, Third World Quarterly 40, 18 (2019)
8. S. Majumder, M. Rahman, Journal of the Social Sciences 48, 3 (2020)
9. A. Raihan, D. Muhtasim, F. Sadia, et al., Energy Nexus 8, 15 (2022)
10. N. Momen, H. Faruque, B. Marzina, New Global Development 21, 8 (2005)
11. M. Asadullah, Z. Wahhaj, Journal of Asian Economics, 58, 9 (2018)
12. M. Rahman, M. Mokhlesur, B. Rahman, South Asia Economic Journal 17, 20 (2016)
13. S. Ahmed, Z. Sattar, World Bank Policy Research Working Paper 34204, (2004)
14. UNICEF, Levels and Trends Child Mortality Report 9, 19 (2019)

Analysis of Investment Policies in China and the U.S. and the Impact of FDI on China's Economy

Shizhuo Zhang*

School of Business, East China University of Political Science and Law, Shanghai, 201620, China

Abstract. With the acceleration of the globalization process and the increase in international links, global trade and transnational investment are growing rapidly, and a clear and sound investment policy system can provide clear guidance and support to domestic enterprises and investors, while also influencing investment decisions and willingness to cooperate of other countries or regions. This paper presents a concise summary of the investment policies of China and the United States. It highlights that the United States' investment policies primarily consist of outward foreign direct investment (OFDI) policy and the safeguarding of domestic industries and capital, while China's focus remains on attracting foreign investment, with continuous OFDI policy improvement. This paper also analyzes the positive impacts and risk challenges of FDI on China's economy. FDI generally promotes China's economic growth, provides employment opportunities, improves the quality of labor, promotes technological progress, and enhances innovation, but it also faces a series of problems, especially the negative side of economic stability, market competition, and coordinated social development. Improvements in all these issues require timely adaptation and guidance from national investment policies.

1 Introduction

Foreign Direct Investment (FDI) is one of the most important forms of capital internationalization in the modern global economy. According to the IMF and OECD definitions, direct investment reflects the aim of obtaining a lasting interest by a resident entity of one economy (direct investor) in an enterprise that is resident in another economy (the direct investment enterprise).

Over the past few decades, the pattern of global outward investment development is undergoing great changes, and the world has entered a "great change not seen in a century": under the traditional international direct investment pattern, developed economies represented by North America and Western Europe have long been dominant, but in recent years, emerging markets have continued to rise, and have become more and more important outward investment source countries; investment direction, industry diversification, in addition to the traditional resource-based industries, more and more enterprises involved in manufacturing, services, high-tech fields, especially in the science and technology industry, many multinational corporations through outward investment to seek technological and innovation advantages; regional economic integration, effectively promoting the growth of outward investment, such as the free flow of the European Union within the industry chain and the formation of the industry chain; diversification of the form of investment, cross-border Diversification of investment forms, cross-border mergers and acquisitions, equity investment and other forms provide more and more efficient investment channels for enterprises, and so on. FDI is also facing more risks and challenges.

The development pattern of global FDI is closely related to the global economic pattern, which to a certain extent reflects the comparison and change of economic strength between different countries and regions. China and the United States are the two largest economies in the world, so the investment policies of the two countries have been receiving a lot of attention.

This paper tries to analyze the changes in the investment policies of China and the United States and their impact on the economic development of their countries, to summarize some regular conclusions and propose an outlook.

2 Literature review

In recent years, new trends in international direct investment have emerged, and the pattern of world outward investment has changed: Wang and Liu link the pattern of international direct investment with the global national and regional economic strength, paying special attention to the changes in the pattern of traditional international investment [1]. Zhang focuses on the pattern of international direct investment under the impact of the new scientific and technological revolution and the new crown epidemics [2]. Yao Shumei, in the Evolution of the Pattern of International Capital Flows, Trend Prospects and Related Yao Shumei, in "Evolution of International Capital Flow Patterns, Trend Outlook

* Corresponding author: 22052901219@ecupl.edu.cn

and Related Initiative Suggestions", focuses on analyzing the complex and severe situation that the global FDI will continue to show weak growth in the long run since 2022, the turbulence of international capital flows, and the steep increase in the difficulty of cross-border capital flow management in emerging economies [3]. All three of them put forward some reasonable suggestions on how to cope with the situation in China.

During the past forty-five years, i.e., since China's reform and opening up, China's outward foreign direct investment policy has continued to evolve and change, and Liu made a specific stage-by-stage analysis in "The Evolution of China's Outward Foreign Investment Policy since Reform and Opening Up", noting that "outward investment policy is one of the clues to the reform of the domestic market-oriented system, and outward investment policy is becoming one of China's participation in global economic governance one of the important ways" [4]. Gao et al. conducted a comparative study of Chinese and international outward investment policies, pointed out the gaps, and put forward the government's policy suggestions for the development of outward direct investment by drawing on the successful experience of outward direct investment in the United States and other countries and taking into account China's national conditions [5, 6].

Regarding China's policies related to attracting foreign investment, Shen Jiawen and Wang Yuandi analyze the trend of China's foreign investment policy evolution during the 30 years of reform and opening up, while Jin Fang focuses on the adjustment trend of China's foreign investment policy after China acceded to the WTO [7, 8].

Previous studies have explored the relationships between foreign investment policy and different aspects of the Chinese economy. breakdown areas such as the impact of FDI on economic growth. FDI has a significant positive impact on the quality of economic growth of the host country. Qi adopts R language and uses the ARIMA model, Holt-Winters model, and nonlinear BP neural network model to predict the value of FDI and derive a better prediction model and the role of appropriate import tax incentives [9]. Secondly, Zhang and three others analyze the important role played by China's foreign investment policy on industrial restructuring based on the flow and direction of foreign investment, to give full play to the role of foreign investment policy in promoting industrial restructuring [10]. Again, regarding the role of FDI on China's technology and innovation capacity, He and Jiang discuss the relationship between FDI technology spillovers and China's absorptive capacity threshold and economic transformation, while Zhao Wei and three others study the analysis of the mechanism and attempted empirical evidence of outward FDI and China's technological progress [11-13].

3 Investment policies between China and US and the impact on China

3.1 U.S. investment policies

The investment policy of the United States can be broadly divided into two parts: OFDI policy and the protection of domestic industries and capital. The OFDI policy system can be analyzed from three aspects: the legal system, the policy system, and the management and service institutions. In terms of the legal system, the United States, as one of the earliest developed capitalist countries in the world to carry out OFDI, has a fairly complete legal system of OFDI, and the U.S. government has enacted the Economic Cooperation Act, the Foreign Assistance Act, the Common Security Act and other relevant laws in the area of OFDI to protect the safety and interests of OFDI in the country and protect OFDI through the granting of tax, credit, and investment insurance to investors in line with the provisions of the Act. The United States also regulates overseas investment and the industrial layout by giving tax, credit, investment insurance, and other preferential policies to investors who meet the requirements. Meanwhile, the U.S. has also signed bilateral investment agreements with several countries to provide excellent environmental protection for U.S. enterprises investing in overseas markets.

The OFDI policy system can be analyzed from three aspects: the legal system, the policy system, and the management and service institutions. In terms of the legal system, the United States, as one of the earliest developed capitalist countries in the world to carry out OFDI, has a fairly complete legal system of OFDI. The U.S. government has specially formulated the Economic Cooperation Act, the Foreign Assistance Act, the Common Security Act and other relevant laws in the area of OFDI to protect the safety and interests of OFDI in the country, and to regulate and control the industrial layout of overseas investment by granting preferential policies on taxation, credit, investment insurance and other aspects to investors in compliance with the regulations. The United States also regulates overseas investment and the industrial layout by giving tax, credit, investment insurance, and other preferential policies to investors who meet the requirements. Meanwhile, the U.S. has also signed bilateral investment agreements with many countries to provide excellent environmental protection for U.S. enterprises investing in overseas markets. The policy system includes three major aspects: foreign exchange management, policy support system, and after-the-fact supervision and monitoring, while the policy support system includes an overseas investment insurance system, tax protection policy, financial support, and provision of information and counseling. The U.S. rarely restricts OFDI unless there are special political needs and economic conditions. Since the mid-1980s, when all countries relaxed their OFDI restrictions and the trend of liberalization intensified, the U.S. has actively adopted a series of policies and measures to encourage and promote its own OFDI, which has led to a large number of U.S. enterprises investing in OFDI and conducting cross-border operations, and a large number of multinational corporations of great strength have been formed.

Among the management and service agencies, the Department of Commerce is one of the major comprehensive economic departments of the United States, and the International Trade Administration and the Bureau of Export Administration are the main executive agencies responsible for the management of international trade and the promotion of exports. To ensure the implementation of policies and the realization of goals, the United States Government has set up the United States Overseas Private Investment Corporation (OPIC), the United States Trade and Development Agency (USTDA), and the United States Small Business Administration (SBA), and other specialized agencies, on top of the existing Export-Import Bank (Ex-Im).

The protection of domestic industries and capital is mainly reflected in foreign investment access policy, industry regulation, intellectual property protection, trade policy, and so on. As one of the earliest countries to legislate on the security review of foreign investment, the United States has always been at the forefront of the world's foreign investment security review system. With the trend of more frequent international economic and trade exchanges and the commercialization of cutting-edge scientific and technological research and development related to national defense and security, the Committee on Foreign Investment in the United States (CFIUS) has gradually expanded its traditional review focus – transactions involving core national security such as national defense, transportation infrastructure, energy, and government supply chains – to the technological and financial fields. From The Exon-Florio Amendment by the U.S. Congress in 1988 to the U.S. legal framework for national security review of foreign investment, The Foreign Investment and National Security Act of 2007, CFIUS has also expanded its traditional review focus-defense, transportation infrastructure, and government supply chains – to technology and financial sectors. And National Security Act of 2007, the U.S. has sought to strike a balance between keeping investment open and safeguarding national security in different international situations. The United States is one of the world's largest trading countries, and its trade policies also have a great impact on investment, such as the protectionist policies practiced by the United States Government, including tariffs on certain imports and anti-dumping measures.

On August 9, 2023, U.S. President Joe Biden signed an executive order severely restricting U.S. investment in China's sensitive technology sectors, limiting the scope to three major areas: semiconductors, quantum information, and artificial intelligence. This presidential decree has become a new change in the U.S.-China investment relationship.

3.2 Chinese investment policies

China's investment policy is mainly based on the policy of opening up to the outside world and attracting foreign investment, in the context of the continuous development of outward foreign direct investment.

The Chinese government has been committed to promoting opening up to the outside world and attracting foreign investment. Since the reform and opening up, China has gradually relaxed the restrictions on foreign investment and provided favorable policies and a good investment environment for foreign enterprises:

3.2.1 Industrial policy

China has formulated a series of industrial policies to guide and support foreign investment in priority development areas. These areas include high-tech industries, modern service industries, and green and low-carbon industries. The government also encourages foreign investment in key areas and weak links through tax incentives, land use concessions, and other measures.

3.2.2 Investment facilitation policy

The Chinese government is committed to simplifying the investment approval process and improving the level of investment facilitation. In recent years, the implementation of the "release of resources, management and service" reform, it has significantly reduced the number of approvals matters for foreign investment projects and improved the efficiency of the approval process. At the same time, a one-stop investment service platform has been set up to provide convenient investment services for foreign-funded enterprises.

3.2.3 Regional policy

Numerous special economic zones and development zones have been established to provide a more convenient policy environment for foreign investment. In order to promote coordinated regional development, the Chinese government has implemented a series of regional preferential policies, such as the policy of attracting foreign investment to the central and western regions.

3.2.4 Talent policy

The Chinese government attaches importance to the introduction and cultivation of talent and provides talent support for foreign investors. It attracts and retains outstanding talents by setting up business parks for foreign students returning to their home countries and introducing high-level talents from overseas, so as to provide talent security for foreign-invested enterprises.

3.2.5 Financial policy

The Chinese government encourages financial Institutions to provide financing support for foreign-invested enterprises. Through the establishment of a risk compensation mechanism for loans to foreign-invested enterprises and the expansion of the cross-border use of RMB, it will reduce the financing costs of foreign-invested enterprises and improve the convenience of financing.

3.2.6 Optimizing the investment environment

The Chinese government continuously optimizes the investment environment and protects the legitimate rights and interests of investors. For example, it has improved the intellectual property rights protection system and intensified the crackdown on infringement and illegal acts; it has strengthened the convergence with international investment agreements to provide a fairer and more transparent investment environment for foreign investors.

3.2.7 Cooperation and exchanges

The Chinese government actively participates in international cooperation and exchanges, and promotes bilateral and multilateral investment cooperation. By organizing events such as the China International Import Expo and the World Internet Conference, it has built a platform for investment cooperation between China and the rest of the world.

In terms of the legal system, China's legislation on outward foreign direct investment is lagging behind, and there is currently no specialized legislation on overseas investment; relevant legal norms are mainly found in a number of regulations and ordinances issued by various ministries and commissions under the State Council. In terms of international law, there are mainly a series of bilateral investment agreements, tax agreements and other bilateral treaties concluded between China and other countries, as well as international conventions to which China has acceded and concluded. The policy system mainly consists of three parts: OFDI approval policies, regulatory policies, and service and promotion policies. China's OFDI management and service institutions mainly include commerce departments, development and reform departments, finance departments, state-owned asset management departments and industry management departments, etc., which delineate the approval authority; foreign exchange bureaus, which carry out foreign exchange registration and filing for domestic institutions' OFDI and the assets and related rights and interests that they have formed; and service organizations, which include the Export-Import Bank of China (Exim Bank of China), China Export and Credit Insurance Corporation (CECIC), state-owned commercial banks, and policy banks. Commercial banks and policy banks, etc.

In response to the Biden administration's investment restriction order, the State Council issued the Opinions on Further Optimizing the Foreign Investment Environment and Increasing Efforts to Attract Foreign Investment on August 14, 2023, proposing 24 measures to increase the attraction of foreign investment, to promote a high level of opening up to the outside world, construct a new system of an open economy, and welcoming international investors to explore the Chinese market.

3.3 The impact on China's economy

3.3.1 Economic growth and employment

The rapid economic growth of China is inextricably related to FDI. Since 1993, China has long ranked first among developing countries and second in the world in terms of the amount of foreign capital utilized. The actual amount of foreign capital utilized has increased from 920 million US dollars in 1983 to 173.48 billion US dollars in 2021, with an average annual growth rate of nearly 15%. China's absorption of foreign capital has made a remarkable breakthrough in terms of scale and quantity and has entered a period of high-quality development. FDI has become an important force in China's economic and social development. Table 1 shows the statistics on GDP and real foreign capital utilization in recent years.

Table 1. GDP and amount of foreign capital actually utilized in recent years.

Subjects / Year	2001	2004	2007	2010	2013	2016	2019	2022
Gross Domestic Product (GDP) Unit: billion dollars	1211.33	1955.35	3550.33	6087.19	9570.47	11233.31	14279.97	17963.17
Amount of foreign capital actually utilized Unit: ten billion of dollars	468.8	606.3	835.2	1147.3	1239.1	1337.1	1412.2	1891.3

Source: China Foreign Investment Statistics Bulletin 2023 - Ministry of Commerce & Trading economics.com-World Bank.

In the long run, FDI can contribute to the easing of regional and urban-rural inequalities under the regulation of national policies and population flows. FDI mainly flows into secondary and tertiary industries in cities, and less FDI flows into rural areas and primary industries, which promotes the concentration of resources, talents and technologies in cities. The inflow of FDI promotes the upgrading of China's industrial structure, which in turn leads to the tendency to widen the gap between urban and rural areas and between regions in China. There is a limit to the widening of the gap. When the level of economic development of cities reaches a certain level, the economic development of cities will show the phenomenon of external diseconomies. This is where government policy regulation is needed. At the same time, the inflow of FDI has gradually changed the employment structure of China. On the one hand, it encourages farmers to work in non-agricultural industries and earn higher wages; on the other hand, FDI tends to flow into labor-intensive industries, and the manufacturing industry occupies an overwhelmingly dominant position in labor-intensive industries, absorbing more rural surplus labor, thus narrowing the income gap between urban and rural residents.

3.3.2 Technology transfer and innovation

The impact of FDI on technology transfer and innovation capacity is mainly a matter of capital outflows to capital inflows. MacDougall first proposed that FDI would have spillover effects on the technological progress of the host country, and according to scholars' opinions, the technology spillover effect of FDI refers to the involuntary diffusion of technology to domestic firms due to a series of resources brought by FDI, such as advanced production technology, business concepts, R&D capabilities, etc., or "quasi-rents" generated by correcting the original distortions of domestic firms due to FDI's entry, whereas TNCs are not able to capture all of the benefits, thus generating externalities. Thus, FDI facilitates the transfer of advanced technology and management knowledge from TNCs to Chinese firms. Through joint ventures and technology licensing agreements, Chinese firms acquire new knowledge and skills, thereby increasing their innovative capacity. Large-scale FDI also brings more capital factors needed for production to the host country, facilitating the inflow of capital and promoting the formation of economies of scale and capital accumulation, which plays an important role in supporting China's R&D activities. MNCs often allocate large amounts of resources to establish R&D centers in China, thereby creating new technological solutions and products. At the same time, FDI has stimulated competition in the domestic industrial market, prompting Chinese firms to invest more in R&D and to innovate to remain competitive. This competitive pressure has led to the adoption of advanced technologies in production by enterprises and has boosted the overall level of technological innovation in China, promoting the transformation and upgrading of China's industrial structure from labor-intensive to capital- and technology-intensive.

Therefore, FDI has played an important role in the optimization and upgrading of the industrial structure of the Chinese economy. The technological innovation and technology spillover effect brought about by the introduction of FDI has improved the productivity and product quality of Chinese enterprises, promoted the upgrading of the entire industrial chain, and contributed to the optimization of the industrial structure, e.g., the automobile manufacturing industry, etc. FDI has also brought about a higher level of the industrial division of labor in China and promoted the extension and integration of the industrial chain. Foreign-funded enterprises usually invest in core technology fields, while Chinese enterprises invest and develop in supporting industries. This division of labor and cooperation in the industrial chain promotes the synergistic development of internal and external links in Chinese industries and accelerates cross-industry industrial integration, typical examples being China's electronics manufacturing industry. Finally, FDI expands the scale and scope of Chinese exports, stimulates the competitive awareness and market development ability of domestic enterprises, spawns the development of local enterprises, and improves the international competitiveness of Chinese enterprises.

3.3.3 Risks and stability

First, the impact of FDI on technological innovation in China is not without its challenges, such as the problem of technological dependence triggered by FDI (excessive reliance on foreign technology, development constraints, and inability to develop domestic innovation capacity), the uneven distribution of benefits from FDI on China's regional and urban-rural development imbalances, and the risk of brain drain, among others. So it is imperative for China to strike a balance between leveraging foreign expertise and fostering indigenous innovation capabilities. This can be achieved through strategic policies that promote knowledge transfer, investment in human capital, and the equitable distribution of technological benefits across regions.

Second, the impact of FDI on inequality. From a spatial perspective, China's FDI is unevenly distributed. Regionally, the eastern and coastal developed areas have absorbed more FDI, of which Jiangsu, Guangdong, Shanghai, Shandong, Zhejiang, and Beijing provinces are the most intensive, and 86.6% of the number of new foreign-invested enterprises will be established in the Eastern Region in 2022; while the FDI inflow into the populous and resource-rich central and western provinces is less, and the regional distribution of FDI shows the obvious characteristic of "more in the east and less in the west". At the urban-rural level, cities are the main FDI inflows.

FDI has brought about unequal regional development in China. Coastal areas have attracted the majority of FDI, leading to rapid economic growth and industrial development, while inland and western regions have lagged based on the above data. This has widened the income and development gaps between different regions, exacerbating the unequal distribution of wealth and resources. The same applies to the widening gap between urban and rural areas. FDI will first flow to the more developed urban areas and provide more capital and resources to the cities, thus widening the gap between urban and rural development.

To emphasize coordinated and fair development, the government will guide and tilt its policies, make reasonable adjustments and arrangements to the industrial structure, and create employment and knowledge training for the less-developed regions to bring about an increase in the incomes of the labor force in these regions, thus reducing the gap between the urban and rural areas, This will lead to an increase in the income of the labor force in these regions, thus reducing the urban-rural and regional disparities.

4 Conclusion

This paper gives a brief overview of the investment policies of China and the United States, pointing out that the investment policies of the United States mainly include the OFDI policy and the protection of domestic industries and capital, and that China is still focusing on the policy of attracting foreign investment, and the OFDI policy is still on the way of improvement. At the same time, it is divided into three parts: Economic Growth and Employment, Technology Transfer and Innovation, and Risks and Stability to elaborate on the impact of the FDI investment policy on China's economy. To sum up, FDI can not only upgrade the technical level of China's industries, promote economic growth and increase financial income but also reduce the regional and urban-rural income gap by promoting the optimization and upgrading of industrial structure, increasing the total employment in China, improve the quality of labor force and improve people's livelihood.

To maximize the positive impact of FDI and meet the challenge, The Chinese government should formulate reasonable policies and regulations, such as continuous market opening and protection of intellectual property rights, to provide a favorable investment environment, and actively guide the flow of FDI to the region and improve the quality of labor; while enterprises should actively take advantage of foreign investment to enhance their core competitiveness and accelerate their development, and should also focus on the construction of internationalized human resources, to make joint efforts to effectively utilize FDI and to promote the healthy development of China's economy. The enterprises should actively take advantage of foreign investment to improve their core competitiveness and accelerate their development.

The defects of this paper, firstly, did not use economic models for analysis, rigor needs to be improved; secondly, the impact of FDI has a lag, so the analysis must be a long-term process; thirdly, some points are not specifically explored such as the specific impact of FDI on the development of various industries.

References

1. W. Wang, Z. Liu, China Finance 24, 2 (2021)
2. Y. Zhang, International Trade 6, 9 (2022)
3. S. Yao, China Investment (in Chinese and English) Z4, 3 (2022)
4. W. Liu, Shanghai Economic Research 4, 10 (2022)
5. P. Gao, W. Sun R. Hu, International Trade 5, 9 (2019)
6. Y. Chen, Master's Thesis of Beijing Jiaotong University (2010)
7. J. Shen, Y. Wang, China Science and Technology Forum 2, 5 (2009)
8. F. Jin, World Economic Studies 6, 5 (2000)
9. X. Qi, Research World 5, 4 (2019)
10. W. Zhang, Y. Bai, Z. Yin, Journal of Theory 2, 7 (2014)
11. X. He, Y. Ou, W. Shi, et al., World Economy 10,25 (2014)
12. D. Jiang, C. Zhang, Economic Research 7, 13 (2008)
13. W. Zhao, G. Gu, Y. He, Management World 7, 8 (2006)

Research on the Trade Imbalance between China and the United States

Fan Lyu*

Department of School of Economics and Management, North China University of Technology, Beijing, China

Abstract. This paper analyzes the phenomenon of RMB depreciation on the basis of trade inequality between China and the United States. It is concluded that the causes of the trade imbalance between China and the United States are mainly related to the transfer of the global industrial chain, the highly complementary trade structure of China and the United States, the international dollar credit standard, etc. This paper puts forward some suggestions and measures to solve the pressure of RMB exchange rate and Sino-US trade imbalance. This paper argues that China should actively promote the internationalization of RMB and improve the formation mechanism of RMB exchange rate. In addition, China should promote the deep integration of the Chinese market into the global market and accelerate industrial innovation and upgrading. It also recommends the cultivation of foreign-related economic and rule of law talents to promote the easing of the relationship between the two sides and the common economic growth.

1 Introduction

With the continuous improvement of China's comprehensive strength and the expanding degree of opening up to the outside world, the internationalisation of the RMB has been gradually promoted and has become a new system of financial openness. The continuous acceleration of the internationalisation of the RMB will inevitably affect the international monetary hegemony of the US dollar, coupled with the great role played by the economic strength expressed by the level of trade and the stability of the currency expressed by the exchange rate fluctuations, the internationalisation of the RMB affects the balance of trade in a certain mechanism. In recent years, as the trade surplus between China and the US keeps growing, the United States has repeatedly said that the yuan is undervalued, and constantly taken measures such as tariffs, anti-dumping investigations and other measures to force the yuan to appreciate, to reverse the unfavourable situation between the two sides of the trade to their own. In this regard, in the context of the trade imbalance between China and the United States and the serious trade friction between the two sides, exploring the reasons for the trade imbalance between China and the United States, and taking targeted measures is of great practical significance.

2 The elements influencing the disparity in trade between the US and China

Over the years, the U.S.-China trade imbalance has been the focus of the debate between the two sides in the economic field, the trade deficit with China has been the United States of America's pressure on the appreciation of the RMB is the most important basis. The trade imbalance between China and the U.S. is only a symptom, a concrete manifestation of the objective economic laws.

As shown in table 1, since 2005, China's trade surplus with the United States has continued to expand, as seen in the import and export trade of goods from China and the United States. During the 18 years from 2005 to 2022, China's trade surplus with the United States rose from $114.269 billion to $404.139 billion, a 253 per cent expansion of the trade surplus.

Table 1. Trade Surplus with the United States, 2005-2022 (US$ billion)

Year	Surplus	Year	Surplus	Year	Surplus
2005	1142.69	2011	2023.24	2017	2757.85
2006	1442.39	2012	2188.79	2018	3232.73
2007	1632.86	2013	2160.64	2019	2957.68
2008	1710.24	2014	2370.02	2020	3164.78
2009	1433.42	2015	2614.05	2021	3964.74
2010	1811.88	1016	2508.26	2022	4041.39

Source: China Statistics Bureau

According to the balance-of-payments theory of absorption, when the national revenue of a nation exceeds what it consumes internally, the balance of payments is in surplus; conversely, when national income is less than domestic absorption, the international balance of payments is in deficit. At this point there are two ways to correct the deficit, one is through tight fiscal and monetary policy to reduce the demand for imported goods, but at the same time will inhibit economic growth; the other is the devaluation of the currency expenditure

*Corresponding author: xyw@ncut.edu.cn

transfer method. The United States is a consumer-led economy, and in recent years, to stimulate economic growth, it has been implementing a low-interest rate policy, with high consumption, high spending and low savings, and constantly breaking the U.S. debt ceiling. According to figures released by the U.S. Treasury, as of September 2023, the U.S. debt has exceeded $33 trillion. With domestic policies unable to break through, there is only a choice on the external path.

Due to China's enormous US trade surplus, the US authorities believe that the RMB is undervalued and chastise the RMB exchange rate issue. However, due to the income elasticity of commodity imports and the income elasticity of exports between China and the US, the former is significantly larger than the latter. Given the terms of trade, as long as this asymmetry in income elasticity exists, there will be unrelenting and maybe increasing trade deficiencies between the People's Republic of China and the United States of America. Based on this reference can be concluded that the main factors affecting the disparity in trade between the United States and China are:

2.1 The global industrial chain transfer is a key factor in the trade imbalance between China and the United States

Over the decades, because of China's surrounding nations and areas for industrial structure upgrading and adjustment, the domestic has lost its comparative advantage of labour-intensive industries transferred to China, the formation of China's import of components and raw materials originating from these nations and areas, processing and assembly in the country and subsequently shipped to the US and other European nations of the processing trade pattern. China by its large-scale market, low-cost factors of production, strong industrial supporting capacity, better infrastructure preferential foreign investment policies and other comprehensive advantages, attracted a large number of foreign investments, including U.S. enterprises, and gradually formed a processing and assembly, the competitive advantage of the manufacturing sector, China has become the "factory of the world". The Asia-Pacific economic restructuring was brought about by changes in the international division of labour patterns so the United States reduced imports from Japan and South Korea and other countries, increased imports from China, the United States and China continued to expand the surplus [1].

2.2 The trade structure of China and the United States has a high degree of complementarity, which is the primary cause of the disparity in trade between China and the US

Trade between China and the US development imbalance to some extent has its inevitability. This inevitability is determined by the characteristics of the economic development of developing and developed countries themselves.

China and the United States as the largest developing and developed countries, and the two countries have strong economic complementarity. The comparative advantages of the United States are: capital-intensive, high level of technology, industry and product brand effect is stronger. Comparative disadvantages are: high labour factor costs, and labour-intensive general manufacturing products are relatively less competitive. China's comparative advantage is: abundant labour resources, low labour factor costs, and labour-intensive manufacturing products are more competitive. The comparative disadvantage is: that the technical level of the industry is lower, and the brand effect of the product is weaker. China's exports to the United States are mainly labour-intensive, items requiring a lot of resources, while the majority of American exports to China are capital- and technology-intensive goods. The two countries have strong complementarity in product structure [2].

Looking at the areas where the U.S. has raised taxes on China in recent years, the main focus has been on the high-tech industries planned for major development in Made in China 2025, including aviation, new energy vehicles, and new materials. These areas are not the most important source of the U.S.-China deficit; China's exports to the U.S. are mainly labour-intensive products and mid-range technology products, whereas more than half of the US's exports to China are capital- and technology-intensive. The reason why the United States did not resolve to take the main source of the deficit in the field of the knife is that the United States is very clear that the United States-China trade deficit is a structural problem, the United States in the balance of payments of the trade deficit capital inflow of outward investment cycle is a beneficiary of the party [3].

2.3 The international dollar credit standard is the international monetary system of China and the United States trade imbalance balance of reason

The dollar is the international standard currency, on the one hand, the dollar privilege guarantees the United States to maintain a growing trade deficit without the constraints of foreign exchange reserves shortage and the threat of financial crisis, on the other hand, but forced other countries to pursue trade surplus and increase dollar reserves to get rid of the unfavourable situation, and thus from the supply and demand for the dollar, both promote the expansion of the U.S. trade deficit [4].

Because the RMB is not an international local currency, in recent years, to promote increased employment, and economic growth, avoid exchange rate risks, stabilise domestic price levels, and improve international payment capacity, objectively also prompted China to pursue a surplus in trade with the United States, and reserve a large number of US dollars. Although the United States has the name of the deficit, but helps the United States' domestic balance of payments, to ensure its normal domestic and foreign investment.

https://doi.org/10.1051/shsconf/202418802010

2.4 U.S. export control of China is the policy the cause of the discrepancy in trade between the US and China

The United States has two major export advantages, one is service goods, and the second is high-tech products. The theory of comparative advantage states that in international trade, the United States should export service goods and high-tech products, while importing labour-intensive products, to maintain trade balance. At present, in the Sino-US trade, China's comparative advantage in labour-intensive industries has been fully released, while the United States, to suppress China, has never released high-tech exports to China. If the United States does not change the high-tech embargo policy, the trade deficit will be difficult to solve [5].

2.5 U.S. savings and investment imbalance is caused by the economic background of the U.S.-China trade imbalance causes

The United States' national income distribution is not reasonable, low savings and high consumption lead to demand exceeding supply, higher investment share and lower savings share, in the trade balance of payments in the performance of imports than exports, a deficit. Although China's investment expenditures have been maintained at a high level due to the need to develop the economy, China has maintained a high national savings rate relative to investment due to traditional habits.

3 Suggestions for countermeasures to resolve the pressure on the exchange rate for RMB and promote the trade balance between China and the US

In dealing with and resolving issues such as the trade imbalance between the United States and China, bringing the two countries together should take measures to find solutions to the problem. The U.S., should actively abandon the Cold War thinking of containing China, abandon trade protectionism, control excessive imports and relax export controls. For China, the following measures can be taken to promote the smooth development of China's economy.

3.1 Actively and steadily promote the internationalisation of RMB

Based on strengthening economic cooperation between countries, strengthening regional monetary cooperation and effectively controlling the growth of foreign exchange reserves. This will not only stabilise trade relations but also reduce the impact of exchange rate fluctuations. Through the settlement with the neighbouring region's currency, the stability of the neighbouring economy and trade has been maintained, and the systemic risk brought about by large exchange rate fluctuations has been avoided, which is conducive to the improvement of foreign trade conditions [6].

3.2 Further improve the RMB exchange rate formation mechanism

Renminbi exchange rate problem China's economic strength and the growth of total foreign trade are born with each other. In the case of the international financial crisis continues to develop, scientific analysis of the exchange rate, import and export and economic development of the relationship between the current managed floating exchange rate policy at the same time, to improve the micro-amplitude, two-way, steady climb in the control technology, appropriate enlargement of the floating range, with other policies, through the market mechanism to achieve the level of the exchange rate level to the equilibrium level of the adjustment to resolve the financial crisis of the transmission of the economic growth smoothly [7].

3.3 Promoting the deep integration of China's market into the global market

Actively develop partnerships with other countries to enhance economic exchanges and maximise economic benefits on an equal footing. Promote the construction of the "Belt and Road", deepen cooperation with countries along the route to achieve mutual benefit and win-win results, and continue to expand trade routes other than the United States [8]. Make full use of the "Belt and Road" to promote China's extensive international market integration, and maximise economic benefits. Give full play to the role of platforms such as the China International Import Expo, the China International Fair for Trade in Services, and the China International Consumer Goods Fair, and improve the quality of imported products in expanding the Chinese market.

3.4 Vigorously develop the domestic demand economy

With the rapid development of China's import and export trade, over-reliance on external demand departs from the general law of large countries based on domestic demand, objectively restricting the sustainable growth of domestic demand, worsening the deterioration of the external terms of trade, also resulting in an unfavourable international transfer of wealth to China [9]. While building a higher-level open economy, China will further deepen its domestic demand and, based on strengthening economic growth drivers such as investment and exports, further cultivate and expand the consumption structure of new domestic demand, including consumption of non-durable goods such as automobiles, credit consumption, final consumption in rural areas, consumption of leisure services, and investment in human resources, to promote the healthy and stable development of the economy.

3.5 Accelerating industrial upgrading in an innovation-driven manner

Continuously increase investment in scientific research, promote technological progress, facilitate product diversification and diversification of export methods, create our own brands and core competencies, and increase the added value and competitiveness of Chinese products.

3.6 Strengthening foreign-related domestic legislation and cultivating foreign-related economic and rule-of-law talents

To cope with the challenges and prevent risks, on the one hand, China, based on complying with international rules, further improves its foreign-related domestic legislation, builds a legal system for the extraterritorial application of Chinese law and the blocking of inappropriate extraterritorial application of the laws and measures of other countries, and improves the system of state immunity, choosing whether or not to respond to a lawsuit according to the actual situation of the case, etc., to further defend the legitimate rights and interests of Chinese nationals, corporations, and other groups [10]. On the other hand, strengthening the training of foreign-related economic rule of law talents, better mastering the ability to apply international rules, to guide power in the topic set, persuasive power in the discussion of rule-making, retaliatory power for hegemonic tendencies, explanatory power for the questioning, to serve the portal to the external environment at a higher level, and to push forward the construction of a new development pattern of domestic and international double-cycle.

4 Conclusion

The main conclusions drawn in this paper are as follows: in the disparity in trade between the US and China, the United States view that the RMB is undervalued, the causes of the trade imbalance between China and the United States are mainly related to the transfer of the global industrial chain, the trade structure of China and the United States is highly complementary, the international credit standard of the U.S. dollar, the U.S. export control of China, as well as U.S. savings and investment imbalance and other reasons. Continuing the trade war between the two sides is not a good choice for both economies. To ease the pressure on the exchange rate for RMB and encourage the United States-China trade balance, relevant suggestions have been put forward, which are to actively promote the internationalisation of the RMB, improve the RMB exchange rate formation mechanism, promote the in-depth integration of China's market into the global market, accelerate the innovation and upgrading of industries, and strengthen the cultivation of talents in the rule of law in the foreign-related economy. The U.S. side needs to put aside its Cold War thinking towards China and relax its export control, which will promote the détente of the two countries and the common development of their economies.

References

1. S. H. Yang, J. Liu. In and Eco Re 1(01):46-53 (2010).
2. X. L. Xia, Soc Sci Liter (2011).
3. B. B. Liu, Jilin University (2021).
4. D. M. Yuan, J.J. Liu, Contem Econ Research, 208(12):28-32 (2012).
5. X. F. Liao, Guangdong University of Finance and Economics (2011).
6. J. Y. Lu, Fin The and Tea, 181(05):1-7(2023).
7. Y. M. Chen, M. Zhang, Contem Fin Re 6(10):66-75 (2023).
8. D. W. Tian. People's Fo, 771(20):36-39 (2023).
9. J. N. Zhu, Yanbian University (2014).
10. W. Shen, Shanghai Jiao Tong University Press (2023).

Impact of the 2015 Stock Market Crash on China's Stock Market: Evidence from Moutai and China Construction

Hao Luo*

The University of Sydney Business School, The University of Sydney, New South Wales, Sydney, 2006, Australia

Abstract. The stock market crash in 2015 had a significant impact on China's finances, some researchers focus on the causes of the stock market crash, however, its impact on stocks does not seem to have a uniformity of trend, perhaps there are different inspirations for investors. Therefore, this paper achieves the goal of exploring the impact of the 2015 stock market crash on Chinese stocks by collecting a total of four sets of stock data on daily and weekly closing prices of Moutai and China Construction and performing ARIMA model analysis on the data to predict the logarithmic returns of the four sets of data. It was found that Moutai seemed to be less affected by the crash than China Construction. Meanwhile, after an in-depth analysis of the coping strategies and business environments of these two stocks, the study highlights that in addition to the financial position and risk management capabilities, a company's brand and product quality, as well as market resilience, are key factors in coping with market risk. This provides investors with a more comprehensive perspective when making investment decisions.

1 Introduction

The stock market crash of 2015 was a watershed moment not only in China's financial history but also in the world's. It exposed the vulnerability of the global financial system and highlighted the importance of risk management [1]. The collapse of Lehman Brothers in 2008 was a harbinger of the 2015 financial crisis, and before the 2015 stock market crash, global financial markets experienced a period of prosperity. Easy credit and lending encouraged risk-taking and leveraging as investors turned their attention to equities [2]. The Chinese stock market, in particular, saw a huge increase in assets under management by hedge funds and private equity funds. At the same time, the use of derivatives such as credit default swaps (CDS) and exchange-traded funds (ETF) increased [3].

The course of China's stock market crash can be traced back to a period of extremely rapid stock market bubble expansion. The source of this bubble was a series of favourable economic policies proposed by the central government, such as the Internet, Industry 4.0 and universal entrepreneurship. These policies aimed to revitalise the economy by stimulating the stock market. However, due to over-interpretation of the policies, a large amount of hot money flowed into the stock market, accompanied by a large proportion of brokerage financing and over-the-counter (OTC) funding. Before the stock market crash, the total market capitalisation was RMB 60 trillion, the amount of financing announced by securities firms was RMB 2.4 trillion, and the size of over-the-counter financing was estimated to be about RMB 4 trillion. Within a short period, the market rose directly to over 5,000 points, led mainly by new technology companies, especially Internet stocks in the Growth Enterprise Market (GEM). However, share prices were significantly higher than valuations and the market was in a bubble [4].

After the Shanghai Composite Index touched a high of 5,178.19 on 12 June 2015, the market began to fall sharply. The government began to adopt a series of measures to stabilize the market, including reducing new share issuance, restricting short selling and adjusting trading rules [5]. However, these measures did not stop the market's downward trend. By 26 August 2015, the Shanghai Composite Index fell to 3,188.90 points, a drop of more than 40%. Many stocks experienced substantial declines, resulting in large numbers of investor losses.

Looking at the overall course of the 2015 stock market crash, its causes were intertwined with multiple factors. The 2015 stock market crash had several primary causes. Excessive leveraged trading was a significant factor, with large influxes of funds through leveraged channels propelling the market upwards in the bull market. However, these funds were unable to withstand losses once the market declined, leading to an accelerated crash. Investors' emotional volatility also played a crucial role, with extreme optimism during the market's rise and insufficient risk awareness [6]. This optimism swiftly turned to pessimism, causing investors to sell stocks and further exacerbate the market decline. Additionally, the accelerated issuance of new shares added pressure on the market, while the shorting mechanism for stock index futures fueled market instability. Listed companies' concentration on reducing holdings also contributed to the crash, with executives

* Corresponding author: hluo0934@uni.sydney.edu.au

cashing out in the face of substantial market gains, undermining investor confidence. Lastly, the implementation of deleveraging policies and the unstable global economic environment, exemplified by the Greek debt crisis, further impacted the global price of risky assets and drove the market down [7].

In summary, the 2015 stock market crash was the result of a combination of factors. Highly leveraged trading, investor sentiment volatility, accelerated IPOs, shorting of stock index futures, concentrated reductions by listed companies, as well as the implementation of deleveraging policies and an unstable global economic environment all played a significant role. The interaction of these factors ultimately led to the market crash and the stock market crash.

The crash dealt a huge blow to the Chinese stock market and also had an impact on the global economy. In addition, the 2015 stock market crash had significant implications for financial theory and practice. It challenged the efficiency of financial markets, a core principle of modern economic theory. It also highlighted the importance of risk management and investor behaviour in determining market outcomes. It is therefore necessary for regulators to closely monitor financial markets and take proactive measures to prevent similar crises in the future [8]. The crisis also has important policy implications that call for a rethinking of the monetary policy and regulatory framework that can ensure financial stability while promoting economic growth.

Certainly, the stock market crash had a profound impact that merits deep consideration. Nevertheless, does the adverse influence of the general atmosphere extend to all investment prospects? Are there stocks capable of evading the downward spiral or even surpassing the market's performance? What are the hallmarks of such stocks? What kind of perspective can they offer investors? As the overall environment experiences an economic downturn, exploring these questions holds paramount importance for investors engaging in scientific stock research. This examination delves into the reaction of individual stocks to the 2015 stock market crash. The study's premise was to employ the ARIMA model to model two sets of stock data from 2010 until the end of 2016 and predict the future values of these two sets of stocks. Additionally, the impact of stock market crashes was quantitatively assessed by comparing the actual prices of the two groups of stocks.

2 Research design

2.1 Data source

The empirical analysis data for this paper is sourced from Investing, a website known for its authoritative and comprehensive stock market data, which aids in the selection of representative stocks for research. After comparing various industries and companies, two stocks - Moutai and China Construction - were chosen. The daily and weekly closing prices from five years before the 2015 stock market crash until December 2016 were extracted, resulting in four groups. Using Stata data analysis software, the closing prices of each group were used to generate a logarithmic stock index series, and the first-order difference was done to obtain logarithmic return series, respectively. It should be noted that daily closing prices had some missing data in early years such as 2010 to 2012, but these missing data were omitted due to their minimal impact on the empirical study. Subsequently, using the updated edited data, Stata was employed to analyze the data and construct the ARIMA model with the logarithmic return data before the stock market crash on 15 June 2015 for further stock price forecasting and to investigate the impact of the 2015 crash on individual stocks.

2.2 ADF unit root test

After completing the initial data processing for the model, the first step is to perform a unit root test on the model. The ADF (Augmented Dickey-Fuller) test statistic is based on the null hypothesis of the presence of a unit root. It compares the absolute difference between the actual time series data and its linear trend at different time points. If the time series dataset is non-stationary, there will be a significant difference between the actual data and its linear trend, resulting in a large ADF test statistic value. On the other hand, if the time series dataset is stationary, the actual data and its linear trend will remain close, resulting in a small ADF test statistic value [9]. After running the ADF test in Stata, it can be seen from Table 1 that the p-value of the log returns for all four groups of data is 0, which is less than 0.1. Therefore, the null hypothesis can be rejected, which means that the model is stable and feasible. It is worth mentioning that three sets of data in Table 1 have been done with second order differences, which is to facilitate the subsequent work of order fixing.

Table 1. ADF test

	t	p
Moutai, daily		
Ln index	-0.971	0.9479
1st order difference	-20.424	0.0000
2nd order difference	-34.183	0.0000
Moutai, weekly		
Ln index	-1.449	0.8459
1st order difference	-11.937	0.0000
2nd order difference	-22.124	0.0000
China Construction, Daily		
Ln index	-0.014	0.9941
1st order difference	-20.839	0.0000
China Construction, weekly		
Ln index	-0.599	0.9790
1st order difference	-9.868	0.0000
2nd order difference	-18.901	0.0000

2.3 ARIMA model

ARIMA model is a method for predicting future outcomes based on historical time series. It is based on the statistical concept of serial correlation, where past data points influence future data points [10]. The full name of the ARIMA model is the Autoregressive Differential Moving Average Model (ARIMA). The ARIMA model consists of three main components, which are the Autoregressive model (AR), Differential process (I) and moving average model (MA) [11]. In ARIMA (p, d, q) model:

p stands for "Autoregressive": this part describes the lagged values of the observations used in the model (i.e. the values of the previous p periods). The starting point of an autoregressive model is to consider the observation as a linear combination of the p values that precede it. The exact mathematical form is as follows:

$$x_t = \varphi_0 + \varphi_1 x_{t-1} + \varphi_2 x_{t-2} + \ldots + \varphi_p x_{t-p} + \varepsilon_t \quad (1)$$

q stands for the "Moving Average" part: this part describes the lagged value of the error term used in the model (i.e. the value of the previous q periods). The Moving Average model is a relationship between current values and past white noise. The exact mathematical form is as follows:

$$x_t = \mu + \varepsilon_t - \theta_1 \varepsilon_{t-1} - \theta_2 \varepsilon_{t-2} - \ldots - \theta_p \varepsilon_{t-p} \quad (2)$$

d is the order of the difference. The goal of differencing is to transform a non-stationary series into a stationary series.

Specifically, in this paper, the AR model uses the daily and weekly logarithmic returns of the two companies' stocks before the crash on 15 June 2015, while the MA model uses the error term to predict the future.

3 Empirical results and analysis

3.1 Order determination and residual test

In this section of the paper, it is first necessary to use the PACF and ACF pairs to order the daily and weekly logarithmic returns of the two stocks respectively, the results of which are shown in Fig. 1.

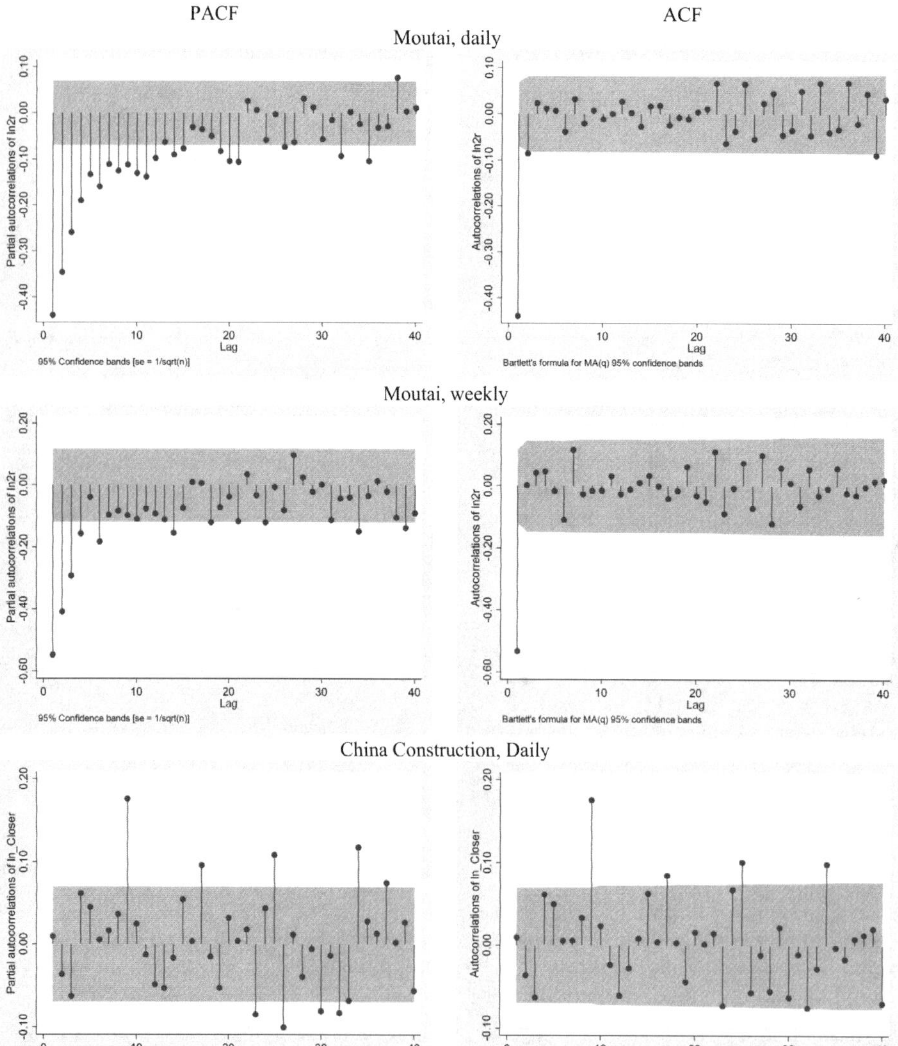

China Construction, weekly

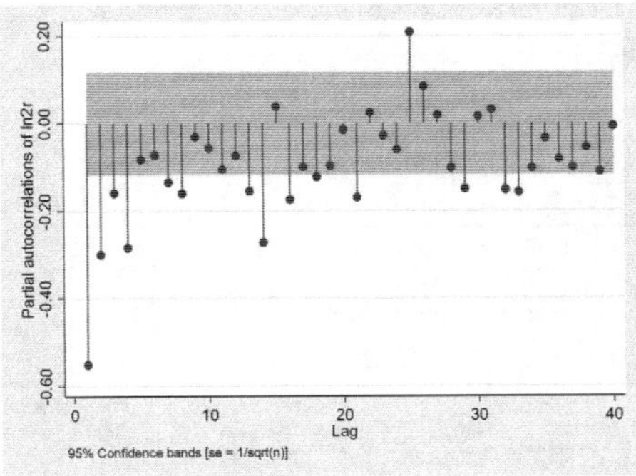

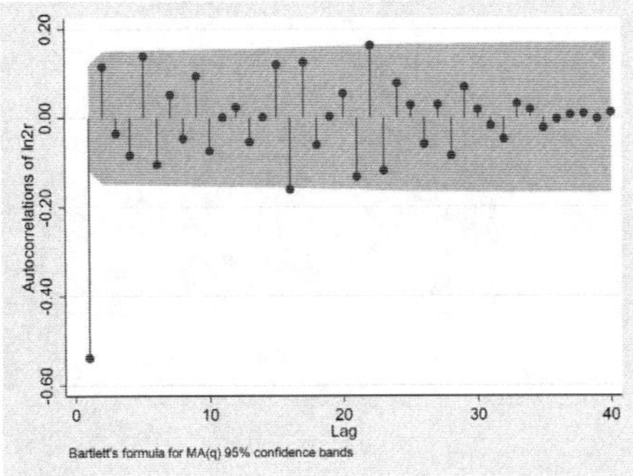

Fig. 1. ARMA (p, q) identification

Photo credit: Original

For any time series, when the ACF image exhibits a trailing tail and the PACF image exhibits a truncated tail, the AR model applies to the current time series and the lag order of the PACF truncation is the desired value of the parameter p. For any time series, when the PACF image presents a trailing and the ACF image presents a truncated state, the MA model is applied to the current time series, and the lag order of the ACF truncation is the desired value of the parameter q [12]. Therefore, these four sets of data can be fixed order and build an ARIMA(p,d,q) model respectively. After the model is built the residual test is performed as shown below:

Table 2. Residual test

Model	Portmanteau (Q) statistic	Prob > chi2
Moutai, daily-ARIMA(10,2,1)	45.9837	0.2382
Moutai, weekly-ARIMA(6,2,1)	20.7290	0.9949
China Construction, daily-ARIMA(9,1,9)	90.2043	0.0000
China Construction, weekly-ARIMA(8,2,1)	43.4285	0.3274

Note: Even though the Chinese building daily data does not pass the residual test, the trend characteristics of the series are still available and the effect of its error term can be ignored by considering its order.

According to the Table 2, these ARIMA models have passed the residual test, i.e., it shows that the error term is consistent with the white noise series, which is unpredictable [12].

3.2 Forecast results and interpretation

After both the ARIMA model building as well as the residuals test were completed, the data prediction was continued using stata for the period after the stock market crash of 15 June 2015, the results of which can be summarised as shown below:

Table 3. Moutai daily forecast results, ARIMA (10,2,1)

	Actual value	Fitted value	difference	Average bias (%)
2015-06-01	246.54			
2015-06-02	242.28			
2015-06-03	238.8			
2015-06-04	234.46			
2015-06-05	230.74			
2015-06-08	240.54			
2015-06-09	235.01			
2015-06-10	237.09			
2015-06-11	236.46			
2015-06-12	241.82			
2015-06-15	237.09	243.116	-6.026	
2015-06-16	230.88	243.4547	-12.5747	
2015-06-17	231.82	244.1673	-12.3473	
2015-06-18	221.82	244.2153	-22.3953	
2015-06-19	214.54	244.9887	-30.4487	

Table 3. Moutai daily forecast results, ARIMA (10,2,1) (Continous)

2015-06-23	229.36	245.3811	-16.0211	
2015-06-24	237.55	245.7781	-8.2281	
2015-06-25	228.71	246.1273	-17.4173	
2015-06-26	221.27	246.6769	-25.4069	
2015-06-29	224.54	247.3481	-22.8081	-7.09%

Table 4. Moutai weekly forecast results, ARIMA (6,2,1)

	Actual value	Fitted value	difference	Average bias (%)
2015-05-10	222.88			
2015-05-17	250.78			
2015-05-24	239.85			
2015-05-31	230.76			
2015-06-07	241.82			
2015-06-14	213.92			
2015-06-21	220.41	216.4044	4.0056	
2015-06-28	227.1	213.7779	13.3221	
2015-07-05	241.45	214.1417	27.3083	
2015-07-12	228.29	213.7323	14.5577	
2015-07-19	219.21	213.6963	5.5137	
2015-07-26	206.83	217.3854	-10.5554	4.20%

Table 5. China Construction daily forecast results, ARIMA (9,1,9)

	Actual value	Fitted value	difference	Average bias (%)
2015-06-02	10.06			
2015-06-03	9.98			
2015-06-04	9.7			
2015-06-05	10.15			
2015-06-08	10.46			
2015-06-09	10.1			
2015-06-10	9.95			
2015-06-11	9.79			
2015-06-12	9.76			
2015-06-15	9.66	10.03418	-0.37418	
2015-06-16	9.01	10.12349	-1.11349	
2015-06-17	9.23	10.09522	-0.86522	
2015-06-18	8.81	10.12394	-1.31394	
2015-06-19	8.07	10.08044	-2.01044	
2015-06-23	8.32	10.07413	-1.75413	
2015-06-24	8.47	9.968959	-1.498959	
2015-06-25	8.27	9.807189	-1.537189	
2015-06-26	7.72	9.868864	-2.148864	-13.99%

Table 6. China Construction weekly forecast results, ARIMA (8,2,1)

	Actual value	Fitted value	difference	Average bias (%)
2015-04-26	7.79			
2015-05-03	6.98			
2015-05-10	6.79			
2015-05-17	7.35			

Table 6. China Construction weekly forecast results, ARIMA (8,2,1) (Continuous)

2015-05-24	6.65			
2015-05-31	7.25			
2015-06-07	6.97			
2015-06-14	5.75			
2015-06-21	5.51	5.934398	-0.424398	
2015-06-28	4.84	5.73098	-0.89098	
2015-07-05	6.21	5.869217	0.340783	
2015-07-12	5.81	5.978944	-0.168944	
2015-07-19	5.72	5.8791	-0.1591	
2015-07-26	4.97	6.076956	-1.106956	
2015-08-02	5.14	6.18845	-1.04845	
2015-08-09	5.46	6.296992	-0.836992	-8.96%

Table 3, 4, 5 and 6 provide daily and weekly actual and fitted values for each stock, as well as the difference between the two values. The data highlighted in yellow in the tables is the average of the difference divided by the average of the fitted values, which directly reflects the extent to which the crash affected the individual stocks. This value is tentatively referred to as the impact coefficient.

It is observed that the closing prices of both stocks are greatly affected in the short period after the outbreak of the crash. before July 2015, the impact coefficients of the daily data for Moutai and China Construction were -7.20% and -13.99%, respectively. However, Moutai is significantly less affected. On the other hand, the weekly data stretches the time to late July and early August, when Moutai's weekly closing price reversed dramatically, less than a month and a half after the plunge impact coefficient turned positive to 4.20%. The data for China Construction even extends to early August, when the impact coefficient is still negative at -8.96%, albeit with a slight convergence compared to the impact at the beginning of the outbreak of the crash.

The analysis provides insights into the short-term impact of the stock market crash on individual stocks. The impact coefficients offer a measure of the extent to which each stock was affected by the crash, with Moutai appearing to be relatively less affected than China Construction.

The provided table offers insights into the daily and weekly actual and fitted values for each of the two stocks under consideration, alongside the difference between these values. This comprehensive data presentation allows for a nuanced understanding of the stocks' performance, both in absolute terms and relative to the predictions generated by the model. Notably, the section of data highlighted in yellow in the table merits particular attention. This figure represents the average of the difference divided by the average of the fitted values, offering a direct quantification of the extent to which the crash impacted the individual stocks. For this analysis, this value is tentatively referred to as the impact coefficient.

A careful examination of this impact coefficient reveals some intriguing insights. It is observed that in the immediate aftermath of the crash, the closing prices of both stocks experienced significant disruptions. More specifically, before July 2015, the impact coefficients of the daily data for Moutai and China Construction were -7.20% and -13.99%, respectively. This negative value indicates that the actual prices of these stocks were lower than the predicted values, a clear reflection of the downward pressure exerted by the crash. However, it is worth noting that Moutai, while not immune to the market turbulence, was significantly less affected compared to China Construction.

Zooming out to a weekly perspective, the data stretches the time to late July and early August, providing a broader temporal context for understanding the stocks' recovery trajectory. During this period, Moutai's weekly closing price underwent a dramatic reversal, less than a month and a half after the plunge. Remarkably, its impact coefficient turned positive to 4.20%, suggesting that the stock not only recovered but also surpassed the predicted values, possibly indicating a strong resilience or effective mitigation strategies.

On the other hand, the data for China Construction paints a somewhat different picture. The impact of the crash on this stock extended to early August when the impact coefficient was still negative at -8.96%. This persistence of negative impact coefficients underscores the magnitude and duration of the crash's influence on China Construction's stock price. While there is evidence of a slight convergence compared to the impact suffered at the beginning of the outbreak of the crash, this convergence is not yet sufficient to push the impact coefficient into positive territory.

These divergent trajectories observed in Moutai and China Construction's impact coefficients highlight the importance of considering individual stock performance in the aftermath of a market crash. While some stocks may demonstrate resilience and quick recovery, others may experience more protracted downturns. Such nuances are critical for investors to consider when assessing risk, formulating investment strategies, or re-evaluating portfolios in the wake of market volatility.

4 Discussion

Based on the observation that in the short term, the impact on Moutai seems relatively smaller than that on

China Construction, the two companies can be analysed for the different strategies they adopted in response to the 2015 crash.

Moutai adopted various measures to cope with the stock market crash, including strengthening brand marketing, launching new products, and adjusting sales strategies. These measures helped to enhance Moutai's brand value and market share while reducing the impact of market volatility on its performance.

On the other hand, China Construction may have focused more on internal management and cost control, adopting measures such as improving efficiency and reducing costs to respond to market fluctuations. In addition, China Construction may have strengthened its strategic cooperation with partners to expand business opportunities and market influence.

However, it has been proven that Moutai's brand value is the key to its outstanding performance in the market. As the representative brand of high-end Chinese liquor, Moutai has a high reputation and popularity that give it a strong competitive advantage in the market. At the same time, Moutai has also done a lot of brand marketing to continuously enhance its brand value and market influence.

The quality of Moutai is the foundation for gaining consumer trust. Moutai's brewing process, raw material selection, and storage conditions are all at the forefront of the industry, making its quality highly recognized and trusted by consumers. At the same time, Moutai also continuously innovates and improves its quality to meet consumers' demand for high-quality liquor.

Moutai's marketing strategy is also an important factor in its success. Moutai focuses on brand image and consumer experience in its marketing strategies and uses various methods to interact and communicate with consumers to enhance their brand identification and loyalty. In addition, Moutai has actively expanded into international markets to enhance its brand influence internationally.

The relatively complex financial situation of China Construction is another important reason for the huge difference in their response to the stock market crash. With a higher debt ratio and tighter cash flow, China Construction relies more on external financing compared to Moutai. This difference in financial situation also affected the ability of China Construction to withstand the impact of the stock market crash.

Overall, Moutai and China Construction adopted different strategies and measures in response to market changes and the stock market crash, which is related to their respective characteristics and industry trends. As investors choose investment targets, they should pay attention to the characteristics of companies and industry prospects to make more informed investment decisions.

5 Conclusion

The core objective of this study is to delve deeper into the impact of the 2015 Chinese stock market crash on individual stocks and to provide investors with insights on how to make informed investment decisions amidst such market turmoil. To achieve this objective, two representative stocks were selected for comparative analysis to observe their reactions during the stock market crash.

During the research, the ARIMA model was utilized to quantify the impact of stock market crashes on stocks and predict their log returns. This approach enabled a more accurate measurement of the extent to which each stock was affected by market movements. Additionally, a new impact coefficient was introduced to further quantify the magnitude of this impact. The study indicates that Moutai appears to be less affected by the crash than China Construction.

Upon conducting an in-depth analysis of the two stocks' coping strategies and operating environments, some interesting conclusions emerged. Firstly, it was observed that a stock with a stronger brand influence and excellent quality exhibited greater stability during market turbulence. This finding suggests that a company's brand and product quality have a significant impact on its ability to withstand market risks. Secondly, companies with flexible market resilience were able to recover and grow faster following stock market crashes. This observation indicates that a firm's ability to adapt and innovate in a rapidly changing market environment plays a crucial role in its long-term competitiveness.

Based on these findings, several conclusions with significant implications for future research can be derived. Firstly, the study emphasizes that a company's brand and product quality, along with its market resilience, are critical factors in dealing with market risks, in addition to its financial position and risk management capabilities. This provides investors with a more comprehensive perspective to consider when making investment decisions. Secondly, this paper utilizes empirical analyses to carry out the study, hoping to offer new ideas and methods for future quantitative models to more accurately measure the impact of market movements on stocks. This will enable further in-depth examinations in the future on the strategies and performances of stocks in different types of companies, industries, and market environments in response to market risks. In this way, investors can be provided with more practical investment insights and advice. Additionally, exploring the development of advanced quantitative models and methodologies is also an important avenue to pursue. This will enhance the accuracy of forecasting market movements and provide investors with more effective risk management and investment decision support tools. Collaboration and exchanges with scholars and researchers in other fields to explore and study new issues and challenges in the field are also expected. Through these efforts, it is hoped that more valuable insights and guidance will be provided to investors and market participants to promote the stability and development of the capital market.

References

1. L. Laskai, The stock market crash. ANU Press. Laskai, Lorand. (2016)

2. A. Li. Tumbled stock market, RMB devaluation and financial reform in China. CP, **4**(104), 63–68 (2015).
3. L. Dittmer, L. Asia in 2015: the year of the China crash. AS, **56**(1), 1–7 (2016).
4. Y. Li, & L. Zhou. The Chinese stock market crash of 2015: causes, consequences and policy responses. JM, **47**, 243-263 (2016).
5. X. Guo, & L. Zhou. "The impact of the 2015 stock market crash on corporate governance: evidence from China. JBFA, **45**(5-6), 698-735 (2018).
6. Z. Wang, & L. Zhou. The causes of the 2015 Chinese stock market crash: a quantile regression approach. JEF, **35**, 17-36 (2016).
7. A. Posen. The Greek debt crisis: what went wrong and how to fix it. PIIE, (2016).
8. K. Chan, & J Sung. The 2015 Chinese stock market crash: lessons for financial market regulation and monetary policy. AEPR, **12**(1), 49-64 (2017).
9. D. Dickey, & W. Fuller. Distribution of the estimators for autoregressive time series with a unit root. JASA, **76**(373), 494-507 (1981).
10. R. Hyndman & Y. Khandakar. Automatic time series forecasting: the ARIMA way. CSDA, **52**(12), 5080-5096 (2008).
11. A. Söderström, A., & P, Athanasopoulos. "Forecasting with univariate ARIMA models: understanding the assumptions and assessing the validity. IJF, **24**(4), 760-775 (2008).
12. S. Billah, & P. Chaudhuri. Model selection and residuals analysis for time series data". JASA, **99**(467), 629-641 (2004).

Case Analysis and Future Expectations of Chinese Enterprises Suffering Heavy Losses in the International Futures Market: Take the Bank of China and Tsingshan LME as Examples

Jialei Liu*

School of Economics, Zhengzhou University, Zhengzhou, 450000, China

Abstract. Affected by various factors such as COVID-19 epidemic and war, the world economic situation changes more frequently, which leads to increased instability in the international and domestic financial derivatives market. For the substantial changes in the international and domestic financial derivatives market, how to deal with sudden changes and analyze the failure cases in the change of financial derivatives is of far-reaching significance to the rapidly developing domestic financial derivatives market. By taking the Bank of China "crude oil treasure' margin call liquidation case and Tsingshan LME Nickel Futures Squeeze Case as the core of the study, this paper uses case analysis method to deeply study the possible problems and failures in the futures market under the condition of financial derivatives market instability and puts forward suggestions on how to deal with these problems. This paper analyzes the attributes and characteristics of China's 'crude oil treasure' products and nickel futures products, restores the event process, describes the impact of the event on investors, trading institutions and banks, and puts forward suggestions for improvement. The suggestions in this paper are as follows: First, the company and the regulatory department should strengthen risk supervision and management; Second, companies and investors should improve their professional capabilities.

1 Introduction

Financial derivative covered futures, forwards, swaps, options and exotics, financial derivatives are opposed to traditional financial commodities, based on the development of traditional financial commodities, whose price depends on the change of financial asset. With the deepening of economic globalization, investors have increasingly strong demand for financial derivatives, so the types and scale of financial derivatives are increasing. As shown in Figure 1, the volume of global on-floor futures and options trading has been on the rise in the past five years. The volume of global futures and options transactions in the first half of 2023 was 55.782 billion lots, an increase of 44.75% year-on-year and a record high growth rate compared with the same period last year.

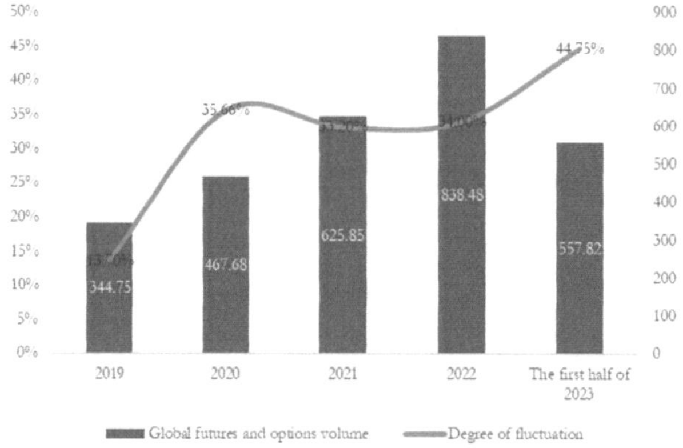

Fig. 1. 2019-2023 Global options and futures trading volume
Data source: Futures Industry Association [1-5].
Photo credit: Original

* Corresponding author: liujialei@ldy.edu.rs

With the continuous growth of global futures and options transaction scale, the types of financial derivatives related to futures and options are also constantly increasing. Compared with European and American countries, although China's domestic futures market started late and developed relatively backward, the continuous opening of the financial market and the rapid development of the network economy have made the domestic futures market develop relatively rapidly, and the booming trend of the futures market makes more Chinese enterprises invest money in futures products. However, with the continuous development of the futures market, the uncertainty and complexity of the futures products are enhanced, and the risks of the futures products are increased. Correspondingly, the defects of the futures market are gradually emerging. Due to the lack of strict risk management system corresponding to the rapid development of the futures market and regulatory departments, as well as a large number of innovations in futures products but the lack of matching degree of specialization, the lack of professional ability of investors, together led to the occurrence of China's 'crude oil treasure' margin call liquidation event and the Tsingshan LME Nickel Futures Squeeze Case. In the past, most scholars started their studies with one case event, but this paper started from two events, carried out in-depth analysis from the two opposing situations of cornering futures markets, and made a more comprehensive analysis of the causes and effects of Chinese enterprises' losses in the futures market, so as to provide more in-depth suggestions for Chinese enterprises to avoid risks from multiple angles. Therefore, this paper chooses China's 'crude oil treasure' margin call liquidation event and the Tsingshan LME Nickel Futures Squeeze Case as typical cases to analyze, hoping to deeply analyze the causes and impacts of the cases under the background that the booming development of futures products does not fit the risk management level of the futures market trading institutions and regulatory departments, and provide ideas for Chinese enterprises to avoid risks in the diversified and unstable futures market. At the same time, it is hoped that the conclusions drawn from these two case studies can help the emerging and rapidly developing domestic futures market to better improve its risk management system, so as to make the healthy development of China's domestic futures market.

The remaining sections are arranged as follows: Section 2 is literature review and main body, including the analysis of China's 'crude oil treasure' margin call liquidation event and Tsingshan LME Nickel Futures Squeeze Case. Section 3 is conclusion.

2 Literature Review

With the expansion of the scale of the futures market, the relationship between the futures derivatives and the economy is getting closer and closer, and the fluctuation of the futures price has an increasing impact on the economic market and spot price. In view of the high-risk characteristics of futures, the academic community has also begun to pay close attention to the risk management field of futures.

Hilary Till argues that futures traders must implement strict risk management procedures [6]. The key factors to consider are the risk tolerance of investors, ensuring that customers do not exceed this tolerance, and understanding the price behavior of commodity futures prices and their potential explosive behavior to manage risk [6]. Moreover, Xianhua Fang and Wenya Lou proposed the concept of "risk corridor", which quantifies futures risk by analyzing the interval between the maximum risk and the minimum risk that investors can accept for financial derivatives contracts, so as to guide investors to reasonably assess risks and do a good job in risk management [7]. After that Sabri Boubaker, Zhenya Liu and Yaosong Zhan proposed that in the case of the rapid decline of crude oil futures prices, timely selling to control the risk is a better risk management method to avoid losses is a better risk management method to avoid losses [8].

To sum up, in terms of futures risk management, in-depth analysis is mainly carried out from investors and futures trading institutions. Therefore, based on such multiple perspectives, this paper adds the perspective of regulatory authorities, studies two typical cases, and puts forward effective suggestions. On the basis of theoretical analysis, more detailed conclusions are drawn through case analysis.

3 China's 'Crude Oil Treasure' Margin Call Liquidation Event

In January 2018, following the crude oil products of other banks, Bank of China launched the crude oil investment product - "Crude Oil Treasure" investment product based on the US WTI and the UK Brent crude oil futures respectively, all are denominated in US Dollar (USD) and Chinese Yuan (CNY), and began to provide domestic and foreign individual customers with personal account crude oil trading services linked to overseas crude oil futures.

3.1 Crude Oil Treasure" Product Basic Information and Characteristics

From the announcement on the official website of the Bank of China about the "crude oil treasure" product [9], it can be summarized that a major feature of the "crude oil treasure" product is non-leverage trading. It takes the form of margin trading and investors need to deposit 100% of the margin account of the "crude oil treasure" product investment trading opened by the Bank of China, and then they can carry out investment trading activities. The second feature is that it can be a two-way choice between long and short, so it is a better choice for investors who are new to futures investment. At the same time, unlike other futures products, it does not support physical delivery of crude oil, only cash delivery. This is related to its trading process. The crude oil futures products are CFD products, and the Bank of China earns potential profits by trading CFD. Therefore, after

* Corresponding author: liujialei@ldy.edu.rs

investors choose to go short or long, the Bank of China will first hedge the risks of the long and short transactions it receives. The remaining long or short transactions that cannot be hedged are carried out by Bank of BOC International Commodity Futures Co., LTD.

In the Chicago Mercantile Exchange (CME), and under the constraints of the relevant domestic legal system, "crude oil treasure" products only support cash delivery. In addition, compared with other futures products, it is more suitable for investors who are new to the futures market. The minimum trading unit of "crude oil treasure" futures investment product is 1 barrel, and the additional sale unit is 0.1 barrel, which is very small compared with the trading volume required by crude oil futures contracts. At the same time, the convenience and diversification of its purchase channels are also one of the major features suitable for novice investors. Moreover, the "crude oil treasure" product is T+0 trading which means it can be traded several times a day.

3.2 Crude Oil Treasure" Product Operation Process and Profit Model

Bank of China acts as a middleman in the trading of "crude oil treasure "products. First of all, after obtaining the overseas crude oil futures trading prices in CME, the bank quotes the futures prices for investors and discloses the risks of related products to investors. If the investors accept the risk content informed by the bank, they sign a short or long contract. After the Bank of China hedges the balance, real transactions are carried out through BOC International Commodity Futures Co., LTD.

The profit model of "Crude Oil Treasure" products is that Bank of China can earn profits by charging handling fees or transaction fees; secondly, because crude oil products can be traded in RMB and US dollar at the same time, it can earn profits through the exchange rate fluctuations between RMB and US dollar; thirdly, through the difference between crude oil products and WTI crude oil futures margin, it can use the remaining margin for savings or loans to generate income.

3.3 China's 'Crude Oil Treasure' Margin Call Liquidation Event Process Motivation

From the perspective of market supply and demand to analyze, the COVID-19 pandemic has led to a sharp global recession, and global demand for crude oil continues to decrease, resulting in a decline in crude oil prices and crude oil futures prices in the international market. As can be seen from Figure 2, due to the serious oversupply of the global crude oil market, the international crude oil futures price has fallen from above 50 US dollars.

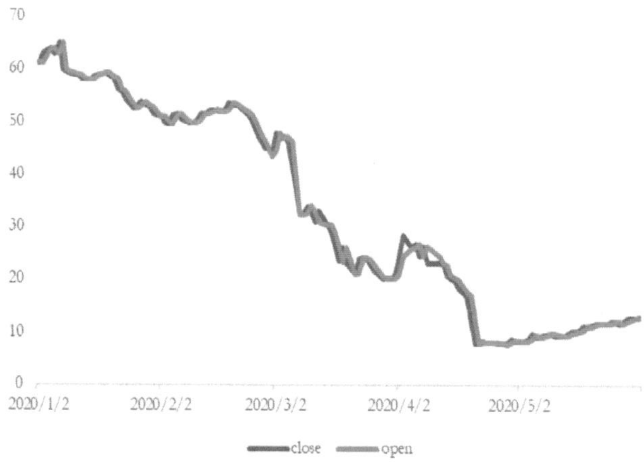

Fig. 2. WTI crude oil futures price
Data source: Investing [10]
Photo credit: Original

To stabilize crude oil prices, in early March, OPEC, led by Saudi Arabia, proposed "OPEC +" 23 countries to jointly reduce production to support oil prices. At the beginning, Russia underestimated the huge impact of the COVID-19 pandemic on oil prices, or refused to reduce production as a bargaining chip to bear less of the production reduction share [11], or after economic sanctions oil exports as its main domestic economic driving force, crude oil production will have a huge impact on the Russian economy and other reasons [12], and the negotiations broke down. Subsequently, Saudi Arabia unilaterally increased crude oil output, the balance of supply and demand was broken, and the supply exceeded the demand, which made the crude oil market price continued to fall, resulting in the price of crude oil sold by Saudi Arabia to Europe as low as \$10.25 / barrel [11]. Due to the continuous decline in oil prices, countries take advantage of low oil prices to store a large number of crude oils, supply more demand less countries crude oil storage quickly tends to be full, by the middle of April, almost all crude oil storage facilities in the United States are full of crude oil. From the perspective of individual investors, due to the high cost of preserving crude oil and its permit transportation, it becomes difficult to deliver crude oil when the crude oil storage in various countries is about to be full, and the long bulls who have bought the bottom before need to sell the contract in the last trading day to close the position, but the institutions with the physical delivery capacity will not buy crude oil because the inventory is full, so the investors of crude oil futures prefer to sell the contract at a negative crude oil price [12]. As a result, oil prices fell again [12]. A large number of WTI crude oil futures contracts for May delivery were closed regardless of the cost, and on April 20, the WTI crude oil May contract closed at -37.63 US dollars/barrel, the first time in history there was a negative oil price, and the spot market fell to the lowest of 10 US dollars/barrel [11].

From the perspective of the Chicago Mercantile Exchange and the Bank of China, the Chicago Board of Trade changed the circuit breaker price for crude oil futures on March 19, allowing for greater price volatility in crude oil futures contracts during trading [12]. Since then, the CME has made a series of changes to the trading rules, first changing the trading system code so that crude oil futures can be traded at a negative price, but the following days after the operation went into effect, the content of this change was stress tested [12]. The Chicago Mercantile Exchange's practice of giving investors a short time to react when futures contracts are traded is inappropriate compared to past practice. However, due to the lack of sensitivity to risks, the Bank of China did not pay attention to and react correctly when the CME clearing house revised the trading rules, which led to the failure to respond in time when the crude oil futures price continued to fall, resulting in heavy losses for investors.

From the perspective of regulatory authorities, the Financial Stability and Development Committee held the 28th meeting after the crude oil treasure incident and proposed to pay attention to the risk of financial derivatives, prevent and control the risk of related financial products, and the administrative penalty decision of the China Banking and Insurance Regulatory Commission on the crude oil treasure product incident to the bank of China and warning fines. However, the punishment measures of the regulatory authorities are relatively delayed, the regulatory mechanism is not perfect, and the risk loss of crude oil products is not timely monitored, and the risk of crude oil products is not regulated.

3.4 Economic Consequence

Investors suffered heavy losses. Over 60,000 investors purchase the Bank of China's "crude oil treasure" products. However, the percentage of long and short investors is extremely out of balance, with only 5% of short orders and up to 95% of multi-orders [12]. As a result, the majority of long investors have experienced significant losses. Incomplete data indicates that approximately 60,000 customers own "crude oil treasure" products from the Bank of China, of which roughly 20,000 have an investment amount of less than 10,000 yuan, roughly 20,000 have an investment amount of between 10,000 and 50,000 yuan, and roughly 20,000 investors have an investment amount exceeding 50,000 yuan [12]. A signed agreement between the investors and the Bank of China states that over 60,000 investors lost roughly 4.2 billion yuan in their margin accounts [12]. In addition, the agreement requires investors to return 5.8 billion yuan to the Bank of China, meaning the total amount of losses incurred by investors is approximately 10 billion yuan [12].

At the same time, the credit of Chinese banks has been questioned by the public, and the bank's credit and economic profits have been reduced.

3.5 Optimization Suggestion

According to the in-depth analysis of the causes of this incident, the main suggestions are put forward. For commercial banks, the high-risk characteristics of financial derivatives need to be paid attention to. Commercial banks should strengthen their sensitive perception of risks in the futures market, be alert when the futures market price fluctuates greatly, and timely remind investors to reduce losses. In terms of the design of futures products of commercial banks, banks should first disclose the risks of futures products in detail, continue to follow up, and carry out forced liquidation operations when the balance of investors' margin accounts falls to a certain amount to reduce investors' losses. Commercial banks need to be aware of how liquidity risk affects the futures market. Bank of China is expected to hedge investors' long and short positions around one week prior to the contract settlement date in accordance with standard trading procedures for the market [12]. The remainder of the time will be devoted to actively finding trading partners for the unhedged net position on international exchanges [12]. But because the "crude oil treasure" product's trading end was set for April 20, which is near the linked futures contract's delivery date, and because there was very little market activity at that time and almost all investors had found a trading partners, it was challenging to close the position at the normal prices[12]. Therefore, the futures products of commercial banks should take into account the liquidity risk of futures market in the design of the trading day, and strengthen the identification and management of liquidity risk.At the same time, in terms of product marketing of commercial banks, it is necessary to strengthen the supervision of influence strategies, clearly classify the risk of financial products, and sell financial derivatives of different levels to investors of corresponding levels.

For investors, investors should strengthen financial literacy, timely identify risks, correctly understand the suitability of their professional ability and financial derivatives risks and choose financial derivatives that are compatible with their professional ability and risk bearing ability.

For regulatory departments, risk supervision and management should be strengthened, the risk fluctuations of financial derivatives should be discovered in time, and the risk should be punished in time to reduce investor losses.

4 Tsingshan LME Nickel Futures Squeeze Case

4.1 Introduction of Tsingshan Group

Tsingshan Group controls a large amount of nickel resources, its Indonesia nickel mines alone accounts for about 10% of the world's nickel production. In 2021, Tsingshan Group's nickel ore production has reached 600,000 tons, accounting for a quarter of the world's nickel ore production [13], which also makes it necessary to hedge such products in the futures market. (1) Tsingshan Group produces nickel, and shorting can hedge risks, manage the risk of their spot positions [14] and avoid price declines. Because the LME market is liquid, shorting the LME international market can have enough trading partners to absorb the short orders it creates, while the domestic futures market cannot absorb this amount of nickel [13]. (2) If the futures market requires spot delivery, Tsingshan Group only needs to use electrolytic nickel from Russian customers for delivery, eliminating the operation of currency exchange [13] and reducing costs. Therefore, Tsingshan Group chose to hedge about 200,000 tons of short orders in the LME market, and the delivery time was March 9 [14].

4.2 Event Process

After the conflict between Russia and Ukraine, the LME was affected by political sanctions that banned the delivery of Russian nickel [14], so Russian nickel could not be supplied to the market.

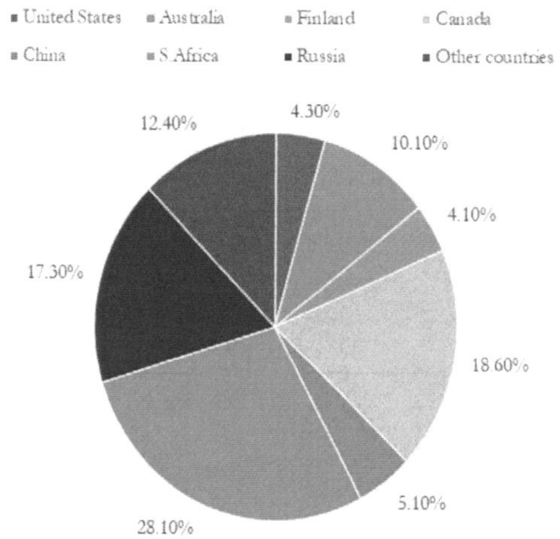

Fig. 3. Nickel ore distribution proportion
Data source: China Business Information Network [15].
Photo credit: Original

From the global nickel ore production and storage scale and nickel ore distribution chart (Fig. 3 & 4), it can be seen that Russia's nickel ore accounts for a large proportion of the world. As a result, after Russian nickel could not be supplied, demand exceeded supply and nickel prices continued to rise. At the same time, the international capital represented by the world commodity giant Glencore of Switzerland is using the panic of nickel supply shortage caused by the conflict between Russia and Ukraine to implement capital sniping to Tsingshan Group with a huge nickel short order [13], through the large purchase of pure nickel in the international market, so that Tsingshan Group cannot buy spot nickel in the market, which also leads to Tsingshan Group cannot carry out spot delivery, then International capital forces continue to buy more positions, making futures nickel prices continue to rise. Thus, on March 8, the LME nickel price opened at just under $50,000 and then soared to $101,365 / ton [14]. Within three hours, the price of nickel almost doubled, rising 274.3% from the opening price on March 4, reaching the highest price ever on the LME. This is a nickel price action that the LME has never seen before in its history [14].

Although Tsingshan Group has rich nickel resources, the high-ice nickel produced by Tsingshan Group is inconsistent with the spot varieties required by the delivery of LME futures contracts, which cannot form a perfect hedge and cannot sell its group's commodities directly to multiple parties. In order to solve this short force, Tsingshan Group needs to pay more margin to buy more short orders to cope with the long attacks. That has put Tsingshan under enormous financial pressure.

However, after the crisis of a sharp rise in nickel prices, LME took a series of countermeasures. It repealed all transactions on March 8 and postponed nickel trading from March 9, and limited the decline and increase of nickel prices (5%), The margin that Tsingshan Group needs to make up also decreases, and the delayed delivery date also gives Tsingshan Group more time to convert products into directly deliverable spot. The Chinese government has also helped Tsingshan raise some spot nickel for delivery.

After that, through active negotiation, Tsingshan Group reached a silent agreement with the syndicate of creditors of the Futures Bank. With the recovery of nickel futures prices in the market, Tsingshan Group needed to reduce its holdings in a reasonable and orderly manner, and Tsingshan Group's losses were effectively controlled [17]. The agreement buys Tsingshan Group more time to resolve its problems. If the nickel price falls in the subsequent market, Tsingshan Group can reduce its position at a suitable point, and if the subsequent nickel price remains high, Tsingshan Group can also sell its nickel products at a high price to minimize its own losses [17].

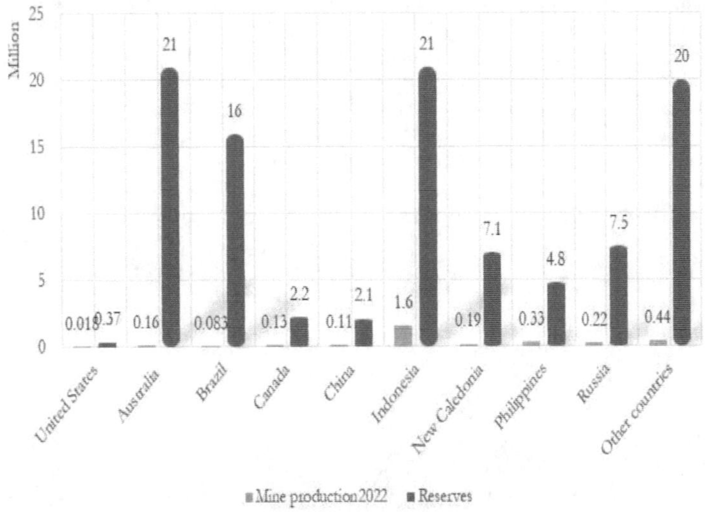

Fig. 4. Global nickel production and reserves
Data source: United States Geological Survey [16].
Photo credit: Original

4.3 Economic Consequence

Tsingshan Company capital loss at the same time London nickel price fluctuations also affected the domestic Shanghai nickel futures price fluctuations, affecting the domestic nickel futures market. It has a huge impact on the financial derivatives market and the real industry related to nickel.

4.4 Optimization Suggestion

As for the company, the company should strengthen risk management, improve the company's risk management system, pay close attention to the domestic and foreign situation and the conduct of financial derivatives, and improve the sensitivity of risk identification. It should have a deeper understanding of futures expertise, participate in the hedging of appropriate futures varieties, and can transfer risks or hedge transactions in a timely manner.

For the futures exchange (LME), it is necessary to strengthen the sensitivity of market risks, enhance the awareness of prevention, and pay attention to the risk events that have a trend in time. Then, it should strengthen the prior risk prevention work, when the LME's own nickel inventory continued to decline and the extent was large, it did not give enough attention to the market warning in February 2022 when there were related reports of nickel futures confrontation between the two sides, which shows that the LME should strengthen the prior risk prevention work [17]. Moreover, it should strengthen the supervision of abnormal capital sniping transactions and follow the example of other exchanges (CME) to strictly identify and manage some trading activities that may cause or accumulate the risk of short-selling.

5 Conclusion

Although the international and domestic futures markets have been in a stage of rapid development, and the types of futures products continue to increase, the development history of risk management measures for the high-risk characteristics of futures is too short, the risk management system is not strict enough, and there are some flaws and problems in investors, banks, regulatory authorities and futures exchanges. This paper adopts the case analysis method and takes China's 'crude oil treasure' margin call liquidation event and Tsingshan LME Nickel Futures Squeeze Case as examples to analyze the problems in risk management during the volatility of the futures market, and makes an in-depth analysis of these problems from the perspectives of the market, investors, banks, futures trading institutions and regulatory authorities, and puts forward the following suggestions: First, institutions and investors should strengthen financial professional capabilities, identify risks in a timely manner, and choose futures products that match the risk level of their own capabilities; Second, banks should strengthen risk supervision in product design, sales strategy, risk disclosure and other aspects to improve the sensitivity to risk; Third, futures trading institutions should strengthen pre-risk prevention work; Fourth, the regulatory authorities should improve the risk supervision system.

Finally, previous scholars paid more attention to futures risk management from the perspective of investors and futures trading institutions, but as mentioned in this paper, the regulatory authorities also have risk management defects in the aspects of pre-risk management and prevention, futures product design and other aspects. In the future, the above perspectives can be further refined to promote in-depth research on futures risk management. To help the international and domestic futures markets develop healthily.

References

1. Financial world, Click here for a more detailed analysis of the global derivatives market landscape in 2019. https://baijiahao.baidu.com/s?id=1669070771103587208&wfr=spider&for=pc
2. Z. Tianmiao. Global futures and options trading volume hit a new high in 2020. Futures daily (2021).
3. Z. Tianmiao. Global futures and options trading rose 33.7 per cent last year from a year earlier. Futures daily (2022).
4. C.Lei. Global futures and options trading volume has set a record for five consecutive year. Futures daily (2023).
5. B. Ren. FIA: Global futures and options turnover in H1 was 55.782 billion lots. Futures daily (2023).
6. H, Till. Commodity risk management. JGR, 5(3):11-18 (2016).
7. F. Xianhua, L. Wenya. Risk management analysis of the commodity futures trading. TS, 15: 88-91 (2023).
8. S. Boubaker, Z. Liu, Y. Zhan. Risk management for crude oil futures: an optimal stopping-timing approach. AOR, 313(1):1-19 (2021).
9. Bank Of China, Description of the Bank of China on the business of Crude Oil Treasure. https://www.bankofchina.com/fimarkets/bi2/202004/t20200422_17781867.html?keywords=%E5%8E%9F%E6%B2%B9%E5%AE%9D
10. Investing, WTI/USD Historical data. https://cn.investing.com/currencies/wti-usd-historical-data
11. H. Hong. Research on the Largest Crude Oil Production Reduction Agreement in History Under the Influence of COVID - 19 ——— Analysis Based on the Game Process of Stakeholders. PTP, 6: 21-24 (2020).
12. W. Jingchuan. Case Analysis of ZG Bank's "Crude Oil Treasure" Incident. Guangxi Normal University (2023).
13. H. Yutong, D. Mulan. London Nickel "epic" forced short risk event reflection and prospect. MC, (03):96-100 (2023).
14. Z. Taihao. The revelation of the Lunni incident to China's financial market. TF, (11):51-54 (2023).
15. China Business Information Network, Analysis of global nickel ore production and distribution in 2022. https://baijiahao.baidu.com/s?id=1726425220370289472&wfr=spider&for=pc
16. United States Geological Survey, NICKEL. https://pubs.usgs.gov/periodicals/mcs2023/mcs2023-nickel.pdf
17. R. Heyun. Research on Hedging Risk of Commodity Futures Metal Products -- Based on the Short Squeeze Case of LME NI Futures. Wuhan Textile University (2023).

The impact of the US-China trade war on the global macroeconomy

Hongcheng Chen[1,*]

[1]School of Economics and Finance, Massey University, Palmerston North, New Zealand

Abstract. In recent times, one of the major issues currently affecting the global economy has been the trade war between the United States and China. This paper examines the impact of the US-China trade war on the global macro economy, including U.S. tariffs, real exports, macroeconomic indicators, and production structure. This paper finds that increased U.S. tariffs on China not only reduce the welfare of U.S. consumers and firms but also cause a domino effect throughout other regions that significantly impact the global trade structure. The US-China trade war, with its complexity regarding taxes and extensive geopolitical implications on current economics, proves itself to be an interconnected entity dictating the course of the present world economy. Based on examining some essential elements, from real exports macroeconomic parameters, the trade conflict has merely exceeded the bilateral dimension and now marks even the global economy. Therefore, the dynamics of this trade war call for global collaboration and advanced planning to guard against its wide-ranging implications.

1. Introduction

In recent times, one of the major issues currently affecting the global economy has been the trade war between the world's largest economies, the United States and China, which has seen highs and lows due to escalating tariffs and trade restrictions. This paper discusses the impact of this trade war on the global macroeconomy, including U.S. tariffs, real exports, macroeconomic indicators, and production structure. Through this analysis, this paper endeavor to reveal the complex structure of the trade war's significant impact on the world economy.

The U.S.-China trade war is rooted in severe trade deficits, intellectual property infringement, and suspicion of fair competitive practices. Growing tensions have led to tariffs, including tit-for-tat tariff escalation between the U.S. and China. The World Trade Organization (WTO) recognized that the cumulative effects of these tariffs were at peak levels, involving many industries and disrupting global trade lines [1]. The initial impact on the economies of both countries was enough to affect production processes, complex supply chains, and reduced trade volumes. According to the International Monetary Fund, the trade war has slowed the world's economic growth and increased uncertainty in financial markets where investor confidence is low [2]. Concerns about the growth of the trade war became widespread, and some analysts even warned that the escalation of tariffs could exacerbate their adverse effects globally, leading to increased volatility in international markets.

2. The Impact of U.S. tariff increases on the domestic economy in the context of the U.S.-China trade war

In turn, raising tariffs as a sales tax on foreign products fundamentally reshapes the global business economy. Tariffs can be thought of as tariffs levied on all imported goods, which directly affect these companies and local consumers involved in foreign trade [3]. Tariffs are like general taxes because they cover multiple items that enter the U.S. territory. It affects the cost of imported goods and extends from manufacturers to retailers. As a result, complex and diverse economic adjustments are intertwined and reflected in different sectors and regions complicating the consequences of trade wars.

The impact of higher tariffs on U.S. producers is a double-edged sword. For example, high prices of imported intermediate input products such as raw materials and components place an additional burden on production costs [4]. As a result, this may lead to a decrease in firms' profitability. The second thing that needs to be considered is the rise in the cost of production in the US industry, which becomes higher than international competitors whose products do not attract such high tariffs. This may reduce the competitiveness of the US products and thus affect the export-oriented industries. Amiti et al. found that the tariffs imposed by the U.S. on China in 2018 were fully passed on to domestic U.S. prices of imported goods, while Chinese exporters did not lower commodity prices. As a result, the price of goods at U.S. ports of entry has risen in line with the

* Corresponding author: 23019994@massey.ac.nz

tariff hikes. The study also found that every 10 percent tariff imposed led to a 43 percent reduction in import demand.

Complex supply chains pose major difficulties in shifting exports and changing the origin of imports. As a result, many United States industries have close relationships with global supply chains; they therefore need help to rapidly change the routes of production and exchange. As a result of the interconnectedness of the various steps within the supply chain, disruptions have occurred, making it difficult for the companies involved to adapt to the new trade realities. Long-term agreements and relationships in these supply chains add to this complexity; therefore, change will take time.

Table 1. U.S. tariff costs

Tariffs in 2018	Pay taxes	Unnecessary loss	Total cost to the consumer
Monthly cost	$3 billion	$ 1.4 billion	$ 4.4 billion
Annual cost	$ 36 billion	$ 16.8 billion	$ 52.8 billion
Annual cost per family	$ 282	$ 132	$ 414
After a 15 percent increase in tariff rates on $200 billion of Chinese goods			
Monthly cost	$ 2.245 billion	$ 6.594 billion	$ 8.84 billion
Annual cost	$ 26.942 billion	$ 79.132 billion	$ 106.674 billion
Annual cost per family	$ 211	$ 620	$ 831

Note: Data from analysis of six U.S. tariffs in 2018 [5]. The annual cost per household is based on 127.6 million U.S. households in 2018.

Comparing the estimated cost of the 2018 tariffs with the estimated cost of the recently announced tariffs on $200 billion of Chinese goods shows that two factors are at play. As can be seen in Table 1, in November 2018, importers were paying an additional $3 billion per month in taxes and $1.4 billion in needless losses, for a combined total cost of $4.4 billion per month. When annualized, the total annual cost to consumers is $52.8 billion and the annual cost per household is $414. Nonetheless, the unnecessary loss of $132 per year per U.S. household means that the net loss to the U.S. economy exceeds any tariff revenues collected by the government [5].

Based on these estimates, it is possible to extrapolate the estimated cost of a $200 billion increase in tariff rates on Chinese goods from 10 percent to 25 percent. As can be seen in table 1, the cost of paying taxes per household declined from $282 to $211 because the taxed price of Chinese imports was so high that consumers began to purchase substitutes from countries such as Vietnam. As the U.S. imported more goods from countries other than China, firms were forced to pay higher prices for similar goods without tariffs. In principle, consumers could shift their spending to domestically produced goods, and domestic firms might benefit from the lack of foreign competition. In practice, however, studies have found that other developing countries tend to fill much of the gap in goods from the taxed country. However, whether consumers choose more expensive alternative foreign suppliers or domestic suppliers, the needless efficiency losses inevitably rise [6].

3. The impact of U.S. tariff increases on the economies of other countries

The effect, for example, of US tariffs on China shows up as the consumers' goods and producers' in the country. The prices of various Chinese exports traded in the United States rise as retaliatory tariffs are established. This decreases American consumers' domestic demand for products from China, thus affecting different industries like electronics, textiles, and manufacturing [1]. Despite this, the Chinese government selectively excluded some intermediary products from the tariffs to ease costs for local manufacturers and lessen the immediate effect on the prices. However, the overall increase in consumer goods prices is a problem for those Chinese industries relying on exporting products to the American market [7].

In reaction to these tariffs, China is responding strategically by moving its exportation away from the US, increasing its presence in other global markets. Diversification among exported destinations is aimed at reducing the impact of reduced access to the US market. The diversion of exports towards these markets has meant a renewed emphasis on Europe and countries from the East and Southeast Asian sub-regions [8]. With the success of the Chinese invasion in these markets, there is an increase in Chinese exports into all such regions, which increases total exports in them. Therefore, countries in these regions export more products to the United States, leading to a complex web of changes in international business with a ripple effect on world trade.

This causes a chain reaction, leading to several interrelated events that significantly impact the global trade structure. Compared to other nations that are more agile about trade adjustments, it has been difficult for the US to change its import sources or divert its exports because of the complexity of its supply chains [9]. On the other hand, changes occurring in China's export concentration also contribute to international trade flow alterations. Such a dynamic process demonstrates that world trade has a complex web, where events in one region cause a domino effect throughout other regions.

4. Variables and their impacts within the U.S.-China trade war

Considering significant parameters within the U.S.-China trade war contributes to revealing the changing circumstances of the international economics sector. Using the detailed tariff data helps analyze all aspects of determining how the current dispute affects global trade [10].

4.1 Real exports

Real exports, indicating the volume of cross-border physical transactions, are one of the most important indicators of economic activities and trading relations among nations. Tariffs significantly affect the volume and composition of goods exported by the United States, China, and other countries. A detailed analysis of actual export statistics helps us notice changes in trading patterns and discover fast-developing economic sectors and their consequences on the world economy, as ahown in table 2.

Table 2. Impact of the tariffs on the real exports from the rest of the world to China and the U.S between June 2019 to December 2019

Country Exporting	June 2019 United States	December 2019 United States	June 2019 China and Hong Kong	December 2019 China and Hong Kong
United States	0.00	0.00	-7.32	-14.38
Canada	0.23	0.31	-0.29	-0.84
Mexico	-0.06	-0.02	-2.63	-3.18
Europe	1.51	2.21	-0.98	-0.89
China and Hong Kong	-5.61	-10.69	1.49	2.71
Japan	2.57	3.14	-1.03	-1.15
South Korea	2.02	3.17	-0.55	-0.91
Other high-income Asia	1.82	3.44	-0.24	-0.68
Low-income Asia	0.61	3.56	-0.04	-0.76
Central America	0.28	1.40	-0.70	-2.03
Latin America	0.04	0.24	1.58	1.55
India	-0.05	2.20	0.69	0.02
Africa	0.21	0.56	-0.03	-0.36
Russia	0.28	0.56	-0.11	-0.42
Middle East and North Africa	0.21	1.19	-0.31	-0.75
Other countries	-3.07	2.67	0.70	-0.19
All countries	-0.33	-0.59	-0.85	-1.64

Figure 1 is a graphical presentation of the impact of the tariffs on the percentage change of exports from other countries to the United States and China. In June 2019, when the tariffs were relaxed, the line graph showing the percentage change in exports for the United States was higher compared to December 2019. Consequently, the line graph for China between June and December 2019 displayed the same results. Both lines show that between June and December of 2019, exports from most nations to the United States and China fell. During this period, exports to China and Hong Kong fell at a greater rate than exports to the United States, suggesting that the former were hit harder by tariffs. Therefore, China felt the significant impact of the tariffs imposed due to the trade war between China and the United States.

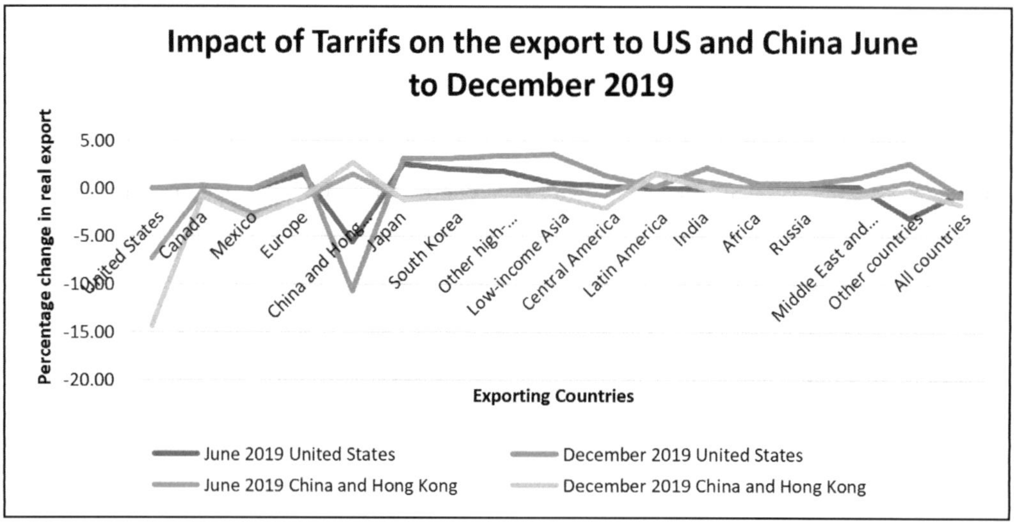

Fig. 1. Impact of the tariffs on the percentage change of export from other countries to the United States and China (Picture credit : Original)

4.2 Macroeconomic Indicators

Regarding the ongoing trade war between the US and China, it is prudent to look into macroeconomic factors to unearth the more profound economic implications. The changes in the indicators are analyzed based on the drawn detailed tariff schedules and reveal new insights into the ongoing trade war.

4.2.1 Impact on GDP

The trade war between the US and China is an essential indicator of GDP strength. With tariff restructuring trade moves and consumption patterns changing, their influence can become the most critical indicator showing the health status of two countries and an ability to cause external negative consequences for the world economy [4]. Through analysis of the GDP figures, one can identify the size of economic shocks and better understand each country's strategy to face trade hostility.

4.2.2 Effects on Final Demand

Trade war goes far beyond production and consumption to affect final demand, an essential element in economic activities. Tariff-related disruptions affect consumer behavior, altering demand for goods and services [3]. The above variable presents a more sophisticated perception of how people feel about the dispute as they shift their preferences, markets adjust dynamically, and households persevere amid all these challenges by sustaining homebound demand.

Table 3. Impact of Tariffs on GDP and Final Demand for Different Countries

Country	GDP June 2019	GDP December 2019	Final Demand June 2019	Final Demand December 2019
United States	-0.02	-0.07	-0.08	-0.21
Canada	-0.02	-0.02	0.25	0.21
Mexico	-0.08	-0.09	0.43	0.39
Europe	-0.01	-0.01	0.04	0.04
China and Hong Kong	0.02	0.01	-0.68	-0.95
Japan	-0.01	-0.02	0.07	0.07
South Korea	0.00	0.00	0.20	0.18
Other high-income Asia	-0.01	-0.01	0.12	0.08
Low-income Asia	-0.01	-0.03	0.18	0.15
Central America	-0.01	-0.04	0.17	0.15
Latin America	0.00	-0.01	0.11	0.09
India	0.00	-0.01	0.08	0.09

Africa	0.01	0.01	0.15	0.12
Russia	-0.01	-0.01	0.09	0.06
Middle East and North Africa	-0.01	-0.01	0.08	0.05
Other countries	0.02	0.00	0.11	0.10

As can be seen from Table 3, a negative effect (-0.02 to -0.07) was seen in U.S. GDP between June and December 2019. Countries like Mexico, Japan, Russia, and the Middle East/North Africa might see similar unfavorable tendencies. GDP fell somewhat in both Canada and Europe. At first, China and Hong Kong's GDP showed some improvement, but by December 2019, the decline had become more pronounced.

Regarding final demand, most nations appear to have witnessed a reduction in ultimate demand. China and Hong Kong had a significant drop in final demand between June 2019 and December 2019 (-0.68 to -0.95) due to the trade war, as shown in figure 2. Final demand fell in Canada, Mexico, Central America, and low-income Asian nations, but the extent varied by region.

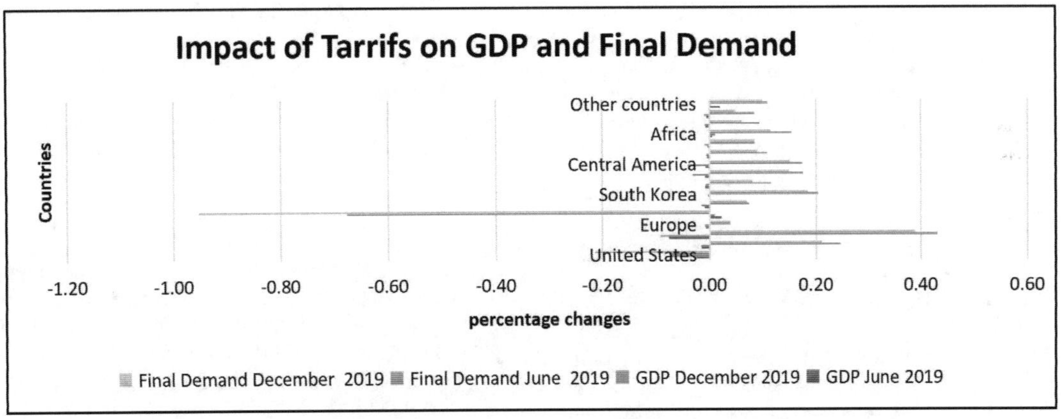

Fig. 2. Impact of Tariffs on the GDP and Final Demand for other Countries (Picture credit : Original)

5. Conclusion

Ultimately, the U.S.-China trade war, with its complexity regarding taxes and extensive geopolitical implications on current economics, proves itself to be an interconnected entity dictating the course of the present world economy. Based on examining some essential elements, from real exports macroeconomic parameters, the trade conflict has merely exceeded the bilateral dimension and now marks even the global economy. Therefore, the dynamics of this trade war call for global collaboration and advanced planning to guard against its wide-ranging implications.

References

1. K. Itakura, Asian Economic Policy Review, 15(1): 77-93 (2020)
2. D. Steinbock, China Quarterly of International Strategic Studies, 4(4): 515-542 (2018)
3. G. H. Hanson, Business Economics, 55: 69-72 (2020)
4. T. T. L. Chong, X. Li, Economic and Political Studies, 7(2):185-202 (2019)
5. A. Mary, J. Stephen. Prices and Welfare, NBER Working Paper 25672 (2019)
6. E. Lovely Mary, L. Yang, Policy Brief, 18-12 (2018)
7. A. Mary, M. Di, C. Robert. F. J. Romalis, NBER Working Paper, 23487 (2017)
8. S. Kumagai, T. Gokan, K. Tsubota, I. Isono, K. Hayakawa, Journal of Asian Economic Integration, 3(2): 127-143 (2021)
9. C. Li, C. He, C. Lin, Emerging Markets Finance and Trade, 54(7): 1557-1577 (2018)
10. Steinberg, D.A., Tan, Y, The Review of International Organizations, 18:145-167 (2023)

Development of Sino-US trade relations and employment of labor force

Huirou Bai[1,*]
[1]Department of School of Economics and Management, Huaibei Normal University, Huaibei, China

Abstract. International trade needs healthy and balanced development, and so does labor employment. There are some connections between the two, so both need to be taken into account in development. In terms of international trade, Sino-US trade is a hot topic at present. Based on the development of Sino-US trade relations and the correlation between the development of Sino-US trade relations and the employment of the labor force, this paper makes a summary. This paper mainly studies the development stage and changing trend of Sino-US trade relations, and discusses the influence of the development of Sino-US trade relations on labor employment. This paper mainly analyzes the impact of Sino-US trade relations in a relatively stable state, including positive and negative impacts. In addition, this paper mainly discusses the relationship between trade relations and labor employment and strives to achieve a balanced development of the two, promote the healthy development of trade, and stabilize employment and people's livelihood.

1. Introduction

After Trump took office, he insisted on the ruling philosophy of "bringing manufacturing back to the United States" and launched trade wars against China many times. In 2018, Trump instructed American representatives to impose tariffs on goods imported from China, and the Sino-US trade war began. In this war without smoke, China and the United States fought fiercely. Many people began to study the development trend of Sino-US relations and have a heated discussion on whether China and the United States can decouple. However, on November 15, 2023, Xi Jinping, President of the People's Republic of China, had a meeting with Biden, the president of the United States in Filoli Manor, San Francisco, USA, China and the United States have reached a consensus in many fields and aspects, which has attracted worldwide attention. The development of Sino-US relations is the focus of world attention, among which the development of Sino-US trade relations is an important factor affecting Sino-US relations. Since the founding of New China, Sino-US trade relations have experienced ups and downs, with cooperation in hostility and friction in communication. Employment is the biggest livelihood, stable employment, and, trade and employment has become an important topic in contemporary international trade research, and the relationship between trade and employment is different in different countries and regions [1]. For some countries, the prosperity of trade may bring positive effects on labor employment, while for other countries, the prosperity of trade may lead to negative effects on labor employment. As far as the information is concerned, a large number of domestic documents have thoroughly studied the background, changes, trends, and prospects of Sino-US trade development, and there is still much room for research on the impact of Sino-US trade development on labor employment. This paper will sort out and sort out the development of Sino-US trade, study its impact on the labor employment market, and then explore the balance of interests between Sino-US trade development and employment development, grasp the relationship between trade development and employment, stabilize employment while developing trade reasonably, and build a solid foundation for people's livelihood.

2. Current situation of trade between China and the United States

Nowadays, the connections between countries around the world are constantly strengthening, and even under the impact of anti-globalization and unilateralism, economic globalization is still developing in depth. No country can leave international trade, completely independent of the international division of labor and trade, achieve complete self-sufficiency, and thrive.

In the context of economic globalization, as two major economies, China and the United States, their trade relations and development have always been a hot topic of global concern. This section of this article will elaborate on the current development status of China-US trade relations in recent years.

The current trade between China and the United States shows strong complementarity and dependence, with frequent trade exchanges between the two sides. The United States is one of China's largest trading countries, and the bilateral trade volume between China

* Corresponding author: 1910841104@mail.sit.edu.cn

and the United States continues to expand, increasing from 2.451 billion US dollars in 1979 to 587.62 billion US dollars in 2020, an increase of nearly 238 times in 41 years. The 2021 bilateral trade data released by the General Administration of Customs of China shows that even against the backdrop of many restrictive policies imposed on Sino-US trade, the total trade volume between China and the United States still reached a historic high - from the perspective of total trade volume, the total trade volume between China and the United States reached 755.645 billion US dollars in 2021. Among them, China imported $179.531 billion from the United States and exported $576.114 billion to the United States. From the perspective of complementarity, China is a typical developing country, an industrial powerhouse with a complete industrial system, and its most typical feature is "large and comprehensive", As a developed country, the United States has a technological advantage, and its manufacturing industry is mostly high-end. The commodity trade between the two countries is both complementary and competitive. At the same time, China is an important foreign investment market for the United States. The United States has technological advantages and numerous high-tech products. China has abundant labor resources and low costs. American companies investing in China can reduce costs and enhance their international competitiveness with the reduced costs. China utilizes American investment to obtain technological and financial support, thereby improving its technological level and enhancing its strength [2].

At present, there are continuous trade frictions between China and the United States. Since March 2018, the trade frictions between China and the United States have officially begun. The United States has repeatedly provoked trade disputes and initiated tariff measures on Chinese goods, and China has also implemented countermeasures against the United States [2]. Trade frictions are gradually showing characteristics of diversification, comprehensiveness, and concealment; In addition, the politicization of economic and trade issues has led to investment protectionism in developed countries such as the United States, mainly targeting emerging markets and developing countries, to protect emerging advantageous industries such as steel, automobiles, communication equipment, and chemical products. The imperfect foreign trade management system in our country and political factors in the United States have become the reasons for trade friction [3].

From the various data on Sino-US trade and the development of Sino-US trade relations, the current situation has the historical characteristics of the development of Sino-US trade relations, with constant friction between the two sides. However, the degree of trade dependence is extremely high and cannot be easily decoupled. Meanwhile, looking at the current situation, it is in line with the general trend of the development of Sino-US trade relations, with fluctuations in stability and a tendency towards stability after fluctuations.

3. Sino-US trade development relations fluctuated locally and were generally stable

On the whole, Sino-US trade relations show twists and turns and spiral development trends. First of all, China and the United States have close trade relations. As of 2007, according to Chinese statistics, the United States is China's largest trading partner, and according to US statistics, China is the second largest trading partner of the United States [4]. By 2017, the trade data between the two sides fluctuated slightly. The United States has become China's second-largest trading partner, the fifth-largest source of imports, and the largest export market. China is also the second-largest trading partner, the largest source of imports, and the third-largest export market of the United States [5]. According to the data, the trade between China and the United States is close and stable. From 2007 to 2017, after ten years, the trade between China and the United States still accounts for a large proportion of each other's total trade, showing a stable trend, reflecting the interdependent economic and trade relations between the two countries. Today, although the United States has launched trade wars with China many times, it is obvious that it is still difficult to "decouple" Sino-US trade relations. At the beginning of the founding of New China, the United States imposed a blockade on China; Nowadays, with the rise of anti-globalization and new trade protectionism, the trade between the two countries is facing many difficulties, but it is still very close and difficult to "decouple". So how did Sino-US trade relations develop? The following summarizes and combs the views of some scholars.

The development of Sino-US trade can be divided into several stages. Yang Zhihuang and Yang Nanlong believed that Sino-US trade is characterized by "long-term politicization", "long-term friction", "asymmetry" and "complementary competition", and the development of Sino-US trade relations from 1949 to 2019 can be divided into six stages. They are the "freezing isolation period" (1949-1970), the "thawing and ice breaking period" (1971-1978), the "growth honeymoon period" (1979-1988), the "fluctuation rising period" (1989-2000), "the golden period of joining WTO" (2001-2016) and "head-on confrontation period" (2017-2016). During the "frozen isolation period", due to the intensification of the Cold War between the United States and the Soviet Union, the United States adopted various means, such as strict trade control with China and prohibiting import and export trade with China, to block the new China; During the thawing and ice-breaking period, the United States was deeply mired in the Vietnam War, which led to one after another domestic anti-war voice. At this time, the hegemony between the United States and the Soviet Union was in a stalemate, and the United States did not have an advantage. At this time, the relationship between China and the Soviet Union deteriorated after the Treasure Island incident in 1969. During this period, the relaxation of relations and trade development between China and the United States was in the interest of both sides, thus breaking the 21-year isolation, relaxing restrictions on China by the United States, and greatly increasing the trade volume between China and the United States. From 1979 to 1988, Sino-U.S. trade relations entered the honeymoon period of growth. After the formal establishment of diplomatic relations between China and the United States in 1979, economic and trade cooperation between China and the United States expanded, and Sino-US trade developed rapidly. After the disintegration of the Soviet Union, the United States lost a big threat, China lost its value of balancing the Soviet Union, Sino-US trade relations declined, a series of proposed agreements were canceled, and sanctions were imposed on China. The two sides held several rounds of negotiations on MFN treatment, a period of rising fluctuations. Sino-US trade relations faced many problems and challenges, but the areas of cooperation continued to expand and economic exchanges continued to deepen. In the golden age of China's entry into WTO, competition and cooperation coexist in Sino-US economic and trade relations, while friction and cooperation coexist. In the period of confrontation that began in 2017, the United States kept pressing, and China was forced to deal with it [6]. The author believes that this study carefully divides the stages of Sino-US trade development, completely combs the context of Sino-US trade development, and reflects the characteristics and changes in different periods. However, the division is more general, and the development of Sino-US relations is observed from a macro perspective, and the influence of events on the development of relations is not analyzed in detail. At the same time, the basis for division and the signs of transformation are not clarified.

Ding Xiayang divided Sino-US trade after 1949 into three stages. One is the comprehensive isolation stage marked by the United States' comprehensive embargo on China in November 1950, which lasted from 1950 to 1969. The second is the limited recovery stage with the Nixon administration's announcement of the partial lifting of the ban on trade with China in July 1969; The third is the all-round development stage that took China's reform and opening-up in 1977 as an opportunity and continued to this day [7]. This study, marked by specific events, analyzes in detail the influence of specific events on the changes and even turning points of Sino-US relations and divides the development stages on this basis.

Song Hong thinks that the development of Sino-US trade is ups and downs, which is roughly divided into the interruption of economic and trade relations (1951). The Embargo, the period of mutual isolation (1952-1971); The deepening period of recovery and mutual communication (1972-present) [8]. Based on the data of trade itself, this study analyzes the development of Sino-US trade relations through a large number of data.

The development of Sino-US trade relations is long and has ups and downs. There are exchanges in competition and frictions in cooperation. It is not static, but it is difficult to make substantial changes. For the sake of various interests, Sino-US trade will be stable for a long time. As Song Guoyou believes, after the collision of the Trump administration, Sino-U.S. economic and trade relations still show the fundamental characteristics of strong complementarity and mutual benefit. Among the new development characteristics of Sino-US economic and trade relations, re-integration, strong competition and weak decoupling are the three most typical trends. As for Sino-US trade relations, this paper holds that their development is generally stable, but there are local fluctuations. Throughout the development process, there was no extreme confrontation or deep cooperation except for the isolation of Sino-US trade relations in the early days of the founding of the People's Republic of China, and the overall trend is stable. This paper divides the development of Sino-US trade relations into three stages. First, from 1949 to 1979, before the formal establishment of diplomatic relations between China and the United States, there were few economic and trade ties between the two countries, and after 21 years of " no contact ", economic and trade exchanges were not frequent. Second, from 1979 to 2017, Sino-US trade exchanges were frequent, and Sino-US trade relations fluctuated, but the overall development was relatively moderate. Third, from 2017 to today, the development of Sino-US trade relations has been severely collided and hindered.

4. The influence of Sino-US trade relations development on labor employment

Employment is the biggest livelihood, and trade has a direct impact on employment. Trade affects supply and demand, thus affecting related jobs, enterprises, and industries. The development of labor employment is closely related to the development of trade. This chapter discusses the relationship between the development of Sino-US trade relations and labor employment by summarizing the influence of the development of Sino-US trade relations on labor employment.

China and the United States are highly complementary in industrial structure, and the two countries have complementary advantages in economic and trade cooperation, forming a large-scale and extensive international division of labor cooperation [9], international division of labor can promote industrial development, help enterprises expand their scale, increase employment resources, and stimulate employment to play a positive role in employment. Li Kaijie takes the wage level as the breakthrough point mainly studies the influence of export trade on labor employment, and thinks that export trade has a significant regional labor market effect, which will affect the wage level of floating labor. Mainly reflected in the following four aspects: First, the scale of export trade has a significant positive impact on the wage level of migrant workers, from benefiting low-income groups to benefiting high-income groups. Second, export trade widens the wage gap within the floating labor force. Third, the impact of export trade on the wages of migrant workers gradually decreases with the increase in age. Fourthly, export trade has a positive effect on the wage level of migrant workers with different inflow durations, and this effect increases with the increase of inflow duration [10]. The author believes that the scholar's research clearly and intuitively analyzes the influence mechanism of trade on labor employment in terms of wage level.

Some scholars believe that the development of Sino-US trade hurts labor employment. This paper mainly sorts out the impact on labor employment caused by the current Sino-US trade relations. Song Guoyou believes that in terms of employment, due to tariff pressure, some domestic manufacturing industries have experienced outflows, which has led to the outward transfer of corresponding jobs [11]. Zhou Shen and Yu Linke believe that after World War II, trade liberalization became the dominant orientation of trade policies of major economies in the world. In recent years, anti-globalization thoughts have emerged, and American trade policy has gradually shown the color of trade protectionism. This change in trade policy has worsened Sino-US trade relations and hurt China's labor market. Specifically, on the one hand, the U.S. government, to protect its enterprises and workers, will curb the import of some industries through trade policy measures, especially by reducing exports from China, which will directly reduce employment in China. It has inhibited the export of Chinese enterprises to the United States and then destroyed some of the original export employment pulling effects. On the other hand, the shift in American trade policy has brought about an increase in the uncertainty of trade relations between China and the United States, which will hurt the export decision-making of Chinese enterprises and impact China's employment by affecting the business decision-making of Chinese enterprises [12].

The development of Sino-US trade has positive and negative effects on the employment of both sides. When the relationship is good, the positive effect is greater than the negative effect. When the relationship is good, it will promote industrial development, expand the industrial scale, and develop high-tech industries in the United States. When the Sino-US trade relationship is good, it will accelerate the industrial transformation and upgrading in China, which will help increase employment, such as foreign trade and product production. At the same time, it is also conducive to improving the quality of labor employment and improving the overall employment level. When the relationship deteriorates, it will lead to a series of negative effects, such as the increase of foreign trade costs and the decrease of profits, which will lead to the contraction of the foreign trade industry, the difficulty in developing related industries in this field, the decline of employment rate and wage level in this related industry, and people are not optimistic about employment in this industry. But there are also positive effects, capital and labor will flow to other industries, thus stimulating the development of employment in other industries.

5. Conclusion

As for the future development of Sino-US trade relations, this paper holds that the United States is bound to suppress China to prevent China from profiting more from trade, and China will not sit still and fight back. Therefore, the future development of Sino-US trade relations will not be "calm" and it is difficult to deepen cooperation greatly, "by going up one flight of stairs". However, the development of Sino-US trade today has a long history, and the industrial dependence and complementarity between the two countries are high, so it is difficult to reduce the relationship.

In the face of the changes in Sino-US trade relations, society should pay full attention to them, and adjust countermeasures in time while conforming to the changing trend, and make countermeasures. For example, when the relationship is improving, foreign trade enterprises can expand investment and production, and relevant employees can tend to develop in the direction of trade, especially trade with the United States; When the relationship deteriorates, enterprises reduce their investment in trade with the United States, reduce the scale or avoid the trade of certain specific commodities, and reduce losses. The employment of related labor can develop in other trade directions or transfer to other industries, thus maintaining the relative stability of labor employment and building a solid foundation for people's livelihood. At the same time, grasp the influence of labor employment on the development of Sino-US trade relations and promote the stable and positive development of Sino-US trade relations.

References:

1. X. P. Xu, M, Wang. Journal of Hebei University of Economics and Business, 43(06), 83-91 (2022).
2. K. Wang, Modern business, (23): 128-131 (2023).
3. H. Zhang, C. L. Zhan,Modern commerce and trade and industry, 21(24): 105-106 (2009).
4. S. J. Zhou. Research on international issues, (02), 7-9 (2007).
5. strategy, 33(06), 192-195 (2017).
6. Y. H. Yang, Yang Nanlong. Journal of Hebei University of Economics and Business, 41(02), 45-53 (2020).
7. X. Y. Ding. Slim, (02), 62-73+184+218 (2023).
8. S. Hong. International Economic Review, (06), 74-99+6 (2019).
9. Song Guoyou. Fudan Journal (Social Science Edition), 62(04), 125-131 (2020).
10. K. J. Li. Industrial Economic Research, (01): 99-113 (2022).
11. G. Y. Song. Fudan Journal (Social Science Edition), 63(05): 176-182 (2021).
12. S. Zhou, L. K. Yu. Journal of Jiangsu Administration College, (01), 42-48 (2023).

The influence of unsure trade policy for China

Xiao Bao[1], Zelin Cai[2, *], Xiaozhe Liu[3]
[1] School of Economics, Zhongnan University of Economic and Law, Wuhan, China
[2]Nanjing-Bond International College, Nanjing, China
[3]College of Economics and Administration, Hunan Institute of Science and Technology, Yueyang, China

Abstract. With the complex world political economic situation, the influence of unsure trade policy for trade, microeconomics, and macroeconomics gained a lot of attraction, which become an up-to-date topic in the political research industry in recent years. This article from the microeconomic of a Chinese entrepreneur perspective, which based on introduces the concept of the unsure trade policy (TPU), its theoretical mechanism, and empirical measurement to have further analysis of unsure political trade ' s influence on Chinese companies: First of all, the influence of trade policy uncertainty on the export of Chinese enterprises includes four aspects: the export scale of enterprises, the quality and price of export products, and the technical complexity of export; Second is that the Chinese companies deciding TPU influence, the result may wait and delay investment, evaluate and carefully choose investment projects, adjust supply chains, prudently treat overseas investment and choose to stabilize the market. The end of the article concludes the influence of unsure political trade for Chinese entrepreneurs and expanding the future situation.

1 Introduction

With President Donald Trump announcing retreat from TPP, the UK's exit from the EU, and the crisis of European immigration, these events happened, the international political and economic situation became more and more complex, and instability increased significantly. From an international trade perspective, the China-American trade war, these kinds of reverse globalization events gradually upgrade. It has become a popular topic for observers to analyze whether should invest. With the flourish of trade protection, Chinese trade policy faces an increasing majority of uncontrol situations every year, which affected the stability of Chinese companies' exports seriously. While trade policy unsure (TPU) exists in international trade widely, trade friction or operational risks will directly or indirectly influence the export companies ' distribution ways or production decisions, etc. In this way, the TPU is closely related to the export behavior of enterprises, and relevant research needs to be improved.

The existing essay on trade freedom, exchange rate fluctuations, financing restrictions, and a lot of other perspectives talks about export expansion and export upgrade in different ways, but the essay on TPU is not enough. As a result, this article from microeconomics connects the TPU with Chinese entrepreneurs to use a new version to explain the behavior of Chinese companies' exports, to help the companies more systematically, understand the entrepreneurs' export problems well-rounded under the TPU background, to know the future direction of the companies.

2 An overview of TPU research

2.1. The original research

With global political and economic changes, TPU already become an important issue in the international trade research industry. TPU is a type of economic trade uncertainty. Economic trade uncertainty includes trade policy, financial policy, currency policy, industry policy, etc. Most trade perspectives are always mainly focused on the effects of actual trade policies on trade prices and flows. But in recent years, some researchers have tended to change their concentrations, and begin to pay more attention to researching some connected questions about TPU, which will have an important influence on some participating international trade companies, then further affect the export trade and other relevant economic variates.

The academic research on the uncertainty of trade policy is gradually deepening. The creators of this are Professor Handley from the University of Michigan and Professor Limao from the University of Maryland [1-3]. They started talking about the effects of TPU after coming up with a method to quantify it. These studies fall into two categories of perspectives: the first examines the direct effects of TPU on trade and other economic variables, while the second looks at the effects of TPU reduction brought about by a variety of factors, particularly trade agreements, on trade and other economic variables. The other is researching how trade and other economic variables are affected when TPU is reduced for a variety of reasons, particularly trade

* Corresponding author: 201010130325@stu.swmu.edu.cn

agreements. The impact of TPU on Chinese enterprises is the main topic of this article.

2.2 The definition of TPU

Some foreign professors started to discuss how to define TPU, and what is uncertainty. From an economic perspective, Jurado& Ludvigson believe that uncertainty is that some policy fluctuations or future economics cannot be predicted [4]. Handley & Limao extend this mechanism to TPU. What is TPU? Handley believes that when trade policies are likely to change, especially when they are likely to become worse, they will significantly affect enterprises' decisions on irreversible investment [1]. In particular, Handley and Limao contended that, about the United States' Permanent Normal Trade Partnership with China, TPU pertains to the degree to which Chinese export companies' earnings will decline if China is not awarded the MFN designation [3].

This topic also attracts a lot of domestic trade professors' attention and followers, which makes it a popular research topic. Tong Jiadong and Li Shengqi defined TPU as a state without rules and legal protection in inter-country trade [5]. Nonetheless, TPU, according to Yu Miaojie and Zhu Guanghui, refers to potential changes in trade policy that are not predictable by the institutions or businesses that are in place at the moment [6]. Begin Match, according to Gong Lianmei and Qian Xuefeng , is the fourth source in the source list. submitted to the University of Birmingham on September 11, 2019 uncertainty is defined as the state of ambiguity around investment environment information, encompassing policy, economic, and Begin Match uncertainties to source 4 in the list of sources. Factor market price, product market price, end match, and begin match to source 4 in the source list were sent to the University of Birmingham on September 11, 2019: submitted on 2019-09-11 to the University of Birmingham; additional end match details [7].

According to a tidy analysis of the essay, it is clear to summarize the commonality, change, unknowability, unpredictability, irreversibility, and loss between different people's different expressions, and the concept of TPU. Based on these words, the whole article makes the concept and definition of TPU: In the absence of rules and laws, future trade policy fluctuations that cannot be predicted by institutions, enterprises, or other economic variables may cause certain economic losses.

3 Research basis

3.1 Theoretical mechanism

The study of TPU has its origins in the general study of uncertainty in the economic environment, and the focus of this study of uncertainty in the economic environment has been to explore the impact of uncertainty in the external environment on the investment decisions of firms. The theoretical mechanism by which TPU affects trade is derived from the mechanism by which external environmental uncertainty affects firms' investment as articulated by Bernanke [8] and Dixit [9], who are pioneers in the study of uncertainty in the economic environment, and who laid out the theoretical foundations of corporate investment decisions under environmental uncertainty. Among them, Bernanke explored the risks caused by uncertainty in the economic environment (including uncertainty in the market prices of products and factors, and the operating state of the macroeconomy) [8], while Dixit explored the non-recoverable nature of firms' market entry costs [9].

According to their idea, a company should begin matching to source 13 in the source list if its investment costs are irrecoverable sunk costs and its external environment is unpredictable. submitted on September 7, 2022, to the University of Bristol will postpone investing until the business climate improves or the investment risk is removed. Put simply, a firm's investment is delayed by uncertainty in the external environment Match. In the case of uncertainty in the external environment, enterprises are faced with the choice of investing immediately or postponing investment: the cost of investing immediately is that once the external environment deteriorates, its return may be lower than the cost of investment; the cost of postponing investment is that if the external environment does not deteriorate, it will lose the benefits of the current investment. Enterprises make decisions based on whether the enterprise expects future returns higher than the cost of investment, it will choose to invest immediately, otherwise, it will choose to postpone investment. Uncertainty in the external environment can cause the firm's expected future returns to be lower than the cost of investment, thus causing the firm to postpone investment.

Handley and Handley & Limao extend the application of this mechanism to the impact of TPU on trade [1-3]. At this point, the external environmental uncertainty evolves into TPU, and the firm's investment is an investment in the export market. Under external TPU, firms face the choice of entering export markets immediately or delaying entry. It decides that if the firm's expected future earnings are higher than its cost of entering the export market, it will choose to enter the export market immediately, otherwise, it will choose to delay entry. TPU, on the other hand, can cause a firm's expected future earnings to be lower than its cost of entering the export market, which can lead to a firm's delayed entry into the export market.

According to the above mechanism, when TPU increases, that is, when the probability of an unfavorable change in trade policy increases or the magnitude of the change increases, the firm's expected returns will decrease. In contrast, the firm's cost of entering the export market will not change, which will lead to the fact that only a smaller number of firms with their efficiency higher than a certain threshold will be able to enter the export market, and some of the less-efficient ones that have already entered the export market firms in the export market will exit the export market. If TPU is reduced, this leads to the opposite result. In sum, TPU affects exports by influencing the choices of firms in entering and exiting export markets (trade breadth, i.e. the margin of expansion of trade).

3.2 Empirical measurement

TPU is measured by an empirical measure of TPU, which is established based on its theoretical mechanism. According to its theoretical mechanism, the impact of TPU depends on the probability of an unfavorable change in trade policy and the magnitude of its change. The empirical measure of TPU has the following two main methods: text extraction method and difference estimation method.

The text extraction method focuses on measuring the probability of an unfavorable change in trade policy. The metric for this approach is represented by the "uncertainty index". This metric is derived from the "economic policy uncertainty index" constructed by Baker et al using the frequency of news reports approach [10], which was extended by Handley & Limao to construct the "TPU index" [11]. The basic idea is to combine the news reports of newspapers or news websites in a certain period that mention "trade", "economy", "policy", "laws and regulations", "uncertainty", and "TPU index". The idea is to standardize the number of articles in a certain period in a newspaper or news website that mention the keywords "trade", "economy", "policy", "laws and regulations", "uncertainty", "deficit", and so on. This is a relatively intuitive measure, but the problem is that the accuracy of the metrics may be greatly affected by the fact that the selection of newspapers, news websites, and keywords is highly subjective and may not accurately reflect changes in a specific trade policy and that there are problems with the multiple distribution and re-dissemination of news stories.

The second difference-in-differences estimation method focuses on measuring the magnitude of unfavorable changes in trade policy for firms. This method uses the difference in tariff changes as a measure of TPU, and this measure is widely used. For example, Handley states that TPU arises from the difference between WTO members' tariff ceilings (bound tariff) and actual tariffs (applied tariffs), which may be raised to the tariff ceilings, and therefore the difference between the two is used as a measure of tariff uncertainty [1]. Handley & Limao note that TPU stems from the possibility that Portugal loses the preferential tariffs it enjoyed before EC accession and returns to general MFN tariffs, and therefore measures tariff uncertainty in terms of the difference between the two [2]. Handley&Limao, and numerous others discussing the uncertainty of U.S. trade policy towards China before China acceded to the WTO point out that this uncertainty stems from the possibility that the U.S. could remove China's MFN trade treatment and raise its tariffs on China to the historical Smooth-Hawley tariffs, and therefore use the difference between the two as a measure of tariff uncertainty [3].

The second measure mentioned above sometimes directly uses the algebraic difference between the two tariffs and sometimes makes some technical adjustments according to the theoretical model of the article. Yu Miaojie and Zhu Huihuang, on the other hand, introduce these metrics with technical adjustments as a separate method [6]. However, no matter what the specific metrics are, the core idea is the same, which is to measure the size of the magnitude of possible tariff changes. This measure is simple, easy to calculate, and more accurate, which is significantly better than the first method, so its application is more common.

3.3 The impact of TPU on Chinese firms' exports

As the direct target of TPU, and as the world's largest manufacturing exporter, China has a strong export base and market diversity, so Chinese exporters are usually able to adapt to different trade policy environments. Still, in general, TPU will have a certain negative impact on the exports of Chinese enterprises, but China is capable of adapting to and coping with such challenges. Many scholars have conducted in-depth research on the impact of TPU on enterprise exports, and the research direction mainly focuses on the following three directions: the scale of enterprise exports, the quality and price of enterprise exports, and the technical complexity of enterprise exports.

First, Wei Xi conducted an empirical study on the impact of TPU on China's exports, taking into account the type of enterprise. The study found that TPU significantly negatively affects China's enterprises' export behavior, which is specifically manifested as follows. The study was based on China's enterprise level and used customs data, industrial enterprise data, and WTO tariff data from 2007 to 2016. A more notable detrimental effect on Chinese businesses' export values, as well as the kinds and quantities of goods they export [12]. Wang Yannan et al. attempted to explain China's export expansion and export upgrading from the new perspective of TPU based on the policy background of China's conclusion of free trade agreements. They did this by introducing TPU into the quality heterogeneity model and reasoning out the equation of the relationship between TPU on export expansion and export upgrading. They found that a decrease in TPU is conducive to the expansion of the export scale and that TPU reduction has become a new strategy for Chinese enterprises looking to expand their exports [13].

Secondly, in terms of the quality and price of export products, Wei Yueyue Antelope and Zhang Hongsheng used the double difference method and triple difference method to find that when TPU is reduced, State-owned enterprises, private enterprises, and foreign-funded enterprises have seen a significant decrease in the export prices of their products., so it can promote the enhancement of the productivity of enterprises, and the construction of stable foreign trade environment is an important way of stabilizing the growth of foreign trade, and when trade friction is intensified The negative impact of rising uncertainty can be hedged by accelerating domestic reforms [14]. Sun Lin and Zhou

Kechuan conducted an empirical test by using nearly 15 years of micro enterprise-level data for the China-ASEAN Free Trade Area, pointing out that the decline in TPU is conducive to the introduction of advanced technology and equipment by enterprises, thus further improving the quality of product exports [15].

Finally, in terms of the technical complexity of enterprise exports, Liu Meixiu found that the decline in TPU has a significant contribution to the improvement of the technical complexity of enterprise imports, and this effect changes with the size of the enterprise, its age, whether it exports, and the different forms of enterprise ownership, and the decline in TPU affects the improvement of the technical complexity of imported technology through the export effect of the enterprise, including the export-induced scale-up effect and the export learning effect [16]. Han Huixia put forward the impact of trading partner unsure trade policy on the technical complexity of a country's high-tech industry exports, the study found that the rise of trading partner unsure trade policy will inhibit the deepening of the complexity of a country's high-tech industry exports, and the unsure trade policy caused by the technical barriers to trade initiated by the trading partner on a country's high-tech industry export technical complexity is more than that of the tariff changes brought about by the unsure trade policy.

3.4 The impact of TPU for Chinese entrepreneurs on investment decision

The general study of uncertainty in the economic environment, which focuses on the influence of uncertainty in the external environment on business investment decisions, is the source of research on TPU. Chinese corporate investment decision-makers are significantly impacted by TPU. The impact of TPU on Chinese corporate investment decisions has been examined in prior research using four different influencing elements. They are as follows: modify supply chains, assess and pick investment projects carefully, postpone investment and wait, and use caution when selecting stable foreign investment markets.

First, TPU increases the prudence of enterprises in investment decision-making, which leads to enterprises choosing to postpone or cancel originally planned investment projects, because decision-makers of enterprises worry that the change of trade policy will adversely affect the feasibility and return of investment projects, so enterprises will choose to wait and see and delay investment. However, prudent decision-making does not mean that enterprises give up opportunities altogether. Enterprises can also cope with uncertainty through flexibility and agility, for example, by diversifying trading partners, adjusting product mix, and exploring emerging markets to diversify risks and seek growth opportunities.

Secondly, TPU increases the risk of investment. TPU will lead to changes in market access conditions, tariff increases, export restrictions, etc., which will have an impact on the feasibility and expected returns of an enterprise's investment projects. Enterprises will assess the policy risks and choose investment projects carefully to minimize the risks. However, enterprises can mitigate the investment risks associated with TPU in several ways, for example, they can diversify their trade to reduce their dependence on a particular market or trading partner, and they can look for more stable investment opportunities, long-term partners and reliable suppliers.

Third, TPU can prompt firms to reassess their supply chain strategies. Increased TPU can lead to trade frictions or export restrictions, so in some cases firms may need to adjust their supply chains to reduce their dependence on markets, thereby reducing the impact of policy uncertainty on their business.

Fourth, increased TPU may be influenced by geopolitical factors in different countries, i.e. policy uncertainty may increase geopolitical risks, including intergovernmental tensions, trade frictions, and sanctions against foreign firms, which would force firms to be more cautious about investing abroad and encourage them to choose stable and relatively low-risk markets.

4 Conclusion

TPU refers to the uncertainty of the degree or probability of possible changes in trade policy in the future, trade policy is a policy measure formulated by national and regional governments to manage and adjust international trade activities, including tariffs, trade subsidies, changes in trade barriers, etc. TPU can originate from government adjustments, trade frictions, changes in tariff policy, and other factors. In this paper, we sort out the literature on the impact of TPU on Chinese enterprises and study the impact of TPU on Chinese enterprises from the impact of TPU on Chinese enterprises' exports and the impact of TPU on Chinese enterprises' investment decisions.

Chinese enterprises will make the following four adjustments in response to the increase in TPU: increase innovation investment and technological upgrading, adjust investment choices, strengthen international cooperation, and policy trade agreement adjustments.

Firstly, as TPU will have an impact on the exports of Chinese enterprises, Chinese enterprises will, in the face of this challenge, increase their investment in innovation and technological upgrading to improve the competitiveness of their products and reduce their dependence on imports, and to cope with the more intense international trade competition by improving production efficiency, product quality, and technological level. Chinese firms can work closely with the government to better cope with and respond to the impact of policy uncertainty while maintaining and increasing their competitiveness in an uncertain environment to seek more development and growth.

At the same time, Chinese companies will adjust their investment choices, turning their attention to the domestic market or looking for other relatively stable markets to reduce the impact of TPU on their business. As China strengthens its policy of guiding domestic demand and diversifying its market layout, Chinese companies are likely to continue to look for opportunities in the domestic market and increase their investments in emerging markets and developing countries. At the same time, Chinese companies need to establish effective investment risk management mechanisms to cope with risks and enhance internal resource allocation to ensure changes in an uncertain environment.

Secondly, in the face of TPU and the challenge of unilateralism, Chinese enterprises will advocate strengthening international cooperation and support multilateralism by actively participating in and promoting the negotiation and signing of free trade agreements, establishing more trade partnerships, and strengthening economic cooperation with other countries and regions, thereby creating more opportunities and market access for Chinese enterprises. Reduce dependence on a single market and explore new international markets to share risks and find more opportunities in more diversified markets. At the same time, we should actively transmit our national values and business ethics and maintain confidence in our market based on a good corporate reputation to increase the trust of domestic and foreign consumers.

Finally, in the face of the development trend of the global economic community, Chinese enterprises need to make changes in policies and trade agreements, and actively adjust and plan according to the maximization of benefits and the needs of multinational markets. In addition, governments need to break down trade barriers between countries and actively promote economic integration, including changes in tariffs and trade agreements, to open to the principle of mutual benefit in trade.

Authors Contribution

All the authors contributed equally and their names were listed in alphabetical order.

References

1. K. Handley, Journal of International Economics, 94(1), 50-66 (2014).
2. K. Handley, N. Limao, American Economic Journal-Policy ,7(4), 189-222 (2015).
3. K. Handley, N.Limao, American Economic Review, 104(12), 2731-2783 (2017).
4. K. Jurado, S.C. Ludvigson, S.Ng, American Economic Review, (3), 117-216 (2015).
5. J. D. Tong, S.Q. Li, American Economic Review, (06), 25-32(2015).
6. M. J. Yu, H. H. Zhu, Journal of Chang'an University (Social Science Edition), 21(01), 1-8 (2019).
7. L. M. Gong, X. F. Qian, Economic dynamics, (06), 106-116 (2018).
8. B. S. Bernanke Irreversibility, The Quarterly Journal of Economics, 98(1): 85-106 (1983).
9. A. K. Dixit, Journal of Political Economy, 97 (3), 620-638 (1989).
10. S. R. Baker et al. Quarterly Journal of Economics 131(4), 1593-1636 (2016).
11. K. Handley, N. Limao, Economics and Policy in the Age of Trump, (2017).
12. Q. Wei. Price Monthly Journal, (07), 46-50(2017).
13. Y. N. Wang, H. C. Wang, H. Su, Audit and economic research, 35(01), 111-119 (2020).
14. Y. L. Wei, H.S. Zhang. Economic science, (01), 57-68 (2019).
15. L. Sun, K. X. Zhou, International economic and trade exploration, 36(08), 97-112 (2020).
16. M. X. Liu, W. Xu, X. M. Zhu, et al. Macroeconomic research, (12), 70-83(2020).

China-US Trade War Unveiled: Analyzing the Root Causes and Effects

Paerhati Maidinuer*

School of International Economics, China Foreign Affairs University, Beijing, 100000, China

Abstract. The China-US trade war has emerged as one of the most significant and complex issue in contemporary international trade. It affects not only the cooperation between the two countries, but also the global economy. Therefore, the analysis of China-US trade war has significant meaning in understanding the global trading system and making economic forecasts. This paper analyses the causes of trade war from the perspective of trade deficit, globalization, and property rights, indicating that the US started trade war for its own interest and felt the stress from the development of China. Apart from causes, the effects are also crucial. This paper analyses the import and export volume, investment effect, economic effect, and political effect, showing that the impacts of China-US trade war are widespread. Based on the analysis above, this paper gives several suggestions in the hope that China and US could strengthen exchange and cooperation, reduce trade disputes, and contribute to the development of global economy.

1 Introduction

Nowadays, the global economy is recovering with the end of the COVID-19 pandemics, but the economic growth is slowing down. According to the International Finance Forum (IFF)'s Global Finance and Development Report 2023, the global economy is expected to grow by 3.1% in 2023, down from 3.4% in 2022. Developed economies are expected to grow by 1.5% and developing economies by 4.1%.

At the same time, due to geopolitical conflicts and inflation and other factors, the development of global economy is full of uncertainties. A growing number of countries are using trade restrictive measures in the name of "national security", and the global economy is experiencing the countercurrent of "deglobalization" [1].

As one of the most important economic and trade relations in the world, trade frictions between China and the US are bound to affect the situation of global economic development.

This paper analyses the China-US trade war from the import and export volume, the relationship between the two countries, and the economic development of the two countries. Most importantly, this paper gives some reasonable and feasible suggestions based on the analysis.

According to the existing literature, whether in trade, investment or financial relations, the decoupling trend between China and the US is expanding, and the degree of interdependence is decreasing [2].

Some scholars believe that trade frictions are detrimental to both China and the US, along with the escalation of trade frictions, the losses to both countries would be greater [3, 4].

Many other countries apart from China and the US are being directly involved. For developing countries, on the one hand, China-US trade war have had a great negative impact on global economic integration and on the export and employment of developing countries. On the other hand, it has brought new opportunities to developing countries, including attracting foreign investment, and expanding export markets.

Therefore, this article explores the causes and effects of trade frictions and puts forward countermeasures and suggestions.

2 China – US trade war

2.1 Background

The relations between China and the US, as one of the most significant bilateral relationship, have been developing in frictions and twists since the establishment of trade between the two countries.

The China-US relations began to take shape and have entered a new stage of development since the establishment of People's Republic of China in 1949. However, the relationship between the two countries was strained during the Cold War, and the outbreak of the Korean War in 1950 further soured the China-US relations. Meanwhile, there was little cooperation between the two nations in various fields because of their divergent ideologies and moral standards.

Since China's reform and opening up, China-US relations have greatly improved. In 1978, Deng Xiaoping visited the US, opening a new chapter in China-US relations. Since then, there has been a growth in the two

* Corresponding author: maidi@mail.cfau.edu.cn

nations' economic and trade, cultural and educational interactions as well as collaboration. With the signing of many agreements, such as August 17th Bulletin and September 3rd Statement, the relationship between the two countries has become more stable and friendly [5, 6].

However, due to the diverse conflicts of interests between the two sides, there are still many unstable factors in China-US relations. For instance, the scientific and technological advancements in China have garnered attention from the US. Against this backdrop, the China-US trade war broke out.

2.2 Process

In March 2018, US President Donald Trump announced tariffs on steel and aluminium imports from China, triggering the first wave of the trade dispute. Subsequently, China also imposed tariffs on some imports from the US to counter its action. There followed a period of tension as both sides started to impose tariffs on each other. Despite the trade agreement, there are still some areas of friction in China-US trade. Refer to Table 1 below, which describes the key points in time of China-US trade war.

Table 1. The process of China-US Trade War.

Time	Events
Jul, 2018	China-US Trade War begins
Dec, 2018	Call a truce in the trade war at the G20 summit
May, 2019	US adds Huawei to 'entity list'
Jan, 2020	Phase-one trade deal signed
Sept, 2020	US issues restrictions on import of Xinjiang cotton
Mar, 2023	The US Department of Commerce decided to re-exempt 352 categories of Chinese imports from tariffs
Sept, 2023	The Customs Tariff Commission of The State Council released the 12th list of goods subject to additional tariffs imposed by US

2.3 Causes

2.3.1 Reducing the US trade deficit

A trade deficit is when the value of goods and services imported by a country or region exceeds the value of goods and services exported. A trade deficit is often considered a sign of a country or region's declining economic strength, as it reflects an over-reliance on external resources and a lack of competitiveness in domestic industries.

The US has trade deficits for a long time [7]. According to the data of the US Department of Commerce in 2017, the US imports of goods and services in 2017 were $2,895.3 billion, exports were $2,329.3 billion, and the annual trade deficit was $566 billion, a new high since 2008. Among them, the trade deficit with China and Ireland are at record highs. The US government has been trying to narrow the trade deficit through various means, such as launching a trade war, promoting the return of manufacturing, and raising tariffs.

Figure 1 below shows the trade balance between China and the US from 2017 to 2022, indicating the trade balance of two countries has fluctuated with the beginning of trade war.

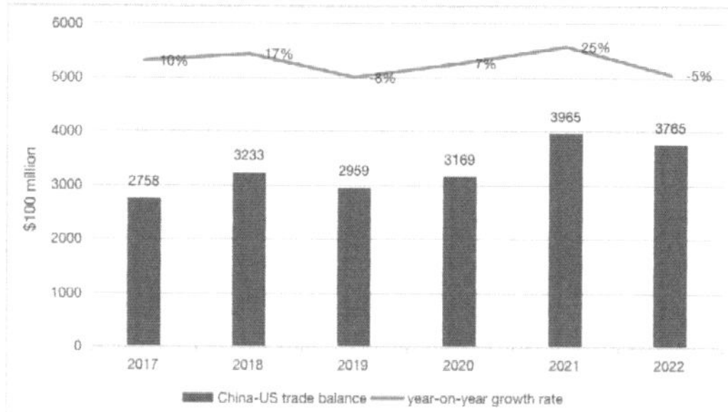

Fig. 1. China-US trade balance (Source of data: US Department of Commerce, General Administration of Customs of China; Picture credit: Original)

2.3.2 Slowing down globalization

As globalization continues, many countries have benefited greatly. For developing countries, cheap labor attracts a lot of investment and foreign companies, while for developed countries, they can enjoy low costs and accelerate economic expansion [8].

In the past, US's global advantage was concentrated in three areas, which includes industrial advantage, technological advantage, and the dollar and military hegemony. Nevertheless, these advantages are gradually disappearing with the development of globalization. Owing to globalization has boosted global trade and capital flows, it has given other countries more opportunities to participate in international markets. In addition, developing countries have pushed for local currency settlements to reduce price pressures on their exports, which has undermined the dollar's global role.

As the world's largest trading country and the second largest economy, China's development process of capital globalization has triggered concerns and reactions from Western countries, especially the US. From the beginning of President Trump campaign, he has slightly shown support for "America First" ideology and may advocate slowing down the globalization of the US. Therefore, the US launched a trade war in an attempt to decouple China-US trade, undermine the stability of the global industrial chain, and achieve its purpose of anti-globalization.

2.3.3 Protecting US property rights

The rapid development of China's economy and technology has made the US worry that China would change the world order, and President Trump and his administration have been worrying about China for it may threaten US's high-end technological property. To safeguard US's intellectual property rights, particularly in the realm of advanced technology, the US implements sanctions and restrictions on China. On August 13, 2018, the President of the US signed the Export Control Reform Act and the Foreign Investment Risk Review Modernization Act. These measures aim to reinforce restrictions on high-tech exports and limit foreign companies' access to technology through investments. Meanwhile, the $50 billions of Chinese exports that the US has imposed tariffs on are mainly targeted at the high-tech sectors outlined in the "Made in China 2025", reflecting the intention of the US to curb China's efforts to close the technological gap.

2.4 Effects

2.4.1 Import and export volume

The proportion of China-US trade in the foreign trade of the two countries has also dropped significantly. According to the data released by the General Administration of Customs of China, the trade volume between China and the US from January to July 2023 was 381.514 billion US dollars, down by 15.4% year-on-year, of which China's exports to the US fell by 18.6% to 281.655 billion US dollars, and China's imports from the US fell by 4.7% to 99.859 billion US dollars. China's trading relationships have shifted, with the US now ranking as their third largest trading partner, trailing behind the Association of Southeast Asian Nations and the European Union.

In terms of specific trade items, China-US trade in high-tech products continued to shrink. According to the statistics of the US Department of Commerce, the import and export volume of high-tech products in the US has increased in 2022, but the proportion related to China has decreased. In 2022, the US imports of high-tech products from the Chinese mainland decreased by 0.4% year-on-year, accounting for only 23.7% of its total imports. The US exports of high-tech products to the Chinese mainland also decreased by more than 30 billion yuan, a year-on-year decrease of 2.4%. Among them, the optoelectronics and information and communication industry are the largest decoupling between China and the US. The total amount of optoelectronic products exported by China to the US has gradually declined, and the total amount of optoelectronic products imported by the US has shrunk seriously. In 2016, China's total exports of optoelectronic products to the US reached 5.6 billion US dollars, and by 2022, it fell by 67.6%, and its total imports fell from 22.39% to 6.35%.

The US has been the world's largest exporter of soyabeans and China's biggest importer for a long period of time. However, after the outbreak of the China-US trade war, US soybean exports to China have also fallen. In July 2018, the US imposed 25% tariffs on $50 billions of goods shipped from China, including soybeans. In response, China has imposed 25% tariffs on $50 billions of goods shipped to the US, including soybeans. This has led to a sharp drop in soybean trade between China and the US. According to customs data, China imported only 16.73 million tons of soybeans from the US in 2018, more than 50% less than in 2017.

Due to trade friction, China and the US have to carry out trade diversion, importing other countries' goods at relatively high prices to meet their own needs. For example, US imports from China may be diverted to Mexico, while China mainly transfers imports to countries such as Brazil.

2.4.2 Investment effect

In recent years, the US has gone further and further on the road of "safety" of economic and trade issues, and its investment security review mechanism for Chinese enterprises has become increasingly strict, which has directly led to the precipitous decline of Chinese enterprises' investment in the US [9].

Moreover, trade frictions have led to an unstable investment environment, and the restrictive measures and tariff policies of the US have made foreign investors insecure about China's investment environment. Simultaneously, China's additional tariffs on US products have increased the production costs of US companies and weakened the competitiveness of US companies in the Chinese market. All of these factors ultimately led to a decline in investment inflows to China.

Large US multinational corporations are responsible for the majority of US investment in China, whereas smaller and medium-sized US companies are hesitant to include China in their future investment strategies. This also indicates that the overall level of US investment in China is lower compared to similarly sized economies in other countries.

Trade frictions between China and the US have also increased the pressure on the depreciation of the RMB exchange rate. Investors may reduce their investment in the risky currency like RMB because of the fear of trade tensions, especially under the circumstance where trade frictions may cause uncertainty. In other words, they would choose to buy more stable currencies, such as the US dollar, and this may lead to the decline of the RMB exchange rate.

2.4.3 Economic effect

China and the US are the world's two largest economies, and trade frictions between them are bound to have a significant and far-reaching impact on the global economy [9]. According to estimation by the World Bank and the International Monetary Fund (IMF), the China-US trade friction could reduce global economic growth by 0.5% to 0.8%.

Not just for the global economy, trade frictions are also detrimental to both China and the US, and with the escalation of trade frictions, the losses to both countries could be greater. The combined impact of the two rounds of trade frictions shows that the real GDP, employment, social welfare and trade of China and the US have deteriorated [10].

GDP is the core index of a country's economic activities, which reflects the total value produced by a country or region in a certain period of time. There are many factors that affect GDP. For example, the level of investment is one of the main factors affecting GDP. An increase in investment means that more funds are available for production and operation, which will promote economic development and increase GDP. The previous analysis of the trade war led to a decline in investment, which in turn affected GDP.

Trade war has an impact on the economies of China and the US by affecting their international trade. International trade refers to the cross-border exchanges and transactions of goods, services and capital between countries or regions. In 2019, the total foreign trade of the US accounted for 19.7% of GDP, while China's total foreign trade accounted for 31.87% of GDP, higher than that of the US. This shows that China is more dependent on foreign trade. Therefore, in the short term, the trade war is likely to have a greater impact on China than on the US. As the data shows, the escalation of the trade war has reduced the GDP of China and the USA by 1.41% and 1.35% respectively [11].

Figure 2 shows the GDP of China and US, and the economic growth of the two countries both slowed down slightly after the trade war began. It also shows that China may suffer more than US based on the 2021 and 2022 China's GDP.

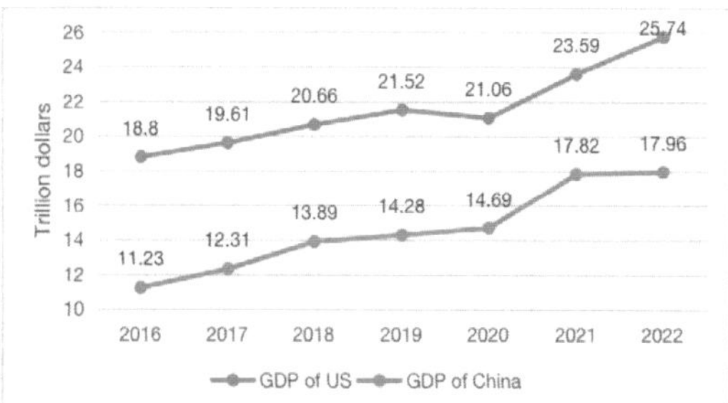

Fig. 2. China and US GDP (Source of data: National Bureau of Statistic, US Bureau of Economic Analysis; Picture credit: Original)

2.4.4 Political effect

As the China-US trade war continues, international trade rules will be affected, which includes the impact on the World Trade Organization (WTO). WTO is a global organization that oversees and regulates international trade rules. Its primary goal is to encourage and facilitate the liberalization and growth of global trade. It strives to create a fair-trading environment for its member nations and guarantees the fairness, transparency, and predictability of trade regulations. However, the unilateralism of the US and the pursuit of its own interests run counter to the WTO.

Since World War II, the US government has adhered to the principle of most-favored-nation treatment, which applies the same tariff and non-tariff barriers to all WTO members. However, the Trump administration has withdrawn from the Trans-Pacific Partnership Agreement (TPP) and imposed tariffs and other restrictions on China, violating the principle of most-favored-nation treatment. Such unilateral actions not only caused a huge impact on China's exports, but also caused other WTO members to worry that the unilateral actions of the United States would undermine the global trade order [1].

Moreover, the US has used "Section 301" to impose huge tariffs on China. The "General Section 301" refers to a provision within Section 301 of the Trade Act of 1974 in the US. This provision originated from the Trade Expansion Act of 1962 and was subsequently modified by the Trade Act of 1974, and it mainly takes unfair measures against trading counterparties. Its main purpose is to protect the rights of the US in international trade practices and to prevent other countries from engaging in unfair or unjust trade practices. Under this provision, the US has the authority to conduct trade investigations on other countries and may also implement various measures, including import restriction, tariff increases, and the suspension of relevant agreements. In order to suppress the Chinese economy, the US government has imposed tariffs on Chinese imports through the "301 tariff" in the name of "national security". This act has worsened and complicated relations between the two countries [3].

3 Discussion and suggestion

A growth in trade between China and the US would positively impact the overall well-being and prosperity of both nations, while a decrease in trade will only reduce the collective welfare of both countries, creating a lose-lose situation in which there is no winner in a trade war.

To minimize trade conflicts between China and the US and establish a mutually beneficial trade atmosphere, both sides could make joint efforts and cooperation.

For the US, it is hoped that the US government can abandon its "decoupling" strategy and hegemonism, and no longer launch a trade war because it is worried about China's development. It is suggested that the US return to rationality and cooperation and work together with China to reach a fair and reciprocal trade agreement and achieve a win-win situation, also learn to respect each other's core interests and major concerns.

China could also make some adjustments to achieve its goal of self-development. To start with, China can stick to reform and opening up, attract the inflow of technology and capital from other countries, and not go on the road of self-isolation. China can also strengthen cooperation with other countries, especially Southeast Asia and Europe, to promote the construction of a common market. In addition, China should also pay more attention to high technology, continuously strengthen scientific and technological innovation, improve the ability of independent creativity, strengthen the training of scientific and technological personnel, encourage innovation and entrepreneurship, and keep core technologies firmly in its own hands.

For both countries, China and the US should strengthen their own economic restructuring, reduce their dependence on each other's markets and reduce the risk of trade frictions by increasing domestic demand, enhancing technological innovation capacity, and strengthening the development of the service sector.

4 Conclusion

The global economy is slowing down and full of uncertainty. As one of the most important economic and trade relations in the world, trade frictions between China and the US are bound to affect not only the domestic economies but the complex situation of global economic development. This paper aims to analyze the China-US trade war from different dimensions, start with the background and process of it, and discuss the causes for trade war, including trade deficit, globalization, and property rights. Meanwhile, this paper also studies the impacts of trade war from different angels, such as import and export volume, investment, economy, and policy. Most importantly, this paper gives some reasonable and feasible suggestions that helps to reduce the trade conflicts between two counties and form a friendly trade environment based on the analysis, and suggests China and US could both make joint effort and cooperation.

The limitation of the present study is that there is a lack of reliable data on imports and exports of specific categories of goods in the China-US trade war, for example, electronic components. Additionally, the analysis lacks the application of data and econometric models. The longer-term impact of the China-US trade war still need to be watched continuously, and may yet turn around as global trade patterns change. In further study, several questions still remain to be answered, for example, how can the trade war come to an end, what is the long-term effect of trade war, which country may suffer more. The usage of econometric model could also be considered in future analysis.

References

1. J. Liu, Y. Yang, Investment and Cooperation, **6**, (2023)
2. J. Tong, X. Ju, China Opening Journal, **5**, (2023)
3. L. Guo, S. Wang, N. Xu, EPS, (2021)
4. S. Hosain, S. Hossain, IJBE, **1**, (2019)
5. A. Dang, K. Krishna, Y. Zhao, NBER, (2023)
6. X. Tu, Y. Du, Y. Lu, C. Lou, Journal of Chinese Political Science, (2020)
7. L. Kapustina, L. Lipková, Y. Silin, A. Drevalev, SHS Web of Conferences 73, 01012 (2020)
8. M. Anam, ICSS, (2023)
9. G. An, World Affairs, **21**, (2023)
10. Z. Xiao, J. Yang, China Academic Journal Electronic Publishing House, **5**, (2019)
11. K. Itakura, JCER, (2019)

De-globalizing Trade in the Wake of the COVID-19: Impacts and Changes in the US-China Relation

Xing Li*

LNU-MSU College of International Business, Liaoning Normal University, Dalian, Liaoning, 116029, China

Abstract. The purpose of this paper is to explore the impact of the COVID-19 epidemic on global trade and its transformation of trade relations between the United States and China. The outbreak of the epidemic triggered a huge restructuring of the global trade system and accelerated the trend of global trade de-globalization. As the two largest economies, the trade relationship between the United States and China plays an important role in this process. This paper analyzes the causes of deglobalization, which are mainly caused by the fracture of industrial chain, trade protection and industrial upgrading. At the same time, the paper focuses on the factors that have caused the deglobalization trend in the post-COVID-19 era, such as changing trade agreements, poor cross-border investment environment, and the challenges and uncertainties brought by e-commerce. Finally, it concentrates on the changes of the US and China bilateral trade in the post-COVID-19 era. Affected by the epidemic, the bilateral relationship between these two countries has become more conflictual and focused on technological competition. Finally, the trend against globalization has led to inefficient economic development and the regionalization of trade because of the necessity of communication.

1 Introduction

Global trade has faced unprecedented challenges since the outbreak of the COVID-19 in early 2020. International flows of goods and services have been restricted as never before, and supply chain disruptions have led to a significant decline in the scale of global trade. At the same time, countries have begun to reassess their dependence on foreign trade, accelerating the trend of de-globalization of global trade. Under this trend, the trade relationship between the US and China faces unprecedented opportunities and challenges.

Indeed, the de-globalization has been affecting global trade since 2008, and the COVID-19 accelerates the trend towards de-globalization due to the halt in trade [1]. As this trend spreads, trade protectionism is also sweeping across the world. Hence, the COVID-19 reshape the global trade so that every country has to alter their trade modes to adapt the new trade tendency. At the same time, as one of the largest trade relationships in the world, changes in trade between the US and China have a profound impact on the global supply chain in the post-epidemic era, which in turn affects the global trade pattern and the development of the international economy. The stability of the relationship between China and the United States affects the global trade pattern, and the well-being of the people of China and the United States, and even the interests of the people of the world, are closely linked to these two great powers [2]. Therefore, changes of both countries' trade relations have a geopolitical impact that cannot be ignored. By studying this change, trade policy makers, enterprises, and investors can formulate adaptive trade policies to cope with potential trade barriers and supply chain changes, and safeguard economic security and national interests.

The epidemic has caused immeasurable pain and loss to the world economy and trade. However, while every country is recovering, the impact of the de-globalization trend in the post epidemic era on the world economy is more worthy of investigation and deep thinking, especially the impact of de-globalization on the US-China trade relations. In fact, from the beginning of the epidemic to now, countless experts and scholars have carried out in-depth exploration of this issue from different perspectives. Meanwhile, because of the dynamic nature of international trade, there are constantly new influencing factors in the research process. Therefore, in order to make the impact of de-globalization clearer, this paper focuses on the causes and influencing factors of de-globalization based on summarizing the views from different perspectives, as well as the future direction of US-China trade relations on this basis.

2 Why de-globalisation take place

Indeed, the trend towards de-globalization has a long history. As globalization continues, geopolitical security, inefficiencies in transnational transport and trade protectionism have all provided impetus for de-

* Corresponding author: xl67s@login.missouristate.edu

globalization. When the COVID-19 cut off the global supply chain, this huge impact on the economy once again made countries rethink the need and urgency of taking the initiative in their own economies. Therefore, this section analyses the causes of de-globalization in three main areas: the severance of global supply chains, the rise of trade protectionism, and industrial upgrading.

2.1 The severance of global supply chains

The supply chain disruption brought about by COVID-19 is not local, but global. This widespread disruption has led more and more countries to start changing their supply chains and trade patterns. COVID-19 is different from other epidemics in that it originated in a specific location and could spread widely, even to more than 200 countries around the world, seriously affecting the world economy and international trade [3]. Besides, many countries have strong links with China for the supply of raw materials, components and manufactured goods for export [3]. Hence, as a country that is deeply dragged down by COVID-19 and an important link in the global supply chain, China has become an important cause of paralysis in the global supply chain.

Due to the widespread paralysis of supply chains, the global supply chain is re-structuring. For China, it has increased its own productive capacity, promoted supply chain diversification and placed greater emphasis on the development of consumption in its domestic market. In the case of the United States, the government has supported its industries in an effort to reduce its trade dependence on China, while reassessing its trade policies and international trade agreements. Overall, in order to help their countries through this difficult phase of the late epidemic, countries are redirecting production to domestic markets.

2.2 Trade protectionism

Protectionism is not a new term, and the start of the 2018 trade war between the US and China was the embodiment of protectionism. However, at this stage of COVID-19, the global recession, mass unemployment, and supply chain risks have resulted in governments having to resort to trade protection policies, such as tariff hikes, to protect their industries and job markets in order to address the economic crisis, which has also meant that countries have become less dependent on each other.

To counteract the economic impact of the epidemic, most countries have chosen to impose tariffs to support their industries, for example, the US and China have adjusted their tariffs on each other, while China has tightened its regulations on foreign firms in specific areas. These measures are de-globalizing world trade. In the short term, this approach protects national industries and responds to economic crises. However, in the long run, it is detrimental to the overall well-being of the world's people and to economic efficiency, especially for businesses. For example, many multinational enterprises will choose to go to countries with lower labour costs to set up branches in order to reduce costs. Others will establish companies in countries with specialized technologies. In fact, this is not only good for these countries to develop a competitive advantage, but also a good time for the country to promote employment and develop its economy. However, de-globalization will lead to the reduction of such development opportunities [4]. Therefore, post-2018 trade protectionism has profoundly affected the market as a whole, and going forward, in response to the economic impact of the epidemic, countries will still need to think carefully about adopting trade policies rather than deepening the level of trade protection.

2.3 Industrial upgrading

In response to the instability of the global economy in the aftermath of the epidemic, global trade chains have begun to reorganize, so countries devoting more resources to the reconfiguration of their supply chains. In this process, in order to gain a competitive advantage, national industries had to improve efficiency and upgrade their industries. At the same time, some countries may undertake technological innovation and digital transformation to enhance global competitiveness.

In fact, the technological development of China has threatened for the US. In recent years, China has increased its investment in high-tech fields such as telecommunications, artificial intelligence, robotics, chips and military. Although China's official stance is to pursue peaceful development, its massive investment and impressive performance in high-tech fields in recent years has forced the US to reconsider its attitude and strategy towards China [5]. During COVID-19, China's manufacturing sector developed significantly, especially in the field of medical devices and life sciences, such as the production of vaccines, respiratory machines, masks, etc. The Chinese government has been working on a number of projects in the field of medical devices and life sciences. At the same time, the United States has increased its foreign restrictions in high-tech sectors to improve its competitiveness. These initiatives have led to greater independence between countries, but on the other hand, restrictions between countries in the field of science and technology are not conducive to the advancement of science and the development of mankind.

3 Factors contributing to de-globalization

International trade is a dynamic process, so in addition to some of the fundamental factors in the previous section, real-time changes in the trade environment during the epidemic deepened the process of de-globalization. Changes in the trade environment are mainly categorized into changes in trade agreements, changes in the environment for cross-border investment, and developments in digital trade.

3.1 Trade agreements

After COVID-19, countries gradually realized the importance of integrated supply chains and industrial systems, and made efforts to adjust in their economic and trade relations to reduce their dependence on global supply chains.

In this process, the US response was more intense because of its large industrial system and foreign dependence. In order to reduce its external dependence and promote the repatriation and development of its own industries, the US is constantly searching for bilateral relations that are favourable in their current form. The United States has even given up on upholding the rules of the international trading system, even though some of them were established and championed by the United States [6].

Hence, many new trade agreements have been developed, such as the regional comprehensive economic partnership (RCEP), the new Korea-US Free Trade Agreement (KORUS), the United States-Mexico-Canada Agreement (USMCA), and the UK-EU trade agreement. The emergence of these trade agreements has led to a degree of de-globalization, with some industries becoming increasingly localized and regionalized. However, this also reflects that complete industrial localization is difficult to continue currently, and that globalization is still an inescapable issue in global economic development.

3.2 The cross-border investment environment

During the COVID-19, global supply chains broke down and countries refocused their development efforts domestically. Until now, when the epidemic is more subdued, the global economy has still remained depressed, all of which contributed to the high risk of cross-border investment and rising investor caution. At the same time, geopolitical tensions have been exacerbated by frequent trade conflicts, and some countries have increased investment and regulation in key technology areas.

For example, the United States has tightened technology export controls on China, such as Huawei's inclusion in the list of entities. The United States has also stepped up its scrutiny of Chinese investments, in particular by expanding the authority of the Committee on Foreign Investment in the United States to prevent technology transfers and improper acquisitions. Recently, the Committee on Foreign Investment in the United States (CIFUS) has had a more stringent review of Chinese direct investment in the United States, particularly in high-tech industries. As a result, this unusual strict scrutiny has brought more uncertainty to investment. This unfavourable investment environment has made many domestic and foreign investors more hesitant and even lose their confidence [7].

In this context, it may be that regionalised trade is more responsive to today's economic development, and even if it brings about a certain amount of de-globalisation, the delineation of special economic zones may give transnational investors more confidence, thus laying the foundations for the re-globalisation of trade.

3.3 Challenges of digital trade for international cooperation

The convenience of the digital economy, with services such as e-commerce, online platforms, digital payments, and cross-border finance facilitate international cooperation. In China, e-commerce retail density increased from 35 per cent to 50 per cent, and even during the Wuhan closure, it only declined by 5 to 11 per cent. In Southeast Asia, the Internet economies of India and Vietnam even increased by more than 40 per cent in 2020 [8]. However, as an alternative to offline trade chains, it is still a new type of development, which has partly led to the deglobalization of trade.

In the aftermath of the COVID-19, many countries implemented embargo policies, which led to a lack of development of the real economy. In this context, the digital economy became an alternative way for international trade to continue. However, as a substitute for the broken global supply chain after the epidemic, the digital economy has greatly helped the survival and development of the global supply chain, and has an important impact on the reconstruction and recovery of the global economy. However, its incomplete relevant systems and unbalanced development regions have led to the development of trade in some regions with advanced information technology, and for some regions lacking information technology, it is impossible to rely on the digital economy to promote economic development.

For example, some international organizations, such as the United Nations Conference on Trade and Development and the International Chamber of Commerce, do not have a consensus on digital trade rules. At the same time, there is a lack of active international organizers to help entrepreneurs participate in this digital trade, especially focusing on some undeveloped countries and some small and medium-sized enterprises [8].

This institutional and informational imperfection in the field of digital economy, especially e-retail, leads to e-retail can only be carried out in some relatively developed regions, which is not conducive to the recovery of the global supply chain, and even helps the development of economic regionalization and deglobalization.

4 The discussion of US-China trade relations

As one of the world's largest bilateral trades, the US-China trade relationship has a significant impact on the trend of de-globalization. While trade between the US and China spans the industrial chain of many transnational corporations and affects the trade development of many countries, industrial complementarities and technological exchanges between the US and China are crucial to global industrial development. Finally, the trade relationship between the US and China has an important position in global governance, and the stability of the trade relationship between the two countries is conducive to the development of global trade rules and systems. Therefore, it is important to explore the direction of US-China trade relations.

4.1 Changes in the level of bilateral trade frictions

The degree of de-globalization is profoundly affected by the level of the bilateral trade conflict between the US and China. The US-China trade friction in the run-up to the 2018-2020 pandemic has led a number of firms and countries to reassess the risks and vulnerabilities in global supply chains. During the epidemic, some firms favoured their home markets. Until now, the US-China trade war is still ongoing, so the role of de-globalization is still shaping the global trading system. For example, the United States has increased its investment in Mexico to reduce its dependence on China. China, on the other hand, has actively pursued regional economic cooperation with international organizations in Asia, such as Singapore, South Korea and Japan.

However, governments should still recognize that the intensification or easing of trade frictions between the US and China has not completely de-globalized in the post-epidemic era. In fact, what has changed is more the direction and scope of trade, and the global economy still needs to be open and cooperative. Closure and trade protection do not lead to the long-term development of national economies, but rather to the detriment of their own interests and the well-being of their people, and even to the degradation of the global economy. According to the World Trade Organization, there was a 5.3% decline in the volume of global merchandise trade in 2020 (compared to 2015). The value of global exports in 2020 fell by 7.5% to USD 17.6 trillion. Merchandise imports saw a 7.6% decline in value to USD 17.8 trillion [9].

4.2 New patterns of technological competition and cooperation in innovation

In the post-epidemic era, the US-China trade relationship has taken a new step forward. The Biden administration has eased restrictions on certain sectors, but still maintains extremely high tax rates on most important areas, such as high technology. This also means that competition and cooperation between the US and China have become sharper and more intense in the face of the epidemic despite COVID-19 proving once again that complete trade closure and de-globalization are not conducive to economic development and reinforcing the importance of global cooperation [10].

There is intense competition between the US and China in a variety of areas and both countries focus on the autonomy to the larger extent. For example, in high-tech areas such as semiconductors, artificial intelligence, and 5G, competition and cooperation continue to be increased. This bilateral relationship with the coexisting of competition and cooperation has profoundly affected the world trade landscape, stimulating further de-globalization, but also providing opportunities for global technological innovation and development.

5 Conclusion

In short, the main purpose of this paper is to analyse the cause of the deglobalisation trend and the dynamic of the US and China in it, so as to judge whether the deglobalisation is a good trend and find a more suitable method for the development of global trade. This paper analyses the causes of deglobalization, the factors that accelerate the trend of deglobalization, and the dynamics of China and the United States in the process of deglobalization.

In general, the post-pandemic deglobalization trend is mainly caused by the severing of global supply chains and the rise of trade protectionism. At the beginning of the epidemic, countries all over the world suddenly cut off their supply chains due to epidemic prevention and control reasons, and then countries began to strengthen the development of their own supply chains, which also caused that although countries were gradually closer in the later period of the epidemic, the tightness of the supply chain could not be compared with that before the epidemic. In addition, trade protectionism, typically represented by the United States, has been affecting the world trade system. After the epidemic, in order to accelerate the recovery of domestic employment and industry, countries around the world have retaliated against each other and promoted trade protectionism.

Factors of deglobalization are then discussed in this paper. First, under the post-epidemic situation, the trade policies of various countries tend to be conservative, such as some trade agreements, which intensifies the trend of deglobalization. Second, the unsatisfactory cross-border investment environment has led investors to turn inward. Third, the immaturity of e-commerce exacerbates the de-globalization trend. As an alternative to global supply chains, the immaturity of the institutional system of e-commerce makes it impossible for some underdeveloped regions and small businesses to participate.

At last, this paper analyses the changes of US-China trade in the post-epidemic era. In the post-COVID-19 era, trade conflicts between the US and China have become more acute, but many are still necessary. At the same time, trade is gradually shifting to competition based on technological competition. In short, the deglobalization trend in the post-epidemic period was caused on the one hand by the overall economic downturn in the world, and on the other hand by the desire of all countries to profit from increased trade protectionism. Therefore, in the short term, the deglobalization trend is good for countries, especially big countries, which can better develop their own industries and raise trade taxes. However, in the long run, this leads to inefficient trade on a global scale because production cannot take advantage of global advantages. Therefore, deglobalization is not a final form of trade, but because communication is essential, it forms regional trade.

People should realize that only greater openness and cooperation is a necessary way to achieve development.

However, the analysis of deglobalization is still one-sided, and there are many factors that this article still does not take into account. For example, some East Asian countries have now started a new round of prevention and control policies, and the long standoff between Russia and Ukraine has also had a huge impact on international trade. As a result, world trade is dynamic and not treated in a fixed way. However, the most important thing is that isolation is not the most effective means to deal with the bad international economic situation, and openness and cooperation remain the themes of economic development in the 21st century.

References

1. D. Marin, Will Deglobalization Fuel Inflation?, Project Syndicate, https://www.project-syndicate.org/commentary/1, (2021)
2. N. Yuan, China Int. Strategy Rev, **2**(1), 14-23 (2020).
3. P. Kumar, A. Gupta, Strategic Management During a Pandemic, Routledge (2021).
4. M. A. Witt, J. Int. Bus. Stud, **50**(7), 1053-1077 (2019).
5. N. Gur, S. Dilek, The Chinese Journal of International Politics, **16**(1), 61-83 (2023).
6. F. Kimura, Seoul J. Econ, **34**(1) (2021).
7. L. J. Lau, China Rev., **20**(4), 1-38 (2020).
8. Johnston, L. A. China Review, **21**(2), 65–86 (2021).
9. K. Starzyk, China-United States trade in the long term, Implications for the world economy. https://depot.ceon.pl/handle/123456789/23242 (2022).
10. F. Haikal, Covid-19: Towards Reviving Economics & New Normal Development Strategies, Trend Research and Advisory (2020).

Research on the Influence of FDI on China's Economic Innovation Development

Yuning Zhao[1,*]

[1]Department of Finance and Trade, Liaoning University, Shenyang, China

Abstract. Foreign direct investment (FDI) and outward foreign direct investment (OFDI) are the primary methods through which capital moves internationally. They serve as significant conduits for technological spillover, which is vital for the progress of countries and regions. Through the combined impact of the growth in foreign direct investment and the two-way flow of FDI, China may enhance its access to various production resources, including labor, capital, and energy. Additionally, this enables China to improve the distribution of intangible assets such as knowledge and technology. Consequently, there is an urgent need to establish and implement a strategy that prioritizes innovation-driven development.This study utilizes China's provincial panel data from 2000-2020 to examine the relationship between the expansion of foreign direct investment (FDI) and the level of innovation. The regional innovation index is used as the dependent variable, while the FDI scale is used as the independent variable. Additionally, a model is employed to test the impact of China's FDI scale expansion on regional innovation capacity. Simultaneously, this study takes into account the disparities in development between the eastern region and the central and western regions, as well as the influence of the Pilot Free Trade Zone policy. Consequently, the sample is further categorized into the eastern region, central region, and western region for a more detailed analysis. Relevant countermeasures are provided based on the results of the empirical analysis mentioned above.

1 Introduction

Based on data from the National Bureau of Statistics, China's research and experimental development investment in 2021 amounted to 2.8 trillion yuan, marking a 14.2% increase compared to the previous year. This growth represents six consecutive years of double-digit expansion, positioning China as the world's second-largest investor in this field. Furthermore, the increase in investment intensity reached a record high in 2010. Record-breaking level reached, surpassing previous year's starting point. China's investment in research and experimental development in 2021 amounted to approximately 5.72 million full-time equivalent personnel per year. This represents 25.3% of the global total and positions China as the leading country in this regard. China's investment in innovation is among the highest globally, and its degree of innovation has made significant advancements.

However, there remains a discernible disparity between China and industrialized nations in terms of effectively translating innovation breakthroughs into practical applications [1]. Based on the data published by the World Intellectual Property Organization, China was positioned as the 12th country in the Global Innovation Index for the year 2021. Despite an improvement in its ranking, China's performance still falls short of meeting the anticipated impact of investment in innovation [2]. Hence, it is imperative that we enhance our innovation capabilities in order to rectify the issue of disproportionate input and output. China's vigorous promotion of the "Belt and Road" program and the creation of pilot free trade zones have propelled the coordinated growth of two-way foreign direct investment (FDI) in China into a new phase. The equilibrium model of two-way direct investment has now achieved stability. What will be the effect of FDI development on the innovative capacity of the region? China's formulation of policies based on scientific and rational principles, along with the promotion of innovation, holds immense practical importance in achieving high-quality economic development.

2 Theoretical analysis and research hypotheses

Over the past few years, there has been a significant influx of foreign direct investment on a huge scale, resulting in a substantial increase in capital inflows to the country [3]. This has played a crucial role in providing robust economic backing for innovation. These investments not only give financial support for research and development, production, and marketing activities of enterprises, but also foster the growth of innovative businesses [4]. Investing in research and trial costs is crucial for innovation, and FDI offers

* Corresponding author: 4032240311@smail.lnu.edu.cn

dependable financial backing for businesses, expediting the innovation process and propelling technological advancement. The increase in foreign direct investment has enticed international firms from various sectors to enter the local market, resulting in the transfer of technology and expertise. Foreign firms typically possess sophisticated technology and extensive management expertise, which can be transferred to local enterprises via FDI, thereby fostering the advancement of innovation [5]. Domestic firms have the opportunity to participate in technological collaboration with international enterprises, gaining insights into their cutting-edge technology and management strategies, so strengthening their own capacity for innovation and competitiveness. Simultaneously, the increase in FDI has resulted in greater market accessibility and heightened competition, thereby fostering the growth of an innovative economy. The influx of foreign firms has heightened market competition, compelling local enterprises to bolster their innovation capacities in order to endure and thrive in the market. Increasing competition compels firms to consistently innovate and offer superior products and services to attract consumers. Simultaneously, the free market offers prospects for domestic firms, enticing increased investment and collaboration, and fostering innovation. The presence of international firms has attracted highly skilled professionals and infused local enterprises with fresh inventive energy [6]. These talented individuals who work for and establish businesses in domestic firms not only introduce new ideas and methods to the company, but also enhance the pool of skilled individuals in creative organizations. Simultaneously, the existence of foreign firms has also incentivized domestic enterprises to intensify their endeavors in fostering talent, resulting in the establishment of a more favorable environment for innovation. The proliferation of foreign direct investment has had a beneficial impact on fostering the growth of creative economies. It facilitates the infusion of cash, technology, and expertise into firms, so significantly fostering innovation and encouraging market openness while intensifying competitiveness. Furthermore, it expedites the movement of skilled individuals and the cultivation of a dynamic and inventive environment. This article presents the following assumptions:

H1: Increasing the scale of FDI can generally stimulate the growth of an innovative economy.

Nevertheless, extensively advanced locations frequently allure a substantial influx of FDI, which might impact neighboring areas via the diffusion of technological knowledge [7]. Technology spillover is the spread of superior technology, management expertise, and industrial methods resulting from foreign investment, which improves overall innovation capabilities. In contrast, less developed countries may struggle to completely assimilate the innovative components introduced by foreign investment due to a dearth of sophisticated technology and managerial expertise. The growth of FDI is intricately linked to the improvement of innovation capacity and the appeal of human resources. The presence of highly skilled individuals is essential for fostering innovation. However, in economically disadvantaged areas, the ability for talented individuals to move and be sought after may be restricted. Consequently, these places may have a limited capacity to attract FDI, resulting in a comparatively deficient ability to innovate. FDI development and innovation can be influenced by several factors such as varying levels of regional development, policy contexts, and economies of scale. Advanced regions typically possess a more extensive policy framework, encompassing measures such as tax reduction, intellectual property protection, and other factors that enhance the attractiveness for an influx of FDI [8]. Simultaneously, the presence of economies of scale in these locations enables them to efficiently offer resources and markets, thereby attracting a greater amount of FDI and fostering innovation. Consequently, regions that are highly developed are generally more capable of effectively incorporating and utilizing elements like technology spillovers, talent, and the regulatory environment resulting from FDI, thereby improving their ability to innovate. Underdeveloped regions may have constraints in adopting new technologies and lack sufficient skilled workforce, leading to reduced capacity for innovation. According to this, this article puts out the following suppositions:

H2: The influence of FDI on innovation is different depending on the level of economic development in a region and shows diversity.

3 Research Design

3.1 Variable Description

Innovative economic development is the dependent variable, calculated using the entropy method [9]. This article draws on previous research experience to construct indicators for measuring the development of innovative economies, as shown in Table

The FDI scale is the explanatory variable, expressed as the total investment of foreign-invested enterprises.

Control variables: This article draws on previous research results and selects common factors that affect the development of innovative economies as control variables [10]. Economic development (GDP), R&D investment intensity (R&D), financial market development level (finance), technology market development level (technology market), urbanization level (urbanization), regional education level (edu).

3.2 Data sources

This article uses provincial panel data from the past 20 years for analysis, and the dependent variable is calculated using the entropy method. All other data is sourced from the National Bureau of Statistics.

Table 1. Indicator description.

First level indicator	Second level indicator	Description	Attributes
Innovation	R&D	Proportion	positive
	Research investment intensity	Proportion	positive
	Patent grants	Patent grants per million people	positive

4 Empirical analysis

4.1. Descriptive statistics

This article conducted descriptive statistical analysis on each variable, This paper selects the provincial panel data from 2000 to 2020 for descriptive statistics, and the variables involved include the year, foreign direct investment, innovation index, GDP, financial market development degree, and the results are shown in Table 2.

Table 2. Descriptive statistics

	(1)	(2)	(3)	(4)	(5)
VARIABLES	N	mean	sd	min	max
code	315	8	4.327	1	15
year	315	2,010	6.065	2,000	2,020
II	315	90.10	9.962	57.05	100
FDI	315	528.4	475.7	7.449	2,257
GDP	315	18,838	17,707	1,401	102,719
Finance	315	0.259	0.125	0.0663	0.704
RD	315	0.0171	0.0132	0.00227	0.0644
edu	315	0.0205	0.00574	0.00805	0.0425
Urbanization	315	0.589	0.134	0.228	0.896
Technology market	315	0.0151	0.0296	0.000322	0.175

4.2 Correlation analysis

According to Table 3, there is a positive correlation between the development level of innovative economy and FDI scale, indicating that the larger the FDI scale, the higher the development level of innovative economy. H1 has been preliminarily verified.

Table 3. Correlation analysis.

	II	FDI	GDP	Finance	RD	edu	Urbanization
II	1						
FDI	0.508***	1					
GDP	0.524***	0.731***	1				
Finance	0.113**	0.185***	0.104*	1			
RD	0.598***	0.421***	0.314***	0.288***	1		
edu	0.094*	-0.098*	-0.169***	0.321***	0.434***	1	
Urbanization	0.0620	0.0380	0.0320	0.684***	0.383***	0.636***	1
mkt	0.361***	0.154***	0.0600	0.215***	0.857***	0.553***	0.427***

https://doi.org/10.1051/shsconf/202418802018

4.3 Regressive analysis

Table 4 shows the benchmark regression results, which show that the regression results of the FDI scale on the development level of innovative economies are significantly positive, and the regression results are significant at the 1% level, indicating that the introduction of FDI has a promoting effect on the development of innovative economies. Hypothesis 1 is valid. After adding control variables, the positivity and negativity of the regression coefficients did not change, and the difference in the size of the regression coefficients was not significant. The regression results of analyzing the control variables show that the regression coefficients for economic development level, R&D investment, urbanization level, and technology market development level are significant, while the impact of education level and financial market development level on innovative economic development is not significant, which may be related to data processing and selection. Therefore, while expanding the scale of FDI, a region or country should also focus on developing the urbanization level of the region and promoting the development of the technology market.

Table 4. Regressive analysis.

VARIABLES	II
FDI	0.000
	(0.19)
GDP	0.000***
	(5.07)
Finance	1.408
	(0.31)
RD	599.563***
	(8.31)
edu	153.560
	(1.50)
Urbanization	-13.821***
	(-2.69)
Technology market	-105.322***
	(-3.43)
Constant	82.700***
	(37.13)
Observations	315
R-squared	0.526

t-statistics in parentheses
*** $p<0.01$, ** $p<0.05$, * $p<0.1$

4.4 Heterogeneity test

This article examines the potential variation in the influence of FDI on innovation, based on the level of economic development in different regions. The analysis focuses on cities located in the eastern area (A), central region (B), and western region (C), and using group regression techniques. The regression findings are displayed in Table 5. Table 5 indicates that there is no statistically significant association between the level of innovation and the scale of FDI in the central and western areas. The magnitude of FDI in the eastern region has a substantial influence on fostering regional creativity. There is a strong positive connection at the 1% significance level, suggesting that as the FDI scale increases in the eastern region, the innovation index in that area also rises. Hypothesis 2 is confirmed

Table 5. Heterogeneity test.

	A	B	C
VARIABLES	II	II	II
FDI	-0.000***	0.027	-0.030
	(-3.73)	(1.60)	(-1.09)
GDP	0.000***	0.001***	0.002***
	(5.45)	(3.17)	(3.62)
Finance	4.214***	4.371	-27.711
	(4.68)	(0.04)	(-1.01)
R&D	-0.340***	-3.289	-1.102
	(-4.20)	(-0.87)	(-0.58)
edu	-3.658**	-31.158	-10.446
	(-2.78)	(-0.88)	(-0.35)
mkt	-93.186**	-10.839	628.916
	(-2.18)	(-0.02)	(1.10)
Urbanization	-42.238***	7.954	31.468
	(-6.95)	(0.04)	(1.24)
Observation	156	236	143

4.5 Robustness check

To further demonstrate the reliability of the conclusion, this article conducts robustness tests on the regression results by replacing variables. The explanatory variable FDI scale is represented by the total import and export volume of foreign direct investment enterprises, and the data is sourced from the National Bureau of Statistics. Regression analysis is conducted again, and the results are shown in Table 6.

From Table 6, it can be seen that after replacing the explanatory variable, the FDI scale and innovation index still show a positive correlation, further proving the validity of hypothesis 1.

Table 6. Robustness check

VARIABLES	II
FDI	-0.008*
	(-1.87)
GDP	0.000***
	(6.15)
Finance	-36.335**
	(-2.40)
R&D	-0.246
	(-0.38)
Edu	7.940
	(1.55)
mkt	584.845***
	(3.04)
Urbanization	21.178
	(1.39)
Observations	315
R-squared	0.553

5 Conclusion

According to the research findings mentioned above, this article offers the following recommendations:

Firstly, leveraging the high-level opening up to the global market as a chance and prioritizing the coordinated growth of two-way foreign direct investment to strengthen regional innovative capabilities. In order to achieve this objective, it is imperative for regions to proactively establish an equitable, transparent, and predictable business climate. This can be accomplished by streamlining procedures for foreign investment access, minimizing the list of restrictions on foreign investment, and eliminating any policies that hinder foreign investment access. It is imperative to exert efforts in order to encourage investment facilitation and guarantee equitable market competitiveness as means to attract foreign investment. Simultaneously, promote the expansion of firms into foreign markets and encourage their participation in foreign direct investment, so enhancing their ability to withstand risks and increase profitability in overseas ventures. Offer crucial assistance and assurance in improving regional innovation capacity.

Furthermore, the free trade zone should effectively utilize its policy advantages of experimentation and learning from mistakes, fully exploit the influential role of foreign direct investment and overseas investment by Chinese enterprises, foster the harmonious development of two-way direct investment, and attain mutual benefits and mutually advantageous outcomes. Simultaneously, it is crucial to have a precise comprehension of one's functional positioning and unique comparative advantages, taking into account various reform tasks and development objectives. Furthermore, we will actively facilitate economic integration and synchronized development between the regions encompassing the free trade zone and the adjacent areas. We will expedite the cross-regional movement of innovative components, enhance the efficiency of resource allocation, and bolster regional innovation capabilitiesEquations should be centred and should be numbered with the number on the right-hand side.

References

1. S. Jun, Z. Kai, M. Minjie, Kybernetes, 53, 410-423 (2024).
2. S. Deepika, M. Rahul, SN Business Economics, 4, 55-59 (2023).
3. J. Wei, W. Yaqin, S. Churen, Emerging Markets Finance and Trade, 59, 3671-3688 (2023).
4. G. Renato, A. Veneziano, M. Suelene, International Regional Science Review, 46, 98-122 (2023).
5. W. Qizhen, L. Suxia, Energies, 15, 9209-9209 (2022).
6. H. Yu, Md.Qamruzzaman, Sustainability, 14, 15732-15732 (2022).
7. W. Dongni, C. Carmen, Insight on Africa, 16, 46-72 (2024).
8. C. Yongmin, J. Haiwei, L. Yousha, Journal of Comparative Economics, 50, 917-945 (2022).
9. L. Shengnan, L. Zhouzhou, L. Dezhi, Systems, 10, 230-230 (2022).
10. Z. Meng, L. Lihang, Z. Fangyi, Processes, 9, 1264-1264 (2021).

https://doi.org/10.1051/shsconf/202418803001

Research on the Factors Analysis and Strategies of LVMH's Profitability

Kexin Wang[1,*]

[1]Manangment School, University of Sheffield, Sheffield, S10 1FL, United Kingdom

Abstract. Moet Hennessy Louis Vuitton (LVMH) has been expanding its territory in the group through mergers and acquisitions. The success rate of the group's acquisition is very high, and through excellent management and operation, many unknown small brands can return to the market and even give the brand life again. During the pandemic, when the world was in an economic downturn, LVMH's luxury goods, as non-essential goods for most people, LVMH's still demonstrated remarkable profitability resiliency. Through the analysis of LVMH's financial data and market data, this paper summarizes the four main factors affecting LVMH's profitability and analyzes the formation reasons behind these factors. Eventually, based on these factors, the author will put forward the company's internal countermeasures and the enlightenment of LVMH on the profit mode in the industry.

1 Introduction

1.1 Research background

Luxury consumption and the industries associated with it keep playing an important role in today's economy and society [1]. The group's shares and share prices have risen rapidly in recent years. In 2023, the company's CEO, Arnault, also successfully ranked the world's richest man. The influence of the luxury empire has penetrated countries and regions, especially in the United States, Europe, and Asia (excluding Japan) [2]. Growing consumer tastes, new technology, industry trends, and the expansion of the global luxury market make room for new players in the luxury market and new business models, which in turn means more competition [3].From then on, the development of LVMH was remarkable, and it steadily gained a significant position as a dominant player in the market. This article will further discuss the influencing factors and causes behind these remarkable figures by analyzing the group's operating conditions and important indicators. For the company and related industries, the article would put forward LVMH's advantages and potential problems about profitability and further provide business ideas for luxury goods and related industries. For society, the content of this paper can also provide diversified management perspectives and profit methods to help relevant enterprises and managers think deeply about the business strategies that suit the enterprise.

1.2 Literature review

In strategy, Chatterjee described the current situation of LVMH with the PEST model and SWOT method and listed the advantages and disadvantages of LVMH and other market factors affecting the company's operation. The author emphasizes that LVMH's success cannot be separated from its excellent diversification strategy and proposes that LVMH may face challenges and competition in new markets in the future. At the same time, the author also proposed that the economic environment and digital transformation should not be ignored, which will not only directly affect the sales effect but also may affect the development of the company in the long term [4]. In addition, Mira analyzed the company's operating conditions in detail by establishing models and analyzing data during the merger and acquisition of Hermes. The authors pointed out that although it is very positive to analyze the merger of the two companies from the data, the difference in management and business philosophy led to the failure of the merger in the end. This also highlights the importance of management mergers in acquisition risks [5]. Meanwhile, Li provides different levels of thinking for the study of this paper in the Tiffany merge case [6]. The Hermes case provides more guidance for the analysis of finance and financial data for this paper, while the Tiffany acquisition comprehensively introduces the relationship between the management and relevant partners in the acquisition and further helps to analyze the advantages and disadvantages of the company's decision-making and strategy.

1.3 Research gap

In recent years, there have been many studies and analyses on LVMH Group, and most of the articles focus

* Corresponding author: Kwang63@sheffield.ac.uk

on the analysis of various company acquisition cases For example, the synergy effect after some major mergers and acquisitions, and the process of mergers and acquisitions. At the same time, it also includes some analysis the marketing strategy of the Group and Arnault, that is, some excellent operation methods of the group. However, in these academic analyses, few scholars have analyzed the reasons for LVMH's continuous growth in recent years: its profitability. Although scholars will mention many companies' marketing strategies, they do not integrate data and strategies closely. At the same time, these strategies' specific manifestations and influencing factors in various important data are not mentioned.

1.4 Research framework

Therefore, this paper will discuss the profitability of the company in the past five years, and its realized strengths and weaknesses. And further, discuss the development direction of LVMH in the future market. The analysis will be divided into excellent profitability and problems and challenges. The strengths will include core data analysis, product line analysis, and consumer behavior analysis. Then, it puts forward the profit problems and potential risks the group may face. Finally, combined with the problems reflected in LVMH's earnings, this paper summarizes the company's advantages and merits, as well as some suggestions for future risks, and discusses the opportunities and possibilities of the company in the huge economic market in the future.

2 Case Description

LVMH is the world's largest e-luxury group, with more than 75 brands, and Mr Arnault will become the world's richest man in 2023. It has a wide range of sectors, including wine and spirits, fashion and leather goods, perfumes and cosmetics, watches and jewelry, and selective retail. LVMH traces its roots back to the early 19th century. The founder, Mr. Arnault, started running a construction company and aimed to build a luxury empire. Therefore, he first obtained financing funds through his family background and French financial institutions and acquired Boussac, which is a famous French brand, Christian Dior. Meanwhile, Arnault also obtained ownership of this famous French fashion house. This was the first step in the establishment of the group. It was not until 1971 that Louis Vuitton merged with Moet Hennessy to form the LVMH [7]. In 1987, after the formal establishment of the LVMH, Arnault began a long road of mergers and acquisitions. Among them, the development of LV is very rapid. Louis Vuitton was still making high-end luggage at the time, which the French royal family and European aristocracy favored. As the group grew and expanded, it introduced more lines of fashion, accessories, and stores around the world. In 2021, LVMH officially acquired Tiffany for 15.8 billion US dollars. LVMH is now one of the world's leaders in luxury goods as its brands continue to grow and its reach expands. LVMH now employs more than 196,000 people worldwide and generated sales of 79.2 billion euros in 2022. In the past five years, except for 2020, which suffered the impact of COVID-19, the net profit and company value has been increasing year by year every year, and from 2020 to 2021, the net profit soared from 49.5 billion euros to 126.9 billion euros, which almost tripled and was higher than the net profit in 2019 [2]. However, the company also has some potential problems. With new changes in people's consumption behavior after the pandemic, the profitability of companies and the profit risks generated after mergers and acquisitions are facing constant changes. The entire luxury consumption industry is also facing new challenges in the market.

3 Analysis on the problem

3.1 The profitability advantages

3.1.1 Analysis of important indicators related to profitability

In recent years, various indicators of the company have changed in different dimensions with the market and the company's operation. The advantages and drawbacks of the LVMH Group's recent profitability can be examined using key metrics. First, the group's overall sales rose yearly from 2020 to 2022. And it continues to rise from 446.51 million euros in 2020 to 79,184 million euros in 2022. Secondly, the company's net profit is rising year by year. The profits even tripled between 2020 and 2021 due to a post-pandemic rebound in consumption and national open-door policies. Meanwhile, there has been a general rising trend in the gross profit margin. Despite a 0.1% decline in 2022 over the prior year, margin profit has essentially been consistent over the previous three to five years. This represents that the company's core business's profitability remains stable [2].

3.1.2 Impact of product lines on profitability

The impact of different product lines on profitability is the most intuitive. First, as the largest product segment in total sales, Leather Goods has maintained a growing trend. Although there was a slight decline in 2022 compared to the previous year, the overall trend is upward. Besides, retail earnings are rising as well. In addition to the official opening of the Chinese market in early 2023, tourism and post-epidemic revenge consumption have also greatly boosted consumption. Moreover, as the mid-end product segment in the company, the consumption of many middle-class consumers cannot be ignored. After Tiffany's acquisition, jewelry's operating profit has changed qualitatively, soaring from 302m to 2079m. The stock price rose rapidly, the first time in nearly five years that it rose above 500 euros [2].

Combined with these data, the brand matrix and product diversification provide a strong resilience for the company. The LVMH products not only cover different fields but also seize a variety of consumer groups and then construct a multi-dimensional brand space. In the product category, there are long-established brands that attract core high-end customers, while many young people prefer fast-selling beauty retailers, such as Sephora and DFS duty-free stores. "E-commerce has been predominant during the COVID-19 pandemic, and retailers have put much effort into building, improving, and promoting their online stores [8]." Thus, the group quickly shifted its online purchasing channels, which helped the group make up for some offline losses. To sum up, multi-dimensional brands and diversified consumer groups could help companies better balance profits and losses and create synergies between brands.

3.1.3 Impact of consumer psychology and pricing strategy on profitability

During the economic downturn, the company grasped the psychology of consumers and raised the prices of some products to cope with inflation and gain profits for the company. Factually, the sales of the group continued to grow in 2021-2022 as the product prices were raised. There are three main reasons for such a strategy. The first reason is related to Veblen's pricing theory. In theory, the luxury market is different from the ordinary market. The demand for luxury goods increases with the price rise to meet the buyers' psychology of conspicuous consumption [9]. Another factor is the support from the core group of luxury goods. For the rich, their price response is not sensitive, which may not affect the core purchasing power. Thirdly, raising prices could somewhat stimulate post-pandemic spending by the middle class. Middle-class customers' incomes have taken a hit because of the pandemic. Therefore, with the rise of prices, people might consider that getting the product before the price increases is a good deal. They may not lose too much if they are later resold as second-hand goods. For the cautious middle class, this allows for both temporary consumption and long-term investment. Eventually, LVMH can remain profitable as long as there is consumption.

3.2 The problem with LVMH's earnings

3.2.1 The impact of Tiffany &CO's M&A risk on profitability

Although the acquisition of Tiffany has brought a lot of benefits to the group and contributed to further occupation in the US market share, such acquisition also has underlying risks in the long run. To begin with macroeconomic risks, according to the 2023 third-quarter report, the currency had an impact on product lines, and jewelry products had a 4% decrease in value because of the weakening US market and inflation issues [2]. The second issue is the risk of return. LVMH's initial acquisition purpose is to make up for the group's weakness in the jewelry field, and the group is optimistic about Tiffany's potential. Although the merger between Tiffany and LVMH helped the company initially, as the post-pandemic impact slowly faded and the market gradually returned to normal, TIFF did not bring an outstanding market performance to the company. The last point is market reaction and stock price volatility. From the third quarter data, Tiffany's long-term growth is not very significant. Although the group achieved share price growth in 2022 after the acquisition, such gains were not sustained in 2023, and the growth rate of jewelry products shrank by four times in the third quarter as the share price fell during the third quarter, with Bulgari performing even better. In general, M&A may not be as impressive as expected with these underlying risks.

3.2.2 The dissipation of the post-pandemic consumer Boom

Loyal consumers of hard luxury are calming down as the post-pandemic spending frenzy winds down. According to the third-quarter report, growth in many product lines slowed significantly from the previous year. More specifically, except that the growth rate of retail remained stable, the growth rate of other product lines decreased by half compared with the growth rate of the year's first half [2]. According to the data, in the second half of 2023, LVMH's stock price has been falling continuously, from 900 euros or even all the way to the lowest point of about 675 euros, and the growth rate of perfume and cosmetics has gradually slowed down. One of the major reasons is the fierce competition in the market. With the rise of new brands focusing on cosmetics production and the increase of the number of competitors, LVMH's fragrance & cosmetics has gradually lost its important position in the market. Another reason behind this is the slower pace of innovation. So far, the group has always relied on classic products rather than launching new ones. Nevertheless, with the development of media and fast fashion, the speed of change in consumer preferences and the speed of product updates are increasing. Gradually, more and more substitutes have emerged, and the concept of good quality and low price has slowly penetrated the market. As a result, many customers are no longer blindly paying for the "premium".

4 Suggestion

4.1 The excellent strategies for the industry to learn from

Brand diversification is a key strategy to help LVMH Group achieve significant profit margins. While the percentage of these groups in the luxury market is low, and there are few replicable examples, comparable businesses can still benefit from studying how brands are deployed. First and foremost, the diversification of the application fields of substitutes and products is very important. For instance, for small and micro enterprises, despite the fact that they cannot have diversified brands like LVMH, they can still learn from and derive profit structures suitable for small enterprises. For one thing, companies can capture different groups of people by producing different products. Similarly, companies can optimize their sales channels based on their internal consumption patterns and build complementary functions along the supply chain as much as possible. When the organization is faced with some uncontrollable external factors, it can also quickly change the production or sales mode to minimize losses. Moreover, digital supply chains are more significant than offline ones, and supply chain management can help businesses reduce labor costs, increase profit margins, and enhance operational effectiveness.

4.2 Capture the needs of future market consumers

Seizing the core of the new consumption generation is the focus of the group's profit optimization direction. According to the KPMG report, "Gen Z will soon become China's major purchase force. Gen Z is leading the adoption of immersive technologies such as AR, VR, and the metaverse [10]." For one thing, it illustrates the significance of the Z era for the Chinese market going forward. Controlling the Z generation's purchasing patterns would be essential to meeting the demand of the Chinese market in the future. Furthermore, this exposition demonstrates the Z era's strong emphasis on the idea of innovation. With the third section of this paper, LVMH's perfume product profitability and update speed have gotten slower. This means LVMH must innovate its products to adapt to the interests of future customers to enhance the profitability of its fragrance line eventually.

According to The Influencer Marketing Benchmark Report 2023, "The influencer-marketing industry is forecast to reach $21.1 billion in 2023, up from $16.4 billion in 2022 [11]." Therefore, the company can fully utilize the publicity effect of the media band by establishing a cooperative connection with bloggers. This has two benefits: first, it reduces the cost of cooperation. For corporate finance, only the sample cost and minimal reputational risk. Such a partnership could save many fixed costs and advertising space expenses compared to internal advertising and placement, thus further improving operating profits. For brand effect, cooperation can indirectly benefit the market performance. People are using and consuming more media and online content because of the growth of new media. By working with various content creators who share the brand's values, many brands can effectively raise their visibility while quietly influencing customer behavior and controlling the consumption path.

4.3 Optimize post-merger profitability

Regarding the Tiffany acquisition, it is undeniable that the benefits since the acquisition have been significant. Tiffany not only enhances the value of the group and makes up for the group's weakness in jewelry but also contributes to the company's organic growth. However, from the perspective of the jewelry market alone, it still cannot compete with the top jewelry, and the subsequent explosive power is insufficient. The company should make timely adjustments to the profit plan to retain sustainable value after the acquisition. More specifically, it includes further innovation and continually tracks changes in inflation, exchange rates, and other economic issues. For the time being, while the Asian market recovers from the epidemic, the rise in marriages and travel will likely give the jewelry business more purchasing power. Nevertheless, the jewelry segment of LVMH was also significantly impacted by exchange rates, which indirectly affected LVMH's profits in the third quarter of 2023. In conclusion, despite the overall positive situation in the market, there are still potential risks in the follow-up performance of the Tiffany acquisition.

5 Conclusion

5.1 Key findings

When studying the profitability of LVMH Group, this paper mainly expounds on the main factors affecting its profitability by studying the company's profitability advantages and challenges. One of the major advantages is that the company's profit advantage is the diversified product layout. This strategy has been throughout the core layout of the group, and it has greatly improved the synergies between different products, thus greatly improving the profitability of the group. Another advantage is capturing core customers and pricing strategies. Since LVMH's core customers are relatively special and mainly of the upper class, it certainly provides the group with significant core purchasing power. These two factors have made the group resilient in the global health crisis, especially during the pandemic. Meanwhile, the group may also be exposed to ongoing risks after the merger and acquisition due to changes in market trends and consumption patterns. Therefore, the company needs to maintain sharp insight and precise strategy to face the market update speed. To sum up, even though the group faces different challenges, LVMH still has strong profitability potential through its years of profit experience, mature team, and positive market consumption signals.

5.2 Research significance

Based on data and analysis, this article summarizes the positive and adverse factors influencing LVMH's profitability and puts forward corresponding solutions and thinking extensions for different problems. This paper analyzes the profitability of the group from a macro perspective that provides ideas for the relevant managers in the industry to apply to the management of the enterprise reasonably. At the same time, this research enables people who are new to the industry to intuitively and quickly understand LVMH's profit method.

5.3 Limitation and future study

The analysis in this paper mainly focuses on the major profitable segments of LVMH group's business instead of all the business segments within the group. Besides, the paper is mainly based on the combination of financial data and related strategies and does not involve the analysis of the financial model and corporate management structure. In the future, the authors will explore other potential factors affecting the profitability of LVMH Group by combining relevant models and corporate structure analysis.

References

1. Chevalier, M., Mazzalovo, G. Luxury Brand Management in Digital and Sustainable Times. United Kingdom: Wiley (2021)
2. 2022 full year result. Retrieved from https://www.lvmh.com/shareholders/agenda/2022-full-year-results/ (2022)
3. Chevalier, M., Mazzalovo, G. Luxury Brand Management in Digital and Sustainable Times. United Kingdom: Wiley (2021)
4. Chatterjee, A. B. Asian Journal of Multidisciplinary Studies, **8**, 5 (2020)
5. Mira, I. A. M. Mergers & acquisitions: a case of a merger between LVMH and Hermès (Doctoral dissertation) (2015)
6. Li, J. Analysis on the Acquisition of LVMH on Tiffany& Co. In 6th International Conference on Financial Innovation and Economic Development (ICFIED 2021) (pp. 426-430). Atlantis Press (2021)
7. Tfl. Retrieved from https://www.thefashionlaw.com/lvmh-a-timeline-behind-the-building-of-a-conglomerate/ (2023)
8. Koch, J., Frommeyer, B., and Schewe, G. Online shopping motives during the COVID-19 pandemic—lessons form the crisis. *Sustainability*, *12*(24), 10247 (2020)
9. Bagwell, L. S., & Bernheim, B. D. Veblen effects in a theory of conspicuous consumption. *The American economic review*, 349-373 (1996)
10. Bisagni, A., Chiu C., Chocano, J. M., and Gardner J. Luxury Redefined (2023)
11. Amed, I., Berg, A., Balchandani, A., and D'Auria. G. The State of Fashion 2024 (2023)

Analyze the Development of Meituan and Fantuan to Promote the Culture of Food Delivery Platforms in the US

Weihao Weng*

College of Liberal Arts & Sciences, University of Illinois at Urbana-Champaign, Illinois, 61820, US

Abstract. In recent years, the food delivery industry has had significant growth. In 2020, COVID-19 pushes this industry to be general for society. The food delivery industry helps customers' lives be convenient. In China, Meituan is at the leading position in the food delivery market. Their business model has a huge effect on other food delivery companies. Fantuan is a food delivery company in Western countries, they usually work with local Chinese restaurants and deliver food to the customers. This paper analyzes both Meituan and Fantuan in macro, meso and micro way, to find out their status. This paper analyzes the governments' politics, country economy, society and technology to find out how external factors affect companies' business. This paper can depend on their competition mechanism to explain the reason for Meituan being the top food delivery company in China. Plus, this paper provides advice for Fantuan to improve their business in the Future.

1. Introduction

1.1 Meituan

Meituan is a company focused on the native consumer products and providing services to the customer by the e-platform. The services include dining, hotel, traveling and livelihood service. It was founded in 2010 by Wang Xing [1]. Meituan is the largest food delivery service and online-to-offline(O2O) service provider in China [2]. In 2010, it was the time for global digitalization, and there has been a surge in smartphone users. Meituan caught the chance. They made a platform for their group buying. Customers can use lower prices to buy the food or other items through the app on smartphones. In 2012, Meituan started to expand their market, which is the movie market [1]. Meituan created a company called Maoyan entertainment [1]. This company helps users buy the movie ticket, choose the seat, and write a response for the movie on their smartphone. The movie service of Meituan gives customers a convenient way to enjoy the movie. After 2012, Meituan expanded their market at an amazing speed [2]. In 2013, they had a hotel booking service and food delivery service [2]. In 2014, they had sightseeing ticket reservations. In 2015, customers can buy air and train tickets by using Meituan [2]. In 2017 and 2018, Meituan had fresh food and daily use item service, car-hailing service and bicycle-sharing service [2] (please see Fig. 1.).

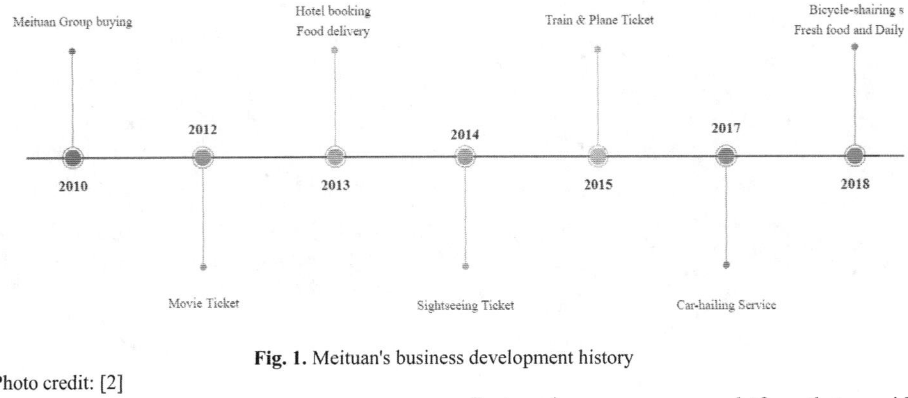

Fig. 1. Meituan's business development history

Photo credit: [2]

1.2 Fantuan

Fantuan is an e-commerce platform that provides food delivery and fresh groceries. It was founded in

* Corresponding author: weihaow3@illinois.edu

Vancouver, Canada in 2014 by Randy Wu [3]. In 2014, the food delivery culture in Western Country was phone calls. People need to remember many restaurant numbers and call for food. Fantuan caught the chance to provide a platform to give a place for the native Chinese restaurant to sell their food [4]. It is convenient for international students to use their own language to order their food. In 2016, Fantuan started their business in Toronto [4]. In 2017 and 2018, Fantuan updated their app [4]. Customers can order online and self-pick up, and they can write the review on the app [4]. In 2019, Fantuan expanded the American market [4]. In 2022, they opened up the Australian market and the British market (please see Fig. 2.) [4].

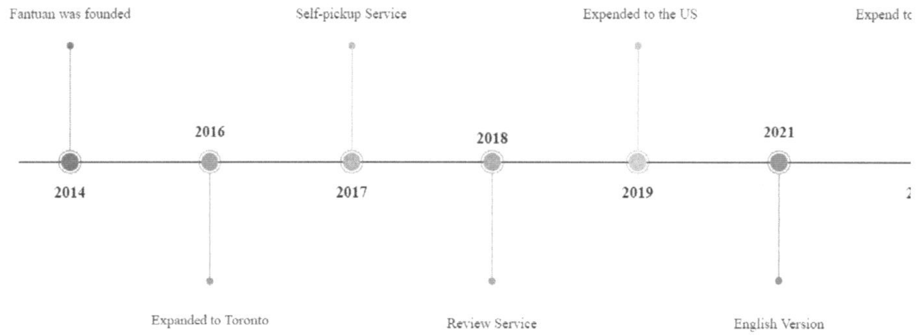

Fig. 2. Fantuan's business development history

Photo credit: [4]

1.3 Purpose

Meituan and Fantuan are two different types of food delivery apps in different countries. They have similar functions at the beginning, but different directions of developments. Meituan is one of the most popular apps in China. Meituan provides not only food delivery functions, but also movies, hotels, traveling, bicycle-sharing service, and etc. Meituan focuses more on people's life and one app provides multiple functions. Fantuan is a food delivery app in Western countries. Fantuan focuses on international students and expands the market in many different countries. This paper compares the differences between Meituan and Fantuan. Based on analyzing the reason why Meituan is popular in China and the potential of Fantuan, this paper provides suggestions to improve Fantuan's competitiveness and business model in the future.

1.4 Paper structure

The rest of the paper is organized in three sections, which are macro, meso and micro. Section 2 analyzes two companies in the macro layer; section 3 compares them in the meso layer; section 4 analyzes two companies in micro.

2. Macro analysis

2.1 Meituan

2.1.1 Politics

Meituan operates in China. The politics in China influences the business of Meituan. State Administration for Market Regulation (SAMR), which is a government agency to manage and supervise the market, published anti-monopoly laws [5]. This law limits companies from using their market position to harm market competition and consumer interests. This law also prevents companies from collecting customers' data to make differential trading prices, which causes damage to the interests of consumers [5]. Meituan is one of the companies targeted by China's anti-monopoly probe. In the competition between Meituan and other food delivery platforms, Meituan uses their leading position and limited platform merchants actions to prevent them from using other platforms, like Ele.me. Therefore, Meituan was fined 3.442 billion Chinese yuan in 2021 [6].

2.1.2 Economy

The Chinese food delivery industry is gradually rising. In 2010, many platforms were created to help people have more convenient lives. The Chinese food delivery platform started at this time. Digital content development makes music, book, movie shopping and other production digitized. People can easily share and trade on platforms [7]. With the popularity of digitalization, smartphones improved the digital platform and made the food delivery industry improve on a large scale in a few years. In 2021, The size of the food delivery market is 811.7 billion Chinese yuan, and market growth is 18.12% (please see Fig. 3) [8].

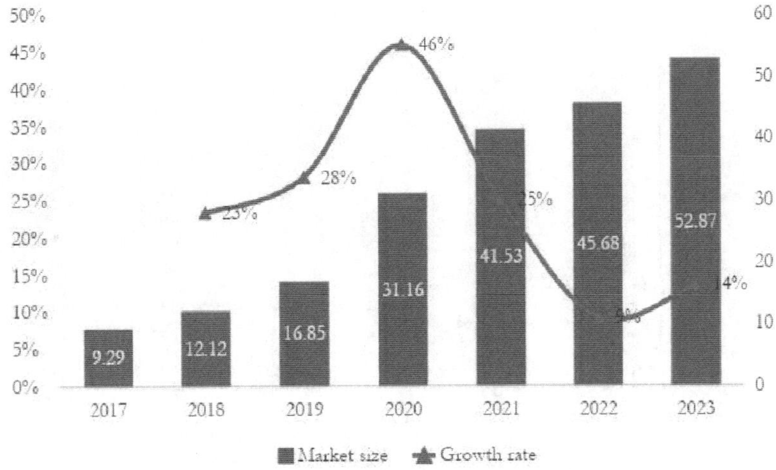

Fig. 3. Chinese food delivery market size and growth rate

Data source: [8]
Photo credit: Original

2.1.3 Society

Meituan's target customer is the young generation. To attract the attention of customers, Meituan's strategy can be explained in the AISAS model [9]. A, which is attention, Meituan advertises through the Internet and celebrities, which attracts people to know there are discounts and vouchers with Meituan. Customer's I, interest, is piqued. Meituan's discounts are not only in food delivery, but also in their other services, such as traveling and hotels. Then, the platform depends on S, search, to classify the discounts and vouchers. Meituan have different types of vouchers that can satisfy the one people's order and group of people's order. After that, customers can take A, action, to order the food and enjoy it. Last, customers can share, which is S, the platform and attract more customers to use their app.

2.1.4 Technology

Meituan uses big data analytics and predictive models to improve the sales and customer satisfaction to be the biggest food delivery platform in China. Meituan analyzed history order, location, and weather of consumers to predict the demand in different areas with different times [10]. Meituan can depend on the prediction and provide accurate services to help merchants' sales and customers enjoy the services.

2.2 Fantuan

2.2.1 Politics

Fantuan is a food delivery company in many countries. This industry is influenced by laws and politics. Take labor laws as an example, in the early food delivery period, the delivery guy did not have specific benefits and protections [11]. Most of the time, they need to bear the cost of the accident themselves [11]. When there is not a certain law related to the food delivery industry. The business of the company can be affected.

2.2.2 Economy

American food delivery is increasing. Before 2020, most food delivery in the US is pizza and Chinese food, which remember the number of restaurants and order through phone call. In 2019, the market size of food delivery was 16.9 billion dollars [12]. However, the market size of food delivery was 31.2 billion dollars in 2020 (please see Fig. 4) [12]. The reason is COVID-19 lets many people stay in their house, and they have a demand for a lot of food, which is a big chance for online food delivery. It's a big increase for the food delivery market.

https://doi.org/10.1051/shsconf/202418803002

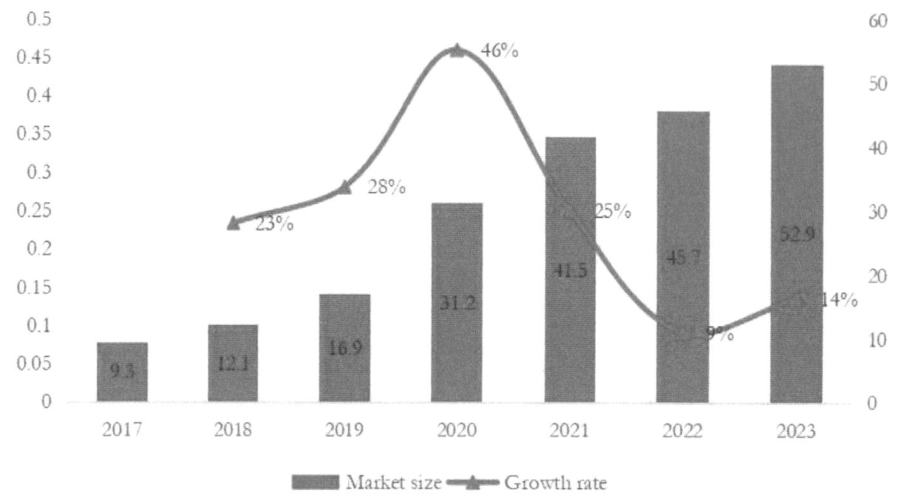

Fig. 4. food delivery market size and growth rate in the US

Data source: [12]
Photo credit: Original

2.2.3 Society

Fantuan targets the Asian community, to be more specific, the international students. They work with local Chinese restaurants, and university international student associations. By using the AISAS model to explain Fantuan's strategy [9]. They work with local restaurants and international student associations to catch more international students' attention. Most international students in foreign countries want to eat their home country's food. They can be interested in this food delivery platform. Then, Fantuan searches for the average price of the Chinese restaurant and provides the voucher and discount for students. Students use the app and enjoy the service and share the platform. Also, they focus on the English market. Fantuan makes an English version app to help more people that are not Chinese to enjoy Chinese food.

2.2.4 Technology

Technology related to platform creation is important to Fantuan's business. The function of the mobile application can affect the user experience. Plus, as a Chinese food delivery app, the payment type includes visa, debit card, Alipay and Wechat pay [4]. This function is great for the international student to use the familiar payment type. Also, it depends on data analysis to find customer's favorites. As a digital platform, Fantuan uses big data to analyze and help to understand customer behavior and optimize the service. They can depend on location, price, packaging, discount, etc to restaurant marketing and make discounts.

3 Meso analysis

3.1 Market share and competition

Meituan is the most leading digital platform in China. They provide many services, including delivery, car-hailing, hotel, traveling, movie, etc. Meituan held about 67.3% of the food delivery market in China [13]. Competitor companies, like "Ele.me", is another big food delivery platform in China which holds around 30.9% of the food delivery market (see Fig. 5) [13]. Ele.me has a similar function as Meituan, but the difference between these two food delivery companies is huge. Meituan and Ele.me both are the leading companies in food delivery in China. Ele.me is focused on food delivery and it extends to the whole country [14]. Meituan also focuses on food delivery and extends to the whole country, but they also extend other life services. They also have movies, hotels and some other services related to people's lives. Meituan focuses on people's lives.

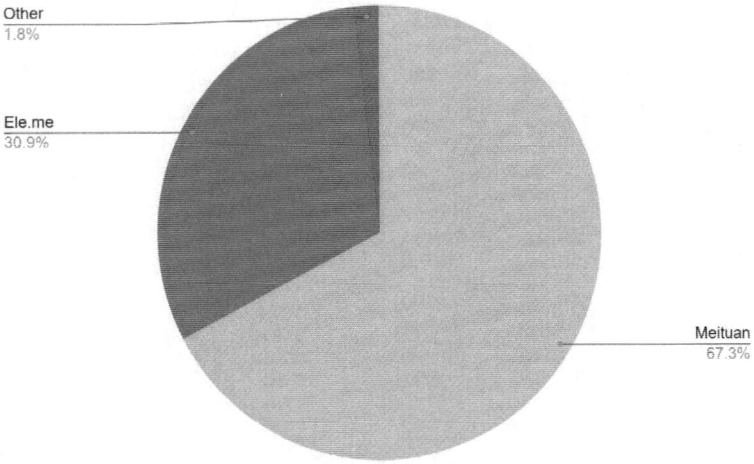

Fig. 5. Market Share in China

Data source: [13]
Photo credit: Original

Fantuan is a food delivery platform in Canada, America, Australia and Britain. Fantuan's target community is the Asian community which is over 40 million people [15]. The market size is over $36 billion [15]. Since Fantuan is in an international market, take the US market as an example. In the US, Doordash, Uber eat, Grubhub held most of the food delivery market (see Fig. 6) [16]. There is only 1% that is some other food delivery company [16]. Since Fantuan focuses on international students, their business is hard to compare with the company's focus on all of the people in the US. In the same Asian community market, there are other two platforms that do the same jobs, HungryPanda and Chowbus are also focused on international students and provide similar services [17].

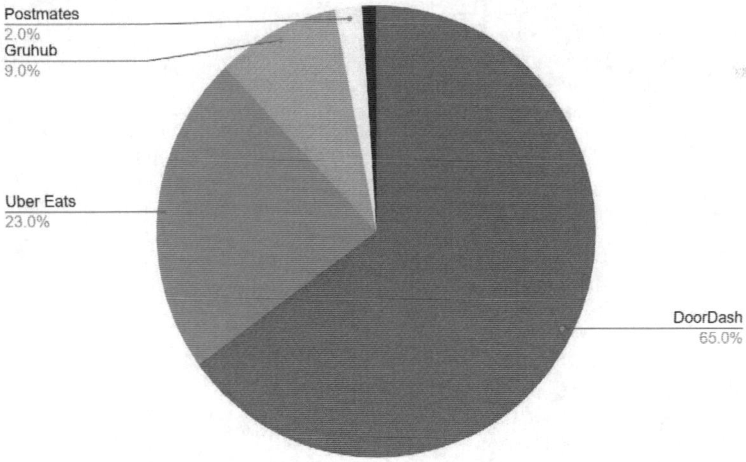

Fig. 6. Market Share in the US

Data source: [16]
Photo credit: Original

3.2 Competition mechanism

Meituan's strategy is retail and technology. They combine retail and technology. The food delivery is the main part of their strategy. Also, some other food delivery companies are also a challenge for Meituan. The point is, after Meritain is stable in the food delivery market, they start to extend other markets, like travel and hotels. By providing more service and targeted ads and personalized messages, they can make users keep using their app. Ele.me only focuses on food delivery and it's hard to compete with Meituan, since Meituan has more functions. Meituan occupies many markets related to people's lives. People only need to have one app in their cell phone and can do almost everything related to their lives.

Fantuan is focused on Chinese food, and more focused on the international student from China. However, not only one company does the same thing. Hungry Panda, and chowbus is also the company which provides the platform. Their consumers are all focused on the international students. The service of Fantuan about reviews and rate is still a big advantage. How to extend the user.

4 Micro analysis

Meituan depends on big data analysis to provide the user the service they want, what they like. People always want a cheap price with high quality service. Meitian is given a consumer voucher to make them think they can have a cheap price and have great food. That can attract more customers and fosters loyalty by fulfilling the expectation of saving money and getting more food. Meituan is in an absolute leadership position in Chinese food delivery market, since their voucher activity, and other diversity services related to people life can satisfy most of people's desires.

Fantuan's main consumer is international students. For international students, they always want their own culture's food. Fantuan is focused on this point, and provides a platform for consumers, they have more choice for food. This way can raise customer satisfaction and be the only platform for international students. Although Fantuan is a good app for international students and the Asian community to use, the market share of Fantuan still needs to be improved. The most popular food delivery app in the US is Doordash, whose target community is all the people in the country. If Fantuan wants to improve their market share, they need to improve their service, like Meituan. Fantuan may work with cinema, hotel and traveling companies. This might help Fantuan to be a muti-functional app in the US.

5 Conclusion

Meituan is absolutely in a leading position in the Chinese food delivery market. They hold more than half of the food delivery market share. Although Meituan is the company targeted by China's anti-monopoly probe, and gets the punishment, their leading position in the market is still stable. Meituan does not only focus on food delivery service, but also provides many other services, like team buying, selling tickets, traveling, and etc. Their business helps people to get a better life by providing good food and good multi-service. Fantuan is an expectable company in Western countries. Western Countries, take the US as an example, the food delivery market is growing rapidly. In 2020, the growth rate was almost double that of last year because COVID-19 made people increase their demand for food. Food delivery apps can satisfy people's needs for all kinds of food. Fantuan is a company that comes to the US market in 2019. They focus on international students and extend to more local families. They provide food delivery, self-picking, reviewing service for customers. This paper compares Meituan and Fantuan to find out the advantage for Meituan, and how to prove Fantuan to improve their business in western countries. Fantuan needs to notice more about politics, extend business in the future. Fantuan works in many countries, in which each country has their labour laws. Fantuan needs to focus on the law related to the food delivery guy and help them have good welfare. Plus, take Meituan as an example, Meituan success would not be possible without their muti-service. So Fantuan can try to work with local cinema or government to provide ticket or bicycle sharing in the future.

References

1. Zichanxinxi. Meituan and its industry chain research report in 2022. Of Week. https://mp.ofweek.com/Internet/a356714211347
2. S. Zhang. The Compound Financial Instruments and Disclosure of Alternative Performance Measures, Southwestern University of Finance and Economics) (2022).
3. Crunchbase. Fantuan - Contacts, Employees, Board Members, Advisors & Alumni. https://www.crunchbase.com/organization/just-order/people
4. Fantuan. About Fantuan. https://fantuan.ca/zh/#aboutus
5. Xinhua. China introduces supporting regulations for anti-monopoly law. The State Council of the People's Republic of China. https://english.www.gov.cn/statecouncil/ministries/202303/25/content_WS641e4728c6d0f528699dc2c8.html
6. State Administration for Market Regulation. SAMR imposed administrative penalties on Meituan for its monopolistic behavior in the Chinese online food delivery platform service market in accordance with the law. https://www.samr.gov.cn/xw/zj/art/2023/art_31910760066b4f69aa119a20dee250ad.html
7. W. Li, & X. Li. The history and trend of global digital transformation and the Chinese promotion path. E, (05): 36-47 (2022).
8. C. Guo, M. Zhang, & J. Zhao. Research and Outlook of Chinese food delivery industry in 2023. China Lianhe Credit Rating Co., Ltd (2023).
9. S. Wang. Research on Differentiated Promotion Strategy of Homogeneous Catering Platform based on AISAS Model, Guilin University of Electronic Technology) (2023).
10. Y. Liu. Research on the Impact of Big Data Analysis on Corporate Marketing. NET, (12),123-126 (2023).
11. A. N. Press. Food Delivery Workers' Labor Conditions Are Abysmal. Jacobin. https://jacobin.com/2023/04/food-delivery-workers-labor-conditions-are-abysmal

12. Statista. Online Food Delivery - US. https://www.statista.com/outlook/dmo/online-food-delivery/united-states
13. Y. Huang, Y. (2021, July 23). The market status of China's online food delivery industry in 2021. Forward-The Economist.
14. Alibaba. Ele.me. Alibaba group. https://ali-home.alibaba.com/about-alibaba-businesses-1492020506872774656
15. Fantuan. Fantuan Raises $40 Million Series C Round, Led by E-Commerce Platform GrubMarket. PR Newswire. https://www.prnewswire.com/news-releases/fantuan-raises-40-million-series-c-round-led-by-e-commerce-platform-grubmarket-302006255.html
16. Beyrouthy, L. U.S. online food delivery market share 2023. Statista. https://www.statista.com/statistics/1235724/market-share-us-food-delivery-companies/
17. PitchBook. Fantuan Company Profile: Valuation, Funding & Investors.

Research on Business Strategy Based on New Culture and Entertainment Industry

Xiwen Zhang*

The High School Affiliated to SUSTECH, 518109 Shenzhen, China

Abstract. The Disney Company and Warner Brothers have long played an important role in shaping and disseminating American popular culture. With the gradual development and improvement of the Internet and the information technology these days, they are quietly subverting the traditional culture and entertainment industry. Disney and Warner Brothers, as two large and classic film and television companies, their success from their founding to today cannot be separated from their own business strategies. As Disney gradually became bigger and bigger, it acquired many famous companies as its subsidiaries, and Warner Brothers also developed many peripheral products, or cooperated with other companies for their marketing. However, in the process of continuous development, the two companies also faced different problems. This paper studies and analyzes the development status and business strategies of these two companies. At the same time, it also provides some suggestions that are beneficial for the two companies. This paper uses the comparison method, and uses the tabulator data to more convincingly reflect.

1 Introduction

Because of the epidemic, people's online office scenes have gradually increased, and everything online has developed more and more rapidly. At the same time, this has brought huge challenges to the film and television industry, and made the box office of many big-name companies much worse than the expected revenue. Many companies are on the verge of bankruptcy at this stage, but there are still many giant companies that are still strong, Warner and Disney are typical examples. Disney is the first giant in Hollywood, was originally just an animation studio, but the depressed economy after World War II forced Disney to produce a theatrical version of Snow White. And the plot of the Mickey Mouse series they made brought joy to people and also cheered them up in a difficult situation during the depression, while the determined and optimistic animated characters also gave people the motivation to overcome difficulties. The Boston American noted that Mickey Mouse arrived at the beginning of the Great Depression, when the country needed him most, and helped people laugh, forget their creditors, and keep their spirits up [1]. With the gradual development and growth of their subsidiary Marvel Studios, Disney's market share can almost reach 25% of Hollywood, almost monopoly. Warner Brothers, the classic "WB" logo is its abbreviation, the company produced and distributed the world's first true sound film, "The Jazz singer", the success of the film was undoubtedly a blockbuster in the year. After the 1970s, it launched "The Matrix", "Harry Potter" and "The Lord of the Rings" and other series of films, "Harry Potter" films have been "the world's most profitable series". A lot of people have done research on the two companies' marketing strategies, but they are not meticulous enough. The research done in this paper will increase or expand the existing foundation of the film and television industry, which has practical significance for the future development of companies.

2 Description of Disney

In terms of earnings and marketing strategy for the two companies, people have to admit that Disney is outnumbering Warner Brothers. Disney is a "non-stop" Hollywood giant, in other words, the frequency with which its films hit a billion worldwide. Taking a look at the other four studios, Warner and Paramount have managed to make a $1 billion movie worldwide, and they do not know when they are going to make another good one. Universal and SONY have recently had a global movie that broke $1 billion in a few years, but all are concentrated in a series, the former's Jurassic dinosaurs have come to the end of their time, the latter's Spider-Man is to rely on feelings card, all belong to their own troubles. Only Disney, not only the frequency is high, but also are different series flowering, which is obviously much better than the other four. Looking at Disney's films, which have exceeded $1 billion worldwide, its comprehensiveness is very strong. For example, the Marvel Universe, which belongs to the global IP, as long as Mickey Mouse does not add some elements which make audience uncomfortable to the films, then it is basically a victory. Under the strong influence of the Marvel brand, superheroes meet the hero complex in the hearts of young people around the whole

*Corresponding author: dugengchen@hsas.edu.cn

world, so this IP is versatile and popular in most areas. Star Wars, the IP main region is North America, it is in the United States belongs to a unique existence, the American fanaticism for Star Wars is beyond imagination. In fact, it can also be seen from the data of the Table 1. However, all Star Wars movies, the North American box office is very high, "The Force Awakens" is still the only film in North America with a box office breakthrough of 900 million US dollars, and several other films clearly have a bad reputation, but the box office is still a level with "Avengers", and even an external transmission has 500 million a lot of box office.

Table 1. Box Office Figure for Disney Films

Film title	North America box office (dollar)	Chinese box office (RMB)	Global box office (dollar)	Film production cost (dollar)
Avengers: Endgame	858m	4.25b	2.797b	357m
Avengers: Infinity War	678m	2.391b	2.048b	316m
Avengers	623m	568m	1.518b	220m
Panthers	700m	663m	1.347b	200m
Iron Man 3	409m	775m	1.214b	200m
Captain America: Civil War	408m	1.244b	1.153b	250m
Episode VII	936m	82.4m	2.069b	245m
Episode VIII	620m	268m	1.332b	317m
Pirates of Caribbean 4	241m	464m	1.045b	250m
Frozen	400m	298m	1.304b	150m
Frozen 2	477m	861m	1.45b	150m
Toy Story 3	415m	118m	1.066b	222m
Toy Story 4	434m	201m	1.073b	222m
Finding Dory 2	486m	254m	1.028b	200m

Data source: China statistics network: www.itongji.cn

A global Marvel, plus a specialized local Star Wars, have these two cards is basically equal to breaking the game, but Disney has others. PIXAR animation department, a variety of "General Mobilization" animated films, specializing in the global children field, from the box office results can also know how popular, and even the "award machine". From the perspective of film and television production, the intercultural communication of Disney animated films is mainly due to the packaging of its universal value. Universal value can be regarded as global, and Disney is very good at tapping into local content and value. Specifically, the first is in the reference of other countries' stories; The second is in the localization of the role and scene setting [2].

However, in recent years, because the direction of Disney has changed, it especially likes to add some "uncomfortable" elements to the film, like black Little Mermaid and Latino Snow White. It is not that this is bad, but it breaks people's previous cognition and makes people difficult to accept, so it will lose many overseas markets, especially China, the world's second largest film market. Of course, a lean camel is bigger than a horse. On August 9, The Walt Disney Company released its results report for the third quarter of fiscal 2023 ending July 1, 2023. Financial data show that Disney's operating revenue in the third fiscal quarter of 2023 was about $22.3 billion, up 4% from the same period last year, and its overall operating profit was $3.559 billion, which was flat compared with last year, but its net profit plunged, from $1.502 billion in the same period last year to a loss of $153 million. Among them, restructuring and impairment charges surged to $2.65 billion as one of the main reasons for the loss [3]. And with the capital accumulated in the first three stages, the seriousness of the problem will not explode immediately. But in the long run, it is clear that Disney needs to think about these issues. Also, when the Internet and the media are fully developed, Disney's previous content-driven animation linkage model was broken, and a new IP creation method without story background, such as "Stella Lou" and "Lina Belle", appeared [4].

3 Description of Warner Brothers

Warner Brothers as an established company, has a variety of marketing methods, which are well worth people's analysis. Warner Media starts from the strategic level, tactical level and business level, they adapted, made some changes, fused them, and evolved. Warner Brothers has long adhered to the strategy of "taking video content as the center, developing new technologies and business models to enhance the value of content", divesting non-core businesses, reorganizing and optimizing the organizational structure and management system, and enhancing its competitiveness in the new media business represented by streaming media video. Moreover, based on the rich content resources and brands, the company looks for the application opportunities of new technologies and new media, improve consumers' insight ability, upgrade the content production and distribution process in an all-round way, and deeply cultivate, deposit and develop valuable head IP [5]. "Friends" is getting an official sequel. Behind the fanaticism, it was a big marketing move. After a fierce battle between the two major media platforms, the streaming show is about to change its home. From 2015 to 2018, the famous Netflix bought the rights to show "Friends" for 30 million dollars a year, and it proved that the investment was worth it. "Friends" has remained at the top of the viewing charts, winning Netflix a large number of young users, and even in 2019, Netflix paid 100 million dollars to stream it for another year. But today, Friends' producer, Warner Brothers, is launching HBO Max. It found out that Disney+ has three major subsidiaries which can all bring a lot of benefits, Disney, Marvel and Lucas film, so it decided to pay 425 million dollars for the rights to show "Friends" and invest in a special sequel.

In recent years, "IP marketing" is a popular phenomenon. Many TV dramas have become film and television IP because of their high-quality content. Friends is considered one of the most influential and popular TV shows in the world. From the dissemination and reuse of content to the production and creation of content, the ultimate goal of various forms of marketing activities around the IP of Friends is to promote the emotional identification of the audience and thus trigger consumption [6]. As a detonating marketing topic, this is of course a good thing for all the fans of the series, 16 years later to see the actual official sequel, Warner can make a lot of money by this action. This is their latest effort to attract more users in the face of competition for users. Next is "Barbie viral marketing". On July 21, 2023, the live-action film "Barbie" was released simultaneously in China and North America. The film, produced by Warner Brothers, has been a worldwide sensation since its official release. Strong linkage products, immersive interaction, as well as the major brands of integrated marketing, Barbie's overall strategy is a "omnipresent". Whether you like her or not, Barbie is without a doubt the most familiar virtual character [7]. Perhaps some people want to sigh Warner's extravagance, but they might not know that behind this, but also the production of Barbie toy brand -- Mattel in a big chess game. In fact, Mattel through the cooperation with Warner, in the realization of the brand IP (IP is short for Intellectual Property). It is often the result of intellectual and creative labor, rather than a bent product that reflects the popular culture and emotional resonance of consumers. Although a brand carries a product, brand IP can help a brand develop a distinct, vivid personality and engage with its target consumers through stories and brand content. Why is Warner spending so much money to build Barbie's IP? The advantages of branding IP can be boiled down to these two keys. First is improving brand identification and communication. IP is essentially through the continuous output of concrete and personified content, so that the brand is easier to be divided and remembered, so as to maintain the communication power and influence like the classic film and television image. Second is enriching the expression of brand value, enhance consumer loyalty, and provide consumers with not only the functional attributes of the product, but also a carrier of emotions. IP will expand the expression of the brand in culture and value, produce emotional connection with consumers, and ultimately enhance consumer loyalty, turn them into big fans.

4 Comparision of Disney and Warner Brothers

From the perspective of the production styles of the two companies, Warner Brothers focuses on the dark style. Their films are always interwoven with the theme of the struggle between light and darkness. They have a thorough understanding of the chaos, darkness and ugliness of the world, and their works emit a tragic heroic temperament like Akira Kurosawa [8]. So it is much worse than Disney in terms of audience. In the survey, it was found that 99.67% of the audience knew the Avengers, and 92.03% of them knew the main selling point of Iron Man. It can be seen that the dissemination of the Avengers has succeeded in occupying a certain position in the minds of the audience. Those who have seen the Avengers or not will be impressed Iron Man in his red and gold high-tach robot armor [9]. Disney films are more down-to-earth, for example, many of the places of the stories can often be found on the map, whether it is the American Civil War or World War II, there are traces. Moreover, Disney's style is relaxed and humorous, and the characters are amiable, like some heroic roles, which can make the audience feel strongly. Take some well-known superheroes for example, whether it is Spider-Man, Iron Man or Captain America, they feel like everyone's neighbourhood, and these are undoubtedly suitable for all ages. But in contrast, many Warner Brothers' films are set in fictional places, with empty characters, empty stories, and often "cold" characters. Take "Gotham City" as an example, this city can basically be said to be a monopolistic city, but also a place "abandoned by the sun", giving people the feeling that it is cold and damp, evil and rampant, ordinary people live in deep water all day, exploitation at the bottom are repeatedly forbidden. The Batman movie: The first release of the Dark Knight caused a heated discussion. At the same time, the Joker played by Heath Ledger in the film has numerous fans, and many people began to follow the craze of clowns. It is because of this craze that the film Joker, starring Warner Joker, was screened at the Venice Film Festival in August 2019. The film recreates Warner's clown image in the form of the protagonist, realizes the successful construction of the clown's self-value from the perspective of others, and completely depicts the clown image, making DC "clown" widely spread as a cultural symbol representing the bottom and full of darkness [10]. It would be better if Warner were willing to change their old style and try some positive and sunny films with happy endings. Because in terms of acceptability, most audiences still like light-hearted, humorous and down-to-earth movies, and they are also willing to pay for such movies. Or it can be said that Disney's movies are a little more commercial, but there is no denying that many of Warner's movies have a lot of depth, but it is truly difficult for mainstream audiences who yearn for a better life and like happy endings.

Back to today's point of view, when Warner Brothers was so powerful, now why is it not powerful than Disney in film? Focusing on the 21st century Marvel Cinematic Universe and the DC Extended Universe. Most people agree that DC's dark style has more depth than Marvel's in terms of connotation, but there is no denying that in recent years, Warner Brothers' films have been less popular than Disney's films. So, if Warner is willing to cater more to audience preferences, it will make their market bigger and have a better response. There is also some advice for the bosses of the two companies. An old company like Warner Brothers has a problem with bureaucracy -- executives are obsessed with controlling power. So for the creators of their subsidiaries, there are too many constraints and too much interference. In contrast, Disney's management of subsidiaries is relatively loose, so subsidiaries have a lot of freedom in content creation. So, Warner's leaders would do well not to interfere too much in the creation of films unless necessary. For Disney, in recent years, they changed the settings of some works, like the wheat skin color of Snow White, which was against people's original cognition and affected the market in some regions. If they do not change these characters' settings, the effect will be better.

5 Conclusion

In the era of the gradual development of the Internet and social media, the film and television industry has become an indispensable entertainment industry in people's lives. Most people only care about some films, TV series and other film and television products they watch, or peripheral products they buy, but they do not care much about the marketing strategies and publicity methods used by the companies behind these. Understanding and learning to apply the marketing strategies of large companies such as Disney or Warner is important to many businesses and can help them grow better. With the gradual growth of the industry, Disney has created more and more rich characters, its audience is also large, and its income is also the most, but at the same time, it also has some shortcomings exposed, they should keep their own original will, and pay attention to the audience's preferences to produce works. Warner Brothers' work have always been deep in content, but the painting style is relatively dark, and their audience is not very broad, they should pay attention to some concerns and preferences, and do some products according to their preferences. Many other studios can take a look at this research and achieve effective growth by drawing on development experiences. The experience of Warner which can think of and adapt to the trend of media convergence, can be learned by various film and television companies or media companies around the world, so that they can develop and improve.

Of course, the research done in this paper also has shortcomings. The whole paper tends to case analysis, and less uses quantitative research, modelling and calculation research methods. The future can be more in-depth research, but also can expand more cases.

References

1. Z. Xu. Cross-cultural management strategy analysis of Disneyland. Master's thesis, Xinjiang, (2023).
2. C. Q. Song. The Practice and Exploration of Disney Entertainment Industry from the perspective of IP. Master's thesis, Hunan, (2019).
3. S. Tu. Computer newspaper. **11**, (2023).
4. Y. X. Ren. Disney's new IP marketing model under the perspective of new media. PHD thesis, Xian, (2023).
5. L. Ting, L. F. Xu. Transformation, upgrading and Integration Development of Western media publishing field.Take Warner Media as an example. Wuhan, (2020).

6. J. W. Weng. The Connection between Commerce and Emotion: A Study on IP Marketing of American TV Series -- A Case Study of Friends. Master's thesis, Hefei, (2021).
7. J. L. Li. Modern Advertising. Barbie marketing universe, a global pink storm. 20-23(2023).
8. W. J. Yan. The Dark Knight in the author's view -- Nolan. PHD thesis, Pingdingshan, (2019).
9. V. Zhang, K. Xue. Disney brand communication research -- Based on Marvel's Avengers movies. Master's thesis, Shanghai, (2018).
10. C. H. Yang. From the Perspective of the Other to Self-Worth: The Construction of Identity symbols for DC clowns -- Take "Batman: The Dark Knight" and "The Joker" for example. Master's thesis, Enshi, (2022).

https://doi.org/10.1051/shsconf/202418803004

Research on Marketing Strategies of Domestic Movies under the Perspective of 4V Theory: Taking "Full River Red" as an Example

Xiaoyan Zheng*

Maynooth International Engineering College, Fuzhou University, 350100 Fuzhou, China

Abstract. With the increasingly updated development of Chinese domestic movies, China's future movie market has great potential for development. More and more Chinese people tend to walk into cinemas in their free time and pick interested domestic movies to watch. This article argues that effective marketing strategy is an indispensable tool for each movie to reach the audience and improve the market competitiveness, and the 4V marketing theory represents a novel approach to marketing that optimally addresses the varied and individualized growth requirements of the modern age. Based on 4V marketing theory, this article analyzes the successes of the marketing strategy and makes suggestions for the shortcomings of the movie "Full River Red" based on the four aspects of "Variation", "Versatility", "Value" and "Vibration", taking the movie "Full River Red" in the Spring Festival of 2023 as an example. Suggestions are put forward, hoping that this paper can provide a reference for domestic movies to enhance their core competitiveness.

1 Introduction

1.1 Research background and motivation

Beginning at the close of the 20th century, as China's film industry evolved and expanded continuously, the status of Chinese films in the world's film industry has also continued to rise, especially on the first day of the Lunar New Year every year, to go to the cinema to watch a Chinese New Year domestic film with family members has increasingly become the first choice of the public. In recent years, China's movie industry has been developing rapidly, and the market is gradually showing a diversified trend. In the face of such fierce market competition, marketing has become an important magic weapon for movies to stand out. According to Cat Eye Pro App, since its release on the first day of the Lunar New Year in 2023, the movie "Full River Red" has captured 1,743 hot searches on the whole network, creating a cumulative box office of 4.544 billion yuan, and taking the top spot in the box office of mainland movies in 2023, generating a phenomenal landscape of domestic movies with a double harvest of heat and box office. In the fast-paced era of "even fragrant wine is afraid of a deep alley", the success of a movie cannot be separated from the meticulous production of the director, screenwriter, actors, and other personnel, and even more so from the skilful planning and execution of the marketing team.

As the high-tech industry, company, product, and service surfaced, the marketing concept and marketing method are enriching and evolving, and the formation of the own style of new concepts. The third-generation marketing model, the "4V" marketing mix view, was coined by domestic scholar Wu Jinming. The so-called "4V" denotes to "Variation", "Versatility", "Value" and "Vibration" (see Figure 1) [1].

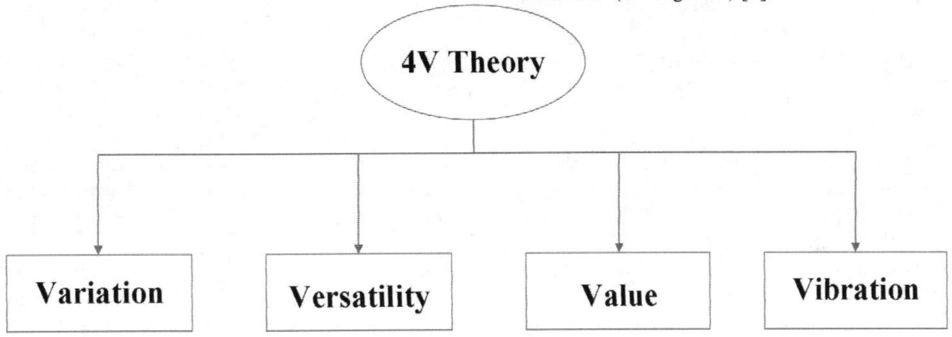

Fig. 1. 4V theory [1]

*Corresponding author: XIAOYAN.ZHENG.2022@MUMAIL.IE

A key aspect of the 4V theory is the concept of "incomplete substitution" in variation marketing, meaning in aspects like product functionality, quality, service, and marketing, the offerings a company makes to its customers are unique and cannot be replaced by other competitors. Variation marketing, aiming to differentiate itself, is typically categorized into product variation, market variation, and image variation. The concept of versatility implies that a company's image in the consumer's perception encompasses three tiers, with the primary role being the product's existence, primarily based on its fundamental features. The second aspect involves expanding the function, meaning the function evolves towards greater depth. Thirdly, extra roles, like those related to aesthetics. Briefly, an increase in the product's features correlates with a rise in its cost, and the reverse is also true. The "value" of 4V marketing theory lies in maximizing value creation. Analyzing the value structure of modern business products reveals two key elements: the fundamental value and the additional value. The first aspect is influenced by the creation and marketing of a product's physical and active labor, while the second encompasses technological enhancements, marketing or service improvements, and the evolution of corporate culture and brand identity. Analyzing the present developmental trajectory reveals a steady decline in the share of living labor usage, centered on product consumption and essential social labor time within the value framework; yet, the share of high-tech added value, including brands like "famous products", "celebrities", "famous enterprises", and corporate culture, that contributes value and marketing value in this value structure is substantial and is set to rise. "Vibration" constitutes the final segment of the 4V theory, denoting the enhancement of value for consumers or customers through ongoing market dominance and competitive edge by businesses, alongside the enterprise's pursuit of "profit maximisation." This highlights the link between a company's capacity to innovate and the consumer's perceived value, aiming to enhance consumer contentment via innovative value. Businesses must focus not just on generating value but also consider the overall customer cost while buying products and services. Customers agree to cover the entire cost only if the customer's total value is at its peak; and it's only upon fulfilling the customer's "value delivery" criteria that the company can ascertain the customer's total cost to "maximize profit" and ensure a balance between supply and demand. Employing the 4V theory to scrutinize film marketing tactics aids companies in comprehending and molding their brand's traits and reputation, boosting its value and competitive edge, and fulfilling their marketing objectives.

The application of 4V marketing theory in the film and television industry is of great significance. Through differentiated content innovation, functional product design, and added value expression, as well as resonance with the audience, enterprises can better meet consumer needs and improve market competitiveness. However, there are still some challenges and problems in the application of 4V marketing theory in the film and television industry, such as how to accurately grasp consumer needs, how to balance commercial interests and social responsibility, etc. Therefore, enterprises need to constantly explore and innovate in practice to achieve the maximum value of 4V marketing theory in the film and television industry.

1.2 Research contents

Based on the characteristics of the film industry and the current social and technological background, this paper will analyze the marketing and distribution strategy of Full River Red from the perspective of the 4V theory, and discuss how Full River Red is different from traditional Chinese New Year movies from the perspectives of variation marketing, versatility, maximizing added value and vibration marketing, and achieve a breakthrough in the box office, and put forward a reference and feasible proposal for brand breakthrough [2]. Finally, this paper presents general conclusions, as well as research limitations and directions for further research.

2. Variation marketing: precise positioning and fine production together to make up for the market gap

Variation marketing aims for "difference" through the "incomplete substitutability" of products, meaning in aspects like function, quality, service, marketing, etc., the offerings for customers are unique and cannot be replaced by competitors. From the movie producers, whether the movie is welcomed by the audience, the most important thing is to be able to distinguish their movies from the competitors, so that moviegoers fall in love at first sight. Therefore, in a sense, to create an audience is to create differences [3]. There is a difference between having a market, to being invincible in the strong players in the same industry competition in the movie. For example, some successful film and television works attract the audience's attention through unique themes, storylines, and character settings, thereby achieving good market performance. In addition, innovation in production techniques is also an important manifestation of differentiation, such as the use of advanced shooting techniques and unique editing methods, making the work unique in visual effects and narrative style.

Zhang Yimou directs and Shen Teng, Jackson Yee, Lei Jiayin, Zhang Yi and Yue Yunpeng star, the movie Full River Red has a strong line-up of big names and is a luxurious cast with a large fan base. With the help of various elements, the movie is a perfect blend of comedy, suspense, and costume, which is a rare combination of elements in the current market. Its novel elements have attracted the interest of many viewers, making it a unique movie in the 2023 Chinese New Year slot. The traditional Chinese New Year is characterized by family reunions and joyful celebrations, which is why the film's comedic style is one of the most colourful parts of the film. The movie's publicity focuses on the slogan of "the first day of the Lunar New Year, suspense is enough, laugh until the end", in which the joyful atmosphere of the holiday of family reunion can stimulate the audience's enthusiasm for watching the movie, and the comedy genre and banter style are extremely popular with families in the Chinese New Year slot; secondly, the element of the suspenseful costume makes the movie appeal to a younger audience and fans of costume films and TV shows willing to watch the movie [4]. Secondly, the suspenseful costume elements also make the movie attract more young audience groups and costume film and television fans willing to go to the theatre to find out what's going on. It is also the consideration of a mature commercial movie that a genre-integrated movie can satisfy the viewing needs of various audiences at the same time.

3. Versatility: integrating aesthetic expression and emotional flow to create an immersive viewing experience

In the 4V theory, the focus is on linking the company's ability to innovate with the values that consumers hold dear. The aim is to maximise consumer satisfaction by providing them with value innovations, emphasizing the personalized needs of consumers, that is, based on the core function of the product, by the consumer's consumption habits, acceptance of habits and other needs, to select the product that suits them [5]. The positioning of a product in the customer's mind has three levels: one is the core function, which is the reason for the product's existence, mainly by the basic function of the product; the second is the extension function, that is, the function of developing the depth direction; the third is additional functions, such as aesthetic function. In the context of the increasingly fierce competition of Chinese New Year movies, movies should not only stay in the plot presentation, but also provide aesthetic expression, spiritual support, and immersive viewing experience while conveying the leisure and entertainment attributes it possesses [6]. For example, movies targeting children may focus more on fun and education, while movies targeting adult audiences may focus more on emotional expression and depth of thought. In addition, with the development of digital technology, the functionality of film and television works has been further expanded, such as new forms of film and television works such as web dramas and microfilms, making film and television works more interactive and participatory

The beauty of "Full River Red" is not only in the image and the use of color but also in the strong visual impact. Zhang Yimou condensed all the scenes in an ancient-style building complex, and at the same time using the traditional art of "walking lanterns" concept, so that all kinds of characters in the corridors walking through, and supplemented with audible bold innovation: the soundtrack used after the adaptation of the traditional Yu Opera, and a blend of rock, electric sound, the characters of the film fast marching when the rapid drums and gongs, transitions fast running board singing makes the film has a strong "Chinese style" [7].The rapid drums and gongs of the characters in the film and the fast-flowing Yu Opera singing during the transitions give the movie a strong "Chinese style", which, together with the use of rock and electro music, makes the soundtrack extremely magical and brings the audience a full movie-going experience. The excellent language rhythm, performance rhythm, plot rhythm, etc. show the core of the story very well, bringing the audience a strong sense of immersion in the process of watching the movie, a sense of release after getting out of the cinema, and a strong desire to swipe the second brush and the desire to share.

4. Maximizing added value: taking offline promotion into account and keeping up with demand across borders

According to the 4V marketing theory, with the change in China's consumer market structure, the constant emergence of high technology has gradually reduced the proportion of necessary labor consumption of products, while services and corporate brand marketing are contributing to the continuous enhancement of the added value of products. In the case of film and television dramas, the basic value of the product is determined when the filming and production are completed, and the subsequently added value focusing on service, management, brand building, etc. can produce sustainable value benefits, realizing a win-win situation for the film and television drama itself, the actors, the director, and the producer.

As the screenwriter of Full River Red, Peking University professor Chen Yu introduced that the creative team, represented by director Zhang Yimou, initially wished to create a film highly related to space, and for this purpose, a complete mansion was specially built in Shanxi. After the release of the movie, its location - Shanxi Taiyuan Full River Red Film and TV Base has also become one of the locations where the majority of fans hit. The popularity of the movie has also brought considerable traffic to the ancient city of Taiyuan, driving the development of the local tourism industry and many other related industries [8]. In addition, the "Full River Red Online Theme Run", which was organized by Full River Red and Gudong App, was carried out from 12.01.2023 to 12.02.2023, and the number of participants reached 220,000. By freely choosing a participant group and completing the running race, people were able to receive a beautiful commemorative medal inspired by the token in the movie. This joint activity strengthened the brand image of the movie while crossing the border to keep up with the demand and meet people's additional needs and expectations.

5. Vibration marketing: character image breaks through the shackles and resonates with the times

4V marketing theory, vibration is the enterprise to continue to capture the market and maintain the competitiveness of the value of innovation to consumers or customers to bring the "maximization of value", as well as the resulting enterprise's "profit maximization", emphasizing the enterprise's ability to innovate with the values valued by consumers, through the provision of value innovation for consumers to maximize their satisfaction. The focus is on linking the company's ability to innovate with the values that consumers hold dear, and maximising their satisfaction by providing them with value innovations. As a special commodity with both economic and cultural benefits, movies need to awaken the emotional memories of the public through the cohesion of the special symbols in the movies, to realize the release of cultural values and promote the development of the cultural economy at the same time. Therefore, from this point of view, the marketing team is bound to need to create an emotional resonance between the movie and the users when marketing the movie [9].

Although "Full River Red" is a commercial genre movie, the characterization of its protagonist breaks through the traditional shackles [10]. The movie has the same title, "Full River Red", its author Yue Fei as a generation of patriotic generals has been celebrated throughout the ages, but the movie does not directly depict the heroic deeds of Yue Fei against the Jin army, and does not take Yue Fei, who is directly related to "Full River Red", as the main object of expression. Instead, the movie focuses on a group of small people at the bottom of the hierarchy - soldiers and pawns, singing and dancing girls, night watchmen, carriage drivers, etc. The movie places the small people in a broad historical background, and through the civilian perspective of the small people, the movie tells the story of the pursuit of Yue Fei by Sun Jun, Zhang Da, etc. to restore and outline the memory of the family and the country, and restore and show the national hero Yue Fei's loyalty and righteousness and his resistance to the Jin Dynasty. It also restores and displays the national hero Yue Fei's loyalty and righteousness and the spirit of fighting against the Jin Dynasty, and awakens people's historical memory and collective patriotic feelings.

6. Conclusion

In the context of China's national conditions, movies are an important communication medium with the function of cultural accumulation. With the continuous progress and development of China's domestic movies in recent years, more and more excellent movies have appeared in front of the people. In order to study the marketing strategy of domestic films and gain insights into the key for films to stand out among competing films, this paper analyzes in detail the film "Full River Red", which was the No. 1 film in the box office of the Spring Festival in 2023, from the perspective of 4V marketing theory. It is found that the movie has outstanding performance in all four aspects of the 4V theory.

In terms of variation, Full River Red has a lavish cast and a large fan base even before the screening. Its skilful use of various elements, the perfect integration of comedy, suspense, ancient costumes, is a rare combination of elements in the current market, its novel elements with attracted the interest of many viewers, so that it has become a distinctive film in the 2023 Spring Festival slot. In terms of versatility, the movie expresses Chinese aesthetics to the fullest, with both visual and auditory sensations, and traditional innovations coexisting, bringing the audience the best movie-going experience. The excellent plot rhythm of the movie shows the core of the story and the flow of the main idea very well, bringing the audience a strong desire to watch and share the movie. In value aspects, the movie Full River Red takes into account the offline promotion and cross-border publicity, keeping up with the demand, the success of the Full River Red film and television base and the Full River Red online theme running activities have a good offline publicity effect, so that its intellectual property can be more deeply rooted in the hearts and minds of the people. In vibration aspect, the character image of the movie breaks through the shackles of the traditional film's protagonist halo, starting from the perspective of a small person, shaping the role of flesh and blood, resonating with the times. It is believed that this paper can provide suggestions and references to the current movie production team and help the domestic movie market get better and better.

The shortcomings of this paper are: due to limited resources, only a single film Full River Red is chosen as a typical case study; this paper is mainly based on theoretical analysis, based on the perspective of the 4V theory to analyze the film, and does not carry out specific quantitative measurements. Therefore, in the future, more cases will be included based on the 4V theory for more comprehensive and in-depth analysis. At the same time, with the availability of data resources, in the future, the author will consider combining real data to quantitatively calculate market valuations and further expand the research achievements in this field.

References

1. J. M. Wu. China Industrial Economics. **(06)**, 70-75, (2001)
2. X. Y. Huang, X. Zhou. Forum Of Arts. **(03)**, 13-18 (2023).
3. S. Y. Zhu. Time Honored Brand Marketing Magazine. **(15)**, 15-19, (2023).
4. Y. N. Huang, Y. F. Ling. Voice & Screen World. **(13)**, 93-95, (2023).
5. Y. Kang. Research on marketing communication of domestic film Tiktok, PhdThesis, Liaoning, (2022).
6. J. Cheng, X. Y. Liu, Y. H. Sun. Radio & TV Journal. **(04)**, 61-64, (2023)
7. L. Zhao. China Film News. 005, (2023).
8. X, Q. Guan. China Film News. 007, (2023).
9. W. Yang. China News Publishing Radio and Television News. 008. (2023).

https://doi.org/10.1051/shsconf/202418803004

10. L. F. Zhou. Research on Li Ning brand marketing optimization strategy, PhdThesis, Beijing, (2023).

Analysis of the Influencing Factors of Marketing Strategy on Consumer Purchasing behaviour: A Case Study of Apple

Qingyan Cai[1,*], *Shi* Chen[2]

[1]College of Business Administration, Capital University of Economics and Business, 100070 Beijing, China
[2]School of Economics and Trade, Xinhua College of Sun Yat-Sen University, 523133 Dongguan, China

Abstract. This passage provides an analysis of Apple Inc.'s marketing strategies, focusing on its advertising and product marketing tactics, as well as its approach to celebrity and film marketing. It highlights Apple's emphasis on simplicity and minimalism in its advertising campaigns, utilizing short, memorable slogans and a clean design aesthetic. The passage also discusses Apple's use of secrecy and mystery surrounding product launches to generate consumer curiosity and anticipation. Additionally, it addresses Apple's engagement with filmmakers to feature its products in movies and TV shows, further enhancing brand visibility. The passage concludes with suggestions for Apple, including the importance of understanding consumer needs, maintaining brand loyalty, and developing a comprehensive marketing strategy that addresses various factors influencing consumer behavior.

1 Introduction

Apple Inc. is a technology company known for its innovative products and services. It was founded in 1976 by Steve Jobs, Steve Wozniak, and Ronald Wayne. After four years, Apple soon went public and became the world's most valuable company for multiple consecutive years. Apple has evolved into a frontrunner in the consumer electronics sector. The company is famous for its widely acclaimed range of items, including the iPhone, iPad, Mac, and Apple Watch. It also offers software and services such as iOS, macOS, and the App Store. Apple has cultivated a devoted following of customers by placing a strong emphasis on design, quality, and user experience. This approach has firmly established Apple as a significant player in the global tech market. Apple's brand marketing revolves around three marketing concepts written by one of its founders, Mike Markkula: empathy, focus, and impute. Apple incorporated the pursuit of brand building, value resonance and product marketing into the whole process of Apple product launch before, during and after. With product innovation as the core, combining humanized communication planning such as copywriting, advertising, content and celebrities, as well as experience store marketing that brings consumers a sense of participation, and then integrating a sense of corporate social responsibility with great value, integrated reach and touch users.

Apple has positioned itself as a leader in high-end technology brands, not just a hardware company, but a technology company that provides total solutions. Apple achieves its market positioning by creating a unique brand image and providing high-quality products. Through their positioning, it is not difficult to see that Apple's target market is mainly middle and high-end consumers, that is, people who have higher requirements for product quality and design and have higher purchasing power. Apple has focused more on young and professional consumers, who typically have a greater interest in and demand for technology products.

In 2023 Apple's brand value is estimated to be around $880.5 billion. The brand has been named the winner of CMO's Best Marketing Survey Award for 10 consecutive years. Forbes Global CMO List is highly recognized in the marketing and business circles, which is an important means to measure the effectiveness of corporate marketing strategies. The 22 indicators to measure CMO influence include personal, brand, marketing and activity attention, emotion and prominence [1]. On a global scale, Apple is influencing the fate of this industry and even the world itself with its unparalleled marketing strategies.

The study of how Apple Inc.'s marketing strategy affects consumer behavior is crucial in the marketing field. Apple, a highly successful and innovative technology company, has transformed the consumer electronics industry with its iconic products like the iPhone, iPad, and Mac. The company's marketing strategies, including brand positioning, product design, advertising campaigns, and customer experience initiatives, have played a vital role in shaping consumer perception and purchase decisions.

Understanding the influence of Apple's marketing efforts on consumer behavior is important for researchers and businesses alike. For researchers, it provides valuable insights into the effectiveness of different marketing strategies and their implications for

* Corresponding author: yomioki0721@cueb.edu.cn

consumer behavior theories. It allows for a deeper understanding of how marketing messages, brand image, and product features impact consumers' attitudes, preferences, and intentions to purchase.

For businesses, comprehending the impact of Apple's marketing strategy on consumer behavior offers valuable knowledge for developing effective marketing plans and strategies. By studying how Apple's branding, advertisements, and product innovations resonate with consumers, companies can gain inspiration and learn best practices to enhance their own marketing efforts. Furthermore, understanding the specific elements of Apple's marketing strategy that drive consumer behavior can inform businesses about potential areas for differentiation and gaining a competitive advantage in the market.

The focus of the following content is to provide a detailed analysis of Apple's marketing strategies. Our analysis will encompass various aspects of the marketing domain such as advertising methods, marketing concepts for product development, celebrity marketing, and film marketing. The purpose of this analysis is to gain insights into how these diverse marketing behaviors are connected to consumers' purchasing behavior and their potential impact. By the end of this analysis, we aim to provide a comprehensive understanding of how Apple has been successful in capturing the market and maintaining its position as one of the world's leading tech companies.

2 Marketing strategy analysis

2.1 Advertising market

Apple's advertising and marketing is a model worth learning from in the whole industry. The marketing tactics every time Apple uses, brings about phenomenally successful results. Here, we will analyze this advertising marketing strategy's impact on consumer behavior from three parts: above-the-line advertising and product launch.

2.1.1 Above-the-line advertising

Apple has always communicated the product features and the ideas behind them in the simplest way, letting their products speak louder than anything, and keep their visual representation and information straightforward. Apple believes that their devices don't need expensive advertising to sell. This strategy is also reflected in Apple's copywriting and color scheme. Whether it's the product introduction itself or the promotional copy for a new product launch, it appears in the form of a short sentence that is easy to remember. At the same time, Apple also has a well-received fashion and simple design of the colour scheme. By simplifying the composition and colour scheme of website, Apple tried hard to reduce misunderstanding. The choice of using large fonts with simple words directly emphasizes the characteristics that consumers need most. This is Apple's successful content marketing strategy, which focuses on creating high-tech products without using technical jargon. Instead of highlighting specifications and features, Apple's marketing and advertising approach revolves around how their products can enhance people's lives.

In 1997, when Jobs returned to Apple, he believed that a fierce advertising campaign aimed at consumers was crucial for the company's temporary stagnation. Under the leadership of art director Lee Clow, Apple completed its first publicity campaign from advertisement publication to screening, with the slogan "Think Different" that has since taken deep root in many people's hearts. It is this simple slogan which has brought great influence to Apple at that time [2]. This advertisement also gave consumers a powerful impact, Apple's "Think Different" image was strengthened into the user's brain, become a creative synonym. The success of this advertising strategy is well reflected in the sales data of iMac launched in 1998. iMac has a clear target group of users, suitable for personal life groups, rather than students or company staff professional computer. Before the official launch of iMac, there were 150000 pre-sales in the United States, and in the six weeks after the official sale, its sales reached 278000 units, more than 128000 units, almost doubled [3]. Many stores have been open late at night, and it rose to the top of the computer sales list 14 days after its release. The focus of the iMac advertisement is not on the introduction of technological progress, but on highlighting consumer demand, reflecting the simplicity of operation and convenient Internet function, and the slogan "I Think, therefore iMac" has been very well continued.

2.1.2 Product launch

Typically, when a company introduces a new product to the market, the marketing team discloses all the details and information about it. This is done to inform customers thoroughly and generate excitement, ultimately building anticipation. However, Apple has adopted a unique approach by deliberately keeping the mystery surrounding their new products. By revealing less information, Apple manages to ignite people's curiosity and generate even greater interest. This strategy of creating suspense during product launches has proven to be one of Apple's most effective marketing tactics. It cleverly converts the target audience into loyal fans because it sparks their curiosity, motivates them to seek out additional information, and encourages them to share everything they discover about the product.

There was once a research team that did a brainwave experiment on the degree of response of different brands. From the study, EmSense chose 200 people, which ages 18 to 54, lived in New York and San Francisco. Neuroscience can provide "a more accurate way to figure out what consumers really like," Mr. Stagliano said in the report, which helps to produce the ADs that "break through the clutter" rather than contribute to it. This study tested their biosensor responses to 19 commercials that won awards last year at the International Advertising Festival in Cannes, France, and Ads that won Effie Awards last year. According to the study, they looked at the spots like a commercial for Apple with characters playing "PC" and "Mac"; the "I Feel Pretty" spot for Nike, with Maria Sharapova, and a commercial for Tide with a talking stain on a man's shirt. People when hear "Apple" "tend to be a little less emotional and use rational claims a bit more". We all know that this result means that people has little reaction to negative news or things about Apple. It can be seen that everyone's trust in Apple has been unshakable [4].

In recent years, Apple has struggled to build a community which is full of their loyal users, customers, and fans around the world [5]. Apple's marketing strategy includes making customers want to join the community that is considered "cool." Apple has cleverly exploited the universality of this self-perception, which has convinced its customers that the brand understands them and likes them. Apple also created a fantastic bond between potential customers and brands, they created a lasting connection for existing customers. The company still focuses on the "emotional economy", that is, changing the "rational economy" to the "emotional economy". This amazing approach mobilizes communication and understanding between consumers and businesses, emotionally connecting products, consumers and businesses.

Even small brands can build a community of loyal users and customers by building a strong, engaged user community that clarifies your company's brand values and personality. And Apple officially used its legendary marketing in advertising to establish a "fruit fan empire".

2.2 Product Marketing

Apple's core competence lies in the production of exceptional products that appeal to consumers. This principle forms the basis of its marketing strategy. Since the debut of the iMac personal computer in 1998, Apple has been a pioneering force in the technology industry. This was followed by the introduction of the iPod music player in 2001 and the MacBook in 2006, which further solidified the brand's reputation for innovation. In 2007, Apple launched the iPhone, which revolutionized the smartphone market, while the iPad, introduced in 2010, set new standards in the tablet market. Apple's unwavering commitment to technology advancement has enabled the brand to maintain its position as a leader in the industry. Apple has been at the forefront of promoting software and hardware development in the field of artificial intelligence. Steve Jobs once stated that "Apple's key is to develop inspiring products", a philosophy that the company has certainly upheld. In conclusion, Apple's unwavering focus on developing high-quality products that resonate with consumers has been the driving force behind its success. Its innovative approach to product development, coupled with a strong marketing strategy, has set it apart from its competitors and cemented its position as a leader in the technology industry [6].

2.3 Celebrity marketing

In the contemporary mobile phone market, characterized by intense competition and rampant entertainment marketing, Apple has refrained from associating with a celebrity spokesperson. Nonetheless, this does not imply that Apple has abandoned its celebrity strategy. Rather, the company seeks to identify individuals whose values and product beliefs align with Apple's. Steve Jobs, the former CEO of Apple, had a distinctive approach to presenting the organization's products to consumers. By conveying his paranoid yet perfect, rebellious yet innovative personality to the world, he infused this persona into Apple's culture and carried it to the market. This culture that Jobs established has garnered widespread recognition and deeply ingrained itself in the hearts of consumers. For many, Apple series products are no longer solely communication and entertainment tools but instead represent a carrier of faith and character. Consequently, they take pride in being part of this culture.

2.4 Film marketing

Phil Schiller, former SVP of global marketing at Apple, revealed that the company collaborates with Hollywood to integrate its products in TV shows and movies. Director Ryan Johnson recently disclosed two pieces of information pertaining to the use of Apple products in movies. Firstly, Apple permits the use of their products in films; however, they do not provide any financial compensation for this usage. Secondly, filmmakers must adhere to Apple's guidelines when featuring their products, which include a prohibition on the use of their products by negative or villainous characters. This approach presents a lucrative opportunity for companies to leverage software services as a cost-effective alternative to hardware manufacturing. By offering these services at no cost, businesses can effectively curtail advertising expenditures associated with TV and film budgets, while simultaneously increasing the product's visibility to millions of people. The resultant economies of scale and cost savings can translate into enhanced profitability and competitiveness for the business. During the 1990s, Jon Holtzman served as the marketing director for Apple. At that time, many filmmakers expressed an interest in using Apple products as props in their movies but often encountered difficulties obtaining the latest models. Holtzman successfully lobbied Apple's management to prioritize filmmakers, as well as media and relatives of employees, in the distribution of Apple products. Subsequently, Apple products - particularly the latest models - have regularly made appearances in Hollywood movies at no cost.

In 1996, Apple entered into a collaboration with the film production company responsible for the first installment of the Mission Impossible series. Holtzman attests that this partnership "saved nearly $500,000 in production costs and received commercials directed by Brian De Palma and starring Tom Cruise." In the fourth installment of the series (2011), Apple products were featured for over eight minutes. Market research firm

Smallwood estimated the value of these scenes to be an impressive $23 million.

3 Suggestions

As one of the premier corporations in the domestic consumer electronics industry, Apple possess the capability to adapt to the swift changes and intense competition within the market. Currently, the challenges they confront revolve around sustaining a stable growth trajectory, countering the encroachment of foreign behemoths in the domestic market, and expanding the presence of their branded products in international markets [7].

Consumer purchasing behavior is influenced by a multitude of factors, including personal, social, cultural, and psychological factors. Personal factors, such as age, income, and lifestyle, are significant determinants of consumer behavior. Social factors, such as family, friends, and social media, also exert a substantial impact on consumer decision-making. Moreover, cultural factors, such as values, beliefs, and customs, shape consumer preferences and influence their purchasing decisions. Lastly, psychological factors, such as motivation, perception, and learning, also hold significant sway on consumer behavior. Businesses that take the time to understand and analyze these factors can gain a competitive edge in the market and develop successful marketing strategies that resonate with their target audience [8].

The concept that "Customer is God" is always right and suitable in any circumstance. For Apple, they should pay attention to user needs in a timely manner, so that the product design would have the viability to arouse the users' surprise. Recently, Apple released a new model, the iPhone 15, but the effect was not as expected. Only one month after its release, sales fell by 6%, and everyone said that they "don't satisfy with the new product" [9]. The worst-case scenario is that people are no longer obsessed with Apple products, so Apple should continue to maintain user stickiness and increase brand loyalty to form the core competitiveness.

Given the complexity of the decision-making process, it is imperative that Apple develops a comprehensive marketing strategy that addresses each of these factors. This strategy should focus on building a strong brand image, enhancing the personalization of products, augmenting the level of online and offline marketing, and strengthening the marketing team's core competencies. By doing so, Apple can create a marketing approach that effectively targets each of these factors, ultimately leading to increased consumer purchasing behaviour [10].

4 Conclusion

Apple is a technology giant that has been dominating the global market for several years and has established itself as the most valuable company in the world. This unparalleled success can be attributed to various factors, including its innovative product designs, exceptional customer service, and a monopolistic market position. However, what sets Apple apart from its competitors is its unique marketing philosophy which has enabled the company to make effective purchasing decisions and achieve unmatched prosperity. Apple has an in-depth understanding of its customers' needs and preferences and has demonstrated a strong commitment to meeting them by employing cutting-edge marketing techniques. The company's marketing strategies have played a crucial role in building a loyal customer base that is willing to pay a premium price for Apple products. Moreover, Apple has maintained its dominant market position by leveraging its marketing expertise and staying ahead of the competition. This article delves into the theoretical aspects of marketing while highlighting Apple's successful marketing strategies and providing valuable insights for other companies looking to formulate their marketing strategies. The article suggests that companies can learn from Apple's marketing philosophy, which includes creating a brand image that resonates with their target audience, delivering exceptional customer experiences, and employing data-driven marketing strategies.

However, the article acknowledges that there is a lack of data provision, which limits the depth of the analysis. Nevertheless, with more relevant and specific data made public in the future, it is expected that more in-depth research can be carried out to explore the richer significance behind Apple's marketing approach. To sum up, Apple's marketing philosophy has been pivotal to its unprecedented success, and businesses can learn from its unique marketing strategies to achieve growth and market dominance. By implementing the right marketing strategies, companies can create a loyal customer base and establish themselves as industry leaders in their respective markets.

Authors Contribution

All the authors contributed equally and their names were listed in alphabetical order.

References

1. K. M. Getchell, L. S. Beitelspacher. Business Horizons. **(63)**, 607-617, (2020).
2. N. B. Omelechko. Antonymy in an Advertising Slogan. (2021).
3. Q. X. Wei. Research on Apple's marketing strategy in China, PhdThesis, Tianjing, (2018).
4. S. Bostanshirin. Proceedings of SOCIOINT14- International Conference on Social Sciences and Humanities, Istanbul, September. 2014, 8-10(2014).
5. B. Hu. International market strategy for the Apple brand. PhdThesis, Dalian, (2014).
6. B. B. Feng, A. D. Hu. Research on Transmission Competence. 1, (2018)
7. J. Ken Corley,Zack Jourdan,W. Rhea Ingram. Electronic Markets. **(23)**, 177-204, (2013).

https://doi.org/10.1051/shsconf/202418803005

8. T.T. Yang. China Market. 3, (2023)
9. J. R. Brown, J. L. Crosno, P. Y. Tong. Industrial Marketing Management. **(77)**, 155-169,(2019).
10. H. Y. Zhang. Apple's brand research from the perspective of consumerism. Phd Thesis, Heilongjiang, 2017.

The Impact of Social Media on Consumer Sentiment

Mengyuan Sun*

One Direction Academy, M3C1V9 Toronto, Canada

Abstract. With the wide use of network media, consumers' information acquisition and communication methods have undergone significant changes. Network media not only provides them with a fast and efficient way to obtain information, but also provides them with a broader social space and communication platform. Therefore, the popularity of social media has brought some negative effects, such as low mood and depression among consumers. This paper will first study the impact of social media operation strategies on consumer sentiment. Secondly, the author will examine how social media self-control affects mood, which includes how users control their emotions and behaviors on social media, and the impact of this self-control on consumer mood. This paper will discuss and study through the research methods of psychology and sociology. Finally, this study aims to analyze the problem of information overload between social media and consumer sentiment by focusing on the comments made by consumers on social media. At the end of the study, the research results need to be summarized and analyzed in order to provide useful references for social media platforms to manage consumer emotions, so as to provide useful references for lawmakers, academics and practitioners.

1 Introduction

Using social media has developed to be one of the primary methods that people in today's society may connect, obtain information, and have fun as The Times has expanded. Social media is a subset of social media platforms that let users create accounts, communicate with others, upload movies and photographs, and share content. The foundation of it is Internet and mobile communication technology. People's social habits have changed immensely as a result of social media's broad usage and simplicity of use, making it an indispensable tool for exchanging concepts, knowledge, and day-to-day experiences. In the digital age, social media provides a new channel for communication. Before, the only options for people to socialize were in person, over the phone, or through letters. Through the connections it makes with people of all backgrounds, interests, and cultures, social media also provides people with an avenue to rapidly expand our social network. Like any other technology, social networking is not without its problems, though. On the other side, some people may disseminate falsehoods and incorrect information on social media, which will have a negative impact on other people and society as a whole. These individuals may overly pursue vanity and comparison on social media and seek out others' attention and admiration. Because of this, consumers must exercise reason when using social media to avoid having negative emotional effects. As a new way of communication, social media has two sides: on the one hand, if the operator adopts appropriate operational strategies, social media can positively affect the emotions of consumers; On the other hand, factors such as information overload, authenticity of information, ease of use of features and use of multiple platforms can also negatively impact consumer sentiment.

To reduce the emotional impact of information overload on users, operators need to take measures. This study aims to improve the negative emotions and anxiety depression caused by social media by paying attention to consumers' statements posted on social media to conduct emotional sentiment analysis. Through real-time monitoring of social public opinion and user sentiment, it can also provide strong support for the government and enterprises to better serve the public.

2. The impact of social media operation strategies on consumer sentiment

In the age of information explosion, people's time is becoming more and more fragmented. Social media such as Twitter, Instagram, Wechat, Weibo, Tiktok are becoming more and more popular because they are diverse, rich and easy to use. For example, with the popularity of Wechat public accounts, people used to spend a lot of time on traditional media to get information, but now they only need to pay attention to a few public accounts to get information easily. So, the Wechat public account has become a form of "We Media" that people like to browse. People also pay close attention to Wechat public accounts.

According to the CNNIC China Internet Report, the number of people using Wechat worldwide has exceeded 1.5 billion, and the number of Wechat users is huge. In the three months of operation of the public account, the

*Corresponding author: funcheesesun@ldy.edu.rs

survey found that the number of articles read in the days after the publication of a significant increase. This shows that the targeted content and users of Wechat public accounts remain basic, and the users are basically stable. According to user data, the content quality and user needs of public accounts are key factors in attracting and retaining users. This shows that some public accounts can attract new users and meet the needs of old users [1]. Display content has an effective impact on consumers.

By spreading positivity, these social media can enhance consumers' purchase intention and loyalty, bring positive emotions, and can also increase social media mobile online payments [2]. Peter Drucker introduced the concept of "consumer perceived value" in the 1990s.The concept describes consumers' perceptions of the value of goods, and these perceptions determine whether they buy goods or not. This concept includes consumers' overall evaluation of a product's quality, desire, convenience, and pleasantness. Rafael et al. point out that by using a perceived value system, consumer purchases and choices can be predicted and evaluated. Li Weiqing et al. developed a consumer preference prediction model based on perceived value. The model shows that consumers have an impact on the quality, reviews and price of products, and these effects ultimately influence their purchase decisions [3]. For example, some social media allow consumers to feel the advantages and value of products by publishing user evaluations and sharing experience, thus enhancing their sense of trust and security in these social media. Since most social media information is modified, embellished, or even exaggerated, it is easier for social media users to make upward social comparisons. Social media upward social comparison is when a person compares themselves to others who are superior to them in terms of appearance, ability, etc., by browsing information on social media [4].

3. The self-control of social media is emotional

Compared with traditional media, social media has stronger openness, interaction and immediacy, which attracts the participation and attention of consumers [5]. Some researchers believe that social media use can make people lack self-control and lead to feelings of stress, depression, anxiety and other emotions. From the perspective of gender, according to the gender difference analysis of social media intensity, self-control and emotion, men's social media intensity is slightly lower than that of women, but the difference is not obvious. This shows that men and women rely on social media to a similar degree in modern life, perhaps due to the popularity of the Internet, people can use mobile phones at any time, a variety of social media emerge in an endless stream, can meet the needs of men and women, and increasingly become a daily necessity. In terms of self-control, men scored significantly better than women [6]. Thus, women are more emotionally affected than men. In terms of age, people of different ages show great differences in self-control. This may be due to psychological maturity and temptation at different ages, leading to different self-control abilities. The over-55s scored above average among all age groups, and compared with other age groups, they gradually gained control and were able to resist impulses and adapt to social situations. Middle-aged people aged 35 to 44 scored the most, perhaps because they faced more life problems and financial pressures [6]. It is easy to be emotionally negative. This is followed by 15 to 24 years old, when many big decisions need to be made, while living in a fast lifestyle and fierce social competition can lead to confusion about the future, inner depression, and depression. From the perspective of education level, the study of Li Qiaoling et al. shows that there are significant differences in the use of social media in different education levels, which is related to different knowledge levels, information contact and dependence on social media [6].

However, with the popularity of social media, people at every cultural level are likely to be affected. The study found that undergraduate and graduate students scored highest in social media use and used social media more frequently, and no significant differences in self-control were found among people of different cultural levels, suggesting that these people showed an upper to average level of self-control and were able to effectively control their behavior. However, with the popularity of social media, people at every cultural level may be affected, and people may develop negative emotions that affect their social and lifestyle. Therefore, frequent use of social media is associated with factors such as social comparison and social isolation [6]. Consumers' psychological empowerment is influenced by social support and information quality, which leads to information avoidance behavior. Perceptual overload and social comparison have significant effects on consumers' cognitive dissonance. When people may be displayed in the lives of others, it can lead to dissatisfaction and anxiety about their own lives. Because it requires more time and energy to process this information, it can also lead to anxiety and stress [7].

4. Social media and consumer sentiment information overload

When people use social media too much, it leads to information overload. Information overload is usually due to conflicts between individuals with limited information processing capabilities. System function overload occurs when the complexity of the use of technical resources exceeds the addition of new functions [8]. A survey of 298 social media users by the University of Salford found that 66% felt anxious after using social media [8]. The effects of social media on emotions can be studied medically, psychologically, and sociologically. Current research has made some progress on the effects of anxiety on social media users. However, many researchers classify social media anxiety as information anxiety or social anxiety. Bozionelos' research shows that when people generate too much anxiety about information systems such as social media,

https://doi.org/10.1051/shsconf/202418803006

users may resort to evasive behavior, which leads to less frequency and efficiency of use. Physical and psychological stress are the most common manifestations of anxiety among social media users. Naveed found that users' uncertainty about information utilization led to their high expectations of information benefits; Second, high expectations lead to anxiety. Bad social media management and communication leads to users being oppressed and isolated [8]. Because of the huge amount of information and uncertainty of social media, users must be useful or interesting from a large number of information. The "information island" of social media reduces the efficiency of users to receive more homogenized information, resulting in information redundancy, which turns into self-compulsion and anxiety [8]. Four speculations about the impact of information overload on consumer sentiment.

4.1 Information redundancy affects consumer sentiment

Driven by commercial interests, social media is flooded with advertisements and junk information. These spam messages make social media consumers feel tired and anxious [8].

4.2 Information authenticity affects consumer sentiment

Because social media has many functions, it can confuse consumers. At first, customers made the mistake of using features they were not familiar with. For example, older children need to learn the intricacies of social media before they can use it. However, users may find social media difficult to use due to factors such as unstable and slow response of websites or mobile apps. This can lead to psychological symptoms such as anxiety and anxiety [8].

4.3 Functional ease of use affects consumer sentiment

According to the survey, from 2013 to 2014, the number of people using two or more social media apps increased by 10 percent in one year. On the one hand, using multiple social media platforms increases the amount of tasks undertaken by users, leading to anxiety and cognitive impairment; On the other hand, since each social media platform has its own rules, it's easy to master using one social media platform alone; However, as the number of social media platforms increases, users can feel difficult to control, leading to negative emotions [8].

4.4 Using multiple platforms increases user anxiety.

Fig. 1 shows the research model of the influence of external factors of social media on consumer sentiment built in this paper based on the above analysis and hypothesis [8].

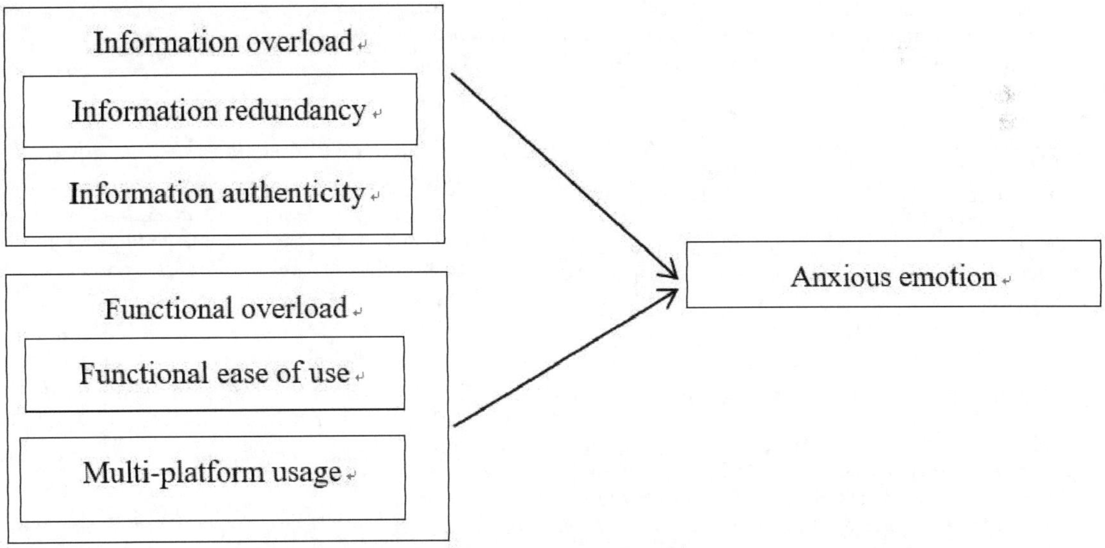

Fig.1. Influencing factor model of social media users' anxiety [8]

5 Suggestions

Although social media is a valuable source of information, it is evident that information variables have an impact on users' emotions. This is primarily because over 70% of the content on social media is duplicated, and there is a severe information silos problem. These factors make it harder for users to locate relevant or important information while also increasing the likelihood that they will forget it [8]. This means that social media companies must actively offer psychological therapy and intervention services to users in order to encourage the increase in the user base of relevant issues.

In order to reduce the impact of information overload on users' emotions, operators in social media need to provide higher quality information, such as improving the information filtering mechanism and raising the threshold for authoritative information to publish accounts. Through the user's communication behavior, location information and other data, operators can mine the needs and preferences of consumers, and provide services and recommendations for consumers. It indirectly affects the relationship between social media use and consumer sentiment [9]. The degree to which a person is affected by stress in a particular environment depends mainly on the traditional perception of the individual, followed by the environment. A person shows carrying through perception and behavior. Psychological stress should result in a response to physical burden [10].

In order to better control their stress and anxiety, consumers can focus on the following areas: First of all, people ought to use social media more responsibly, acknowledge that it is only one aspect of their lives, and stop viewing it as the entirety of it. Second, in order to lessen tension and worry, individuals ought to focus more on their mental health and acquire methods of relaxation like deep breathing and mindfulness meditation. Thirdly, users need to be mindful of how they handle social media. By listening, voicing their own thoughts, and respecting those of others, people may learn to prevent disputes and misunderstandings. To guarantee that users may more readily profit from social media on the platform, social media companies should fortify their content management methods. These should include early blocking of unlawful short films and frequent screening of offensive comments and videos. Furthermore, it is recommended that social media platforms enhance their user reporting procedures in order to incentivize users to proactively report offensive information and guarantee prompt resolution of such reports. Furthermore, it is important that social media platforms consistently enhance and optimize the management of content to facilitate users' enjoyment of social media's ease and fun.

6 Conclusion

With the rapid development of new media, social media platforms have gradually become an important channel for the public to obtain information and express ideas. Social media platforms provide consumers with a place to vent their emotions, let them share their lives and some emotions, which also allows consumers to have a sense of participation and satisfaction, while relieving their emotional pressure from different aspects, such as study and work pressure, using social media to distract their attention and relax properly. In short, social media has become an indispensable part of modern society. However, consumers must also be aware of the negative issues that social media can bring, namely when people with different views argue on social media, it can lead to emotional polarization and negative emotions. These problems deserve people's attention. Serious negative emotions can lead to anxiety and depression, if the impact of negative emotions is not paid attention to, anxiety and depression will become more and more serious. Prolonged exposure to negative emotions can lead to physical ailments, such as depression and irritability. Therefore, consumers should pay attention to the impact of negative emotions, learn to control their emotions, maintain an optimistic attitude and a positive attitude. In addition, if consumers feel that their emotions are out of control or having a negative impact on their lives, they should seek professional psychological counseling and treatment immediately. Through this series of studies, it is found that social media is a double-edged sword that affects consumer sentiment. Consumers need to take its positive and negative effects seriously and take certain measures to avoid the negative effects. When consumers make better use of social media platforms, it will become an important force to promote social progress and development. In the future, with the continuous development and application of technology, social media platforms will be more personalized to provide consumers, major media and businesses with better experience, and the positive development will also bring positive emotions to consumers.

However, this article also has certain limitations in terms of comprehensiveness and depth of content analysis. In the future, with available resources, the author will conduct in-depth research around this topic, quantifying the correlation between social media and consumer emotions.

References

1. S.Y. Hu, H.H. Yin. Journal of Economic Research. 30,123-124 (2020).
2. S. Q. Yang. Research on influencing factors of consumers' willingness to use third-party mobile payment, Master's Thesis, Nanchang, (2019).
3. J.Y. Luo, R.Chen. China Merchants. 22, 41-44 (2023).
4. S. H. Huo, F. Yin, J. Q. Cong, M. T. Li, J. Q. Cao. Chinese Journal of Health Psychology, 1-9 (2023).
5. L. H. Ding, News Research Guide, 23, 41-43 (2023).
6. K. Xu, B, Yang. International Public Relations, 09, 167-169 (2022).
7. T. Zhou, Y. Y. Xie, S. L. Deng. Modern Intelligence, 1-17, (2023).
8. L.C. Liu, B.Q. Zhang, L.Xu. Journal of information resources management, 02, 66-76 (2019).
9. G. Chao. Communications Industry News, 08, (2023).
10. Y. T. Zeng, L. J. Cui, Journal of Educational Biology. 03, 168-173 (2014).

Success Factors Influencing Commercial Movies in the Hollywood Model and Limitations: Based on Superhero Movie Series

Yueting You*

NOIC Academy, Markham, ONL3S2H4, Canada

Abstract. Commercial films have always been the mainstream choice for filmmakers and film and television companies to invest in and produce in the film industry, especially films adapted from comics and novels. Even if there is a strong fan base of the original book, whether it is the original fans or the fans of the movie, there are both positive and negative reviews for these commercial films. It can be said that there are limitations on the bases of good development. This study focuses on Spider-Man, an outstanding Hollywood film series, and examines the marketing methods of this series to explore the factors that contributed to its success, as well as the shortcomings that existed in the back, and finally made recommendations for these shortcomings. According to this study, the success of commercial films under the Hollywood operating model is mainly due to Hollywood's excellent marketing methods, and the recommendations of this study for the future of commercial films are conducive to reducing audience losses and maintaining their profitability in the film market, which will contribute to the progress of future films. The point is to balance the commercialization and artistry.

1 Introduction

With the continuous growth of Hollywood films, as the world's commercial film giant, its companies and films have been widely recognized by the public. Hollywood, as a signature of the film industry, has a unique and complete mode of film production and marketing, and today's film industry is generally categorized into commercial films and art films. In the literature of Hollywood movie industry operation mode, it is written that "commercial movie is a type of movie whose main or only purpose is to make money"[1]. The difference between and art movie is only in the different proportion of commercial and artistic content. With the booming of Hollywood movie industry, especially the commercial movies make the industry thriving, the commercial movies are successful but also face challenges. This paper will be based on the literature of Hollywood movie industry operation mode on the study of Hollywood movie industry operation mode and Marvel Enterprises, Inc. for the Spider-Man series of movie research points reflecting the advantages of the current commercial movie and the challenges and problems faced by the study. This study will analyze the following cases and give relevant recommendations after the study and analysis. According to this study, the success of commercial films under the Hollywood operating model is mainly due to Hollywood's excellent marketing methods, and the recommendations of this study for the future of commercial films are conducive to reducing audience losses and maintaining their profitability in the film market, which will contribute to the progress of future films. The point is to balance the commercialization and artistry [1,2].

2 The movie Spider-Man series

The movie Spider-Man series stands out as a commercial movie success story among the many superhero franchises. The reason behind this is attributed to the marketing techniques also, the fan base, and the excellent movie making of good Hollywood [3,4].

The superhero movie series is one of the typical commercial movie genres, and its commercial purpose is greater than its artistic purpose. Spider-Man series of films by Marvel Studios and Sony Pictures Columbia Pictures co-distribution, the first series of Spider-Man by Columbia Pictures distribution and production, the Amazing Spider-Man series and the new Spider-Man series Marvel Studios is involved in the distribution of the new Spider-Man series by the Marvel Sony together.

Spider-Man this IP was originally under the banner of Marvel, there are a total of three series, in 1985 Marvel sold its filming movie rights to other film and television companies for film production, and finally in 2002 by Sony's Columbia Pictures release to produce the first Spider-Man movie series and release, in the consecutive completion of the trilogy after the release of the Sony release to produce the Amazing Spider-Man series.2017 Spider-Man Heroes Returns was released in

*Corresponding author: Rileyyou0712@ldy.edu.rs

theatres announcing both the addition of Spider-Man to the Marvel Universe and the return of Spider-Man to Marvel.

Spider-Man has also linked up with other characters in other movies since joining the Marvel Universe. Peter Parker, played by Tom Hyland, first appeared in the Marvel Universe in Captain America 3 Heroes of the Civil War, and then joined the Avengers, and was also involved in a very important part of the character in Avengers 4 and 5. Continued Heroes Return followed by the release of sequels 2019 Spider-Man Heroes Expedition, 2021 Heroes Without Returns [5].

3 Distributing company

The Spider-man series made such success could literally thank to the movie production companies Marvel Studios and Columbia Pictures(whose parent company is Sony picture).The distributing companies are mainly from Hollywood, playing a vital rule in being the strong background of those commercial movies. The firms have systematic and professional film producing procedures.

3.1 Marvel studios

Marvel started out as a company that produced comics, so it has nearly 4,700 characters under its belt, and has produced several movies from the time the first comic book came out in 1939 to the present day. Its lineup covers original characters Captain Marvel, Thor, Spider-Man, and other popular IPs, and these character series of movies are distributed by most of them by the Walt Disney Company. Marvel Studios is involved in the production of three series of films x-Men, Spider-Man and Marvel Universe. It joined Walt Disney Studios as a subsidiary in 2015.

Marvel Studios' products include spin-off TV series in addition to movies. Characters from the Marvel Universe who do not have solo movies have developed TV series that focus on them personally, such as the TV series Loki, Scarlet Witch, which was released on the streaming medium" Disney+".

3.2 Columbia pictures

Columbia TriStar Pictures Group, one of the eight major Hollywood studios, is the film sales company of Sony Pictures Entertainment, responsible for selling, distributing and promoting film products in the United States and 67 countries and territories worldwide.

Columbia was founded in 1924 to produce 30 films a year and over the decades has grown to become one of the core Hollywood studios with 12 of its films winning the Academy Award for Best Picture [6]. Columbia Pictures took over the production and distribution of Spider-Man, and after its release the Spider-Man series won the highest box office of any superhero franchise.

3.3 Synopsis

The Spider-Man trilogy, directed by Sammy Rehm, tells the story of Peter Parker, who was inadvertently bitten by a mutant spider and gained special powers, falling in love with Mary Jane at one point, and fighting the villain. During the period lost self also lost their important relatives uncle Ben, also in the struggle to grow back to find their own story.

The Amazing Spider-Man tells the story of Spider-Man and Gwen Stacy, and unlike Peter Parker and Mary Jane ultimately Spider-Man ends up losing Gwen Stacy.

The new Spider-Man joins the Marvel Universe as a member of the Avengers and also meets Mary Jane. The plots of the first two movies were much the same as the other Spider-Man movies but due to the joining of the Marvel Universe, linkages with other major characters also appeared. In Heroes Without Returns, Doctor Strange joins the fray so the concept of parallel universes is involved and there is also a storyline where all three generations of Spider-Man appear on screen at the same time.

3.4 License

In addition to the comics, Spider-Man also released the games Marvel Spider-Man 1 and Marvel Spider-Man 2. In addition to this they license IPs to businesses to produce peripheral products such as toys, t-shirts and sweatshirts.

4 Analysis of the marketing strategy

Why exactly are commercial movie superhero movies, one of the falling movie genres in Hollywood, so profitable? The commercial movie model in Hollywood, marketing techniques, script adaptations, and a certain Hollywood fan base for the series are key to the success of these superhero movies.

In the beginning Marvel sold the rights to Spider-Man to Sony as a solution to Marvel's debt crisis, and the first series of Spider-Man movies were distributed and produced by Columbia Pictures. In the usual sense, Hollywood commercial movies are characterized by the following four aspects: i.e., internationalization of capital, scripted assembly line work, highly commercialized products and prioritization of entertainment [7].

Hollywood spin-offs are sold all over the world as the movie spreads and the movie becomes an advertising spot for these goods, while games, toys, books, and records adapted from the movie are all sources of high profits [7]. Licensing and Hollywood spin-offs all bring in a lot of profit to the movies, ensuring that they have additional ways to make a profit besides the box office. For example, the Marvel superhero print clothes in Uniqlo and the Lego toys for the members of the Avengers. Superhero movies, as comic book adaptations, have a strong fan base of their own; in addition to the original book fans of the comics, their popularity grows dramatically for a particular character's popularity after the movie is released, and a lot of fans of the movie will go on to learn more about the source material as a result.

One could also argue that all superhero movies are promos for comic book characters. As well, every great movie requires a soundtrack and casting under a producer-neutral system, where the producer-promoter hires popular singers and actors who fit the image and are also well known to increase the quality and popularity of the movie. For example, the new Spider-Man series cast Zendaya as Mary Jane.

Usually, it is known that the Marvel Studios on the works are adapted from the comic book released by Marvel, so since it is a comic book adapted into a movie, there will be commercial adaptation. There are hundreds of issues of a comic book, and the script is continuously updated according to the author, whether from the perspective of drawing art or script writing angle, the whole process is less commercially oriented compared to a movie release. Compared to movies, the production cost of comics is much lower. According to Dai Luyao, production management in Hollywood under the producer-centered system goes through three stages: In the first stage, the studio's studio managers give the scripts they receive to script reviewers, who then decide whether or not to give them to the story writers, and the scripts they get can only be shown to the story writers if they have passed the review process [7]. The second stage is when the movie project is polished and the script has to be polished. The third stage is that the script is acquired by the studio and then the studio will ask the producer to transfer the rights about the script. In Hollywood's producer-centered system, the producer pays more attention to commercial returns, and in the development of the project, the producer will pay more attention to the certainty of the genre, the combination of the actors and the market response, and the commerciality of the film elements from the audience's point of view. To prevent the phenomenon of self-indulgence in the movie [7]. Commercial movies pay more attention to commercial returns. From the viewpoint of superhero movies in recent years, most of them have already fixed the plot pattern of this genre: a protagonist with supernormal capabilities or strong abilities who saves the world, and a villain with the same abilities as the protagonist, and the ending is to save the world. At the same time, the protagonist will also face sacrificial situations and experience brief failures, but in the end, it will be the protagonist who succeeds in saving the world.

5 Suggestions

From the perspective of the movie, with the development of the times, the electronic information industry is so advanced in the twenty-first century in general the number of movie viewers is greater than the audience of the comic book, so that the movie script adaptation to be popular enough, and to be reasonable enough. The measure of quality for Hollywood movies is the box office, based on its own commercial positioning. The first Spider-Man script went through twists and turns eventually directed by Sami Rehm and was a huge success. The crew had to have a deep understanding of the character as well as great artistry and a strong enough business acumen to go back to a producer-cantered system to polish the script. One thing that all these superhero movies have in common is that they all have sequels. Hollywood gives these comic book adaptations a sequel, which is also a good means to make the IP popular and commercialized. For example, the James Bond series, the Mission Impossible series, and the Matrix series.

Table 1. The box of the movie series Spider-Man [8].

Cinematic	Distribution company	Box office performance (worldwide)
Spider-Man 1	Columbia Pictures	$821,708,551
Spider-Man 2	Columbia Pictures	$783,766,341
Spider-Man 3	Columbia Pictures	$890,871,626
The Amazing Spider-Man 1	Columbia Pictures, Marvel Studios	$757,930,663
The Amazing Spider-Man 2	Columbia Pictures, Marvel Studios	$708,294,944
Spider-Man: Heroes Return	Columbia Pictures, Marvel Studios	$175,000,000
Spider-Man: Heroic Expedition	Columbia Pictures, Marvel Studios	$160,000,000
Spider-Man: No Return of Heroes	Columbia Pictures, Marvel Studios	1,921,847,111

All of the Spider-Man movies have been successful in terms of the box office performance mentioned in Table 1, and all three trilogies are among the top 5 highest grossing Marvel Comics adaptations in the U.S., with Spider-Man listed at number two, Spider-Man 2 at number four, and Spider-Man 3 at number five. The trilogy is also one of the ten highest grossing movies of all superhero movies in U.S. history, with Spider-Man fourth, Spider-Man 2 sixth, and Spider-Man 3 seventh. In addition, the Spider-Man trilogy is also the three highest-grossing Sony Columbia Pictures movies. After the release of the new Spider-Man, Spider-Man: Heroes Return ranked second among all Spider-Man movies. SPIDER-MAN: HEROES RETURN NO MORE the three spiders together became the highest grossing Spider-Man movie of all time. It ranked 7 at the world box office and 3 in North American movie history. Especially Spider-Man Heroes Without Return has been released to achieve the seventh in the world and the third in North American movie history. Series of film adaptation is also a technical job; most sales series of films is through the last film left in suspense as well as to capture the audience's love for the characters and reluctance to give up.

However, under such a model, certain limitations emerge. Firstly, although the box office figures are impressive, the audience's comments on the movie are not always impressive. A part of the audience also appeared aesthetic fatigue. From the public' comments on the plot appeared on the satisfaction is not high. The same assembly line script mode the audience seems to have no great expectations for the plot of the movie. There are also cases where the audience who went to see the movie because of sentimentality found that the movie was no longer heart-warming, and slowly became disappointed. Secondly, movies that are too commercialized will lose some of their audience. If a movie is forced to have a sequel, then the audience will be over-consumed. In addition, the audience will easily lose their enthusiasm for the movie because they can guess the plot just by looking at the promotional trailer, so they will not choose to watch the movie [9].

The advice given to the above situation is that Hollywood commercial movies can polish the plot, a good story lays the foundation of a good work, and a classic Hollywood movie that sells well needs a gripping story. Avengers 4 and 5 are unusual in terms of plot, not only echoing other series but also breaking the superhero movie formula. The publicity has been appropriately toned down to create suspense for the audience. There is also the cultivation of actors and actresses, the new Spider-Man actor Tom Hyland has been spat out by the audience that the phenomenon of acting is not good. The last is to enhance the level of film production, the movie is a visual art, despite the strong commercial, but also a visual commodity, commercial movies are essentially no different from art movies [10].

To summarize, commercial movies under the Hollywood model rely on sequels and marketing techniques and scripts and fan bases to achieve success. But at the same time, there are some limitations, such as excessive packaging and marketing, and the single plot makes the audience produce aesthetic fatigue and other problems. A good work needs a good director, a good actor, a good crew and a good production, so don't let commercialization ignore the artistic attributes of the work itself.

6 Conclusion

In summary, according to Hollywood's producer-centric system and the commercial nature of commercial films, the producers and crews of commercial films should pay attention to this research, good movies must be indispensable to good scripts, and make certain innovations to the scripts, scripts need such diversity, no one wants to watch the plot under the same formula for more than ten years. Commercial films are also films, and they should not be left behind. In other words, the film itself, as a work of art, is not a product of assembly line mass production, and there is no difference in the essence between commercial films and art films. Producers need to keep an eye on it, because the producer is the key to whether a film can be invested and profitable, and under the operation of a producer who has both artistic skills and business acumen, the film can avoid losing money to the greatest extent. There are certain limitations in the development of Hollywood films today, the most obvious is that the plot is too cliché, and the blunt story will gradually make the audience lose enthusiasm, resulting in a film with a high production cost but a loss. In the long run, if no changes are made, the future of commercial films will be bleak, and the artistic connotation of film as a work of art itself will be lost, deviating from the fact that film itself exists as a work of art. There are some limitations to this study, as the case study is a comic book adaptation of a Hollywood film, but there are many different forms of commercial film. In the future, the research direction will be to dig deeper into the specific balance between the commercial and artistic aspects of film.

References

1. M. C. Oxoby. Interdisciplinary Studies in Literature and Environment, 1, 233-234 (2011).
2. S. F. Dong. Cinematic Literature, 22, 3 (2016).
3. G. F. Li. Tradition and Breakthrough - A Study of Typologized Narrative in Hollywood Superhero Movies. Phd Thesis, Shanhai, (2023)
4. J. Liu. Journal of Hubei Radio and Television Universit, 33(12), 2 (2013).
5. L. N. He. Film Review, 16, 3 (2015).
6. L. P. Shi. Cinematic Literature, 24, 3 (2015).
7. L. Y. Dai. Hollywood movie industry operation model. Phd Thesis, Chengdu, (2021).
8. T. H. Zhang. Cinematic Literatur, 13, 3 (2017).
9. X. L. Zhou. Journal of Yuxi University (Social Sciences Edition), (2002).

https://doi.org/10.1051/shsconf/202418803007

10. Z. Y. Xiao. Literary and Art Life: Midday Magazine, (2015).

Application of Game Theory to Business Decision-making

Yuecheng Xu[1, *]
[1]Faculty of Science, The University of Nottingham-Ningbo (315100), Ningbo, China

Abstract. How to make correct business decisions has become a hot issue that entrepreneurs are concerned about. Some researchers have found that game theory greatly impacts business decisions. However, there is still a lack of a unified explanation of the formation mechanism behind using game theory to make correct business decisions. Therefore, this article explores the use of game theory to make correct business decisions by collecting data on business competition, organizing the data into a benefit matrix, and comparing to conclude, through which the benefits of business cooperation and business competition can be demonstrated. Through research, it is found that game theory plays an important role in business decision-making, which makes a significant difference in planning the future development path of the enterprise. By using game theory models such as the Prisoner's Dilemma and boxed pigs, entrepreneurs can make optimal business decisions. Through an in-depth understanding of the relevant knowledge of game theory, entrepreneurs can know the timing and maximum benefits of business cooperation and competition, which provides important tips for enterprise reform and development in the new era.

1 Introduction

How to make correct business decisions has become a focus of concern for entrepreneurs. With the continuous development of the times, the business environment has become more and more complex and competitive. The modern business environment is highly competitive and fast-paced. With the development of technology and the drive for globalization, the market has become more complex and diverse. Businesses need to constantly innovate and adapt to change to stay competitive. At the same time, consumer needs and behaviors are constantly changing, and they have higher requirements for product quality, service, and sustainability. In addition, the rise of social media and the Internet has made it necessary for companies to pay more attention to brand image and consumer experience. In this environment, businesses need to be flexible, innovative, and agile to proactively respond to challenges and seize opportunities. In this era of rapid change, making the right business decisions has never been more important. Correct business decisions can help companies seize opportunities, cope with challenges, and achieve sustained competitive advantage. It can not only increase a company's revenue and profits but also improve its reputation and brand image. Wrong business decisions may cause enterprises to face huge risks and losses. Therefore, for enterprises, making correct business decisions is the key to staying competitive and achieving sustainable development. According to the existing literature, the application of game theory in business decision-making is very extensive. Business decisions often involve competition and cooperation among multiple parties, and game theory can help analyse the interests, strategies, and results of each party.

Moreover, game theory provides a theoretical basis and decision-making tools for business decisions, helping companies develop smarter strategies.

However, there is still no unified understanding of the specific mechanism of application of game theory in business decision-making. This article will explore the principles behind using game theory to make correct business decisions and its impact on future enterprise development by exploring two specific game theory problems, the Prisoner's Dilemma and the Boxed Pigs. This article first provides a detailed introduction to the prisoner's dilemma concept and its workings. The application of the prisoner's dilemma to commercial price battles reveals the significance of cooperative efforts and ideal pricing tactics for the sound growth of the business. Additionally, this page describes the concepts and best practices and deduces the full procedure of the boxed pigs. Both large and small and medium-sized businesses have developed distinct business strategies and development plans by examining the corporate innovation ideas offered by the boxed pigs.

In the context of enterprise pricing, for example, the optimal strategy of the Prisoner's Dilemma suggests that a price war must ultimately result in both losers and no winners. Thus, it can be concluded that win-win collaboration is the safest way for firms to profit and that enterprise cooperation is the only option to overcome the price war conundrum. For another, tiny and medium-sized businesses will opt to wait and copy, while huge corporations can only decide to keep innovating, according to the best strategy of the smart pig game. This will ultimately have the effect of making it more

* Corresponding author:smyyx10@nottingham.edu.cn

difficult for small and medium-sized businesses to thrive in the quickly evolving modern world unless they pursue innovative development and implement progressive improvements. Generally speaking, game theory is used to inform business decisions in more ways than just these two. Future investigation and study into company strategies is eagerly anticipated, as is the growth of firms in the future. Game theory techniques for use in corporate decision-making are also anticipated.

2 Application of game theory to business decision-making

2.1. Pricing strategy--price wars

According to the prisoner's dilemma model in game theory, the result of a continuous price war is that both sides will lose, so win-win cooperation is the correct business decision in pricing [1]. The following is the traditional prisoner's dilemma: Although A and B, two suspects, were taken into custody by the police, there was insufficient evidence to prosecute them. Thus, the suspects were detained individually by the police, who also held separate meetings with them and gave them the following options:

• If one pleads guilty and selects "confess" (a term that is connected to "betraying" the other party), and the other selects "don't confess," the guilty party will be released right away and the other will receive a 10-year prison sentence.

• Both of them will receive a one-year prison sentence if they decide to "don't confess" (applicable phrase refers to joint "cooperation").

• Should they both select "confess," they will both receive a six-year prison sentence [2].

Table 1. Prisoner's dilemma's payoff matrix

A / B	don't confess	confess
don't confess	(-1, -1)	(-10, 0)
confess	(0, -10)	(-6, -6)

Table 1 shows the payoff in this prisoner's dilemma. Confess is the dominant strategy among the two strategies. Both players betray each other. As a result, both players serve 6 years in prison. In terms of overall interests, if both participants cooperate and don't confess, both of them will only be sentenced to 1 year in prison. The overall interests are higher, and the result is better than if the two betrayed each other and were sentenced to 6 years in prison. But based on the presumptions mentioned above, it appears that they are both reasonable people who just look out for themselves. Ultimately, both inmates made the decision not to confess. Consequently, the overall advantage was less than that of cooperation, and the verdicts of both inmates were greater than those of cooperation. The "dilemma" is located here [3].

This study now applies the "prisoner's dilemma" model to market rivalry. This study assumed that Suning and JD.com are the only two oligopolistic firms engaged in the price war. They provide consumers with uniform products to grow their market share and profits [4].

Both parties have access to the following four pricing strategies: high-priced, high-priced, low-priced, high-priced, and low-priced, low-priced. This analysis was conducted under the assumption that should JD.com and Suning choose to implement the costly policy, each would be able to generate 100 units of revenue. If both of them choose to adopt low-cost policies, they can each make 70 units of income. The firm that lowers prices can make 150 units of income, whereas the firm that doesn't lower prices can only earn 20 units if one firm chooses high-priced policies and the other takes low-priced policies [5]. The payoff in this price war is demonstrated in Table 2.

Table 2. The price war's payoff matrix

JD.com / Suning.com	high-priced	low-price
high-priced	(100, 100)	(20, 150)
low-price	(150, 20)	(70, 70)

According to "Prisoner's Dilemma", the dominant strategy for two companies is to continue to reduce prices, which will lead to a loss on both sides compared with both high prices. Therefore, thanks to the prisoner's dilemma of game theory, the right business decision in pricing is cooperation, which can provide an effective and efficient approach for all enterprises to gain collaborative development and common benefits.

2.2 Innovative strategies

Scientific and technical innovation has progressively supplanted conventional production variables like labor and capital in the global framework of world economic globalization and expanding regional economic integration, rising. It is now a crucial foundational resource for business development. Thus, the initial strategic decision should be to center technology innovation on the enterprise's overall development [6]. Based on the smart pig game in game theory, large companies are like big pigs. They invest a lot of money in technological innovation and develop new products, while small and medium-sized enterprises are like small pigs. They may not be able to carry out large-scale technological innovation for a while, but they can adopt a follow-up strategy and wait for big companies to develop new products. When a company's new products open new markets, imitations of large companies' new products begin to be sold [7].

With an exit on one end and a button on the other, the manager is incredibly lengthy. Once the button is pressed, 10 units of food can be obtained, but 2 units of payment are required. Therefore, depending on whether they choose to "press the button" or "wait" in terms of their gambling methods, the outcomes will vary. The small pig can only obtain four food units whereas the giant pig can receive six when the big pig clicks the button while the small pig waits, however, after subtracting the cost, the big pig can only receive four units. If the big pig waits and the small pig presses the button, when the cost is subtracted, the big and small pigs can receive 9 and -1 units. If they press the button synchronously, when the cost is subtracted, they will receive 5 and 1 units. If neither press the button, there can be zero food available. Here are the specifics of the traditional Boxed Pigs [8]:

Table 3. The boxed pigs' payoff matrix [9]

Small pig / Big pig	press	wait
press	(5, 1)	(4, 4)
wait	(9, -1)	(0, 0)

Table 3 displays the reward of the big pig as the first component and the payout of the small pig as the second player for each payoff vector. The payoff matrix indicates that "wait" is the small pig's dominant strategy. The big pig's best course of action when the small pig selects "wait" is to "press the button," and thus creates a Nash equilibrium in the game when the big pig clicks the button and the small pig waits [9]. Therefore, the small pig may incur a high cost with a benefit level of -1 if it is unable to accurately assess the circumstances and selects "the button" hastily. When there is unequal bilateral strength, a game theory known as "boxed pigs" is played; the strong player initiates, while the weak player hitches and waits. According to the gambling model, we should choose a betting strategy that suits the situation and the opponents [8].

In the real market, due to the inequality of enterprise strength, or even large differences, different enterprises have different choices of technological innovation strategies - large enterprises have a large market share, and the effect of innovation is more obvious; small enterprises have a small market share, and the motivation for innovation is insufficient. In addition, the size of the enterprise will have a great impact on innovation efficiency. For example, the innovation costs (investment costs and operating costs) of large enterprises are easier to digest than those of small enterprises. Suppose A is a large enterprise and B is a small and medium enterprise. If A's technological innovation contribution rate is higher than B, then the behavior of the smart pig game will occur which is displayed in Table 4 [10].

Table 4. The return matrix of the two enterprises

B / A	innovate	not to innovate
innovate	(5, 1)	(4, 4)
not to innovate	(9, -1)	(0, 0)

Due to the constraints of scale, capital, talent, risk resistance, and other factors, in the process of competing with large enterprises, small and medium-sized enterprises will not spend money on technological innovation. Instead, they wait for the successful development of new products by large companies and then carry out imitation production. Large companies know that small companies will choose "not to innovate", so they can only choose to "innovate" first. Because of "no innovation", the income is 0. Therefore, the Nash equilibrium currently is (Innovation, not Innovation) [10].

The smart pig game illustrates that when large and small enterprises coexist, only large enterprises have sufficient incentives to carry out technological innovation. And the proactive innovation of large enterprises will lead to the development of an industry [11].

2.3 The solution to price wars

Businesses need to work together to put an end to reckless, harmful competition behavior when it reaches a particular level so that the industry won't suffer from significant losses [12].

For instance, in the building industry, there is a distinct perception that quality generally comes at a lower cost. In the slim chance that they may be awarded a contract, contractors often rush to the bottom with their prices, and tender quotes are not thoroughly investigated. Roberts feels that charging less than what is required for the job will ultimately leave the trader and the consumer out of money, notwithstanding this incentive. However, if subcontractors cooperate and allocate resources reasonably, a win-win situation will be formed. There is evidence to suggest that subcontractor earnings increased in 2019 by up to 7%, which is three times the annual rate of inflation. Regrettably, some subcontractors tarnish this by underselling themselves and putting themselves in a lose-lose scenario. Not only do they lose out on possible higher income, but by underselling and producing mediocre work for clients, they damage the industry's worth and reputation overall [13].

In conclusion, if the company's strategy is known to competitors and it should be clear to competitors that the company is prepared to cooperate but will retaliate against betrayal, then the company will ultimately win the competition and the gains from cooperation will be large. Companies may significantly lower the likelihood of damaging competition, such as price wars, by thoroughly analyzing the competition, accurately predicting its potential responses, and having a desire to collaborate and share.

2.4 The solution of Innovative strategies

According to the conclusion of the smart pig game theory, the best strategy for small businesses is to wait. However, practice tells us that this is only a theoretical optimal, and rational choice. In fact, due to the influence of many factors such as internal and external environment, for many small businesses, this passive waiting is not the best choice [14].

Firstly, small and medium-sized enterprises should promote innovation through imitation.

In the process of imitation, small and medium businesses should gradually digest and absorb advanced technologies, through which they can improve the market competitiveness of our products, strengthen, and develop corporate strength, and lay the foundation for independent innovation. Don't just be satisfied and simply imitate, they should set their goal to catch up with the pioneers. Given that small and medium-sized enterprises are weak and have insufficient innovation resources, small and medium businesses can form strategic alliances with other enterprises, taking advantage of each other's advantages to jointly develop new technologies, share risks, and benefit from each other. Additionally, Small and medium-sized enterprises must clarify their market positioning. In the boxed pigs model, the best strategy adopted by small pigs is to wait, so small and medium businesses position themselves in the market. In terms of marketing strategy and marketing mix, small and medium-sized enterprises should keep a certain distance from companies that are pioneers in technological innovation and should not follow too closely. Otherwise, it will trigger a counterattack from large companies. If large companies react violently, they may suppress imitation innovators in all aspects. On the other hand, the early preparation of large enterprises in the market can save imitators a lot of market cultivation and development costs, and followers can also learn from their experiences and lessons [15].

In a word, small and medium-sized enterprises should reposition themselves and unswervingly pursue an independent innovation path, through which they can transform the enterprise development model, and use technological progress to solve resource and cost bottlenecks that restrict enterprise development [16].

3 Conclusion

In conclusion, this study found that game theory can help entrepreneurs make correct business decisions, not only in terms of business cooperation and business competition but also in terms of future reform and development of enterprises. First of all, this article introduces the principle of the prisoner's dilemma and its operating mechanism in detail. By studying the application of the prisoner's dilemma in commercial price wars, the importance of optimal pricing strategies and cooperation for the healthy development of business is discovered. Besides, this article completely deduces the entire process of the boxed pigs and explains the principles and optimal strategies. By exploring the strategies provided by the boxed pigs for corporate innovation, large enterprises, and small and medium businesses have obtained different business strategies and development plans. Additionally, this article infers two important strategies for enterprise development by studying the conjecture of the Prisoner's Dilemma strategy on the consequences of price wars and the impact of the Boxed Pigs strategy on the corporate innovation market. For one thing, according to the optimal strategy of the Prisoner's Dilemma, it can be inferred that in enterprise pricing, the result of a price war must be that both losers and no one can benefit. Therefore, it can be inferred that enterprise cooperation is the only way to break through the dilemma of price war, and win-win cooperation is the safest way for enterprises to benefit. For another, according to the best strategy of the smart pig game, large enterprises can only choose to continue to innovate, while small and medium-sized enterprises will choose to wait and imitate. In the long run, the consequence of this is that it will be difficult for small and medium-sized enterprises to survive in today's rapidly developing era unless they make gradual changes and seek innovative development. In general, the application of game theory in business decision-making is not only reflected in these two aspects. More business strategies are waiting for future exploration and research, and the future development of enterprises is waiting for more game theory strategies to be applied in corporate decision-making.

References

1. J. Y. Pan. Shopping Mall Modernization, (27): 38-40 (2008).
2. B.C. Li, J. Li. Communications on Dialectics of Nature, (04): 25-32 (1996).
3. Z. N. Huang. Chinese Business Theory, (01):86-89 (2022).
4. Y. J. Yang. Modern Business, (10): 39-42 (2023).
5. Y. Liu. E-commerce Price War Based on Game Theory. (2021).
6. M. F. Yu. Chinese Business Theory, (13): 147-148 (2019).
7. W. J. Wang. China Collective Economy, (15): 65-66 (2012).
8. X. T. Peng, S. T. Peng, IEEE, 401-404.
9. Y. Gong, Q. Liu, Y. Xu, Y. Feng. (2022).
10. L. M. Cai, Y. Liu. Popular Science and Technology, (06): 298-301 (2013).
11. W. H. Yan. Publishing and Distribution Research, (11), 20-23 (2015).
12. S. Eilon. Omega, 21(6): 619-627 (1993).
13. M2 Presswire, (2021).
14. W. Z. Yang. Business Economics, (17): 47-48 (2010).
15. W. J. Yang, X. H, Liu. " Technology and Market, (09): 101-102 (2012).
16. X. Lan, Y. T. Lu. Learning Monthly, (17): 16-17 (2010).

The Investigation on The Factors Influencing Lady Dior Handbag Consumption in China's Luxury Market: Whether Price is The Dominant Factor

Sijia Chen[1,*]

[1]Gabelli School of Business, Fordham University, 150W. 60th St, NY, New York, USA

Abstract. The luxury industry is full of challenges especially under the COVID-19 pandemic, business has been struggling through, such as logistics problem. Despite the difficult economy background, China's luxury market experienced a double-digit growth while Dior increased the price of Lady Dior handbag. According to the law of demand, quantity demand falls as price increases. Luxury goods are not necessities, thus in economics, luxury goods are defined to have an elastic demand. It is predicted that total revenue falls when price of Lady Dior rises. This is because of the elastic demand will lead to a fall in quantity demand but proportionately larger than the rise in price. However, the financial report of Dior has shown a rises total revenue and increase in demand for luxury goods. This paper explains why consumers are still willing to buy luxury goods even though price increases and the value of price elasticity of demand (PED) of Lady Dior handbag. PED is a numerical measure of the responsiveness of quantity demand of a product following the change in price of goods.

1 Introduction

Luxury goods are often expensive and scarce, with high quality. The Chinese luxury market has always been the dominant market for luxury brands. Chinese customers have a desire to pursue extravagant lifestyle and develop the increasing desire as more western luxury brands has entered China [1].

During the COVID-19 pandemic, the price of Lady DIOR handbag is increasing constantly since January 2020 [2]. The price increased 17.65% throughout the period. However, it is expected that the total revenue of luxury goods to decrease since they are not necessities. The Chinese luxury market benefit from the reduction of international travel, which created exponential boost in domestic spending. Chinese luxury market has a 48% growth [3]. As a major luxury brand, the total revenue of Dior has also been increasing.

This paper is going to figure out the price elasticity of demand of Lady Dior, the determining influence of price, and what other factors influence consumers' decision in luxury consumption.

2 Literature review

Chinese luxury consumption behaviours, the influencing factors and economic effects have been investigated. In this part, it introduces the basic concept of luxury and relevant theories, include the background of the research followed by the basic economic concepts related to the research and finally the key effect that are used to explain the influence of price in luxury market.

2.1 Luxury goods

Luxury goods has a fastly growing demand while consumer's income increases at a much lower rate [4]. Etymologically, luxury has two meanings: luminosity and sumptuousness. Luxury is usually related to exclusive, high status and quality [5]. What kind of product is luxury has changed throughout the period. In the past, people usually consider that piano is a luxury in 1900, but now space tourism is a luxury [6]. Usually, there are some characteristics of luxury goods:

- Brand history
- Goods that have the highest quality
- Goods that are very expensive, which are distinct from essential goods
- Goods that are unique and scarce
- Goods designed with unique creativity

2.2 PED in economy

Price elasticity of demand (PED) is the numerical measure of the responsiveness of the quantity demand following change in the price of the product, ceteris paribus [7]. The value of PED reflects the sensitivity of consumers towards the price of the product. When PED>1, people have a relatively elastic demand towards the good, products with this kind of PED has a high proportion in consumer's income and often has many

* Corresponding author: schen440@fordham.edu

substitutes. When PED<1, people are relatively inelastic towards the change in price of the product, product with this kind of PED only take up a small proportion of consumer's income and often has few substitutes. In real life, the PED is not that extreme. However, when PED is infinite, the demand for the product is perfectly elastic. If the PED=0, the demand is perfectly inelastic. Usually, the expense on luxury goods take up a large proportion of consumer's income and they are not necessities, thus consumers usually have a relatively elastic demand towards luxuries, then PED>1. As price increases, the quantity demand decreases which falls proportionately greater than the rise in price, as price elasticity of demand is elastic. Therefore, total revenue should decrease when luxury goods are more expensive. However, the annual financial report of Dior shows a rise in total revenue, while the price of Lady Dior handbag raises. This research will discuss whether price is the dominant factor influencing the luxury consumption.

2.3 The Veblen effect

Veblen effect is a popular theory in microeconomics, which it means consumers will follow the luxury consumption of rich people [8]. The sociologist Thorstein Veblen studied the phenomenon of conspicuous consumption, called this effect as the Veblen effect. It explains the purchase of conspicuous consumption, the demand for the good rises as the price increases [9]. The important economics feature helps explain that The Veblen effect divided price into two categories: the utility from a product is consist of both qualities and the price paid for it. Conspicuous price is the price others think people paid for these goods; it also determines conspicuous utility. Some consumers may even stop purchasing when conspicuous price decrease since the utility falls [9].

2.4 The Bandwagon effect

Bandwagon effect means people's demands can lead other people to consume the same products. This theory means that people have a desire to purchase the same goods as others, but they initially do not have the desire to buy it. One's demand can be more affected by the demand of others.

2.5 The Snob effect

The last effect is the snob effect, which means that people's demand for the goods decreases when others consume lots of them. Consumers may feel threatened when seeing other people wearing the same or similar luxury goods as they do [10]. Therefore, some consumers choose unfamiliar brands or stop consuming popular brands with common items. The need for uniqueness allows consumers to engage in distinguishing among all consumers. Different consumers have different response to the change in price [11-15].

2.6 The materialism

Materialism is a tendency to consider material possessions and physical comfort as more important than spiritual values. Materialistic consumers are interested in finding ways to make their social status outstanding by using luxury goods to symbolize their personal standing and getting effective response from others. There are extrinsic goals, which is to achieve financial accomplishment, social recognition, and social image. In other words, materialism is an explanation for luxury consumers because of their intrinsic motivations and other motivations, according to previous research. Intrinsic motivations derive from a macro-theory of people's motivation. Intrinsic goals, such as the desire for enjoyment, fulfilling personal needs, and physical fitness. Luxury consumption is tied to the idea of physical appearance and achievement vanity in luxury.

3 Methodology

This part explains the methodology used in this research, including which methods are used, how the data is collected, what kind of data, and the limitations of these measures, and how they are used to answer research questions of this project.

3.1 Research methods

The methods used in this project cover qualitative and quantitative methods. Specifically, in order to find the background information of this project, secondary data collected from Google scholar, Jstor will be used. Also, official statistics from Christian Dior Official Website is used as resource to find out the change in total revenue.

3.2 Questionnaire

Using questionnaire, a quantitative data, as my research method is because responses are standardized with closed-form questions. The results of questionnaire can show the proportion of attitudes of the respondents, while the answers are fixed. Questions includes their basic information, their attitude towards the price of luxury goods, and their thoughts of reason for purchasing luxury. The questionnaire is mainly sent to consumers who have stable and high income, or consumers who are in wealthy families.

3.3. Interview

By using the quantitative data, questionnaire, it is also necessary to use the qualitative data— Interview. By interviewing Dior's salesmen and consumers helps to explain and gain better understanding on the behaviours of consumption. Also, interview has open-ended questions so that answers are not limited. The answers from interview will be more accurate than that of questionnaire and maybe even unexpected. The questions include people's change of attitudes towards the increase of price, the strategies that company uses to maintain consumer loyalty, and his own interpretation of luxury consumption during the COVID-19.

4 Findings and discussion

In this part, the essay will explain the data from questionnaire and interview, followed by a conclusion of the research question. Eventually, the results based on the real response will also be evaluated (Table 1 to Table 8).

4.1 Results from questionnaire

Table 1. Respondents' Gender Frequency Table

Gender	Frequency	Percentage	Gender
Male	44	22.34%	Male
Female	153	77.66%	Female
Gender	Frequency	Percentage	Gender
Total	197	100%	Total

Table 2. Respondents' Age Proportion Bar Chart

Age	Proportion
41-7	21.83%
31-40	26.40%
19-30	18.78%
10-18	32.99%

The questionnaire has a total respondent of 197, in which there are 77.66% of the respondents are women, and 22.34% of men respondents. respondents are covered form teenagers to elderly, a range from 10 years old to 70 years old. Half of them occasionally purchase luxury goods, 41.62% of them purchase luxury goods at a low rate, only 8.12% of the respondents often buy luxury goods.

Table 3. Respondents' Frequency of Luxury Pruchasement

Frequency	Proportion
Barely	41.62%
Occasionally	50.25%
Frequently	8.12%

The questionnaire also covers their preferred determining factors whether buy the luxury good or not, each respondent is allowed to choose two influencing factors. The most determining factor is the style (including the colour, the sense, the decorations of the product), which nearly 83% of the respondents think this is the most important factor when choosing luxury goods. The next top choice is the brand of the luxury goods, where there are almost 62% of the respondents chose this. On the other hand, only 49% of the respondents think price is a determining factor when deciding to purchase luxury goods. Although the proportionate of choosing 'price' as the determining factor is not small, it does not show a high connection between price and the quantity demand.

Table 4. Respondents' Attitude about Luxury Consumption Factor

Category	Proportion
Limited edition	1.52%
Practicability	55.84%
Price	49.24%
Style	82.23%
Brand	61.93%

Since the research question mainly focus on the price of the luxury goods, respondents were asked to choose the determining level for one about the price of the good. The results show that most people consider price as an important or not-that-important factor, each with 32.99% and 39.09% proportion respectively. Only less than 20% of the respondents think price is crucial, and 10.15% of them think that it is not important.

Table 5. Respondents' Attitude about The Importance of Price Factor

Level	Proportion
Not important	10.15%
Not care	39.09%
Important	32.99%
Very important	17.77%

Furthermore, since this paper discusses about Lady Dior handbag, respondents were asked to whether they would choose to buy Lady Dior with the increase of its price. Over half of them decide to purchase the Lady

Dior handbag, but they need to consider other factors as well. Less than 10% of them will buy it and 32.99% of the respondents refuse to purchase Lady Dior.

Table 6. Respondents' Choices

Choice	**Proportion**
Perhaps	32.99%
I will not	57.36%
I wil	9.64%

Previous research and new report show that many consumers rush to boutiques to purchase Lady Dior before it become more expensive, thus respondents were asked to choose their reasons in explaining why an increase in luxury goods may even stimulate the desire for people to purchase it. Over half of them, 62.44% of them, prefers the choice of 'Price is not the most determining factor when purchasing luxury goods. Some respondents said that they may want to get the luxury goods before the next increase in price, and some said consumers may be forced to buy the luxury goods but to their own needs. Others said that the increase in desire may be a result of a thought that an increase in price means increase of the item's value and scarcity.

Table 7. Respondents' Attitude about the Price Factor

Attitude	**Proportion**
Price is not the determining factor when purchasing luxuries	30.96%
Worry the product will increase price again	62.44%
Others	6.6%

Lastly, respondents were asked to answer why most people has the desire to own luxury goods. 55.84% of the respondents think having luxury goods is a symbol of high-quality lifestyle. 25.38% of them thinks it represents personal taste and 13.2% of them think it represents social status.

Table 8. Respondents' Attitude about What Luxury Means

Hat Luxury Means	**Proportion**
Symbolises superior	55.84%
Symbolises taste	25.38%
Symbolises social status	13.2%
Others	5.58%

4.2 Key findings of interview

In December, the author has interviewed a manager in Chongqing Dior. He used to be the salesman in Dior located in Chongqing IFS mall, and now he is the manager of the Chongqing district. During the interview, the author has asked questions about his attitude towards the luxury market in China and Chongqing, his answer towards the price factor in consuming luxury goods, his understanding of Chongqing people luxury consumption, how sales are trained and other relative questions.

'During the COVID-19, as China has been locked down, many cities forbid citizens to travel abroad. Since most Chinese consumers are into purchase luxury abroad, their luxury consumption has changed from foreign countries like France and Italy to their local city. This switching consumption has greatly increased the Chong Qing's Dior consumption.' This is what the salesman mentions that the total economy of Dior has increases, despite price of all goods increases. This is because of the proportion of the increase in price is greater than the proportion of the decrease in consumer quantity.

Furthermore, he also suggests that Dior and other luxury brands will increase their product price approximately 2 times a year, usually the increase percentage is about 10% to 20%. The manager of Dior mentions that consumers will consider factors such as style, colour, raw material, scarcity, limited edition, and product value. Moreover, some consumers even have different purchasing objective. Granted, most consumers purchase luxury goods for themselves because they like the product. Some consumers buy luxury goods simply because they have been influenced by social media, as well as social trends. Others consume luxury goods as a present to themselves since they have worked so hard for a long time. These consumers think they will feel satisfied and encouraged from luxury goods. Some of them buy luxury goods as a present to others.

4.3 Discussion

4.3.1 Price elasticity of demand

The questionnaire has only shown a low percentage (17.77%) of respondents that they think price is a dominant factor when consuming luxury goods [16]. Concluding that consumers are less responsive to the change in price. Moreover, there are no close substitutes for the specific Lady Dior handbag. For consumers especially fascinated about Lady Dior handbag, they cannot use other handbags to substitute the more expensive Lady Dior. Lady Dior handbag has its own unique style and design, so it is hard for consumers to find a similar handbag in the luxury market. Moreover,

Dior has used a variety of valuable, scarce, and expensive raw materials to produce Lady Dior. Fabrics such as lizard skin, cattlehide, sheepskin, crocodile leather, and ostrich skin. Dior has also collaborated with world artists, allowing them to design limited edition Lady Dior handbag. With the variety of raw material and style, the market of Lady Dior handbag has lots of choices, increasing the choices for consumers to purchase. In this way, Dior has continued to expand its Lady Dior handbag market.

Moreover, the manager claimed that Dior has a stable consumer base, who have stable and high-income resources, and these consumer groups are usually careless towards the change in price. Normally, the price of Lady Dior is between 30 thousand RMB to 60 thousand RMB. The price of one Lady Dior handbag only consists of a small percentage of the total income for wealthy consumers. Therefore, a fluctuation in Lady Dior handbag will not be a serious problem for wealthy consumers. They are careless of the change in price, thus price elasticity for most Lady Dior handbag's consumers is inelastic, less sensitive to the change in price.

Lastly, the accessibility of luxury consumption is limited by the pandemic. Many cities have locked down in 2020, and even in 2022 some cities, like Shanghai, are not totally free to travel around. Therefore, choices of shops have greatly decreased due to COVID-19 restrictions, Chinese consumers can only purchase luxury goods local. Choices are limited, thus demand for Lady Dior is relatively more inelastic than before the epidemic.

4.3.2 The Veblen effect

This theory refers to the positive impact of the price of a product on the quantity demand of that product. Where quantity demand increases as price increases. The luxury consumption in this effect is called as conspicuous consumption, quantity demand is conspicuous demand, and price of the luxury is conspicuous price. The theory represents the change in quantity demand after the turning point of the demand curve of consumers represent below (Figure 1).

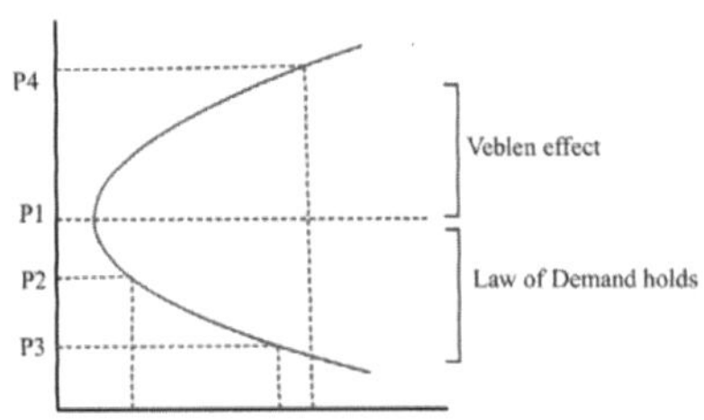

Figure 1. The Veblen effect [16]

The curve of the demand curve is 'C' shape. When price is below P1, the demand follows the law of demand, where quantity demand falls as price rises. When price rises from P3 to P2, the quantity demand falls from Q3 to Q2, follows the law of demand.

However, when price is above P1, the demand obeys the law of demand. The quantity demand rises as price rises, which is the Veblen effect. Thus, quantity demand rises as price rises after the turning point (P1) of demand curve.

In the case of the increase in total revenue of Lady Dior can be explained by the Veblen effect. The Lady Dior handbag is a Veblen product where the change in quantity demand does not follow the law of demand (Figure 1).

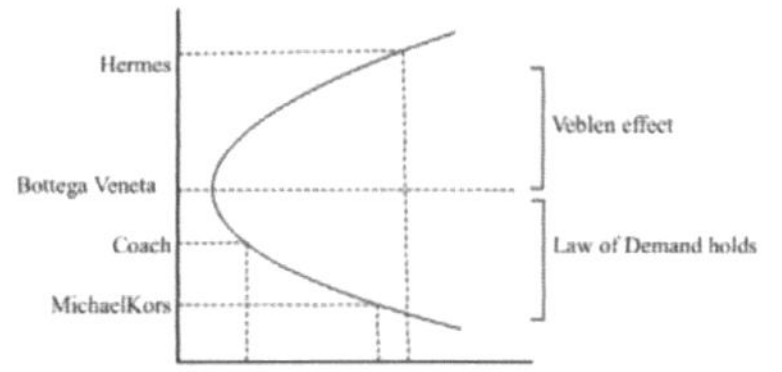

Figure 2. The Veblen Effect in Luxury Market [16]

In the figure 2, there are 5 **brands,** and the y-axis represents the price of each of their price in increasing order. Coach and MichaelKors are considered as quite affordable brands, where consumers are attracted to the low price. For these two brands, the law of demand holds. If price of Coach and MichaelKors falls, handbags are more attractive to consumers, consumers are more willing to buy the handbag, thus the quantity demand for the brand's handbag will increase. However, Bottega Veneta is considered as the turning point of the demand for luxury handbag, because BV has both expensive and relatively more affordable products. Brands above Bottega Veneta, like Hermes, the law of demand does not hold. For these brands, price is not only a demand factor, but also a monetary value of the symbol of luxury goods. Price of a Hermes Birkin or price of a Lady Dior represents status, wealth, and power. The higher the price, the stronger the symbol of these identities. Therefore, consumers' quantity demand for handbag rises as price of the product increases.

Therefore, the Veblen effect is the theory for explaining the phenomenon of the luxury consumption. As Lady Dior handbag's price increases, the quantity demand rises, leading to a rise in total revenue. After the price have reached a certain high level, the law of demand does not hold anymore. The price factor is different from what people thought before, but the price has other meanings. The price after it reached P1, it also represents status, wealth, power, and symbol. The price after P1 is a monetary value of these symbols. Therefore, when the price of a product is high enough, price is a symbol of those identities, where other factors like intrinsic needs, external goals, and psychological needs influences the quantity demand, which explains the increase in demand for Lady Dior as it becomes more expensive.

4.3.3 The Bandwagon effect

This effect is a psychological phenomenon in behavior economy where people do something because others are doing it, even though they intentionally don't want to do it.

In luxury consumption, the Bandwagon effect explains luxury consumption psychologically why quantity demand for Lady Dior rises. Consumers can easily be influenced by comments of others. Chinese consumers often evaluate the quality and value of a product by relying on the opinions from other consumers. Under the environment of this thinking, consumers are indirectly accepting this misleading information. For example, consumers are influenced by celebrities and popular culture. The certain style celebrities wear, or the certain item famous person wear is a symbol of themselves. People are influenced by the status of the wearer, and consumers may think that buying the same item or wearing the same style can be like that person.

The Bandwagon effect can happen positively and negatively. If people's initial preferences are similar, consumptions are rational, and they have accurate information of the quality of product. Therefore, it makes sense for consumers to follow the trend and make consumption. However, the bandwagon effect in luxury consumption can be misleading because it indirectly gives consumers the signal to purchase goods that they intentionally do not want to buy. Luxury goods are not necessities thus there is no need for consumers to buy extra expensive handbag. Also, some consumers are not that wealthy, and they probably do not like the Lady Dior handbag, but they still buy one at the store. Additional consumption of Lady Dior handbag may be considered as a waste of resources. Rationally, consumers do not need extra handbag. Nevertheless, consumers in practice are irrational and their motivations for buying luxury goods is not juts marginal utility anymore.

All in all, the Bandwagon effect explains the luxury consumption psychologically, through explaining the consumer behaviour. Meaning that people can be influenced by others, can following the consumption if others are buying too. Though the influence may be rational, but in luxury consumption it is often seen as irrational and misleading.

4.3.3 The Snob effect

The Snob effect refers to the phenomenon that quantity demand for certain consumer falls because others are increasing their demand for a product. It explains the psychological reason of the fall in quantity demand is due to the feeling of being unique. Thus, these types of consumers pay less attention towards popular brands and popular products. Therefore, as Lady Dior is getting more and more popular, some consumers are decreasing their demand for Lady Dior.

4.3.5 The desire to achieve psychological goals: symbolism, self-satisfaction and perfectionism

Other factors may influence luxury consumption more--Materialism. Luxury goods does not only present to other people about the wearer's social status, also provides hedonistic effects and psychological satisfaction. Materialistic consumers mainly consider the symbolism of luxury goods, and what luxury goods can represent them.

The Chinese luxury consumption motivations mainly includes individuals internal desire and external stimulations. In research done by Silverstein and Fiske, it has a result that many consumers who purchase luxury goods are not rich, but they still spend a large amount of money on luxury brands. This motivation from these consumers can be explained by individuals' self-esteem. Although consumer do not consider luxury goods as necessitates, they still spend a large proportion of their income to purchase on of them.

Chinese consumers care about the feeling during the consumption and what the product can bring them, such as superiority, self-satisfying, recognition, and 'saving face'. There is a strong connection between the motivation of luxury consumption and psychological satisfaction. Chinese consumers are obsessed with luxury goods and often consume luxury goods to satisfy themselves, for internal needs, or to satisfy their desire in owning one of it.

Furthermore, Chinese consumers luxury consumption is also relevant to social needs rather just only internal demands. Many job now requires employees to dress up, for instance, job in a fashion industry and business industry. Having a delight suit of Dior or having a classic Lady Dior handbag may give the business partner or employers a good impression. Moreover, Chinese care about their figure in public and their reputation among people. Self-recognition is one of the motivations for luxury consumption. When others give effective response towards luxury clothes, shoes, or accessories, this satisfies consumers' psychological needs and increases consumer's recognition. Thus, Chinese tries to present themselves by owning luxury brands. Chinese purchase luxury goods because they think luxury goods is a symbolic of an extravagant lifestyle. In order to directly show they are rich and live in an affluent lifestyle, Chinese are particularly interested in well-known brands with obvious logo on the products. The other motivation is the specific term, often use only in China, is 'saving face'. Saving face always occurs in social occasions and even in daily-get-along between friends and families. Consumers depend on the well-known brand, expensive price, and the symbolic meaning from luxury goods to show-off or use luxury goods as a communication.

Purchasing luxury goods provides consumers hedonistic rewards. Consumers are interested in satisfying their own thoughts and feelings, which factors other than price influence on decision making more.

Thus, price is one of the factors that consumers will consider whether to purchase luxury or not, but it is does not cover most of the decision making. The rises in price of Lady Dior handbag will lead to a fall in quantity demand but proportionately smaller than the rise in price. Overall, the total revenue increases.

5 Conclusion

5.1 Main findings

The reason why an increase in the price of Lady Dior handbag led to an increase in total revenue is due to the Veblen effect, the Bandwagon effect, and the luxury consumption behavior of Chinese consumers. The paper also draws conclusion that consumers have price inelastic demand for Lady Dior. Though price influences the quantity demand of Lady Dior, it only has a small impact on the change in demand. demand of Lady Dior, it only has a small impact on the change in demand.

Price has always been the demand factor, either when price of the product is low or high. What the Veblen effect meant is that when price is high enough, the price factor also represents more. The price is not only a demand factor, but also a monetary value of the internal symbols of the Lady Dior. Furthermore, price is an indicator of the quality. Thus, consumers may think products with higher price has better quality.

Other motivations for consuming luxury include fulfill self-satisfaction, materialistic motivations, achieve intrinsic and external goals, and 'saving face'.

5.2 Limitations and suggestions

Both questionnaire and interview have shown tendency about the importance of other factors for consumers to consider during luxury consumption. Motivations for Chinese consumers to purchase luxury goods contains their desire to satisfy their psychological needs and their desire to be served, as well as to enjoy the sale's services. Besides these needs, consumers buy luxury goods as a reward to themselves.

However, the result coming from questionnaire may be inaccurate and biased. Since the answers are previously set by the questionnaire designer, respondents can only choose the closest answer, but not the most accurate one. Thus, the results are inaccurate. Future researchers can avoid this problem by not providing any choices and let respondents to type down their answers. Nevertheless, this will lead to disincentive to answer the questionnaire.

Moreover, questionnaire is only answered by limited numbers of people, the sample subject is not large enough, so the answers are not representative. Researchers can use big data or random sample to improve the representative.

Also, interview is time consuming and it needs time to analyse the answers given by the respondents. Also, it is difficult to practice in large scale, thus the answers may be not representative and subjective. One of the solutions is to interview more managers with high status. Therefore, there are more answers, and their answers are more objective.

Lastly, the turning point of the Veblen effect is inaccurate and hard to measure. Everyone has different standards of the level considered as a start of the Veblen effect.

Though the reasons for the increase in sales can be predicted before the study, the investigation is surely worth it. The study can provide information to firms in what problems do firms have if their promotion failed, how to adjust business strategies and what firms need to do to have greater opportunity to success. The research of Dior provides a great example for how business should do to improve their product and enhance consumer loyalty. Dior has designed a variety of colors and fabrics of Lady Dior. And collaborated with famous artists in the world, to make Lady Dior more various so that most consumers can buy one of them. Thus, the research suggests that luxury firms should also find ways to make their supply more flexible and elastic, in order to face different kinds of demand.

References

1. C. Bamford, S. Grant, C. U. P, F 8(2014)
2. M. Kasztalska, I. M. M. I. I. S. E-J, 2, 77-87 (2017)
3. Y. Chan, K. To, C. Chu, J. R. C. S., 27, 1-10 (2015)
4. Y. Truong, R. McColl, J. R. C. S.,18, 555-561 (2011)
5. E. Ko, M. Megehee, J. B. R., 65, 1395-1398 (2012)
6. D. Bochanczyk-Kupka, L. G. E. E. S. D. B. P., 122-127 (2019)
7. H. Leibenstein, T. Q. J. E., 64, 183-207 (1950)
8. M. Husic, M. C. J. F. M. M. A. I. J. (2009)
9. S. Bagwell, D. Bernheim, T. A. E. R.,349-373 (1996)
10. Y. Wang, S. Sun, Y. Song, J. P. M., 17, 345-359 (2011)
11. Q. Zhou, L. *Market in China* (2011)
12. B. Trigg, J. E. I., 35, 99-115 (2001)
13. L. Zhan, Y. He, J. B. R., 65, 1452-1460 (2012)
14. S. Nwankwo, N. Hamelin, M. Khaled, J. R. C. S., 21, 735-744 (2014)
15. J. Choo, H. Moon, H. Kim, N. Yoon, J. F. M. M. A. I. J. (2012)
16. S. Chen, L. Lamberti, Q. M. R. A. I. J. (2015)

Exploring Current Trends and Strategies in Online Marketing for National Beauty Brands: A Case Study of Perfect Diary

Xi Chen[1,*]

[1]Western language and culture, Beijing Language and Culture University, Haidian District, Beijing, China

Abstract. Focusing on The Perfect Diary, this article discusses the rise of national beauty brands and delves into the significance of online end-to-end marketing. The context of the article highlights the rise of national brands globally and emphasises the growth of the Chinese beauty industry. The Perfect Diary is used as a case study because of its historical importance and online marketing success. The development of national beauty brands reflects the rise of the Chinese economy and the evolution of consumer preferences. The analysis includes the evolution of online marketing. Perfect Diary's strategy and the role of online marketing in the beauty industry. Challenges include increased market competition, changing consumer demands, and the evolution of the online marketing environment. Perfect Diary's strategy includes innovative marketing on emerging platforms, interaction experiences, and enhanced brand storytelling. The analysis also emphasizes the importance of adapting to the dynamic digital landscape, where Perfect Diary must continually assess and integrate new technologies and trends in social media and e-commerce to maintain a competitive edge in the rapidly evolving beauty industry. In conclusion, Perfect Diary's success is due to its adaptability, innovation and consumer-centric approach. The article recommends that domestic beauty brands continue to innovate, enhance their brand culture, adopt a diversified marketing strategy and develop a long-term growth plan in order to thrive in a dynamic market.

1 Introduction

In the vibrant global landscape of beauty, domestic brands are increasingly capturing the limelight. As Chinese consumers' tastes evolve and the calibre of homegrown products rises, we're witnessing an unprecedented surge in the sector's growth. This study intends to delve into the background and the importance of online terminal marketing to the rise of national beauty brands, as well as the reasons for choosing The Perfect Diary as a case study.

The emergence of national beauty brands in the global market not only reflects the new image of Made in China, but also reveals the significant increase in Chinese consumers' trust and recognition of local beauty brands. Behind this trend, a series of key issues have emerged, the most noticeable of which is the key role of network terminal marketing in the beauty industry.

As an indispensable part of the beauty industry, network terminal marketing has greatly shaped brand image and promoted product sales. Against this background, Perfect Diary is chosen as a case study, aiming at revealing its successful experience and strategy in online terminal marketing through an intensive study of a representative national beauty brand with a long history. This not only helps to deeply understand the development path of the national beauty brand, but also provides valuable experience reference for other brands.

The objectives and scope of this study include a comprehensive analysis of the present conditions of national beauty brands with respect to online terminal marketing with the aim of exploring effective online marketing strategies. Through in-depth research in this area, the author hopes to provide useful insights into the development of national beauty brands in network era and to facilitate the sustained expansion of the beauty trade.

2 Overview of the development of national beauty brands

2.1 The development of national beauty brands

In the evolution of China's beauty industry, national beauty brands have gone through a period from a start to a rise. What started as an analogue of international brands has gradually evolved into a process of forming their own unique style. This evolution is attributed to the rise of China's economy and consumers' pursuit of quality and local culture.

National beauty brands occupy a growing share of the domestic market, not only dominating in 1st and 2nd tier cities, but also making significant progress in 3rd and 4th tier cities and rural markets. Consumer groups are gradually diversifying, attracting widespread attention and support from the younger generation to the

* Corresponding author: 202111059035@mail.bnu.edu.cn

middle-aged group. With the development of science and technology, the online terminal marketing has become a key driving force for the rapid expansion of national beauty brands. Through e-commerce platforms, social media and live broadcasting, brands are able to interact directly with consumers and increase brand awareness. The convenience of online sales channels provides brands with a wider range of market opportunities.

2.2 The development of online marketing

2.2.1 The rise of online marketing

With the booming development of Internet technology, online marketing has gradually emerged. In the last 20 years, the explosive development of the population of Chinese Internet users has provided a broad space for the development of Internet marketing.The beauty industry realises brand promotion, product promotion and sales through online platforms.

2.2.2 Online Marketing Strategies in the Beauty Industry

Beauty brands have adopted a variety of strategies for online marketing, including promotion through social media, using microblogging, WeChat and other social platforms to build their brand image and interact with users. There are also signing cooperation with online celebrities such as famous beauty bloggers to increase brand exposure [1]. Equilibrium theory can explain the way in which clients assess business information obtained through digital communication in order to provide potentially useful insights[2].Specifically, shoppers (followers) rate messages higher if they feel a good match with the influencer and when the influencer appears to be a good match within the context of the substance it is promoting (e.g., product, brand, clothing).If any of these elements do not evoke a sense of fit, the convincing process of communication aimed at encouraging consumers to accept the attractiveness and suitability of the marketed brand or product for their spending is probably going to fail. Also, the research verifies that when the degree of influence and consumption are fixed and relatively high, a high degree of influence and product fit (low fit) leads to a high degree of consumer-product fit (low fit). Greater levels of consumer-product fit are linked to a better relationship with the sponsored product and a higher willingness to buy and refer to the product.At the same time, beauty brands show the effect of product usage through live broadcasting platforms, interacting with viewers in real time and prompting merchandise sales.

2.3 The role and influence of online marketing in the beauty industry

Online marketing provides a wider brand communication channel for national beauty brands. Through content creation and brand storytelling, brands can better communicate their core values and attract the attention of potential consumers. The data of 2021 Tmall Golden Makeup Award shows that of the 8,000,000,000 shoppers on Ali Tmall's platform, nearly 200 million are post-95 consumers, 40% of whom buy highly aesthetic and cost-effective Chinese national cosmetics, including products with distinctive Chinese content, such as Perfect Diary National Geographic Colour Cosmetic Collection, Flower Xizi Sculpted Flower Lipsticks, and Maogoping Oriental Collection, among others. In addition, among young consumers nowadays, people's sense of ethnic proudness has gradually increased after the Pandemic, and Gen Z has keen and diverse sense of identity with the trend of ethnic culture consumption and personalised vision[3].

Internet marketing provides diversified sales channels for beauty brands. In addition to traditional offline shop sales, brands can directly reach consumers across the country or even around the world through e-commerce platforms, social media direct sales and other means to achieve the expansion of sales channels. Livestreaming is particularly effective in the introduction and sales of experiential products such as clothing and cosmetics. For instance, clothing and makeup account for nearly 60 % of Taobao's livestreaming sales in 2019[4].

Through social media and online live streaming, beauty brands can establish closer interaction with consumers. Responding to users' questions and feedback in a timely manner and listening to their needs can help improve the brand's user satisfaction and form a good reputation.

3 Analysis of the current situation of the perfect diary network terminal marketing

3.1Perfect Diary Introduction

Perfect Diary is a native beauty brand originating from China, founded in 2017. The brand was created with the aim of providing cost-effective, innovative, and fashionable make-up products for young women. Since its establishment, Perfect Diary has been expanding its market with its unique positioning and innovative products, and gradually become one of the leaders in China's cosmetics industry. Perfect Diary's market positioning mainly focuses on young, fashionable and individuality-seeking consumer groups. The brand is committed to providing colorful make-up products to meet the needs of female consumers of different age levels and make-up levels. Through close-to-consumer product pricing and diversified product lines, Perfect Diary has successfully attracted a wide range of target consumers.

3.2 Analysis of online marketing strategies

Perfect Diary actively carries out product promotion, brand activities and interaction with users through media platforms for communication and entertainment (SMEs) such as Weibo and Xiaohongshu. Through the release of new product information, make-up tutorials, user sharing and other forms, it increases brand exposure. At the same time, it cooperates with major e-commerce platforms, providing a convenient shopping experience and expanding sales channels through online sales channels such as the Tmall flagship shop and Jingdong Beauty Zone. Perfect Diary has signed cooperation with famous beauty bloggers and fashionistas to promote its products through their influence. These collaborations have increased brand awareness and conveyed the effects and characteristics of product usage.

Perfect Diary has created an attractive brand image through creative content production, including short videos, pictures and stories. Brand storytelling enhances the emotional connection with consumers, and the sensory appeal, vivid content and character interaction of short videos are significant factors in enhancing the sentimental enjoyment of the experience, which in turn promotes consumer recognition and fidelity to the brand. [5]. There is also the combination of products and traditional Chinese culture here. As national self-pride and ethnic sentiment increase in the aftermath of pandemics, the tendency to nationalise cultural consumption grows in popularity, and this predilection for ethnic goods creates a sense of nationhood, which is shaped by the consumer's love of his or her homeland as a citizen of the country [6]. Ethnocentric orientation and individual acculturation of consumers have a significant impact on their intention to purchase ethnic goods [7].

Through sales data and market feedback, Perfect Diary can evaluate the effectiveness of different marketing strategies. For example, whether the launch of new products is popular or not, and whether the marketing activities have increased sales. It also analyses consumer reviews and feedback to understand the product's strengths and points of improvement. Also, monitor the brand reputation through social media and other platforms to maintain a good brand image.

Perfect Diary comprehensively covers social media, e-commerce platforms, KOL cooperation and content creation through diverse online marketing strategies. These strategies have effectively increased brand exposure, expanded sales channels, and built a positive brand image through interaction with consumers. However, brands still need to continuously focus on user feedback, innovation as well as adapting their policies and tactics to meet the changing dynamics of the market.

4 Challenges and problems

4.1 Increasing competition in the market

With the trend of Globalization, the entry of international beauty brands has sharpened competition in the market. These brands have strong resources and extensive international influence, posing competitive pressure on local brands. The fierce competition in the beauty market has led to national beauty brands, including Perfect Diary, needing more competitive products and innovative strategies to stand out in the market At the same time, the rise of emerging brands has had an impact on the market. The emergence of new local brands such as Flower Knows may break the existing market landscape and increase the intensity of competition. These new brands are competing for consumer attention through innovation and differentiated strategies, with hedonistic and the value of meritocratic purchases[8]driving buyer behavior, which poses a challenge to traditional beauty brands. This will require established brands such as Perfect Diary to be more flexible in responding to changes in the market and continue to innovate and optimize their product lines. In order to increase the uniquely assumed willingness to purchase cosmetics m-commerce while shopping online, various factors, such as visual attractiveness, inter-personal impact and accessibility, are crucial.

4.2 Changes in consumer demand

4.2.1 Characteristics and needs of young consumer groups

The current consumer group of cosmetic products is showing a trend of youth. The younger generation of consumers have more diversified and personalised needs. Their expectations of products do not only remain in the basic functions, but also focus more on the emotional empathy of the goods as well as the sociality of brand, also the brand's social responsibility, sustainability and other aspects. Perfect Diary needs to adapt to younger consumers' pursuit of brand image and culture, with hedonistic and utilitarian browsing likely to be the core determinants driving consumer intent [9].

4.2.2 Consumers' expectations of quality and innovation

Consumers' expectations of national beauty products do not only stop at price, but also focus on product quality and innovation. Brands need to continuously improve their product development capabilities to meet consumer demand for high-quality beauty products. Displaying goods/services can have a major impact on make-up. Websites with good graphical screens and appealing colour schemes will engage shoppers [10].Visual appeal is as important as making a first impression.Therefore, the authors advise make-up merchandising executives to give adequate attention to their online visionary information.

4.3 Changes in the online marketing environment

4.3.1 Changes in social media platform policy

Policy changes in social media platforms may have an impact on brand promotion and interaction. Frequent changes in policies may affect the effectiveness of brand promotion and publicity on these platforms. Perfect Diary needs to be flexible to respond to platform policy adjustments, maintain a good social media presence and find new ways to promote.

4.3.2 Online marketing regulations and ethical issues

As online marketing evolves, regulatory and ethical issues are of increasing concern. Brands need to ensure that they follow relevant regulations and ethical guidelines in online marketing, and deal with ethical issues in advertising, privacy, false advertising, etc., in order to avoid potential legal risks and safeguard the brand's legal rights and reputation. For example, the Advertising Standards Authority in the United Kingdom has set out a fresh guidance to assure the legality and honesty of influencer communications by revealing the influencer's possible commercial relationship with the brand [11]. In the wake of the ban, the amount of Netflix content that publicly indicates a sponsored nature increased by a massive 200 per cent for the period between 2018 and 2019[12]. Social media users are also more aware than ever of the substance of influencer's adverts.Therefore, marketers must be aware of how social media users interpret sponsorship disclosures and influence advertising effectiveness.

5 Strategies and recommendations

5.1 Innovative marketing strategies

5.1.1 Using emerging social media platforms

It can try to build up the brand image on emerging social media platforms, such as posting interesting and creative content on short video platforms and emerging social applications to attract more young users. As the internet has become more popular, online media is now an invaluable method for online campaigns [13], describing the connotations of a destination from a civilian's point of view is a practical approach, as vivid content also positively affects the emotional experience of consumers. Purposeful short videos can be combined with narrative communication strategies to evoke the user's emotive energy. For example, sitcoms, science fiction and blogs can be used.Building an emotive link with buyers through characterisation as well as story threads can give a destination brand a unique connotation. Brand identity and core loyalty to the destination will be rapidly developed, a key to facilitating the transition from temporary churn to permanent branding of the destination's identity [5].

5.1.2 Innovative interactive and experiential marketing

To create unique online and offline interactive activities, such as virtual make-up try-on experiences and online make-up teaching, in order to enhance user engagement and product experience. Online interaction is increasingly emerging as an essential way to improve the transmission of commercial web sites [14].

5.1.3 Strengthen brand story and cultural connotation

Create a stronger storytelling brand image by digging deeper into the history and cultural connotations of the brand to enhance the emotional connection with consumers. Research has shown that consumers' tendency towards ethnocentrism and individual acculturation orientation impacts positively to their desire to purchase ethnic goods. Brand familiarisation is related to and influenced by consciousness of the ethnic product, meaning that ethnic brands that are well known better represent the national identity in the mind of the consumer [7].

5.2 Enhancing product and service quality

5.2.1 Strengthen product development and innovation

Increase investment in product research and development and launch more innovative and differentiated products to meet consumers' pursuit of quality and uniqueness in beauty products.

5.2.2 Improve service quality and customer satisfaction

Establish a perfect customer service system, strengthen the training of the online customer service team, improve the service level, better meet customer needs and enhance customer satisfaction.

5.3. Sustainable development strategies

5.3.1 Integration of environmental protection concepts and social responsibility

Pursue an environmentally friendly packaging policy to reduce the use of plastics, advocate sustainable consumption, and work with consumers to focus on environmental protection. The notion of sustainability has been adopted recently for worldwide consistency of both consuming and producing to achieve the United Nations goals for sustained progress to be realised by 2030[13-15]. Make-up organisations are expected to respond to such threats by making the transition to sustainable development,challenges in pursuit of economic profitability, preservation of the environment and protection of public health[16].Therefore, the cosmetics industry needs a long-term sustainable perspective on the green transition[17], as well as the necessity to reconsider and reintroduce solutions for more environmentally and sustainably produced and consumed goods and services.

6 Conclusion

In reviewing Perfect Diary's successes and challenges in online end-to-end marketing, it can be seen that this national beauty brand has excelled in adapting to changes in the market, innovating its marketing strategies, and focusing on consumer needs. Its proactive response to changes in social media platforms and creative use of emerging social media, as well as its success in attracting the younger generation of consumers by strengthening its brand story and improving product quality.

However, as market competition intensified, national beauty brands faced new challenges. The rise of emerging brands, changing consumer needs and the complexity of the online marketing environment require brands to maintain keen insights and continuous innovation.

Predictions and suggestions for the future development trend of national beauty brands are as follows:

1. Continuous innovation and differentiation

In the future, national beauty brands need to continuously strengthen their investment in product research and development, push forward new ideas, and provide more innovative and personalized products to meet changing consumer needs.

2. Strengthen brand culture and social responsibility

In brand building, focus on deepening the brand story and cultural connotation, so that consumers can better understand the core value of the brand. At the same time, it integrates the concept of environmental protection and social responsibility, and actively participates in public welfare undertakings in order to enhance the brand image.

3. Diversified online marketing strategy

In the face of changes in emerging social media platforms, national beauty brands should maintain flexibility and continuously adjust their online marketing strategies, including exploring new platforms and innovating interactive experiences, to stay connected with young consumers.

4. Long-term development plan:

Develop a clear long-term development plan, including international market expansion and sustainable development strategies, to ensure that the brand has a more robust competitiveness in the future market.

In future development, national beauty brands can learn from the experience of successful brands such as Perfect Diary, insisting on innovation, focusing on consumers, quality and social responsibility, in order to meet the challenges of the future market and continue to grow their influence on the international stage.

Reference

1. F. Heider, J.P **107**,12 (1946)
2. S. van Dam, E. van Reijmersdal, J.P.R. C **13**,2 (2019)
3. K. Xue, M. Yu, FUP, 09 (2021)
4. A.Wong, K.Itrungrueng, N.Assarut, J.B **117**, 543-556
5. Z. Li, J. Zhang, J. D. M. M **30**, 100825
6. L. Zhu, S. Wang, X. Lu, J. M. W 9, 122-128
7. Y. Li, J. Sun， L. Zhu, T. I **10**, 100046
8. B. J. Babin, R. William, J. C. R **20**, 644 – 656
9. J. Park, S. Ha, J. R. C. S **28**, 310-316
10. W.K. Chen, D.S. Chang, C.C. Chen, J.E.M **13**,193-220
11. A. Arnold, Transparency In Influencer advertising: Are We There Yet. https://www.forbes.com/sites/andrewarnold/2018/10/25/transparency-in-influencer-marketing-are-we-there-yet/?sh=160fec4175e1
12. C. Wilson, Social bakers Reports Influencer-Sponsored Posts Surge by 150% on Instagram. https://www.businesswire.com/news/home/20190430005386/en/Socialbakers-Reports-Influencer-Sponsored-Posts-Surge-by-150-on-Instagram
13. S. Chen, C. Lin, T. F. S.C **140**, 22-32(2019)
14. K. Chen, D. Yen, I. M **42**,217-226 (2004)
15. T. Suphasomboon, S. Vassanadumrongdee, S.P.C **38**, 225-240(203)
16. U. Amrina, A. Hidayatno, T. Yuri M. Zagloel, J. O.I. T. M. C **7**,225
17. R. Rocca, F. Acerbi, L. Fumagalli, M. Taisch, C.W.S **3**,100057 (2022)

Decoding Disney's Marketing Mastery: A Strategic Analysis

Wanying Zhu[1,*]

[1]Urban Culture and Communication College, Suzhou City University, Jiangsu, 215000, China

Abstract. Nowdays, the Walt Disney Company is one of the most influential entertainment companies in the world, which is famous for its creativity and unique marketing strategy.Disney used to be just a small animation studio but now it has influence all over the world. To investigate the key factors which made Disney's successful global expansion and development,this paper did this following reserach.This research is mainly about Disney's core business and the marketing strategy used by Disney.The study was conducted through a meticulous analysis of Disney's primary business segments, its overarching business strategies, and its management practices. Furthermore, it examines Disney's brand positioning, market penetration tactics, and customer engagement techniques that collectively forge its competitive advantage. By dissecting the synergy between Disney's content creation and its promotional tactics, this research aims to unravel the intricacies of Disney's approach in nurturing a loyal consumer base and securing its status as an indomitable force in the entertainment industry.

1 Introduction

The Walt Disney Company was created by Walt Disney and his business partner in 1923. It was first named as Disney Brothers Cartoon Studio in Hollywood. At that time, it began to make animated films and short films. In 1937, Disney released its first animated film called Snow White, which not only set box-office records, but also established Disney's position in the field of animation.In the following decades, Disney produced a series of well-known animated classics, such as Dumbo, Cinderella, and The Lion King.In 1955, Disney opened its first Disneyland in California,which started the era of the Disney theme park kingdom. Since then, Disney has opened several theme parks around the world. In the 1990s, Disney began acquiring large media companies and gradually expanded into television shows, movies, and music. In the early 2000s, Disney began to focus on digital entertainment with the launch of Disney Online and Disney Games. Since 2005, Disney has made a series of acquisitions. First Marvel, then Lucas film, and after that, a majority stake in 21st Century Fox [1]. In 2019, Disney became one of the biggest entertainment corporations in the world, further expanding its reach into new areas including film, TV, streaming media. Now Disney is a multinational company integrating entertainment production, theme parks and media networks.

2 The core business of Disney

2.1 Disney's animation and films

To begin with, the typical structure of Disney knowledge is distinguished by the preponderance of the cinema media [2]. At present, Disney's content landscape has six parts: Disney, Pixar, Marvel, Star Wars, 20th Century Pictures and National Geographic. Each segment has a large number of audio and video entertainment content and IP, expanding the scope of product coverage from children and teenagers to more diverse audiences. Disney invests most of its time and capital in creating high-quality content, while at the same time maximizing its embrace of technology, first using technology to create conditions for high quality products and using more advanced and precise ways to reach more consumers. Creation is a key factor in the success of Disney animation. The rise of various animation industries has made the audience's vision more demanding than the past, only continuous innovation can attract people. Disney is aware of this point, so it constantly increases the cost of technological innovation.

Consumer demand is an important aspect in the development of businesses. Disney not only constantly responds to market needs, but it also prioritizes the development of new markets. Disney broadens the consuming style and audience for animated films, ensuring that its animations are not only liked by children, but also reflect the aesthetic and depth of the younger generation. Disney has created wonderful, animated films that are liked by people of all ages. For example, many people like the animated film "COCO", particularly the family values it included [3]. As a truly global enterprise, Disney also pay attention to the values of globalization in content creation. Disney has put a lot of emphasis on international sourcing in its animated films. In Disney, people can see all kinds of different stories by people from different regions.

* Corresponding author: Xqq.@szcu.edu.cn

2.2 Disney theme park

According to Smith, travel and tourism is the world's largest industry in terms of employment, and it ranks in the top two or three industries in nearly every country on practically every measure [4]. The Walt Disney Company operates theme parks in addition to its media company [5]. In the eyes of many people, Disney Park is the best tourist attraction. Disney parks and products include park tickets, meals, hotel accommodations, and surrounding areas, among other things. There are currently six Disney parks in the world, located in California, Orlando, Tokyo, Paris, Hong Kong, and Shanghai. These six Disney parks are summarized in table 1.

Table 1: Disney resorts in the world

	City	Year	Area (Acre)	Theme parks
Disneyland resort	California	1955	512	2
Walt Disney World	Orlando	1971	30500	4
Tokyo Disney resort	-	1983	494	2
Tokyo Disney Sea	-	2001	-	-
Disneyland Resort Paris	-	1992	4800	2
Hong Kong Disneyland	-	2005	310	1
Shanghai Disney	-	2016	287	8

Disney holds a significant position and has an edge in the worldwide theme park industry. There were 501 million visitors to the top 10 theme park groups in the world in 2018, with 31.39% of those visitors coming from the Disney Group, which had 157 million more visitors than the second-ranked Merlin Entertainment Group. Disney has a significant impact on the global theme park industry and has a much larger market share than any other company, having been the industry pioneer and explorer.

Disney theme park can always bring the most interesting experience for visitors. Disneyland's theme changes throughout the year. It consistently provides a fresh experience and is a major lure for return tourists. For instance, fans of Elsa are the target audience for the Frozen theme. After the popularity of the Frozen movie faded, the theme was quickly replaced by a new trend theme. Disney Parks implement a business strategy of continuously adding new services, facilities and attractions to attract repeat customers.

In recent years, the development and industrialization of information technology has prompted the theme park industry to gradually form its own development trend. Science and technology are becoming more and more significant. With the acceleration of science and technology and the increasing popularity of information technology and virtual technology, Disney continues to improve the technological content of products and enhance the interaction between technology and tourists. For example, projection-based augmented reality (AR) remains an important technology in Imagineering's toolbox, helping to bring structures to life in theme park entertainment shows.

2.3 The streaming media of Disney

During the COVID-19 epidemic, streaming video became a part of many people's daily life at home, and consumption is still growing [6]. Disney deeply integrates the internal resources of the group, upgrades online communication channels by acquiring media and building streaming media platforms. Disney+, Hulu and ESPN+ are the online media streaming platforms launched by Disney Streaming Services. In 2019Disney formally acquired 21st Century Fox to enhance its content. Since then, Disney, Pixar, Marvel, Lucasfilm, Fox, and National Geographic have all joined the content system. This differentiated content makes Disney+ the second largest streaming platform in the world by subscribers, with its three streaming platforms, Disney+, Hulu and ESPN+, reaching a combined 221 million subscribers.

3 Disney's IP

Currently, Disney has six content divisions: 20th Century Pictures, Pixar, Marvel, Star Wars, Disney, and National Geographic. Each part contains a significant amount of intellectual property (IP) and audio-visual entertainment content, broadening the product coverage beyond kids and teens to include a wider range of audiences.

Disney's primary competency is strong IP. Disney can strengthen its intellectual property through acquisitions and mergers as well as independent research and development. The company's autonomous intellectual property is primarily founded on thorough market segment study, with a particular emphasis on the topic of love and family, as well as a precise understanding of the demands of the female and child markets. For example, The Disney Princess line was launched in 2001 as an advertising and marketing effort aimed at young girls [7]. Simultaneously, the firm sought to address the gap in the male intellectual property demand market by acquiring Marvel and Lucasfilm. This move served to elevate the status of heroes, accentuate the allure of men, and bolster Disney's brand recognition. Disney developed a comprehensive IP segmentation strategy and progressively widened its consumer base through in-depth market segment analysis.

Disney devotes the great majority of its resources including time and money to producing branded content of the highest caliber. At the same time, it makes the most of technology, first utilizing it to establish the framework for superior products and then employing increasingly sophisticated and focused methods of reaching more audience.

4 Disney's 4P marketing strategy

4.1 Products

When people talk about Disney, the first thing that springs to mind are movies, but Disney has expanded to offer a wider range of products, such as: entertainment and music product line (including films, music, theater plays, etc.),media networks (including TV interviews, programs, radio broadcasts, etc.),theme parks and resort hotels (such as Disneyland and Disney-themed hotels), publications (including comics, games, etc.), accessories (such as keychains, hairpins, clothing, candies, etc. Entertainment and music product line is the most well-known form of Disney products, with its rich story content and beautiful pictures deeply loved by the audience. As an offline theme park, Disneyland offers interactive entertainment experiences that bring audience face to face with animated characters. Games, derivatives, hotels, parks and software applications built around IP, toys and other merchandise based on movies and TV shows all make up a significant portion of Disney's revenue.

4.2 Price

Disney adopts market-responsive pricing and perceived-value pricing models for its offerings. Disney Cinematic and Broadcast: Competitive pricing approach - aligning prices with the prevailing market norms. Disney Recreation and Lodging: Experiential pricing model - setting rates based on the visitors' appraised value of the overall experience.

4.3 Promotion

Disney's promotional strategies extend beyond traditional outlets like Disney Stores and movie theaters to embrace digital platforms, including its official website, accessible through popular e-commerce giants like Taobao and Jingdong. Additionally, Disney leverages technology through apps and mini-programs, enhancing consumer engagement. Crucially, Disney's success is amplified by licensing its intellectual properties (IPs). It owns five of the top 10 global IPs, underscoring its supremacy in the IP licensing arena. With over 3,000 licensees globally, Disney licenses out its beloved characters for a multitude of products, generating significant revenue. To feature Disney characters, groups must secure authorization, a process that has proven lucrative for Disney. In fiscal 2022, while revenue from Disney's derivatives business slightly dipped by 1.1% to $5.28 billions, operating profit saw a healthy increase of 4.7%, reaching $2.81 billions. This strategic approach to promotions and licensing illustrates Disney's adaptive and profitable business model in the ever-evolving entertainment industry.This strategic approach to promotions and licensing illustrates Disney's adaptive and profitable business model in the ever-evolving entertainment industry.

4.4 Place

Disney uses many sales strategies based on the audience and the product, such as: advertising sales (open screen advertising, outdoor advertising, etc.), direct sales (store direct sales, APP direct sales, official website direct sales) sponsorship(Increase brand exposure through sponsorship) and discount sales (such as Ole stores, through box sets). As to public relations marketing such as holding activities, celebrity endorsement, public opinion and event marketing, is the most successful part of Disney's marketing strategy. Disney's many public relations marketing has become a classic case of marketing. With the popularity of Disney princess culture, Disney launched an activity quickly called witness the power of princesses. This event invited 19 female photographers from 15 different countries to use great women as role models to create a positive image, such as the youngest woman to address the United Nations and the surfing World champion from Brazil.For every photo shared online, Disney donated $1 to Girl Up.

In 2016, Disney released the trailer: Reboot from The Book of the Forest, and simultaneously released stills of the actors voicing the characters and a few seconds of film clips. The nostalgic movie immediately appealed to parents, helping it stay at the top of the box-office for three consecutive weeks. In 2018, to celebrate Mickey Mouse's 90th birthday, Disney opened a stunning immersive art exhibition - held at the Museum in New York, which in addition to introducing Disney's history, mainly showcases Mickey-themed artwork by contemporary artists. Interactive activities are also arranged: ice cream making and steamboat parade. In addition, Disney also took the opportunity to co-branding with fashion brand Vans and Forever 21, expanding Disney's visibility in the fashion field.

5 Disney's marketing strategy

5.1 Brand management strategy

Brilliant brand images are becoming increasingly important in today's marketplace for the longevity and success of items [7-9]. The Walt Disney Company is at the cutting edge of multinational entertainment branding. First of all, the Disneyland brand is instantly associated with happiness, creates a positive perception of the company and its products, and builds a solid international reputation—all of which contribute to a broad variety of customer aggregation effects. Second, brand management creates the benefit of industrial aggregation by quickening the group's growth. One of the key and efficient ways to hasten Disneyland's growth is through brand management, which can eliminate geographic constraints, increase the enterprise's counter-exhibition space, and grow the brand's market share in order to support the company's quick growth and start down the path to scale management.

5.2 Service winning strategy

Disneyland is well-known for its high degree of service excellence, and its service concept and standard have become a model for all types of businesses to emulate. In any event, guests' safety is Disneyland's fundamental value proposition. During holidays, when an increase in tourists flow causes congestion and disruption, personnel will take steps such as reducing the number of visitors and tourist mobility to ensure that visitors receive adequate service standards and for safety reasons. Disneyland is fastidious when it comes to employee courtesy. Disney expects its employees to be friendly, polite, and considerate when they serve their guests. In short, Disney has polished every detail of the service.

5.3 Product innovation strategy

Disney makes updates and changes all the time. Disneyland parks have been following the "three-three system" for a long time, which involves replacing one-third of the hardware equipment annually, starting one-third of new projects, and continuously bringing in new employees. Disney parks actively integrate their own intellectual property (IP) with regional features and cultures, updating their entertainment offerings and facilities annually to maintain their allure and offer visitors a novel experience. This bolsters the company's tagline, "the Disneyland that will never be built" [10].

5.4 Flexible pricing strategy

A low pricing is appropriate for theme parks near the resort region. Disneyland's pricing model is quite adaptable. The park uses differential pricing, regional pricing, and price adjustment strategies depending on multiple factorise such product sort, sales times, and location to make sure that the ticket price is reasonable for target customers. This strategy ensures that prices remain attractive and competitive, catering to different segments of the market. For example, during peak seasons or for exclusive attractions, prices might be higher to reflect the increased demand. Conversely, during off-peak times or for less popular attractions, prices might be reduced to encourage attendance. Additionally, residents of the region where the park is located might enjoy special discounted rates, fostering local patronage and community goodwill.

5.5 Marketing management strategy

Disney has a distinctive approach to marketing management, emphasizing "external marketing" to consumers after stressing "internal marketing" to staff. Disney tries to use internal marketing management to create a wonderful workplace where employees "enjoy work and work happily" in order to motivate them to provide exceptional customer service. Disney Park spends a fortune on traditional media like radio, television, and newspapers for external marketing, which is then supplemented by a range of marketing methods.

6 Conclusion

As to the part of global marketing, it is necessary to make appropriate adjustments to each marketing element according to the special factor of the market environment. Trying to use some localization decisions will be very important. For example, Europe Disney theme park's sale is much lower than other Disney theme parks in terms of food and drink because it does not conform to the living habits of European people.

Disney is now the world's biggest producer of live-action and animated films. Disney is also widely regarded as the most powerful film company in Hollywood. The total number of Disney films that have broken 1 billion dollars worldwide is now 25, which is more than three times that of Warner and Universal, which rank second and third. Currently, Warner is Disney's main competitor in the North American market. As a veteran film production company, Warner also entered the field of animation at an early age. What's more, Warner still owns the rights to the once-popular fantasy film Harry Potter. Although Harry Potter has ended, Warner can use its prequel and other stories to shoot another animation, which will undoubtedly enhance the status of Warner Company in the field of animation production.

What's more, Disney also had to contend with a number of rivals in the amusement park industry such as Universal Studios, which has grown in popularity recently. There are numerous offline theme parks under the Universal Studios umbrella. Maybe they will be more exciting than Disney in the future.

References

1. J. Shen, M. Xu, S. Yang, AP,203,764-770, (2021)
2. W. Disney, AoS, 8(2002).
3. D.Dan, W.Putri, N A. Sophia, M. B.Simanjuntak, W.Ridwan, *EDUCATIONAL VALUE OF DISNEY FILM "COCO" BY WALT DISNEY PICTURES,* in Proceedings of Undergraduate Students'National Seminar, USNS,219
4. B.Francoeur, JOUR, 4(1),1-8, (2004)
5. W Y.Li, BP,3(1),12-21, (2022)
6. D.E.England, L.Descartes, M. A. Collier-Meek, S. S. 64, 555-567(2011)
7. M. Mine, D. Rose,B. Yang,J. Van Baar, A.Grundhofer,IEEE, 45(7): 32-40.（2012）
8. M.Braun, NEURUS, November 21,1-121, (2001)
9. M.J. Robbins, TRACE,5,1-31, (2014)
10. A.Bohas ,GS, 29(1): 23-41, (2015)

SHS Web of Conferences **188**, 03012 (2024) https://doi.org/10.1051/shsconf/202418803012
ICDDE 2024

A Study on the Game Strategy of Chip Price Behavior at the Background of the US-China Trade War

Minghao Ma[1,*]

[1]Department of Humanities and Social Sciences, University of Nottingham Ningbo China, Ningbo, China

Abstract. The US-China trade war has had a profound impact on the game strategy and price behavior of chips in the semiconductor industry. This study aims to analyze the influencing factors, strategic shifts, and game theory dynamics of chip prices in the context of the trade war. The asymmetrical relationship between the United States and China in chip supply and demand, coupled with the imposition of tariffs and restrictions, has disrupted the supply chain, which leads to fluctuations in chip prices. The study highlights the artificial inflation of demand and oversupply of certain chip types because of stockpiling and entity list disruptions. It also examines the impact of tariffs on the cost structure of semiconductor manufacturing and the subsequent adjustments in pricing strategies. Furthermore, the study explores the localization strategies and shifts in global semiconductor production that have been prompted by the trade war and their implications on chip prices. Lastly, the study analyzes the repeated game perspective and its influence on the strategic choices and behaviors of the parties involved in the trade war. Overall, this study provides insights into the game strategy and price behavior of chips in the background of the US-China trade war, contributing to a better understanding of the dynamics and implications for the semiconductor industry.

1.Introduction

The research by Zhang and Zhu suggests that there are significant opportunities for further development and expansion of international trade relations in various segments of the chip industry chain between countries [1]. However, in an era marked by the rise of techno-nationalism, the process of technological decoupling is intensifying, leading to intricate implications where technological capabilities become closely intertwined with a country's national security and geopolitical influence [2]. For instance, the US-China trade war had a profound impact on the semiconductor industry, specifically in terms of the behavior and price of chips. As two global economic powerhouses, the United States and China have engaged in a trade conflict that has resulted in tariffs, restrictions, and supply chain disruptions in the semiconductor trade. The semiconductor trade between the two countries has always been characterized by an asymmetrical relationship, with China heavily relying on the United States as its main supplier of chips.

The imposition of tariffs and restrictions on semiconductor imports and exports has caused significant disruptions in the supply chain, leading to increased costs for manufacturers. Additionally, political tensions and economic uncertainties have resulted in fluctuations in both supply and demand for chips. These factors have contributed to the volatility in chip prices, creating challenges for companies operating in the semiconductor industry.

The objective of this study is to analyze the game strategy behind the price behavior of chips in the context of the US-China trade war. The study aims to identify the key influencing factors that have led to fluctuations in chip prices, including the supply and demand dynamics, tariffs, and strategic shifts in semiconductor production localization.

Additionally, the study will examine the implications of the trade war on the semiconductor industry, both in the short term and the long term. It will analyze the impact on leading US semiconductor companies, as well as the challenges faced by China's high-tech sector. The research will explore the effects on equipment and material procurement costs, international collaboration, talent acquisition, and other business risks. Furthermore, the study will investigate the potential benefits and risks of domestic semiconductor chip production and other high-tech products resulting from localization policy incentives.

Moreover, the study will examine the role of intellectual property (IP) rights and licensing in the semiconductor industry and how they have been affected by the trade war. It will analyze the enhanced scrutiny of IP and trade secret protections, as well as the increased legal and administrative costs for safeguarding technologies. The study will also explore China's response to these protections, emphasizing the development of independent IP and its potential impact on licensing costs and the global pricing ecosystem for semiconductors.

Furthermore, the study will consider the perspective of a repeated game to understand the strategic choices and

* Corresponding author: hmymm3@nottingham.edu.cn

behaviors of the parties involved in the US-China trade war. It will analyze the tit-for-tat and trigger strategies commonly observed in this trade game and their implications for cooperation and non-cooperation between the two countries. The study will examine the long-term benefits of maintaining cooperation and the conditions under which participants may choose non-cooperation.

In summary, this study aims to provide a comprehensive analysis of the game strategy behind the price behavior of chips in the context of the US-China trade war. By examining the influencing factors, strategic shifts, implications, and game theory dynamics, the research seeks to shed light on the underlying drivers of chip prices and their influence on the semiconductor industry.

2.Game strategy of chip price behavior at the background of the US-China trade war

2.1 Influencing Factors of Chip Prices

Firstly, from a supply and demand perspective, the semiconductor trade between the United States and China reflects an asymmetrical relationship. China heavily relies on the United States as its main supplier of chips, with over one-third of total US chip sales being exported to China annually. Additionally, due to its technological leadership in high-tech production, the United States has consistently maintained dominance in the US-China semiconductor trade [3].

The US-China trade war has led to tariffs and restrictions on semiconductor imports and exports, causing supply chain disruptions and increased costs for manufacturers. Additionally, political tensions and economic uncertainties have impacted investor confidence and demand for chips. These factors have contributed to fluctuations in chip prices.

The first and most immediate effect of the trade war on chip pricing was through the lens of supply and demand. As Chinese companies anticipated the worst, they began to stockpile essential chips, fearing prolonged restrictions or embargoes. This artificial inflation of demand led to a corresponding increase in prices. Conversely, the entity list disrupted the supply chain, leading to an oversupply of some chip types, reducing their market price.

Furthermore, tariffs on Chinese goods affected the cost structure of semiconductor manufacturing. Many elements of the production process involve a complex global network; a chip might be designed in the US, manufactured using equipment from Europe, and assembled and packaged in facilities in Asia. Tariffs imposed inefficiencies on this process, which sometimes resulted in a significant enough disruption to alter pricing strategies as companies sought to mitigate increased manufacturing costs or shifts in demand.

The imposition of tariffs during the US-China trade war disrupted the supply chain of the semiconductor industry, causing both short-term and long-term fluctuations in chip prices. As Chinese companies anticipated potential trade restrictions, they began stockpiling semiconductors, resulting in an artificial increase in demand. This surge led to a corresponding increase in prices. However, as the trade tensions continued, the semiconductor market experienced a correction, with prices returning to normal levels.

2.2 Strategic localization and shifts in global semiconductor production

The trade war prompted a strategic shift in the localization of semiconductor supply chains. The United States sought to reduce reliance on Chinese semiconductor products by incentivizing domestic production and research. The US CHIPS and Science Act passed in 2022 is an example, which is aimed to solidify its leading position in the semiconductor industry [4]. The passing of the Act, combined with the escalating strategic competition between the US and China, underscores the recognition by both superpowers regarding the paramount importance of the technological revolution in an era marked by fragmented globalization [5]. Simultaneously, China implemented the " National Integrated Circuit Industry Investment Fund" initiative as a policy instrument [6] and invested heavily in its domestic chip industry to achieve self-sufficiency and reduce dependency on imported chips.

The impact of such localization strategies and shifts in global semiconductor production on chip pricing can be multifaceted. As companies invest in domestic manufacturing facilities and R&D, it may lead to increased costs that can influence pricing strategies to recover these investments. Additionally, the relocation of production or adoption of alternative supply sources in response to trade barriers could introduce complexities to market competition.

2.3 Impact of the Trade War on the Semiconductor Industry

The US-China trade conflict not only imposes profit losses and marketing obstacles on leading US semiconductor companies but also inflicts a severe impact on China's high-tech sector, which is unavoidable and irreversible in the short term. Chinese firms will encounter increasing equipment and material procurement costs, a flight of international orders, challenges in international collaboration, and talent acquisition, among other business risks. The semiconductor industry, in particular, will bear a more substantial brunt. However, in the short term, domestic semiconductor chip production and other high-tech products can benefit from localization policy incentives, domestic design, and equipment and materials, which are expected to absorb domestic demand orders, providing direct benefits [7].

In the future, the domestic semiconductor industry faces long-term risks such as product blockades, technological monopolies, and heightened international competition. Overseas cooperation and mergers and acquisitions may also be inhibited. However, concurrently, the trade war fosters domestic enterprises' independent research and development, encourages close collaboration within the local industry chain, enhances industrial ecology, and promotes industry growth [7].

The trade war resulted in an acceleration of technological advancements as Chinese firms sought to "leapfrog" to the next level of semiconductor technology. The US restrictions on technology transfers prompted China to invest significantly in research and development to achieve self-reliance in chip production. This aggressive push for indigenous innovation in China's chip industry not only impacts the market competition but can also potentially lower prices as Chinese-made chips become technologically competitive.

2.4 The Role of Intellectual Property and Licensing

Intellectual property (IP) rights play a considerable role in the semiconductor industry, with patents protecting much of the technology that goes into chip design and manufacturing. The trade war led to enhanced scrutiny of IP and trade secret protections. On one end, the fear of loss of IP to Chinese companies under potentially relaxed enforcement conditions led to higher pricing due to increased legal and administrative costs for safeguarding technologies. On the other end, the Chinese response to these protections was to develop independent IP, potentially reducing licensing costs and impacting the global pricing ecosystem for semiconductors.

The intricacies of intellectual property (IP) rights and their protection—underscored in the World Intellectual Property Organization (WIPO)'s reports on the patent landscape—demonstrate a battleground beyond tariffs and trade restrictions. The semiconductor industry heavily relies on a complex web of IP rights and licensing agreements to operate globally. Moreover, the costs associated with IP litigation and the creation of new IPs as a reaction to the trade war likely resulted in some price adjustments within the industry, reflecting increased operational costs.

The protection of intellectual property and trade secrets has long been a critical aspect of the semiconductor industry. However, the US-China trade war heightened concerns over the loss or misuse of IP, resulting in increased legal and administrative costs for safeguarding technologies. Additionally, to reduce licensing costs, China has also emphasized the development of independent IP. These factors have implications for chip pricing as costs associated with IP protection and licensing influence overall product expenses. According to Liu, China currently occupies the low-end sector of the global trade division [7]. Li also points out that China's high-tech industry is currently lacking strength and is vulnerable [8]. As a result, in the event of sanctions being imposed by both sides, China is likely to experience greater losses. Therefore, Li suggests that China should prioritize the development of high-tech industries and proactively prepare for potential sanctions [8].

For instance, under the condition of strong capital and talent reserves, Huawei offers a strategy for other high-tech enterprises in China to manage the risk of supply chain disruption, which is independent R&D and production. This approach is the optimal choice to mitigate the impact of supply chain disruptions [9].

3.The perspective of the repeated game

3.1 Two model of repeated game

A repeated Game is a dynamic game where the same structure game is repeated multiple times. In daily life, people usually tend to chase short-run payoffs for the following three reasons:

1. Psychologically, People want to enjoy something today rather than in the future

2. The sooner people get the payoff, the more flexibility and options for people to use it

3. Financial payoffs can be reinvested, so money now is worth more than money in the future

Repeated games can lead to cooperation because they can change participants' space of strategic choice. Both reality and theory show that tit-for-tat and trigger strategies are the most used strategies.

As mentioned above, now we have two strategies in the repeated game ——tit-for-tat and trigger strategy.

The former means that each player's action is based on their opponent's previous move.The latter means that if one person cooperates with the other and the other does not break the cooperation, the person will continue to cooperate; but if the other breaks the cooperation, the person will never cooperate with them again. For instance, once the US side behaves in a way that breaks cooperation in China-US trade, China will refuse any further cooperation, leading to the complete collapse of cooperation.

To calculate the long-term benefits, a general prisoner's dilemma game can be described using table 1;

Table 1: Prisoners' Dilemma matrix in the short run

	player B		
player A		cooperate	not cooperate
	cooperate	T , T	S , R
	not cooperate	R , S	P , P

In a one-shot game, if players A and B cooperate, they both get a payoff of T. If both do not cooperate, they both get a payoff of P. Suppose one cooperates and the other does not. In that case, the one who cooperates gets a payoff of S and the one who does not cooperate gets a payoff of R. We can easily conclude that R > T > P > S. At the same time, the total value for both players is greater than the total value of one player cooperating and the other not cooperating, as well as the total value of both players not cooperating, i.e. (T+T) > (S+R), (T+T) > (P+P).

Now suppose that player A and player B play an infinitely repeated prisoner's dilemma game. If they never cooperate, the payoff for each player in each period is P.

Now imagine that both players have cooperated until a certain point in time t. What is the value of continuing to maintain cooperation forever? To calculate this value, the concept of discount factor will be introduced, which represents the value of tomorrow's money compared to today's money. The writer will use $0 < \theta < 1$ to represent the discount factor, which reflects the patience level of the participants. A larger θ means a greater emphasis on the future. Therefore, the discounted value of maintaining long-term cooperation is:

$$V = T + \theta 1T + \theta 2T + \theta 3T + \theta 4T + \ldots \quad (1)$$

Mathematically, we know that this value equals T / (1-θ). θ is vital here.

3.2 Model analysis of repeat game

3.2.1 Tit-for-tat

This strategy constitutes a Nash equilibrium. In the trade game between China and the United States, if both sides adhere to the tit-for-tat strategy, an ideal situation is that no one initiates non-cooperation, and both sides will receive a payoff of T in each period, resulting in a total payoff of T/(1-θ) after discounting. A more likely scenario is that the US side initiates non-cooperation at stage t, and then China implements this strategy by choosing not to cooperate with the US in stage t+1 as a punishment for its non-cooperative behaviour. The actions of both sides from stage t+1 onwards will be as follows:

US side's actions: Cooperate, Not cooperate, Cooperate, Not cooperate, ...

China's actions: Not cooperate, Cooperate, Not cooperate, Cooperate, ...

China's expected payoff stream will be R, S, R, S, R, S (2)

This pattern continues. But if China chooses to forgive the US, cooperation will resume from stage t+1 onwards, and China's expected payoff stream will be T, T,T,T,T, (3)

Comparing equations (2) and (3), it is clear that the sum of the latter is significantly larger than the former. In theory, given that the US initiates non-cooperation at a certain stage, as long as China believes that the US is implementing the tit-for-tat strategy, China will not have the motivation to implement punishment and will choose to forgive the US and continue to cooperate.

3.2.2 Trigger strategy

The main idea behind the trigger strategy is that once the other one makes a mistake, you will never forgive them.

It is easy to prove that if θ is sufficiently large, the trigger strategy not only constitutes a Nash equilibrium but also a subgame perfect Nash equilibrium. Specifically, assuming that both China and the US choose the trigger strategy, meaning that if the US breaks cooperation in a period of good cooperation, China will never cooperate with the US again. Suppose that both parties cooperate consistently and China can receive a payoff of T in period t and afterward, the discounted value of the payoff stream is $T / (1-\theta)$. But if the US chooses to break cooperation which causes China to suffer a loss in the current period, then from the next period onwards, China will never cooperate with the US again.

In this case, the best outcome the US can achieve is to never cooperate again, and it will only receive a payoff of P in each subsequent period. The total value of the payoff stream is then $R + P\,[\theta / (1-\theta)]$. If the condition $T / (1-\theta) \geq R + P\,[\theta / (1-\theta)]$ is satisfied, the US's best choice is to always cooperate rather than initiate non-cooperation midway. In other words, as long as $\theta \geq (R - T) / (R - P)$, both players choosing the trigger strategy (not initiating non-cooperation) is the best choice.

The above condition can be restated as $\theta\,(T - P) / (1-\theta) \geq R - T$, where the right side of the inequality represents the increase in current income brought by choosing non-cooperation in a certain period, and the left side represents the discounted value of future loss caused by this non-cooperative behavior (where T - P is the loss in each period).

Therefore, whether participants will cooperate or not depends on whether the long-term benefits outweigh the immediate benefits and the level of patience. Specifically, given the level of patience, the greater the temptation of non-cooperation, the greater the immediate benefits brought by non-cooperation compared to the long-term benefits brought by cooperation, and the greater the possibility of participants choosing non-cooperation. In addition, given the temptation of non-cooperation and the long-term benefits of cooperation, the importance of the future, the greater the possibility of cooperation.

In this case, research by Liang also suggests that China will not take action at first because China is more dependent on this bilateral trade than the United States [10].

4.Conclusion

In conclusion, the US-China trade war has had a significant impact on the game strategy and price behavior of chips in the semiconductor industry. The asymmetrical relationship between the two countries in terms of chip supply and demand, along with the introduction of tariffs and restrictions, has disrupted the supply chain and increased costs for manufacturers. This has led to fluctuations in chip prices, with artificial inflation of demand and oversupply of certain chip types.

The trade war has also prompted strategic shifts in the localization of semiconductor production, as both the United States and China have sought to reduce reliance on each other. This has resulted in increased costs associated with domestic manufacturing and research, which can influence pricing strategies in the industry.

Furthermore, the protection of intellectual property (IP) rights and licensing has played a crucial role in the semiconductor industry and has been a battleground in the trade war. The trade war has brought about enhanced scrutiny of IP and trade secret protections, leading to higher pricing due to increased legal and administrative costs. However, it has also spurred China's development of independent IP, potentially reducing licensing costs and impacting global pricing of semiconductors.

In terms of game theory, the repeated game perspective has shed light on the strategic choices and behaviors of the parties involved. Both the tit-for-tat and trigger strategies have been observed in the trade game between China and the United States. The choice of strategy depends on factors such as patience levels, the balance between short-term and long-term benefits, and the need for cooperation or non-cooperation.

As the trade war continues to evolve, it is important for stakeholders in the semiconductor industry to understand the driving forces behind chip price behavior. This study has provided insights into the influencing factors, strategic shifts, and game theory dynamics, which can inform pricing strategies and decision-making in the industry. Moving forward, it will be crucial for industry players to adapt and navigate the changing landscape of the US-China trade war while also considering long-term risks and opportunities in the global semiconductor market.

Reference

1. Y. Zhang, X. Zhu. Heliyon, 9(6), e17092 (2023)..
2. H. Farrell, A. L. Newman. Foreign Affairs, 99, 70 (2020).
3. D. Keller, J. Goodrich, Z. Su, Semiconductor Industry Association, (2020).
4. Y. Luo, A. Van Assche. Journal of International Business Studies, (2023)
5. R. L. Tung, Journal of International Business Studies, 54(1), 1–10 (2022)..
6. X. Tong, X. Wan. Journal of Innovation & Knowledge, 8(1), 100319 (2023).
7. L. Liu, Y. Chen, Journal of Capital University of Economics and Business, 23(2), 34-49 (2021)..
8. X. Li, J. Wang, J. Liu et al. Journal of Changsha University of Science & Technology (Social Science Edition), 35(3), 113-122 (2020).
9. L. Wang. China's Huawei in the Us-China Trade War in the Communications Sector Game. Proceedings of the 2022 2nd International Conference on Enterprise Management and Economic Development (ICEMED 2022).
10. C. Liang, N. Liu, Y. Liu. The Game Between China and the United States Based on Trade in the Epidemic Era. Proceedings of the 2022 2nd International Conference on Enterprise Management and Economic Development (ICEMED 2022).

Analysis of the Interfering Factors about Auction Games

Shengjie Cao[1,*]

[1]Shanghai Pinghe School, 201208 Shanghai, China

Abstract. This essay simply explores the complex world of auctions and how they basically work. Start with a brief summary of auction's history, from the Babylonian era to the present, the essay shows how auctions have evolved over the history. Then, four typical auctions are introduced by listing their rules and how they are played. Most importantly, at the main body, the essay revealed various factors that have impact on how an auction is played, such as sunk cost fallacy, information dynamics, auction rules, and the existence of bidders with distinct motivations. In addition, Candle and dollar auctions are used to show the impact of information and rules on an auction respectively. In the end, the essay argues that auctions are complicated rather than just contests for riches and emphasizes the significance of comprehending these factors. The essay aims to inform people to make wise decisions in both auctions and everyday life.

1 Introduction

There are many movies and stories that have similar scenes: one or a group of millionaires gather and are bidding for a treasure, such as "Batman and Robin" or "Willy Wonka & the Chocolate Factory". They are eager for the bidding items, so they call enormous numbers trying to be the auction leader and then finally get that treasure. Moreover, the mental activities of these bidders are emphasized by their exaggerated movements or by the narrator's narration about their inner thoughts. This is really a good method to attract readers or audiences' attention because these scenes are usually tense, full of rich emotional descriptions, and can make the story more complex and interesting. However, these stories cause people to misunderstand about auctions although it clearly states the basic idea about how an auction works. By knowing these stories people may think that bidding is as easy as just calling out numbers and competing for the highest price they can afford. That's just an auction's basic principle, not the full complexity of auctions. There're much more details of auction types that makes them different and special. Auction is not only an easy game of wealth competition, but it will also be affected by various factors, such as nature of the auction or tactics that bidders used. This essay aims to give a simple introduction to auctions and discover some decisive factors that play important roles on affecting auctions. Therefore, this research can also explore some solutions to avoid the effects brought by these factors. Players' internal factors, auction rules, players' purposes that bring auctions great effects will be analyzed and clarified.

2 History of auction

To discuss factors of irrational biddings, the concept of auction should be claimed first. The Cambridge dictionary provides a clear statement: "*a usually public sale of goods or property, where people make higher and higher bids (= offers of money) for each thing, until the thing is sold to the person who will pay most.*" Fabio mentioned that players call bids is to discourage their opponents to stay the game [1]. The earliest auction recorded happened at about 2500 years ago, which is around 500 BC. The auction was described by the Greek historian Herodotus, who claimed that it was utilized in Babylon to sell women for marriage. The order in which the women were to be sold was decided by the auctioneer's subjective assessment. People aim to help their sisters to find a husband by sending them to this auction.

The earliest auction played a role as a tool, helping people to reach their purpose. Its essence is a market, a way people trade "the ownership of wife" for money. Then modern auctions emerge, bringing new rules and features to auctions. Their origin can be traced back to Roman Empire. At that time, because of the increasing number of wars, soldiers seized loots, including weapons and commodities. After they picked things they want and satisfied with, they will sell extra things for money. Auctions were existed from that time. There might be a possible explanation of the existence of auction is that the soldiers want to earn as much money as they can. If they sell things like marketing with a fixed price, their income will have a maximum quantity. The money they earn depends on the quantity of things sold. However, by holding auctions, soldiers can possibly have higher income. Since the price is called by bidders, the money the person who finally paid for that item would increase as the bid increased. People clearly know the price is increasing, but they didn't give up and kept calling bids because they were emulous. The auction increased the

* Corresponding author: caoshengjie2023@shphschool.com

price of the item by using this identity, which could bring the soldier a great profit.

This is a milestone in the history of human auctions. It identified the basic form of modern auction and laying the foundation for modern auction.

3 Types of auctions

As time goes, the method for auction develops and finally there are four main forms play a dominant role.

3.1 English auction

It is the simplest and the most understandable form of auction. The price is gradually increased in an English auction from a low price, until there is only one bidder left, and that bidder pays the auctioned item's final bid amount. The first cost represents the reservation amount. The good is not sold if no one bids more than the amount reserved. This auction can be conducted in one of three ways: the seller announces the prices, the bidders announce the prices themselves, or bids are made electronically, and the top bid is posted. Since in an English auction, bidders' bids are public, it is also called an Open ascending auction.

3.2 Dutch auction

It is a variant of English auction. Unlike a standard ascending-price auction such as English Auction, where the auctioneer starts at a lower price, bidders increase their bids to compete to be the auction leader, Dutch Auction is totally different. In a Dutch auction, the auctioneer sets a very high offering price initially. Then the auctioneer gradually lowers the price until there's a buyer places a bid and wins the item. Hence, the item is won by the first bidder who calls for the bid. This prevents a bidding battle that could impede the auction process, making Dutch auctions a dependable and efficient method for products that must be sold quickly. This form of auction was popular in Holland, where producers utilize this method to sell their flowers quickly. Therefore, Dutch Auction is usually used to sell something that need fast sales, such as fresh flowers and produce.

3.3 First price sealed auction

This type of auction is similar to Dutch Auction. In this auction, bidders submit their sealed bids to the auctioneer. The bidder who bids highest will win and pay his bid for the item. The two main components of a sealed-bid format are typically the bidding period, during which players submit their bids, and the resolution phase, which involves opening the bids and selecting the winner. Bids in this case are sealed, hence bidders should determine their bids by themselves instead of adding money based on bids from others.

3.4 Second price sealed auction

Second Price Sealed Auction, which can be also called a Vickrey Auction, can be considered as an updated version of First Price Sealed Auction. The principle of the auction doesn't change, which is bidders still seal their bids in this auction. What is different, however, is that when the high bidder wins, he only needs to pay for the second highest price. Because of its special rule, it is easy to be affected by some factors (see Table 1).

Table 1. How different auctions work.

Auction Type	Price determination	What the winner pays
English Auction (Open ascending price)	Starts from a low price, moves higher	Their own bids
Dutch Auction (Open descending price)	Starts from high price, moves lower	Their own bids
First-Price Sealed Bid Auction	Everyone submits their bid privately	Their own bids
Second-Price Sealed Bid Auction	Everyone submits their bid privately	The second highest bid

4 Influence factors

4.1 Sunk cost fallacy

Martin Shubik had introduced dollar auction in his *The Dollar Auction game: a paradox in noncooperative behavior and escalation* [2]. The game's rule is to bid for one dollar. Each bid should increase for 5 cents. Moreover, there's a special rule in the game that makes it different to other types of auctions is that the second highest bidder should pay their own bid even though he doesn't win the game and get the one dollar. Hence, the second bidder is the biggest loser in this auction. Let's assume there's only 2 people are bidding at the end of the auction, when the bid comes up to 90 cents. Player 1 bid for 95 cents because he is eager to win. At this time, player 1's playoff will be 5 cent if he wins the game.

Then player 2 will bid for 100 cents because until then if he wins the game, he will have no gains or losses, which is an acceptable consequence for him. But then player 1 will lose 95 cents if he doesn't win the game, therefore he decides to bid for 105 cents, which is higher than 1 dollar, to decrease his loss. His net loss will be 5 cents if he bids 105 cents, which is far less than the loss of 95 cents. As the bids increases, player's decision is not to bid for the 1 dollar anymore. However, their final purpose is to minimize their net loss, so their best choice is to bid higher. The final price is inevitable. The individual choice seems irrational because nobody will pay more than 1 dollar for a dollar. In this case, players always make an irrational decision based on a sequence of apparently rational choices made throughout the game.

One reason of this phenomenon is the sunk cost fallacy [3]. The propensity for people to persist in a project or course of action when giving it up would be preferable is known as the "sunk cost fallacy." It is the main motivation why players don't give up when the price for a dollar comes higher than 1 dollar. In their thoughts, they considered that if they give up, they will pay an amount of money which is far higher than they price they need to pay if they win. In order to minimize their loss, they prefer to bid higher and strive to win the game.

There are many famous examples in our life, such as eating dessert and watching movies [4]. Most people will choose to eat dessert although they taste bad or keep watching the movie though it is boring. People continue what they are doing to ensure the money they paid earlier won't be wasted. In their mind, "paid but not do" is a failed investment, leading to a waste of money. However, the money they paid can't return. What really wasted is their time which can be used to create other beneficial outcomes. Sunk cost fallacy is inevitable because people don't treat gains and losses equally and often ignore opportunity costs.

4.2 Information

The information possessed by players can be considered as an important factor. This can be proved by comparing open and sealed auctions. Maskin and Riley's work proved showed that sealed biddings tend to favor weaker bidders [5]. In the open auction, player who has the highest wins. However, in sealed bid auctions, bidders are more incentive to shade their bids below their true valuations, because they hope to optimize payoffs by reducing the chance of winning. This leaves an opportunity for weak bidders to win the game, hence the attraction to weak bidders are stronger than that to strong bidders.

Sealing bids is beneficial to weaker bidders, however, there's another variable will both affect strong bidders and weak bidders. Time is an important factor in an auction. Candle auction is a variant of English auction which time is restrained – the auction ignites a candle for time recording. The candle flame expires to indicate the end of the auction. This was done to make sure that no one could bid at the last minute and know exactly when the auction would end. This increases the difficulty for bidders to determine whether to bid or not.

The lack of access to information can mentally affects players to be anxious. Anxiety arises from uncertainty about a potential threat because it interferes with our ability to prevent it or lessen its negative effects [6]. In candle auction, a lack of time awareness increases bidders' anxiety, leading them make irrational decisions. In this case, bidders will feel difficult to decide when to bid or bid how much. Moreover, the value of the bid can also have great effect. If the bid called by previous bidder who coincide with another player's expectation, then more time will be taken by the player to consider whether his next choice is beneficial or not. In English auction, the person who called the highest bid finally gets the item. However, in this variant auction, winner doesn't need to call very high price to win. What they need to do is to ensure their bid can be the highest until the candle extinguish. Hence, the essence of candle auction is not to compete who has more money or can afford larger price, the tactics players used are more important. In this situation, a bid that is bided at the correct time and for an appropriate amount is better than bidding as much money as the player can.

4.3 The rule of the auction

Different types of auctions will bring various results. As two major auction types, first price sealed-bid auction and second price sealed-bid auction have distinct bidding methods. The only difference between them is that First price sealed-bid auction's winner should pay the amount that person paid, while in Second price sealed-bid auction, the winner only needs to pay the amount called by the second highest bidder. Since their bids are all sealed, they should determine how much they should bid. In First price sealed-bid auction, the amount that bidders prefer to bid is lower than their valuation because bidders want to get a profit. In this case, people who have more money or have higher valuation of the item have a bigger chance to win. However, if other bidders are rich or there are lots of people participating, bidders should shade less their bids for winning the auction. This is because rich people often have higher value than normal people based on their abundant finance. Moreover, large participants base will increase the competitiveness because it's hard to know each of their information and background to predict how much they will bid.

In second bid auction, the condition is more complex. The winner should pay the second highest bid, so the decisions of other bidders are the decisive factor of what premium the winner can get. In order to win the game, bidder should bid at least the value of the item to ensure his possibilities to win. Assume that there are several people are bidding for an item by using the form of Second price sealed bid auction. At last A and B are competing for the item. To analyze this case, focusing on the behavior of second highest bidder is necessary.

The difference of auction rules has an important impact on strategy selection and results. This can be shown in a simple example.

The item's value given by the winner is $100. The first circumstance is that B bid less than the value, for example, $80. When A bids $150 which is higher than the value, his profit will be $100-$80=$20. If A bids the value $100, his profit will still be $20 because he only needs to pay for the second highest bid. In this condition, bidding the value or bidding high are equally good. The second circumstance is that B bids more than the value, for example, $120. If A bids $100, his surplus will be 0 because he doesn't win the auction. If A bids $150, his surplus will be -$20. Thus, the dominant strategy for A in this case is to bid the true value. The last circumstance is that if B bids higher than A's bid, A's surplus will always be $0 because he doesn't win the auction. Both bidding the true value and bidding high are equally good. Combine these three results together, the conclusion would be bidding true is the Second price sealed-bid auction's dominant strategy.

In different auctions, players will select diverse bidding strategies based on consideration of different auction rules. Therefore, auction rules can greatly affect players' tactics, which leads to distinct results.

4.4 Bidders who have special purposes

A fun phenomenon was mentioned in Tegar's "*Too much invested to quit": The escalation of commitment in individual and group decision-making.* Tegar mentioned that in an investigation, the final two competitors are a pair of girls who have never gotten along in life. It turns out that their animosity of each other originated from their simple desire to prevent the other from winning [7]. There's such kind of participants in auctions. They increase the bid intentionally because they only aimed to make troubles to other bidders instead of creating their own premium. Some are losers from the previous rounds, the loss of their money cause them changing their minds from a rational bidder into spiteful players. Waniek found that these players will be stimulated by both the loss of their own interests and the desire to harm their opponents. In this case, the balance point of the auction is determined by these players [8].

There's another type of special player whose action will bring a big effect to the auction. This kind of player will call a high bid at the beginning of the auction to show their determination for this auction [9]. Their purpose is to win the game, just like what others' are. However, they choose this specific method to ensure they can achieve their goal more easily. The method they used will cause others' hesitation because others may think that their initial high bid means they have great amount of finance can be used in bidding. Although this can only bring these players a small premium if they win, it's still an effective method for them to take the initiative. Wall had concluded this kind of behaviour as "people show up at an auction to see and be seen" [10].

5 Conclusion

Auctions have evolved over centuries. From Babylonian auctions to four main types of auctions today, auctions are gradually developing themselves. By listing four common auctions – English auction, Duction auction, First price sealed-bid auction, and Second price sealed-bid auction - rules of auctions are basically introduced and clarified. Then, some critical factors that have special effects on auctions are stated. The sunk cost fallacy, which is dominant in the Dollar auction, illustrates how people sometimes make irrational decision because they want to minimize their loss of payoffs. Sunk costs fallacy not only affect biddings in auctions, but it also influences the decision makings in our daily life. Another key factor is information, which plays an important role in affecting players' decisions. Time constraint, exemplified by the candle auction, can likely affect player's mentality. This further causes players to be anxious and make inappropriate decisions. Difference in information can be clearly seen by comparing open and sealed-bids auctions. Moreover, the internal reason of different auctions is their rules. By analyzing first and second price sealed-bid auctions, results of different circumstances are concluded, and dominant strategy is determined. Although they are both sealed-bid auctions, the difference of the amount of money the winner should pay changes the strategy of each game. Finally, one external factor is mentioned – special bidders. The presence of these specific players breaks auctions from working systematically. These players can break the balance and reshape the dynamics of the auction, whether they are motivated by unsatisfied or resentment, as Tegar's study found; or by a planned display of strength at the beginning of the auction to show their determination to win. In conclusion, auctions are complex social and economic events impacted by psychological tendencies, information dynamics, historical foundations, and strategic considerations, rather than just being competitions of wealth. Some factors in these auctions may also affect our decision-making in our daily lives. Although further research and analysis are needed for discovering the intricacies in these factors, it is necessary for everyone to have a brief understanding about auctions and considering how to avoid getting troubled with these factors, conversely, think about how to use their effects to make better decisions in their lives. By doing this, they can improve their life satisfaction.

References

1. M. Fabio, University College London, (2007).
2. M. Shubik, J Conf Res **15**, 109-111 (1971).
3. Dodge, R. V. Oxford University Press (2012).
4. K. A. Dijkstra, Y. Hong, PLoS One **14**, e0209900 (2019).
5. S. Athey, J. Levin, E. Seira, Quar J Eco **126**, 207-257 (2011).
6. D. W. Grupe, J. B. Nitschke, Nat Rev Neuro **14**, 488-501 (2013).
7. G. R. Whyte, Yale Uni Pro Disserta Publi, (1989).

https://doi.org/10.1051/shsconf/202418803013

8. M. Waniek, L. Tran-Thanh, T. Michalak, N. Jennings, AAAI **31**, (2017).
9. M. Broom, J. Rychtář, Dyn Games Appl **8**, 211-231 (2018).
10. Wall, C. Eighteenth-Century Studies **31**, 1-25 (1997).

Game-Theoretic Analysis of Live-Streaming E-Commerce on TikTok

Zhifei Li[1] and *Xinyue* Lin[2,*]

[1]Shenzhen Zhengde High School, 518000 Shenzhen, China
[2]Shenzhen Foreign Language School, 518000 Shenzhen, China

Abstract. This paper analyzes the application of game theory in live streaming sales from three models: prisoner's dilemma, British auction, and Nash equilibrium. Firstly, using the prisoner's dilemma to analyze cooperation and competition in live streaming sales, using charts to analyze that competition appears to be the optimal strategy, but cooperation is more common. In the process of signing contracts with internet celebrities, the company also used English auctions for analysis. During the bidding process, it is necessary to avoid the curse of the winner, maintain fairness in competition, and reduce the minimum bidding increment. Finally, the application of Nash equilibrium was explored to find the balance of interests between sellers and buyers, while meeting their expectations. Overall, this research provides valuable insights into strategic decision-making in e-commerce, enhancing understanding of the interplay between influencers and brands and guiding them towards mutually beneficial outcomes in the evolving market of live-streaming commerce.

1 Introduction

In recent years, the evolution of social networks and media has provided wider access to various goods for consumers, coupled with the convenience of shopping from home. These factors have undeniably propelled the growth of e-commerce. Among various formats, live-streaming commerce, which involves influencers or celebrities introducing and selling products through online live broadcasts, has emerged as a significant form in the e-commerce market. In countries like the United States and China, live-streaming sales platforms such as Amazon Live, TikTok Live, and Taobao Live have attracted millions of viewers [1, 2]. Investigating the principles of live-streaming commerce is crucial for understanding this innovative sales approach and thus fosters the further development of e-commerce.

This paper aims to explore and analyze the application of game theory models in the process of live-streaming sales, mainly focusing on three key steps: live-streamers strategies for product promotion in live broadcasts, the competition among brands for advertising fees to live-streamers, and the dynamic process of finding a balance between price, product display, and market strategies by sellers and buyers. The "prisoner's dilemma model," "English auction model," and "Nash equilibrium model" will be used to analyze these stages respectively.

In this paper, section 2 will explore the application of the prisoner's dilemma model in the decision-making process of live streamers when promoting products during live broadcasts. Section 3 will discuss the use of the English auction model in the price bidding process among brands offering live-streamers advertising fees. In Section 4, the Nash equilibrium model's application in the dynamic process of sellers and buyers striving for balance through pricing, product presentation, and market strategies in live sales will be explored. Finally, Section 5 will summarize all sections and provide a comprehensive overview of the findings.

2 Prisoner‘s dilemma behind live-streaming

The Prisoner's Dilemma (PDG) is a classic model in game theory, primarily used to analyze the strategy of individuals when making decisions. This model basically involves two participants, each facing the decision to either cooperate or betray the other. If both choose to cooperate, they can achieve a relatively better outcome; if one betrays while the other cooperates, the betrayer gains maximum benefit at the expense of the cooperator; if both choose to betray, they both receive a relatively worse outcome. The Prisoner's Dilemma reveals the contradiction in individual decision-making: how to make a balance between personal interests and collective interests. In live-streaming commerce, every influencer faces the choice of either cooperating to promote each other's products or competing independently, which is similar to the cooperation and betrayal dynamics in the Prisoner's Dilemma.

2.1 Theoretical predictions of influencers' strategies

The payoff for different strategies chosen by influencers is represented numerically. For instance, mutual cooperation, symbolized by (5,5), benefits through an

* Corresponding author: Zhifei-Xinyue@hualial.com

https://doi.org/10.1051/shsconf/202418803014

increased range of promotion, creating a win-win situation. When either influencer opts for betrayal, potentially by disparaging others' products to better promote their own, audience credit may decrease due to perceived drawbacks in all products, thus harming both influencer's interests, represented by a payoff of (1,1) (see Table 1).

Table 1. Blogger B.

	collaborate	compete
collaborate	5 , 5	0 , 10
BloggerA	10 , 0	1 , 1

In a scenario where one chooses cooperation and the other betrayal, the betraying influencer, benefiting from others' recommendations and their disparagement of another's product, receives a payoff of 10, higher than mutual cooperation, while the cooperating influencer suffers with 0 payoff, lower than mutual betrayal (see Table 1).

How will influencers make their choices? Assuming a single-game scenario where influencers are rational and aim to maximize their interests, if an influencer believes the other will compete, he will also choose to compete as 1 (compete) > 0 (collaborate). Similarly, if he believes the other will collaborate, they will still choose to compete as 10 (compete) > 5 (collaborate), making the rational decision to always compete (dominant strategy). As a result, both parties end up with a payoff of (1,1).

2.2 Influencers' strategies in the real world

Contrary to theoretical predictions, decision-making in the real world is often more complex than simply relying on the payoff obtained in a single-game scenario theoretically; cooperation can sometimes be achieved and more common in specific scenarios [3].

In reality, the decisions of cooperation and competition among influencers tend to be interpreted as a practical application of the Iterated Prisoner's Dilemma model. In this model, participants engage in multiple rounds of the game, making decisions based on the strategies of their counterparts and the specific context. This approach accounts for long-term interactions and payoff. While choosing to betray may offer short-term benefits theoretically, long-term cooperation can yield greater potential advantages in terms of brand development, audience credibility, and sales growth [4]. Consequently, influencers in their practical decision-making process tend to favor cooperation to achieve long-term gains.

In addition, this can also be analyzed by calculating the relationship between influencers' expected payoff and the probability of cooperation:

If both choose to cooperate (C, C), each receives a payoff of R.

If one chooses to cooperate and the other betrays (C, D or D, C), the cooperator's payoff is S, while the betrayer's payoff is T.

If both choose to betray (D, D), each receives a payoff of P.

Here, T > R > P > S [5].

A cooperation probability p ($0 \leq p \leq 1$) can be set, representing the likelihood of each participant choosing to cooperate. Thus:

The probability of both cooperating is p^2, and the probability of both betraying is $(1-p)^2$, and the probability of one cooperating and one betraying is $p(1-p)$, and vice versa.

The expected payoff for an individual player is calculated as the probability of these scenarios occurring multiplied by the corresponding payoff value:

(1) $R \cdot p^2$ represents the expected payoff when both players cooperate.

(2) $T \cdot p(1-p)$ represents the expected payoff as a betrayer (with the other player cooperating).

(3) $S \cdot p(1-p)$ represents the expected payoff as a cooperator (with the other player betraying).

(4) $P \cdot (1-p)^2$ represents the expected payoff when both players betray.

Therefore, the expected payoff for an individual player at any given cooperation probability p should be expressed as:

$$E(p)=R \cdot p^2+T \cdot p(1-p)+S \cdot p(1-p)+P \cdot (1-p)^2 \quad (1)$$

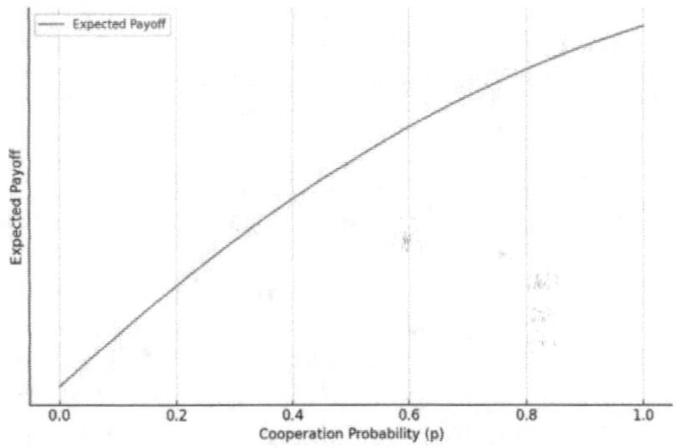

Figure 1. Expected payoff vs cooperation probability (Picture credit: Original).

As indicated by Figure 1, as the probability of cooperation increases, players' expected payoffs show an upward trend [6]. This suggests that even though competition might seem more beneficial in the short term, the expected payoff for influencers increases with the likelihood of cooperation. This means that in ongoing interactions between influencers, long-term cooperation can lead to more stable and sustained benefits, thus encouraging them to choose collaboration over competition. Therefore, from the perspective of long-term cooperative decision-making, influencers' tendency to cooperate is based on a logic of maximizing long-term benefits, supporting the idea that cooperation could be a more advantageous strategy in certain contexts.

2.3 Market dynamics and strategic adjustments

Furthermore, influencers must closely focus on market dynamics, including audience responses and competitors' strategic changes. Based on this information, they may adjust their live broadcast content, promotional activities, or partnership choices to attract more viewers, increase sales, and maintain market competitiveness. Such dynamic strategic adjustments help influencers maintain an edge in the competitive live-streaming market and achieve long-term success.

3 English auction behind live-streaming

3.1 English auctions belong to dynamic games.

In English auctions, players will continuously bid, and each player will see the bids of other players and adjust their bids based on their own strategies and goals. In the process of live streaming sales, there are also applications of English auctions.

English auctions start from the direction that bidders are most likely to accept and gradually move towards the target price of the auctioneer. In live sales, starting from the lowest price, most bidders are willing to accept it and then proceed to the next round of price increases until the price reaches a certain level. At this point, only one bidder is willing to accept, and the English auction ends. When combining English auctions with live streaming sales, there are three aspects that need to be noted here.

3.2 Avoiding the winner's curse

As shown in Figure 2, if the actual value of the auction project (profit x) is lower than the bid (loss y), the psychological perception of profit and loss v (x) v (y) will inevitably lead to the curse of winner 1; If the actual value (profit x) of the auction project is equal to the winning bidder's bid (loss y), and the psychological feeling of losing the same value is equal to the winning bidder's bid. The psychological feeling is still V (X). If the actual value of the auction item (income x) is greater than the winner's bid (loss Y) but lower than their actual valuation of the item before the auction, then the curse of winner 2 will still occur. When and only when the actual value of the auction project (profit x) is significantly higher than the bid of the winning bidder (loss y), resulting in the influence of the winning bidder's curse, the psychological feelings of the winning bidder [7].

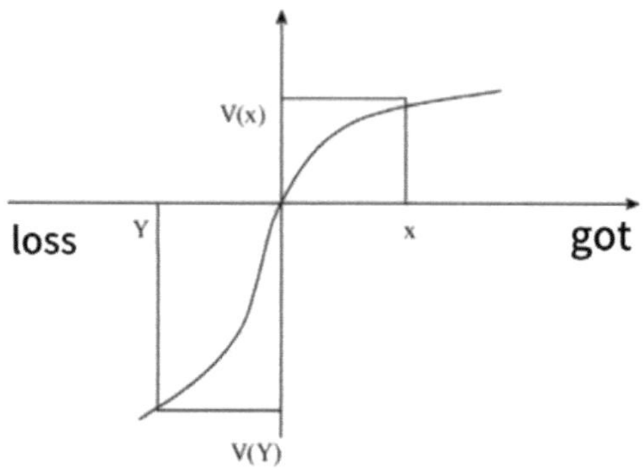

Figure 2. Encoding rules for the "gain and loss" of the value function (Picture credit: Original).

Given the strategies for dealing with the winner's curse, current strategies for dealing with the winner's curse mainly include joint bidding and sharing information, enjoying and learning. Collaborating with the rest of bidders can decline the number of bidders after the alliance, the bidders' bidding power is stronger, so their ability to effectively avoid the curse of the winner is also stronger. Another way to reduce the curse effect of the winner is to share information with your competitors, including both feedback and situational information. Feedback information refers to providing the average profit or loss information of all participants to the participants after each round of the experiment so that they can realize that they will suffer losses no matter how hard they try, so what they need to do is how to narrow the gap between their bid and the actual value of the product. Be careful when determining information about the winner's curse. The information on the occurrence of the winner's curse in existing research mainly includes the degree of uncertainty in the value of bidding products and the number of contractors. Individuals must first clarify the credibility of this information and gain a deeper understanding of whether the information they have obtained can be used for bidding activities. In addition, learning can also be used to avoid the curse of winners. Learning the curse of the winner requires a long process. If a person has a gradual process and multiple bidding experiences, bidders can gradually learn to reduce the losses caused by the winner's curse [8].

3.3 Minimum price increment

In the design of English auction, the most important part is how to design the minimum price increment, which is the minimum change of each round of price. During the bidding process， we need adjust the minimum price increase to maximize the value of the bidder.

3.4 Avoiding unfair agreements

When conducting online live streaming sales, the platform interacts with sellers should avoid unfair competition. Taking Amazon as an example, as a leading online shopping platform, it has provided trading opportunities for countless small and medium-sized platform operators, but at the same time, it is also suspected of using data collected from operators on other platforms to replicate similar products for self sales, thereby improving Amazon, with high self operated business sales, was investigated for antitrust by the European Commission in July 2019 At the same time, the Austrian Federation. The Bureau of Competition (BWB) has also issued a document stating that it has received multiple complaints over Amazon's favoritism towards its own services in the past three years. December 2018.In the month, the Austrian Retail Association also filed a lawsuit against Amazon on behalf of platform retailers. Currently, the Austrian Federal Competition Agency has been launched the antitrust investigation procedure against Amazon. In addition, Amazon has signed unfair agreements with other platform operators, which allow for Xu Amazon unilaterally modified the terms of the contract or closed its seller account without explanation, resulting in being banned by France in September 2019 The Li Commercial Court fined 4 million euros [9]. It is important to reduce the occurrence of unfair competition through policy restrictions

4 Nash equilibrium in live-streaming sales

4.1 An model for Nash equilibrium

Regard the Nash equilibrium problem in general. GNEP expanding the classical Nash equilibrium problem by assuming the feasibility of each participant. The strategy of competitors determines this set. N players, and each player v controls the variables x v ∈ ℜnv .

We use x to represent the vectors formed by all these decisions variable:

$$x \equiv \left(\begin{Bmatrix} x^1 \\ \dots \\ x^N \end{Bmatrix} \right) \tag{2}$$

Which has dimension n: $= \sum_{v=1}^{N} n_v$ and by X^{-v} the vector formed by all the players'decision variables except those of player v. Each player's strategy should be included in a set Xv(x^{-v}) ⊆ $\Re^{n^v}$ that depends on the rival players' strategies. Player v's aim, given the other players' strategies x^{-v} is to choose a strategy x^v that solves the minimization problem.

$$minimize_{x^v}\ \theta_v(x^v, x^{-v}) \tag{3}$$

$$subject\ to\ x^v \in X_v(x^{-v}) \tag{4}$$

For every x^{-v}, the solution set of this problem is denoted by Sv(x^{-v}). The GNEP is the problem of finding a vector $\bar{x}$ such that

$$\bar{x}^v \in S_v(\bar{x}^{-x}) \tag{5}$$

Point $\bar{x}$ is named a (generalized) Nash equilibrium [10].

4.2 When it comes to Nash equilibrium in the context of live streaming sales

Considering seller expectations, the seller hopes to achieve maximum profit and sell the most products. Sellers need to make timely price and inventory adjustments to cater to market and customer needs. Sellers need to find Nash equilibrium between pricing, product display, and audience groups. Then, considering customers' expectations, customers hope to buy high-quality and affordable products, and hope to receive more preferential policies and benefits. The Nash equilibrium of customers may need to consider factors such as product quality, discounts, and marketing methods. In the process of live streaming sales and customer purchasing, it constitutes a dynamic process, because the factors that need to be considered in the Nash equilibrium of customers include those determined by the seller, and the factors considered in the Nash equilibrium of sellers include those influenced by the seller. Therefore, sellers will make better choices based on the buyer's behavior, and buyers will also search for the most suitable product among multiple sellers. To achieve Nash equilibrium, neither buyer nor seller has a better choice.

5 Conclusion

In conclusion, in live-streaming commerce, influencers need to choose between cooperation and competition, and the Prisoner's Dilemma model helps explain the complex dynamics behind these decisions. While competition may seem likely to be the dominant strategy theoretically, cooperation is more common in the real world and can bring more long-term benefits. Also, this paper discusses the bidding strategies of brands for advertising fees in collaboration with influencers by applying the English auction model, this auction model emphasizes the importance of dynamic pricing, where brands must consider how to avoid the "winner's curse" to balance expected profits and actual costs. The setting of the minimum bid increment is important in attracting potential bidders. Additionally, maintaining the fairness and transparency of auctions is vital for protecting consumer rights and sustaining market competition. This process is dynamic and interactive, not only involving strategic decisions between brands and influencers, but also the ongoing adaptation to market evolving and consumer behavior. Finally, by analyzing the application of the Nash equilibrium model in live-streaming sales, this paper explores how sellers can predict optimal pricing points and product promotion strategies, finding a stable strategic balance in a highly competitive market, satisfying both sellers' and buyers' expectations. This dynamic process involves factors determined by sellers and choices made by buyers, creating an interactive game scenario.

This research applies the Prisoner's Dilemma, English auction, and Nash equilibrium models to the context of live-streaming commerce, offering new perspectives for understanding and analyzing strategies used in the e-commerce market. These theoretical models reveal the dynamics between brands and influencers, providing insights into effective strategies in a competitive market.

However, as the e-commerce market continuously changes, existing models may not be enough to accurately predict future rapid market changes. Therefore, continual exploration and development of these theoretical frameworks are necessary for adapting to new market trends and ensuring long-term market prosperity. Additionally, while this research offers deep insights into live-streaming commerce, its generalizability may be limited due to a focus on specific social media platforms or region-specific influencers. Future research should expand the sample range and explore more diverse live-streaming platforms to enhance the broad applicability of the study's conclusions.

Authors Contribution

All the authors contributed equally and their names were arranged in alphabetical order.

References

1. A. Day, C. DiLella, CNBC (2023).
2. T. S. Robertson. Harv. Bus. Rev., September-October, (2022).
3. Heuer, L., Orland, A Royal Soci Open Scien **6(7),** (2019).
4. FasterCapital, Benefits of collaboration and partnerships in content distribution, (2023). Retrived from : https://fastercapital.com/content/Benefits-of-collaboration-and-partnerships-in-content-distribution.html
5. S. Kuhn, Stanf Ency Philo (SEP) (1997).
6. Ng, G.T.T., Au, W.T. Psychon Bull Rev **23**, 353-360 (2016).
7. Z. Hongfei, X. Fuming, L. Tengfei, Z. Junwei, J. Duo, Pro Psyc Sci **19(5)**, 664-672 (2011).
8. R. H. Thaler, J Eco Pers **2(1)**, 30-30 (1992).
9. W. Jian, J. Haozheng. Adva Psych Sci 19(5), 664–672 (2021).
10. F. Facchinei, C. Kanzow, Comm SIMAI Cong **5**, 173-210 (2007).

Environmental accounting information disclosure from the perspective of game theory

Liuxin Yang*

RCF Experimental School, 100101 Beijing, China

Abstract. In reality, environmental accounting information disclosure still faces a series of issues, such as information asymmetry and lack of transparency. This results in discrepancies in the information held by both buyers and sellers. The party with information advantage may conceal their known information as a means of profit, while the other party takes various actions to obtain information to avoid losses. This article primarily introduces the background of environmental accounting information disclosure and its importance in market operations and management. It then analyses the motives behind accounting games and the potential dynamics of decision-making processes in non-cooperative relationships and conflicts of interest.In the study, qualitative research methods were mainly employed, including literature reviews, specific case studies, and mathematical measurements. Additionally, data on environmental accounting information disclosure from typical publicly listed companies were collected to construct a model of the bargaining relationship and consider its depth quantitatively. The research results indicate that in accounting games, the factors influencing the bargaining of both parties are not singular but are affected by various situations and conditions. Because of the divergent interests pursued by both parties, the intended outcomes of environmental accounting information disclosure, such as information symmetry and transparency, are compromised. Based on these findings, this article presents some optimization suggestions and actionable plans to prevent publicly listed companies from exploiting policy loopholes and to encourage them to more actively fulfill their obligations in disclosing accounting information, thus improving the stability of the domestic market.

1 Introduction

Game theory, as a theory that analyses strategic interactions among decision-makers, has a powerful explanatory and analytical capability for the gains and losses experienced by most publicly listed companies. It also possesses a good predictive ability for their future development and trends. This strong guiding role has made game theory widely used in the business and financial sectors [1].

This article focuses on the combination of game theory and environmental accounting information disclosure, explaining how game theory elucidates how decision-makers strive for maximum rights and benefits through environmental accounting information disclosure. The article mainly employs a targeted research approach, involving literature reviews and specific business cases, to gain a deeper understanding of the motivations and outcomes of intentional environmental accounting information disclosure by publicly listed companies in different contexts. In an era of information explosion and intensifying business competition, the ability to identify the effectiveness of disclosed information not only serves as valuable guidance for companies themselves but also mitigates potential investment risks, maintains the stability of formal markets, and ensures the sustainable development of social resources [2].

The merger of game theory and environmental accounting offers a novel perspective on how companies navigate the complex landscape of information disclosure, balancing their economic objectives with environmental responsibilities. This approach is not only relevant for understanding corporate strategies in environmental management but also crucial in highlighting the role of accounting in sustainable development and ethical business practices.

2 Practial analysis of environmental accounting

2.1 Definition and scope of environmental accounting information disclosure

Environmental accounting information disclosure refers to the public presentation by publicly listed companies, through financial statements or other public information channels, of their performance in fulfilling environmental responsibilities, the real impact of their products on the environment, and other related information. These pieces of information manifest in the

* Corresponding author: yangliuxin@rdfzcygj.cn

https://doi.org/10.1051/shsconf/202418803015

specific environmental policies followed by the companies, the cost investments made to minimize environmental impacts, and the disclosure of risks along with the measurement of performance [1]. Moreover, the importance of environmental accounting information disclosure cannot be denied. For companies, having sound environmental accounting data helps establish a positive corporate image, enhance their reputation in society, and attract investors to purchase stocks, thereby increasing profits. For investors, it enables effective assessment of a company's sustainability and enhances the accuracy and scientific basis of specific investment decisions [3].

2.2 Game theory in environmental accounting information disclosure

Game theory is a discipline that studies decision problems involving conflicting interests of both parties. In the context of environmental accounting information disclosure, the key stakeholders include publicly listed companies, investors, and government regulatory authorities. These three parties have differing specific interests, but they often come into conflict and constraints. Analyzing this issue from multiple perspectives is beneficial for understanding its underlying causes and proposing solutions.

As such, when game theory is applied in the context of environmental accounting information disclosure it simplifies what seems to be an inconceivable meshwork of relationships and rivalries between different stakeholders with contrasting interests. In this world there are various players ranging from companies, shareholders and regulatory bodies all seeking their own ends. For instance, corporations are more concerned with the profit maximization; shareholders will demand all information to inform their investment decisions that would yield profits for them and not losses while government agencies strive to ensure compliance on matters like environmental conservation.

The complex dance between these entities significantly influences environmental disclosure practices, driven by government incentives and representation of environmental problems through mass media. From a game theory view of these interactions, we can be able to understand the underlying motives and limitations all parties had. This enhanced insight can enable building more efficient and cooperative environmental disclosure strategies.

Moreover, game theory can provide more in-depth analysis of strategies applied by different stakeholders concerning disclosure of environmental accounting information. For instance, corporations may be engaged in a game of "green-washing" where they strive to employ an image that suggests them as being environmentally friendly without instigating significant alterations on how businesses are performed. This can form a dilemma for investors who are seeking actual data on sustainability.

On the other hand, shareholders can adopt types of what it with Scrutiny and activism by using their economic resources to persuade corporations in reporting more transparently and responsibly concerning environmental issues. It would therefore become a strategic game in which corporations need to decide whether they should want these demands or oppose them.

Government agencies equally hold an important place within this dynamic environment. They can establish their rules and regulations kind of "rules to the game" that motivate or punish specific behaviours. In addition, the government agencies could engage in cooperative games with corporations and investors by providing rewards for responsible practices toward environment or through promoting cooperation among stakeholders.

Media portrayal makes the landscape even more complicated. Public opinion which could be influenced by media reports may influence the strategies of all parties involved. However, corporations might engage in such activities with some motives to consciously influence media narratives or the way things happen while investors will use those same reports as an analytical tool for assessing corporate performance.

Hence, by looking at these intricate game situations more profoundly we become well aware of the various strategies as well as anti-strategies that emerge in this world of concealment accounted for environmental accounts. This in-depth insight allows us to build stronger and more productive initiatives that promote collabouration, openness, as well as environmentally responsible practices for all stakeholders. So, game theory is a very helpful instrument in this important field that could provide some help to adequately analyse the intricate network of interests and interactions.

2.3 Analysing the causes of environmental accounting information disclosure issues from a game theory perspective

From the perspective of publicly listed companies, their primary objective is to maximize profits and attract more investors to increase their disposable capital and resources. Therefore, when disclosing information, company executives tend to exaggerate their compliance with relevant environmental protection policies in the primary and secondary industries and the achievement ratios [4]. They may also downplay or even conceal the extent of environmental pollution in the production process and the costs incurred in this area. Such non-genuine reporting can attract more individuals to become shareholders of the company and invest in it, even though this behaviour is detrimental to both the nation and individual shareholders' interests when the true information is not known.

Furthermore, another significant factor is that the cost of violating information disclosure policies is often too low, or the regulatory efforts of relevant government agencies are weak. In such cases, a game of mutual bargaining between publicly listed companies and regulatory authorities may occur. Some companies may engage in information disclosure with a gambling mentality because, due to the current imperfect state of the law, they are confident that the chances of detecting false disclosures are minimal. Even if violations of relevant provisions are discovered, the substantial investments and profits generated by false disclosures far outweigh the punishment imposed by regulatory authorities. Therefore, many companies choose to ignore regulations, even repeatedly crossing the line, simply because the deterrence is too weak [5]. To enhance the standardization of public information, relevant authorities continuously strengthen and improve related laws and policies, increase penalties, and prevent further resource losses and potential risks and harm to the environment caused by false disclosures [6].

Expanded Scenario and Strategies

Strategies for Company A:

Fully Truthful (FT): Full and accurate disclosure of environmental information.

Partially Misleading (PM): Partial disclosure, some information is obscured or altered.

Completely Misleading (CM): Entirely false or misleading information.

Strategies for Regulator B:

Strict Regulation (SR): High level of scrutiny and strict enforcement.

Moderate Regulation (MR): Some oversight but not very strict.

Lenient Regulation (LR): Minimal oversight and enforcement.

Additional Payoffs

For Company A: The payoffs increase from Fully Truthful to Completely Misleading, assuming higher risks for higher gains.

For Regulator B: The payoffs are higher for stricter regulation, assuming better environmental protection but also higher costs.

Multiple Payoff Matrices are shown below (see Table 1, Table 2 and Table 3):

Table 1. Company A vs. Strict Regulation

	SR	MR	LR
FT	(2, 4)	(3, 3)	(4, 2)
PM	(0, 4)	(4, 3)	(5, 2)
CM	(-4, 4)	(1, 3)	(6, 2)

Table 2. Company A vs. Moderate Regulation

	SR	MR	LR
FT	(1, 3)	(2, 2)	(3, 1)
PM	(-1, 3)	(3, 2)	(4, 1)
CM	(-5, 3)	(0, 2)	(5, 1)

Table 3. Company A vs. Lenient Regulation

	SR	MR	LR
FT	(0, 2)	(1, 1)	(2, 0)
PM	(-2, 2)	(2, 1)	(3, 0)
CM	(-6, 2)	(-1, 1)	(4, 0)

Nash Equilibrium: For each matrix, identify the Nash Equilibrium by looking for cells where neither player can unilaterally improve their payoff. For example, in Matrix 1, (CM, LR) might be a Nash Equilibrium if Company A values potential gains more than the risks of penalties.

Company A's expected payoff for a strategy can be calculated as the weighted sum of payoffs under different regulator strategies, considering the probability of each regulatory approach.

Example: If the probabilities of SR, MR, and LR are 0.2, 0.5, and 0.3 respectively, and Company A chooses FT, the expected payoff = 0.2*(2) + 0.5*(3) + 0.3*(4).

Mixed Strategy Nash Equilibrium: If no pure strategy Nash Equilibrium exists, we may consider mixed strategies where players randomize over their strategies. The equilibrium can be found by equating the expected payoffs of different strategies for each player and solving the resulting equations. This expanded model with multiple matrices and more strategies offers a deeper understanding of the strategic interactions between Company A and Regulator B. By examining the payoffs under different scenarios, we can identify potential Nash Equilibrium and predict how changes in strategy or external factors (like changes in regulatory environment) might shift these Equilibrium. Keep in mind, however, that these models are simplifications and real-world scenarios may require more complex considerations.

2.4 Impacts of game theory models applied in environmental accounting

Using such game theory models as discussed through the payoff matrices presentation gives not only a theoretical foundation for understanding interactions between corporations and regulatory bodies but also practical stiffness. These models focus on the subtle balance it holds concerning strategies that create revelation of disclosure towards environmental accounting contriteness. For instance, high levels of transparency in the disclosure plus differential imposition ranging from tight to loose regulatory measures can create solid reasons behind a move towards balancing strategy as one implements an environmental policy [6].

Furthermore, such game theory models illuminate possible consequences of strategic decisions made not only by companies but also regulators. By reviewing a variety of situations and approaches, they help in identifying the potential strengths and weaknesses. This data can be useful in shaping policies and regulations that promote more accurate and comprehensive accounting of the environment. Further, the use of game theory models helps in understanding motivations and behaviours better from various stakeholders concerned with environmental accounting. It elucidates the logical decisions that entities could make while pursuing their self-interest and can impact overall environmental disclosure environment [7].

In conclusion, the usage of game theory models in environmental accounting brings not only theoretical benefits but also makes it possible for policymakers and practitioners to utilize these helpful instruments while operating on such a complicated land side related to the practise of environment disclosure that is developing better-informed yet more effective policies aimed at safeguarding our planet from harmful human activity.

3 Strategic recommendations based on game theory analysis

Further from the possible Nash Equilibrium identified, it is a crystal clear fact that if there are higher level of regulatory stringency (SR), increased climate transparency in disclosure always improves. Hence, it is necessary for regulatory authorities to introduce more comprehensive and enhanced regulator frameworks that accentuate punishment towards companies. However, this strategy would create strong pressure on companies that will force them to adopt more explicit disclosure practises. This enhanced regulatory framework should incorporate various elements to enhance its effectiveness. These may include tougher enforcement strategies, larger punishment fees and a stronger focus on proactive surveillance. Considering the above considerations, it is evident that regulators must address problems from various sides and use a range of punitive incentives in regulatory frameworks.

In summary, the study of Nash Equilibrium highlights that one way to strengthen regulatory systems baselines truthful disclosure practices by corporations. Through the conscious blending of these interventions, regulators can guide environmental accounting to a future where it is ethically and responsibility-aware.

There is a chance for regulatory bodies to introduce new incentive structures that would allow moving this equilibrium towards the state of Full Truthful FT disclosure. For instance, the provision of tax reductions to firms that maintain high levels of accuracy in disclosure might be one such reward. Through reductions in the taxes owed by such compliant entities, regulators would encourage responsible behaviour while giving financial reward to businesses that make a point of correct reporting. Public recognition system for firms that do well every time about their environmental accounting could also be initiated by the regulatory bodies, but in addition to tax incentives. This could involve the giving out of awards or certifications, even a publication that lists those companies which do more than simply pay lip service to transparency. Acknowledgment of this type is not only an advantage for companies that comply with it but also proves to be a strong reputation booster.

Furthermore, these incentives could be enhanced when linked to long term performance. For example, companies that make truthful disclosures in every reporting period might qualify for more tax advantage or higher ratings of public recognition. This approach would promote long-term interest in the conduct of open accounting practises. If regulators use these incentive structures strategically, they can make the balance tip towards Full Truthful disclosure and create a rule structure that encourages ethical reporting when corporate interests do not conflict with larger agendas of environmental transparency and accountability. This in turn also contribute to a more responsible and sustainable corporate atmosphere as far as environmental accounting is concerned. These models do not only give the notion on what can be made for effective regulation but they also raise a cautionary note against over-regulation. Investors may also prevent investors and stifle innovation if they view the regulations in place as being stringent. Thus, it is very attractive that there should be managed a fine balance between the opportunities of economic growth and compliance. Firstly, it must be noted that an over stringent regulating environment may lead to a number of negative outcomes. It may prevent firms from adopting environment friendly technologies or practices for the fear of strict compliance requirements. This, in turn slows down the progress to achieve sustainability goals as well prevents developing eco-friendly practices [8].

Another aspect is that over-regulation can impose financial burdens on businesses especially smaller ones which may not be in the position to satisfy compliance with high cost requirements. This may lead to less competitiveness of industries affected, job losses and economic slowdowns. Regulators, therefore, have the challenge of forming laws that encourage truthful disclosure and environmentally prudent businessmen without unnecessarily crippling their businesses [9]. A responsive regulatory framework that changes with changing situations in the industry and fosters an interactive relationship between regulators and businesses can make this possible. In a field where markets are frequently changing, it is crucial to find that balance between innovation and taking business forward with calls for sustainability whilst providing strong benefits which will motivate compliance without stifling development [10].

4 Conclusion

These models identify Nash Equilibrium and possible changes in strategic behaviour as a result of adjustments that occur within the regulatory environment. Such research, however implies that regulators should prescribe an integral and well rounded approach between punitive sanctions and incentives to encourage truthful disclosure. Acknowledging the dangers of over-regulation, it highlights that regulatory framework should be dynamic and balanced to encourage compliance without stifling economic growth[10]. Potential areas of future research include incorporation behavioural game theory, empirical validation studies tests, design dynamic games models and international comparative analyses to improve understanding environmental accounting practices globally.

References

1. X. Kan, H. Yan, J. Xiong, Front Busi, Econo Mana **4(3)**, 59-63 (2022).
2. R. Sellah, Inter J Econo Perfor **6(01)**, (2023).
3. S. Schilizzi, J. B. Lesourd, Aus Aus Agricu Reso Econo Socie, (2001).

4. P. K. Ray, Spring Scien Busi Med, (2012).
5. N. Avogadro, R. Redondi, Rese Trans Econo **100**, 101304 (2023).
6. W. H. Kloezen, Wagen Uni Res, (2002).
7. M. S. Siddiqui, Uni Ottawa (Canada), (2011).
8. T. P. Zis, H. N. Psaraftis, Sustain Ship, 249-284 (2019).
9. D. Hess, T.W. Dunfee, Busi Eth Quar **17(1)**, 5-32 (2007).
10. M. Malheiros, S. Preibusch, M.A. Sasse, In Trust and Trustworthy Computing: 6th International Conference, June 17-19, 250-266 (2013).

Profit mechanisms in penny auctions: Unraveling the impact of sunk costs

Han Wang[1,*]

[1] School of Accounting , Guangdong University of Foreign Study, 510420 Guangzhou, China

Abstract. This study provides a distinctive perspective on the intricate dynamics of penny auctions, which are characterized by incremental bid costs and potential sunk costs, constituting a significant area of research in existing literature. Our research takes a unique approach by specifically delving into the profit mechanisms inherent in penny auctions, with a focused examination on the profound impact of the sunk-cost fallacy on bidder behavior. To achieve this, we employ a custom model built upon the structural elements proposed in previous works, aiming to scrutinize the dynamics of bid costs and bid increments. In the course of our investigation, we uncover counterintuitive strategies employed by bidders that have a substantial impact on auctioneer profitability. This revelation contributes to a deeper understanding of bidder decision-making processes and their consequential influence on auction outcomes. By shedding light on these nuanced aspects, our study provides valuable insights that extend the current understanding of the intricate dynamics governing penny auctions. The implications of our findings have relevance not only for academic researchers seeking to expand their knowledge in this domain but also for industry professionals involved in auction platforms, offering practical considerations for optimizing profitability in this unique auction format.

1 Introduction

Penny auctions, often hailed for their profitability, have long captivated researchers seeking to understand the behavioral intricacies of participants. Prior studies by Augenblick and Brünner et al. have laid a robust foundation by dissecting the unconventional nature of pay-per-bid auctions and introducing prospect theory into the analytical framework. Building upon these insights, our study shifts the focus to the core of auction profitability, unraveling the mechanisms that drive lucrative outcomes for auction platforms [1, 2].

Intriguingly, our investigation reveals that the setting where bid costs surpass bid increments engenders counterintuitive bidder strategies. We explore scenarios that challenge traditional economic models, providing a comprehensive understanding of how the sunk-cost fallacy amplifies auctioneer profitability. The work by X. Zhang et al. contributes a rich empirical perspective by studying the bidding behavior on DealDash [3]. The findings reveal a significant optimization of bids aligned with the pay-per-bid structure, with a notable pattern of bids being placed just before the timer expiration. This predictability in bidder behavior, as highlighted by the study, provides a valuable foundation for understanding the strategic aspects of penny auctions. By integrating empirical data from DealDash, we validate our model's predictions against real-world auction dynamics, solidifying the significance of our findings.

As we navigate through the intricacies of bidder decision-making, our study not only contributes to the academic discourse on auction dynamics but also offers practical insights for auction platforms aiming to optimize their profitability. The subsequent sections delineate our model framework, incorporating insights from Augenblick and Brünner et al., and delve into empirical evidence, providing a comprehensive analysis of penny auctions' profit dynamics [1, 2].

2 Literature review

The profitability of penny auctions has been a subject of enduring interest among researchers, driven by the intricate behaviors of participants in these auctions. Augenblick and Brünner et al. have provided foundational insights by dissecting the unconventional nature of pay-per-bid auctions and incorporating prospect theory into the analytical framework. Expanding on these foundations, our study directs attention to the core of auction profitability, unveiling the mechanisms that underlie lucrative outcomes for auction platforms [1, 2].

Our investigation uncovers counterintuitive bidder strategies in scenarios where bid costs surpass bid increments, challenging traditional economic models. This exploration provides a comprehensive understanding of how the sunk-cost fallacy amplifies auctioneer profitability. Zhang et al.'s empirical contribution, focusing on bidding behavior on DealDash,

* Corresponding author: 20221504106@gdufs.edu.cn

 https://doi.org/10.1051/shsconf/202418803016

adds a valuable perspective [3]. The study highlights a significant optimization of bids aligned with the pay-per-bid structure, particularly emphasizing a notable pattern of last-minute bids just before the timer expiration. This predictable bidder behavior, as illuminated by the study, establishes a crucial foundation for comprehending the strategic aspects of penny auctions. The integration of empirical data from DealDash serves to validate our model's predictions against real-world auction dynamics, reinforcing the significance of our findings.

As we delve into the intricacies of bidder decision-making, our study not only contributes to the academic discourse on auction dynamics but also offers practical insights for auction platforms aiming to optimize profitability. Beyond Augenblick and Brünner et al., our analysis draws on additional literature that enriches our understanding of penny auctions [1, 2].

2.1 Dynamic volunteer's dilemma and war of attrition

A dynamic volunteer's dilemma, where risk arises from others' decisions, mirrors a general war of attrition [4, 5]. This scenario, described by Bulow and Klemperer in various contexts such as natural monopoly markets, bargaining, and election campaigns, highlights the prevalence of risk in interpersonal interactions [6]. While Brünner et al. emphasize the limited application of prospect theory (PT) in such scenarios, our study bridges this gap by proposing a dynamic game-theoretic model incorporating endogenous risk from interpersonal interactions, utilizing PT preferences [2].

2.2 Applications beyond penny auctions

Building on Platt et al., Hinnosaar, and Augenblick, our study extends existing models by incorporating PT into the analysis of pay-per-bid auctions [1, 7, 8]. These auctions, often termed penny auctions, deviate substantially from traditional formats like eBay, featuring an open-end structure and requiring bidding fees from all participants. The anomalies observed in bidding behavior, such as average auctioneer revenues surpassing the retail price and the sunk cost fallacy, present a unique context for testing PT.

2.3 Empirical insights into bidder behavior

Caldara and Wang and Xu offer alternative explanations for bidder behavior in pay-per-bid auctions [9, 10]. Caldara's laboratory experiments indicate that auction revenues surpass the values of products, even with revealed information [9]. Wang and Xu empirically show that bidder sophistication and experience positively affect consumer surplus [10]. Our study incorporates these insights to provide a unified explanation for anomalies, demonstrating that PT effectively describes bidder behavior in pay-per-bid auctions.

In conclusion, our study bridges the gap in the literature by applying PT to dynamic scenarios where risk arises from interpersonal interactions, focusing on pay-per-bid auctions. The empirical findings support the effectiveness of PT in describing and predicting bidder behavior, offering valuable insights for both researchers and practitioners in auction settings.

3 Model framework

Our model follows the structure proposed by Augenblick [1]. Like Table 1, there are n+1 players, including a non-participating auctioneer (player 0) and n bidders. There is a single item for auction. Bidders have a common value v for the item. There is a set of potentially unbounded periods t, each period is characterized by a publicly observable current leader "Lt", with L0 = 0. In each period t, bidders simultaneously choose Bid or Not Bid. If any of the bidders bid, one of these bids is randomly accepted. In this case, the corresponding bidder becomes the leader for the next period and pays a non-refundable cost c. If none of the players bids, the game ends at period t and the current leader receives the object

In addition to the bid costs, the winner of the auction must pay a bid amount. The bid amount for the good at time t is t_k. Therefore, at the end of the game, the auctioneer's payoff = t_k+t_c.

Table 1. Model description.

Parameter	Description
Players	Non-participating auctioneer (Player 0) and Bidder (Player 1)
Valuation	Common value for the item (v) = $1
Bid Increment (k)	Increment in auction price with each bid (k1 = k2) = 15 cents
Bidding Cost (c)	Non-refundable cost incurred for each bid = 10 cents
Sunk-Cost Effects	Considered in bid decisions, influencing bidder behavior
Bid Amount (tk)	Represents the bid amount for the item at time t
Dynamic Bidding	Simultaneous bid decisions in each period
Bid Acceptance	Random acceptance of bids if placed
Cost Incurred	Winning bidder pays cost (c) in addition to bid amount
Parameter Settings	Adjustable bid increment and cost for scenario exploration

Then this paper simplified this model by assuming only two players, one item, and both players valuing the item at $1. The bidding stages are denoted as p1, p2, p3..., with each bid increment (k1=k2) set at 15 cents and a bidding cost (c) of 10 cents per bid. In analyzing returns based on surplus, factoring in sunk costs makes it harder for players to exit the auction, even exceeding their initial valuation of the item. (Fig. 1) By controlling variables in scenarios one and two (Fig. 2), considering with and without sunk costs, we observed that it actually change the equilibrium, if seem it as player 2 left when the surplus is 0. There is a shift from an auction resembling an English Auction (the highest price win, but pay the second highest price) to a auction that benefits the auctioneer. This illustrates that sunk costs alter the original player equilibrium, significantly impacting outcomes.

In the third scenario, seem in Fig. 3, this research set the bid increment (k) to be less than the cost (c), aligning with the notion that, when treating cost c as a fixed cost, minimizing losses and maximizing surplus often involves smaller bid increments. However, through the same sequential game analysis, we discovered that compared to the case where k is greater than c, people exhibit greater stickiness in auctions when k is less than c. The sunk cost fallacy has a more pronounced effect, exacerbating losses and revealing a counterintuitive and intriguing phenomenon.

This paper believes that, in addition to the perspective of increased risk and enhanced risk-bearing capacity due to a heightened estimation of product value, there is also a sensitivity issue. Our assumption is that people's sensitivity to sunk costs is higher than their sensitivity to existing surpluses.

In real auction platforms, the common practice of setting bid increments lower than the bid cost to some extent supports the validity of this situation. Auctions, by capitalizing on individuals' sunk costs and leveraging this mindset, significantly increase their profitability.

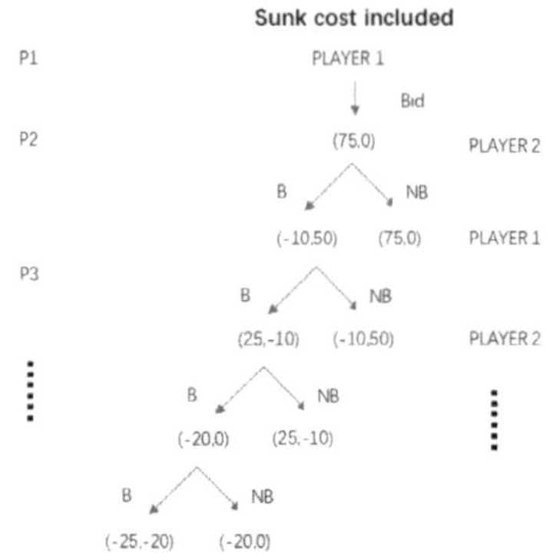

Fig. 1. Sunk cost included (Picture credit: Original).

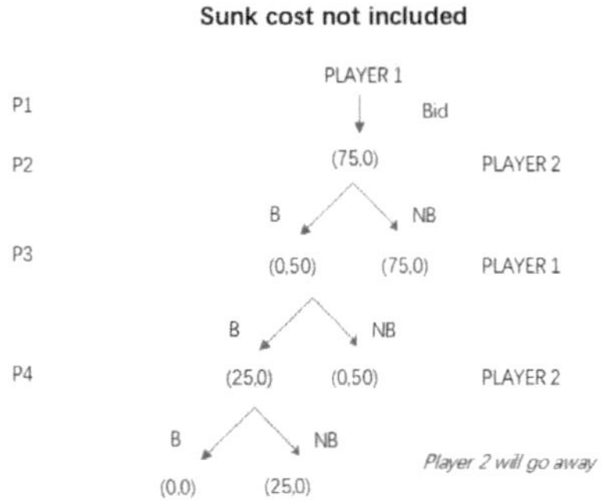

Fig. 2. Sunk cost not included (Picture credit: Original).

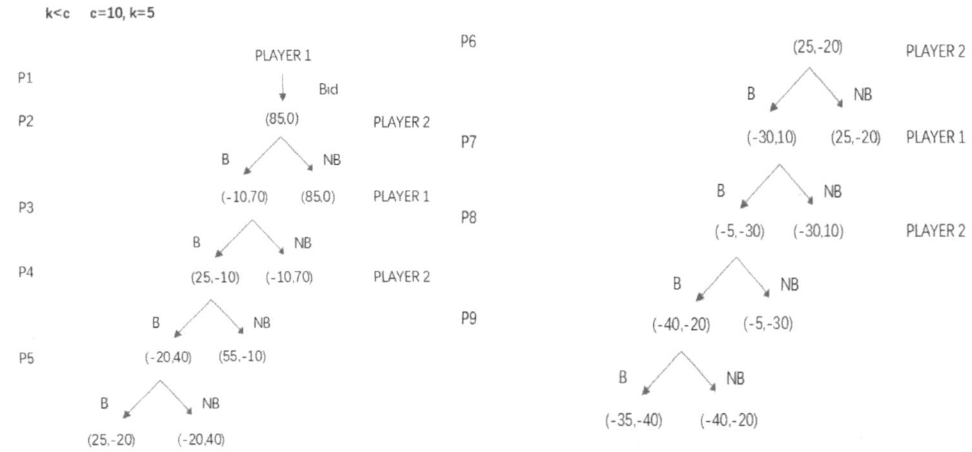

Fig. 3. Model when k < c (Picture credit: Original).

4 Empirical validation

To validate our model, this paper leverages data from DealDash, one of the largest penny auction platforms. Our empirical analysis supports the counterintuitive finding that higher bid costs relative to increments enhance auctioneer profitability. The observed bidding patterns and outcomes align with our theoretical predictions, confirming the impact of sunk costs on bidder behavior.

In the case study of DealDash, researchers aimed to gain insights into bidding behavior and patterns within the unique structure of penny auctions. DealDash, one of the largest and oldest penny auction websites since 2009, operates with distinct features: a bid fee of 12-15 cents, a fixed price increment of 1 cent, and a countdown clock that expires in 10 seconds. The platform also supports a buy-it-now function and a BidBuddy helper script.

The empirical analysis covered a 166-day period, from October 19th, 2017, to April 3rd, 2018, and included a total of 134,568 auctions with 174 million bids from 101,936 unique users. The researchers sought to answer two key questions: first, to understand the bidding patterns and their predictability, and second, to identify common bidding strategies and their quantifiable outcomes.

The findings from the case study revealed several significant aspects of bidding behavior:

(1) Optimization of Bids: Users tended to optimize their bids in alignment with the pay-per-bid auction structure. The majority of bids were placed at the last possible second before the timer expiration, indicating a strategic approach to maximize their chances.

(2) Repetitive Bidding Behavior: Users exhibited repetitive bidding behavior across auctions, leading to highly predictable sequences of bids. This pattern suggests that participants followed specific strategies influenced by the auction mechanics.

(3) Clustering of Bidders: Using similarity analysis, bidders were clustered based on their bidding behavior into five key categories, each defined by the dominant bidding strategy observed. Aggressive and persistent bidders were found to win a disproportionately high number of auctions, earning significant gains per auction.

(4) Low-Activity Bidders: Bidders with limited activity or constrained by budget won fewer auctions per user and faced challenges recouping losses from bid payments, resulting in a net loss.

Overall, the case study provided valuable insights into the predictability and strategies employed by users in the DealDash penny auctions. The findings contribute to understanding the dynamics of bidding behavior in the context of specific auction mechanisms and serve as a foundation for further research and analysis.

Shown as Fig. 2, through this paper's analysis of data from Swoopo, a similar characteristic is evident [11]. Similarly, prices exhibit predictable trends. However, according to my model analysis, when the bid fee is relatively low, individuals tend to increase the number of bids. Consequently, this leads to a higher final price for the same product. In empirical validation, this confirms the theoretical framework this paper has proposed.

5 Price predictability in Swoopo data

Similar to the observations in DealDash, the analysis of Swoopo data reveals a notable characteristic of price predictability. This consistency across different penny auction platforms strengthens the generalizability of the observed phenomena.

5.1 Impact of bid fee on bidding behavior

Diverging from DealDash, my model delves into the specific influence of bid fees on bidding behavior. In instances where the bid fee is lower, my analysis suggests a tendency among participants to increase their bidding frequency. This is a nuanced understanding that goes beyond the generic predictability of prices and sheds light on the factors influencing bidding strategies.

5.2 Correlation between bidding frequency and final price

Building on the bid fee influence, the analysis indicates a corresponding impact on the final price. With increased bidding frequency, a higher final price is likely to be observed. This correlation is a crucial insight that aligns with the theoretical framework proposed in my model.

5.3 Empirical validation of theoretical propositions

The empirical validation of my model involves scrutinizing real-world data from Swoopo, providing tangible evidence supporting the theoretical ideas presented. This not only strengthens the validity of the proposed model but also adds a layer of robustness through cross-platform consistency.

6 Further analysis emphasizing penny auctions and sunk-cost theory

In delving deeper into the realm of penny auctions and the sunk-cost theory, it is crucial to highlight the counterintuitive effects generated by auction platforms when setting bid fees higher than the incremental price 'k.' Additionally, understanding player stickiness, or the persistence of certain behaviors, adds a layer of complexity to the analysis.

Counterintuitive Effects of Bid Fee Setting:

One of the key focal points of our analysis is the auctioneer's decision to set bid fees higher than the incremental price 'k.' Conventionally, one might expect that increasing bid fees would deter bidders, as it raises the cost of participation. However, our empirical findings, consistent with theoretical predictions, reveal a counterintuitive phenomenon.

When bid costs surpass bid increments, bidders exhibit a strategic response rather than withdrawal. This counterintuitive behavior challenges traditional economic models and underscores the intricate dynamics at play in penny auctions. It suggests that participants, influenced by the sunk-cost fallacy and potential losses, intensify their commitment, hoping for a favorable outcome despite rising bid costs.

Player Stickiness in Penny Auctions:

Player stickiness, or the persistence of certain bidding behaviors, becomes a critical aspect to consider. In the context of higher bid fees, our analysis indicates that bidders tend to exhibit stickiness in their strategic approach. Rather than abandoning the auction, participants adjust their bidding strategies to align with the new cost structure, showcasing adaptability and persistence.

The sunk-cost fallacy, wherein individuals continue investing resources based on prior commitments, plays a pivotal role in player stickiness. Bidders, reluctant to abandon their investment in bids, adjust their behavior to mitigate perceived losses, contributing to the observed stickiness.

Strategic Adaptation and Optimizing Outcomes:

Bidders, faced with higher bid fees, strategically adapt to optimize their outcomes. The empirical evidence from DealDash and Swoopo showcases a pattern where participants intensify their bidding activity, especially as the auction approaches its conclusion. This strategic behavior aligns with the goal of maximizing gains, even in the face of escalating bid costs.

Understanding the interplay between bid fees, sunk-cost considerations, and player stickiness provides a comprehensive framework for explaining the observed dynamics in penny auctions. It also emphasizes the need for auction platforms to carefully consider the setting of bid fees to influence bidder behavior and overall profitability.

In conclusion, our extended analysis underscores the multifaceted nature of penny auctions, where bid fee decisions interact with psychological factors, resulting in counterintuitive bidder strategies and persistent player behaviors. This nuanced understanding contributes to both the academic discourse on auction dynamics and offers practical insights for auction platforms seeking to navigate the delicate balance between profitability and bidder engagement (see Fig. 4).

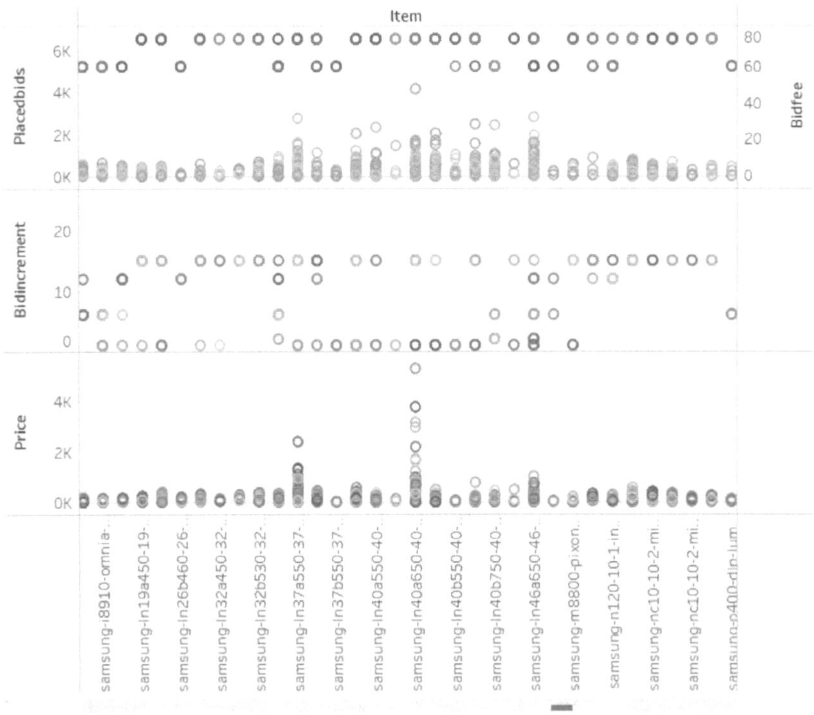

Fig. 4 Place bids, bid increment and bid fee comparison chart (Picture credit: Swoopo site)

7 Conclusion

In conclusion, the exploration of penny auctions, particularly within the context of the DealDash platform, sheds light on the intricate dynamics of user behavior and the underlying mechanisms that contribute to the profitability of such auctions. By integrating insights from the literature, model analysis, and the empirical case study, several key takeaways emerge.

Firstly, the empirical analysis of DealDash auctions reaffirms that users tend to strategically time their bids to maximize their chances of winning. The optimization of bids, especially observed in the last seconds before timer expiration, underscores the influence of the pay-per-bid auction structure on participants' decision-making.

Secondly, the identification of repetitive bidding behavior across auctions suggests that users develop and employ specific strategies in response to the unique features of penny auctions. This predictability in bidding sequences highlights the role of auction mechanics in shaping user interactions.

The clustering of bidders into distinct categories based on bidding behavior provides a nuanced understanding of the diverse strategies employed by participants. The dominance of aggressive and persistent bidders in winning auctions and achieving substantial gains emphasizes the competitive nature of these platforms.

Furthermore, the case study brings attention to the challenges faced by low-activity bidders or those constrained by budget limitations. Their struggle to win auctions and recoup losses underscores the potential risks and financial implications for participants engaging in penny auctions.

Drawing from the literature, the analysis aligns with previous discussions on the exploitation of human psychological tendencies, such as risk-seeking behavior and the sunk-cost fallacy, in penny auctions. The study contributes empirical evidence to the ongoing discourse on the profitability of penny auctions and the potential predictability of user behavior within these environments.

In the broader context, these findings have implications for both users and platform operators. Users may benefit from a more informed approach to bidding, considering the observed patterns and strategies. For operators, understanding the dynamics revealed in this study opens avenues for refining auction mechanisms or developing strategies to enhance user engagement and platform profitability.

While this research provides valuable insights, it also prompts further inquiries. Future studies could delve into the development of predictive models based on the identified bidding patterns, offering potential applications in designing adversarial bidding algorithms or refining auction platforms.

In essence, the multifaceted analysis presented here contributes to the evolving understanding of penny auctions, enriching the discourse on user behavior, predictability, and the intricate interplay between auction structures and participant strategies.

References

1. N. Augenblick, Rev Econ Stud **83**, 1 (2016)
2. T. Brünner, J. Reiner, M. Natter, B. Skiera, J Econo Behav Organ **164**, (2019)
3. Z. Xinyi, S. Shawn, T. Shiliang, Z. Haitao, Z. Ben Y., HT '18: Proceedings of the 29th on Hypertext and Social Media, (2018)
4. C. Bliss, B. Nalebuff, J Public Econ **25**, (1984)
5. H. Otsubo, A. Rapoport, J Confl Resolut **52**, (2008).
6. Bulow, Jeremy, Klemperer, Paul, Am Econ Rev **89**, 1 (1999).
7. B. C. Platt, J. Price, H. Tappen, Manag Sci **59**, 9 (2013).
8. T. Hinnosaar,. Penny Auctions. Northwestern Uni Working Paper, Dec (2016)
9. M. Caldara,. Uni Calif Irvine Working Paper, Dec (2013)
10. Z. Wang, M. Xu, Inf Econ Policy **36**, (2016)
11. J. Byers, M. Mitzenmacher, G. Zervas, Compu. Sci., Mar, (2010)

Analysis of big data push and Nash Equilibrium: a case study of live commerce on TikTok

Yixuan Tang[1,*]

[1]Trinity College, University of Melbourne, 265200 Yantai, China

Abstract. In this growing field of digital marketing, integrating big data strategy and modern commerce has become a revolutionary sales method. The goal of this article is to explore the profound connection between big data push strategies and Nash equilibrium in modern business. Taking the TikTok as an example, I will analyze how big data push is used to influence consumers' shopping decisions. The article will also explore how this effect reflects the Nash equilibrium principle in game theory. Based on these goals, this study examines in detail how to collect, process and analyze user information on the data platform to create accurate user portraits. The platform can perform targeted push based on user portraits to attract consumers who are most likely to purchase the pushed products. The importance of this study is that it analyzes the combination of big data-driven marketing strategies and game theory concepts to gain a deep understanding of the key role of big data in shaping consumer behavior, as well as the practical application of game theory in current Internet commerce. , filling the gap in the academic field in the field of cooperation between classic economic models and modern marketing, and has far-reaching significance for modern economics research.

1 Introduction

In the rapidly developing field of digital sales, the combination of big data analysis and real-time commerce has become a revolutionary marketing method, widely used by platforms like TikTok. The use of big data can not only be applied as a new approach of advertising and promotion, but also influence the shopping decisions and behaviors of consumers on the platform by analyzing consumer data, ultimately increasing consumers' enthusiasm for shopping on the platform and increasing consumers' "brand loyalty" to the platform. This behavior can be viewed as the platform's analysis of consumer behavior in order to form a strategy that the best responds to consumer actions. Therefore, it can be regarded as the mature application of Nash equilibrium in the field of modern marketing. This represents the application of Nash equilibrium in the field of digital marketing. This article will take TikTok as an example to provide a comprehensive analysis of the application of Nash equilibrium in the live streaming industry. Through this research, I aim to gain a better understanding of the significant impact of big data on consumer behavior, the role of game theory in business during the Internet era, and the potential risks associated with personalized big data push for society and consumers.

2 Situation of live streaming

"Live" appeared on November 2, 1936 as a television program [1]. Its real rise as a business model began during the epidemic, when the contradiction between users' demand for shopping and the difficulty of going out to shop during the epidemic prompted e-commerce platforms such as TikTok to quickly become important business platforms in the Internet era. In recent years, despite the end of the COVID-19 epidemic, live streaming is still in a stage of rapid development and has become an important means for modern people to shop. Taking TikTok as an example, its diverse content, including big-name beauty, technology products to affordable food, cheap daily necessities, etc., has attracted all kinds of user groups, providing a broad potential customer base for live streaming, real-time feedback from anchors, and a model of direct interaction with consumers, which also increases the shopping experience of consumers. Most importantly, the platform is personalized through accurate big data. Successfully convert potential consumers into consumers.

Taking the performance of live streaming in China as an example, Taobao, the largest e-commerce platform, generated sales of 498.2 billion yuan during China's Double 11 shopping festival alone, of which TikTok, as a non-traditional e-commerce platform, has created a unique form of personalized push with big data and live streaming that is superior to other platforms. With sales of 100.9 billion RMB, it has gradually become one of the most important e-commerce platforms in China as a social platform [2]. Live streaming also provides a huge development opportunity for personal development.

*Corresponding author: 2015141075030@stu.scu.edu.cn

Since 2021, "Crazy Brother Yang" (Qingyang Zhang) has transformed from a short video expert to a streamer with goods, relying on the tens of millions of popularity accumulated by his funny short videos, and the platform to accurately push potential users among short video fans, and finally achieved great commercial achievements, and its annual sales in 2023 are estimated to reach 15 billion yuan. At the same time, TikTok's precise push to potential users on all platforms has also caused a crazy increase in the number of fans of "Crazy Brother Yang", as of now. The number of fans of the account has reached about 180 million, and the huge number of fans has formed a virtuous circle with the platform's precise big data push, which has promoted the expansion of its sales.

At the same time, live streaming contains certain potential risks . Since the relationship between the media is in a winner-takes-all mode in the information cocoon, all platforms will choose to push the best response to consumers in that time period to get the best benefit in the short term, which will lead to a situation similar to the "prisoner's dilemma", so that the "best response" is not the dominant strategy, in other words, not the best choice in the long term [3]. Big data personalized push is based on the behavior of each individual user on the platform to best respond to it. This means that the push to each individual user is almost similar, and the content of the best reply to the user will increase the user's shopping experience in the short term, and increase the likelihood that the user will make a short-term purchase. In the long run, an information cocoon will be formed, which not only limits the scope of users' information exposure, but also reduces the diversity of consumption, making the platform's business less dynamic, and more importantly, from the perspective of the long-term development of the platform, the information cocoon will gradually make users feel "bored" and exacerbate the risk of permanent loss of users. In addition, big data push has also promote the user's subjective preference, topic concern, and content expression of browsing content to show a homogenization trend, greatly affected the shopping experience of consumers [4].

3 Game theory and Nash equilibrium

Game theory, also affectionately known as strategy theory, is a nascent branch of modern mathematics and one of the most important elements in the field of operations research. His primary research focus is on the interaction between different incentive mechanisms and the thorough analysis of the balanced response process. Game theory is committed to digging deep into complex phenomena, such as competition, and examines the strategies individuals should adopt to maximize benefits when responding to external environmental stimuli. Furthermore, this theory helps to interpret biological evolutionary processes and in predicting potential future outcomes. Moreover, game theory has become an essential research tool in the field of economics. So far, this theory has been widely applied in various fields, including finance, securities, biology, economics, international relations, computer science, political science, and military strategy.

The Nash Equilibrium describes a combination of strategies in which all participants are in a state where they must maintain the original strategy in order to achieve maximum returns. On the other hand, if any participant attempts to change their strategy, it will immediately result in a corresponding decrease in their own returns. Therefore, every rational participant must strive to maintain a strong strategy and should not adjust their strategy lightly unless they encounter a very exceptional situation. The "equilibrium even" refers to a specific type of game environment. It assumes that Party A and Party B choose their optimal strategies A* and B* respectively. If Party A chooses B* again and Party B encounters Party A's adjustment to the original strategy A, then the cumulative profit of the cache confession will exceed the situation when the two parties initially chose their strategies. Similarly, this rule also applies to Party B.

4 Case study – Take Oriental Selection as an example

"Oriental Selection" is a live streaming platform for agricultural products launched by New Oriental. Its parent company, New Oriental, was originally an educational institution, but after implementing the "double reduction" policy in China to reduce the burden of education, it announced its transformation on December 28, 2021, and established "Oriental Selection" to officially enter the live broadcast e-commerce industry on the TikTok platform. In June 2022, "Oriental Selection" became popular overnight with its unique live broadcast model, with 470,000 followers in one day and 19.5 million followers in a whole month, and 6 live broadcast accounts were opened, forming a live broadcast matrix [5].

The following chart shows the revenue of Oriental Selection's business from 2016 to 2023. Specific business areas include university education, middle and high school education (K12 education), nutritious catering and live streaming e-commerce.

As can be seen from Figure 1, although the revenue of each business has almost increased in different years, the growth of live broadcast e-commerce is the most significant. It can be said that the growth of live broadcast e-commerce is the driving force for the company's revenue growth. Especially during 2021 and 2022. Live streaming e-commerce's viewership in fiscal year 2022 appears to account for the largest share of all businesses.

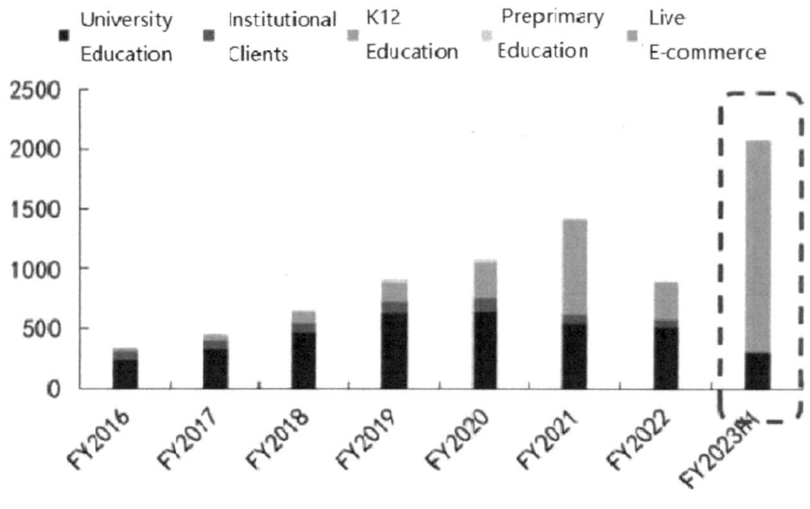

Figure 1. Starting from fiscal year 2023, e-commerce business has become the main driving force for the company's growth (Picture credit: Original) (Data source: Company announcement, Guoxin Securities Economic Research Institute).

The part framed with a red dotted line on the right side of the chart predicts the revenue in fiscal year 2023. Although the specific figures are not shown, judging from the trend, live broadcast e-commerce is expected to have huge growth and be ahead of other business lines. . The text description at the bottom mentions that the data in the chart comes from company announcements and the Securities Research Institute, and the data is extremely reliable.

It is essential that live streaming is of great significance to New Oriental, accounting for an important part of the company's main revenue, and it still has huge room for growth. Therefore, Dongfang Selection can be used as a typical research case in this topic.Therefore, the analysis of the relationship between the big data push strategy used by "Dongfang Selection" in live streaming on the TikTok platform and the Nash equilibrium is not only helpful to understand the specific embodiment of game theory in the contemporary Internet economy, but also provides a profound example for the study of micro-economy, and has certain significance for further analyzing and summarizing the innovation of the live streaming model, and providing reference for the development of e-commerce using big data push.

The mode of live streaming is inseparable from the correlation of game theory. Under this business model, the application of big data provides in-depth insight into the market, as a profound practical manifestation of the theory of game theory: all players (such as sellers, platforms, buyers) formulate strategies based on the collected information to maximize their own interests. For example, sellers can analyze consumers' likes, favorites, and purchase behaviors through big data to understand their preferences and needs, so as to customize their promotion strategies to gain an advantage in the highly competitive market [6]. This kind of strategy development involves not only responding to current market conditions, but also predicting future market trends after collecting and building massive data models. Game theory provides a theoretical support here, enabling all parties to find the best strategy point in the ever-changing market environment and achieve the optimal decision with different information at each stage. Through this approach, the live streaming model not only improves sales efficiency, but also provides participants with a way to compete and cooperate based on big data strategies. Under the framework of game theory, Dongfang Selection gives full play to personalized marketing by analyzing the big data model provided by the TikTok platform. Highlight Dong Yuhui's personal IP, create a diversified way of live content, shape the cultural experience of customers, and accurately penetrate the emotional and cultural needs of customers [5]. In the study from Liu, Zhao and Long, the excellent shaping of IP can effectively enhance the image positioning of the company and related products (goods or services) in the minds of consumers [7]. This personalized marketing method can be regarded as making the best response to customer needs at that moment under the framework of game theory, and can also ensure that in the subsequent push, the big data model will recommend it to the brand's potential customers, achieve mutual benefit and win-win results with consumers, and reach the Nash equilibrium point in that time period.

The dynamic relationship between competition and cooperation is particularly critical in the game theory analysis of the live streaming model, where the concept of Nash equilibrium provides a framework for understanding and predicting market behavior. Participants, whether sellers, buyers, or platforms, are seeking to maximize their own interests [8], and this pursuit involves not only competition with competitors, but also potential collaborations with other market participants. In this multi-party environment, each role needs to constantly evaluate and adjust their own strategies in response to the actions of other actors. For example, when deciding on product pricing, promotion strategies, and live content, sellers must not only appeal to consumers, but also consider the likely reaction of competitors. In this case, reaching a Nash equilibrium means finding a state in which neither side will benefit more, whether it is an increase in inputs, a change in marketing strategies, or an adjustment in price. Through in-depth analysis of big data, participants are able to more accurately predict market trends and counterparty behavior, thus more effectively reaching or approaching this equilibrium state. In this process, the live streaming market has become more efficient and stable, and all participants have jointly promoted the development and progress of the entire market through continuous strategy adjustments and market feedback. Under the Nash equilibrium, Dongfang Selection seeks a win-win cooperation point with customers, and maintains personalized and pure content to ensure that it is specialized and non-generalized under the big data algorithm, so that the target customers who are really interested in New Oriental culture and Dongfang Selection can see it [9]. It not only reduces the cost of pushing (push fees and publicity fees for the platform), but also ensures that the entire market is more diversified and strives for long-term development by approaching the Nash equilibrium point.

The Nash equilibrium point is always changing, and it changes with the market and consumer Xi. This means that Dongfang Selection needs to constantly explore new Nash equilibrium points to respond to the changing market and make the best response. By analyzing the constantly updated data, seeking new market changes, and finding new Nash equilibrium points, this process is a dynamic and continuous game process. If the platform only pushes the previous "best response" to the user for a long time, the customer will quickly feel bored, which will not only make Dongfang Selection lose customers, but the platform will even permanently lose the user, so that all merchants on the platform will lose a potential customer. What's more serious, Fu worried about that the push of big data in the media age makes it easier for people to fall into the trap of consumerism, reducing the vitality of the market economy and damaging the long-term earnings of the company [10]. Therefore, in the future development, Dongfang Selection should not only give full play to its existing advantages, but also explore new consumption tendencies through the user data provided by the platform, make new responses to consumer preferences, and push it to the audience with changing tendencies through big data, which can not only expand its own customer base, but also consolidate the loyalty of user groups to the brand.

To sum up, the analysis of Dongfang Selection reflects the role of big data push in live streaming, the theoretical basis of Nash equilibrium in big data push, and the vivid practice of game theory in modern Internet business. Through the theoretical combination of big data push and game theory, merchants similar to Dongfang Selection can use big data push to accurately define target customers and transform their potential advantages into market competitive advantages.

5 Limitation

This research has certain limitations due to various reasons such as platform attributes and research direction. First of all, because the research direction is focused on the TikTok platform, it lacks the breadth of the entire live streaming field. Second, because big data analysis relies on obtaining large amounts of user data, data access to TikTok and other live streaming platforms may be restricted by privacy policies and commercial confidentiality. Due to the restrictions and protections of the privacy policy, it is difficult for researchers to obtain accurate data for deeper research. Moreover, TikTok's recommendation algorithm is not public, which further limits understanding and analysis of its inner workings. At the same time, there is no variable control in this study. Various factors (such as anchor popularity, product quality, private domain traffic management, fan activity, etc.) may affect sales and operations, making it difficult to evaluate the role of big data push alone.

6 Conclusion

In conclusion, this article takes TikTok as an example, discusses the basic attributes of live streaming in modern e-commerce, the important position of big data models in it, and discusses the theoretical foundation of game theory based on Nash equilibrium. Then, taking Dongfang Selection, a delivery company on TikTok, as a case, the application of Nash equilibrium in the field of big data personalized push in e-commerce is discussed, and its positive effects and potential risks are discussed. This article can broaden understanding of the relationship between modern e-commerce and economic theory, understand the strategy of marketing in the context of the modern Internet, and understand the positive significance of big data push for modern business.

References

1. H. Zhang, V. S. Golik (Ed.), A. N. Varaksin, (2022)
2. Huachuang Research, Res report, Huachuang Securities, (2023)
3. H. Xu, Z. Chen, R. Li, C.-J. Wang, arXiv, (2020).
4. X, Xu, J. Yu, J Beijing Inst Tech (Soc Sci Edi) **25**, 4 (2023)
5. Z. Guo, Yantai Uni Facul Liter J Commu **12**, (2023)
6. H. Li, Mana Tech SME **36**, (2020)
7. Z. Liu, X. Zhao, W. Long, China Busi Market **8**, (2020)
8. Y. Lu, J. Tao, J Math Com Sci, Jilin Normal Uni, (2023)
9. Y. Gao, G. Sijia, West China Broad TV **7**, (2023)
10. S. Fu, Theor Stud Liter Art **2**, (2007)

The collapse of Kyoto Protocol: An analysis based on Game Theory

Ziyu Peng [1,*]

[1]Shenzhen College of International Education, Shenzhen, China

Abstract. Everyone is a stakeholder in environmental issues. Contemporarily, climate change is incrementally imposing threats to human development, making multilateral cooperation necessary to minimise the impacts of climate-related risks. The Kyoto Protocol was a significant internationally binding agreement that aimed to reduce greenhouse gases emissions, whereas its signatories failed to achieve its target to a large extent. This paper analyzes the reason behind the failure of the Kyoto Protocol through a game-theoretic literature. The main factors that contributed to the collapse of the Kyoto Protocol include the complex nature of the environmental issue and strategic interest in the treaty ratification procedure. The global environment is defined as a public good, therefore, each country has a free-rider incentive to take advantage of others' actions in pollution reduction, which is analyzed through a single prisoners' dilemma game. When such a game is extended to a repeated prisoners' dilemma game with an infinite horizon, there is a possibility that nations adopt a cooperative strategy in the long run. Simultaneously, the ultimatum game provides a representation of the treaty negotiation and ratification process, highlighting the importance of fairness and reciprocity of the treaty for its signatories. Potential solutions include trade sanctions, tax on exports, and the measure of cumulative emission has been evaluated at the end of the paper.

1 Introduction

1.1 Research background and motivation

The compatibility between economic growth and environmental consideration is always a challenge for human development. Under rapid technological advancement, the exposure to unforeseen climate-related risks would interrupt economic activities intermittently. Hence, climate issues have increasingly raised concerns among different countries. They have realised that multilateral collective action is inevitable to address climate change.

In December 1997, the Kyoto Protocol was adopted in order to limit six anthropogenic greenhouse gases emissions. Through a convoluted ratification procedure, the terms of the Kyoto Protocol officially entered into force in February 2005. A binding agreement had been reached among the developed and industrialised countries. However, several non-negligible limitations entail the collapse of the Kyoto Protocol. Foremost, the major carbon emitters were not encompassed in the treaty--the United States, the second-largest emitter of carbon dioxide, rejected the ratification and Canada ultimately withdrew from it. In addition, the Kyoto Protocol exempted developing countries such as China and India, who also contribute to a large proportion of global greenhouse gas emissions. The absence of those vital greenhouse gas emitters, it seems effect-free to obey the terms within the treaty. Therefore, although the Kyoto Protocol was recognised as a significant landmark of multilateral cooperation to combat climate change, most signatories failed to meet their targets and it ultimately became ineffective.

The culprit that entailed the collapse of the Kyoto Protocol was considered as an internal scheme design failure [1], including the scope of its signatories, the standard of setting its target, and the lack of a punitive mechanism. The external factor of nations' incentives to deviate from their commitment is also responsible for its failure. In the language of economics, climate change mitigation is a global public good [2]. The alleviation of global warming would make everyone individually better off, whereas it also underlying the free-rider problem where everyone has the incentive to take advantage from others' actions of reducing carbon emissions, and the advantages brought by the mitigation of irreversible climate-related risks are non-excludable, non-rival, and non-rejectable for everyone, which underlying the complex nature of climate issue. As a significant branch of economics, game theory is ubiquitous in real-life applications. It provides an analysis based on a payoff matrix that examines individual or group decision-making in a strategic setting. With the help of game theoretical methods, it gives us an insight into the international dispute over environmental policies, and helps us to comprehend the deep-rooted reasons, or motivations that countries have to escape from environment-protection treaties. Based on such an analysis, this research can therefore resolve

* Corresponding author: s21102.peng@stu.scie.com.cn

the issues and reformulate a more effective international treaty.

1.2 Literature review

In recent years, environmental issues have drawn more attention to economic researchers and there is a numerous game theoretical literature in this field. Foremost, Osborne & Rubinstein in 1994 discussed the repeated game and compared it with finite and infinite horizon. Further, in 2001, Finus integrated real-world situations into a game theory model, showing that these theoretical results are helpful in the analysis of climate negotiations, specifically, the Kyoto Protocol. In terms of solutions of these complex environmental issues, Barrett in 2003 suggested that trade sanctions may be a useful measure to bind international cooperation. Game theoretically, there will be a preferable equilibrium where all countries are signatories of the treaty, which can be achieved through the introduction of a minimum participation level in the treaty. Admittedly, there is a lack of consideration and evaluation of the willingness of those countries who are responsible for imposing trade restrictions. Overall, these previous works were summarised by Peter John Wood in 2010, who combined mathematical equations and real-life examples. He examined different cases investigated previously, relating to climate change and the negotiation to alleviate it, with non-cooperative game theory. In this paper, it provides an overview of the factors that contributed to the collapse of the Kyoto Protocol, analysing this specific case with game theory, and proposing possible prescriptions to improve international environment agreements in the future. Nevertheless, the assumptions of each model of game theory always have to exclude some factors from analysis--whether the players have full information, whether the players are making their decisions independently, the number of players and their variable payoff, etc. Therefore, the games that analysed in this paper may not perfectly represent all the elements in the real circumstance, but the simplicity of the model would offer a useful insight into the fundamental reasons for the failure of the Kyoto Protocol.

1.3 Research framework

This paper is structured as follows: The first section includes an introduction to the basic terms of the Kyoto Protocol, and the phenomena that indicate its failure; the second part provides detailed case descriptions of the two deep-rooted reasons: the complex nature of environmental issues and countries' profit-related considerations. These analyses are based on the game theoretic analysis, including single prisoners' dilemma, repeated prisoners' dilemma, and the ultimatum game respectively; in the third part, the paper further applies the results of these cases to the difficulties in climate-related negotiations, and discuss how the results are useful for us to make improvements. The potential prescriptions include trade sanctions, taxation on exports, and taking cumulative emissions into account. Towards the end, this paper draws a brief conclusion of the application and usefulness of game theory approaches in international cooperation to combat climate changes, and discusses several limitations of the current solutions.

2. Case description

2.1 Prisoners' dilemma

2.1.1 A Single prisoners' dilemma game

In the simplest way, a circumstance of international negotiation to mitigate greenhouse gas emissions can be represented by a non-cooperative, static situation of prisoners' dilemma [3]. We assume that there are two players—Player 1 and Player 2, who are making their decision independently. Both of them have two possible strategies {Pollute, Abate}. Table 1 portrays a payoff matrix of the possible outcome for two players, with Player 1's payoff listed first. The transverse columns display two strategies for Player 1 and the longitudinal columns represent Player 2's options in the same way (see Table 1).

Table 1. Prisoners' dilemma game

Decision		Player 2	
		Abate	Pollute
Player 1	Abate	100,100	0,101
	Pollute	101, 0	10,10

Intuitionally, the strategy pair (Abate, Abate) seems to be an optimal solution for two players since it maximizes the payoff for each player as (100,100). The economic term Nash equilibrium refers to a situation where each player is best responding, making the optimal choice, and has no intention of unilaterally deviating from its strategy. However, in this case, the Nash Equilibrium of this game gives them a payoff (10, 10). First, concerning the strategy for Player 1, when Player 2 chooses to play Abate, he will be better off by choosing to play Pollute and get a payoff of 101 instead of choosing Abate and get 100. Whereas in this situation, Player 2 will obtain a payoff of 0, thus also giving him a profitable deviation to shift to play Pollute and acquire 10, which is greater than 0. The same argument applied when we considering the strategy for Player 2. Eventually, regardless of what the other player does, none of them will be better off by shifting from Pollute to Abate [4], thus making Pollute the dominant strategy for the two players, and the strategy of (Pollute, Pollute) reaches a static Nash Equilibrium. As long as the game is on a finite horizon, (Pollute, Pollute) is the only Nash Equilibrium consisted.

This is a reflection of the real-world situation where each country is expecting others to take action to mitigate global warming, since a limitation in pollution will inevitably accompanied with a sacrifice of their total output and damnify short-term economic growth. It gives countries an intrinsic incentive to escape from taking their responsibility.

2.1.2 Repeated prisoners' dilemma game

In reality, combating climate change is a long-lasting and multigenerational event. When the game becomes infinitely continuous and repeated, the players' strategies may alter to a collectively more favorable outcome for both of them [5]. Therefore, we can consider this situation as a repeated prisoners' dilemma game in extensive form.

Fiugre 1 illustrates a game which is similar to a single-stage game in Table 1, whereas in this circumstance, we assume that players are making their decisions over an infinite period, with unlimited subgames. The payoff for the game will be the sum of the stage-game payoffs. In this case, cooperative behaviour may occur from a long-term perspective. Both players recognize that their payoff would be maximized when they play Abate simultaneously. In each game, Player 1 and Player 2 play a static stage game and independently select their actions. There is a possibility that both of them play a simple "Trigger Strategy", which is, if one player ever defects, another player will deviate from their cooperative outcome forever. This strategy will initiate a large amount of subgame perfect Nash Equilibrium in each stage game since it de-incentivizes players' profitable deviation. Alternatively, a "Tit for Tat" strategy is also available for the players. In this case, players are forgiving, meaning that even if the other player had defected, it is possible to shift back to cooperation if that player stops defective behaviour. The "Tit for Tat" strategy seems more practical in real life, but it is less enforceable than the "Trigger Strategy".

In a nutshell, a deviation from cooperative behaviour will destroy the player's reputation and trigger a punitive profile with less payoffs. For instance, if in one subgame a player defects and leads an outcome of (0,101), their payoff for the next stage of the game will be (10,10). For the one who committed defection, his total payoff would be 121, but ideally, he can obtain a sum payoff of 200 from cooperation. As a result, when they perceive that once they defect in a single game, the cooperation in the rest of the games will be terminated, and the game will continue for additional periods, then a mutually desirable outcome of (Abate, Abate) will stably occur in each period [6]. The reason is that the long-term losses in their payoff caused by the defection outstrip the short-term gains by playing defection.

This game demonstrates that in the long-term multilateral negotiation and the following treaty implementation process, a design of a punishment mechanism that impairs the signatories' payoff when they deviate, could effectively bind the nations' cooperative behaviour.

2.2 Ultimatum game

The absence of the United States and the withdrawal of Canada from the Kyoto Protocol significantly marks its failure. In fact, the United States was unsatisfied with the fact that only Annex B countries (developed countries) had to commit to greenhouse gas emission reduction. Also, there was a tremendous opportunity cost for Canada to meet the carbon reduction target under the terms of the treaty. The reason why those countries rejected the ratification of this environmental-friendly treaty can be analysed by an ultimatum game [7].

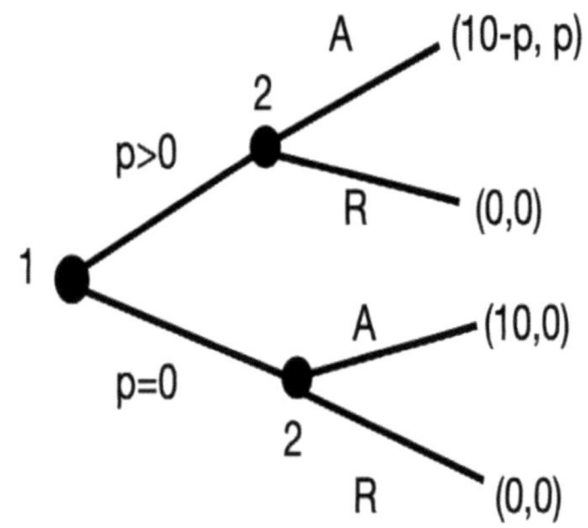

Figure 1. Ultimatum game (Picture credit: Original)

As shown by Figure 1, there is a money offer which valued 10 in total. Player 1 and Player 2 are dividing the offer. Stages 1 and 2 are denoted in this extensive form, where "A" and "R" represent Accept and Reject respectively. In Stage 1, Player 1 makes the choice first, meaning that he could choose to offer Player 2 any amount of money where $p \in [0, 10]$. Player 2 further chooses to "Accept" or "Reject" the offer at Stage 2. If Player 2 chooses "Accept", then he will get the money that Player 1 offers, and Player 1 could retain the rest of the money. Whereas if Player 2 chooses "Reject" that offer, then both players will not get anything.

In this case, when Player 1 chooses p=0, Player 2 will be indifferent between "Accept" or "Reject", as he always gets a payoff of zero. Rationally, player 2 will always choose to "Accept" the offer when p>0, because there is a positive payoff for him. Consequently, the outcome will be (10-p, p) as shown in Figure 2.3, where p is a positive constant. Therefore, considering the strategy for Player 2, he will always "Accept" the offer regardless of Player 1's choice, since it is the best response in every subgame.

The ultimatum game can simulate the ratification process of a climate-related treaty. In Stage 1, the leading countries negotiate the terms of the treaty; In Stage 2, the countries decide whether to ratify the treaty or not. If they refuse to sign it, the entire treaty would be pointless. However, in a realistic setting, there are more factors affecting the choice of Player 2 (i.e. the signatory countries). They also value the fairness and reciprocity of the offer [8,9].

3. Results and discussion

First, to address with the complex nature of environmental problems, the result of a single prisoners' dilemma indicates that countries are intrinsically lack of an incentive to collectively protect the environment, which is reflected in the failure of the Kyoto Protocol. This issue is an obstacle for nations to reach an agreement to mitigate global warming collaboratively. It provides an explanation to the fact that several countries refused to sign the treaty to limit their greenhouse gas emissions, as they are considering their economic output and an escape from the responsibility to protect environment is seemingly uninjurious in the short-term. Nonetheless, such a single-shot game with solely two players, each with only two choices, is overly restrictive in capturing crucial real-world factors comprehensively [10]. Therefore, when the game is extended to an infinite period, forming a repeated prisoners' dilemma, it is likely that players develop a cooperative outcome as they are concerned about the long-term benefits. Also, the "trigger strategies" in the repeated prisoners' dilemma game create a punitive action that deters the countries from deviating from their promise [6]. From the perspective of institutional design, a punishment mechanism, for instance, a trade sanction or taxation levied on the fossil fuels that are exported to those non-cooperative nations, might be an effective solution to restrict the number of non-cooperating countries [11].

Furthermore, for those signatories, the process of negotiating and ratifying the terms of the treaty is also difficult. As shown by the ultimatum game, although it is a rational strategy that always accepts the "offer" since it generates positive payoffs, in reality, the countries also value the fairness and reciprocity of the terms designed in the treaty. Hence, in order to enhance the countries' willingness to ratify environment-related treaties, the terms can be improved to be more equitable for every signatory. From the perspective of treaty designers, they could treat the desired outcome as given, and then further design the terms to reach this outcome [12]. One solution for them could be to take the historical emissions into account, and each country should have an equivalent cumulative emission [13]. The deterioration of the environment is a cumulative process rather than an immediate effect of pollution. Hence, the greenhouse gas emissions could be measured over time, and the countries' cumulative emissions illustrate their responsibility for pollution proportionately, thus this method could redistribute the emission capacity and make every country have an equal emission amount in total. However, this measure is less preferable for those industrialised countries since their historical emission would be much greater than those developing countries, meaning that they would have less permission for carbon emission now. Therefore, how to make such a term acceptable for those developed countries is still debatable.

4. Conclusion

Overall, the failure of the Kyoto Protocol is instructive to design an environment-related treaty in the future. The free riding problem of mitigating climate change is essentially a prisoner's dilemma game with Nash equilibrium, where all countries have a profitable pollution bias. In the long run, an implementation of punishment could be potentially useful to bind the countries in cooperation in an infinitely repeated game, such as trade sanctions and taxation on exports. Further, the ultimatum game demonstrates that during the treaty negotiation process, paying more attention to the fairness and reciprocity of the treaty is necessary to increase countries' willingness of participation. However, this paper does not evaluate the effectiveness of trade sanctions, since it will damnify the economic gain of the countries who imposed sanctions as well. They may consider a retaliatory trade war would be triggered. It leaves us with the question that who should be responsible for imposing the sanction and the extent it would be. Also, there is controversy over how precisely the improvement in the equity of the treaty could be made so that it is generally acceptable. As a result, these areas are still open for more investigation, and more efforts are needed to improve the global environment.

References

1. A. M. Rosen, Politi & Policy **43(1)**, 30-58 (2015)
2. P. J. Wood, Annals of the New York Academy of Sciences **1219(1)**, 153-170 (2010)
3. A. Endres, Poies & amp, Praxis **3(1–2)**, 123-139 (2004)
4. D. M. Kreps, P. Milgrom, J. Roberts, R. Wilson, J Eco The **27(2)**, 245-252 (1982)
5. J. Watson, Nort & Comp, 175-182 (2013).
6. M. J. Osborne, A. Rubinstein, The MIT Press, 133-160 (1994).
7. R. N. Stavins, S. Barrett, SSRN Elec J (2003).
8. E. Fehr, S. G achter, J Eco Persp **14(3)**, 159-181 (2000).
9. M. Finus, Cheltenman UK Northampton, MA (2001).
10. D. Snidal, Amer Polit Sci Rev **79(4)**, 923-942 (1985).
11. S. Barrett, Resour Ener Eco **19**, 345-361 (1997).
12. M.O Jackson. Soci Cho Welf **18**, 655-708 (2001).
13. J. Pan, Y. Chen, W. Wang, C. Li, Working Paper. Chin Aca Soci Sci (2000).

https://doi.org/10.1051/shsconf/202418803019

Analysis of the energy trade game between major countries under the background of "carbon neutrality": A case study of the photovoltaic industry in China and the United States

Yixuan Wang[1,*]

[1]School of Economics, Management and Law, Jilin Normal University, 136000 Jilin, China

Abstract. With the global climate change poses a major threat to human society, more and more countries begin to "carbon neutral" as a national strategy. As a major country in the global carbon emissions, China and the United States focus on the development of the clean industry - photovoltaic industry to increase investment, in order to deal with global climate problems. At the same time, China and the United States for the photovoltaic industry game also presents a two-way interaction situation, on the one hand, the two countries for the "carbon neutral" energy strategy affects the two countries' trade borders, on the other hand, the two countries' trade strategy also affects the global "carbon neutral" process. This article will be based on the current stage of the two sides of the energy use, the development of photovoltaic industry strength comparison and other aspects of the photovoltaic energy game between China and the United States to discuss.

1 Introduction

1.1 Background of "carbon neutrality"

At present, countries are emitting about 51 billion tons of greenhouse gases into the atmosphere every year, and these greenhouse gases have a serious impact on the global climate and ecological environment. In order to avoid severe climate disaster, the Paris Agreement signed by many countries in Paris requires the parties to the United Nations Framework Convention on Climate Change to immediately specify nationally determined contributions to mitigate climate change, peak carbon emissions as soon as possible, and zero net carbon emissions by mid-century. To achieve by the end of this century, the global surface temperature relative to the pre-industrial Revolution rise of 2 degrees Celsius. In addition, since the reform and opening up, China's manufacturing industry continues to take off behind the need for more energy support, the use of traditional fossil energy in the decline of air quality, but also because of the inadequate use of energy restricts the further development of China's manufacturing industry. As the largest developing country and the largest coal consumer in the world, China's carbon emissions peak as soon as possible and work with other countries to achieve net zero carbon dioxide emissions by the middle of this century are of Paramount importance to global climate response. To this end, in 2020, based on its inherent requirements for sustainable development and its responsibility to build a community with a shared future for mankind, China announced the goal and vision of carbon peak and carbon neutrality.

1.2 Changes in energy industry structure guided by "carbon neutrality"

In order to achieve the goal of "carbon neutrality", China has proposed to take low-carbon energy as the starting point, optimize the energy structure, promote the clean and efficient use of coal, rationally develop natural gas, safely develop nuclear power, vigorously develop hydropower, wind power, solar energy, biomass and other non-fossil energy generation, produce and utilize green hydrogen energy, and improve the capacity of energy transmission and distribution networks and storage facilities. To build a safe, clean, low-carbon, efficient and economical energy system energy development path [1].

Under the vision of "carbon neutrality", the development idea of traditional energy is mainly "low carbonization", starting from the aspects of improving energy utilization rate, using chemical means such as secondary combination, and recycling combustion products, etc., to carry out the "carbon reduction" utilization of traditional energy.

The clean energy development goal will be based on the "new energy" + "smart energy" system, so that it has the characteristics of intelligent, clean and efficient energy system, through the energy form will be from high carbon emissions of fossil energy to low carbon or no carbon emissions of new energy; In terms of energy technology, the transformation and upgrading of the

* Corresponding author: wangyiiixuan@ldy.edu.rs

energy resource-based market into an energy technology-based market, the use of technological innovation to make up for the lack of energy reserves and other means, the carbon neutral science proposed "energy saving and efficiency", "low-carbon fossil energy", "clean energy scale", "electrification of terminal energy use", "intelligent energy system" and other carbon reduction paths are gradually implemented. Is the only way to achieve carbon neutrality [2, 3].

2 Comparison of energy situation between China and the United States

2.1 Energy use in China and the United States

With the rapid development of the global economy, energy consumption has become an important support for national economic development. China and the United States occupy a pivotal position in the world energy consumption market.

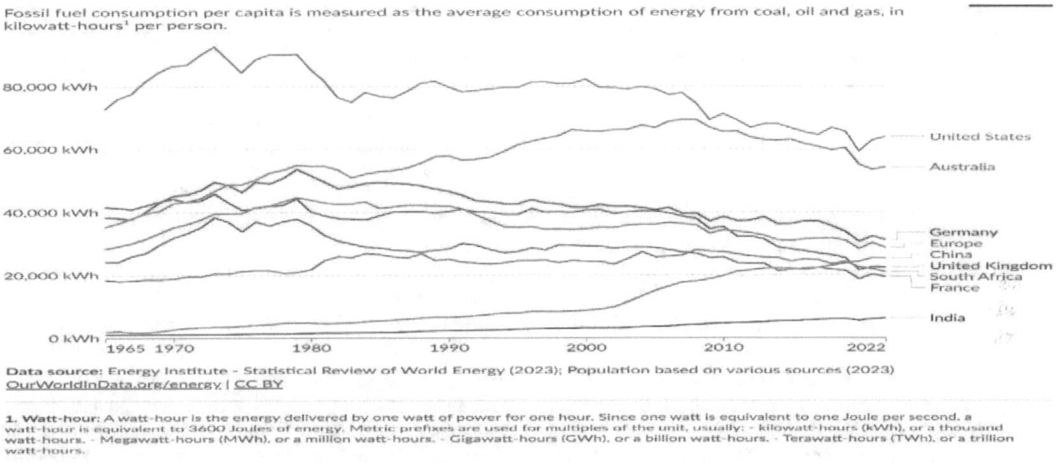

Fig. 1. Per capita consumption of fossil energy in major countries and regions of the world, 2023 [4].

As Figure 1 shows, overall, China's total energy consumption has continued to increase over the past decade, and the growth rate has been relatively fast. In contrast, total energy consumption in the United States is also increasing, but at a relatively slow pace. This is mainly due to China's rapid economic development, which has led to its growing demand for energy. At the same time, the United States is paying more attention to technological innovation and the development of clean energy, and its energy consumption structure is gradually transforming to clean.

From the perspective of energy consumption structure, in order to meet domestic production needs and improve its power generation, transmission and storage capacity, China still takes fossil fuels as the main energy, that is, traditional energy such as oil, natural gas and coal. The United States, due to its rapid development of science and technology and the perfect development of high-end industries in the local, pays more attention to the development and application of clean energy, and clean energy also accounts for a large proportion in the country's energy consumption.

From the perspective of per capita energy consumption, China's per capita energy consumption is relatively low and growing fast. Due to the large population base of China, the resources per capita are relatively small. In contrast, the United States has a higher per capita energy consumption, which also reflects the differences between the two economic development models and paths.

2.2 Development of photovoltaic industry in China and the United States

As an important part of clean energy, the volt industry has been widely developed and applied in the world. According to the "World Energy Outlook" report released by the International Energy Agency (IEA) and relevant public information, this paper makes a comparative analysis from the macro perspective, the production of photovoltaic components in the country, the proportion of photovoltaic enterprises in the global energy industry, and the export of photovoltaic components overseas, in order to have a more in-depth understanding of the development of the photovoltaic industry in the two countries.

From a macro point of view, China's photovoltaic industry has developed rapidly in the past decade. China's PV installed capacity continues to increase, and the growth rate is relatively fast. In contrast, the growth rate of the photovoltaic industry in the United States is relatively slow. The reason is that China's huge population size, the vast domestic consumer market has led to its huge demand for energy, in the past few years, by the epidemic and the changes in the international situation such as the Russia-Ukraine conflict, oil and gas and other traditional energy import costs continue to rise, but the application of the photovoltaic industry is limited to lower-end models at scale.

From the perspective of photovoltaic components and other production in the country, in China, the photovoltaic industry has a very wide range of applications, including the production of solar panels, installation, power generation and other fields. Among them, the production of photovoltaic panels is one of the largest markets, accounting for nearly 70% of the global market share. In addition, China is also actively promoting the construction and operation of photovoltaic power plants to improve the efficiency of renewable energy utilization. The United States focuses on the development of cutting-edge technologies in the photovoltaic industry, and there is still a certain distance for the mass production and large-scale market use of high-end photovoltaic components.

In terms of the global proportion of photovoltaic enterprises, with the strong support of national policies, China has emerged in the solar panel manufacturing and research and development area, a number of high-end photovoltaic enterprises with a high technical level and market share, such as Longi Shares, JA Technology and other enterprises in the global market have a high visibility and influence. The United States' First Solar (First Solar) ranks seventh among global photovoltaic module manufacturers and is one of the world's leading solar photovoltaic module manufacturers. Unlike e Chinese PV companies, First Solar is taking the thin-film solar cell route.

Starting from the export of photovoltaic components overseas, in the past decade, China has been one of the world's largest exporters of photovoltaic components. With the increasing demand of the domestic market and the continuous improvement of the technical level, the export value of China's photovoltaic components is also rising year by year. Among them, the export volume of key components such as silicon wafers and battery wafers is large, leading the global photovoltaic industry trading market. In order to limit the further development of Chinese enterprises in the international photovoltaic industry, the United States said that photovoltaic components produced in China and photovoltaic components "with Chinese ancestry" are applicable to the "Section 301" when imported, in order to suppress the Chinese photovoltaic industry and maintain local enterprises.

3 Sino-us energy trade game with photovoltaic industry as the core

3.1 The Sino-US energy trade game leads to changes in the international power pattern

From the coal era to the oil and gas era, the transformation of energy structure has been the driving force for the change of international power pattern. With the proposed goal of "carbon neutrality", the historic substitution of clean energy for fossil energy is accelerating, and mankind is entering a new era of electric energy. This shift not only has a profound impact on the environment, but also brings new challenges and opportunities to the international political, economic and security landscape.

In the oil and gas era, the United States ensured its dominant position in the international oil and gas political game by controlling key oil and gas producing areas and establishing the petrodollar system [5]. However, as the goal of carbon neutrality advances, this power structure is changing. On the one hand, the geopolitical influence of traditional fossil energy exporters and international organizations that depend on these resources is gradually diminishing [6]. On the other hand, because clean energy is widely distributed and resources are relatively even, most countries are able to secure their own energy supplies, thus greatly improving energy security.

Although the United States retains technological advantages in certain "carbon neutral" technologies, such as carbon dioxide capture and electrochemical energy storage, these technologies are still far from commercial application. China, by contrast, has made remarkable progress in renewable energy. Taking the photovoltaic industry as an example, China not only occupies a global leading position in output, but also has made major breakthroughs in technology research and development and market application.

With the influence of multiple factors such as economic globalization, political integration, and the continuous development of China's photovoltaic industry, the American hegemonic system dominated by oil and gas resources continues to decline, but the energy game between China and the United States may be in a strategic balance for a long time. On the one hand, the US is likely to remain ahead in some areas of technology; On the other hand, China's technological and industrial advantages in the field of renewable energy will be further highlighted. This balance is not only conducive to the cooperation and competition between the two countries in the energy field, but also may become an important factor in stabilizing the global energy political pattern. In this context, countries need to re-examine their policies and strategies to adapt to this series of changes.

3.2 The Sino-US energy trade game leads to changes in the international trade pattern

At this stage, the turnover of international fossil energy trade accounts for about 15% of the total global trade [7]. In the future, affected by the global "carbon neutral" development strategy, this part of the market share will be gradually replaced by the solar photovoltaic industry, hydrogen energy, combustible ice and other clean energy. Based on its own development needs and long-term strategic vision, China has established diversified import channels for oil and gas resources to ensure domestic energy security. In 2020, China's import of oil and gas resources is about 270 billion US dollars, accounting for about 13% of China's total annual import. In the same period, China's photovoltaic product exports were about 20 billion US dollars, and the cumulative installed capacity and new installed capacity continuously ranked first in the world [8]. At present, the year when most countries are expected to reach the "carbon peak" is gradually approaching, the global market demand for clean power equipment will continue to increase, and the market prospects at home and abroad are very broad. This also points out the development direction for China's photovoltaic industry. With the gradual depletion of traditional oil and gas energy and the continuous optimization and adjustment of energy consumption structure of various countries, if China and the United States still basically maintain the current energy trade structure, the United States, which focuses on oil export industries such as Mobil and Shell, will further aggravate its trade deficit.

The proposal of the EU's carbon border regulation mechanism highlights the far-reaching impact of climate policy on international trade. The implementation of this mechanism will directly affect the export of electricity, steel, cement, aluminum and fertilizer to the European market in five areas. This not only means that the products of these industries need to meet new requirements on carbon emission standards, but also may trigger the implementation of a global carbon tax, thus changing the pattern of international trade [9].

With the decline of oil and gas trade, the global energy mix is undergoing profound changes. Traditional oil and gas trade routes, such as the Straits of Hormuz and Malacca, are becoming less important. In contrast, the construction and interconnection of regional power grids is becoming a new focus. This not only means that countries in the region will become more dependent on each other for energy supplies, but it could also lead to a reshaping of the global political landscape. Countries such as the United States, Japan and the European Union have been promoting the construction of regional power grid interconnection. The rise of power infrastructure not only provides countries in the region with a more stable and efficient energy supply, but also may become a new field of competition among great powers [10, 11, 12].

3.3 Sino-US energy trade shows a "Two-Way Interaction" situation

Taking "carbon neutrality" as the development strategy will not only bring a new round of revolution in the development of the energy field, but also affect the global trade border and economic pattern to a certain extent, and change the current global power pattern. In today's world, there will be a two-way interaction between "carbon neutrality" and the international political landscape with climate diplomacy as an important factor.

3.3.1 "Carbon neutrality" affects the Sino-US energy trade border

(1) Increased risk of trade conflicts

With the gradual withdrawal of traditional fossil fuels, Sino-US oil and gas-related trade is likely to decline at this stage. In the long run, countries will adopt a series of policy measures to achieve the goal of "carbon neutrality", some of which may go beyond the simple climate scope and have an impact on trade, economic and other issues. This could lead to a trade conflict between the two countries, particularly in the area of a low-carbon economy. For example, Mr Biden's proposed carbon tax on some high-carbon imports could hurt the competitiveness of Chinese exports. If the United States agrees to the carbon border adjustment mechanism proposed by the EU, it will further link international trade and carbon emissions, increasing the risk of trade conflicts around carbon emissions on a global scale.

(2) New points of conflict regarding overseas infrastructure investment.

In a "carbon neutral" era, infrastructure investment is critical to achieving emissions reductions. Developing countries have huge investment needs, and the competition between China and the United States in this area is becoming increasingly prominent. The Building a Better World Initiative (B3W) proposed by the United States is intended to counterbalance China's Belt and Road Initiative. While the specifics of how B3W will be financed and carried out are unclear, the United States has demonstrated its ambition to compete with China in overseas infrastructure investment. Such competition may give rise to new points of conflict and affect the cooperation and exchanges between the two countries in this field.

3.3.2 The Sino-US energy trade strategy affects the global "carbon neutrality" process

As the world's largest economies, China and the United States play a pivotal role in technology research and development, equipment manufacturing and business model innovation. The United States is known for its advanced research and development capabilities and innovation system, especially in the digital information technology and digital technology industry has a strong strength, and has a number of globally competitive leading enterprises and rich market experience. In addition to China's remarkable technological and industrial advantages in the fields of photovoltaic, battery and electric vehicle manufacturing in recent years, it also relies on its complete manufacturing system and huge market size to make full use of the advantages of scientific and technological industrialization and economies of scale to reduce the cost of energy conservation, emission reduction and pollution reduction.

Looking ahead, China and the United States have formed many potential complementarities in the field of renewable energy, namely, China's strong wind equipment industry and manufacturing capacity, the potential huge demand of their respective markets, as well as the United States in the intelligent, materials and other aspects of high-end research and development capabilities. Once these advantages are combined and cooperation obstacles and blockages are removed, China and the United States will carry out joint technological research and development in green industries, reduce trade barriers, encourage mutual investment, and exchange and coordinate industrial policies and standards, which will greatly reduce emission reduction costs and accelerate the global and bilateral energy transition. Achieve a win-win situation of climate change mitigation, industrial and economic green development for both sides and even the world [13]. To ensure the well-being of mankind, China and the United States should go hand in hand, actively engage in dialogue, jointly promote global energy transformation, and create a new situation of green economic development.

4 Conclusion

The "carbon neutrality" strategy is still in its infancy, and it will redefine the relations between major countries in the future and have a profound impact on the international pattern. However, at the same time, the diversified path to achieve "carbon neutrality" should not be divorced from the current political situation, and the objective development law focusing on promoting global economic development and building a community with a shared future for mankind must be firmly grasped.

As important economies in the world, China and the United States play an increasingly prominent role in global climate governance, and their "carbon neutral" actions will have a decisive impact on global climate change. This makes cooperation and competition between the two countries in the field of climate especially critical. On the one hand, the climate issue may further exacerbate strategic tensions between China and the United States and expand the scope of strategic competition between the two sides. On the other hand, it also provides a new cooperation platform for the two sides to find new points of cooperation by jointly addressing the challenges brought by climate change, and thus inject new vitality into China-Us relations. However, the development of things is always in twists and turns, in the context of "carbon neutrality", Sino-US relations are also facing a series of risks and challenges. With the growing competition between the two sides in trade, investment and other areas, the climate issue may become a flashpoint for more economic and trade frictions. Especially in the field of overseas infrastructure investment, the two sides may engage in fierce competition for resources and market share. Such competition is likely to further fuel bilateral recriminations, undermining the already fragile political trust between China and the United States.

Despite the many challenges, China and the United States share the same long-term vision and goals in addressing climate change. With the return to the political scene of former key figures in climate cooperation, the possibility of climate engagement between the two sides has increased. This is not only expected to ease tensions in Sino-US relations in the short term, but may also become an important means to manage the risk of further decoupling of relations between the two sides. In the long run, climate cooperation has the potential to transcend the political disturbances brought about by the change of parties in the United States and become an important pillar of stable Sino-US relations.

In addition, if China and the United States can carry out healthy competition in low-carbon technology research and development and "carbon neutral" business models, jointly guide global climate governance, reduce the cost of countries to achieve "carbon neutrality", and accelerate the process of "carbon neutrality", it will be of great significance to maintain global climate political stability.

References

1. Z. Y. Ouyang, S. Zuo-Ting, Shi Min-Jun, et al. J Hebei Uni Busi Econ, 5 (2021).
2. Zou Caineng, Chen Yanpeng, Xiong Bo, et al. Bull Chin Acad Scien, 1 (2023).
3. Zou Caineng, Wu Songtao, Yang Zhi, et al. Petro Explor Deve, (2022).
4. Energy Institute·Statistical Review of World Energy, (2023).
5. M. Zhongquan, M. Jikang, Glob Ener Inter **20**, 3(5), 518-525 (2020).
6. VAN DE GRAAF T. Ener Res Social Scien 23, 182-188 (2017).
7. World Trade Organization.World trade statistical review[R/OL]. (2018-11) [2021-07-10].
8. C. Yu, Z. Wenbo. Global Energy Internet, 6 (2021).
9. D. Yue, Z. Xiaohan, Z. Wenbo, China Petroleum & Chemical Industry Insight [R/OL] (2021-07-19) [2021-07-20].
10. US Department of State. Advancing a free and open Indo-Pacific [N/OL] (2018-07-31) [2021-07-19].
11. Association of Southeast Asian Nations. Master plan on ASEAN connectivity 2025 [N/OL] (2016-09) [2021-07-20].
12. European Union. Connecting Europe & Asia: the EU strategy [R/OL] (2018-09-26) [2021-07-20].
13. M. Qi, C. Jingjing, P. Linan, X. Jiannan, Z. Ji. China Energy News, November 27, (2023) (5th edition).

Game Theory and Game Mechanics Design

Jiasheng Pi[1,*]

[1]High School Affiliated to South China Normal University, 510000, Guangzhou, China

Abstract. This paper focuses on the significance of game balance in games and explores the application of game theory concepts for designing and analyzing balanced gameplay. When analyzing instances of games, the paper initially presents the renowned prisoner's dilemma, a prominent problem in game theory, and delves into diverse strategies along with their corresponding advantages, thereby enabling readers to appreciate the captivating essence of game theory. After that, the paper respectively mentions two individual cases from two different forms of games. The well-known game Rock-Paper-Scissors is a simple strategy game. FPS (First Person Shooter) game is a sort of video game that is a complex strategy game. In analyzing this type of game, the paper draws images to show the imbalance in the game. In the end, the article puts forward the prospect that game theory can contribute to game design. The approach adopted in this study integrates existing research in game theory with practical insights from game design, without delving into extensive theoretical derivations or complex formulas.

1 Introduction

Games are already like literature or anything else that's becoming a fundamental part of life. When playing the games, the most essential thing is the balance. The concept of balance is not novel. In a two-player competitive game, game balance refers to a scenario where both players have an equal 50% chance of winning in multiple rounds if they possess the same skill level and comprehensive understanding of the game rules [1]. However, when it comes to confrontations involving "n" individuals or teams, the situation becomes slightly more intricate. Nevertheless, from a victory standpoint, each person or team should ideally have a win rate of "1/n." Balance serves as a parameter for evaluating whether the game can achieve its intended design win rate. At this point, it can think of game theory. The primary objective in game theory is to analyze the solution of a game, commonly referred to as the strategy of game equilibrium. A "balanced" game implies that when the game reaches equilibrium, the players' payoffs should be equal. Regardless of whether the payoff is positive, negative, or zero, equality signifies "balance" [2]. Therefore, this paper is going to talk about the application of game theory in the strategy design of games

2 Analysis

2.1 Introduction of game theory

There is a famous problem of game theory called the Prisoner's dilemma. This is about the cooperation and betrayal of two prisoners. Each prisoner is given the choice to either remain silent or betray the other. If they choose silence, they will receive a sentence of 1 year; if they betray each other, the sentence is reduced to 0 years; however, if both prisoners remain silent, they will be sentenced to 3 years. For this game, assume that there are two people, A and B, who each have two choices, cooperate or betray. A supposed to choose between the two that give me more benefit, and then A is going to have to think about which of these two choices A's going to make, and A's going to have to weigh. At the same time, how much A benefit depends not only on own choice but also on the choice of the other person, so each person has two choices, 2*2. There are four situations, and then in each of these four situations. As shown in table 1, it can evaluate A's benefit and the other person's benefit.

Table 1. Mutual benefit assessment form (uncompleted)

B A	Silent	Betray
Silent		
Betray		

For convenience, denoting it as (0,0), where the first element represents A's payoff and the second element represents B's payoff. Moreover, cooperation is often characterized by mutual benefits; thus, considering the outcomes to be (1,1). Firstly, since betrayal implies

* Corresponding author: pijs.peter2022@gdhfi.com

profitability, the gains from a successful act of betrayal are often greater than those from cooperation. Simultaneously, the losses incurred by the betrayed party are typically more severe compared to mutual betrayals which people perceive as -1. Henceforth, a table can be constructed in this manner, as shown in table 2.

Table 2. Mutual benefit assessment form (completed)

B A	Silent	Betray
Silent	(1, 1)	(-1, 2)
Betray	(2, -1)	(0, 0)

In this scenario, assuming effective communication between the two individuals, remaining silent becomes the optimal solution for them. If Prisoner A chooses silence, he faces the possibility of being sentenced to either 1 or 3 years; on the other hand, if he opts for betrayal, he may receive a sentence of either 0 or 2 years. Therefore, regardless of Prisoner B's choice, betrayal remains the best strategy for Prisoner A in what is famously known as the Prisoner's dilemma.

The application of game theory provides a robust framework for analyzing optimal strategies in both two-player and multiplayer games. Simultaneously, it enables the development of more equitable game mechanics.

There are many types of games in the world, and their rules are different. Games are activities of a recreational nature that usually involve a set of rules and objectives, as well as some degree of interaction and competition. Games can be played in a variety of scenarios, such as video games, board games, and sports.

2.2 Simple strategy games

The most common games played by children are often the simplest ones. These games can be played anytime and anywhere. From an early age, it learned that in a game against others, if the rules or participants are not balanced, the game will lose its meaning. For instance, in the famous game rock-paper-scissor, imagine a scenario where scissors become an invincible tool capable of defeating all defenses. In such a case, all players inevitably choose scissors. Consequently, no one has a chance to win and the unpredictability of the game at this point emphasizes the joy it brings to people. The core idea of game theory is the Nash equilibrium. If each player in a policy configuration cannot obtain a higher return by changing his or her strategy alone, this policy configuration is called a Nash equilibrium. However, there is no real Nash equilibrium in the rock-paper-scissor game, because it is a symmetrical game where all players have the same function. Games with mutual restraint of functions like rock-paper-scissor form a triangle pattern. Therefore, the
rock-paper-scissor mode eliminates the Nash equilibrium. The probability of rock, paper, scissors is 33.3%.

2.3 Complex strategy games

The rock-paper-scissor is one of the simplest games, but for most games that require strategy, the problem gets more complicated because different outcomes have different payoffs.

A video game is a form of interactive entertainment that involves player engagement with a virtual world or simulated environment. It typically includes elements such as graphics, sound effects, and gameplay mechanics to provide an immersive experience. There is a classic type of video game, which is a good example to explain balance in complex strategy games. That is FPS (First-person Shooting game). As the name suggests, a first-person shooting game involves shooting from the player's subjective perspective. Unlike other games where players control virtual characters on the screen, in this genre they experience the immersive visual impact of the game, thereby significantly enhancing their agency and sense of realism.

As mentioned in the introduction, balance is the foundation of adversarial games. In the perspective of game theory. A completer game should encompass five key elements: firstly, the game participants; secondly, the game information, which refers to the strategic decision-making information available to players; thirdly, the set of all possible behaviors or strategies that can be chosen in the game; fourthly, the order of play, indicating the priority for participants to make strategic choices; and finally, the payoff structure for each party involved in terms of gains and losses after making decisions [3]. In FPS games, the player assumes the role of a participant; Players acquire game information through learning the rules and battlefield intelligence; The choices made by players represent their behaviors and strategies in game theory; The sequence of players' actions falls under the concept of game order; Within game theory, the achievement of the game goal by a player is contingent upon their chosen strategy, resulting in a payoff. The traditional two-team PFS game aims to ensure that the game equilibrium represents a zero-sum outcome, where winners and losers are determined through level design, gameplay design, and matching systems. In other words, there must be a clear distinction between a winner and a loser. However, when the game reaches a state of equilibrium, all rational players are inclined to maintain the status quo rather than alter their actions, as any changes would result in a disadvantageous outcome. Therefore, how does the game progress? It's all about game mechanics. Mechanisms such as victory conditions force the player out of the game equilibrium.

 https://doi.org/10.1051/shsconf/202418803020

In game design, game designers need to consider the game mechanics that will facilitate the game without creating an imbalance. There are many kinds of imbalances in FPS games. One of the most common imbalances is imbalance caused by different incomes. For example, a level designer always need to think about the placement of cover in the scene; Cover is the gameplay element that makes the most immediate difference to the player's revenue.

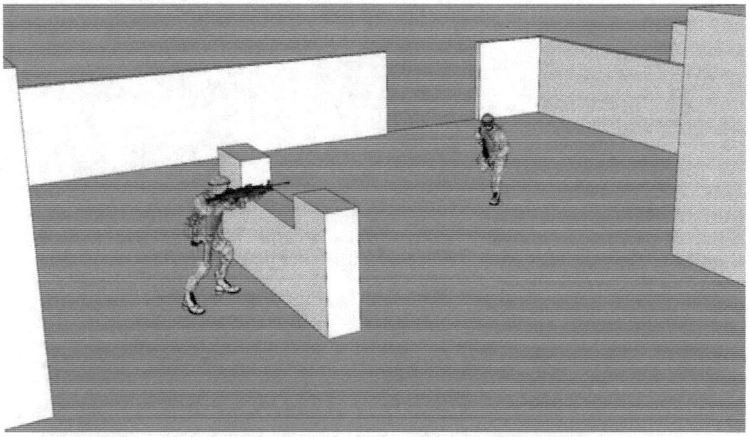

Fig. 1. Unbalanced area design (Photo/Picture credit: Original)

In the situation shown in figure 1, the player standing behind the bunker has a clear advantage. In this situation, the one who can seize the position behind the bunker first will have a greater probability of killing the enemy player, which is a typical unbalanced design. If you want to balance this scene, there are many ways. The simplest is to place an identical bunker in a symmetrical position within the space, as long as the player enters the bunker for the same amount of time, the spatial symmetry must be balanced [4]. But in the design of most games, such a crude approach is often not adopted. This is not true, and easily causes the player to be confused about its position [5].

The role of the information gap is also significant in achieving a well-balanced design. A common manifestation of the information gap in life can be likened to single-sided glass. In FPS games, the most common design imbalance caused by inadequate information (in this case mainly parallax) is channel corners.

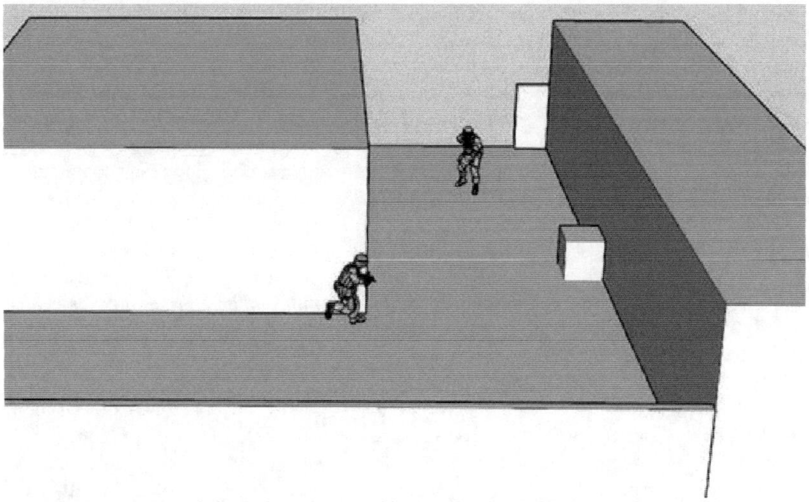

Fig. 2. Unbalanced channel Angle caused by parallax (Photo/Picture credit: Original)

Assuming that Player A must pass the corner and that the enemy on the right also knows this information, Player A's perspective will be as figure 2 when Player A's path is narrow.

https://doi.org/10.1051/shsconf/202418803020

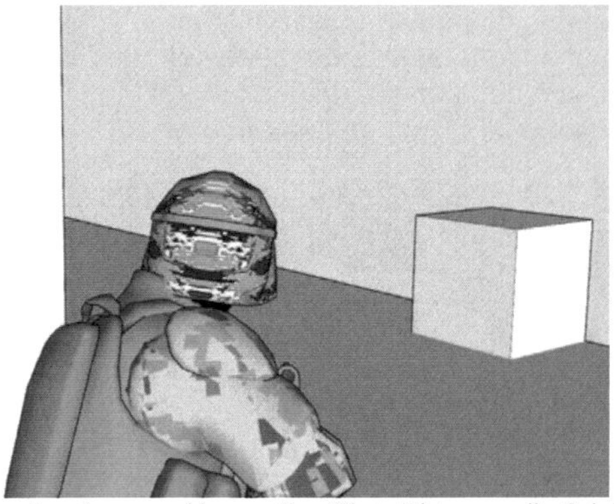

Fig. 3. Unbalanced channel angles caused by parallax (Photo/Picture credit: Original)

Fig. 4. Unbalanced channel angles caused by parallax (Photo/Picture credit: Original)

In other words, before Player A turns to see Player B, Player B has already seen Player A's exposed position. As shown in figure 3 and figure 4, this situation often exists in real combat, resulting in the Close Quarter Battle corner strategy, that is, when passing the channel corner, it must be close to the outside of the corner, and put away weapons to reduce the impact of parallax [6].

Most FPS battle maps are unbalanced [7]. However, it is important to be clear that all levels are designed to avoid absolute imbalance. As mentioned in the rock-paper-scissors example above, scissors can always win, if the players are rational and can choose scissors, then the game becomes a never-ending draw. In game theory, this situation is called a superior or inferior solution [8,9]. To experience a rich variety of games, that can be carried out normally, so that the game in addition to competing marksmanship, there is a certain strategic (branching, specific weapon advantage points, standing positions, etc.), local relatively unbalanced design necessary. Overall balance is also necessary to reduce the map's dependence on game mechanics [10].

3 Conclusion

The level design of a designer's ideas and abilities is most prominently manifested through a combination of partial unbalance and overall balance. Within the intricate 3D space, the gameplay area is meticulously planned, incorporating key elements that seamlessly integrate with the game mechanics. Ultimately, creating an immersive experience for players within an ostensibly raw environment stands as one of the paramount objectives for a level designer in such games.

For a complete game mode gameplay, levels alone cannot guarantee balance. External mechanisms, such as matching, Ban&Pick, and internal mechanisms, such as random position resurrection and half side change, jointly build a complex dynamic incomplete information game system that does not let any party dominate. The game pushes the player away from the game balance through the victory condition so that the participating players can build their information greater than the strategy is greater than the income cycle according to their understanding of the game, and constantly battle with the opponent players according to the dynamic scene.

In the practical design application, not only the balance of scenes and levels should be judged qualitatively, but also the quantitative analysis and practical statistics of the balance data information related to the model through user research, online testing, and other methods. With the development of AI technology in recent years, the use of machine learning agents to simulate the behavior of human players, and the solution of discovering the problems of maps and modes that are not online in advance has also been applied in many games.

References

1. D. Sniper, Balance evaluation, (2019).
2. R. Gibbons, In Princeton University Press eBooks. (1992).
3. J. Kneer, D. Munko, S. Glock, G. Bente, Cyberpsychology, Behavior, and Social Networking 15(5), 251–256 (2012).
4. J. Wood, Gaming Xiuhpohualli: A (Chicano) Theory of Game Design. Design Issues, 39(1), 42–54 (2023).
5. S. Gök, S. Ergün, B. Kırlar, I. Özcan, A. Tayman, International Journal of Uncertainty, 31(06), 891–915 (2023).
6. C. Battle, In Routledge eBooks, 61–66, (2018).
7. F. Coutinho, R. O. Prates, L. Chaimowicz, Deaf Players Experience (2021)
8. M. Khalid, F. Al - Obeidat, A. Tubaishat, Neural Computing and Applications, 34(11), 8295 - 8308 (2020).
9. J. Wood, Design Issues, 39(1), 42–54 (2023).
10. A. Pasqualotto, J. Parong, C. S. Green, International Journal of Human-Computer Interaction, 39(11), 2211–2228 (2022).

Exploring the Synergy Between AI and VR: Advancing Film, Gaming, and E-Learning

Zhiyao Zhang[1,*]
[1]Department of Economics, College of Arts and Sciences, University of Washington, Seattle, Washington, 98105, United States

Abstract. The main thrust of this essay is to delve into the impact of virtual reality on traditional industries, especially in the fields of entertainment and education. In an age where technology and information go hand in hand, traditional ways of working have changed dramatically, with the aim of increasing efficiency and creating entirely new results. The study focuses on two companies that are utilizing virtual reality technology for innovation in the entertainment and education sectors respectively. A comparative analysis of the approaches of these two companies provides insight into the significance and innovative applications of virtual reality technology in these areas. As a revolutionary and innovative technology, virtual reality is having a wide and far-reaching impact on people's lives. It shows great potential for improving efficiency and outcomes, but is still in the early stages of exploration and experimentation. Therefore, more advanced technical support is urgently needed and the application of virtual reality technology is constantly being improved. Virtual reality technology is at the forefront of innovation in this day and age, and it opens a door to the future.

1 Introduction

People live in similar, repetitive scenes and life dramas every day, seeing with their eyes, hearing with their ears, and feeling the real, familiar world with their bodies. As people continue to imagine boldly, and with the rapid development of technology, human beings gradually begin to explore other ways to feel the things around us, to find new worlds.

Thus, virtual reality was discovered step by step. Virtual reality uses advanced technology, including computers and various multimedia peripherals, to create a simulated environment that makes users feel like objects and events in the real world [1]. The first reference to the concept of virtual reality glasses was in a novel called Pygmalion's Glasses, published by author Stanley G. Weinbaum in the 1930s.

WWhen people wear these glasses, even if they don't experience many of the scenes and stories first-hand, they can still immerse themselves in the world that these glasses create for them. Because the person wearing the glasses can hear, see, and feel the things that the virtual reality glasses present to them. It is worth pointing out that the term "virtual reality" has multiple meanings, covering the simulation of some aspect of the real world, the symbolic world, and the imaginary world [2].

When it comes to experiencing virtual reality, immersion is crucial. When participants perceive that the simulated world has a strong sense of reality and veracity, making them feel like the real world, they will generate a sense of spatial immersion, making them feel like they are in it [3].

Many movies involve elements of virtual reality. For example, Neo, the protagonist of the classic movie The Matrix, is made to live in virtual reality through sensory stimulation so that he can't tell if it's the real world or a created world. Because all his feelings are very real. There's also the movie Valerian and the City of a Thousand Planets where the protagonist is surrounded by just a normal empty space before they put on their glasses, but once they do, they enter another world entirely. They can communicate with the people there and can touch objects in that world.

When movies involve sci-fi elements such as virtual reality, this allows people to use their best imagination to create this whole new world in the movie. Because there is no upper limit to human imagination, human power is also unlimited. If the people making the movie dare to think, they can bring the audience into a brand new, exciting movie scene. So that people begin to long for having the virtual reality glasses in the movie.

Unfortunately, all these elements are currently a figment of people's imagination, and today's virtual reality technology such as virtual reality glasses simply allow people to be more immersive to watch and listen. Only most recently have humans been able to interact with artificial worlds via simulations or expertly designed multimedia programs. In the future, users will not only be able to interact in the virtual world as themselves, but also take on another role on a psychic level [4]. So if human beings dare to think and do, they will have the technology of virtual reality like the one depicted in the movie and apply it to various fields, such as the field of movies, education and games.

* Corresponding author: zz1129@uw.edu

This thesis focuses on analyzing the significance and innovative applications of virtual reality for two companies in the fields of entertainment and education, respectively. These two companies are Immersion (Beijing) Technology Co., Ltd. and VEDX SOLUTIONS.

With the help of artificial intelligence, the significance of virtual reality for people is becoming more and more significant. People are also gradually beginning to explore how virtual reality can revolutionize traditional industries and traditional ways of working, increasing efficiency while making people more interested in their work in a novel way.

Artificial intelligence and virtual reality also have many innovative applications in education. The use of virtual reality in education is helping students to become more diverse in their learning styles and strategies, to become autonomous with new techniques for accessing information, and to build skills such as independent planning and teamwork. Universities are also responding to the latest scientific trends and looking for solutions to reach students through sight, sound, and touch. There is also a lot of collaboration and co-innovation between the audiovisual media and the education sector, such as educational films and videos and educational digital games, both of which have new institutional frameworks, industry media and rulebooks.

In conclusion, the advancements in information technology have catalyzed a significant evolution in the digital content sector, fostering the development of varied service scenarios and delivering precision-targeted digital content services across multiple domains, including film, gaming, and education.

2 Description of VEDX SOLUTIONS

Despite the significance of virtual reality for education, there aren't a lot of new companies emerging that are focused on using virtual reality to provide more ways to educate and improve the quality of education. But VEDX SOLUTIONS is a company with a clear goal and a strong dedication to virtual reality. VEDX SOLUTIONS wants to make education more diverse and use immersive experiences to drive educational transformation. Their goal is to "deploy immersive learning tools" in every library, school, institution, and distance learning program in the world. VEDX SOLUTIONS strongly believes that immersive learning tools can increase the effectiveness of learning and produce better learners. VEDX SOLUTIONS is also a company that cherishes talent and is willing to nurture it. Their official website introduces every staff member in the company. Each of them is dedicated to VR education and very good at using VR and AR.

VEDX SOLUTIONS has a wide range of products and programs to implement all aspects of education. For example, VR can be used for soft skills training. PricewaterhouseCoopers conducted a study to explore the effectiveness of VR in diversity and inclusion training, an aspect of unconscious bias training. This study shows that virtual reality environments are more effective than traditional classroom and online learning environments in teaching soft skill concepts.

Here are three visualizations of the remarkable effect (Figure 1- Figure 3):

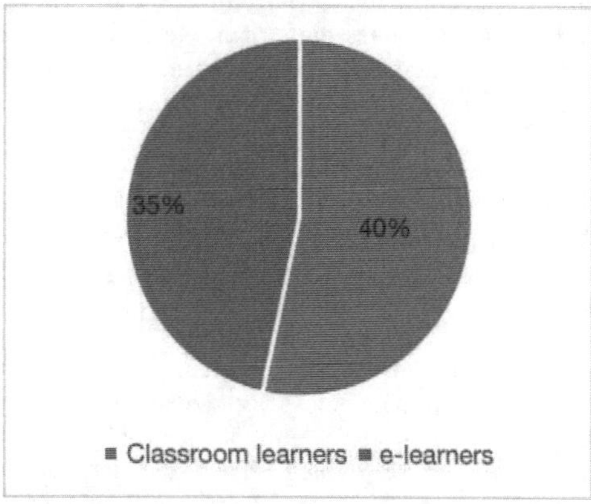

Fig. 1. Percentage of VR learners with increased confidence compared to other learners (Picture credit: Original)

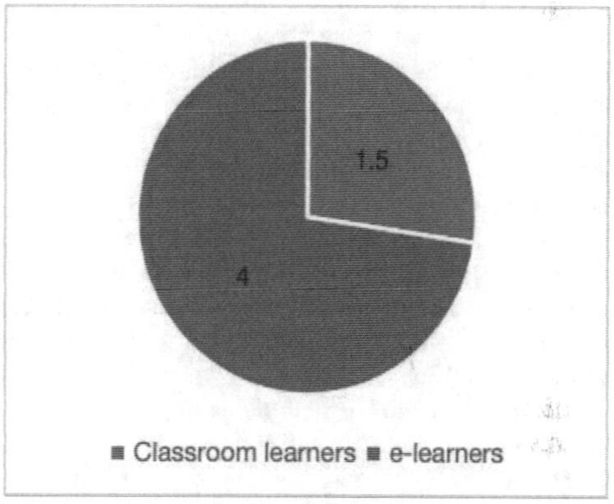

Fig. 2. Multiple increase in attention span of VR learners compared to other learners at the time of training (Picture credit: Original)

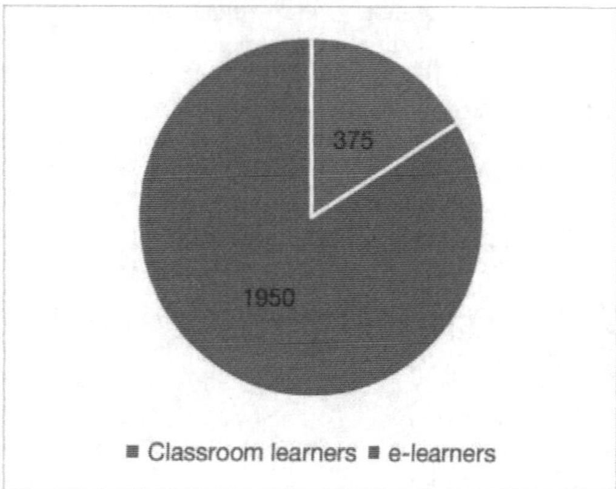

Fig. 3. Number of people who believe that VR learning can be more cost-effective than other learning methods (Picture credit : Original)

In addition to the dramatic results in the three areas of comparison - learner confidence, cost-effectiveness, and attention span - other areas were also very fruitful. V-learners complete training four times faster than classroom training. V-learners made 3.75 times more emotional connections with content than classroom learners and 2.3 times more than e-learners. According to the survey, three-quarters of learners who took part in a virtual reality course suddenly realized that they were not as inclusive as they had previously thought [5].

Jeremy Dalton, Head of VR/AR at VEDX SOLUTIONS, said that Virtual reality will foster people's hard and soft skills in cost-effective, immersive, and efficient experiences, driving a new era of learning, development and education.

Therefore, virtual reality technology is of great significance in the field of education, providing students with a new and immersive learning experience. VR puts students in a virtual environment, an immersive experience that helps them understand and remember what they learn. With the continued development of virtual reality, students can conduct science experiments, simulate historical events, or explore geographic terrain through virtual labs, all of which allow them to understand classroom content more vividly. "Hands-on experience will always be more profound than reading about it in a book. This is just like in the movie Mr. Peabody & Sherman, where Mr. Peabody uses a time machine to take Sherman back in time to teach him about historical events. When Sherman experiences those vivid historical events first-hand, he remembers and understands them much more deeply than his classmates. Although students in the real world can't own a time machine, virtual reality can take students "back in time" to experience historical events, see dinosaurs up close, do chemistry experiments, and more.

Learning with virtual reality can stimulate students' interest and make learning more vivid and interesting. Students will then be willing to take the initiative to learn and spontaneously expand according to the classroom content to get more knowledge. This novel way of learning can increase students' engagement and concentration, and improve the learning effect.

While virtual reality has great potential and scope for development in education and can enable great innovation and change in the field of education. However, it also faces many challenges, such as cost and technical limitations. Emerging technologies such as virtual reality also need more regulations and publicity to regulate their use and promote them widely to students.

3 Description of Immersion (Beijing) Technology Co., Ltd.

Immersion (Beijing) Technology Co., Ltd. has a VR virtual reality entertainment social brand - Immersion World. Immersion world is a VR virtual reality entertainment social brand, its business includes immersive experience software and hardware integrated solutions and virtual reality content production, the company focuses on large space multiplayer interactive VR technology and content development, through the VR large space hardware and software wireless solutions, the player can be in the 100 square meters of the open game field, without weight to achieve 1:1 space walking, and at the same time, feel the VR visual VR visualization brings the depth experience of the real scene.

Chen Xin, founder of 'Immersive World', believes that the iteration of technology represented by VR not only allows content to have a form of expression such as radio dramas, film and television works in addition to text, but more importantly, it enhances the sense of experience of the content in complex scenarios [6].

Immersive Worlds produces a wide variety of genre-rich, large-space VR content, such as VR chambers, shooting fitness games, and more. Founder Chen Xin mentioned that creating virtual reality games to do is also to visualize the scene, three-dimensional form of communication, so that the user becomes a character in the work. In this process, VR technology not only reduces the threshold of the user to receive information, but also enhances the user's memory and sense of presence, and the boundary of this change comes from the interaction, which will make you more and more excited [7].

VR technology allows players to interact with other players in a virtual world, exploring, competing or cooperating together. This immerses players in the world of gaming more than computer and mobile games because virtual reality opens a whole new range of game design and play possibilities. With VR devices, players can operate and interact in a whole new way, allowing them to experience the content of the game in a more profound way through the joint activity of body and brain. Utilizing body movements, gestures, and speech, this innovation makes gaming more intuitive, fun, and challenging. And this real-time multiplayer interaction makes the game more social. Completing the game objectives together in the game can also quickly bring people closer together and enhance their relationship. Players can even interact with other players around the world, enhancing the game's fun and long-term appeal.

Chen Xin said that the three carriages of offline entertainment in China in the past: movie theaters, KTVs, and video game arcades, have gradually become a sunset industry. Therefore, the medium of content dissemination needs to change, and the feelings brought to the user as well as the excitement is not enough to meet the user's needs. The hotness of offline live entertainment, such as escape rooms, has brought about a change in the medium.

VR will inevitably bring great innovation and change to more fields such as movies, games, education, etc. Regardless of age or gender, most people said they had increased their use of VR and agreed that it was good for their physical and mental health and keeping themselves busy [8]. The continuous development and improvement of VR also brings more possibilities for entertainment and education, from hardware equipment to software applications are constantly advancing. The continuous development and improvement of VR also brings more possibilities for entertainment and education, from hardware devices to software applications. More people, such as viewers and learners, have more opportunities and ways to enjoy immersive entertainment and learning. When it comes to virtual reality, the emphasis is on the ability to transcend the limits of reality and accomplish things that are not possible in the physical world [9].

As the technology matures and costs fall, VR devices and experiences will become more popular and accessible, further promoting their use in entertainment and education. Virtual reality has a wide range of applications in primary education that can open new opportunities, increase engagement, and contribute to the efficacy of student learning in higher education [10].

Therefore, there is still a long way to go to make virtual reality widely used in entertainment, education and other fields. Because at present, only the sense of hearing and vision at the same time to get immersive experience. Virtual reality also needs the technical support of various aspects and the participation of composite talents to realize gradually.

VR is seen as a teaching aid for the 21st century, and research has shown that students retain and apply knowledge better after engaging in VR exercises, so researchers and education practitioners are delving into the technology [11]. Overall, virtual reality is an inevitable trend in the development of technology. The development of this technology will also bring great innovative applications to traditional industries.

4 Conclusion

In general, the technology of virtual reality not only improves the efficiency of people in doing traditional and daily work, improves work interest by changing the way they work, but also makes people's lives more fulfilling and promotes physical and mental health.

The potential of virtual reality in both entertainment and education is immense. In terms of entertainment, expect a more realistic and immersive gaming experience in the future. This could involve intricate virtual realms, interactive games involving whole-body engagement, and enriched social interactions, offering users heightened immersion and emotional depth.

In the realm of education, virtual reality holds promise for delivering more dynamic, hands-on learning encounters. Through simulated scenarios, students can conduct experiments, delve into historical events, and grasp intricate concepts, fostering their curiosity and comprehension. Virtual classrooms also hold the promise of providing equitable access to educational resources for students worldwide, bridging gaps in resource availability.

However, hurdles persist in the realm of virtual reality. The technology remains expensive, limiting its accessibility to the wider populace. Furthermore, some users experience discomfort like motion sickness and dizziness, restricting prolonged usage of virtual reality devices. Moreover, there's a pressing need to enhance and diversify virtual reality content to cater to diverse user preferences.

Despite these challenges, as technology progresses and markets evolve, the future of virtual reality applications in entertainment and education remains promising. It's poised to broaden its reach and undergo significant developments in the times ahead.

References

1. P. L. Weiss, A. S. Jessel, V. R. A. W, 11(3) 277-293 (1998)
2. Y. Zhang, H. Liu, S. C. Kang, & M. Al-H. A. C. **118** 103-311 (2020)
3. S. Helsel, E. T. **32(5)** 38-42. (1992)
4. L. Freina, M. Ott, *A literature review on immersive virtual reality in education: state of the art and perspectives*, in Processing to theinternational scientific conference elearning and software for education, 10-1007
5. J. Dalton, PwC's study into the effectiveness of VR for soft skills training, https://www.pwc.co.uk/issues/technology/immersive-technologies/study-into-vr-training-effectiveness.html
6. Y. Lan, focus on VR track, large space VR platform "immersive world" won two rounds of financing in six months, https://36kr.com/p/1801831959217161
7. J. Zhang, Chen Xin, Founder of Immersive World: meta-universe fulfills human nature, China's VR industry lacks imagination, https://36kr.com/p/1425562157006468
8. A. Siani, S. A. Marley, H. T. (B), **11** 425-435 (2021)
9. M. Slater, & M. V. Sanchez-Vives, F. R. AI, **3** 74 (2016)
10. G. Al Farsi, A. B. M. Yusof, A. Romli, R. M. Tawafak, S. I. Malik, J. Jabbar, M. E. Bin Rsuli, I. J. I. M., 15(22) (2021)
11. J. Radianti, T. A. Majchrzak, J. Fromm, I. Wohlgenannt, C. E. 147, 103-778 (2020)

AUTHOR INDEX